Electronic Media Programming
Strategies and Decision Making

McGraw-Hill Series in Mass Communication

CONSULTING EDITOR
Barry L. Sherman

Electronic Media Programming

Strategies and Decision Making

Raymond L. Carroll
University of Alabama

Donald M. Davis
Brenau University

McGRAW-HILL, INC.

New York   St. Louis   San Francisco   Auckland   Bogotá   Caracas
Lisbon   London   Madrid   Mexico   Milan   Montreal   New Delhi
Paris   San Juan   Singapore   Sydney   Tokyo   Toronto

ELECTRONIC MEDIA PROGRAMMING
Strategies and Decision Making

1 2 3 4 5 6 7 8 9 0   DOH   DOH   9 0 9 8 7 6 5 4 3

ISBN 0-07-010298-8

*This book was set in Century Old Style by The Clarinda
Company.*
The editors were Hilary Jackson and John M. Morriss;
the designer was Joan Greenfield;
the production supervisor was Friederich W. Schulte.
Project supervision was done by The Total Book.
R. R. Donnelley & Sons Company was printer and binder.

Library of Congress Cataloging-in-Publication Data

Carroll, Raymond L.
   Electronic media programming: strategies and decision
  making/Raymond L. Carroll, Donald M. Davis.
      p.   cm.—(McGraw-Hill series in mass communica-
tion)
   Includes bibliographical references and index.
   ISBN 0-07-010298-8
    1. Broadcasting—United States—Planning.   2. Radio
programs—United States—Planning.   3. Television programs—United States—Planning.   I. Davis, Donald M.
II. Title.   III. Series.
PN1990.83.C37   1993
384.54'42—dc20   92-46063

About the Authors

Raymond L. Carroll is an associate professor of Telecommunication and Film in the College of Communication at the University of Alabama. He received his Ph.D. in Communication Arts from the University of Wisconsin–Madison. In addition to teaching at the University of Alabama, Dr. Carroll has taught at Texas A&I University, the University of Wisconsin–Whitewater, and the University of Wisconsin–Madison. He is the author of many book chapters and journal publications. Professor Carroll is a member of the editorial boards of the *Journal of Broadcasting & Electronic Media* and the *Journal of Radio Studies.* He is a past editor of *Feedback,* a quarterly publication of the Broadcast Education Association and most recently served as chair of the board of directors of the Broadcast Education Association.

Donald M. Davis is associate professor and head of Communication Arts at Brenau University in Gainesville, Georgia. He received his Ph.D. from The Pennsylvania State University. Davis has also taught at the University of Georgia and The Pennsylvania State University. He has authored numerous journal articles and reports and presented many competitively selected and invited papers. He served as editor of *Feedback* from 1986 to 1989 and has chaired the Mass Communication divisions of the Eastern Communication Association and Southern Speech Communication Association. He is also a founding member of the Media Research Group. From 1986 to 1990 he served as assistant director of the George Foster Peabody Awards.

To Barbara and Donna

Contents

Preface

Writing about radio and television during the 1990s has seemed akin to trying to catch lightening in a jar. It is becoming predictable that events will overtake the established order so often and so quickly that by the time a manuscript is submitted yet another major change will occur. Even so, understanding the bases upon which electronic media programming decisions are made enables practitioners to function more effectively day-to-day and to more astutely anticipate the future—volatile though it is. Although the circumstances are ever changing, the essentials of practice follow consistent principles.

NEED FOR THE TEXT

Our motive in undertaking this book is to impart understanding of the workings of professional electronic media decision making in the greatest breadth and depth possible. We have noted with some dismay that many students seem to have little understanding of the realities of the electronic media industry. This is understandable since each of us focuses on things that we find meaningful, and we are all products of our experience. One of our tasks as professors, though, is to provide experience that will let students know what is needed to be successful practitioners in this fiercely competitive world.

Most of the important work pertaining to electronic media is conducted in offices, not in studios. The real performers are those behind the scenes who make the decisions that determine what "products," as programs are often called, get on the air. We approached this book with the premise that its readers would prefer to be decision makers, able to exert some influence over what is presented to their audiences.

Regardless of whether he or she aspires to a career in management, sales, program production, programming, or some other endeavor related to electronic media, the reader should be served well by an orientation to the bases for programming strategy. Even though the process is imperfect and inexact, the leaders in electronic media seem to apply the concepts we discuss.

FEATURES OF THE TEXT

Current Examples

Despite constant flux in electronic media, we have used examples that are as current as we can make them. The alternative is to illustrate our subject with generalities that would serve neither our intent nor the reader's purpose in using the book. If one or another among our examples or illustrations appears to be a bit behind whatever is in vogue, our readers should recognize the likelihood that what is now current will quickly pass. This is a very trendy business, but illustration through the familiar and the recent should help in circumstances yet to be confronted.

Unity in Approach

We wished to present a unified whole in the book. Each section is intended as a foundation for chapters that follow, although the reader can skip some of the discussion and not lack orientation when turning to another part of the book.

Sections were designed to stand together in spite of occasional repetition of a concept introduced earlier. The different forms of television—independent stations, network affiliated TV stations, local cable system program channels, cable and broadcast television networks, commercial stations, and noncommercial stations—follow similar programming strategies that are adapted to the outlet's unique needs. The comparability of each form is due to a common source of programming. Rather than treat each in a vacuum, we attempt to show where they overlap as well as how they differ.

Seeking Further Knowledge

We want our readers to understand that to advance in their careers they must continue to acquire insight. Consequently, we recommend additional sources of information at the end of each chapter, and we explain how these resources embellish the discussion in the chapter and broaden the reader's awareness and professional perspectives.

The Language of Electronic Media Decision Makers

A career in the electronic media requires the acquisition of its vocabulary and an understanding of how it is applied. Important terms are emphasized in **boldface** in the text because they serve as the shorthand by which most practitioners communicate. The beginner who can carry on a conversation with a prospective employer without need for interpretation has an advantage. To assist in learning this language we have provided definitions of terms where they are introduced in the text. An extensive glossary is included at the end of the book for easy reference.

Program Appeals

Although this book is not about creating programs, many programming decisions depend on projecting the likelihood of their success in attracting and maintaining an audience. Thus, attention is given throughout the book to the ways that program content can attract viewers and how these appeals are applied to programming decisions. Such knowledge is also crucial to radio programming because the elements of music programs are assembled and scheduled by the programmer.

Marketing: A Consumer Orientation to Programming

The plethora of listening and viewing options available to electronic media audiences has made it a consumer's market. This has caused a fundamental shift in strategies, wherein programmers ascertain listener and viewer needs and wants and then attempt to fulfill them. That orientation is emphasized in this book since it is the basis for much of the decision making in programming.

Research: Reducing Risk

Our emphasis in the first part of the book is on audience research since it is used in making many decisions about which programs will be offered. Research can be thought of as a tool for reducing the elements of uncertainty. Procedures for conducting research and interpreting its results constitute the rules of the game in many programming situations. It is incumbent on programmers to understand these rules in order to compete effectively in attracting and maintaining listeners and viewers.

Economics

Electronic media programming success is not measured by the number of people who watched or listened, but by whether the program schedule was profitable. Throughout the book we identify economic considerations that affect programming decisions, including which programs to acquire and when they should be scheduled if they are to achieve economic success.

ORGANIZATION OF THE BOOK

Part One orients the reader to the foundation for decision making in programming: audience research. Chapter 1 provides the context for the book. Chapter 2 looks at the concept of identifying audience needs and wants and providing content that will satisfy them. Since marketing objectives are determined by assessing the attributes of the potential audience, understanding research procedures is integral to determining strategies and evaluating their effectiveness. Chapter 3 looks at how programs are designed to attract and maintain listeners and viewers. Chapter 4 introduces the reader to the fundamentals of research. This foundation is followed in Chapter 5 by a review of the procedures used to determine the size and scope of electronic media audiences. Then Chapter 6 discusses how research is directly applied in programming decisions.

Part Two concentrates on radio programming. Chapter 7 looks at the way radio stations are organized and how radio market attributes—including the facilities and the programming of competitors—influence programming objectives. Chapter 8 reviews the development of modern radio formats, describes the major formats used by stations today, and examines their economic potential and audience appeal. The ingredients in program formulas are described in Chapter 9, where the execution of radio formatting is detailed. Chapter 10 looks at sources of radio program content.

Television programming is considered in Part Three, starting with Chapter 11, where the TV programmer's job is reviewed, along with market influences and the way viewer habits influence programming strategies. Then, in Chapter 12, strategies for attracting and maintaining TV audiences are detailed. Considerations in acquiring programming rights by stations are discussed in Chapter 13. Chapter 14 then discusses the strategies used by stations that not only must acquire all the programs they broadcast but have to compete against the attractive programs offered on network affiliates. The tables turn in Chapter 15, where the advantages of their larger audiences give network-affiliated station programmers more options in acquiring and scheduling the most attractive programs available. Chapter 16 considers program development and acquisition and the problems of networks in competing for the national audience. An important program form for both television stations and networks is considered in Chapter 17, which discusses news programs and how stations and their networks are reacting to a changing competitive environment. Special considerations in programming noncommercial or public television stations are dealt with in Chapter 18, including public station programming sources, competition for audiences, and the way programming costs are covered.

Part Four turns to cable television and its unique programming needs. Chapter 19 reviews the development of cable television systems and how the abundance of channels has affected the structure of the television industry. The factors involved in acquiring program services and assigning their channel placement on local cable systems are considered in Chapter 20, followed by a look at the programming strategies of such cable networks as Nickelodeon, Lifetime, and ESPN in Chapter 21. Chapter 22 reviews the strategies used in programming the major premium cable services.

ACKNOWLEDGMENTS

First, we thank Alan Wurtzel, Capital Cities/ABC who recognized the potential in our proposal and advocated the project. Phil Butcher, then the editor-in-chief of Social Sciences and Humanities at McGraw-Hill, expressed his confidence by striking an agreement with us.

Hilary Jackson, editor, Communications, has been acknowledged by many authors. We know why. Her belief in this project was expressed often and consistently through her interest and encouragement. She not only imparted invaluable instruction that improved the writing but identified astute reviewers who gave us sound feedback. And even when her new son Sam came along to establish his place in her life, she did not forget about us.

During the period following the submission of our manuscript, we had the good fortune to work with a superb copy editor, Eric Lowenkron, a master tutor of clarity and lean writing. We were twice blessed by our assignment to project supervisors Kate Scheinman and Annette Bodzin, who shepherded our project through its transformation from manuscript through publication with a demeanor that consistently conveyed their interest in the importance of our effort.

Our reviewers have our sincere thanks for pushing past the underbrush that obscured our purpose. Robert Bellamy, Duquesne University; John Craft, Arizona State University; Emily Edwards, University of North Carolina, Greensboro; Robert Finney, California State University, Long Beach; Edward A. Foote, University of North Alabama; Brad Gromelski, Iona College; George Heinemann, New York University and Syracuse University; Diane Lamude, University of New Mexico; David Lowry, Pepperdine University; Norman Marcus, Boston University; Marilyn J. Matelski, Boston College; F. Leslie Smith, University of Florida, Gainesville; James R. Smith, SUNY, New Paltz; Daniel Viamonte, North Texas State University; Gilbert A. Williams, Michigan State University; and Michael Wirth, University

of Denver commented on various drafts of the manuscript, identifying many of our lapses, and we took their counsel to heart. Our special thanks to James R. Smith, SUNY, New Paltz, for his encouragement, backed up by his "street smarts," and the time he devoted to drafts of the manuscript. Joseph R. Dominick provided insight that comes only after using a text in a class. The comments of his students at the University of Georgia were similarly useful. Roger Walters, California State University, Sacramento, also provided classroom feedback. His imaginative assignments gave us invaluable access to readers. His students were knowledgeable and frank and gave us reviews that were thorough and specific. Again, their comments were taken to heart and we hope we have done justice to the efforts of all of those so willing to share their insights. Any errors and oversights are our responsibility, and we want to make them right. We hope other readers will be no less shy about communicating their reactions.

The fraternity of authors needs no prompting to appreciate the perseverance required to complete a book. But spouses and other family members know something of the process too, as much is exacted from them. We raise our pens (word processors being much too heavy) to those who endured with us; they were a part of this. Barbara and Donna have our thanks and admiration for putting up with spates of cantankerousness (slavish devotion?) that continued for weeks, if not months at a time. We also thank Jesse, Melanie, Lindsay, and Bryan, who may have wondered why anyone could be so single minded. Heretofore, we could only rely on description as our rationale. We hope what is now tangible serves as a plausible explanation for where we spent those days and nights.

Raymond L. Carroll
Donald M. Davis

PART ONE

Audience and Program Assessment

Before expanding on specific aspects of programming that are dealt with in later chapters, Chapter 1 provides an overview of programming, which includes how people use the electronic media in their daily lives. Their habits influence programming decisions, as do regulations, similarities and differences in the electronic media, and economic considerations like the size of the audience that can be attracted. Putting such knowledge to use requires certain skills and influences the strategies that determine program choices provided to consumers.

The electronic media are in the business of delivering audiences to advertisers. That seems straightforward enough, but presenting program content that will draw desired listeners or viewers is an expensive proposition. Wrong decisions mean that the cash invested in program content is wasted. Equally important, program content that does not attract a sufficiently large audience usually results in a reduction in advertising revenue. Part 1 of this book explains how electronic media programmers reduce risk by relying on audience and program research to guide their decisions.

Research can help reduce risk by identifying audience needs and wants and determining the programming content that will satisfy them. In the past programs could be presented with little risk of rejection because consumer options were limited, but electronic media operation has moved into an era of consumer orientation, and audiences now have a wide range of viewing and listening choices. Chapter 2 looks at how modern programmers approach the challenge of gaining audiences by ascertaining who is available to watch or listen, determining the motivations and needs of different groups of viewers and listeners, and offering programming that serves their wants and needs.

Even with the reduction of risk facilitated by audience research, programming is as much an art as a science. Thus, programmers must evaluate and understand the content of programs in order to schedule them effectively. Chapter 3 discusses the appeals of programs to audiences, explains how television programs are structured to meet the demands of the medium, and goes on to describe the major program types. This chapter also analyzes the structure of radio programs and the important role personalities play in most radio programming.

Chapter 4 presents a review of the elements of research, or the "rules of the research game." A good grasp of the fundamentals of research provides the basis for understanding the procedures used by the audience research services that supply this crucial information to stations, cable operators, networks, and advertisers. In Chapter 5, the electronic media players are described and their respective specialties are introduced. Chapter 6 discusses how research is used in making programming decisions.

CHAPTER 1

Overview of Electronic Media Programming:
Strategies and Decision Making

Like millions of other families across the country, the members of the Jones family arise to the sounds of their clock radios. Suzie, who is 15 years old, always wakes up to the latest rock hits on Power 99 and continues to listen as she fixes her hair and puts on makeup. Her 18-year-old brother, Ted, listens to rap music on compact discs or cassette tapes as he dresses for the day. Their mother and father, who are 40 years old, wake up to an adult-oriented rock station.

Radio has long been an individual medium for its audience members. Television started as a group or family medium because the high cost of TV receivers made it difficult to have more than one set in the typical household, but it too is becoming personalized. Since TV was introduced in the 1940s, the cost of receivers has been reduced dramatically. A majority of American homes today are multiple-set households with receivers in several rooms, accommodating differing tastes.

When Mr. and Mrs. Jones stumble into the kitchen to brew coffee and make toast, they may turn on the TV and watch the *Today* show. Or perhaps they've struck a deal with 8-year-old Bobby, who is an early riser. Bobby can watch animated cartoons while he eats his cereal but must give up the TV in the kitchen when Ted and Suzie show up to watch *Good Morning America*. By that time Bobby has finished breakfast and is happy to go to the basement den, where he can watch *Double Dare* uninterrupted until his mother calls him upstairs to catch the bus for school.

Although many viewers and listeners are available early in the morning, their schedules take them out of the audience as they leave their homes. After the children depart for school, Mrs. Jones enjoys a second cup of coffee during the first portion of *Donahue* before she too must be off to her job. Meanwhile, Mr. Jones has rejoined the radio audience on his way to work, alternately listening to his favorite music station, Easy 102, and to Countrypolitan 104, a station that he doesn't like as well but that provides the best traffic reports. By the time Mr. Jones pulls into the parking lot at work, his high-school-aged son and daughter have stored their *Walkman* radio/tape players in their lockers, where they will remain until the children leave for home that afternoon.

Mr. Jones, Mrs. Jones, and the children are away from the television during the workday. But across town Mrs. Jones's older sister, Aunt Flora, who does not work outside the home, watches *Joan Rivers*. This is not only a relaxing occasion but an opportunity to participate vicariously in a discussion of subjects of interest to those in her peer group. Flora's husband removed himself from the potential audience when he left the house to go to work, and she is part of the predominantly older female audience available to watch during the morning and early afternoon.

Technological developments have had a strong impact on the habits of many people in the radio and television audiences. The clock radio has created a large audience that hears radio programming the first thing every morning. Television viewers have overcome the tyranny of the clock that dictates that programs must be watched when they are broadcast, thanks to the videocassette recorder (VCR). Of course, some people choose not to watch or listen. Ted, for example, prefers recorded music and is therefore unavailable for radio programming at most times of the day.

Even though Mrs. Jones isn't at home when Flora watches soap operas, the sisters eagerly discuss the latest calamities and transgressions of the programs' characters when they get together. Mrs. Jones solved the problem of watching her favorite soap operas when the family acquired a VCR.

With an increasing number of women in the work force, programmers cannot rely on traditional viewing habits. Mrs. Jones's job has limited the hours when she is available to watch TV and affects what she can listen to while at work. She must make choices based not only on her personal preference but on the situation in which she does her listening.

Mrs. Jones has a private office where she can listen to the radio, so she tunes in Easy 102, which features soft rock music. She doesn't mind listening to Power 99 as she and Suzie drive to the mall, but the music and comments of the disc jockeys distract her as she attempts to complete reports at her desk. Suzie, who is not as tolerant, calls Easy 102's programming "elevator music" and pretends she's gagging whenever that station is tuned in on the car radio.

As the day progresses, new members of the radio and TV audiences become available and programming offerings are adjusted to accommodate this influx. As the door to her locker slams shut at the end of the school day, Suzie tunes in Power 99 on her *Walkman*. Bobby arrives home and goes straight to the kitchen, where he turns on the TV and begins watching cartoons while eating an after-school snack. When Suzie arrives, she goes to her room, where she talks on the telephone and watches MTV. Mom arrives a little later and rewinds the videotape recording of her soaps while she gets dinner started. As the casserole is baking in the oven, she fast-forwards through the commercials and the slower scenes in the unfolding drama. After reviewing the soaps, Mom usually tunes in *Oprah Winfrey* or *Geraldo* while completing her preparations for the evening meal.

Programmers adjust their content to cater to people who are available to watch or listen. Few TV stations schedule cartoons before children are out of school, for instance, because cartoons have little appeal to the dominant audience of adult viewers. Since the female audience is much larger than other potential audiences during that period, most afternoon programming is designed to appeal to women.

While Mrs. Jones is watching Geraldo interview men who have married women old enough to be their mothers, Mr. Jones is sitting motionless on the freeway alternately listening to the disc jockey on Countrypolitan 104 suggest that motorists use a different route and punching up Easy 102, which features a breezy announcer and up-tempo soft rock music during the afternoon. He is attempting to relax during a very frustrating part of his day. When he finally arrives home, he and Mrs. Jones watch the net-

work news, but Mrs. Jones leaves early in the program to take care of a last-minute chore because she has already watched almost an hour of local news and little on this newscast seems new. She joins the children, who are in the kitchen watching a rerun of *Alf.*

After dinner, the older children go off to do their homework, accompanied by their radios, their tapes, and MTV. Bobby and his father watch a situation comedy on CBS TV until his bedtime. When Mr. Jones changes the station to watch a nature documentary on the Discovery Channel, Mrs. Jones drifts off to the bedroom, where she will watch a network rerun on Lifetime since nothing on ABC, CBS, or NBC seems especially appealing. The paltry viewing choices on TV remind her that she should stop by the video rental store to pick up a movie she has been wanting to see.

Suzie, who has finished her homework, is listening to the radio again. This is her favorite time of day to listen, since the music and the disc jockeys are much more attuned to the interests of people her age. She has called twice to request her favorite song on Power 99. Ted, who hasn't watched much TV all day, tunes in *Arsenio Hall* for a while to relax after his homework. Mr. and Mrs. Jones will watch a bit of the *Tonight* show on NBC before they go to sleep. Then, with their clock radio alarms set, the Joneses are ready for the start of a similar day the next morning.

This scenario is played out in millions of American households every day. Since potential viewers and listeners have so many alternatives, it is important to develop a strategy to attract some portion of the listening and viewing audiences as they change during the day. Programming is thus a challenging, ever-changing, and essential activity in the operation of any electronic media outlet, whether a radio or TV station, a cable system, a broadcast network, or a cable network. That process is the subject of this book.

This chapter will give the reader an overview of the considerations involved in programming the electronic media. We define programming

Calvin and Hobbes   by Bill Watterson

FIGURE 1-1   *Calvin and Hobbes © 1990 Watterson. Dist. by Universal Press Syndicate. Reprinted with permission. All rights reserved.*

before going on to discuss major influences on programming decisions. We then differentiate among the electronic media and the kinds of markets in which they operate, noting how different audiences can be served. We go on to review the skills needed to program effectively in the modern electronic media environment. Since programmers do not carry out their responsibilities in a vacuum, we raise some of the ethical considerations that they encounter every day. At the end of the chapter we address a fundamental question: Why study programming? This is followed by a chapter summary.

WHAT IS ELECTRONIC MEDIA PROGRAMMING?

Attracting and Maintaining Audiences

Electronic media programming is the planning and scheduling of programs to attract and maintain a specified audience. People spend many hours every day with the electronic media. The question is, *What* do they watch or listen to and *for how long* before they turn to an alternative source or abandon the media altogether? The programmer answers these questions by plan-

ning programming that will attract and maintain the largest possible audience throughout the entire programming day and induce a loyalty to a particular station or program that will motivate listeners or viewers to return day after day.

As we showed in the example of the Jones family, the audience becomes more narrowly defined after the day has started since many of the people who were available to watch early-morning programs are gone, leaving a somewhat older, predominantly female audience at home. Throughout the day, programming changes to address the needs and interests of the available audience.

Programming Strategy

A programmer is the person at a station, network, or cable system who is responsible for determining not only the type of programming but the schedule of program content to be presented each day. Thus, the programmer's job is to create a strategy for scheduling programs that will attract and maintain a specified audience. A **strategy** includes the identification of an objective and the determination of the steps that will contribute to achieving that goal. For instance, the Lifetime Network's strategy has been to create an identity among the myriad alternatives available to television audiences. That network has identified as its **target audience** adult women. Each program in the Lifetime schedule is a step in that plan; each is designed to appeal to women. The Entertainment and Sports Programming Network (ESPN) follows a strategy of specializing in sports programming. Part of ESPN's strategy is to accumulate a large audience over several hours or even several days by repeating programs at different times. ESPN pursues this strategy because few viewers watch a sports channel exclusively.

Each step, or **tactic,** should be orchestrated to contribute to the objective. ESPN once presented reruns of college football games that originally had been broadcast live a few days earlier on a broadcast television network. This tactic offered sports enthusiasts an attractive program even though most knew its outcome. For dyed-in-the-wool followers, the repeat was another chance to see their teams in action. For other football fans, it was an opportunity to see a good game they might have missed in its original showing. Furthermore, the football game was repeated at different times during the week, giving viewers an alternative to less interesting programs on competing channels. Also, ESPN was able to acquire a program with considerable potential appeal at a relatively low cost since the game had already been broadcast. The network could accumulate the audience needed to make that investment worthwhile by offering repeated showings at no additional cost; the fact that it was a big-time college game reinforced ESPN's image as a sports network.

Some tactics don't work as planned. For example, Lifetime acquired the rights to *Moonlighting,* originally shown on ABC, at a fairly low cost because the program's producers could not interest individual broadcast stations in purchasing it to air on local outlets. Programmers at TV stations did not believe the program would have much appeal to their local audiences during the afternoon, when they needed to fill their schedules. Although Lifetime's audience is small by traditional network standards, the tactic of airing *Moonlighting* was logical since it fit the network's strategy of offering shows that appeal primarily to women. Many women had been attracted to the series, starring Cybill Shepherd and Bruce Willis, when it was originally broadcast on ABC. *Moonlighting,* scheduled during the evening prime-time period, was expected to attract a large enough audience to make Lifetime's investment profitable. That tactic failed when *Moonlighting* received disappointing ratings, so Lifetime moved the show to midnight and replaced it during prime time with reruns of the NBC TV series *L.A. Law,* which it promoted on the air with wry commercials that referred to the lawyers in the series as "hunky guys in dark suits."[1] The new program was successful in that time period, supporting Lifetime's strategy of attempting to reach women viewers.

Programming as Part of a System

Stations, networks, and cable TV franchises are systems composed of departments of administration, sales, news, public affairs, engineering, and production. All the members of the station's staff must have knowledge about the other parts of the system so that it can be "tuned up," or fixed when broken.

Whether one anticipates producing programs, wants to work in time sales, or plans a career as a disc jockey or news anchorperson, appreciating the programming objectives of a station or network can only help one's performance and success. It is unrealistic, for instance, to consider news as a separate entity in any system's operation. A newsperson who ignores his or her employer's strategy of targeting a specific audience not only fails to contribute to that important objective but interferes with the likelihood of its success, especially if that newsperson alienates members of the audience. If a radio station is attempting to attract men and women age 25 to 54 and features Country music, broadcasting a news story about Paula Abdul would not be a good tactic, since that kind of information is of little interest to the audience the station is serving. Or consider a situation where a newsperson is preparing a newscast for a station that plays popular rock music. Would that station's audience be concerned with the news that Social Security benefits are being raised by 1 percent? This does not mean that the news staff should ignore the story but that it should not be the lead in a newscast and should be given less emphasis than it would on a station whose primary audience is older listeners.

Like a newsperson, an account executive, or advertising time salesperson, must be aware of the station's strategy and the audience it seeks to attract in order to understand why some commercials are detrimental to achieving that goal. Programmers of successful radio stations are concerned with the quality of commercial messages since listeners may tune out if the ads become too annoying. Thus, the number of commercials, where they are placed in the program, and how well they fit with other content are crucial considerations. The programmer at an easy-listening radio station would probably resist accepting a "hard sell" commercial that used loud rock music, sound effects, and a bellowing announcer because such an advertisement would be jarring to listeners accustomed to a relaxed presentation.

In a similar vein, a television producer must build the program around breaks where advertising messages are inserted at the local level or the network level. If the program does not sustain its audience through the commercial breaks, it will not remain on the air for very long since advertising is the means through which most electronic media outlets generate operating revenues.

INFLUENCES ON PROGRAMMING DECISIONS

Just as a field general has many things to consider in conducting a battle (the terrain, the number of troops, the weather, food supplies, ammunition), a programmer's strategy is affected by a number of factors. Among them are program salability, profitability, competition, management

policy, sponsor availability and interest, social trends, and the technical capabilities of the medium. Each of these influences helps shape programming decisions, and several of them are discussed below.

Salability

Earlier, we defined programming as the planning and scheduling of programs to attract and maintain a specified audience. That is the activity, but the *purpose* of programming is to bring audiences to advertisers' messages. The local appliance dealer wants to avoid door-to-door selling or reliance on word of mouth to sell refrigerators. To let consumers know about his or her line and induce them to make purchases, the dealer "buys" access to potential customers through local radio or television stations or local cable channels. Thus, *salability* is the attractiveness of a program to advertisers as an effective means of reaching potential consumers.

The real business of electronic media: delivering audiences It seems obvious that radio and TV stations and networks are in the entertainment and information business, but that is only the means to an end since the program content is put on the air to attract an audience. Since revenue comes from the sale of advertising time, the electronic media are in the business of delivering audiences to advertisers: The larger the audience they can be expected to deliver, the more advertising dollars they will bring in and the greater profit they will earn.

Advertisers routinely influence what is programmed because they need to reach certain kinds of consumers. Programmers are happy to comply since they depend on advertisers' revenues. Since 25- to 54-year-old women make most of the purchasing decisions for the majority of products, stations and networks present the kind of programs they think will attract this group in hopes of capitalizing on potential advertising revenue. However, no program can be all things to all people. Very young listeners' tastes in music and situation comedies differ from those of teenagers, which contrast greatly with the tastes of parents. No media outlet can hope to attract all these and other **demographic segments,** or audience groups categorized by age and sex. Young men will opt for an action/adventure program such as *Hunter* over a soap opera drama such as *Knot's Landing,* which attracts older viewers, particularly women. Besides, advertisers target various groups: Nintendo needs to reach children and teens with its message, for instance. Consequently, television and radio stations and cable services specialize in their programming in order to attract and maintain a carefully defined segment of the audience.

As Figure 1-2 illustrates, product manufacturers create advertising messages that are delivered to targeted consumers via radio, television,

and cable programs. Stations, cable systems, and networks, knowing the needs of advertisers, design programs to attract particular segments of the audience. Advertisers will select a station or program on the basis of how effectively it attracts targeted consumers.

If one radio station has the lion's share of teenage listeners, a competitor must decide whether to compete for the same audience or identify another one. Rather than attempting to appeal to both teens and adults, the second station may decide to go after an older segment with its program content even though this probably will cause it to be snubbed by younger listeners. Similarly, a local **independent** TV station, or a station that has no network affiliation, may schedule cartoons in order to attract chil-

FIGURE 1-2 Sponsor-program-audience-sales cycle.

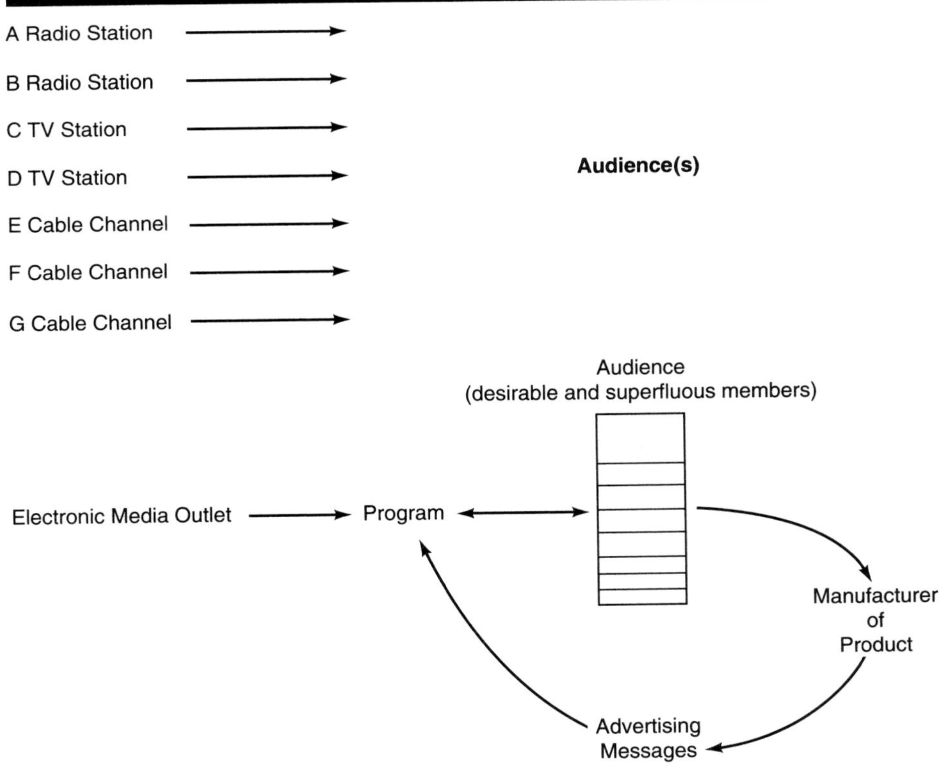

dren in the afternoon. Since the independent station's programmer knows that little can be done to steal the adult female audience from *General Hospital* and *All My Children,* it is better to target an entirely different audience. Thus, the independent station has identified an available audience that is not being served by other TV outlets. The children who are watching the independent station constitute an attractive audience to advertisers who need to reach children with their messages in order to sell products such as toys and candy.

Advertising rates are based on both the size of the audience and how desirable its demographic composition is to the advertiser. Some advertisers seek a very well defined audience for their messages. A BMW automobile, for instance, is probably out of the financial reach of most radio listeners, so a station may adopt a strategy that attracts a narrow audience of **upscale consumers** who are well educated, have high incomes, and are willing to spend money on expensive items. A station that delivers such an audience offers an attractive advertising medium to advertisers whose clientele is basically limited to people for whom such purchases are affordable and whose lifestyles make the acquisition of such luxuries important to them.

A number of AM radio stations specialize in business news. Their programmers know that the audience for business news and investment tips is older and predominantly male. Such a station's audience, though relatively small, is concentrated and therefore is an efficient conveyance for placing advertising for products and services that will be of interest to that audience, such as investment firms, hotels, travel agencies, and car dealerships.

Some companies are more concerned with burnishing their images than with selling products directly to the general public. They are more interested in advertising on prestige programs that appeal to a specialized target audience than in advertising on programs that attract the largest audiences. For many years Mobile Oil supported *Masterpiece Theater* on PBS as a way to enhance its public image because many

"opinion leaders" were among that series' regular viewers. Such strategies suggest that public broadcasters who want financial support will have better luck if they schedule the kinds of programs that appeal to corporate sponsors.[2]

Profitability

The yardstick for determining programming *effectiveness* is the number of people who listen or watch, but having the largest audience does not always translate into making a profit. Many TV stations learned to their financial dismay that the high cost of acquiring the rights to reruns of *The Cosby Show* provided neither the largest audience nor a profit. In many cases cheaper, less prestigious programs attracted about as many viewers, which made them attractive to advertisers. Thus, they could generate enough advertising revenue to make a profit. As will be discussed in detail in Chapter 13, consideration of program costs and projections of revenue from advertising are essential aspects of programming strategy.

Competition

Audiences have increasingly expanding viewing choices among TV and radio stations, cable TV systems featuring 30 or more channels, home satellite receivers, and audio and video recordings. All these choices influence whether enough people can be attracted to justify a particular program. For example, an independent TV station may be on the verge of acquiring the rights to a former network series that it plans to schedule during the evening hours, but if the networks offer programs that are more attractive because they are new, the independent station's programmer must consider whether the investment in reruns can be justified in light of the network competition. Similarly, if a movie has been out for months in video rental, fewer viewers will be interested in watching a network broadcast of that film.

At the beginning of the 1990s the greatest competition for national television audiences was still between ABC, CBS, and NBC, but the Fox Television Network had already emerged as a serious contender, and the traditional balance was disrupted. As a result of inroads being made by raunchy Fox programs such as *Married . . . with Children* and a situation comedy featuring an interracial couple, *True Colors,* the big three networks began to loosen up their traditional program formulas by scheduling imaginative series such as *Twin Peaks* on ABC TV. While radio stations competed primarily with one another in the early 1990s, a number of cable audio services began to vie for audience attention with stereo music services that rivaled the quality of Dolby cassette tapes and compact discs. Radio stations became increasingly concerned about the audio quality of their programming since clarity is a feature that many listeners appreciate.

Management Policy

Station or cable system owners' policies can greatly affect programming decisions. A station may present more news or public affairs programs because its management feels it is in that station's interest to build an image as the news leader in the community. Another manager may decide to minimize such programming because of its great expense.

Some station managers feel an obligation to broadcast an occasional public affairs or cultural program as a service to the community regardless of whether it generates revenue for the station. Other managers are motivated by the potential revenue from such a broadcast. For example, Billy Graham Crusade specials often replace weak network offerings that attract small audiences. News documentaries and cultural programs are typical of programs that are **preempted,** or replaced by another program at the local level. Stations can earn more money by renting the hour to a religious group than by **clearance** of the scheduled network program and airing it when the network scheduled it.

Some managers forbid the use of double entendres and discussions of risqué topics by on-air personalities, whereas other stations actively promote outrageous antics in order to attract listeners. In either case, a policy is at work. The direction that programming will take is influenced by a restriction or by its absence as programmers attempt to gather the largest possible audiences.

Trends

There is an old saying that imitation is the sincerest form of broadcasting. Program types go in and out of fashion, and when imitation reaches a saturation point, a *genre,* or program type, will lose popularity. Doctor shows and westerns have come and gone and may become popular again, although probably in a modified form. Music formats such as Disco were adopted by radio stations desperate to find an audience during the 1970s. A respectable number of listeners were attracted for a while, but the popularity of the format soon declined and most of the stations programming it went on to try something else.

If it works in Houston, it will probably work in Peoria—at least that's how the pattern seems to play out as stations adopt successful ideas and practices. Former WLS, Chicago, program director Art Roberts once remarked that "radio is a license to steal" the ideas of other stations, but imitation does not always work because of regional differences. Country music is a more successful radio format in the south than in the northeast, and *Hee Haw* does better among rural viewers than among urban viewers. Similarly, *Mayberry, RFD,* starring Andy Griffith, continues to enjoy its greatest success in reruns broadcast in southern and rural markets.

Station Facilities

The physical ability of a station's signal to be received by viewers or listeners has much to do with its potential audience and the kind of programming that will be most successful. As Figure 1-3 indicates, an AM radio station's transmitter power and the frequency on which it is authorized to operate have a considerable effect

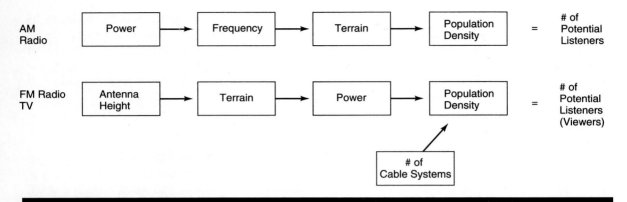

FIGURE 1-3 Signal reach.

on the area its signal will cover. The topography and the conductivity of the soil where a transmitter is located also shape or limit the signal. An AM signal transmitted at 5000 watts in a rural plains area can provide several counties with good reception, but the small number of actual listeners in the area may offset the advantage of wide coverage. The same signal in a heavily populated urban area in hilly terrain may be received with clarity only in the city, but the population there may be many times greater than that in the coverage area of the rural station.

FM and TV signal reach is affected by antenna height above the ground level and by the topography of the coverage area. FM and TV signals travel in a straight line-of-sight pattern, and so buildings and hills can be obstacles, causing the signal to be reflected away. Thus, a household in a low-lying area may have poor reception, especially if the station is some distance away. The signals of stations that broadcast over relatively flat terrain generally go farther, with less interference. In any case, broadcasters attempt to locate their towers on the tallest building or hill possible since the tower itself is a means of elevating the antenna elements from which the signal is radiated.

Whether a station is AM, FM, or TV, the most important consideration is not how far its signal goes but how many people receive it. The prefer-

able facility is a high-powered signal in the largest possible population center. Obviously, that ideal cannot be met in many cases. A number of independent television stations, particularly those operating on ultrahigh frequency (UHF) channels 14 and above, do not get out as far as do very high frequency (VHF) channels 2 through 13, so their over-the-air reception may be marginal. Furthermore, in markets with a high percentage of homes subscribing to cable TV, viewers will not bother to maintain an outside antenna to receive these stations since the cable link makes that unnecessary. Consequently, many such stations depend on cable carriage to reach an audience large enough to be attractive to advertisers. Cable systems are the key ingredient in the existence of **superstations** such as WGN, Chicago, and WTBS, Atlanta; these are independent stations whose signals are transmitted by satellite to cable systems, where they are distributed to millions of households.

Regulation

Sanctions by the federal government and, conversely, the removal of such restrictions affect the nature of electronic media programming. In 1971, for example, the Federal Communications Commission (FCC), the federal agency responsible for licensing and regulating the electronic media, became concerned about the drug-oriented lyrics of many popular songs. Official FCC reminders of licensee responsibility for the content of all broadcasts were mailed to all stations, sending a chill through the broadcast community.[3] During the 1970s and 1980s the FCC went through a **deregulation** phase (it would be more accurate to call it unregulation) in which many specific operator rules and expectations were removed or relaxed. For example, after the FCC abandoned its guideline for a minimum level of nonentertainment programming in 1981,[4] many radio stations cut back on or discarded newscasts.[5] Although their audiences might have listened to news, these stations felt they could eliminate the expense of newscasts without getting much negative reaction from the Commission.

The regulatory pendulum has a way of swinging back, however. National economic conditions, political attitudes, and public sentiment can alter laissez-faire regulation by refocusing attention on the programming responsibilities of broadcast licensees. Members of Congress, perhaps in response to their constituents' grumbling, have introduced legislation that would require stations to restrict sexual content on television, and in late 1989 the FCC began to crack down on radio stations that broadcast sexually explicit songs, skits, or dialogue.[6] More recently, Congress overroad a presidential veto to "reregulate" cable television. The legislation was motivated by an escalation in subscriber costs that had angered many constituents.

Citizens' Groups

Organizations of citizens concerned about the content of broadcasting have been formed over the years. Whereas some groups have been concerned about negative depictions of members of minority or ethnic groups, others have complained about a lack of representation of Hispanics, blacks, and women. Some groups have fo-

cused on the quality of television for children, while others have been concerned with the lack of morality seen in many programs.

The Coalition for Decency in Television attempted a 1981 nationwide boycott of sponsors' products to rid sexually explicit material from offending programs.[7] The organization got the attention of major national advertisers, although it is unclear whether it had any effect on program content.

In 1986 congressional hearings prompted by parents led by Tipper Gore, the wife of Senator Al Gore (D-Tenn.), investigated sexually explicit lyrics in rock music. Recording artists rejected the claims; Frank Zappa, for example, testified before a congressional committee and appeared on TV talk shows to argue against restrictions on artistic freedom.

During the 1970s a small organization called Action for Children's Television (ACT) mobilized enough concern about violence in children's TV programs to result in 80,000 letters to the FCC.[8] As a result of this campaign, each network created a position of vice president for children's programming. However, with the removal of pressure in the 1980s, these officials' functions have largely been abandoned.

Over the years society's tolerance for certain kinds of program content has increased. Subjects that once were taboo are now commonplace. For instance, in 1952, when *I Love Lucy* star Lucille Ball was an expectant mother, the word "pregnant" was never uttered on the series. Just a few decades later television programs were openly depicting sexual relationships, marital infidelity, impotency, and homosexuality, but some groups of people are still offended and concerned. One recent protest was organized by a suburban Detroit homemaker, Terry Rakolta, who heads a lobbying group called Americans for Responsible Television. In 1988 she mounted a boycott against advertisers on *Married . . . with Children* and followed that up with a direct-mail campaign to more than 100,000 households with children. Another group, the American Family Association, headed by the Reverend

Donald Wildmon, monitors television programs and threatens to boycott sponsors of shows determined to be offensive. The result of such pressure is an increasing sensitivity by advertisers, who do not want their products associated with shows containing objectionable words of depictions.[9] Even though the strength of such protests has waned, content dealing with sexual matters and depictions of violence remain controversial, and programmers must deal with those issues as they are raised.[10]

SIMILARITIES AND DIFFERENCES IN PROGRAMMING THE ELECTRONIC MEDIA

While many of the principles of programming and the influences on programming decisions apply to all the electronic media, there are differences that call for separate strategies. Each electronic medium has unique attributes, and audiences use them differently.

Radio

Perhaps the most important attribute of radio is that it functions as a companion to its listeners. Since radio is portable, people listen to it everywhere, usually while doing something else, such as studying, jogging, driving a car, washing dishes, or sunning themselves at the beach. Since most people listen one at a time, programming is aimed at the individual listener, even though she or he is part of a much larger total audience.

There are many radio stations on the air, and they serve smaller geographical areas than television does. Consequently, most radio stations *localize* by concentrating their programming efforts on listeners in the immediate coverage area. Some stations reverse that strategy, particularly if they are located in a large metropolitan area. If their signals are strong enough, they may try to identify with the whole market since that attracts more listeners and thus more advertising dollars. Regardless of size of geographic coverage, radio stations try to establish a strong tie with listeners in their coverage areas.

Most radio formats are made up of a stream of material that continues a single program concept throughout the day. Music is the principle programming fare of most stations. Regardless of music type, radio programs usually incorporate short individual elements such as records, newscasts, weather reports, traffic reports, sports news, and other chunks of information and entertainment. Commercials are integrated with other program content, making them as important a consideration as the kind of music that is played.

Television

Although radio is not cheap to operate, it is much less costly than TV. Television staffs are much larger and have much more specialized responsibilities. Whereas a radio programmer is often an on-air personality and may serve part-time as an advertising time salesperson, a similar concentration of labor for television occurs only in small-market operations.

Not only is television a more technically complex medium, its programming is much more expensive. The upshot is that TV programmers generally take fewer risks since the stakes are higher, and those who do take risks often lose out. Many independent TV stations, for instance, find themselves in financial trouble when the heavy investments they make in programming cannot be covered by advertising revenues. They take a chance in purchasing the rights to broadcast programs because there is much to gain if they are successful and much to lose if they continue to offer programs that are less desirable than those available on other stations.

The Fox Television Network's decision to schedule potentially offensive programs such as *The Simpsons* and *In Living Color* or air a program such as *Beverly Hills 90210* that appeals largely to teens was made because it had nothing to gain by playing it safe. With fewer affiliated stations than ABC, CBS, and NBC, Fox could not hope to attract viewers by scheduling the same cautious programming the other networks offered. The conservative approach of the big three networks gave Fox an opportunity to make inroads into their audiences.

TV programmers focus much more on scheduling than on the production of programming. Radio programmers, by contrast, function as program producers in that they assemble the components of the program and place them in a particular order throughout the day. At the local level, television programmers have little to say about the way programs are constructed. At the network level, programmers exert considerable influence over content but nevertheless are not on the creative side of producing programs. Instead, TV programmers fill half-hour or hour periods of time with programs that come already assembled from their producers.

As was noted earlier, only a few local TV stations serve each viewing area, so their programming has traditionally had a more general appeal than that of most radio stations, which attempt to attract only a portion of the total audience. These stations' audiences, categorized according to age, sex, ethnicity, education, and income, include teenagers and young adults, Hispanics, or those who like Easy-Listening music, to name but a few audience segments. The goal of most TV stations, though, is still to attract 100 percent of the potential viewers in the audience each day. Consequently, shows designed to attract different audience groups at different times or on different days of the week are scheduled because the station will then have a greater chance of gaining a significant portion of the available audience. Most radio stations maintain the same format throughout the day, and their regular listeners recognize it regardless of when they tune in.

Cable

As with radio, narrow-appeal television programs on cable can be profitable if enough of the viewers likely to watch them live in the area being served. Through cable system distribution, newer networks have access to millions of potential viewers across the nation. The Discovery Channel attracts viewers who enjoy nature documentaries, while ESPN serves sports fans who live in different communities that receive cable TV. There is enough demand by companies that want to sell breakfast cereal, candy, and toys to justify Nickelodeon, a cable network that features children's programs.

A television station programmer is concerned with attracting and maintaining an audience for a single channel. By contrast, a cable system programmer's objective is to keep current subscribers and recruit new ones. The two most important attractions of cable are improved signal quality and a greater number of channel choices. In television markets where homes get clear over-the-air reception, the variety of program choices is the most important consideration in deciding whether to subscribe to cable. Thus, cable systems offer MTV because teenagers will ask their parents to subscribe so that they can receive this channel. The father may feel the monthly subscriber fee is justified because he can watch baseball and basketball games carried by WTBS, the Atlanta-based superstation. Both parents may agree that the Disney Channel provides wholesome entertainment for their children.

DIFFERENCES BETWEEN BROADCAST AND CABLE MARKETS

Radio and television **markets** are composed of a cluster of counties served by stations in that area. Every station is assigned to serve a city, usually the largest in the market, which is a focal point for commerce in the area. A few stations whose signals cover two or more cities that are in close proximity use a multiple-city market identification. Whereas a TV market is defined by signal reach, a cable market is defined by the political boundaries of the city it serves, although many systems also serve adjoining municipalities and unincorporated suburban areas. In either case, the size of a broadcast or cable market is determined by its population, not its geographic area. The market indicates the scope of the audience and the facilities required to distribute programming. The options available to programmers depend on the size and thus the diversity of the audience in the market.

National (Network) versus Local Programming

Electronic media, whether at the national level or local level, must spread the cost of their programming over a large number of people. Radio, television, and cable networks have the organizational apparatus and financial backing to develop and distribute a consistent volume of high-quality programming. Thus, the key benefit of network affiliation to stations and cable systems is the provision of high-quality program fare that will attract local viewers or listeners at little or no cost. The affiliates in turn provide access to the local listeners or viewers networks must have to create a large national audience. National cable networks supply programming to cable systems, which offer it to their subscribers on designated channels. The benefit to the cable company is a program service that is desired by the subscribers. Moreover, an increasing number of cable systems are selling local advertising time, which has been made valuable by the growth in the audiences of cable network programs.

Large Markets

The larger the potential audience, the more there is to gain or lose. Media outlets in larger markets stand to make more money, but they must invest more in program material and on-air talent to be competitive. Consequently, the most talented performers and programmers usually gravitate to the largest markets, attracted by higher salaries and the opportunity to participate at the highest levels of competition.

The diversity of large populations enables programmers to identify narrow but significant segments of the audience. While the same segments of the viewing or listening audience may exist in smaller communities, their actual number is usually too small to sustain a programming effort that might appeal to them directly.

The larger the market, the greater a programmer's reliance on audience research in making decisions. The particular audience to be targeted is defined by the attributes of the consumers whom advertisers want to reach and by the level of competition among media outlets for different segments of the audience. Thus, both programmers and advertisers rely on audience research to ascertain whether specific programs will help them achieve their objectives.

Small Markets

As a rule, small communities are more homogeneous than larger ones are. The focus of community life is more centralized, people are more alike, and activities are more widely shared. There is usually less of everything in a smaller market: fewer advertisers, large businesses, automobile dealers, and media outlets. Thus, each media outlet must appeal to a general consumer or audience group in order to survive. This means that some portions of the audience may not be well served. Teenagers and young adults are often dissatisfied with the music played on a small-market station because it is not contemporary enough for their tastes. However, many adults will avoid listening if the program content does not offer them something meaningful, and so programming usually includes a bit of everything.

Moreover, smaller communities are generally less tolerant of program content that pushes at the boundaries of acceptable taste. A disc jockey on a large-market station may be able to get away with raunchy remarks, but that would be much less likely on a small-market station. Community leaders would be more likely to make their disapproval known to the station manager at church, the country club, or the weekly lodge meeting. Community leaders are usually local businesspeople who often base their decisions to advertise on whether they think their customers listen to the same stations and read the same newspapers they do. Thus, they are inclined to refuse to buy advertising if they hold a negative impression of a station. In other words, local outlets must conform to local norms if they want to win the approval of local advertisers.

Many smaller-market radio and television stations face competition from outside their markets. These rivals are usually stations in larger markets whose signals are strong enough to cover part, if not all, of the smaller-market coverage area. Since larger-market stations generally offer more attractive programming and more polished and attractive talent, they can attract a substantial number of listeners and viewers who live in the smaller market, but "out-of-market" stations do not focus on the needs and interests of local audiences. Therefore, a small-market station can be most successful by providing local service, including news and information, that is unobtainable elsewhere. That way, local audiences have a reason to identify with the station and become loyal listeners and viewers.

In some large television markets, cable systems have been successful in offering local news programming that serves communities within the larger market. A New York City TV station that serves millions of viewers cannot focus on local happenings that are of interest only to people who reside in a specific community, for instance, but a cable news program can provide its specific audience with news about the community.

SKILLS INVOLVED IN PROGRAMMING

A programmer in any electronic media outlet needs a variety of skills. A well-rounded programmer understands audience research, is computer-literate, has marketing acumen, appreciates the role of sales, has a strong sense of objectivity, possesses legal knowledge, and has the ability to work effectively with other people.

Audience Research

Creativity is not based on a formula, and there is much to be said for intuition based on experience. However, the intended results of creative

radio or television efforts can be objectively measured. Thus, among the most important qualifications of a program director is knowledge about audience research in making programming decisions.

Research is a means of reducing risk. If a producer creates a TV show that is supposed to attract women, how does she or he know that it actually will? Finding out about audience preferences may provide an answer, as may asking women to watch the show and then react to it. Similarly, a radio programmer faces decisions every week about whether to add new music recordings to the programming. Will the audience like the new offerings? One way to find out is to ask a group of typical listeners to evaluate songs before the songs are introduced on the air. This step can reduce the risk of presenting program content that the station's audience dislikes.

A program idea that was fresh and interesting a year ago may become stale, and the producer or programmer is not necessarily the first to figure that out. To minimize the possibility that the audience will abandon the program, problem areas may be identified by tracking audience reaction over a period of months. For example, if the producer is responsible for writing the jokes or humorous anecdotes used in a program, she or he is unlikely to be objective about how well they are received. Perhaps the humor has a predictability that has become tiresome. This important information, which can improve the program, isn't likely to be recognized unless audience members are asked.

Programmers want to know why certain things are done and why they work as well or poorly as they do. It simply isn't enough to assert, "I don't know much about art (or music or movies), but I know what I like." In an increasingly competitive media world, Hollywood's "golden gut" or "seat-of-the-pants" decision making will not suffice. Consequently, Part 1 of this book deals with the basics of research and then details the kinds of services offered by audience research companies before going on to discuss research that is applied to specific program decisions.

Computer Literacy

Audience research data are increasingly available to station personnel because of inexpensive but powerful personal or desktop computers which provide access to audience ratings data that can be analyzed to learn about the patterns of audience behavior. Computer literacy is a must. A broadcaster who ignores that resource will be left far behind and may not have access to such important information as audience ratings reports since the research companies are phasing out the distribution of printed copies.

Many advances have been made in computer programs that schedule commercials and program events. Several services are available to assist in the advertising sales effort by matching desired audience groups with advertising budgets to compile a proposed advertising schedule.

Computer software is a boon to programmers because it enables them to have greater control over the myriad details that must be considered in making programming decisions. Such programs help radio programmers keep track of the frequency of play, the tempo, and other characteristics important in the placement of songs in music programs.

Marketing Orientation

Just as advertisers have become increasingly sophisticated in identifying their primary consumers, electronic media programmers have developed similar acumen in identifying and attracting various segments of the audience. A successful station or cable service meets the needs of the intended audience. If the audience's desire for serious, thorough local news coverage is not being met, a station or cable outlet can identify that need and fulfill it. Similarly, if a segment of the radio audience is not being served with the kind of music it most desires, a station may be able to meet that need, assuming that the audience has the age, ethnic, gender, or economic attributes desired by advertisers, thus making it worth the station's while.

A programmer with a marketing orientation first identifies an audience and then designs program content to serve its needs and desires. Chapter 2 deals with marketing concepts and their application to programming strategies. This approach is an increasingly important aspect of programming, reflecting a shift in the approach of both radio and television in the 1990s.

Sales Orientation

A programmer's function is to develop and implement strategies to attract and maintain audiences that can be delivered to advertisers. It is virtually impossible to separate programming considerations from sales objectives, and sales departments cannot be expected to sell a poor product. Therefore, in commercial electronic media at least, advertising time sales are always the other half of programming considerations. Throughout this book we consider the influence of sales objectives on programming strategy. The job of selling time to advertisers can be made easier when the programmer understands the electronic media outlet's sales objectives and knows which audience segments are most desired by advertisers. Programming that attracts those audience groups is the easiest to sell.

Objectivity

An engineer at a Texas radio station once remarked that when he wanted to listen to music he liked, he put on a record at home. He meant that he had no business imposing his personal taste on his station's programming, and neither does any other member of the staff. A programmer's job is to determine what the target audience wants regardless of personal preference. Thus, she or he must have flexibility and versatility, coupled with objectivity, to recognize the circumstances of the market and adapt or innovate in order to attract the audience that is available. The programmer may not appreciate the musical artistry of performers such as Bon Jovi and New Kids on the Block but will play their songs because the evidence provided by research shows that targeted listeners want to hear them.

Legal Knowledge

A programmer must be aware of legal limitations and obligations. In radio, it is often the responsibility of the program director to maintain the station's **public file,** a collection of documents pertaining to station ownership, program proposals, and other license-related materials the FCC requires stations to make available to the public during business hours. The program director is also the management person usually charged with ensuring that the station is in compliance with regulations concerning contests, **payola** ("under-the-table" payments to disc jockeys from promoters to play their records), and **plugola,** which is the acceptance of under-the-table payments to on-air personalities to "plug" products without the usual commercial announcement.

People Skill

At radio stations, the program director is often in charge of hiring as well as supervising the on-air personnel. In any medium, the programmer must be able to communicate effectively with all members of the staff, since the news director or sales director's objectives may interfere with the program director's plan to offer listeners a particular blend of music and information. Until they are resolved, such conflicts have a negative effect on the station and the impression it makes to the members of its potential audience.

ETHICS: THE PROGRAMMER'S RESPONSIBILITY

Many people live by a double standard, and broadcasters are no exception (Box 1-1). Even sensitive general managers on commercial TV have approved broadcasts of professional wrestling and other programs that they themselves might never watch. They may even prohibit their children from tuning in. Yet such fare is broadcast because it will attract an audience. Michael Jackson's crotch-grabbing, car-smashing scenes in his "Black or White" video were toned down after receiving much criticism, yet Fox premiered the video with much ballyhoo

---

**BOX 1-1
THE BALANCE BETWEEN RESPONSIBILITY AND PROFITABILITY**

An unethical practice occurred when a station took out an ad in the local paper in which it reproduced a copy of an audience ratings survey form. The station offered to pay people who were participating in the survey if they would bring their survey forms to the station and let station personnel fill them out.

A consulting company advised its clients to run "Nielsen family specials" during local news shows while the ratings were being measured nationally, hoping that this would induce Nielsen families to tune in those news programs. Since each family represents 800 to 1000 others in the community, ratings could be expected to rise sharply if those particular families tuned in.

Another consulting company set up "surveys" for client stations (during the ratings season, of course) in which families were asked to respond to questions about local news. They had to watch a certain station (the client station) for several nights and then answer questions about their news preferences. Of course, this attracted families with ratings diaries and meters in their homes and swelled the clients' ratings. The survey was bogus; the point was to attract Nielsen families to the client's news program.

A radio station sent out a survey/promotional flier in an envelope marked "Audit Department." An eagle emblem helped convince people that the Internal Revenue Service was making an inquiry. Nearly everyone opened the envelope.

Why were such unethical activities allowed to happen? What are the constraints against those who engage in such conduct? Is there an enlightened self-interest that every programmer should apply to similar situations? ∎

Calvin and Hobbes   by Bill Watterson

FIGURE 1-4   *Calvin and Hobbes © 1986 Watterson. Dist. by Universal Press Syndicate. Reprinted with permission. All rights reserved.*

and the original version was run on MTV even though many people who had watched the video thought that some of its scenes were close to pornographic and that others appeared to promote senseless violence.

The need to decide whether to include or reject records for air play on the basis of their lyrics comes up often at radio stations. Pop songs have frequently been criticized for glorifying sexual activity and drug use, and many television programs include violence or sexual content. Every programmer must consider whether material may be deeply offensive or even harmful to members of the audience and if it should be broadcast or cablecast.

A different kind of decision involves choosing whether to schedule a critically acclaimed drama or news program regardless of the probability that it will attract only a small audience. Enlightened electronic media programmers feel their stations, networks, and cable systems can provide at least an occasional service that is above the usual level of quality (Figure 1-5). Presenting extraordinary programs, whether artistic or informative, is a way of giving something back to a community that has supported the station or cable service.

A survey by *Electronic Media* revealed that many people in the electronic media industry seem to be saying, "Can't we somehow have less greed, sex and violence, and still make profits?"[11] The question of how to conduct one's business in a responsible or ethical manner is always countered by the necessity of making programming decisions that will attract and maintain audiences. These contradictions face every programmer who is trying to hold to a standard for conduct.

A responsible operator will not hesitate to take a stand when the situation calls for it. There are role models among the many broadcasters and cable system managers who not only live up to high standards but help set them for the industry. For example, some stations produce and broadcast special reports on issues pertaining to their communities. If a TV station schedules a half-hour program about its city's troubled school system during prime time, it surely will lose money. Why, then, should the station make that sacrifice? The apparent answer is that its

"...So then I said: "Shares? ratings? Who cares, this show has cultural values."

FIGURE 1-5 *Reprinted by permission of* **BROADCASTING** Magazine, *December 10, 1990.* © *1990 by Cahners Publishing Company.*

management is concerned about a problem in the community it serves and is willing to put its money where its mouth is.

A few years ago a CBS Television Network affiliate refused to broadcast a rerun of the Edward R. Murrow documentary *Harvest of Shame,* citing its controversial nature (even though the original broadcast had been made more than 10 years earlier). The manager of the market's NBC affiliate agreed to broadcast the program at 9 p.m. on Saturday night, giving this outstanding piece of television journalism much greater exposure than it would have received if it had been broadcast when scheduled by CBS.

If the choice is between maximizing profit and maintaining integrity, some programmers will go for the program content that seems to appeal to the greatest number of viewers or listeners regardless of its bad taste or the effect it may have on people who listen or watch. However, other programmers take a higher road. Responsible radio programmers avoid the use of vulgarities and contests that require participants to demean themselves to win money. Responsible TV programmers consider carefully whether sexually

explicit content is warranted and stop short of scheduling programs that exploit sensational subjects. This is not being prudish but maintaining a standard that respects the sensibilities of the audience.

Critical standards are important to educated people. Each person has definitions of beauty, quality, and worth in virtually all things. Such standards change with maturation and experience, but largely they are taught either formally (Music Appreciation 101) or informally through the influence of parents, friends, and business associates. Still, in the final analysis, a programmer's decision to include or discard program content is most often made on the basis of its effectiveness in attracting a specific audience (often as large an audience as possible), not its quality as the critic sees it. A responsible programmer must be willing to allow critical standards to supersede the need to attract an audience and deliver it to advertisers. Public service and a commitment to quality are ways to develop a positive image that can pay off in greater audience loyalty and advertiser support in the long run.

WHY STUDY PROGRAMMING?

Whether a person wishes to become a general manager, embark on a sales career, or produce programs for the electronic media, attracting and maintaining audiences is at the heart of the process. Programming knowledge will serve readers in the same way that acquiring performance skills, understanding management concepts, and knowing about regulatory demands and constraints will enhance readers' perspective on the field. Thus, this book's objective is to provide a solid grounding in the basic principles of electronic media programming.

The term "program director" may be overly narrow, especially for television. An increasing number of television stations have eliminated this position, giving most of the responsibilities to the general manager or incorporating programming in a larger marketing and promotion department. Regardless of any organizational shifts, both radio and television programmers are increasingly involved in promotion and marketing. Audience research is an integral responsibility. Moreover, programming decisions usually involve costs. In television especially, program acquisition is very expensive and pro-

motional campaigns require budgetary approval, which directly involves the general manager. Thus the label "program director" is just that—a convenient way to succinctly indicate the *process* of programming a radio or television station, a cable system, or a network.

SUMMARY

Electronic media outlets provide many choices that serve the particular interests of a variety of viewers and listeners. This variety of program choices is available in part because the low cost of radio and TV receivers has made them plentiful. We have become a nation of individual listeners and are rapidly become individual viewers as well.

Audiences are increasingly segmented into different categories based on age and sex as well as demographic considerations such as place of residence, income level, and occupational status because advertisers want to reach the consumer groups that are most likely to purchase their products and services. Programmers must bear in mind the diversity of viewer and listener tastes and interests; the audiences desired by advertisers, who constitute the source of station and broadcast revenues and a major source of cable network and cable system revenues; and the availability of alternative programs as they look for more narrowly defined groups in the potential audience. As audience composition changes during the day, programmers adapt by appealing to the viewers and listeners who are available.

Radio is a portable and individual medium. Moreover, its programming is localized in that stations usually orient their programming to a specific geographic area. Programmers adjust to changes in the composition of the audience throughout the day. Unlike television, which schedules programs in half-hour or full-hour periods, most radio programming is conceived in

3-hour or 4-hour blocks with a steady stream of music recordings, advertisements, announcements, and other brief segments mixed together into a consistent program sound that is available all day.

Cable television is not programmed as broadcast stations are. Instead, cable operators are concerned with the selection of program services, including off-air TV station signals, basic cable networks, and premium or pay services in the channels available on their systems. Their objective is not to attract and maintain audiences but to attract and maintain subscribers to the system.

There are a number of important influences on programming decisions. They include salability, or whether the program attracts the kind of audience desired by advertisers. Programs that cost more than they can make in advertising sales are not a good choice even if they attract large audiences. The nature of the programming offered by competitors also must be taken into account. Sometimes it is more prudent to settle for a smaller audience than to challenge a strong competitor directly. Management policy may dictate that some programming is to be emphasized or avoided. For instance, management may feel that certain program content is harmful to the station or network's image even though it may attract a large audience.

Other influences on programming include program trends. Whether they appear in television detective shows or radio music formats such as Disco, trends eventually run their course and audiences tire of them. Furthermore, program concepts do not always transfer from one market to another, and ideas that are successful in one place may not work as well in another place because of differences in audience composition and interests those audiences have.

Influences on programming also include the technical facilities available to a media outlet. A station's power or frequency assignment may limit programming options. Although the density of the population in the area being served is the single most important consideration, the strength of the signal also affects the number of listeners or viewers who can tune in. Some television stations rely on carriage of their signals on cable TV systems in order to reach an audience large enough to be attractive to advertisers. In addition, the regulatory climate affects the kinds of programs a station includes in its schedule. Finally, groups of audience members organize to try to change program content they find objectionable. These groups make their feelings known through pressure on politicians, regulators, and advertisers, whom they threaten to boycott for sponsoring offensive programs.

Networks operate in a national market, providing programs that are attractive to audiences. This is a valuable service to local outlets because networks have the administrative and financial resources to originate schedules of high-quality programs.

The larger the market, the more intense and diverse the competition. Small-market audiences are usually conservative, and programmers typically emphasize general-appeal programming that reflects the narrow focus of community values.

A modern programmer must understand audience research, be computer-literate, possess a marketing orientation, appreciate the objectives of delivering audiences to advertisers, be objective in evaluating programming situations and coming to conclusions, know the regulatory requirements of the medium, and work well with the other members of the staff.

Programmers have a responsibility to establish a standard of quality even while they attempt to attract and maintain audiences. Responsibility to the sensitivities and taste of the audience, though, should supersede the temptation to maximize an audience by pandering to its base instincts. Moreover, a responsible programmer is willing to occasionally schedule programs of higher than usual critical quality in spite of the ongoing pressure for audience size.

SUGGESTED READINGS

We hope readers will want to learn as much as they can about the aspects of programming discussed in each of the chapters that follow. To help in that process, further readings are suggested to help readers explore each chapter in greater depth.

Since Chapter 1 is an overview, we suggest some general sources that follow issues and trends in programming. The publications described here are important resources for industry leaders. Virtually every successful broadcaster or cable operator keeps his or her ear to the ground by keeping up with news and reports published in trade publications. In other words, part of their success can be attributed to knowing more than the competition knows.

Broadcasting is a weekly trade magazine that covers news about programming, business, and regulatory activities that affect the electronic media industry. Since its editorial offices are located in Washington, D.C., *Broadcasting* gives considerable attention to the lobbying efforts of trade organizations such as the National Association of Broadcasters and the National Cable Television Association and to the regulatory activities of Congress and the FCC. Special reports survey the state of television, broadcast journalism, radio, cable, and other aspects of the industry.

Another weekly publication, *Electronic Media,* covers much of the same ground, but with more emphasis on financial and programming news. *Electronic Media* gives particular emphasis to television programming issues and to business trends in television and cable.

Multichannel News is a weekly publication

that specializes in local and network cable sales and programming activities. It is oriented toward economic and technical developments in the cable industry.

Both *Broadcasting* and *Electronic Media* have special student subscription rates. Readers are urged to get in the habit of scanning these publications every week so that they can become knowledgeable about issues and trends in their field. Many academic departments subscribe to several trade publications, as do many college and university libraries.

NOTES

1. Sara Rimer, "Lifetime Seeks Growth by Targeting Women," *Tuscaloosa News,* Nov. 17, 1991, Sec. H, pp. 20–21.

2. Craig Leddy, "The Commercialization of Public TV," *Broadcasting,* June 23, 1986, pp. 1, 26.

3. William K. Jones, *Cases and Materials on Electronic Mass Media: Radio, Television and Cable,* 2d ed., Foundation Press, Mineola, N.Y., 1979, pp. 284–296.

4. Sydney W. Head and Christopher H. Sterling, *Broadcasting in America: A Survey of Electronic Media,* 5th ed., Houghton Mifflin, Boston, 1987, p. 471.

5. "The Radio News Conundrum: How Much Is Enough?" *Broadcasting,* Sept. 24, 1990, pp. 43–44.

6. See, for instance, "FCC Cracks Down on 'Shock Jock' Indecency," *Radio & Records,* Sept. 1, 1989, pp. 1, 32; "FCC Cleans Out the Pipeline on Indecency," *Broadcasting,* Oct. 30, 1989, pp. 28–29; "FCC Indecency Campaign Reaches New Climax," *Radio and Records,* Nov. 3, 1989, pp. 1, 34; Paul Harris, "FCC 'Decency Squads' on the Prowl Scanning Airwaves for Lewdness," *Variety,* Oct. 11, 1989, p. 171.

7. "Crusade Sets Out to Clean Up TV," *Broadcasting,* Feb. 9, 1981, p. 27.

8. "They've Been Keeping Those Cards and Letters Pouring In," *Broadcasting,* July 12, 1971, p. 47.

9. Bill Bruns and Mary Murphy, "Dirty Words, Racy Pictures . . . Is TV Going Too Far? *TV Guide,* Nov. 10, 1990, pp. 12–20.

10. Doug Hill, "Is TV Sex Getting Bolder?" *TV Guide,* Aug. 8, 1987, pp. 2–5.

11. "Ethical Dilemmas," *Electronic Media,* Feb. 29, 1988, p. 1.

CHAPTER 2

Programming as Marketing

WHAT IS MARKETING?

Electronic media outlets operate in a very competitive environment. For example, even in small markets several radio stations may compete for listeners and advertising dollars. In television, the traditional configuration of three network-affiliated stations per market has given way to a proliferation of independent stations, the upstart Fox Television Network, cable networks, video rentals, video games, and backyard satellite dishes. People don't spend more time with electronic media just because another radio station goes on the air or a new cable TV service is made available. If they turn to a new or improved service, it is usually at the expense of an existing one.

As Figure 2-1 illustrates, the competitive environment of both television and radio is increasingly crowded with options for media consumers. Thus, every outlet must establish and maintain an identity in the increasingly crowded field of choices available to listeners and viewers.

This competition has been accompanied by an increased availability of knowledge about audi-ences. Advances in personal computers have made it possible for any station or advertising agency to have access to audience data for making programming or advertising decisions. As discussed in later chapters, marketing analysts have gone beyond traditional *demographics* (descriptors of the age and sex of audience members) to develop geographic, psychographic, product consumption, and media use information. Advertisers now identify highly specific portions of the total audience as those most likely to purchase their goods and services. Instead of paying a high price to advertise on a very popular program that attracts a general audience, advertisers increasingly buy advertising time on more specialized or narrow-appeal programs. While these audiences may be smaller, they are composed primarily of individuals who are likely to purchase a given product. For example, the makers of denture adhesives know that most purchases of these products are made by men and women over age 55. Consequently, these advertisers place their messages in programs, such as the network evening news, that attract large numbers of older viewers or listeners. Sim-

FIGURE 2-1 The electronic media competitive environment. (*From* Broadcast Marketing and Technology News, *August 27, 1990, p. 39. © National Association of Broadcasters, 1990. Reprinted with permission.*)

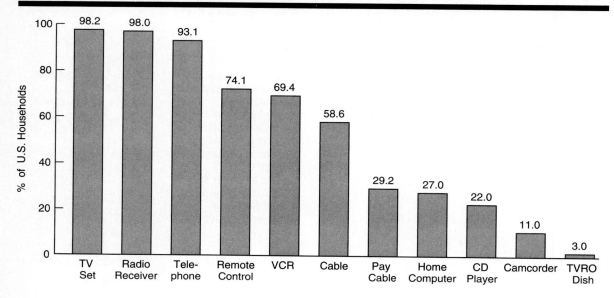

ilarly, toy and candy advertisements appear on Saturday morning children's programs because the audiences they attract are the prime consumers of such products.

On Saturday morning children constitute a large portion of the viewing audience that makes itself available to watch TV. However, later in the day, stations or networks compete for larger, more general audiences by scheduling programming that will appeal to the broader interests of those in the potential audience. For instance, sports programs are presented on Saturday afternoon because of their traditional appeal to male viewers; men are more likely to be at home and available to watch TV during this time period. Other channels may present movies that attract older viewers who do not want to watch sports.

Because only a few outlets can attract a majority of the audience at any one time, some services focus on narrow program interests. During the week, for instance, some stations offer cartoons to children during the afternoon even though children are not the biggest available audience segment. That way, they don't have to compete directly with *Geraldo* and *Oprah Winfrey* in what would probably be a losing battle to attract an adult audience. Stations and other electronic media outlets have discovered that they can prosper by conducting marketing research, identifying advertisers and audiences, and bringing those groups together by promoting their services, which consist of providing programming that serves audiences and identifying the audiences that advertisers need.[1]

The marketing process can be illustrated with an example from another field. IBM is not principally in the computer-manufacturing business but in the knowledge business. That company's slogan, "Machines should work. People should think," says it all. Knowledge can be gathered rapidly through the use of computers. A computer is capable of making rapid calculations and cross-checks, but it has no capacity for understanding or insight. The machine cannot perform a useful task until a thinking person gives it orders and assesses the raw data it provides.

Human input is necessary to reach a conclusion. Similarly, electronic media outlets are not in the advertising sales business or the cable subscriber business but in the entertainment and information business. A station can broadcast programs or can provide recreation and information that is meaningful to audiences. The focus should not be on the product but on the perception of its benefits held by consumers.

In Chapter 1 we pointed out that the electronic media attract audiences to deliver to advertisers. That description could naturally lead to the assumption that the electronic media are in the audience delivery business, selling audiences to advertisers. While that is true, there is more to it. The audience delivery business is a limited concept since it allows for the possibility of attempting to sell something that people do not particularly want. A marketing approach, by contrast, assumes that the electronic media are in the people satisfaction business. If the programming satisfies peoples' needs and wants, they will be on board to be delivered to advertisers.

Marketing versus Selling

From a *selling standpoint,* a television station sells advertising time to manufacturers, stores, and other businesses. From a *marketing standpoint,* an electronic media outlet's sales force provides access to an advertiser's targeted consumers. The marketing concept is expressed by a philosophy of programming in which audience wants and needs are satisfied. Consequently, a programmer's activities are devoted to finding out what the audience wants and then satisfying those wants while making a profit over the long run.[2]

To illustrate, some independent television stations broadcast a local news report at 10 p.m. Eastern time. The programmers at those stations have discovered that a sufficient number of people in the television audience want to watch a local newscast but prefer to go to bed earlier than the late newscast at the customary time of 11 p.m. It's difficult for many working people to stay up until 11:30 at night if they have to get up the next day at 6 a.m. Thus, the independent station's newscast, which is finished by 10:30 or 11:00 p.m., fulfills the audience's desire for information while accommodating its need to get to bed at a reasonable hour. Understanding this, the Atlanta independent WGNX TV uses the slogan "All the news you need at a time you really want it" in its 10 p.m. newscast.

As you can see in Table 2-1, which compares a selling orientation with a marketing orientation, some important distinctions can be applied to programming the electronic media. The programmer as marketer emphasizes customer (audience) wants instead of attempting to sell the audience on the benefits of a previously produced program. The marketing-oriented programmer creates programming after determining the audience's needs and wants. Instead of being concerned with attracting the largest possible audience, this programmer's priority is to achieve the highest possible profit level. Thus, by identifying and serving the needs and wants of a more narrow portion of the total audience and being able to deliver that segment of poten-

tial buyers to advertisers, a station or network service may actually reap a greater profit than it would if it attempted to compete directly with other electronic media outlets for the largest number of people in the whole audience.

A marketing-oriented programmer thinks in terms of establishing an identify and adapting to changing circumstances to maintain the loyalty of the audience. In other words, the programmer anticipates the inevitability of change and is ready when shifts in audience needs and wants occur. The *Tonight* show serves as a good example. Even though Johnny Carson was older than many of his regular viewers, the program adapted over the years. The guests included many performers who were popular with younger members of the broadcast audience, and the subject matter reflected the prevailing attitudes of the audience. A fashion show of scanty lingerie styled by Mr. Fredrick's of Hollywood would not have been presented in the 1960s, but few people would consider that scandalous these days. When Carson retired, a number of important changes were made to increase the appeal of the program to younger viewers. For example, the new permanent host, Jay Leno, has a wide appeal to people of college age. Similarly, longtime band leader Doc Severinson was replaced by Bradford Marsalis, who has a much younger following.

Segmentation and Differentiation

There are many approaches to marketing. For our purposes, the important ones in terms of fulfilling audience needs and wants are product differentiation and market segmentation. **Product differentiation** promotes the differences between the seller's product and those of competitors. In many cases the distinction may lie in the packaging or design. It has been shown in a number of blind taste tests, for example, that most consumers cannot identify their favorite brand of beer by taste. However, they have developed a preferred brand by associating certain attributes with that beer, such as the macho gusto that is associated with former professional

TABLE 2-1   SELLING AND MARKETING

Selling	Marketing
Emphasis is on the product.	Emphasis is on customers' wants.
Company first makes the product and then figures out how to sell it.	Company first determines customers' wants and then figures out how to make and deliver a product to satisfy those wants.
Management is sales volume–oriented.	Management is profit-oriented.
Planning is short run–oriented in terms of today's products and markets.	Planning is long run–oriented in terms of new products, tomorrow's markets, and future growth.
Stresses needs of seller.	Stresses wants of buyers.

SOURCE: From William J. Stanton, Michael J. Etzel, and Bruce J. Walker, *Fundamentals of Marketing*, 9th ed. Copyright © 1991. Used by permission of McGraw-Hill, Inc.

athletes who extol the virtues of drinking Miller Lite: It tastes great and is less filling. Thus, advertising slogans can create distinctions among beer brands.

In a **market segmentation** approach, products are specifically developed for smaller, homogeneous groups in the market. Whereas product differentiation seeks to distinguish a product within a broad, generalized market, market segmentation identifies a limited market and attempts to penetrate it in depth.[3] Market segments are subgroups of a broader market that have different needs, preferences, or buying patterns. Segments of the automobile market, for example, include economy car, luxury car, and import car buyers as well as those who choose to lease a car.[4]

Electronic media outlets and programs are analogous to products. They can be differentiated, and portions of the audience can be identified, or segmented, and served by particular programming services. Since it has a fairly broad demographic appeal, a station that uses a Contemporary Hit Radio (CHR) format may attempt to differentiate itself from the other radio stations in the market on the basis of zany morning personalities who tell jokes and present humorous skits and stunts. Formats with more narrow demographic appeals, such as Album-Oriented Rock and Black Appeal, will probably market themselves on the basis of market segmentation. They will identify a portion of the audience, such as men 18 to 34 years of age, and present music and other program content that has a special appeal to those listeners. A station attempting to segment the African-American population will play the music favored by that audience and present news and information of particular concern to the black community.

Most broadcast stations use a combination of segmentation and product differentiation in their marketing strategies. Radio stations typically target fairly specific audiences because they can compete best by being most popular or second most popular in a specific segment of the audience. The tastes and interests of the narrow group can be specifically served by ignoring the needs and wants of other segments. In other words, attempting to satisfy everyone usually satisfies no one, and so stations generally segment the audience in order to attract a loyal following among a portion of the total possible audience. However, within formats, competing stations must differentiate their programs in order to attract listeners. That is where stations' emphasis on personalities or "much more music" or "fewer commercial interruptions" comes into play.

Television also uses the techniques of market segmentation and product differentiation. Product differentiation is particularly important in distinguishing news shows. Local news programs have broad demographic appeal, and the majority of the available viewers watch them. Therefore, television stations must attempt to differentiate their local news programs from those of competing stations. The most obvious difference is that each station has a distinctive anchor team, or group of news personalities. If a station's anchor is an older individual who has been in the market for a long time, the approach may be to stress the anchor's experience or deep roots in the community. Another station with an especially personable sports anchor may stress his or her knowledge of sports. Yet another station may place great emphasis on the knowledge and qualifications of its weather forecaster, pointing out that he or she holds a master's degree or even a Ph.D. in meteorology.

Similarly, differentiation strategies are used in situations where the audience is narrowly defined. A limited audience makes itself available to watch the morning TV news shows, for example. After a poor showing for several years against *Today* on NBC and *Good Morning America* on ABC, the CBS news president, Howard Stringer, acknowledged that CBS was going to do what NBC was doing, only better.[5] Each of the morning news programs uses the same basic formula of news, celebrity interviews, weather forecasts, and interviews with newsmakers. By hiring Harry Smith and Kathleen Sullivan, who was later replaced by Paula Zahn, the *CBS Morning News* was supposed to become a more attractive program to morning viewers. All three networks target the same audience segments in the morning, but each one hopes that it can show audience members that it is differentiating, or doing it better, through set design, the personalities of the hosts, the type and appeal of guests who appear on the program, and the length of program segments.

Targeting an Audience

If you look on the magazine rack in a news stand at any grocery store, airport, or drugstore, you will see many specialized publications appealing to interests from computers and hiking to body building and needlepoint. In the same way that general-appeal magazines such as *Life, Look,* and the *Saturday Evening Post* have given way to narrow-interest publications, electronic media programming has also evolved in terms of targeting.

The **target audience** is the segment or segments of the audience that the programmer has decided to try to attract. This target should be selected from the *potential audience*, or the identifiable demographic groups that make themselves available to watch or listen. As the audience changes during the course of the day, the target audience may also change as some audience members leave and others begin to listen or view. Other determinants of the target audience include the groups of audience members that are most desired by advertisers.

Today most radio stations attempt to attract a fairly specific segment of the audience. After the general audience abandoned radio for television in the 1950s, many radio stations narrowed their programming to rock 'n' roll music to reach teenagers. As formats were refined, they began to appeal to more specific groups. Teenagers and 35-year-olds may not like the same kinds of music, and some listeners like Country music while others want Easy-Listening tunes. At the same time, advertisers have become increasingly aware that narrow-appeal publications and electronic media outlets are often more efficient vehicles for reaching their most likely customers.

Increasingly, television programming follows a targeting strategy to establish an identity that attracts identifiable segments of the total viewing audience. Certain kinds of television programs have a narrow appeal. Sports programs are more attractive to men than they are to most women, as are specialized programs on fishing and hunting. Cooking shows appeal to men and women who enjoy culinary activities. Home shopping cable channels appeal mainly to women. The programming offered by the Nashville Network (TNN) appeals primarily to viewers who like Country music.

Target and Core Audiences

After languishing in third place for several seasons, in 1981 the NBC Television Network began to attempt to attract a prime-time audience particularly desired by advertisers: affluent men and women age 25 to 49. NBC's new prime-time lineup in 1981 included *Remington Steele, Hill Street Blues, St. Elsewhere,* and *Cheers.* These series were not watched by the majority of the total viewers during their time periods, but they attracted audiences prized by advertisers.[6] Although NBC did not attract the largest overall prime-time audience for several seasons, the network was able to establish itself as a desirable advertising buy because its programs could deliver the *right* audience.

The ABC Television Network has followed a similar strategy of targeting younger viewers for years, most recently with such shows as *The Wonder Years* and *Full House.* CBS, though, has had a continuing problem attracting younger audience groups: Its programming appeals to an older audience which has its strongest base in less-populated, more rural counties. Among the most successful of CBS's current programs are *Murder, She Wrote* and *60 Minutes,* which both attract a predominantly older audience. In an attempt to turn a vice into a virtue, CBS now argues that since the population is aging, advertisers increasingly target older viewers.[7]

By contrast, Fox's success has come through a strategy of scheduling programs that appeal to younger viewers. Shows such as *Beverly Hills 90210* and *In Living Color* have been supported by advertisers because their audiences are composed of prime advertising target groups. Thus, as Box 2-1 indicates, CBS has tried to draw a core audience of older, more rural viewers while Fox has been successful at targeting a narrow segment of the total potential audience.

As Figure 2-2 suggests, the demographic groups that constitute **core audience** may or may not be the **target audience.** Thus, a program that gathers a loyal regular audience dominated by men and women age 55 and over may not be particularly desirable from the standpoint of many potential advertisers, but it is an audience. The programmer is faced with a dilemma: Continue to serve this group or change the programming to attract another kind of audience. However, there is always a risk of alienating the loyal (core) audience and failing to attract another group.

Put another way, the challenge is to increase **light viewers** or listeners (or convert nonviewers or nonlisteners) without alienating the core audience. Since **heavy viewers** and listeners are already attending programs about as much as they can, they offer only a limited potential for increasing audience size.

The conservative approach is to capitalize on what one has (the existing core) rather than abandon it altogether. In this case the programmer tries to expand the appeal of the program in subtle increments. If the change is gradual, core audience members will not be driven away, at least not immediately. The idea is to develop a larger audience by attracting other people who previously did not find the program appealing or were unaware of it as a viewing or listening option.

A bolder go-for-broke approach in targeting a different audience may be the best strategy under some circumstances. A radio station with an Easy-Listening music format may have a loyal but very small audience. By changing to a Country music format, it may be able to attract a much larger audience. However, if the lush orchestration of Easy-Listening music and relaxing ballads is presented along with Reba McEntire and Travis Tritt, neither the original listeners nor the potential new audience will be satisfied. In such a case, the programmer is likely to make a break with the past and start anew.

THE MARKETING ENVIRONMENT

Nonnegotiable Forces

The forces at work in nature shape the landscape and affect the kind of plant and animal life that exists in an environment. Similarly, the marketing environment in which a station or cable outlet exists influences the nature of that station or outlet's programming. The marketing environment is defined by the demographics of the potential audience the station or cable channel serves, the economic conditions in which this population lives, social and cultural influences, political and regulatory forces, technological de-

FIGURE 2-2   Core audience.

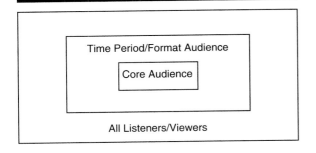

velopments, the technical limitations of the station or cable system, and the attributes of the competing outlets. These forces are not under the programmer's control, but they must be taken into account in setting up a strategy for the station.[8]

Demography   Although the age and ethnic mix of the audience in each market are characteristics that cannot be changed, they are very important in defining the available audience and determining programming strategy. Audiences watch or listen very much as they purchase products. One can't expect to make a profit by selling suspenders or Batman posters unless there is sufficient consumer demand for them. Thus, a programmer who operates the only radio station serving a farming community will probably want to schedule grain and livestock market reports, along with extensive reports on the weather. Moreover, the music presented on the station should reflect the tastes of the *majority* in the area being served. If their needs and wants are ignored, it is not very likely that the station will prosper since the minority that does like the narrow programming content will not be a big

enough audience to be useful to advertisers in the community.

Ethnic Characteristics   Many programs and music types appeal to a broad spectrum of listeners, but the ethnic composition of the market may suggest that certain kinds of programs will have greater appeal. Figure 2-3 shows the top black TV markets in the United States. In such markets, TV programs such as *A Different World, Amen,* and *227* that are known to attract large black audiences will probably be successful.[9] Similarly, radio formats such as Black Appeal and Urban Contemporary may also have great success.

The impact of the ethnic mix of the audience is apparent in southwestern states, where a number of radio stations broadcast in Spanish and play Latino music and where there are Spanish-language television stations. However, this is not limited to Texas, Arizona, and Los Angeles, the largest Hispanic market (Figure 2-4). In Chicago, the fifth largest Hispanic market, an independent TV station, WBBS TV, programs in Spanish, as do stations that serve New York, including WNJU TV, Linden, and WRTV, Patterson, New Jersey. Hispanics constitute a suffi-

FIGURE 2-3   Top black TV markets. *[Copyright 1992 Crain Communications Inc. Reprinted from Electronic Media (July 8, 1991) with permission.]*

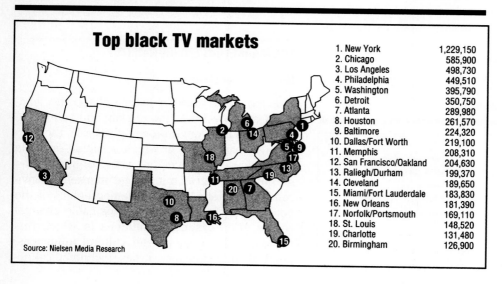

Top black TV markets	
1. New York	1,229,150
2. Chicago	585,900
3. Los Angeles	498,730
4. Philadelphia	449,510
5. Washington	395,790
6. Detroit	350,750
7. Atlanta	289,980
8. Houston	261,570
9. Baltimore	224,320
10. Dallas/Fort Worth	219,100
11. Memphis	208,310
12. San Francisco/Oakland	204,630
13. Raliegh/Durham	199,370
14. Cleveland	189,650
15. Miami/Fort Lauderdale	183,830
16. New Orleans	181,390
17. Norfolk/Portsmouth	169,110
18. St. Louis	148,520
19. Charlotte	131,480
20. Birmingham	126,900

Source: Nielsen Media Research

Top Hispanic TV markets	
1. Los Angeles	1,168,8000
2. New York	895,080
3. Miami/Fort Lauderdale	333,510
4. San Francisco/Oakland	260,940
5. Chicago	260,080
6. San Antonio	256,300
7. Houston	212,350
8. Albuquerque/Santa Fe	180,070
9. Harlingen/Weslaco	157,640
10. El Paso	139,070
11. Phoenix	126,210
12. Dallas/Fort Worth	125,990
13. San Diego	122,920
14. Fresno/Visalia	119,240
15. Sacramento/Stockton	116,170
16. Denver	87,440
17. Corpus Christi	87,420
18. Tucson	68,060
19. Philadelphia	67,690
20. Tampa/St. Petersburg	57,140

Source: Nielsen Media Research

FIGURE 2-4   Top Hispanic TV markets. *[Copyright 1992 Crain Communications Inc. Reprinted from* **Electronic Media** *(July 8, 1991) with permission.]*

ciently large population within these markets to warrant specialized programming that meets their needs and wants. Such programming is valuable to advertisers who specifically wish to reach Hispanic consumers.

Age   A radio property may serve an area, such as Pensacola, Florida, that has a moderate climate and is near a military base with PX privileges for retired military personnel. Such a market may be populated by large numbers of retired people for whom Big-Band, Nostalgia, and Easy-Listening music formats have great appeal. The wants and needs of most persons age 55 and over will not be met by hard rock music.

Older audiences watch more news and public affairs programs as well as more nature programs and other documentary shows, and audiences for religious programs are also generally older. If such needs can be identified, one of the stations in the market will try to satisfy them through its programming. The viewing and listening preferences of older audience members are taking on increasing importance with the "graying" of our society. The baby boomers, those born between 1945 and 1960, have always

represented a large chunk of the population. As this group moves into older age brackets, programmers will respond to the changes in its programming preferences. Also, the notion that older consumers don't spend as much money as younger people do is being abandoned, making an older audience increasingly attractive to advertisers. The financial clout of people age 50 and over is expanding while that of younger groups is shrinking.[10]

Audience Appeals   It is the programming that attracts specific audience segments, and different kinds of programs appeal to a greater or lesser extent to particular audience segments. Thus, *audience appeals,* or the characteristics of programming that make it attractive to specific audience groups, include fulfillment of an audience group's desire for information, its ability to identify with the personalities of program characters, or its representation of a particular way of life. As Box 2-2 indicates, older TV viewers are attracted to news magazine programs such as *60 Minutes* and are also heavy viewers of local news programs. Younger viewers like *Roseanne* and *A Different World* and can identify with the charac-

**BOX 2-2
PROGRAM APPEALS**

Sitcoms (situation comedies) attract the largest audiences of any current program type. They tend to appeal to children (age 2 to 11) and teens (age 12 to 17) but also have the heaviest adult viewing, particularly among women 18 to 49.

Informational programs have little appeal to children and teens but have high appeal to older adult (50 and above) viewers. In addition to news programs, older viewers are especially attracted to nature documentaries like those shown on the Discovery Channel.

Dramas such as *Knot's Landing, Dallas,* and *China Beach* have predominantly female audiences, appealing about equally to younger (age 18 to 49) and older (50 and over) women, but also attract older men (50 and over).

Police/action drama series such as *Hunter* and *In the Heat of the Night* have a broad appeal among men and women of all ages. Some, such as *The A-Team, Knight Rider,* and *Dukes of Hazzard,* have attracted large audiences among children and teens. A fair number of males 18 to 49 were also in the audience, no doubt attracted because their children were enthusiastic and because there was no better action alternative at the time of the broadcast.

Sports programs, particularly golf, tennis, and professional and college football, attract upper-income viewers, notably men. NFL football attracts a large audience of men age 18 to 49 with men 50 and over also in fairly high attendance. Baseball, except for the World Series, attracts a lower-income audience than do some of the other major sports. Female and teen viewing is lower here than it is for other program types. ∎

ters. Conversely, it is not hard to understand why older viewers more readily identify with the mannerisms, values, and problems of the characters in *Matlock, Empty Nest*, and *Golden Girls.*

There are times during the day when narrow-appeal programming is feasible because of who is available to listen or watch. As the hour grows later, older viewers go to bed. Also, the majority of the adult audience abandons radio during the evening hours, making nighttime radio largely the province of younger listeners, and so most popular music stations present youth-oriented program content at night. Rock music is directed toward the tastes of teenagers, and the comments of disc jockeys are aimed at this young audience.

One television station in a midsize market scheduled reruns of Groucho Marx's *You Bet Your Life* during its late-night period. Since most viewers have left the audience by 11 p.m. and prices for advertising are lower, the programming to be aired cannot be costly if the station is to achieve a profit during this time period. The idea worked for several reasons. *You Bet Your Life* was obtained cheaply. Sponsorship by a

pizza delivery service gave this otherwise poor revenue period a financial base. The sponsor, who wanted to sell more pizza, was attracted by an audience that included a large contingent of young people because a major university, a large insurance company, and the state government were located in the market. Young people were seen as more likely to order pizza, especially at night. Furthermore, the desired audience of younger viewers was appreciative of the humor offered in the series.

Television programs vary in their appeal to different demographic groups. A series's demographics can be influenced by its story line, the time period in which it is aired, competing programs, the personalities or cast involved in the episodes, promotion, and other factors. Aside from those influences, the generalizations discussed in Box 2-2, which are represented graphically in Figure 2-5, usually apply.

Regional Characteristics Similarities can be seen in most markets across the country. However, a programmer must look beyond the demographic traits of an audience to be effective in

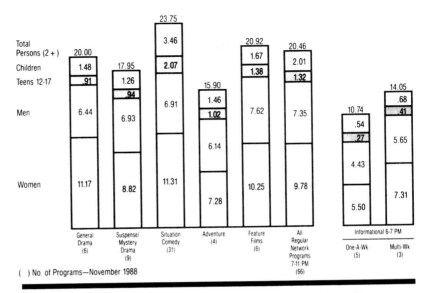

Regularly Scheduled Network Programs 7-11 PM (Average Minute Audiences)

FIGURE 2-5   Audience composition by selected program type. (*From* Report on Television. *Used by permission of Nielsen Media Research.*)

some circumstances. For example, the Tex-Mex influence of south Texas and other border states has created a distinctive kind of Hispanic music. Similarly, there is a distinctive kind of south Texas Country music, as played by Al Dean and the All Stars. This musical style has received little following outside that part of the state except for occasional airplay late at night on WBAP-AM in Dallas. Likewise, polka music can be heard regularly on some stations in Wisconsin because of the large German population there.

While there are people in every population who enjoy fishing, hunting, and other outdoor pursuits, frequent participation in these activities may be more characteristic of certain markets. In areas where the weather supports winter sports activities, snow skiers are interested in the powder reports, particularly as the weekend approaches. Similarly, in regions within driving distance of beaches, sun worshipers, weekend vacationers, and fishers are interested in fishing and weather reports. If there is local significance in such information, the station can capitalize on it through its programming strategy.

Audience Changes during the Day   In the early morning hours, television viewing is dominated by adults, primarily women 55 and over, who watch morning news programs. As Figure 2-6 shows, by 7 a.m. the audience becomes larger, with children watching cartoons and reruns of situation comedies, mostly on independent stations. After 8 a.m. the audience becomes predominantly female and less affluent, since many of the men and working women in double-income households have departed for work. From midmorning through midafternoon most of the audience is older and female. The men in the audience are predominantly age 55 and above. The number of women 35 to 54 in the audience declines, since more of them are in the work force. At about 3:30 children rejoin the audience as they arrive home from school, and some working adults also come home. Between 4 and 6 p.m. viewing levels rise from 30 percent to 50 percent of all households. This audience is composed largely of older women, who watch news and talk programs, and children, who watch sitcom reruns and cartoons.

As more people enter the audience after finishing dinner or arriving home from work, the percentage of *households using TV (HUT)* swells. By 8 p.m. Eastern time, as Figure 2-6 shows, the HUT has reached about 60 percent of the potential households. The audience peaks at around 9 p.m., with older viewers and children leaving to go to bed. A sharp drop begins about 10 p.m., continuing through the end of prime time at 11 p.m., and occurs again at the end of the late evening local news. The decline after 11:30 continues to be sharp, falling at 1 a.m. to about 15 percent of the potential viewing audience.

Programming strategies for both radio and television can be affected by the commuting time of large numbers of audience members. Some radio stations provide traffic and weather information more frequently if their programmers know that the audience will tune in only briefly and wants that type of information. Other stations may provide that information less often so as not to irritate listeners who may hear such reports two or more times during a block of listening. If many individuals are trapped in their automobiles for an hour or more during morning drive time, the programming can be adjusted to appeal to those listeners. During the afternoon drive time programmers adjust their offerings to appeal to listeners who must again endure rush hour traffic after a long day at work.

Television stations plan their schedules according to who is entering the audience at different times. Most stations in the largest markets schedule periods of early-evening local news that often run 2 or more hours. These programs are typically broken into distinctive segments, even though much of the content consists of repeated or updated reports. The individual arriving home between 4:30 and 5:00 p.m. can watch the news, but so can a person who arrives home an hour later. These broadcasts are designed to appear to be fresh to those who were part of the early audience at the same time that they capture the new audience members.

Economic conditions   Economic and demographic information on the areas served by electronic media outlets is often compiled by a bureau of economic research on a university campus. In many instances these data are readily available in a campus library. Reports issued by the U.S. Bureau of the Census and by local chambers of commerce can also be helpful in understanding the economic attributes of the marketplace.

The nature and size of the audience an electronic media outlet can reach affects the advertising revenue that outlet can generate, and profitability has a direct influence on whether certain programming is affordable. Several television stations have found themselves in serious financial jeopardy because they invested in programming inventory only to find out that advertising revenues did not cover the cost of the rights to broadcast those programs. Furthermore, it is a consistent rule of thumb that the best talent can be found in the largest markets because the stations operating there have greater revenues and therefore can afford to pay higher salaries. Thus, expectations in smaller markets must be scaled

FIGURE 2-6   Percent of households using TV. (*From* What TV Ratings Really Mean. *Used by permission of Nielsen Media Research.*)

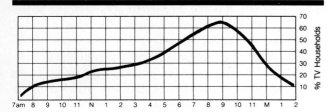

back or the programmer must be willing to hire talent with less experience. If these people have great potential, they will leave for better opportunities fairly quickly because the money just isn't available to keep them in smaller markets.

Another important insight can be gained by assessing the retail outlets in a market. If the biggest store in the market is a Wal-Mart or a K-Mart, that indicates that the majority of the local consumers buy lower-cost, less fashionable clothing and lower-priced electronic items and furniture compared with customers who shop in markets that feature large shopping malls, furniture stores, and automobile dealers. The greater the number and variety of consumer outlets that want to advertise their products and services, the more room there should be for stations to segment the audience for their advertisers. These outlets have advertising dollars to spend but will invest them only in programming that can deliver their target consumers. In small markets that are heavily dependent on agriculture, for example, stations must appeal to area farmers before local seed and feed suppliers, farm equipment dealers, banks, and other businesses will see fit to advertise.

Fewer retail outlets mean fewer advertising possibilities, and so the appeal of programming has to be more general. A program format that has wide adult appeal (e.g., age 25 to 54) will more likely be considered favorably by a potential advertiser in this type of market. In contrast, a station that targets a narrow segment, say, men age 18 to 34, simply won't reach enough people to be attractive to most advertisers.

Yet another important consideration in determining the appeal of a format is whether advertisers like it. The smaller the market size, the more important this becomes, since decision makers are more likely to be the persons who actually run local businesses. The heaviest advertisers in larger markets rely much more on research and have a more abstract conception of who their customers are. By contrast, smaller retailers deal directly with most of their customers and thus have a concrete idea of who those individuals are and what they are like. If these adver-

tisers can't personally identify with the program content, it is not likely that they will expect many potential customers to be reached by it. Thus, from a practical standpoint, stations must position themselves to appeal to advertisers as much as they appeal to audience segments.

Employment Characteristics Big factories and other employers with large numbers of shift workers in the market core have an important impact on programming during different times of the day. Workers who get off work at 2 a.m. will probably want to unwind before retiring. In some markets this allows a local TV station to schedule repeats late at night (especially of the 11 p.m. newscast) to attract this group. While this night owl audience is not nearly as large as that available during earlier hours, it can be served with little additional investment in the program product. Moreover, such an audience is easily defined as a target for potential advertisers. Though these programs might have been presented at other times during the day, it is unlikely that many in the late-night group will have seen them since these people were at work or asleep during the original broadcast.

If a community's work force has experienced layoffs, stations may have to adjust their programming strategies. The unemployment level in the market is another indicator of economic conditions and usually has a direct impact on retail merchants and their ability to advertise. As was pointed out earlier, the revenues from advertising must cover the cost of programming if a station is to prosper.

Social and cultural forces During the past few decades a number of significant societal changes have had an impact on programming decisions. For example, there are now fewer children born per family and an increased number of women are in the workplace. Also, our attitudes about what is acceptable language and which subjects can be openly discussed have changed our reaction to program content. Stations must be sensitive to whether they can—or should—present some kinds of programming content that is consonant with the new or different attitudes they can identify in the audience.

An independent TV station in a small southern market scheduled a series of movies that ran uncut during prime time. One film in the package, *Porkys*, was heavily promoted both on radio and in the local newspaper as the uncut version. Because the sexually explicit content of the movie was well known, the promotion drew the ire of members of a number of local churches, and the film was canceled. It seems likely that if the station had quietly aired this uncut product, as it had with *Animal House*, little if anything would have been said. Instead, the station's attempt to attract an audience backfired, since the program content ran counter to predominant standards in the community.

Political and regulatory forces   For more than a decade the FCC has been engaged in deregulation. In a movement that had its start in the late 1970s, the FCC relaxed or abandoned many of its rules and regulations. For example, the licensing period for TV stations was changed from 3 to 5 years; for radio, it was extended to 7 years. The rules on call letters have been relaxed to the point where all a station must do is provide the Commission with a notice of intent to change them. These and many other rule changes have indicated that the FCC is increasingly willing to let the forces of the marketplace determine the kind of programming that broadcast licensees present.

Nevertheless, programmers need to be sensitive to the legal responsibilities of licensees. Whether or not a station is specifically required to carefully screen song lyrics or movies for offensive material, a programmer should be very careful about when or if borderline material is aired. During the 1988–1989 season, NBC broadcast a three-part miniseries, *Favorite Son*, that included fairly graphic scenes depicting sexual bondage. The negative critical reaction was so strong that NBC decided to increase the number of censors in its standards and practices department. As a result of increasingly explicit lan-

guage and controversial depictions on such shows, Congress has introduced bills aimed at curbing depictions of violence, drug use, and sexual activity on TV.[11]

At the same time, television has relaxed its standards. For example, the Fox Television Network has had a strong impact on the content of network TV shows. In spite of a letter-writing campaign launched by activist viewers in 1988 to protest the raunchy themes in *Married . . . with Children*, the general tone of the show has continued to be risqué That program was acknowledged by CBS Broadcast Group president Howard Stringer as having broken taboos, thus enabling the other networks to present bolder programs.[12]

Regardless of high audience ratings, advertisers apparently got the message that many people in the audience were willing to boycott products manufactured by the sponsors of certain TV programs. Several advertisers left *Nightingales*, a weekly 1989 drama that featured student nurses who spent more time in their underwear than in their uniforms, after it drew protests from members of the nursing profession. Even though the show had high ratings, NBC canceled it. "Hit lists" have been drawn up by advertising agencies, citing television programs on which advertisers refuse to place their messages because of the content. Prominent among them are tabloid shows such as *Geraldo, Hard Copy*, and *Inside Edition*, along with *Married . . . with Children*.[13] Such is the dilemma that the networks and stations face. When advertisers are leery of the negative reaction and withdraw their support, programs may fail to accomplish the dual goals of attracting audiences and generating revenue for the programmer.

Technology   A programmer is either blessed or saddled with the station's technical facilities. There is little one can do to change a frequency or power assignment. These limitations, then, help dictate programming strategy. If the signal can't reach listeners or if certain types of listeners don't tune in classifications of broadcasting services such as AM radio, the programmer should be realistic in identifying the audience that can be served. Operators of stations with a weak signal strength should concentrate on the audience they can reach, providing that segment with a specialized service that is unavailable from stations whose signals cover a much wider and thus more diverse listening population. Increasingly, AM stations across the country have changed their programming to cope with the reality that their signals cannot compete with those of FM stations in the area of sound quality. They acknowledge that music sounds better on FM because FM has a much greater frequency range. Since voice quality is not affected, many AM stations have turned to news and talk programming. Furthermore, informational programming has greater appeal to older listeners, especially those who grew up listening to AM stations.

TV stations are adding stereo audio transmission capability, especially as more people are discovering the benefits of enhanced sound. In 1990 more than 21 percent of American homes were equipped with stereo TVs, and by 1991 more than 2 million stereo VCRs were in American households. A stereo VCR enables any TV viewing to be in stereo if the owner runs the audio through a stereo amplifier.[14] As stations look for ways to appeal to viewers, technological developments such as stereo sound will be offered.

Cable distribution of TV station signals is an important part of this technology. Simply put, if a TV station is not carried on cable, it is likely to miss out on most of the households that subscribe.

Competition   Loyalty to one's employer is commendable, but not if it makes the programmer lose objectivity. It is crucial that the strengths and weaknesses of all the competing electronic media outlets be recognized in order to assess realistically what can be done to compete. If competing stations' weaknesses can be identified, it may be possible to take away audience

members by offering a better service. However, as we have already mentioned, it is sometimes better to acknowledge that another station has an unassailable hold on the majority of viewers or listeners in the desired demographic groups. In such cases the programmer should look for other groups that can be attracted even if it means ceding the bulk of the audience to a dominant station.

Negotiable Forces

Other environmental forces also tend to shape the market, but the programmer can influence them to some degree. Agreements can be negotiated, and the kinds of programming that will appeal to target viewers or listeners can be acquired by perceptive programmers.

Suppliers   For electronic media outlets, the raw materials for making program product are talent, program series, and, in the case of radio, recorded music. With the exception of local news and local morning talk shows, virtually all television programming is produced for national distribution. Stations receive programs through a network or purchase them through distributors, who sell the rights to air programs to individual stations and cable systems. The station or cable system must be prepared to negotiate the purchase of the product, and if a competing outlet has acquired a particular series, that series simply is not available.

Radio stations may be able to hire competent announcers, an important ingredient in a music format, and they must either buy records or rely on promoters to supply them. There is nothing automatic about receiving copies of recordings from record distributors. The program director or music director must communicate frequently with the representatives of recording companies to receive the music the station needs and wants. Recording companies in turn rely on air exposure to sell their products, and so they take into account the quality of exposure offered by a particular station.

Marketing intermediaries Cable has become an important intermediary for television programmers. Traditionally, radio and television stations distributed their service (programming) directly to consumers (audiences), but there have been exceptions. During recent years a number of independent television stations have gone on the air, some in rather small markets where the revenue potential is low. Many of these stations have expanded their potential audiences through cable systems. Cable carriage gives a television station with a weak signal a boost because it improves signal quality to the point where it is generally comparable to that of other stations carried on the system. Moreover, cable carriage also gives such stations a better tuning position. Without cable carriage, the majority of independents, which operate on UHF channels, would be much less convenient to tune in. But with the removal of the FCC's "must carry" requirements for cable TV, some stations are vulnerable to being dropped from cable systems. In addition, audience confusion or lack of awareness of the availability of a signal may occur when a station is assigned a high channel number. A service carried on cable channel 36, for instance, may be overlooked by viewers who do not routinely scan that high when tuning through the offerings on the system. In fact, a recent Nielsen Media Research study showed that lower dial position and placement adjacent to broadcast stations improve the ratings of cable networks.[15]

The importance of the cable intermediary is illustrated by the deal negotiated by the Fox Television Network to get its programming carried by a major **multiple system operator (MSO)**, or owner of a number of cable systems that serve different cities. The Fox deal with Tele-Communications, Inc. (TCI), increased the network's potential audience by almost 1 million households beginning in 1991. TCI agreed to carry Fox programming on its systems in areas that are not served by a Fox TV affiliate. This arrangement provides TCI cable systems with an inexpensive source of programming and en-

ables them to offer their subscribers exclusives of popular Fox shows such as *The Simpsons* and *Married . . . with Children.* An important part of the bargain is the carriage of Fox programming on a VHF channel (2 through 13) on the cable system. This means that the fledgling Fox network has a channel position that is easy for viewers to tune in on each of the systems.

Cable TV networks must also negotiate with cable operators for carriage, which is crucial if they are to reach TV households. In 1988, for instance, Jones Intercable dropped the USA Network from most of its systems, reducing that network's potential audience by a million households.

Cable system operators, aware of the dependence of stations and networks for signal distribution to households, often broker their channel assignments by negotiating with TV stations for compensation for signal carriage. An independent UHF station, for instance, would face a serious limitation in its ability to attract viewers if it were excluded from cable TV system carriage. As was noted earlier, UHF stations are more difficult to tune in, and if a high proportion of households in the market are cable subscribers, they are not likely to switch from the cable to an outside antenna in order to watch stations that are not available on the cable system.

A cable system with a 36-channel capacity is limited to offering its subscribers that many TV stations and program services, and so cable operators choose services on the basis of their attractiveness to subscribers and their potential for selling advertising. Since ESPN and WTBS attract large numbers of subscriber viewers, they are attractive local advertising vehicles, and this increases their value to cable system operators. Independent TV stations, which often reach fewer viewers, have less clout with operators. As a result, a number of independent stations have been forced to pay cable systems to carry their signals. Still, at least one Fox affiliate has attributed part of its success in competing with the more established stations in its market to a willingness to pay cable operators for optimum channel assignments.

POSITIONING STRATEGY

Another important marketing strategy is **positioning**, which has been defined by Stanton, Etzel, and Walker as "the image that the product projects in relation to competitive products."[16] More to the point, positioning is the strategy of establishing a place in the listener or viewer's mind. As Ries and Trout describe it, "positioning is not what you do to a product. Positioning is what you do to the mind of the prospect."[17] In electronic media programming, positioning is the consumer's perception of the station, program service, or individual program series.

Positioning Questions

Positioning is an amalgamation of elements that define the station or service in such a way that it will meet the expectations and needs of the desired (target) audience. These elements are put into place after a number of important questions about the environment in which the station or service is to be positioned have been addressed:

■ What is the current market position of the station or other electronic media service? Equally important, what is the position of the competition? It is crucial to realize that positioning is in the mind of the target audience, not in the management of the station. That is, regardless of how effectively management thinks the programming is being executed, it all comes down to what place that service occupies in the minds of potential audience members.

■ What position does the station or service want to hold? It may be unrealistic for a station to unseat the market leader because of the leader's strong position in the minds of a majority of the audience members. There may not be room for more than one of the services that the market leader already provides. That is, if the audience likes the format of the existing Country music station, it will see no reason to switch its allegiance to another one.

■ What is the commitment to attaining and holding that position? The financial resources of the station or network must be behind the programming if it is to attain a desired position. No network magazine news program has come close to preempting the position of CBS's *60 Minutes* even at CBS. The success of this program finally came when CBS scheduled it permanently at 7 p.m. on Sunday. The program attracted the audience it inherited from NFL football broadcasts, but it was also scheduled in the same time period for several seasons, and so the audience knew where to find it.

■ Will the program be able to maintain its basic positioning plan for the long run? Although *60 Minutes* has not changed markedly since it premiered in 1968, innovations and personalities have been introduced over the years. Similarly, the formats of top-rated radio stations evolve over the years, but their positions in the market are by and large unwavering. The most dramatic changes came when the positions of AM market leaders declined as FM stations ascended in audience popularity.

Articulation of the Key Benefit

Regardless of whether a strategy entails segmentation or product differentiation, it is important to clearly articulate the benefit of listening to the station or watching a particular program. In the case of local television news, a station may emphasize the professionalism or experience of its news staff.

Even in the case of successful **full-service radio stations** such as WGN, Chicago, WTMJ, Milwaukee, and WCCO, Minneapolis, where a variety of services from music to talk shows and news are provided to listeners, a key benefit can be identified. That benefit is a sense of the various station personalities as being "friendly people who are like me." Listeners can relate to the individuals hosting the music, talk, call-in, and news programs and thus get hooked in by this perceived benefit.

Is the station's sound contemporary, youthful, sophisticated, or down-home? Is the talk show or news program produced by a TV station striving for a particular level of audience intimacy? These are benefits that a station could promote.

If the format for a radio station emphasizes the latest hit tunes, how can that objective be expressed and supported with actions? "All music, all the time" should deliver on that promise to listeners. This is not to say that the station must play songs continuously but that there should be minimal interruption of the music. All the elements involved in the station's programming should convey the impression of a steady stream of songs that listeners want to hear.

The benefit may simply be the type of format. If a station programmed heavy metal "head-banger" music, it would probably not appeal to many potential listeners, but it might trigger a positive response from some segments, say, males age 12 to 24, who were looking for hard rock. A programmer must determine if there are enough males 12 to 24 in the potential audience to justify that narrow position by programming hard rock music. These listeners would not find an Easy-Listening format appealing, whereas other audience segments might prefer a format with subdued announcers, light instrumental music, and romantic ballads.

Master Marketing Plan

Every programmer should have a *master marketing plan* in which the specifics and objectives of the program service are spelled out. The key benefit of the program to its potential audience should be described, along with the means of communicating it. A successful positioning strategy comes from such a plan, which is developed over several years. Here are some of the elements of a master marketing plan.

Specify the nature of the media outlet and unsatisfied audience needs that should be met. To the staff members, this statement should clearly describe what kind of station, network, or other service they are working for, who the target audience is, and what the programming is trying to say to the target audience.

Describe objectives to meet specific audience needs and wants that have been identified.

Describe directions for the implementation of tactics that will help meet those objectives. A station that wants to occupy a position as the source of entertainment and leisure companionship for men and women age 18 to 34 in its market could dictate that its newscasts be short and contain news of specific interest to young listeners. Other regularly scheduled information could include announcements of concerts and reviews of movies popular with people in the target audience.

Provide a basis for evaluating the execution of the plan, including the following:

- A precise description of the target audience's demographics and lifestyle
- A precise description of the station's format or program formula
- A section identifying program elements and their role (local versus national news, lengths of radio segments, frequency of occurrence, etc.)
- A statement of the tone and flavor the station seeks to communicate to listeners
- Reasons why a person in the target audience should listen to the station

Establishing and Maintaining a Position

There is so much competition for attention that it is often difficult for audience members to identify the stations or other program services they watch or listen to. It is very important for media outlets to work constantly at building their position in the market not only to reinforce audience loyalty but to stimulate audience awareness of the station they are tuned to so that the station will get credit when respondents complete audience surveys.

It would be very difficult to create a new, unique radio format since most music is being played on other stations in the market anyway. Similarly, a local TV news program cannot be positioned by providing distinctive informational content, since all stations present the latest local news with only slight variations. This means that the programming must offer something that will make the service unique and meaningful to audience members. Instead of looking at the problem as one of selling viewers on the best news program, the programmer should focus on what makes audience members feel that a news program is the best. In a number of cases the crucial element is that the anchor comes across to viewers as being "one of them" rather than an outsider.

Another news program segment—weather information and forecasting—is particularly important to most members of an audience. Is the treatment of the weather report tapping the audiences' perceptions of what is meaningful in their lives? In areas where tornadoes are a frequent threat, there may be a particular station that many people tune in because they feel they will receive the most immediate and complete information on this danger. If this is a radio station, they may become regular listeners because they feel they can depend on that station when they most need it even if they don't particularly care for the music the station plays. Similarly, extensive coverage of high school athletic teams, industrial softball leagues, and local bowling tournaments may be more meaningful than the more glamorous college or professional sports news to many people in the audience. In other cases viewers may be concerned with keeping abreast of developments in the local economy that can affect their jobs.

In the process of attracting a loyal audience, media outlets approach positioning by adhering to several general principles. First, it is difficult to challenge the market leader successfully. Not surprisingly, the station established as the TV news leader or radio format leader is the most difficult to compete against. A station's position is similar to that of a member of Congress: The incumbent's chances of reelection are greater because she or he has established a position. In the electorate's mind, that individual *is* the congressman or congresswoman. Furthermore, a politician who has already been elected has the

opportunity to keep his or her name before the constituency through mailings to voters and appearances on TV and in the newspapers and by being known as the area's congressional representative. Anyone else must work to establish his or her name and identity with the voters. Having had less exposure, the challenger starts at a disadvantage.

To become and remain the top station in a market requires strategic determination and a financial commitment. This means investing in talent and program product that will be at least as attractive as or even more appealing than those offered by the competition. Very importantly, the media outlet must invest in promotion, which is discussed later in this chapter, to reinforce audience perceptions of the station's service.

The leader needs to embrace innovation without abandoning the concept or objective that originally positioned the station. At the same time, the programmer should be assessing the competition and should be looking for potential or real erosion of that station's market share. Otherwise, the market leader may suffer the fate of American auto manufacturers, whose position has been undermined by imports.

To avoid this fate, winners must anticipate their opponents' next several moves in the programming game. Maintaining a position effectively means anticipating new forms of competition. Strong competitive moves should always be blocked. The market or format leader must move rapidly before the challenger gets established. For example, suppose a station changes its format in order to compete more directly against the format leader. The leader should move aggressively against the upstart by offering its audience an even greater incentive to listen. Rather than deprecating the challenger, an astute programmer will assess the strengths and potential of the competition realistically. This way, the threat to the leader can be recognized and appropriate action can be taken quickly. It will be too late if another station has already been able to position itself in the same audience segment. If, for instance, a competing TV station acquires a new local news set or anchor team in an attempt to upgrade its image as a dynamic service that delivers the important news with greater vitality, the market leader can preempt that move by increasing its promotion and placing more emphasis on its own valuable attributes by reminding viewers of how trustworthy, knowledgable, and experienced its news team is.

Radio and television program formats can become stale as artists and producers who were on the cutting edge of creativity get into a rut or when imitators saturate the marketplace, making the original idea seem ordinary. Still, while every television series has a limited life expectancy, some manage to stay on the air longer than others because their producers continue to find ways to add interest. In *M*A*S*H*, which ran for nine seasons on the CBS Television Network, the characters developed so that viewers came to know them as real people. Moreover, none of these characters was a consistent or a perfect human being. In some episodes Dr. Hawkeye Pierce, played by Alan Alda, was noble, idealistic, and brave. In others he was overly righteous, petty, devious, or even cowardly. Also, new characters were added when original cast members left the series, and this introduced new personalities and relationships. These changes were just some of the ways in which the program was continually adjusted and new facets were introduced.

Some radio station programmers have recognized the need to adapt to changing conditions in the market and have adjusted their formats to attract desirable demographic groups that had not been listening. Other factors notwithstanding, the best strategy for the market leader or a strong contender for first place is a subtle, gradual change. One station that featured an Album-Oriented Rock (AOR) music format, for instance, evolved into a CHR format over a period of about a year. The AOR audience consisted predominantly of younger male listeners, and the station realized that it could broaden its audience appeal if more women listeners could be attracted. Because the station moved slowly, those in its original audience were not jarred by the change as more currently popular recordings

were introduced into the format. The station avoided alienating the core audience as it repositioned its content to appeal to a broader range of listeners.

When a change like this occurs, the format leader must deal with a new direct competitor. Such a challenge necessitates a countermove. While that may or may not mean altering the format, the leader should look at how it can freshen the attributes that attracted the dominant share of the audience in the first place. One of the ways in which successful format leaders maintain their position is by increasing their ongoing promotional campaigns to reinforce the place they occupy in listeners' minds and by adding new features or personalities. In this way, the leader does not allow a challenger to take away its audience.

Rewarding the Audience

Providing audience members with a greater **reward** for continuing with the dominant program reinforces their **loyalty**. For example, a station that employs a weatherperson who has a degree in meteorology rewards viewers, who feel they are getting a good grasp of forthcoming weather conditions. Similarly, if the anchor is a mature individual who conveys the idea that he or she has gained wisdom and insight into the news and knows and understands the community because he or she has been in the market for many years, viewers can be rewarded by being informed by a person who understands their problems and relates values important in their lives. Radio audiences can be rewarded by hearing outrageous comments or humorous skits on a particular station. For other listeners, knowing that they will hear a report on traffic conditions within a few minutes of tuning in a station in the morning is a reward.

Brand Character

An important aspect of marketing a product is to maintain some distinction from the competition in the consumer's mind. One can travel across the country, switching from station to station, and hear virtually the same type of music. Since almost all television programming is distributed by one of the major networks or is syndicated and carried during similar time periods, a person can count on seeing virtually the same programs in Philadelphia, Pennsylvania, and Philadelphia, Mississippi.

Since the same fare is available to just about everyone who has access to a TV or radio receiver, what can distinguish one station from another? In radio, it comes down to two things: treatment of program events and personalities. Program **events** are the individual elements that are mixed together to create radio programs, including news reports, music recordings, commercials, humorous skits, and conversations with telephone callers. The principal personalities on most radio stations are the disc jockeys, with newscasters and other sidekicks often in the role of supporting personalities. Combined, they give the station a particular image, that is, a personality or brand character. A radio station that features a "morning zoo" team that emphasizes raunchy humor will evoke a certain image among listeners. To some people it will be shocking or even disgusting, whereas other listeners will consider the mixture of jokes and music very funny and "contemporary."

In the case of television, the equivalent of program events are the various programs that are scheduled, usually on the hour and half hour, throughout the day. The principal personalities in television are often the news anchors since news programs are the single strongest identification that viewers have with specific TV stations and networks. It is no accident that Dan Rather, Tom Brokaw, and Peter Jennings anchor most of the special news coverage presented by their networks. This is one way the networks can keep their anchors in the most visible position possible, not only reinforcing their role as the symbol of the evening news program but bolstering the image of the network as a source of important information.

Other important personalities on a television outlet include the stars of the other programs of-fered on that channel. Fox has capitalized on this and is known as the network that programs somewhat daring material that appeals mainly to younger viewers with such shows as *Married . . . with Children, The Simpsons, Babes*, and *In Living Color*. Similarly, local stations that carry highly popular shows such as *Wheel of Fortune, Oprah Winfrey,* and *Donahue* have something to make them distinctive in their markets. Each of those shows draws viewers on the strength of its individual appeal, but together they help the station establish a distinct position in viewers' minds as being the source of "shows we like."

Finding a Niche

Programming strategy consists of two alternatives: competing for an identified audience segment and establishing a **niche** by finding an unserved segment and developing program content to attract it. Again, only one station can be the market leader. There is always a reason for that dominance, and sometimes it can't be overcome by a competing station. Since most stations are seeking a way to get a piece of the audience action, they should look for unfulfilled expectations or desires in potential listeners' or viewers' minds; that is, they should look for an underserved audience segment.

A station or a cable service can establish a niche in the marketplace by finding a way to provide a unique service to an identifiable though smaller segment of the total consumer population. In the New York City newspaper market, there is only one *New York Times*. The *New York Post*, with its sensationalistic headlines and copy, appeals to a different group of readers, and *Newsday* established its niche by serving the residents of Long Island, adjacent to the city.

The marketers of 7-Up found a niche by positioning the soft drink as a caffeine-free alternative to cola instead of attempting to compete directly against Coke and Pepsi. Similarly, a Beautiful-Music station became number one in the Providence, Rhode Island, market by using as its theme "WLKW, the unrock station."[18] The station achieved its market position by emphasizing what it was *not*; that is, it was neither loud nor distracting. The positioning statement told potential listeners that since the station did not feature rock, it offered a better alternative in music, at least for some people. The soft drink and the radio format both emphasized an attribute in response to an unfulfilled need in the target audience. Neither may have a dominant market share, but each has been able to find a successful niche in a very competitive environment.

The Lifetime Network, which is distributed on cable systems, has positioned itself by emphasizing programs that appeal to women. ESPN, also available through cable, faces competition from a wide variety of services, but no other channel devotes its time exclusively to sports.

Along with celebrity interviews, behind-the-scenes looks at the making of various films, and show business gossip, viewers of the E! (for Entertainment) cable channel can get information on many newly released theatrical movies they may have heard about. Just as ESPN found its niche as a sports service, E! has a found a niche by giving viewers quick, easy access to current entertainment information. In both cases specialization gave a cable network a unique position in the minds of television viewers.

For many years the Public Broadcasting Service (PBS) had an easily defined niche among television viewers with its offerings of educational programs for children such as *Sesame Street*, along with news analysis and cultural and documentary programs. But with the establishment of cable networks such as C-Span, the Cable News Network (CNN), the Learning Channel, the Discovery Channel, Arts and Entertainment (A&E), Bravo, Turner Network Television (TNT), and Nickelodeon, that niche has been under severe attack. Each of these services offers many of the same kinds of programs that were within the traditional purview of PBS. Thus, there has been a **fragmentation** of the television audience in which different viewer segments are dispersed across this greater number of channel choices instead of the whole audience watching the same few programs. Because newer cable networks offer programming that attracts more narrowly defined portions of the total audience, some advertisers have found them to be an efficient means of reaching their target audiences, which include a high proportion of desirable higher socioeconomic status (SES) groups, in a cost-effective way. As a result, the noncommercial public television service is in distress, although its officials state that PBS will continue to offer eclectic programming. Nevertheless, its virtually exclusive position in cultural, public affairs, and documentary programming has been taken away.

After assessing the strengths and weaknesses of the market leader, the programmer of a media outlet may identify where the market or format leader is not serving the target audience well. Rather than taking on the leader directly, the programmer can exploit an area where the leader is vulnerable. One of the ways in which FM stations did this during the days of AM dominance was by minimizing the number of commercial announcements and programming more minutes of music during each hour as a way to establish a clear reward to listeners for changing their listening habits. Actually, many FM stations had little choice, since so few people were listening that their sale representatives had trouble selling commercial time. FM stations thus took what ordinarily would have been a negative and turned it into a positive attribute of their programming. FM radio found a way to position its service as an alternative to AM radio's heavier load of commercials.

In some cases market leaders play it safe. Radio stations may play hit music, but only after the songs have become well established as popular fare. The leader may emphasize music and limit the input of the station's personalities to stating the names of songs and announcing the time and temperature, shortchange news, or schedule a heavy commercial advertising load because its advertising rates generate so much profit. Any of these practices may then be identified by competitors as a weakness.

A positioning failure that was ultimately transformed into a successful niche effort is illustrated by the case of an FM station that languished near the bottom of the ratings during the 1980s. The station decided to change its call letters and replace its AOR format with Country. The reasoning seemed clear enough: Only one other FM station in the market was programming Country, and it appeared that the Country format slice of the audience pie was large enough to permit another station to establish a reasonable niche.

It didn't work, however. The existing Country station was the market leader. It had established its position and continually reinforced it with heavy promotion. Perhaps the challenger needed to make a greater commitment of time and money to be competitive. While some TV promotional spots were aired, the campaign was neither heavy nor long. Also, the challenger's format lacked real personalities. The market leader, by contrast, anchored its position with a strong morning personality duo and featured other friendly-sounding, upbeat personalities during the other time periods.

Stations that cannot take away the market leader's position must find an unfulfilled need or desire in some segment and serve it with the appropriate programming. In the above example, the challenger's format and call letters were changed again after about 6 months as the station made another switch, this time to an adult contemporary "Lite Rock" format. The management felt it had identified an audience segment, women age 25 to 44, not being attracted by other stations, and that became the target audience. This format was maintained for about 2 years with only moderate success. Finally, the station returned to a modified version of its original format. After changing its call letters once again, the station reestablished an AOR format, but with an emphasis on older music to attract men age 25 to 49. These people had grown up listening to rock music, but as they had matured, their interests were bypassed by the existing contemporary music stations. Finally, the station found

a successful niche. Its ratings climbed to near the top because it was able to stake out a position where there was no direct competition.

PROMOTION

Purpose

Stations and other electronic program services can't assume that audiences will come to them. The old adage "You've got to get 'em into the tent before you can save 'em" applies to promotion: You've got to get people to try your programs before they can be counted in your audience. Thus, the first purpose of promotion is to increase the size of the media outlet's audience by enticing new viewers or listeners to tune in. The second purpose is to reinforce viewing or listening in order to build audience loyalty.

Promotion has become increasingly important since the mid-1970s because of the growth in the number of radio and television outlets and the intensity of competition for audiences that comes with targeting program content to appeal to specific demographic segments. Successful electronic media outlets use attention-gathering promotional events and stunts as part of their positioning strategies, along with advertising campaigns through other media, such as outdoor advertising and television ads for radio.

Conducting promotional campaigns in newspapers or in outdoor media may get people to tune in, but the programming itself reinforces and expands on those efforts. If, for instance, a station promotes itself as the "best of the oldies" station, it must deliver on that promise or many of the people who decided to sample the programming will not stay in the audience. Of course, the programmer should have a very clear understanding of the target audience's perception of the best of the oldies. If the best means recognizable hit tunes from the past 5 years but the targeted listeners hear a large proportion of songs that are 6 to 15 years old, many in that audience will reject the promotion, along with the station's programming, because it is not meaningful to them.

Types

Browne, Bortz & Coddington, Inc. (now Bortz & Co.), a Denver-based consulting firm, has suggested three kinds of promotion for developing a TV station promotion strategy, but their methods apply to radio and cable as well.

Background promotion *Background promotion* is conducted constantly and is used to build general awareness of a station among advertisers and audience members. This kind of promotion typically involves community activities such as charity events, parades and festivals, print advertising of programs, and general station promotions through TV, radio, and outdoor media. Steady background promotion has made the superstation WTBS and the sports programming specialist ESPN virtual household words. Similarly, Home Box Office (HBO) is virtually synonymous with pay-cable TV.

Targeted promotion *Targeted promotion* is used when the message is placed during times when potential viewers are watching or in other programs or media that attract the target group. Thus, targeted promotion is used when a station is attempting to increase viewing and share within a daypart or a program. Targeted promotion for television is an increasingly important budget consideration when a station produces its own programming or decides to schedule a first-run syndicated product. Whereas network reruns of series such as *Murphy Brown* and *L.A. Law* have received tremendous promotional exposure during their network runs, new programs, untested in the marketplace, are unknown entities to viewers. Promotional announcements placed in the most established popular programs will alert audiences to the availability of new programs. Similarly, when radio stations first go on the air or change formats, advertisements on TV shows that attract the kind of listeners a radio station is targeting can be effective in promoting the new service.

Opportunistic promotion *Opportunistic promotion* is carried out by tying in with some event that has the target audience's attention. The station should keep a promotional mind-set at all times in order to capitalize on the unanticipated event, such as the success of a local sports team, a local celebration, or another experience that can be shared with the audience. This means that the station should have a contingency fund available to support such promotional activities.[19] A station could prepare to do remote broadcasts from the site of the Little League state championship tournament when a team from its coverage area makes the playoffs, for instance. Or a station could acquire hard-to-get tickets like those for the Super Bowl and give them away after an appropriate promotion.

A station should carefully define its promotional goals and develop a plan for accomplishing them. Identifying the key benefits of radio or TV programming and then finding ways to communicate those attributes through other media has become part of the programmer's responsibility. For example, a locally produced TV talk show might focus on the appearance of a soap opera star who is in town, and another broadcast might feature the author of romance novels as a guest. Such promotion should help position the program as a source of interesting information about people who are of particular interest to women viewers. A radio station could use a similar strategy to position itself among targeted listeners as "the station that plays all hits, all the time" or "plays your Country favorites."

Promotion through Other Media

Outside promotion carries the message through other media in order to attract potential audience members. For example, local television news programs are often promoted on radio stations in a TV station's coverage area. Billboards can be very useful as outside promotion for a broadcast or cable facility. The message must be very succinct—usually no more than seven words and preferably no more than five—so that the reader can absorb it quickly while passing by. In cities with large numbers of mass transit vehicles, placards on taxicabs and buses serve a similar purpose.

The "experience counts" theme used to promote a local TV news program can be reinforced in the introduction to a news program and in promotional announcements placed in other programs on the same station. In addition, promotion can be carried in *TV Guide* ads, in local newspaper ads, in outdoor advertising on billboards, and on bus or taxi placards.

Print advertising for the purpose of radio promotion can inform potential audiences about new personalities, the details of a major contest, or a concert that the station is sponsoring. For television, print advertising is most effective in drawing viewer attention to programs offered on a station or channel. For either medium, print can explain the benefit to potential listeners who may then tune in. Otherwise, those persons may never become aware of the station or the benefits of listening to it. The relative effectiveness of newspapers and magazines hinges on the age of the audience the station is trying to attract and the audience segments most efficiently delivered by the advertising medium. Since young listeners are not heavy newspaper readers, the value to radio stations who are targeting that group will probably be minimal.

Television can be a very effective medium for promoting radio, but it is very expensive. Aside from the cost of buying the advertising time, the station must pay for the production of an effective TV message. Promotional spots should be placed specifically in programs that deliver large numbers of target listeners.

Contests and Giveaways

Faced with the increasing fragmentation of their audiences, television stations and networks are actively seeking new ways to attract viewers. In the past, promotional contests and giveaways were the province of radio, but television sta-

tions and networks are increasingly using these tactics to get people to sample programs they might not otherwise watch. In Dallas, KTXA viewers had to watch between 5 and 7 p.m. to pick up clues in a contest called "the Phrase That Pays." At 7:21 p.m. an announcement appeared at the bottom of the screen, asking viewers to try to win $2,100 a day. As a result of this promotion, the station determined that the audience for this time period increased by 150 percent from the previous year.[20] At the network level, both CBS and NBC ran contests to kick off their fall 1990 prime-time seasons. In the case of CBS, a tie-in with K-Mart required viewers to watch various CBS programs to pick up the clues in a contest. NBC presented the winning numbers in MacDonalds' Macmillions contest, inducing people to watch different NBC programs each evening to see if they had won.

Stations in many markets have fallen into a trap by running straightforward giveaway promotions. By offering thousands of dollars in cash, expensive cars, vacations, and other such prizes, they have caused the costs of promotion to skyrocket. In response to the competition, other stations sometimes offer even more cash and better prizes. If a station drops out of the race, it is likely to lose audience.

Getting listeners involved, making the contest fun, and offering prizes of low cost to the station is a more productive approach. There is general agreement among programmers that cash is the most appealing prize. Although $100 isn't a lot of money, it is substantial enough for the winner to feel she or he has really won something. If the stakes must be higher, winning a month's rent has high appeal among all age groups except those age 24 and younger. Compact disc players appeal to younger listeners, whereas VCRs appeal more to those who are older.

It is important to reward audience members often so that they will not think the contest has no payoff, and if a grand prize is to be awarded, the contest should be structured so that it is not given away during the first few days. Promotion should build anticipation and interest over a period of time so that the station can reap the benefits of increased listening and add new audience members.

While the most apparent benefit is attracting new listeners, contests work best if they also provide a reward for the current audience. Many regular listeners, perhaps the majority, may participate only vicariously, just as viewers play along with the contestants on *Wheel of Fortune*, and the contest should be enjoyable for them, too. In this regard, MTV has capitalized on word-of-mouth promotion very effectively with its "ultimate" giveaway contests. MTV prizes have included an island, a town, and a radio station with Billy Idol as guest disc jockey. Because MTV's prizes are so unusual and play on people's fantasies, people become excited and talk about the opportunity, and this induces other people to watch MTV to get the contest details.

If a contest is promoted well, it can help position the station among the nonlisteners who become aware of it. Not only are outrageous promotions and contests fun, they attract considerable media attention. A number of stations have been successful with tacky contests such as a "weird birthmark" contest inspired by Mikhail Gorbachev, while others concentrate on contests such as scavenger hunts that ask listeners to find additional clues to solving a puzzle or finding the keys to a new car or motorcycle. Other contests ask participants to cover themselves with honey and roll around in a pool filled with dollar bills. The contestant gets to keep all the money that sticks. Usually these antics result in local TV and newspaper coverage, which is the kind of publicity that money can't buy.

Community Involvement

As one travels from city to city around the country, it is easy to spot the similarities in how people live, but every place has a unique history and set of traditions that give it an identity. Getting the station involved in the community achieves greater listener or viewer identification. Many cities located along rivers hold a riverfront festival each summer. In oceanside and lakeside cities, seafood festivals are conducted. Many other communities hold county fairs and similar events during the year. Each of these events presents an opportunity for the station to tie in, creating audience involvement and reinforcing its identity with the target audience. Some TV stations even broadcast their local news programs from these sites; this brings the local news personalities closer to their audience members and focuses attention on the station's commitment to the community.

Even though it is a well-worn technique, having representatives of a radio station cruise the swimming pools and beaches in the market to give prizes to those who are listening to the station is an example of getting personalities involved in the community and reinforcing the station's brand character. Participating in local charities and fund drives by holding contests where the money collected is donated to a specific community cause builds goodwill and listener involvement.

For many radio listeners, the music they hear is the most important aspect of their listening. Stations can become involved in the concerts held in the area. Whether that participation involves sponsorship or simply giving away tickets, current and potential listeners will associate the station with these musical events. Similarly, TV and radio stations can participate in bridal festivals, boat exhibitions, health fairs, and other organized events in the community.

The objective of such efforts is to ingrain in the minds of audience members that this station is an important part of their lives. Consequently, when people turn to a station to keep up with what's going on in the community, they tune in the one which features the most caring, trustworthy personalities. Moreover, audience members feel they have come to know station personalities as real people because they have seen them in person at a shopping mall or during a remote broadcast at the county fair.

Radio Promotion

Radio promotion has two distinct objectives: to attract new members to the audience and to heighten their awareness of who they are listening to so that the station will receive credit during audience ratings surveys; this credit in turn helps the station attract advertisers. Listeners can become confused and have no reason to care which station they are listening to unless the station gives them an incentive. In all likelihood, more than one station in the market can fulfill their needs and wants.

Off-air promotion through other media can be used to attract new listeners, while the station's programming reinforces and expands on those efforts. An example would be a contest in which the station gives away a trip to Hawaii or another exotic locale. Outside promotion may include advertising on television, in newspapers, and on billboards and other outdoor media, but the effort all comes together in the execution of the promotion on the air. The payoff for most new tune-ins will come not from the contest but from an enjoyable radio listening experience.

On-air promotion is most useful in reinforcing the image a station is trying to project. For instance, if a station wants to promote an "all hits, all the time" image, it can use outdoor advertising to reinforce television ads. To reinforce this position in the minds of those who tune in, on-air promotions can include contests that reward listeners who can list all the songs that were played in a row without interruption. The programmer must go even further, though, by minimizing interruptions of the music. Just as important, the songs that are selected for play should be those which the target audience thinks are "hits," whether that means the most recent top-20 tunes or classic rock hits from the past 10 years.

As a part of on-air and outside promotion, many stations use a **positioning line**, or a statement of the unique benefit to the listener, such as "your country favorites" or "the best mix of the '60s, '70s, '80s, and '90s music." To be effective, a positioning line should be clear, simple, and easy to reinforce through outside media. If another station in the market is using the line "your hits station," adopting a positioning line such as "all-hit radio" may lead to listener confu-

sion and potential disaster. Moreover, if the concept being stressed by the station in its liner is not meaningful, the effort will be wasted. As radio program **consultant** Rob Balon has pointed out, a positioning liner such as "KAAA, where we tell you the titles and artists of the songs we play" may seem trite, but for many listeners that is an important benefit for a station to offer.[21]

Station identifiers A brief **station identifier,** or a phrase such as "I-95" or "Magic 106" by which a station is known to listeners, is an effective tool for promoting the station. The frequent mention of the identifier on the air reinforces the promotional efforts made in outdoor advertising and on TV. Since the station identifier is very brief, it can be incorporated in off-air advertising as a symbol of the station and its programming concept.

The identifier was traditionally based on the FCC's requirement for a station identification announcement near the beginning of each hour that states the station's exact call letters and its city of license (e.g., "WPOP, Grand Forks"). However, listeners tune in and out at various times during the hour, and so the station must continually remind them which station they're listening to in order to receive credit in audience ratings surveys. Consequently, stations have applied much effort to creating unique identifying slogans or phrases in the hope that listeners will recall them.

Since the FCC loosened its rules on call letters, changing them has become a frequent practice. Stations have favored Q, X, and Z in call letters because these letters are easy for listeners to remember and report in ratings surveys. Just as television viewers identify the station they are watching by its channel number (e.g., channel 6), radio listeners may think of the station they are listening to by its nickname. In one case an FM station had promoted itself so insistently as Z-102 that some of its regular listeners corrected others by saying, "Oh, you mean Z-102," when its real call letters, WZBQ, were used to refer to the station.

There are only so many combinations of useful or memorable call letters, and the choices are limited. As an alternative, a number of stations have turned to nicknames or slogans such as Easy 102 and Power 95 as a way to position themselves and reinforce the format concept in the minds of listeners. Animal and bird designations such as "the Eagle" and "the Fox" are also popular.

A programmer should never assume that listeners pay much attention to the details so important to those who work in radio. Thus, the identifier should reinforce the brand character of the station in a way that will not confuse its program offerings with those of a competitor. If a respondent to an audience ratings survey correctly indicates that she or he was listening to Power 99 but confuses the call letters with those of another station, the competing station will get credit for the listener.

Data collected by the radio programming consulting firm Paragon Research found that 70 percent of listeners say they remember a station more easily when its frequency is announced (for example, 102.5). In addition, 44 percent of listeners preferred exact frequency identification over rounded frequencies (e.g., 95.7 versus 96) while only 18 percent did not want to be given exact station frequencies. A slight majority (52 percent) of Paragon's respondents preferred a combination of a slogan and the frequency. When the station identifier is trimmed from a word to an alphabetical letter in combination with a rounded frequency (e.g., B-105), 48 percent of the respondents liked this approach to identifying the station.[22] Stations can avoid the awkwardness of stating the exact frequency in conjunction with an identifying slogan by rounding the identifier to a single letter in combination with rounded frequency, such as Hot 96, but a station that calls itself Z-94 on the air will sound very much like another that calls itself Q-104.

There is a danger in being less than exact in identifying a station, however. Radio station consultant Rhody Bosley points out that in signal-crowded markets, several stations may claim the same rounded frequency position. Thus, a station that operates at 95.7 and rounds its frequency to 96 can easily be confused with station operating at 96.3 that also rounds to 96. In Orlando,

for example, four stations used the slogan "105," which naturally created confusion in Arbitron surveys when respondents reported which station they listened to. Listeners do report exact frequency locations, or *addresses*. Technology is helping with this through the adoption of digitally tuned radio receivers. Listener awareness of a station's exact address is reinforced by the tuners' frequency display, which shows the exact dial position.[23]

Promotion through program events Another approach to promotion through programming is to feature events and personalities that cause listeners to recall and discuss the station in conversations with others. Larry Lujak used to do "the cheap, trashy show-biz report" each morning on WLS, Chicago, in which he used news wire copy describing a celebrity's life. He also used to read the "clunk letter of the day," a presumably authentic letter from a fan, to which he made a sarcastic reply. Rick and Bob, the "Goofy White Boys" on WAPI-FM, Birmingham, ran a call-in contest called Barking for Dollars, in which the participants won $10 for every bark they could coax out of their dogs. Bob and Tom of WFBQ, Indianapolis, and Mark and Brian of KLOS, Los Angeles, tell outrageous and often crude jokes. Some listeners in the potential audience find these presentations enjoyable; others find more appeal in lawn and gardening tips provided by a local nursery owner who can tell them how and when to mulch their roses. Whether the bit is outrageous, funny, provocative, or informative, the reward to the listener is enhanced by describing it in a conversation, particularly if other persons participating in the conversation have shared the listening experience. Some of these people may be stimulated to tune in and enjoy similar experiences or see what the fuss is about. Such events can be considered effective if they accomplish the objective of attracting listeners.

Television Promotion

Television stations face the same challenges in positioning themselves with audiences that their radio counterparts have dealt with for years. The television networks' shares are eroding, giving way to other sources of programming. Satellite systems are widely used to deliver program product directly to stations and cable systems. All these changes have created a muddled image for individual TV programming outlets. The reruns of programs originally broadcast over the NBC Television Network may appear on CBS's late-night programming. ABC's *Roseanne* is broadcast by affiliates of ABC and CBS as well as by independent stations, and *Murder, She Wrote, thirtysomething,* and *L.A. Law* can now be found on cable networks such as USA and Lifetime.

At the same time, advertisers have identified more precisely defined audience segments (e.g., men age 35 to 54), and programmers must follow suit, identifying programs that will appeal to these desirable segments. However, a programmer must also take into account the need to promote the availability of the program. If narrowly defined groups are to be attracted to programs that appeal to a relatively narrow audience, a high level of awareness of the existence of the specialized program must be developed.

First-run versus off-network program promotion In developing a programming strategy, human nature must be a primary consideration. Audience members follow routines in their daily and weekly viewing, and so familiarity is a potent influence on viewing patterns. Consequently, television stations face different problems in attracting viewers depending on the viewers' knowledge of the programs that are being offered.

First-run programs are original shows that have never aired anywhere. Game shows such as *Jeopardy* and *Wheel of Fortune* and talk shows such as *Geraldo, Donahue* and *Oprah Winfrey* are examples of first-run shows that are **syndicated** or sold to individual stations or cable systems. **Off-network programs** include shows ranging from *I Dream of Jeannie* and *Mayberry, RFD,* to *M*A*S*H, Cheers,* and *The Golden Girls* that were originally aired on a network. Because first-run programs are fresh, they should

have high viewer appeal. However, they lack an important attribute of off-network programs: a record of appeal to an audience and immediate recognition.

The built-in promotion offered by the network visibility of *The Cosby Show* is powerful indeed. Millions of viewers were exposed to the show during its run on the network, and their awareness has been reinforced by all the network promotion and the related publicity. Consequently, when viewers discover that *Cosby* is available at 6 p.m., they immediately recognize the show's premise and characters. Promotional needs are minimized and may only entail informing potential viewers of the show's availability in the station's schedule.

When a station introduces a new series, though, it must budget promotional dollars to educate potential viewers about its availability and induce them to watch it. Generally, the costs to a station for a first-run syndication product is lower than that for an off-network series, at least until the program has established a record of audience attendance. A much higher promotional budget should be included in the decision to air first-run programs if they are to be fully competitive.

Locally produced programming promotion Local early-evening and late-evening news programs are the most prominent locally originated broadcasts because they are scheduled at times when the largest potential audiences are available. Second in status are morning talk and variety shows. Since they are daily broadcasts and are likely to be sampled by viewers, these programs have a promotional advantage. Moreover, daily talk/variety and news programs have a built-in means of attracting viewers when they cover activities in outlying areas of the market. By covering community activities, the station recoups its investment by gaining greater market visibility and an enhanced image of community involvement. Many stations bolster their image among viewers in outlying areas by establishing news bureaus in other cities within the station's coverage area to help position a station as one that provides a specific service to viewers who live there.

In addition to daily news and talk shows, many stations produce weekly local public affairs, sports, and talk shows. These broadcasts can also generate viewer interest if they include coverage of activities that audience members are involved in as participants or observers. By ful-

filling the needs and wants of viewers and telling them how they are doing so, these stations can increase their audiences. For example, if viewers know that a station's Friday night sports show will include coverage of the high school football, hockey, or basketball game, many will tune in just to see familiar people and places on the screen.

SUMMARY

Programming as marketing is the concept of identifying audience needs and wants and providing content that will satisfy them. The focus of the programming effort should be on fulfilling the perceptions of benefits that are held by the potential audience.

One approach to marketing programs is to differentiate a program on the basis of its featured personalities, level of comedy, seriousness of approach, or another aspect that can make a program stand out from the competition in fulfilling audience needs and wants. With a market segmentation approach, a segment of the total audience is targeted through a service designed to fulfill that group's specific needs and wants.

Positioning is the strategy of establishing a place for a program, station, or cable service in audience members' minds. Positioning works by identifying audience needs and wants and fulfilling them through the program service. Challenges to market or format leaders must be based on fulfilling needs or wants that the current leader does not fill. To remain the leader, a station or network must be able to anticipate challenges and move to reinforce its position. Since only one service or station can be the market or format leader, others may find it more worthwhile to identify niches in the market by identifying an underserved market segment and providing a unique service to a smaller but still significant audience.

A number of forces that shape the market environment must be taken into account. The demography of the market, including its ethnic

characteristics and age, is beyond the control of the programmer. Likewise, the employment characteristics of the community are a reflection of the socioeconomic attributes of its population. Moreover, the social attitudes of the community residents will have an influence on the kind of programming that is acceptable. In addition, a programmer must be sensitive to regulatory trends to keep the media outlet out of jeopardy. Little if anything can be done about the technical facilities of the station except to be realistic about the kind of potential audience they are capable of attracting.

Among the negotiable forces in the market are program suppliers, who can be more or less cooperative about a media outlet's objectives. Financial resources are necessary to attract talent and acquire the most desirable program product.

Every programmer should have a master marketing plan in which the specifics and objectives of the program service are spelled out. The programming objective of the station should be clearly stated. The benefit of the program to its potential audience, such as "providing the most popular music with the least interruption," should be described, along with the means of communicating it. For example, a radio station may meet its marketing objective by playing only the most popular new music as determined by local record sales and by limiting commercial announcements to 4 minutes per hour. In this effort, a brand character, which represents a fulfillment of audience wants and needs, should emerge to occupy a position in audience members' minds.

Without promotion of the programming, many viewers or listeners may never become aware of it. Outside promotion is necessary to reach potential audience members; thus, the use of other media, including newspapers and billboards, TV advertising for radio, and radio ads to promote television programs, can be effective. A radio station's call letters and frequency address, or identifier, and a positioning liner (a statement that conveys the essence of its service, such as "the Country Music Tradition" or "Rock 'n' Roll Legends") can reinforce the position the station is attempting to occupy. Contests and giveaways should be designed to reinforce the loyalty of current audience members while attracting new ones. Audience involvement does not have to include actually participation in a contest as long as listeners can participate vicariously and thus receive some enjoyment or reward.

Television and radio stations can position themselves in the minds of their audiences through their involvement in community activities. Background promotion builds general audience awareness. Targeted promotion attempts to attract an audience for a new program or to a daypart. Opportunistic promotion involves being prepared to capitalize on events that give a media outlet an opportunity to reinforce its position by involvement in community activities and events.

SUGGESTED READINGS

Ries, Al, and Jack Trout: *Positioning: The Battle for Your Mind*, McGraw-Hill, New York, 1981. Ries, Al, and Jack Trout: *Marketing Warfare*, McGraw-Hill, New York, 1986.

Ries and Trout expound a philosophy of marketing based on the premise that success comes to programming services that fulfill a need. According to these authors, a program must occupy a position in an audience member's mind. This is must reading for programmers. These overviews are filled with examples that introduce readers to important concepts in marketing. With this background, much of what you read in trade publications and textbooks will begin to coalesce into an understanding of the marketing concept.

Stanton, William J., Michael J. Etzel, and Bruce J. Walker: *Fundamentals of Marketing*, 9th ed., McGraw-Hill, New York, 1991.

There are many introductory marketing textbooks on the market, but this one is especially clearly written. Excellent graphic depictions of concepts supplement a well-organized and easily understood text. Those who are serious about understanding an increasingly important aspect of electronic media programming will seek a background in marketing fundamentals through this or another introductory text.

Eastman, Susan Tyler, and Robert A. Klein, eds.: *Promotion & Marketing for Broadcasting & Cable*, 2d ed., Waveland Press, Prospect Heights, Ill., 1990.

This is a comprehensive overview of electronic media promotion with contributions by several industry professionals, including coeditor Robert Klein, whose company, Klein &, specializes in station and cable promotion. The book reviews promotional strategies for all aspects of broadcast and cable programming.

Radio & Records, a weekly newspaper for radio programmers, includes many columns written by industry research and marketing consultants. In addition, regular columns pertaining to specific radio formats (Album-Oriented Rock, Contemporary Hit Radio, Adult Contemporary, Urban Contemporary, and Country) frequently discuss marketing and promotion. Regular readers can pick up a great deal of insight into how different programmers develop marketing strategies as they attempt to fulfill the needs and wants of listeners. *Multichannel News* reports on new wrinkles in cable marketing.

Broadcast Promotion and Marketing Executives (BPME), a professional group, publishes a bimonthly magazine, *BPME Image*, that includes tips presented by professionals.

NOTES

1. Victor P. Buell, *Marketing Management: A Strategic Planning Approach*, McGraw-Hill, New York, 1984, pp. 20–31.

2. Ibid., p. 10.

3. Ibid., pp. 201–202.

4. Ibid., p. 19.

5. Merrill Panitt, "Review: 'CBS This Morning,'" *TV Guide*, May 14, 1988, p. 40.

6. L. J. Davis, "How Tinker Turned It Around," *Channels*, January/February 1986, pp. 31–39.

7. Adam Buckman, "CBS: Key Viewers Now 35-to-54, Not 18-to-49," *Electronic Media*, April 23, 1990, p. 38; "CBS Marketing Study Shows Aging Audience," *Broadcasting*, April 23, 1990, p. 64.

8. William J. Stanton, Michael J. Etzel, and Bruce J. Walker, *Fundamentals of Marketing*, 9th ed., McGraw-Hill, New York, 1991, pp. 38–52.

9. "Top Shows among Black Viewers," in Nielsen Media Research's "Television Viewing Among Blacks: The 1989–90 Season," reported in *Electronic Media*, July 8, 1991, p. 42; "Blacks View More TV, Study Says," *Electronic Media*, Sept. 30, 1991, p. 24.

10. Alfred J. Jaffe, "Ballooning Older Demos Are Changing Marketing Landscape," *Television/Radio Age*, June 26, 1989, pp. 34–35; Edmond M. Rosenthal, "The Grey Boom: Agencies Cued—for Tomorrow," *Television/Radio Age*, June 26, 1989, pp. 37–38; Jean Bergantini Grillo, "New Study Sees Gold in the 'Young Old,'" *Multichannel News*, Oct. 2, 1989, pp. 37, 40; "Growing Old Gratefully: Adults 55+," *Broadcasting*, June 3, 1991, p. 48.

11. Steven Beschloss, "Making the Rules in Prime Time," *Channels*, May 7, 1990, p. 26.

12. Richard Zoglin, "The Fox Trots Faster," *Time*, Aug. 27, 1990, p. 65.

13. Marianne Paskowki, "'Hit List' Paints Picture of Advertiser Resistance," *Electronic Media*, Feb. 19, 1990, pp. 1, 31; "HRP Draws Up Latest 'Hit List,'" *Electronic Media*, April 2, 1990, p. 8.

14. "Stereo TV Now the Norm," *Tuscaloosa News TV & Video*, Oct. 21, 1990, p. 23H.

15. "Nielsen Study: Lower Dial Position = Higher Ratings," *Broadcasting/Cable*, Jan. 8, 1990, p. 12.

16. Stanton, Etzel, and Walker, op. cit, pp. 217–218.

17. Al Ries and Jack Trout, *Positioning: The Battle for Your Mind*, McGraw-Hill, New York, 1981, p. 3.

18. Ibid., p. 40.

19. Paul I. Bortz, Mark C. Wyche, and James M. Trautman, *Great Expectations: A Television Manager's Guide to the Future*, National Association of Broadcasters, Washington, D.C., 1986, pp. 127–128.

20. Andrew Grossman, "It's How You Play the Game," *Channels,* Aug. 13, 1990, p. 14.

21. Rob Balon, "Fine-Tuning Positioning Liners: You Are What You Say You Are," *Radio & Records*, Sept. 7, 1990, p. 52.

22. Chris Porter, "You Never Know Until You Ask," *Radio & Records*, May 18, 1990, p. 48.

23. Telephone interview, Nov. 2, 1990.

CHAPTER 3

Analysis of Program Content

What causes people to tune in a particular television show or choose one radio station over another? This is a concern that underlies every programming decision, particularly when one is developing new programs or placing untried program material in the schedule. Moreover, the way in which all the elements in a program are put together is crucial to whether the program is successful or another of many failed attempts.

This chapter describes attributes that appear to a greater or lesser extent in virtually all radio and television programs. After a discussion of basic program appeals, we examine the framework of a television program, its program structure. We then describe a number of specific program types that have appeared consistently during the history of television. This is followed by an assessment of radio programs, including the contributions of personalities and the importance of program structure.

PROGRAM APPEALS

Appeals are the elements within a program that motivate people to watch or listen. As Lichty and Ripley have stated, program appeals can be considered the ways in which the content fulfills people's needs, drives, and desires.[1] Based on the approach taken with a particular program, one or more of these appeals may predominate, but most radio and television programs contain several. The major program content appeals include conflict and competition, sex appeal and personality, comedy, recognition and human interest, and information.

Conflict and Competition

The appeal of conflict can be observed in the attendance at a football game that promises to be a struggle between two powerhouse teams as opposed to a game between a clearly superior team and a weak opponent. When the outcome is in doubt, suspense is heightened. Audience interest is greater, and attendance at the stadium and in the television audience is much higher.

Conflict is inherently interesting because the viewers get to choose sides and root for certain characters over others. They can cheer for justice, for altruism, or for revenge. Conflict of almost any kind fosters involvement in the show and generates suspense or a sense of uncertainty about the outcome.

Direct conflict is easy to dramatize. The themes of good against evil and right versus wrong are easy to understand, and violent solutions can be rationalized as necessary in the fight against evil.[2] Such shows capitalize on people's interest in violence, the same element that draws audiences to boxing matches and auto races.

There is considerable concern, especially among television watchdog groups, about one form of conflict—violence—and its potentially harmful effects on young viewers. The fact remains, however, that violence represents one of television's primary drawing cards.

Conflict does not necessarily mean brutality or murder and mayhem. Personal endangerment is a form of conflict in which characters must survive against the natural forces that threaten them. Nature shows such as *National Geographic* specials follow this form, often showing the struggle of animals to avoid predators.

Some drama and action shows feature avalanches, floods, shipwrecks, and "lost-in-the-jungle" forms of conflict. That sort of setting often serves as a backdrop for a conflict between the characters. They fight themselves and each other as much as they fight nature.

Yet another type of conflict features a man or woman against himself or herself. Such shows dwell on the inner workings of the psyche as characters wrestle with self-doubt and struggle over values, beliefs, and ethics.[3] Such programs are exemplified by shows such as *thirtysomething,* in which the characters agonize over the sacrifices and limitations of having a family while pursuing a career and the dilemma of having to fire a well-liked employee.[4] Many programs feature situations in which a character must decide whether to "do the right thing." For instance, in one situation comedy a teenage girl accepted a date to a big dance and then was invited by the football team's star quarterback. Should she dump the guy whose invitation she had already accepted, never mind how hurt he might be, in order to go out with the "hunk"?

The metaphysical struggle of an individual God tends toward the theological and existential and is characterized by cerebral themes.[5] In the *Family Ties* episode "My Name Is Alex," for example, Alex wrestles with the death of a young friend and must examine his own values and sense of the order of the universe and a supreme being's plan.

Sex Appeal and Personality

Former NBC programmer Paul Klein drew much attention for his quip that audiences tune in to television hoping to see a couple in the throes of mad and passionate lovemaking. "We cannot give them that, of course," he is reputed to have said, "but it should never be far from our minds." Television sex appeal is characterized by more talk than action, although soap operas have become increasingly spicy as the characters hint at what they have done or intend to do.

Some series include contextual sex appeals that are only thinly disguised. In *Charlie's Angels,* for example, the Angels had to solve a number of crimes at beaches and spas which required them to wear skimpy attire to blend in. In the short-lived 1989 program *Nightingales* the nurses were out of their uniforms more often than they were fully attired, which drew criticism from the nursing profession.[6]

The other side of sex appeal is personality. Viewers may be attracted to characters because of their likability. For example, most of the characters in situation comedies are attractive, likable people whom we like to watch as they interact with other characters and deal with the situations presented to them in the plot. Sex appeal may emphasize beauty over eroticism. For example, former Charlie's Angel Jaclyn Smith played a homicide detective in a 1992 "made-for-TV" movie, *In the Arms of a Killer.* Unlike real life and even many other crime/detective movies, where the investigators are ordinary-looking people who wear cheaply made clothing and have plain hairdos, Smith was beautifully made up and coiffed. While the plot was, to quote *TV Guide,* "unreal and gloppy," Smith was beautiful to look at even though her appearance made her far from credible as a detective.

Comedy

Laughter is an enjoyable experience and is especially valued as a way to relieve some of the pressure created by the demands made on our time throughout the day. Thus, most people turn to radio and television for diversion from the tedium of the day or as a way to relax. The silliness offered each night on *Late Night with David Letterman* may not appeal to all viewers, but it works for those who want to relax by watching something that will not tax their intellects and can distract them from whatever kept them up that late.

When we recognize the human foibles of others, we often find humor in those situations. For instance, in an episode of *Coach,* Hayden grudgingly succumbed to pressure to become engaged and, instead of going to a jewelry store, got a deal on the diamond ring, which wasn't delivered on time, forcing him to substitute a fake diamond. The comedic aspects of his cheapskate action were revealed when he tried to make it right.

Recognition and Human Interest

Recognition makes us see ourselves sometimes as we are, sometimes as we want to be, and sometimes as we fear we are. Characters' flaws tend to mirror our own, and we empathize with their feelings and actions. Similarly, we can see some of our better points in them. If most adult males are honest, they can recognize at least some aspects of their own character in Homer Simpson's self-indulgence as he gobbles doughnuts or is distracted at the bar while daughter Lisa awaits his attendance at her recital. Similarly, Bob Newhart's character can evoke an empathic response from most viewers, as we have all felt somewhat awkward in the presence of obnoxious people with strong egos. Most people would like to be as handsome or beautiful and in command as the successful, well-dressed men and women who populate *L.A. Law.* In other words, we identify with characters and the situations in which they are presented.

Most viewers have an innate curiosity about the lives of other people, particularly the well known. Thus, television coverage of the trial of William Kennedy Smith on charges that he raped a woman he had picked up at a Palm Beach, Florida, bar was prompted by viewer interest. The large audiences were motivated approximately equally by voyeurism and interest in the Kennedy family. Two cable networks, CNN and Court TV, provided the nation with gavel-to-gavel coverage, and many talk and news programs turned their attention to the progress of the trial. For similar reasons, programs such as *Lifestyles of the Rich and Famous* attract viewers. That program offers the curious a peek into the way celebrities and the wealthy live. No doubt, those are the appeals that attract viewers to tune in *Geraldo, Oprah Winfrey, Jenny Jones, Maury Povich, Sally Jesse Raphael, Donahue,* and *Montel Williams,* which feature subjects such as nudist camps, 50-year-old women who marry men in their twenties, the children of celebrities, cross-dressing men, and couples who carry on an active sex life after divorce. These and other programs also focus on ordinary people, because viewers can identify with and may share their problems, including how people deal with unemployment, incorrigible children, and meddling mothers-in-law.

Information

Sometimes programs show the audience how to do things or handle situations. Sometimes this is simple information, such as recipes, that are useful for living day-to-day; another program may show a viewer how to cope with life's tragedies. Shows such as *Today* and *Good Morning America* are largely built around this information appeal. PBS, independent stations, and cable networks carry many how-to shows, from cooking to repairing houses.

Programs such as *60 Minutes* and *20/20* have been joined by a host of others that base their appeal in part on information. A *Current Affair, Inside Edition,* and other "reality" shows use many of the appeals described here in combination. Identified heroes and villains, conflict, sex, and recognition are interwoven with information.

ANALYZING TELEVISION PROGRAMS

Television programs are placed in a schedule in order to attract viewers. There is a constant turnover as shows which fail to gain enough viewers to attract advertisers are replaced. In this process, producers and programmers seek the most reliable ways to ensure that the creative process achieves its programming objective. Although a foolproof formula has yet to be discovered, successful programs have many common elements that are consistently effective.

Program Formula

In a show with a **formula,** each episode follows a consistent framework that is used to develop a plot. Formula treatment is a means of anticipating the desires of the audience and asserts a consistent quality control over the product, much in the way that refrigerators and automobiles are manufactured.

Formulaic elements of comedy, for instance, include the misunderstanding, which can be fraught with all kinds of secondary meanings and undertones. Let's say Mom is planning a surprise birthday party for Dad. She enlists the aid of his best friend and subsequently spends much time with the friend. Dad is concerned about their increased chumminess but is not ready to make an accusation until he overhears Mom saying to the friend, "I have had so much fun doing this. It's wonderful. I hope we can do it again in the future." Depending on the show, the sexual implications can be played at varying levels. In *Alf* the laugh would be low on the sex scale, but in *Three's Company* that aspect of the joke would be played to the hilt.

In a comedy, the bad character may try to impose some penalty on the good character, such as the loss of a job, but the conflict is played for laughs and the bad character always fails. In a drama, the hero may be undermined by the villain in a business deal and the conflict may be played out as economic peril, as in *Dallas,* where J.R. was constantly attempting to ruin a rival or keep the enemies of Ewing Oil at bay. In action/adventure, the confrontation is usually more physical, and a bad character may try to kill the good character.

Successful formulas are often adapted to fit the premise of other programs. The success of Archie Bunker's abrasive "social relevance" in *All in the Family* was copied in *Maude,* where actress Bea Arthur, who had played Archie's wife's strong-willed cousin, was given her own series. The conflicts in *Maude,* though, were usually caused by her strident liberalism, not the working-class bigotry espoused by Archie.

In any TV series, the characters maintain a consistent stance and viewers can count on certain behavior from episode to episode. For instance, the sparring marital partners formula of radio's *The Bickersons* has always been well represented on television in a wide variety of shows ranging from Archie versus Edith Bunker in *All in the Family* to more recent series such as *Walter and Emily,* starring Brian Keith as Cloris Leachman's irascible husband. The formula is carried out even on *Golden Girls,* where the four women continually jab verbally at one another.

As illustrated in Box 3-1, the objectives of programs are met by following a set of conventions that efficiently communicate information necessary for audience orientation and enjoyment of a show.

Program Structure

The basic structural elements of television programs include openings or introductions, demographic-specific themes, 8-minute minicrises, teases, bumpers, extended rising action, late climaxes, and an extremely fast ending or resolution to the story (the denouement).

Introductions Regardless of the type of program, an important purpose of the program introduction is to provide viewers with an orientation so that they will easily understand the circumstances in which the plot is to unfold. Thus, at the beginning of each episode of *The Simpsons* the audience is quickly informed that Marge is a mother who does not work outside the home (she is shown driving from a store with her baby daughter), Lisa is a talented saxophone player who does not quite fit society's expectation

---

**BOX 3-1
FORMULA
OBJECTIVES**

A basic formula will do the following:

- Orient the viewers so they quickly understand and accept the circumstances under which the plot will unfold
- Maintain consistency in the series from episode to episode so that viewers will always know what they are tuning in to watch
- Establish the context, roles, and personalities of the characters
- Place the good character (protagonist) in conflict with the opposing character (antagonist)
- Intensify the conflict between the protagonist and antagonist
- Introduce a possible plan for resolution that may include good outside forces
- In a direct confrontation, show good overcoming bad
- Wrap up the details   ■

of conformity, Bart is a devil-may-care kid who virtually blasts out the door of his school on a skateboard, and Homer has a boring assembly-line job that he does not care about performing particularly well.

Thus, in the **exposition** introductions are handled quickly because people have so many program choices. If the program does not grab viewers right away—that is, if they are required to work hard to understand and follow the plot—they are likely to tune to something else. Consequently, a show must attract attention in the first 60 seconds or so. Moreover, a strong **hook,** or compelling reason to remain tuned, must be established in the first few minutes. In action shows, the hook is often a sexual or violent event. In comedy, a big laugh must occur at the beginning. In a drama, the theme of the show must be made evident quickly. In *Colombo,* for example, even before Detective Colombo appears on the scene, the viewer sees that a murder has taken place and knows who committed the crime. Invariably, the perpetrator is a very intelligent individual, a well-tailored and manicured person who usually holds a position that illustrates his or her considerable success in life. The remainder of the episode shows Columbo's coffee-stained, raincoated character ("Oh, by the way, just one more question.") badgering the villain until he or she is finally ensnared by the single mistake in an otherwise perfect crime.

Demographic-specific themes Increasingly, television programs are aimed at demographic groups rather than heterogeneous audiences. Although TV shows appeal to general audiences, their primary direction is demographic-specific, and when they lose that appeal, they lose their central audience identification. The primary audience appeal of *Designing Women*, for instance, is to female viewers. *Golden Girls* has its strongest appeal to women, but it also appeals to older persons.

Younger viewers are attracted to comedies such as *Growing Pains* and *Doogie Howser*. Many children are regular viewers of the situation comedy *Hey Dude* and the game show *What*

Would You Do? on Nickelodeon, while older audiences identify with *Murder She Wrote* and *Matlock*. Men tend to be attracted to action shows such as *Wiseguy* and *Hunter*. In each case, elements important in the lives of the target demographic are integrated into the show's episodes. In every show, consistent themes are apparent. In *The Golden Girls* these themes include both platonic and romantic relationships among older persons and the way in which the attitudes of a youth-oriented culture affect older persons. *What Would You Do?* features lots of whacking the host on the head with a giant powder puff, pie-in-the-face gags, and votes by the studio audience to determine whether a kid eats a snail or sees a bucket of blue goo dumped on his mother's head.

Eight-minute minicrises A **cliff-hanger** occurs when some peril threatens a character or an important development in a relationship is established. The audience is forced to wait to see how the problem is resolved. Whether minute-to-minute, week-to-week, or season-to-season, cliff-hangers bring viewers back to the show.

Commercial blocks are scheduled about every 8 minutes in television. With so many interruptions, the audience may be tempted to go elsewhere during the usual 2-minute commercial breaks that are placed within programs. The remote control comes into play here because it makes it easy for viewers to check out other channels, where they may find something interesting and never come back.[7] Consequently, a **minicrisis** creates the promise of a reward to induce viewers to return after the commercials. As the scene ends, viewers are shown that a character is in a situation that must be resolved immediately. Of course, the screen fades to black at the crucial moment, and the viewer cannot see the outcome until after the ads. Action is frozen at the moment of import, often with a close-up of the protagonist's face as she or he recognizes the peril; this also lets viewers know how important the crisis is.

After the commercial block, the immediate crisis is resolved, only to be followed by another that builds to a critical point about 8 minutes later. At the same time, the overarching plot is being developed and will eventually lead to the major climax in the episode.

The cliff-hanger has proved to be a workable device for enticing the audience back after the spring and summer break in the production of new episodes. For example, in the final scene of the last episode of *Dallas* for the 1979–1980 season, the conniving J.R. was shot by an unknown assailant. The mystery was not resolved until the premiere episode the next season, forcing viewers to wait months to learn whether he would live and who had shot him.

Thanks in large measure to the record-breaking audience for the "Who Shot J.R.?" episode, the producers of *Dynasty* responded by having a mysterious woman appear as a prosecution witness against Blake Carrington at his murder trial in the episode that ended the 1980–1981 season. *Dynasty* took the cliff-hanger to a greater height a few years later with a season finale in which terrorists machine-gunned a crowd that included nearly all the primary characters.

Teases A tease is a hint about what is to come. In a news program, the tease is a brief synopsis of a very interesting story which is mentioned at the beginning of a newscast and perhaps over one or more commercial breaks. It heightens viewers' interest and compels them to stay tuned to the newscast to get the rest of the story. Thus, a tease serves the same function as a minicrisis or cliff-hanger by making people want to see what happens next.

In a soap opera the tease is often the promise of sex or a confrontation between characters. A couple may seem to be on a course that will end in the bedroom, when the scene shifts to another subplot or to a commercial. A newcomer to town may be on the verge of telling the mayor that she is his illegitimate daughter. Teasing thus maintains viewers' interest in the outcome so that they can be held through several commercial breaks or even through several episodes.

In weekly series television shows the tease is usually resolved within the individual episode,

although more and more shows carry teases through subsequent episodes. For example, many of the romantic relationships between the characters in *L.A. Law* were developed over several episodes. Roxanne's relationship with Arnold Becker, for instance, went from faithful and supportive friend, to dismay and then aloofness caused by her disgust over his philandering, then to sexual attraction, and finally to lover over several seasons.

Teases have also been used as running plot lines. In *Cheers* viewers were teased for years with the on-again, off-again relationship between Sam and Diane. Most viewers wanted them to be together, and that made those viewers vulnerable to a long-term tease of relationship and marriage. When Shelley Long, who played Diane, left the program, the source of sexual tension was assumed by Kirstie Alley's character, Rebecca, as she and Sam carried on a similar love-hate relationship. In circumstances very similar to *Three's Company,* where Jack lived with two beautiful roommates, the principal characters on *Cheers* are in titillatingly close contact in the bar. Yet nothing happens as each one is afraid to make a clear commitment to the other.

Bumpers A **bumper** is resolved right after the commercial break, whereas a tease may be carried out much later. On a news program, an announcement such as "When we come back, the story behind the firing of the Mudcats' coach" tells the audience that story will come immediately after a commercial break. Such statements preview the reward to viewers who stick with the program.

Whereas a bumper is content-related and spoken in a news program, it is usually acted out in television drama. For example, character A says, "You want to know what I think of you—well, I'll tell you!" Thus, the bumper comes in the form of a minicrisis that will be resolved right after the commercial break.

Extended rising action The events leading to the climax of a story are called **rising action**. While minicrises are a part of the overall plot, there is a larger theme, and all the action supports it. Let's say the theme of a program episode is that people should be honest. Two of the series characters, Jan and Jim, are friends. Jim is enamored of Susie, who is using him to gain access to his friend George. A minicrisis develops around Jan's awareness of all this as she wrestles with the dilemma of whether to warn Jim about Susie and surely hurt his feelings and endanger their friendship. Other minicrises could hinge on Jim's starry-eyed adventures with the scheming Susie, George's unwitting encouragement of Susie, and Jan's eventual confrontation with Susie and Jim.

These events can be be structured to maximize the importance of truth as each character is involved in a subplot where he or she loses sight of the truth for various reasons. The resolution occurs when the characters and issues come together. For example, if *Roseanne* has a fight with her sister-in-law Crystal over how she should raise the baby, the conflict will be resolved and the women will have patched up their differences by the conclusion of the episode. It is important to delay the resolution until late in the program to hold the audience for the entire episode. Thus, rising action takes up 90 percent or more of the time available in most shows.[8]

Climax   In a drama, the program **climax** is the high point in the program, occurring after the action has built to a point where the situation must be resolved. The climax occurs late in any television program whether it is a 30-minute comedy or a 16-hour miniseries. Since the rising action must hold the viewers' attention until the end of the program, the final confrontation that constitutes the climax must be put off until the last possible moment or audience members may check the viewing alternatives on other channels.

Denouement   The rising action, along with the subplots, holds viewers' attention and motivates their interest in seeing how things turn out. Viewers have learned by now that things will turn out all right (this is television, and major characters cannot be killed off or turn bad), but the question that remains to be answered is how.

A **fast denouement** refers to the unraveling of a mystery, the explanation of the elements that have led to the climax, and the restoration of order. Since the information must be delivered to viewers in a very short time, this places pressure on the writers to foreshadow the resolution or stick to simple elements that can be explained briefly. In some shows the explanation itself holds interest. In the *Columbo* series, for example, the culprit and the crime are introduced early in each episode. The primary appeal of the series is based on how Lieutenant Columbo solves the crime. At the end of one episode, for instance, the detective explained to his adversary, a whiskey-drinking Irishman, that he got the goods on him because of an Irish whiskey bottle left at the murder scene. The villain was undone by a habit of scoring the side of the bottle with his diamond ring to mark the level of liquor consumed. The murder had resulted from a confrontation with the victim, with whom the murderer had been sharing a drink.

Resolution is important in a series because it reestablishes order. Viewers know that everything is back to normal for the main character until the next week, when he or she will be confronted by a new mystery or danger. In the case of *Columbo,* the viewer knows that the case has been resolved and that order has been restored in Columbo's world. In other series, the restoration of normality is accomplished during a final scene in which the characters are together, relaxed and cheerful, with all the tension that contributed to the plot removed. Next week, though, some new force will intercede to set up a conflict that will motivate the development of that plot.

Structural Shorthand

Most shows share the structural attributes of stereotypes and familiarity. The medium must establish and tell stories quickly, usually within 30 or 60 minutes, and that requires the use of some "shorthand," which often includes stereo-types.

A *stereotype* occurs when characters are given a narrow set of attributes that depict a group of people as having common characteristics that do not allow for individuality. Accurate and fair or not, stereotypes abound in television because they communicate information efficiently. A thug can be created simply by dressing a swarthy man who has a permanent five o'clock shadow in a shiny suit and giving him an Italian name. The creation of a fanatical terrorist merely requires the producer to cast an actor with Arabic features. In seconds, viewers recognize both characters.

If the star of a show needs a foil, the easy treatment is to typecast a blond, ditzy woman or man. Viewers immediately understand that the character is an airhead. The writer needs no exposition, as the stereotype does the work.

Unfortunately, stereotypes may represent reality to viewers who have a limited frame of reference for the group that is being portrayed or whose biases are reinforced by the depiction. Many groups have felt stigmatized by the lack of sensitivity in simplistic characterizations.

TV Program Genres

Some types of programs work very effectively when scheduled with other program **genres,** or types of shows, but others stand as islands, not working well with other forms. Thus, genre should be included with program appeals and structure as elements taken into consideration by programmers. Types of television shows come and go, but some genres have remained over the decades.

Situation comedies Chief among the survivors has been the **situation comedy (sitcom).** In the sitcom we are confronted with exaggerated versions of everyday living that range from family relationships to death and taxes. It's the familiarity that makes identification with these shows so easy.

Comedies have excellent scheduling potential and can be blocked with a host of different kinds of programs. Sitcoms use the half-hour program length, which gives them the greatest flexibility in scheduling. Moreover, many sitcoms appeal to a wide range of viewers, and this further enhances their utility in a program schedule. For instance, while children find *Laverne and Shirley*'s Lenny and Squiggy amusing because of their broad characterizations and slapstick humor, older viewers may pay more attention to the dialogue and enjoy Laverne and Shirley's constant quest to find boyfriends in addition to the goofier antics of the other characters on the show. Similarly, *Night Court*'s Bull contributes slapstick humor, while adults may be more attracted to Judge Harry Stone's sardonic quips.

Action/adventure Characterized by car chases, gunplay, and plots involving good guys versus bad guys, **action/adventure** shows are high in action (a euphemism for violence) and sometimes in sex appeal as well. It is easy to figure out who the good guys and bad guys are, and criminals are always brought to justice. These are the modern westerns with a private detective substituted for the marshal. Shows such as *Hunter* and *Quantum Leap* fall into this category.

Drama Focus on interactions and relationships between characters rather than action separates **drama** from action/adventure. One dramatic type—the soap opera—began on radio and has dominated daytime television for decades. In the 1970s a variation of the soap opera flourished during prime time with the introduction of *Dallas, Dynasty, Falcon Crest,* and *Knot's Landing.* Yet another variation on continuing drama, though much less serial in nature, includes *Hill Street Blues* and *L.A. Law,* in which some plot lines are carried out over several episodes. For example, Douglas Brackman's deteriorating marriage was chronicled over a period of time, as was Leland McKenzie's May-December romance with law partner Grace Van Owen.

Reality **Reality** programs focus on real people and events. Programs such as *60 Minutes* and *20/20* follow the traditions of broadcast journalism and are produced by their networks' news divisions. Another popular form is the crimestopper show, such as *America's Most Wanted.* Yet another treatment, *Entertainment Tonight,* deals with entertainment news and celebrity profiles. Tabloid, or "trash news," shows such as *A Current Affair* blur the line between news and blatant exploitation of sex and scandal.

One reason for the rising popularity of reality shows is that they cost little to produce. As the networks have struggled to maintain both audience and profitability, they have turned more and more to reality programming as a solution.

Reality programs are very versatile for scheduling purposes. They can be placed next to other news programs, and many stations broadcast *Entertainment Tonight* after the local late-evening news. Reality shows work well before or after sitcoms, game shows, and court shows.

Documentaries **Documentaries**, which follow a long tradition of presenting information based on actuality footage, come in a number of forms. Some are designed to educate viewers about many sides of an issue and take no position of their own. Others strongly advocate a point of view and supply information to support that view. In terms of issues, they range from abortion and gun control to sex and violence.

Whatever their orientation, documentaries traditionally draw small and narrowly focused audiences. They are not popular with programmers, as they deliver lower ratings. As a result, the broadcast networks, which produced most of the documentaries over the years, dramatically curtailed their production of such shows in the 1980s.

In the late 1980s NBC carried two documentaries that signaled a change. The first was Geraldo Rivera's look into Satanism, "Devil Worship: Exposing Satan's Underground," and the second was Connie Chung's examination of sex in America, "Scared Sexless." Both drew substantial audiences and showed that documentaries about particular subjects can succeed. Even so, such a limited focus can be used only so often, and the documentary form has more and more been relegated to public television and cable networks.

The nature documentary seems to have found a home on the Discovery Channel, which features many programs about animals and nature. Historical documentary series originally produced by TV network news divisions have been scheduled by the Arts and Entertainment cable network. For example, the series *The Twentieth Century,* which was narrated by Walter Cronkite and broadcast during the 1960s on CBS, was later run on A&E, as was the 1950s series *World War I,* also narrated by Cronkite.

At this writing, the only traditional broadcast network that is devoting an appreciable amount of scheduling to documentary programming is PBS, with series including *P.O.V.* and *Frontline.*

PBS has presented a number of special documentary series, including the acclaimed 13-part *Vietnam: A Television History,* originally broadcast in 1982. This was followed by the six-part *Eyes on the Prize,* which chronicled the early civil rights movement in the south. *Eyes on the Prize II* carried the story of the movement into the current period. The critical success of the form was further burnished by the wide audience interest won by the six-part *Civil War.* Although the historical compilation documentary form has had much success, its future is dependent on obtaining the funding necessary to undertake such projects. Producers typically must scrounge for contributions by corporations and foundations virtually up to the completion of production in order to finish these projects.

Miniseries The **miniseries** is a multihour production that is presented over a specific sequence of days. The form came into its own as a television genre with *Roots,* which premiered on ABC on January 23, 1977. That series, which chronicled the history of an African slave and his descendants, was not expected to attract much of an audience but was broadcast to garner prestige. Consequently, ABC programmers scheduled it on successive evenings during a single week to minimize the damage by getting the loss of audience over with quickly. Ironically, the scheduling of the program actually induced more people to watch on successive nights as they heard about the program from friends who had watched the previous evening. The last episode of that miniseries was among the most highly rated in television history, drawing 100 million viewers, a fact not lost on network programmers. Thus, high-cost multinight projects continued into the late 1980s.

The failure of *Amerika,* a miniseries that depicted the United States being overrun by the Soviet Union, harkened a change. This $14^1/_2$-hour high-budget thriller did not draw large enough audiences to justify its expense. By 1990 no miniseries longer than 4 hours were being scheduled. Still, an occasional exception is made. The acclaimed CBS miniseries *Lonesome Dove* proved so popular that even after it had been broadcast twice on the network, it was released on videotape and is still available at video rental stores.

Docudramas Docudramas—dramatic presentations of true-life situations—have been around since the 1950s, when historical reconstructions were common on shows such as *You Are There,* in which CBS News correspondent Walter Cronkite took viewers, in on-location news fashion, to Troy or the trial of Socrates. Moviemakers and television producers have long been fascinated with historical figures and events. But while the ideas are already conveniently in existence, historical figures and events do not always make interesting programming. Often figures of great historical importance lead dull lives. Producers often take dramatic license with the facts to make these programs more interesting, but this practice has generated criticism from historians and critics who point to their inaccuracies and embellishments.

Movies Movies have long been a staple in television programming. A large volume of attractive programming product already exists, and the box office attendance and publicity surrounding a motion picture provide a good indication of the likelihood of attracting an audience on television. Moreover, a compelling movie should maintain its audience, whereas the audiences for programs that end after an hour or half hour are more likely to consider the program choices on competing channels.

Competition for high-quality theatrical releases has intensified as pay-cable services such as HBO, basic cable networks such as Lifetime, and video rental outlets compete as outlets for films. Also, the content of some movies makes them unsuitable for television without extensive editing.

Another important factor for pay-cable services as well as broadcast and basic cable networks is that theatrical releases have been seen by many potential viewers long before they are available on TV. Most movies have had a theatrical run, a home video release, a pay-per-view cable release, and a pay-television release before being made available to basic cable networks or broadcast networks. By that time they have become quite shopworn, and this explains why when a movie is finally shown in a local station broadcast, it is usually in a late-night time period when few people are watching TV.

Television and cable networks and pay-cable services produce some of their own movies, often referred to as **made-fors,** to fill their programming needs. An advantage of custom-produced movies is that both their content and their length can be controlled to accommodate time periods in which programming is needed and to permit the insertion of commercial breaks without destroying the continuity of the story.

In addition to have providing program fare, made-for movies are also useful as prototypes, or **pilot programs,** in developing program series. A movie that attracts a large audience can be further developed as a regular series since the casting has been done and the premise of the program has been demonstrated. Moreover, a 2-hour movie can be repeated, whereas there is little likelihood that a half-hour pilot will have any utility as a program to be scheduled by it-self.

Children's television Some program forms are limited to certain days of the week or particular time periods. Children's programs predominate on Saturday morning. They also turn up in early morning and during afternoons, most often on independent stations and cable networks. Since network-affiliated stations tend to program for adults, other program outlets try to appeal to children, a sizable and underserved audience.

In the past, stations were dependent on Hollywood-produced cartoons, but the inexpensive animation developed by Hanna-Barbara allowed for animated content specifically tailored for the television audience and the time constraints of television. It was no fluke that the Turner Broadcasting System acquired Hanna-Barbara in 1991, since it provides TBS with an in-house programming source that TBS doesn't have to share with any other outlet.

The "Disney Afternoon" package including *Chip and Dale's Rescue Rangers, Duck Tales,* and *Tale Spin* that became available in the early 1990s marked a strong return to animation backed by one of the most important providers of animated product. The Disney Studios' magic, accompanied by the continuing popularity of such series as *Teenage Mutant Ninja Turtles* and Steven Spielberg's entrance into animated television through *Tiny Toons,* has revitalized animation.

Network reruns such as *Silver Spoons* and the even older *Gilligan's Island* have proved successful in transitional periods where it is necessary to appeal to both children and adults. Nickelodeon specializes in programming for children during the day and fills its schedules with cartoons and child-oriented contest programs such as *Family Double Dare,* in which parent-child teams compete in obstacle course races.

Variety **Variety programs,** which combine entertainment acts ranging from singers and dancers to comic skits and stand-up comedians, are a genre that has declined over the years. One of the major variety shows was *The Ed Sul-*

livan Show, which began in the 1950s and ran into the 1960s. Major performers such as Elvis Presley and the Beatles received their first U.S. network television exposure on that show. *The Sonny and Cher Show* was a big hit for several seasons in the early 1970s but failed at about the time the couple's marriage ended. ABC tried in 1987–1988 to resurrect the variety form with *The Dolly Parton Show.* Although critically well received, *The Tracy Ullman Show* languished from 1988 to 1990 on Fox. It was, however, picked up by Lifetime and went back into production there. CBS attempted a revival of *The Carol Burnett Show* in 1991, but the program was canceled after a few weeks.

Like other program forms that wax and wane in popularity, variety may make a successful return in the future. During the mid-1980s some people in the television industry thought that sitcoms were in their death throes, but the genre recovered and is as popular among audiences now as it ever was.

Westerns **Westerns** had their heyday in the 1950s and 1960s, when as many as 25 series graced the prime-time network landscape. But the western declined quickly and died off by the mid-1970s. However, the tales of the old west have been retooled as action/adventure shows which use the same plots set in more contemporary and urban landscapes. The motif of good versus evil has been adapted and the characters have been updated, but the form is very similar.

Following up on the success of the theatrical motion picture, the 1990 series *The Young Riders* premiered on ABC and developed a loyal following. It was the first western in years to make good. On the heels of this success, CBS brought back the canceled *Paradise* in January 1991 and renamed it *Guns of Paradise.*

Generally, when one show of a type succeeds, imitators follow and a trend begins. Eventually, though, program types go out of fashion. However, rather than dying, TV program genre become dormant and can be resurrected later. Or, as in the case of westerns, the genre can come back in another incarnation.

ANALYZING RADIO PROGRAMS

Radio Program Structure

Episodes of television series generally begin with an introduction in which viewers are given an orientation to the characters and the situation they are to be involved in. This is followed by the plot development and then by the climax. Last comes the denouement, where order is restored until the next week's episode.

Such a structure works in radio only for episodic programs or programs of a distinct time length. Formula radio programming continues for several hours. Listeners expect a certain consistency in the music and other events during the daypart. Nevertheless, basic principles of structure apply. Radio programming researcher David T. MacFarland has extended the concept of Aristotelian dramatic structure discussed below by using the psychological drives of listeners to develop a programming concept that is based on the audience's physiological and psychological states at different times during the day.[9] Well-designed radio programs ensure that the format will accommodate all the elements of program structure, including building, pacing, variety, and unity.

Building There is no climax in a radio daypart since listeners tune in and out periodically. Consequently, anticipation should be fulfilled through climaxes in a rhythm of building and ebbing. The objective is to reward listeners with events such as well-conceived and well-produced humorous skits, current news reports, meaningful information such as weather and traffic reports, and, of course, the music that targeted listeners most want to hear.

One kind of building is attained by teasing events. Another method is to program commercial breaks so that they begin with the announcement that is the least interesting, such as a straight-voice announcement, and climax with the announcement that has the highest amount of listener interest, which may include lively music, sound effects, and funny dialogue. When announcements are sequenced in this manner, each can contribute to building to a climax within the set of commercials. Another approach is to schedule the most appealing categories of music strategically throughout the hour.

Pacing Pacing is the listener's illusion of a forward movement of time versus the perception of a static state. If several slow-tempo songs are played in sequence, the station's format will bog down. Conversely, when several fast-tempo records are played, the pace will increase. However, since variety appeals to most listeners (popularity is also important in determining whether a song is played on most stations), programming music according to tempo will permit the program to build in intensity and then to go back down before building again.

MacFarland calls this structure a "composite mood curve" in which the listener is aroused and the music builds to a peak in listener arousal, followed by an adaptation phase in which there is a steady level of arousal for a time. With decreasing arousal comes a period of satiation. There, the listener is relaxed before the next cycle of building to another peak. In other words, a peak in the intensity of the music is followed by an adaptation to that level. Then the listener wants to be relaxed before resuming the stimulation of more arousing music.[10]

MacFarland's approach may be more sophisticated than that followed by most programmers, but the goal is the same: control over mood through careful sequencing of the music that is presented. Tempo is instrumental in a radio program's pacing. At some times of the day listeners may prefer a slow pace because they use the radio as a companion while at work and would be distracted by music that builds to high levels of intensity. But at other times, such as when they get into their cars after a long day at work, listeners may demand a quicker state of arousal because they are seeking a change in the mood they were in while pursuing their jobs. Now they are unfettered by the demands of the workplace and want to relax as they look forward to going home to dinner.

Pacing can bog down when records are **back announced,** which occurs when the disc jockey relays information about artists and titles after songs have aired. While back announcing is effective in certain programming formulas, it may diminish the listener's perception of a continual forward movement of time, even in an Easy-Listening format, where the pace of the program may be intentionally slow. Furthermore, if an announcer interjects a long commentary after a music recording, the digression is likely to be irritating to listeners. For example, if a Jazz announcer goes on at great length about the performers on a piece that was just played, only the most astute Jazz buff will not begin to fidget. Similarly, a Country disc jockey who waxes on about Jerry Lee Lewis's birthday may be telling listeners a fact of mild interest, but what they really want is to hear another song as good as or better than the one by "The Killer" they just heard.

Most popular music stations try to avoid **dead air,** or prolonged periods of silence. In some formats a couple of seconds can seem like an eternity. In such cases disc jockeys are often instructed to talk over the introduction to the record as a way to increase the pacing of the program. In many such stations the disc jockeys are provided with information on the number of seconds of introductory music preceding the vocal and the amount of time at the end so that they will know how much time is available for making comments over each recording's "intros" and "outros."

The absence of sound can also work as an effective pacing device. If the announcer pauses for a beat or so at the end of a record before beginning the next comment, it may contribute to the relaxed presentation an Easy-Listening or other adult-oriented format is attempting to achieve.

The use of a station identification in the form of a **jingle**—a produced musical insertion that usually includes a chorus of singers—that is played immediately after a commercial break is a means of enhancing the pacing because it can be a signature for the pacing goal of the format. Whereas a Beautiful-Music jingle will be smooth and relaxed, a Country or pop music format jingle will be much more energetic, a lively burst of sound to serve notice to listeners that they are about to be rewarded with a record.

Variety Many examples of variety are present in all formats: Every record is different, the comments of disc jockeys are varied, the news changes, and there is a plethora of commercial announcements for a range of goods and services.

Still, variety can suffer if the list of songs played regularly is too short, causing some records to be aired too frequently, or if listeners begin to tire of some of the songs that are played. Records of similar tempo or style played close together can diminish variety; commercial announcements can become stale as well. The production style of commercials may not differ enough for most listeners to distinguish among them. In some stations one individual produces the majority of the commercials. If a single copywriter bangs out a high volume of commercial continuity each day, the spots are bound to begin to sound alike. Also, many a disc jockey has such a limited repertoire that his or her comments soon become redundant to listeners.

Programming music according to each record's tempo and intensity can also contribute to variety. When a music set is built and then dropped off from a peak in intensity, the listener is built up and then brought back down rather than being subjected to a long period of slower songs or songs with high intensity. Music programming resembles the way dance bands and disco jocks work: Slow numbers are presented periodically to give the dancers an opportunity to get close together or take a break from the dance floor. The change of pace provides a form of psychic relief.

Unity Unity is a seeming contradiction to variety, but the two concepts coincide. Although every record on the playlist may be performed by a different artist, there is a unifying theme among most of them, which is represented by the integration of the events in a particular format. In a Country music format, for example, most artists are recognized as Country by the emphasis on guitar accompaniment, the southern accents of performers, and the rhythm of the music.

Another unifying aspect of a format can be the projection of a particular lifestyle by the on-air personalities. In a rock music format, for instance, off-color jokes and other irreverent remarks by on-air personalities may have particular appeal to young listeners. In contrast, Adult Contemporary music comedy bits that skewer elected officials may be lost on young listeners who don't have much interest in local public affairs and may have no idea who the chief of police and the mayor of the city are. However, they aren't the target audience of that format, and the core listener, who is typically 25 to 54 years of age, is much more attuned to such subjects.

Another subtle contribution to unity can be observed in the production style of many commercial announcements. Ad agencies frequently produce different versions to reflect the music format of the individual stations on which the announcement is aired. Programmers have rejected commercials because the product or the production values in the announcement clashed with the concept of the format. Moreover, the use of a jingle following clusters of commercial announcements that was discussed above helps unify the program by tying in the station ID or positioning statement and the unspoken message "Now, back to music!" as the commercial break ends and entertainment programming resumes.

Role of Personalities

The disc jockey, or announcer, is as crucial to radio programming as the anchorman or anchorwoman is to television news. Both fulfill similar functions by introducing the various events that make up the program. In the case of TV news, the variety is great: news reports from different correspondents at different sites about different subjects, sports reports on various teams and events, weather, perhaps a feature or two, and the inevitable commercials. With all this activity, the continuity provided by the anchor is crucial. Without someone in that role, a TV news program would be a string of unrelated events.

Program personalities on radio make a similar contribution to program unity. Just as the anchorpersons in a television newscast provide a focus for the whole program as a link between the various news topics, disc jockeys provide continuity through their personalities and commentary. Both what is said and when it is said are very important for pacing, variety, and tying the listening experience together as people enter and leave the audience.

The performance of the personality must be consistent. If the patter is cohesive, meaningful, and amusing during one interjection but flat and off-tempo during another, unity will suffer. Similarly, if the role of one member of the morning team is that of the straight man who laughs at the comments of the partner, that should be carried out consistently, although not necessarily in every exchange between the two, as that could sound contrived and become irritating.

Depending on the target audience and the nature of the music and other program content the station uses, personalities who are effective in the morning may not work as well in other time periods. The greatest contrast is between the demographic segments represented in the morning audience and those which may predominate during the daypart from 7 p.m. to midnight. On many stations the proportion of listeners 12 to 24 years old is much greater after 7 p.m., and so the disc jockey on duty can be much more attuned to appealing to them. Although a comparable number of teens may be listening in the morning, the total audience for most stations is dominated by people over age 18. Thus, a more adult-oriented personality will probably be much more appealing to the available audience.

In the midday period, from 10 a.m. to 3 p.m., women predominate as listeners since many men are unavailable because of school or work. Nevertheless, the programmer must be sensitive to social changes. Increasing numbers of women are in the work force, and the proportion of the available midday audience they represent is changing. In the afternoon period, from 3 to 7 p.m., teens are out of school and available to listen, but increasing numbers of older listeners are also tuning in as they get off work and make their way home. The afternoon disc jockey is typically upbeat but not as dominant as in the morning period. People want to be entertained more than they wish to be informed. They have spent a long day on the job and are looking forward to arriving home to dinner and relaxing. Moreover, many of these listeners have had access to information all day long. Even if they haven't, the news may not have changed much since they traveled to work.

Monitoring On-Air Talent

Principal among the program director's (PD) supervisory duties is the evaluation and improvement of the air staff's performance. This means conducting frequent talent meetings and providing continual coaching. The PD's people skills include positive motivation of staff members and deft handling of their egos. Critiques should be honest but should be conducted in a way that helps each person see ways to improve his or her performance.

Many program directors monitor the staff's air shifts as a tool for improving the station's programming. Such **air checks,** or samples of on-air personalites' performance, are usually taped so that they can be played back during the one-on-one critiques that are conducted weekly at many stations. The station's engineer can wire a cassette tape recorder so that it begins recording when the announcer's microphone switch is activated. This way, the recording includes a few seconds of the program material that was presented before and after the announcer talked on mike. When the bulk of the prerecorded material, including commercial announcements and songs, is automatically edited, the disc jockey's broadcast shift is thus "telescoped." A telescoped air check enables the programmer to concentrate on listening to the announcer's on-air presentation in context without having to

fast-forward through recorded music and commercials.[11]

In listening to the execution of the format, the program director considers a number of specific questions regarding the disc jockey's performance. Although different program directors may place more or less importance on them, the following considerations are typical:

- Is the format being followed, including maintaining the proper music rotation, talk policies, and jingle placement?
- How well is the disc jockey maintaining the overall flow of the program, including levels of music, transitions from event to event, and smoothness of delivery?
- Is the announcer talking to one person at a time and thus really connecting with each member of the audience, or is she or he addressing "everyone out there in radio land"? The difference lies in whether the announcer is projecting as if talking face to face with the listener. People listen to the radio one at a time even though thousands of others may also be engaged in similar one-on-one listening experiences.
- Does the announcer's delivery project energy? Does the announcer communicate with the listener in a personable, friendly manner? Does he or she use a conversational tone with natural inflection and pacing, or does the delivery sound as if copy were being read?
- In comedy sketches and dramatized bits, does the presentation give the listener a reason for a willing suspension of disbelief in order to enjoy the presentation? In other words, are the characters being portrayed in such a way that listeners will accept the situation as plausible even though they know it is a dramatic fabrication? Even though moviegoers knew that Superman was a fictional character being portrayed by Christopher Reeve and that he really couldn't fly, they were able to suspend their knowledge of these facts for the duration of the movie. On a morning radio show, if a fake telephone call is placed to the President, does the actor sound enough like the Presi-

dent for the listener to visualize him on the other end of the bogus conversation? Equally important, does the actor stay in character and comment in the style of the President so that the listeners' suspension of disbelief can be carried throughout the sketch?

- Is the mood consistently positive, as though the announcer were happy to be on the air? (There are exceptions to this consideration, but they involve unique circumstances and/or personalities.)
- Are there any pauses ("ah," "er," "um") or un- necessary words ("well, let's see") or clichés ("drivin' ya home") that could be eliminated to make the presentation tighter and less dis- tracting in communicating to the listener?
- Are talk breaks kept to one or two items, and are the comments meaningful to the listener? For example, does the announcer repeat the answers to his or her questions during tele- phone conversations or interviews? Could words and phrases be deleted from the an- nouncer's comments without weakening the presentation?
- Are call letters, frequency, and positioning statements announced often and presented clearly so that listeners understand exactly which station they are listening to?
- Is the execution of the format predictable, or does it heighten the listener's anticipation of highlights? For instance, does the announcer tell the listener that a contest will be conduct- ed "at 2:35," which could cause an immediate tune-out after the event, or is the contest run sometime between 2:15 and 3:00 p.m. without ballyhooing the specifics of when, encourag- ing listeners to remain in the audience longer?
- Is the announcer's preparation evident, or has she or he winged it through complete reliance on spontaneous comments to the listener? In other words, does the on-air talent make inter- esting, meaningful comments on items of in- terest to listeners? Successful air personalities typically prepare for their shows by reviewing a variety of newspapers and other sources of information for topical subjects, jokes, and skits. But presentation goes beyond the mere

recitation of something read in the paper or found on the station's news wire. It must be thought out and polished so that it comes out as spontaneous and without awkwardness. Many of Johnny Carson's ad libs on the *Tonight* show were effective because he pre- pared those quips and stored them so they would be at his disposal when they were most appropriate during conversations with guests. Moreover, Carson's or Jay Leno's opening monologue is a good example of topical humor based on items found in newspapers and wire services. Interestingly, many of the same items will be heard on radio stations around the country because the same sources are available to anyone who seeks them out.

- Is the announcer respectful toward people who call the station? Or are these listener- participants treated in an indifferent or conde- scending manner or otherwise unable to fully enjoy their moment on the air? (This rule ap- plies to most situations, but a few radio per- sonalities specialize in acerbic interchanges with callers.)
- Is the announcer distracted by communication with other staff members, such as carrying on private conversations or sharing inside jokes, instead of keeping the focus directly on the lis- tener?
- Is the announcer just mouthing words, or is she or he saying something that is meaningful to the listener? Is it really important, entertain- ing, or informative?[12]

A log of program events as they were present- ed on the air can help the PD analyze patterns in the presentation and look for compliance with station policies and assess strengths and weak- nesses in the execution of the station's program- ming strategy. Programming consultant Ed Shane recommends a form, similar to the one shown in Figure 3-1, that can be made on a legal pad. By developing a system of shorthand, the PD can make notations for later review about the programming, categories of music, announcing patterns, and pacing and intensity of the music and commercials.[13]

Time	Programming	Production/Commercial		Live/Recorded
8:16	"Dust in the Wind "	Good seque from preceding song		
	Kansas			
8:19		Commercial : Van Halen Concert	: 60	"I'll be there" tag sounds insincere
		Commercial : Berwin Furniture	: 30	All talk : bogs down the comm'l break
		Commercial : Frebo Grocery	: 30	"Today's Special" tag sounds rushed
8:21	"Hammer Time"			
	TC Hammer			
8:24	Sports Headlines			Abrupt , No intro
8:25	"Ice Ice Baby"			2 Rap songs back–to–back
	Vanilla Ice			
8:27	"Yesterday"			Back announced title – listeners
	Beatles			already know the song
8:30	Call letters			Calls slurred, hard to understand
	"Bad Feelings"			A new add to the play list
	Noo Groove			Use a "top 10" to start the half hour

FIGURE 3-1 Air check log format.

SUMMARY

Program appeals are the elements that bring viewers into a program's audience. While violence and sex appeal are the most powerful appeals, personality, comedy, recognition and human interest, and information work in combination to entice viewers.

Television programs are designed with mini-crises, cliff-hangers, bumpers, and teases to suit the commercial needs of television. Thus, the specialized television program form places many restrictions on writers, who must introduce characters and situations and develop the plot for each episode in very short order while maintaining the interest of viewers, who can easily tune out to search for something more appealing.

Television program formulas are designed to orient viewers so that they quickly understand the premise of the program they are about to watch and to maintain consistency over the series. The formula establishes protagonists and antagonists for the viewer, carries the plot through to a climax, shows how the situation or conflict can be resolved, and wraps up details within the episode so that the viewer is satisfied that order within the context of the show has been restored.

Television program genres become more or less dominant as popular tastes fluctuate. Today situation comedies, action/adventure, and drama account for most program time. Reality programs have risen in popularity, while movies, docudramas, and miniseries receive limited play. Documentaries receive little air time on the commercial broadcast networks but have been very successful on public television and on cable networks as those program services attempt to attract a more specific group of viewers from among the general audience.

Most radio programs are structured as a continuous presentation rather than having a clear beginning, middle, and end, unlike the structure of television programs. Thus, radio programs build to climaxes throughout the broadcast day to help move the programming forward for the listener. One way this perception of forward movement can be accomplished is by integrating teases into the format; another is by building on the tempo and intensity of music and other events and then bringing the level back down in succeeding songs and commercials. Pacing also moves the programming along and can be controlled by the length of events as well as their tempo and intensity. Variety adds interest to the content and is controlled by rotating the music and altering the tempo and intensity of events.

The personalities heard on the air are usually crucial to the effective execution of radio programming. The most prominent local radio personalities are usually those who are on the air during the morning, since audience ratings for that period usually have a considerable effect on ratings for other time periods during the day. Regardless of the time period, personalities must appeal to targeted listeners and reflect the activities they are engaged in while they are listening.

SUGGESTED READINGS

Field, Syd: *Screenplay: The Foundations of Screenwriting,* Delacorte, New York, 1982.
Even though this book is about screenwriting rather than television and is more than 10 years old, it may still be the best concise book on how to write for any screen. Field helps readers understand the practices and tricks of the screen and shows them how to visually exploit materials for maximum effect. He shows how plot elements can be tied together in a multitude of ways. The information contained in this book is equally useful to student critics who want to dissect and analyze a work.

Chambers, Everett: *Producing TV Movies,* Prentice-Hall, Englewood Cliffs, N.J., 1986.
Like Field, Chambers shows how each element of a production is assembled into a whole. The television movie serves as a wonderful example of structure because of the need to tie its multiple subplots together. This book also shows how to develop characters, scenes, and stories.

Rose, Brian G., ed.: *TV Genres: A Handbook and Reference Guide,* Greenwood Press, Westport, Conn., 1985.
This book assembles a group of authors who, in separate chapters, describe 19 television program genres. In addition to a discussion of their attributes and the presentation of numerous examples, the historical development of each genre is described. In addition, a bibliographic survey of sources of information is presented at the end of each chapter. These descriptions are very helpful to the uninitiated reader who is interested in quickly finding useful sources of information. Furthermore, a videography of major programs and series that exemplify their genres is included for each genre. The listing of series includes the beginning and ending dates as well as the stars or hosts.

Kuhns, William: *Why We Watch Them: Interpreting TV Shows,* Benziger, New York, 1970.
The reader of this book will be struck by how little things have changed during the past two decades of television even though new series and stars are on the schedule. Actually, many of the programs Kuhns describes are still being aired, particularly on cable networks or in local station reruns. *Why We Watch Them* provides the reader with criteria for analyzing the appeals of programs and includes numerous examples to make those points clear. Many program series are analyzed, and so the reader has ample examples of why viewers like the shows that are broadcast. Developing this insight serves the programmer's goal of identifying the attributes in particular series that attract and maintain viewers.

NOTES

1. Many of the ideas expressed here were developed by Harrison B. Summers, professor of radio and television, the Ohio State University; see Lawrence W. Lichty and Joseph M. Ripley II, *American Broadcasting: Introduction and Analysis: Readings,* College Printing & Publishing, Madison, Wisc., 1969.

2. Paul Rubenstein and Martin Maloney, *Writing for the Media,* 2d ed., Prentice-Hall, Englewood Cliffs, N.J., 1988, pp. 81–82.

3. Ibid.

4. For background and many examples, including scripts of nine episodes, see writers of *thirtysomething, thirtysomething Stories,* Pocket Books, New York, 1991.

5. Rubenstein and Maloney, op. cit.

6. Mary B. Mallison, "NBC's Tinsel Handmaidens," *American Journal of Nursing,* April 1989, p. 453.

7. To some extent, television outlets have negated this effect, since most of them schedule commercial breaks at virtually the same time. Thus, restless viewers are confronted with commercial messages on many of the other channels, denying them immediate entry to another program.

8. Robert L. Hilliard, *Writing for Television and Radio,* 5th ed., Wadsworth, Calif., Belmont, 1991, pp. 73–76.

9. David T. MacFarland, *Contemporary Radio Programming Strategies,* Lawrence Erlbaum, Hillsdale, N.J., 1990.

10. Ibid., pp. 44–45, 144–158.

11. Walt Love, "Learning & Winning through Critiques," *Radio & Records,* July 1, 1988, p. 48.

12. "How to Critique a Jock's Aircheck," *NAB Radio Week,* Jan. 16, 1989, p. 6; Dan O'Day, "Aircheck Critique: WHEN's J.B. Louis," *Radio & Records,* April 8, 1988, p. 54; Dan O'Day, "Perfecting Delivery," *Radio & Records,* Oct. 6, 1989, p. 45; Dan O'Day, "Be a Dangerous DJ," *Radio & Records,* May 4, 1990, p. 63; Dan O'Day, "Return of the Dangerous DJ: Building up Your On-Air Arsenal," *Radio & Records,* June 22, 1990, p. 52; Jeff Pollack, "Communicating with Listeners: Don't Speak a Foreign Language," *Radio & Records,* Oct. 20, 1989, p. 29; Ed Shane, *Programming Dynamics: Radio's Management Guide,* Globecom, Overland Park, Kan., 1984.

13. Ed Shane, "Monitor Your Station's 'Sound,'" in Shane, op. cit., pp. 33–37.

CHAPTER 4

Conducting Research

For many people research is a mysterious and complicated endeavor, but for electronic media programmers it is an important fact of life since research reports form the basis for most advertising and thus for most programming decisions. Much information is gathered and reported in the name of research, but its validity may be questionable because some suppliers of information capitalize on their clients' lack of sophistication. In any case, a programmer should consider research and numerical descriptions as a help rather than an obstacle. This chapter covers the fundamentals of audience research. It takes the reader through the basic considerations in conducting research studies, including nomenclature and basic procedures.

PURPOSE OF RESEARCH

The purpose of research is to provide program decision makers with information that can help attract and maintain an audience. Research provides *insight*—a way to identify problems that might otherwise go undetected, such as finding out that people think a station broadcasts too many commercials. However, this knowledge does not automatically mean that one should schedule fewer commercial announcements. Perhaps they should be presented in clusters to minimize the number of interruptions of the programming. Or perhaps they could be arranged so that the most entertaining commercials are aired near the end of the group; that way, their appeal as entertainment and a sense of building toward a climax are enhanced.

More fundamentally, research can help a programmer identify an underserved audience whose wants and needs are not being met, assess the strengths and weaknesses of the competition and of the programmer's own outlet, or establish a better understanding of the motives and habits of members of the target audience. The programmer's objective is to deliver listeners or viewers to advertisers in order to generate a profit through the sale of advertising time. The larger the potential audience and the more intense the competition for it, the higher the stakes. Research can help a programmer reduce the risk in making strategic decisions that will attract and keep listeners or viewers.

What Research Can Do

Most audience research is best considered a "recent history" that reports audience traits during a period of time that has just ended. It describes the present and future only in the sense that people tend to be consistent. If the circumstances for the audience remain the same, a "hot" disc jockey who attracts a large audience during the period from March through May can be expected to repeat that performance during the period from June through August. As a result, the programmer often makes decisions about the future that are based on what audiences have done in the past. If, however, a competing station employs a new personality who is attractive to the audience, history may not repeat itself; the programmer won't be able to determine that until the audience has been given the opportunity to make a choice. Similarly, TV network programmers reason that if large numbers of people have watched a situation comedy that features a family consisting of a teenage brother and sister, a younger sibling, and their working parents, viewers must like that kind of program. Predicting that viewers will watch more programs featuring families, networks have ordered new series based on a similar premise. The only way to know when audiences tire of the imitators is to spot a decline in viewing after these audiences have been measured.

What Research Cannot Do

Research cannot predict the future. Asking people what they will like is not going to elicit satisfactory information. People can't reliably report whether they like something they have not experienced. If one asked a group of individuals whether they would listen to a new station or watch a program that is not currently available, a large number might respond affirmatively. However, a number of things might get in the way of an affirmative response after the fact, not the least of which is audience loyalty to programming that is already a known quantity or habit. It requires more than the mere offering of alternatives to motivate portions of the audience to try new fare. Even when they do, it is often more a matter of apparent curiosity than of long-term dissatisfaction with a competing program.

ATTRIBUTES OF RESEARCH

Research is a systematic, consistent means of finding out about audiences. That is, the results one researcher obtains should also be obtained by any other researcher who follows the same procedure in investigating a question. Thus, electronic media research is *numerical* and *objective,* and its findings are consistently *representative* of the attributes of the group being studied. These attributes are important if the information that is gathered is to provide realistic insights from which intelligent decisions can be made.

Numbers

Audience research involves working with numbers, and it is important to become accustomed to looking at the world in quantitative terms. Numerical description actually makes the programmer's world simpler to grasp. It is far easier to describe a large group of people with a few descriptive statistics than to try to account for every one of the individuals who happens to be included.

Obviously, the larger a group is, the more difficult it is to deal with each of its members. However, several attributes can be selected to summarize information in a more comprehensible form. Take a look around the next time you are in a gathering of people. Whether it is a church congregation, fans in a football stadium, students in a classroom, or members of a TV or radio audience, each individual who is a part of the collection of people may be quite different or may share some traits with the others. It is the rule rather than the exception that is important in describing most audiences. While some of the details get lost, categorizing members of the group provides meaningful yet fairly simple descriptors. For example, a college class may be described as consisting half of seniors and half of juniors; 40 percent of the group is male (leaving 60 percent female); the average age of the group is 20 years; and 70 percent are Communications majors, 10 percent are Theater majors, and 20 percent are Business majors.

Objectivity

Research should help us get outside the assumptions we make about what we think we know on the basis of our own experience. If we want valid knowledge about a group of people and want to know how they feel about the programs they are offered, we must follow an objective, systematic way of finding out. In short, we must research the problem.

The attributes of the college class listed above seem to be straightforward, but there is always a possibility that the describer may interject a research **bias,** or unwarranted influence on the results of the findings. Bias is not always intentional. Still, people want the world to conform to the beliefs they hold and tend to screen out information that contradicts what they think they know. For example, a student researcher may believe that all the students in his or her class are Communications majors. If the student makes that assumption, it will be easy to ignore the one or two people who are not Communications majors. Overlooking or discounting these exceptions to the rule will bias the results of that research just as a person's response can be biased by the way a question is asked.

During the cross-examination of a witness, a lawyer asks, "Mrs. Jones, do you agree that people who have long hair and beards like the defendant are much more likely to have criminal tendencies?" Such a question is going to elicit a biased response. Similarly, asking a person whether he or she listens to the "hot new rocker in town, WXXX" is a self-serving, and thus biased, research question.

Programmers do not conduct their work for their own gratification but for that of their viewers and listeners. It follows, then, that the purpose of audience research is not to support one's illusions or to prove anything but to learn as much as possible about potential listeners or viewers in order to maximize the audience for an electronic media outlet. Programming decisions cannot be based on wishful thinking or a programmer's own response to a program but must arise from a clear, rational, objective, systematic assessment of the facts. Research is worthless if it is designed to tell people what they want to hear. Research is valuable if it can indicate what is real. You may not like what you find out, but you should be able to accept the validity of the measurement and adjust your strategy accordingly.

Representativeness

An important bias occurs when some of the members of the **population**—all the persons who could feasibly tune in a TV station, for instance—are not represented in a study. Objective research is based on the assumption that those who respond to questions about their listening and viewing habits form a composite that represents the whole population. This is referred to as **representativeness.**

Most readers are familiar with the notion of a *normal curve* (Figure 4-1). When the scores on a test are curved, those which are especially high cause students who score lower to receive a lower grade. Conversely, if a large number of students score poorly on an exam, one has a better chance of obtaining a higher grade.

The normal, or bell-shaped, curve represents the distribution of a characteristic in a **universe,** or a population chosen for study, whether it involves the scores for an examination or the viewing habits of the people who live in a television market.

It doesn't matter whether one is interested in weight, age, grades, or TV viewing. If a sample of the population is of sufficient size and has been chosen properly, it should be distributed along a bell-shaped curve, with the majority of the respondents placed at its center. Those with extremely high IQs or weight will be at the right end of the continuum, while those with abnormally low IQs or weight will be distributed on the left side, going farther and farther away from the **mean** (average) of that attribute as it exists in the population represented in the sample. The population ranges from individuals who are extremely obese to those who are anorexic. A few people are exactly the weight they should be; others range from slightly to extremely overweight on one side, and on the other side, they go down the scale to malnourished. Of course, both 500-pound and emaciated individuals are rare in the population. This is indicated by the decline of the curve as the characteristic moves farther from the average.

The implications of a normal curve can be illustrated by the knowledge obtained by keeping a record of information obtained from the people who call a radio station. There is no way to know how well those callers are distributed along the curve of all those in the listening audience. Thus, their answers may be pleasing, but they will almost certainly not be dependable. For example, a disc jockey who asks people who call the station on the request line how well they

FIGURE 4-1 Normal curve.

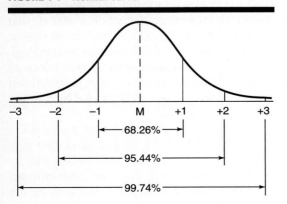

think his new morning program is going may begin to feel very good about his technique. The jokes are very funny, the skits are great, they love the all-hits format, and his frequent put-downs of the mayor are a scream. But what about all the listeners who don't bother to call in? How about the attitudes of those who listen to other stations? These and many other pertinent questions may be ignored while the unsubstantiated beliefs of the programmer are being reinforced.

THE RESEARCH PROCESS

Define the Research Problem

The first step in conducting research is to carefully specify what one wishes to find out. For instance, do you want to find out who is listening or watching, or do you want to try to determine why certain people listen or watch? The purpose of doing research may seem obvious, but it is often commissioned without clearly thought out objectives and needs. As the saying goes, "When you're up to your waist in alligators, it's difficult to remember that your objective was to drain the swamp."

Determine the Appropriate Method

After deciding what you want to find out, the next step is to determine how best to answer those questions. The most prevalent questions asked by both advertisers and electronic media outlets are, What are people listening to or watching? and How many people are in the audience, at what times, and for how long? The most efficient means of finding answers to those questions is by directly asking people to report on their listening or viewing.

Among the potential problems in this approach are that the respondents may not understand you and thus may tell you something that is not exactly accurate, may forget and thus not tell you about all the listening or viewing they have done, or may lie to you, telling you that they watched public television because they think that casts them in a better light than admitting that they were actually watching an R-rated movie on a pay-cable channel.

An alternative is to observe people's viewing and listening. That sounds simple, but it is costly. It would require placing a monitor in every room in the house, the car, and the workplace, or it would require that a researcher camp out in a person's house to observe what channels he or she tuned in. Obviously, neither is a practical means of obtaining the needed information. The expense would be far too great, and there is the question of invasion of privacy. More important, when people know they are being watched, they often change their behavior.

No method is perfect, and clients have to acknowledge the limitations in the completeness of the information they receive. The procedures described below have been developed over the years as the principal means of observing who is listening to radio and watching television.

Establish the Research Budget

The more precisely listening or viewing behavior is described, the more costly that information is to obtain. The client establishes an amount that she or he is willing to spend to obtain information, and the researcher conducts the investigation within those constraints. For instance, if you ask 100 people which station they listen to every morning, the information you obtain will not be as good as it would be if you asked 500 people the same question. Let's say 10 of the 100 respondents said they listened to KWWW but only 2 of them were men. How precise could you expect the study to be in identifying the traits of KWWW's male audience? What the programmer saves in time and expense is compromised by lower accuracy in the responses that are obtained.

Define the Universe

After determining the question and establishing the research budget, the next step is to define the universe. Two different kinds of populations are normally defined for electronic media studies. The first is the potential audience for the electronic media outlet. In the case of a national television network such as ABC, CBS, or NBC, that would include all the television households in the United States, or virtually everyone. In the case of a radio or a television station, that would be all the potential listeners or viewers in the station's coverage area. The second kind of universe would be a target audience defined by the electronic media outlet. A radio station that programs popular music may decide that it wants to attract men and women between the ages of 18 and 34. That target audience can constitute a research population if the purpose of the study is limited to finding out only about those people. It makes sense for a station to focus on the segment of the potential audience that it most wishes to attract.

To draw a sample the researcher must be able to identify who is in the population. For example, one is a student at Enormous State University or is not. The registrar at the institution can provide a list of all currently enrolled students, which should serve as a reasonably accurate **sample frame,** or listing of the members of the population. Still, that sample frame probably has limitations, since the registrar's list might not have been updated to include late enrollees and dropouts. Even with what may be assumed to be an accurate list, errors of omission are virtually assured.

There are other limitations as well. If late registrants (who are not included on the list of enrollees) are sprinkled throughout the universe (in this case, the student body), the effect on the representativeness of the sample will be minimal. But what if most of the students who delayed registering have some attribute in common? Perhaps the late enrollees include a large number of students whose grade point averages were so low that they were placed on academic probation and were required to make a special appeal to be readmitted. Their absence from the sample will distort the representativeness of the population.

Even with such deficiencies, the registrar's list is probably the most feasible way to identify the population being studied. The expense of improving the sample frame would probably be prohibitive, and so a compromise must be made between the highest possible accuracy and one's willingness to pay for it.

The major audience research companies base their samples on telephone listings provided by a Lincoln, Nebraska, company, Metromail, Inc., which maintains computer listings of telephone numbers by state, county, and **ZIP code.** These universes do not include every household in the United States because many people have unlisted telephone numbers and other households do not have telephones. Thus, this sample frame defines the world of radio and television listening and viewing narrowly. Many single women and wealthy people, for example, do not list their telephone numbers. While research companies take extra steps to include households with unlisted numbers, their reliance on telephone listings as a sample frame still represents a compromise.

Select the Sample

Some popular means of obtaining information from people compromise accuracy because far too much is left to chance even though the results are reported as being representative of a group. For instance, some polls conducted on college and university campuses are based on the responses of people who walk up to a table in the student union or the library. The problem here is that the opinions or habits of the students who did not have classes on the day the table was set up cannot be included in such a study. Moreover, after a long, tiring day of attending classes or studying in the library, would you eagerly volunteer to answer questions or avoid the table and even shake your head no if asked to stop?

The same kinds of problems exist in determining the preferences of potential audience members. What kinds of individuals will volunteer to watch a new TV program and answer questions about it afterward? People who happen to be on the street near CBS in New York or in the Los Angeles shopping center where "Preview House" is located are recruited to watch and evaluate TV programs. What might make them different from people who never go near either of those places and those who refuse to participate? It seems likely that people who do not live in these areas would not have an opportunity to watch the programs being tested; nor would people who are very busy, even though many such persons may be in the actual television audience from day to day. The lack of specific efforts to ensure the representation of all members of the potential viewing population and of a means to increase the cooperation of those who were contacted and refused to participate make the results of such research suspect in terms of its representativeness of all the potential audience members.

Similarly, telephone opinion polls conducted by television stations, in which people call in to register their support for or opposition to a question, are not reliable indicators of public opinion. A person has to feel strongly enough about the issue to be motivated to call. Also, if there is a charge for the call, the cost may deter would-be callers. Furthermore, there is nothing to prevent a person from calling again and again to rack up more votes for the side of the issue that she or he supports. In short, the organization conducting this opinion poll has no control over who participates and no means of ascertaining how closely the callers approximate the distribution of the population along the normal curve.

At the least, a sample should be *systematically* drawn to eliminate the biases in the results described above. One common way to establish a systematic sample is to select every "*n*th" person in the sample frame, for example, every tenth name on the list. However, even though that procedure comes far closer to being representative of the population than the methods described above, the representativeness of the sample is still uncertain.

Control over representativeness is provided by **probability sampling,** whose fundamental

tenet is that every member of the population being studied has an equally likely chance of being selected. Consequently, probability sampling is often more accurate and efficient than an attempt to contact every member of a population. That should be easy enough to observe in the typical classroom. If on a particular morning a professor decides to ask her class to complete a questionnaire about the students' radio listening, there is every likelihood that someone will arrive late or that one or more people will not even show up. Thus, the chance of getting a truly representative response is low even in a class where attendance is expected. Which types in this universe are not represented? The commuters? The "party animals"? Those who were unfortunate enough to pick up a virus from a person in another class?

Moreover, a group that constitutes an individual class hardly represents the panorama of student radio listening. A required class in English composition is more likely to include students who are majoring in most of the disciplines offered at the college or university. Even so, there may be a course required of Engineering students that meets at that hour, precluding their enrollment in that particular section of English composition. Even if all college majors are represented, the likelihood of juniors and seniors enrolling in the course is minimal since most students in that group have already completed that requirement. Furthermore, the size of the population of students at most colleges or universities makes interviewing everyone nearly impossible.

Let's say you're interested in finding out who your fellow students think is the best candidate for homecoming queen. What could be more representative of the student body than an election in which every student votes? That might work, except that some students won't bother voting as a result of apathy or perhaps because they take offense at the focus on physical charms. Other students will forget to vote, still others will not be on campus that day because they are sick or were called home for an emergency, and some will vote in droves because they have a particular interest in supporting a friend or sorority sister. Is this election a valid measure of student opinion? That can't be determined since you were unable to exercise any control over who participated and who didn't.

The only reasonable solution to these dilemmas is to use probability sampling, in which each member of the population has an equally likely chance of being included in the sample. In addition, sampling increases the likelihood that all the persons selected will be contacted since their number is small enough to be manageable, at least in comparison to the size of the total population. While a sample can be drawn by other means, only probability sampling can provide an estimate of how accurately the results that are obtained from the sample represent the population.

Once the universe has been identified and defined by means of a sample frame, a probability sample is selected by giving each individual, or unit of measurement, in the sample frame a mutually exclusive number, say, from 1 to 20,000. Then, using a table of random numbers (Table 4-1), the researcher compiles a list of numbers. If these numbers are generated in a truly random fashion, none will have been selected arbitrarily or through some bias such as the person selecting the numbers skipping around or overlooking certain digits. When the randomly drawn numbers are matched with those as-

TABLE 4-1 Table of Random Numbers

67373	44963	48241	22828	07406	47865	92474	86245
92830	34520	78174	24113	73255	26149	17263	57405
98823	93320	95093	24711	41282	17872	76142	70430
07094	96941	45338	99424	68069	41469	58743	15028
72853	06133	70070	32286	59533	66005	62935	63990
60810	45690	15620	48014	77336	09914	63114	96479
18757	53319	23172	84899	14113	45778	96993	28254
11402	53813	70683	18652	64728	44374	39360	31055
40513	84880	70415	47094	21817	47426	27927	20642
56651	71312	22613	38659	80245	25710	37481	68756
37365	50816	39533	15930	37725	20949	05735	80609
73816	47014	21418	99683	78540	03920	07477	70910
93983	46831	80525	81641	68310	16347	65184	37450
60121	50841	17099	82581	35165	32522	93489	94939
22475	45970	75034	94226	12733	46511	15258	41167
43301	32793	25669	37354	18650	01748	29891	80296
72843	97063	35167	03687	72781	95815	00098	53087
73356	88573	06506	17518	92761	24490	25668	56279
95086	70030	76941	22913	98454	54495	86400	30631
31927	91228	71717	13306	12575	81607	37816	72886
05219	14873	28090	32764	41705	10642	82787	13254
31123	85986	98355	74720	41763	83365	87533	91446
30977	27293	78267	86756	19332	45999	87367	30252
20943	53569	92778	14649	30327	45285	30003	69381
54001	80339	11753	75123	81333	61434	47024	31625
98502	68603	75529	69068	61931	03908	81240	52514
64221	02682	43592	11741	79604	11815	06725	40499
78557	76214	57749	57657	21104	75190	19348	31867
17405	33177	07904	13954	28266	84158	56692	11466

SOURCE: From Gerald G. Hartshorn, ed., *Audience Research Sourcebook.* © 1991. Used by permission of National Association of Broadcasters.

signed to each individual in the sample frame, a sample can be drawn in which each member of the population has the same chance of being selected.

Interpret the Results

Even when the universe is identified by a sample frame and a sample is selected, there may be an important difference between the sample size and the number of responses obtained. An **in-tab sample** includes those members of the sample who are actually included in the tabulation of results.

In a sample size of 500, some individuals in the group may never be contacted. To find out what a person watched last night on TV, for example, that person is usually contacted by telephone. Some people might have been out of town or at work. Others who were contacted might have refused to answer the researcher's questions. Some of the responses received may not be useful. It is possible for an individual to become confused by questions about subjects to which she or he has not given any thought or to deliberately give outrageous answers. In such cases, the researcher's only recourse is to discard those responses from the tabulations. Thus, the reported results are based on a smaller **in-tab,** or number of cases, than were in the sample selected to represent the population.

Think again of the normal curve representing the distribution of the members of the universe. If uncooperative or unavailable sample members are randomly distributed in the population, the curve created by the usable sample of respondents should look fairly normal. However, if the uncooperative individuals are mostly older, black, female, or Hispanic, there may be a distinct "hole" in the line that creates the curve. Thus, the sample curve will provide a distorted representation of the traits of the actual population.

The objective of researchers is therefore to elicit the greatest possible cooperation from the respondents selected in the sample. To simply dip back into the pool of population members to fill a quota will negate the "equally likely" premise on which the sample was selected. If the response rate is low, one cannot be sure how representative the results are. In this case, it is reasonable to assume that significant portions of the population were not represented in the reported data.

The number of sample members and the number whose responses were actually included in the tabulation of the results should be provided in every research report. A low in-tab should caution the decision maker against giving much credence to the representativeness, and thus the validity, of the report.

Much of the research available to programmers is obtained from audience **survey research,** a procedure in which people who have been systematically selected to represent all the persons in a universe are asked to describe their listening or viewing behavior. One of the important estimates that is reported is a program **rating,** which is the percentage of all the possible listeners or viewers actually in the audience. For example, in a sample consisting of 500 persons, if 100 respondents report watching or listening to a particular program, then 0.20, or 20.0 percent, of the possible audience members were watching. Thus, that program has a rating of 20.0:

$$100 \div 500 = 0.20, \text{ or } 20.0 \text{ percent}$$

Sampling Error

How large must a sample be to serve as a realistic picture of the audience? Conceptually, the larger the sample size, the more precisely it will represent the detail in the universe. However, there is a point of diminishing returns. Every ratings report includes information on **sampling error,** the statistical estimate of the range of accuracy of the results being reported (Figure 4-2). Smaller sample sizes provide less precise results (that is, a higher sampling error), but research customers are often unwilling to pay for increased accuracy. Obviously, the more precise the measure, the better, but doubling or

FIGURE 4-2 **Sampling and representativeness.** *(From* **What TV Ratings Really Mean.** *Used by permission of Nielsen Media Research.)*

quadrupling the sample size increases the cost of obtaining the information in almost the same ratio.

The ratings game may be poorly played and refereed, but the results determine which stations or programs are the winners in the effort to attract the largest possible audience. Audience ratings are estimates and should always be treated as such. It is neither accurate nor wise to interpret these estimates too narrowly. It is entirely possible that the higher rating of one show compared with that of a competing program can be accounted for by statistical error, negating any clear differences between the two.

With the aid of a simple calculator, the sample error can be determined to interpret the results of a study more accurately.

The formula for sample error is

$$SE = \sqrt{\frac{P(100 - P)}{N}}$$

where P represents the finding and N represents the sample size.

To illustrate, if we surveyed a sample of 500 households and determined a rating of 20 (20 percent of the households had watched a particular TV program), the sample error would be ± 1.79:

$$SE = \sqrt{\frac{20\,(80)}{500}} = \sqrt{3.2} = \pm\,1.79$$

Let us now take into account the in-tab figure. In the original sample of 500, where the results were based on responses from 300 sample members,

$$SE = \sqrt{\frac{20\,(80)}{300}} = \sqrt{5.3} = \pm\,2.31$$

In the first case, where the response was based on a sample of 500, the estimate of households watching a program could range between 18.2 and 21.8 percent of the total households. In the second case, based on an in-tab of 300, the margin of error could range from 17.7 to 22.3.

To reduce the in-tab sample error by half, to 1.15, at least 1200 usable responses would have to be included. Thus, by quadrupling the in-tab we could narrow the sample error to a range of 18.9 to 21.2, but that increase in accuracy would more than double the cost of the estimate based on an in-tab of 300.

$$SE = \sqrt{\frac{20\,(80)}{1200}} = \sqrt{1.3} = \pm\,1.15$$

TABLE 4-2 Sample Error over Ratings Periods

	Sample Period				
	1	2	3	4	5
Rating	20.00	21.50	21.75	21.00	19.50
Sample error	± 1.79	± 1.84	± 1.84	± 1.82	± 1.77
High	21.79	23.34	23.59	22.82	21.27
Low	18.21	19.66	19.91	19.18	17.73

Virtually everyone associated with radio and television has heard horror stories about managers or program directors who fired disc jockeys because there was a drop in their shows' ratings from the previous measurement period. Such drastic action may be justified, but not on the basis of a single ratings report and not without a calculation of the sample error. If a statistical error is involved, the next report may show the ratings up around their level from before the disastrous rating period. Consequently, audience habits may not have changed appreciably. For instance, if a station's **ratings,** or percentage of the possible audience that listened, were tracked over five survey periods, with each estimate based on an in-tab of 500, the results would be like those shown in Table 4-2.

At first glance, the figures indicate that the station had a sharp rise in its audience during measurement periods 2 and 3, with a declining trend in periods 4 and 5. However, the sampling error calculated for the five different samples could mean that no real differences occurred in any of the measurements. Although the results appear to be fluctuating, this could be caused by sampling error. Thus, the ratings obtained for each period could fit within the range of each of the other periods. Before management rushes to cancel programs or fire personnel, that possibility should be taken into account. Many ratings reports include a summary of results of past measurement periods. Trends identified from that information may more cleary indicate a change in audience position than a comparison between the two most recent reports

FORMS OF SURVEY RESEARCH

Audience Measurement Services

At this writing, two audience research services provide survey estimates of television viewing and radio listening: the **A.C. Nielsen Company,** now known as Nielsen Media Research, and its competitor, the **Arbitron Ratings Company.** Most television viewers associate TV audience ratings and "the Nielsens." Nielsen Media Research's high public profile is due to its reports on national, or network, television viewing, but Nielsen provides advertising agencies and stations with estimates of local viewing as well.

Nielsen started out by doing radio ratings, but by the 1960s radio measurement was no longer profitable, and the A.C. Nielsen Company stopped that service altogether in 1964. Since then, the company has periodically considered reentering the radio measurement field, but the decision has always been to remain exclusively in television audience measurement.[1]

Arbitron, a subsidiary of Control Data Corporation, a major computer manufacturer, quickly became the dominant radio ratings service after it began measuring radio market audiences in 1964. Arbitron is presently the only company that regularly supplies a measurement service for local radio audiences. Currently, 260 radio markets are measured by the diary method at least once a year, during the spring sweep.

Arbitron has also measured local television viewing since 1949. Unlike Nielsen, Arbitron does not provide a national television audience measurement service. It has been common practice for stations and advertising agencies to subscribe to both companies' reports of local television viewing. With the current tightening economy, though, an increasing number of stations are opting for only one such service.[2]

Diaries

The **diary** used in electronic media research could more accurately be called a log, since respondents are asked to keep a written record of their listening or viewing for 7 days, usually beginning on Wednesday (Arbitron) or Thursday (Nielsen). It is an efficient means of reaching respondents since the measurement instrument—the diary—can be sent and returned by mail. Arbitron's version of the television viewing diary is shown in Figure 4-3.

To enhance the likelihood of cooperation, a token incentive, usually around $1, but up to $5 for some radio listeners and $20 for some TV households, is included with each diary. Telephone calls are made to remind respondents to fill out the information, and this also improves the chances for a higher response rate.

The unit of measurement for television is still the household. Because of the number of multiple-set households, three or more different programs may be viewed simultaneously in many homes. In households that participate in television viewing surveys, a diary is kept for each TV set. Someone in the household records who is watching and when that person enters or leaves the viewing area. One of the criticisms of television measurement has been that out-of-home viewing is seldom reported. Thus, people who watch TV in hotel rooms and bars are not counted in the audience.

The importance of individual viewing has grown to the point where the National Association of Broadcasters (NAB) has developed an individual viewing diary.[3] The individual may soon become the unit of measurement in television audience estimates since TV is becoming an increasingly solitary activity. That has long been

the case with radio, where individuals constitute the sample units.

Advantages One of the principal advantages of the diary method is the amount of information that can be obtained. Respondents are asked to list the times when they watch television and report who else in the household is watching the set. Arbitron's television diary (Figure 4-3) and Nielsen's version (Figure 4-4) are similar.

Figure 4-5 shows Arbitron's radio diary, in which the respondent reports on where the listening is done (at home, in the car, at work, or in another place). The radio diary provides a record of all listening by a single individual selected for inclusion in the sample, whereas the television diary reports all household viewing for a particular TV set.

Respondents are categorized by **demographic** attributes such as age, sex, race, and household income. Demographic questions in the Nielsen diary cover the age and sex of each member of the household in addition to the number of TV sets and cable subscriber status to help classify television households by socioeconomic status.[4] Some diaries also include a number of questions about household product purchases, occupation, and income status.

Another advantage of the diary is that programmers can inspect the original entries to identify patterns in respondents' answers. If the programmer feels that his or her station did not get credit for all the viewing or listening due it, an inspection of the diaries can confirm or refute that suspicion. For instance, a radio programmer may discover that respondents confused the station's identifying slogan with one used by a competing station. Although there is virtually no chance that credit will be given to the station after the fact, at least the programmer can revise the way the station is identified to assure full credit during the next ratings period.

Disadvantages Diaries must be completed by people who can read and write. This limits the respondents to people who are literate, eliminat-

Keep this page open to assist you while filling out your diary.

1 List your TV channels.

For all channels this set receives clearly:
- List channel numbers.
- Include call letters/channel identification (WADJ, KABS, etc.) or channel names (HTO, Starvision, etc.).
- Include the city of the TV station or cable company.

Channel Number	Call Letters/ Channel Identification	City
33	WADJ	PLAINVILLE
6A	HTO	OAK CITY
12	KABS	PLAINVILLE

Begin Here.

Channel Number	Call Letters/ Channel Identification	City
14	WWOR	
15	WGN	
17	WTBS	
18	WSB	
19	WAGA	
20	WGTV	
21	WXIA	

Channel Number	Call Letters/ Channel Identification	City
22	WPBA	
23	WATL	
24	WGNX	
25	WVEU	
26	MTV	
27	DSC	
29	CNN	
32	NIC	
38	TNN	
42	TNT	

Channel Number	Call Letters/ Channel Identification	City
47	USA	
48	ESPN	
50	LIF	
52	WRCB	

Heads of House	Other Household Members and Visitors				
	John	Sue	Larry	Kay	Visitor

Time	TV Set Off	TV Set On	Channel Number	Call Letters/ Channel Identification	Taped on VCR? (✓)	Name of Program	First Name	John	Sue	Larry	Kay	Visitor			
							Age			14	12	12			
							Sex	M	F	M	F	F			
6:00AM - 6:14															
6:15 - 6:29															
6:30 - 6:44															
6:45 - 6:59															
7:00AM - 7:14															
7:15 - 7:29															
7:30 - 7:44															
7:45 - 7:59															
8:00AM - 8:14															
8:15 - 8:29															
8:30 - 8:44															
8:45 - 8:59															
9:00AM - 9:14															
9:15 - 9:29															
9:30 - 9:44															
9:45 - 9:59															
10:00AM - 10:14															
10:15 - 10:29															
10:30 - 10:44															
10:45 - 10:59															
11:00AM - 11:14															
11:15 - 11:29															

FIGURE 4-3 Arbitron TV diary. *(Used by permission of Arbitron Ratings Co.)*

It's easy to keep a NIELSEN diary!
Just mark as shown in Example:

- WHEN . . . TV set is turned on or off.

- WHICH . . . station and channel are being watched for 5 minutes or longer.

- WHAT . . . program is being watched.

WHO . . . is watching or listening for 5 minutes or longer.

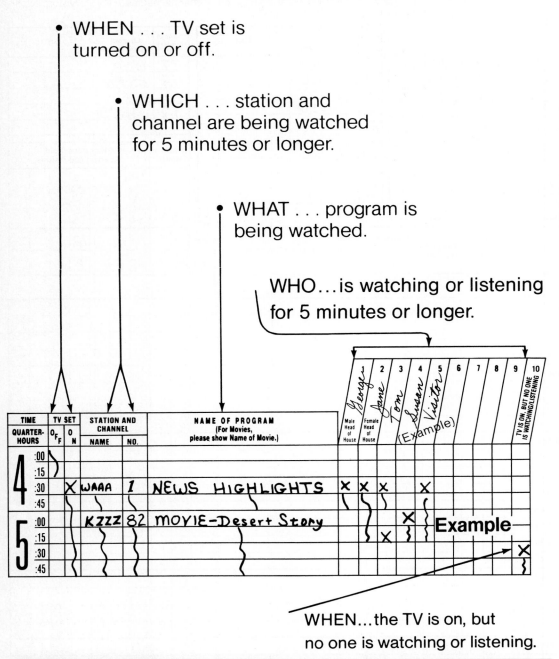

WHEN . . . the TV is on, but no one is watching or listening.

FIGURE 4-4 Nielsen diary. *(Used by permission of Nielsen Media Research.)*

TUESDAY									
	Time		Station			Place			
			Call letters or station name *Don't know? Use program name or dial setting.*	*Check (✔) one*		*Check (✔) one*			
	Start	Stop		AM	FM	At Home	In a Car	At Work	Other Place
Early Morning (from 5 AM)									
Midday									
Late Afternoon									
Night (to 5 AM Wednesday)									

If you didn't hear a radio today, please check here. ☐

FIGURE 4-5   Arbitron radio diary. *(Used by permission of Arbitron Ratings Co.)*

ing a fairly large segment of the population in some markets. However, the diary's greatest shortcoming is that people forget to fill it out or err in logging which programs are tuned in and, in a television diary, who is viewing each set. Respondents start off well in completing their diaries, with Wednesday (Arbitron) or Thursday (Nielsen) viewing being recorded most accurately, but accuracy declines through the 7-day period. Thus, the record may include a fabrication of what was watched or listened to because diary

keepers relied on their recollection over a day or two to reconstruct what they watched or listened to.

Problems of accuracy and completeness are compounded in measuring the audiences in cable TV households because there are many more channel choices for respondents to keep track of. Since it is suspected that many diary keepers try to recall what programs they and others watched, network-affiliated stations may have an advantage over independent stations and cable networks because diary keepers' memories tend to favor the oldest and best known stations.

The limited number of weeks included in ratings periods invites **hyping,** or **hypoing**—the use of unusual promotions to attract listeners or viewers during a ratings period. For example, local TV news programs often save their most sensational and titillating subjects for **sweeps** weeks, as audience ratings periods are known. Special reports on incest, how to quit smoking, the new summer bathing suits, and breast cancer are often given considerable promotion to induce viewers to watch. Similarly, stations or networks may present blockbuster movies or other special programs during sweeps weeks to build up their audiences. When the ratings period has ended, it's back to more usual programming, with a concurrent reduction in the audience.

Further limiting the accuracy of diary responses, only about half the households included in diary samples return diaries that can be used. The low in-tab response to diary surveys raises serious questions about the representativeness of the sample results. In radio, this problem is especially severe among younger male listeners, particularly black and Hispanic males. Of course, the problem is not theirs but that of the researchers and the radio stations and advertisers that subscribe to audience estimate reports (Box 4-1).

Telephone Interviews

The telephone has become an important way for survey researchers to contact respondents. The advent of WATS (Wide-Area Telecommunications Service) lines enables research companies to contact respondents all over the country at a relatively low cost per interview. A large number of interviews can be completed in a short time because of automatic dialing devices that begin to make the call to the next number the instant a field worker disconnects from a completed interview.

Telephone interviewing has become the staple in audience interview surveys because of the low cost of contacting respondents by telephone. In face-to-face interview situations, field workers have to contact respondents by telephone anyway to set up an appointment to complete the interview. Even though much more depth of interviewing is possible in face-to-face situations, the logistics are expensive and the cost of completion is high. Researchers have found that they can keep respondents involved and responding to questions for as long as 15 to 20 minutes in telephone interviews and that is enough time to get a considerable amount of information.

Random-digit dialing   Telephone interviewing offers a means of reaching respondents who might otherwise never be contacted: those with unlisted numbers and households that have had telephones installed after the latest listing was made available. Since the alternative is a sample frame limited to telephone subscribers with listed numbers, **random-digit dialing** studies, which rely on a listing of telephone numbers that are generated randomly, give any working telephone an equally likely chance of being selected in the sample.

The random-digit dialing technique usually relies on a list of four-digit numbers compiled in a random fashion by a computer; this theoretically makes any combination of digits equally likely to be selected. The researcher adds the prefixes and the area codes as necessary to obtain a sample for a given area. Since the prefixes used in a telephone service have different numbers of subscribers, the number of respondents drawn from each one is adjusted to achieve a sample that is in proportion to the distribution of telephone subscribers throughout the area being surveyed. Thus, any person with a working telephone with a specified prefix and/or area code has the same chance of being selected for an interview that any other person with a working phone that uses the same area code or prefix has.

A drawback to random-digit dialing surveys is that only about half the numbers selected for the sample will be usable as working household numbers. The main advantage is that all the members of the population who can be reached

**BOX 4-1
DIARY RESEARCH
METHOD**

ADVANTAGES

- Provides a record of radio listening in cars, offices, and other workplaces and in restaurants and stores in addition to the home.
- Provides weekly cumulative ratings.
- Allows for many demographic breakouts.
- Provides TV household consumer data.
- Are available for inspection by subscribers, providing feedback unavailable with other methods.
- Is reasonably inexpensive.

DISADVANTAGES

- May omit some listening and viewing and may contain inaccurate entries.
- Underreports viewing by children, teens, and young males.
- Response rates are relatively low (40 to 50 percent for TV and 40 percent for radio).
- Cooperation among several important radio audience segments is low, for example, adult males under age 35, particularly blacks and Hispanics.
- Handwritten entries such as radio call letters, dial positions, and station slogans are especially difficult to edit.
- Respondents are influenced by conditioning in their identification of stations and channels. Their tendency to report their "usual viewing" creates a potential bias.
- Respondent fatigue may affect reporting accuracy and response rates toward the end of the diary-keeping period.
- The limited number of weeks surveyed in sweeps invites hyping.
- Serious communication and response rate problems exist among poorly educated and foreign-born respondents.

SOURCE: Hugh Malcolm Beville, Jr., *Audience Ratings: Radio, Television, Cable* (Hillsdale, NJ: Lawrence Erlbaum Associates, Inc., 1985). Copyright © 1985. Used by permission of Lawrence Erlbaum Associates, Inc. ■

by telephone have an equal probability of being included in the sample.

Regardless of whether the sample is based on random digits, is drawn from a sample frame (the telephone listing), or both (random dialing techniques can be used to supplement the listed numbers), there are two principal interviewing methods used in telephone audience surveys: coincidental and recall.

Coincidental interviews In telephone **coincidental interviews,** the respondent is asked about

the radio or television program she or he was watching or listening to at the time the telephone rang. The potential advantage in asking this kind of question is that the person should be able to say with virtual certainty what was being watched or listened to when the phone rang. However, that is not necessarily a reliable assumption. It may seem apparent that everybody knows exactly what he or she is doing at a given moment, but researchers cannot count on it. At the least, one cannot be certain that all the respondents will be able to accurately describe their viewing or listening to an interviewer, especially since they may not have been paying much attention to what they were watching.

There is a distinct disadvantage to the coincidental method: Researchers cannot make calls early in the morning and late in the evening. Some public opinion polling firms will not make calls before 9 a.m. or after 9 p.m.[5] If the coincidental method is to be useful to electronic media programmers, there must be some way to obtain information about viewing or listening done very early and very late in the day. This is particularly important in radio audience measurement, since the morning audience reaches its peak at 7:30 a.m. in most markets.

Regardless of these limitations, this method offers researchers a means of pinpointing audiences in an electronic media outlet's coverage area and determining their awareness of certain aspects of the program. For instance, if a TV station broadcasts a local daytime program that features a different community in the coverage area each day, it would be useful to know whether people who live in that particular geographic area knew about or watched the show. Moreover, it would be helpful to know whether those who were watching could accurately report on what the program featured so that the station could evaluate the effectiveness of its content and the effect that promotion had in attracting viewers (Box 4-2).

Recall In **recall interviews,** the respondent is asked to reconstruct his or her listening or viewing for the past 24 hours. These interviews are normally conducted by telephone because of the

**BOX 4-2
TELEPHONE
COINCIDENTAL
RESEARCH**

ADVANTAGES

- Can be focused on a single program or a block of programs.
- Can be set up quickly, and the results can be reported quickly.
- The cooperation rate is relatively high.
- Potential accuracy is greater because no memory is required.
- Demographic data can be obtained.
- A relatively unbiased sample of listed telephone households can be drawn.
- Nonresponse is relatively low since interviewers can probe for answers.
- The overall expense may be lower than that of other methods since measurement can be targeted to specific programs, time periods, or areas.
- Repeat surveys can provide data for a trend analysis of specific time periods or programs.

DISADVANTAGES

- Does not cover unlisted households unless the researchers use the more expensive random-digit dialing sampling.
- Ratings figures are not generally predictable for the entire general coverage areas of stations or networks.
- Cannot cover early-morning or late-evening periods.
- Covers only in-home viewing or listening.

SOURCE: Hugh Malcolm Beville, Jr., *Audience Ratings: Radio, Television, Cable* (Hillsdale, NJ: Lawrence Erlbaum Associates, Inc., 1985). Copyright © 1985. Used by permission of Lawrence Erlbaum Associates, Inc. ∎

much greater economy in reaching large numbers of respondents compared with face-to-face interviews. In a recall viewing survey, for example, respondents may be asked to report whether they had their TV sets on after they got out of bed, during breakfast, before work, and the like. For each of those periods or other time periods, the person will be asked what she or he was watching. It is generally considered impractical to ask for information beyond that period because of the likelihood that respondents won't remember. Since audience members are creatures of habit, they might not have paid full attention to what was on unless they were particularly interested or otherwise noticed the program, especially if it was on several days before they were asked about it (Box 4-3).

Aided recall   In **aided recall** interviews, the respondent is read or shown a list of programs and asked whether she or he listened to or watched any of them. The rationale for this technique is that most respondents go through a daily routine that becomes fairly predictable. How many times do you remember what you ate for dinner during the past week unless there was something especially good or some other extraordinary event caused the menu to remain in your conscious memory? When a memory jogger is provided, a respondent can recall much more detail from the recent past.

Mall Intercept Surveys

There are many instances in which information about audiences is not provided by Nielsen or Arbitron. There are many other questions about audience habits and interests that are valuable to programmers in their decision making. For example, if a radio station's management is interested in finding out who the most popular disc jockeys, newspersons, or traffic reporters are and which categories of audience members find them most appealing, it can con-

---

**BOX 4-3
TELEPHONE RECALL
RESEARCH**

ADVANTAGES

- Covers out-of-home as well as in-home listening or viewing.
- Produces data at a relatively low cost.
- A relatively unbiased sample of listed telephone households can be readily drawn.
- The sample can be drawn to cover a specific area.
- Can cover all parts of each day surveyed, including early morning and late night.

DISADVANTAGES

- Depends on the respondent's memory, which can affect accuracy.
- There is no satisfactory way to deal with nonresponse. When persons being interviewed do not volunteer that programs were watched, this implies that they were not in the audience. This raises questions about possible bias toward overstating listening or viewing caused by reliance on individuals who did report watching particular programs.
- Does not cover nonlisted homes unless the more expensive random-digit dialing is used.

SOURCE: Hugh Malcolm Beville, Jr., *Audience Ratings: Radio, Television, Cable* (Hillsdale, NJ: Lawrence Erlbaum Associates, Inc., 1985). Copyright © 1985. Used by permission of Lawrence Erlbaum Associates, Inc.   ∎

tract with a research supplier to do a telephone survey.

An alternative method of obtaining that information is the **intercept survey,** or **mall intercept survey,** in which field workers interview a **quota sample,** or specified number of respondents in desired demographic groups. Since shopping malls have become major gathering centers in many communities, they are convenient places to reach an approximate cross section of the population. As was discussed earlier, individuals who go to shopping malls "self-select" their eligibility to be participants in any survey that may be conducted there, and so the researcher has no control over who is present at that location. Since there is no way to know who is at the mall at any given moment or day, the researcher cannot devise a sample frame. Furthermore, the ability to control who is interviewed is greatly diminished. If field workers consciously or unconsciously avoid approaching certain kinds of people (for example, if female field workers are reluctant to approach men), the data will be biased.

Different shopping centers cater to consumers of different socioeconomic levels. People with greater discretionary income gravitate to shopping centers that feature shops with more expensive merchandise. Even chain stores upgrade or downgrade the levels of their goods to meet the purchasing inclinations of the consumers who shop at their various locations. For an intercept survey sample to approximate the general population, shopping centers in all areas of the market must be included in the study.

Depending on the day of the week and the time of day, certain segments of the population may or may not be present in proportion to their presence in the total population. For example, there is an influx of teenage girls in department stores in the afternoon after school lets out. In certain locations, the number of shoppers increases in the evenings since a high percentage of working people do not have the opportunity to visit those stores during the day.

There are other serious potential limitations to quota and intercept studies. If there is no supervision of field workers, falsification can result or the results can be biased because of who is included in or left out of the interviewing process. Another problem is that there is no way to determine with accuracy how closely the results mirror reality.

If every major shopping center in the metropolitan area is included or at least given an equally likely chance of being selected or if shopping centers are chosen on the basis of their geographic distribution, the level of representativeness of those interviewed can be made higher. Nevertheless, intercept surveys can never be considered sufficiently representative to be a worthy substitute for surveys that are based on a random selection of respondents. Intercept surveys permit the gathering of information at lower cost, but this information is compromised by the absence of control over sampling error. This always casts doubt on the accuracy of the research findings (Box 4-4).

Electronic Measurement

Earlier in this chapter we suggested that the most accurate way to find out what people are doing is to watch them, but we also pointed out the impracticality of that method of doing research. An alternative to having an observer in the home is to install an electronic device that monitors when the set is on and who is watching.

Electronic recording devices are impractical for measuring a radio audience because radio is a portable medium. There are so many Walkmans in use and so much listening is done in cars and other places outside the home that it would be impossibly expensive to attach a device to all those receivers. However, this method is used extensively in television audience research.

People meters In 1936, Arthur C. Nielsen, who was already running a successful market research business, acquired the patent rights to the **audimeter,** a device attached to radio receivers that used a coated paper tape to record when they were on and which frequencies were

BOX 4-4
MALL INTERCEPT
RESEARCH

ADVANTAGES

- The geographic residency and some of the shopping preferences of potential or actual listeners and viewers can be pinpointed exactly.
- Some demographic attributes can be observed directly (sex, race).
- Offers the opportunity to ask open-ended questions such as, "Since you are a regular listener, what do you like about WZZZ's morning wake-up radio program?" This enables respondents to express in their own words how they feel about the subject without being restricted to a simple yes or no response. The interviewer can follow up with probing questions that ask the respondents to explain what they mean if they give a vague response such as "They are a great bunch of guys." The interviewer can then ask, "What do you mean?" or "Give me an example of what you mean."
- Offers the opportunity to ask open-ended questions of a large number of respondents.
- The proportion of respondents in the sample can be compared with the proportion in the population. If the number of respondents is sufficiently large, it should resemble the distribution of the actual population.

DISADVANTAGES

- It is necessary to obtain permission from the shopping center and/or store management to conduct interviews on the premises. This may be a problem in areas where store owners prohibit solicitation of their shoppers by fund-raisers for fear that customers will be offended and not patronize their businesses.
- Requires a large staff of field workers who have been trained and who must be supervised closely.
- The schedule for interviewing must take into account the habits and availability of different audience segments.
- Field workers may unconsciously avoid certain kinds of shoppers.
- Customers may be unwilling to interrupt their shopping to cooperate with interviewers.
- The time during which an interviewer can expect a respondent to remain cooperative is very short. ∎

tuned in. After a period of development, the A.C. Nielsen Company began to measure commercial network radio service in 1942. In 1949, Nielsen introduced a 35-mm film audimeter in a mailable cartridge that home set owners could replace and mail back to Nielsen for analysis. Television audience measurement was begun in 1950, and the audimeter was adapted to TV. The audimeter was replaced by the **people meter,** an electronic device that records not only when the set is on and which channel is tuned in but who is watching.

Both Nielsen and Arbitron use versions of the people meter for some of their audience measurements; each member of the household is assigned a button on a small box that sits on the top of the TV receiver or has a designated button on a remote control device. When the person enters or leaves the room where a TV set is playing, his or her button is supposed to be pushed to indicate presence in or absence from the TV audience.

Each people meter is connected by a special telephone line to a central computer. Throughout the day it records and stores information about when the set is on and which channel has been tuned in. Late at night the computer reads the stored information from each box and compiles it.

The advantage of the metered method lies in its reliability. The research company does not have to depend on someone in the household remembering to write down when the set is on and what was watched. The computer faithfully performs its duty every day, and the information is gathered unobtrusively. However, the technology is costly, as is the rental of a separate telephone line for each sample household and the computer that does the electronic sweep of each box every day to gather the data that have been collected there. Furthermore, the set may be turned on as background with no one actually watching it. Regardless, credit for viewing is given because that information has been recorded by the computer.

Since the research company has already recorded information on the age and sex of each member of the household along with other key demographic data, its computers can quickly generate more thorough information about the audiences for programs. This enables the programming sources to deliver more specific audiences that fit the target marketing objectives of advertisers (Figure 4-6).

FIGURE 4-6 Nielsen people meter. *(Used by permission of Nielsen Media Research.)*

The ratings service most often discussed in newspaper and magazine articles is Nielsen's national audience estimates, which are based on a national sample of television viewers. This sample, which consists of about 4500 households, is measured with a people meter.

In addition to national network audiences, Nielsen measures individual television market viewing. Instead of using the electronic recording device, though, viewers keep a diary. Nielsen measures a number of the largest individual TV markets in the country with people meters. The viewing information obtained from these households is fed each evening into a computer that generates an overnight report to stations, advertising agencies, and networks. Although the results are not representative of national viewing, they provide programmers and advertisers with daily information about the success of shows in attracting viewers (Box 4-5).

A people meter sample enables one to track a program's audience accurately over long periods, something that is not possible with diaries. Arbitron and Nielsen diaries are maintained for 7 days, which means that four sets of viewers are typically included in a 4-week ratings period. People meter households, by contrast, are measured on a daily basis and kept in the sample by Nielsen for 2 years before they are replaced.

The problems with the accuracy of people meter measurements are similar to those with diaries. Researchers must count on respondents to push their buttons to indicate their presence

---

**BOX 4-5
PEOPLE METER
RESEARCH**

ADVANTAGES

- Allows more specific and reliable demographic ratings.
- Allows overnight demographic reporting.
- Generates comparable ratings for broadcast and cable stations.
- Credits VCR playback of programs that were **timeshifted,** or recorded and watched at a later time.
- Monitors **zipping,** or fast-forwarding through the commercials when one is watching a taped program, and **zapping,** or the practice of putting the recorder on pause during commercials to eliminate interruptions when the program is played back.
- Eliminates diary respondent fatigue.
- Lowers the nonresponse rate.
- Measures audiences over a long period of time.
- Gives viewing credit to independent stations, cable services, and less popular programming.

DISADVANTAGES

- Measures very specific behaviors based on demographics. For instance, there may be a bias toward viewers who are not intimidated by button pushing. Whereas some people have techniophobia and never get the hang of operating electronic equipment, others seem able to intuitively understand how to operate computers, video games, VCRs, and remote control devices.
- The willingness of respondents to push buttons over a long period of time is questionable.
- It is questionable whether children will remember to push buttons. ■

or departure from the audience. Each of the meter services uses a light that sits on the set or a message that flashes on the TV screen as a reminder to push the buttons, and so participants are continually reminded of their special status as research participants. When people are aware that their responses are being observed, they sometimes alter their behavior. Consequently, people may not watch TV in the way they would if no observations were being conducted.

A suspected bias of people meters was confirmed in a study conducted jointly by Nielsen Media Research and the J. Walter Thompson advertising agency. A coincidental telephone survey of 75,000 calls made in 1989 found that the people meter reports underestimate the viewing of teenagers and children, who do not push the buttons when watching TV.[6] A 2-year study sponsored by the three broadcast networks found that families began to tire of pushing the buttons while watching TV and that procedures for including household visitors in the audience were confusing.[7]

We all know someone who has yet to figure out how to operate a VCR, and some people never use microwave ovens because they can't figure out how to push the right buttons. Thus, there is bias in the technical skills required to respond to metered surveys. Although reading and writing are not necessary for operating people meter response devices, there may be many technically inept respondents in the sample.

People meters versus diaries The use of people meters has been important to the Fox Television Network and to independent stations in general. Since people meters were put into place by Nielsen as its sole means of measuring the national TV audience, the ratings of the big three networks have declined while the ratings of some of the programs on Fox have steadily improved. Because the more narrow, younger audiences targeted by Fox programs are desired by advertisers, the network can sell spots for premium prices in spite of having smaller audiences.

The diary method relies on the diligence of respondents in writing down what the members of the television household watched and how long they were tuned in. Since the details of viewing are easily overlooked, diary keepers often underreport their actual viewing. As a consequence, independent stations have realized higher shares of the audiences in markets where metered measurement is done because of a rise in HUT levels as a result of the people meter giving credit for viewing that was not recorded in diaries. Among the reasons for this are that less important or less popular shows are not as likely to be checked in a diary, the diary measurement does not reflect shorter viewing periods, the diary is not likely to reflect tuning when no viewing occurs, and as the week wears on, diary keepers are less likely to fully report their viewing.[8] In other words, many diary respondents tend to remember the most popular networks because they are more familiar with them and overlook other programs that were actually watched by someone in the household.

Nielsen Media Research The Nielsen Company abandoned its audimeter/diary system for gathering national TV ratings to concentrate on a people meter service in September 1987. In June 1989 Nielsen announced that it was at work on a **passive people meter** which would do away with the need for viewers to push buttons to inform the computer they were in the audience. The Nielsen device, which was expected to take several years to develop, would scan the facial features of the members of the household and thus recognize when any one of them was watching television.[9] Not to be outdone, Arbitron revealed shortly after the Nielsen announcement that it also was developing a passive system.[10]

If passive people meters can be made to work and if people will be willing to have their activities so monitored, they will diminish the problems of viewers who forget to push the buttons indicating they are present. This is especially a problem in getting accurate estimates of the children's audience.[11]

Arbitron ScanAmerica The differences between the Arbitron and Nielsen people meter services may be negligible to programmers except that Arbitron assumes that its service will better identify programs that attract the consumer demographics that particular advertisers want to reach. From a programmer's standpoint, if certain viewers can be identified and if those audiences can be matched with the needs of advertisers, the kind of programs that attract the desired audiences can be scheduled. This could further refine the process of selecting programs that will deliver the audiences for which advertisers are most willing to pay. By providing a **single-source measurement** service which combines data about audience viewing and purchasing habits, Arbitron expects to be able to fulfill the hopes of advertisers.

Arbitron's **ScanAmerica** respondents use an electronic wand to scan the Universal Product Code (UPC) on items they purchase. When the wand is returned to its holster on the people meter box, the information is read into the

storage unit to await retrieval by the Arbitron computer. These data, which Arbitron calls "BuyerGraphics," offer subscribers, whether advertisers or media outlets, the ability to define the people who are watching by what they buy (Figure 4-7).

The ScanAmerica people meter asks viewers to report every 30 minutes by entering information on who is watching. An on-screen prompt is given to remind them to push the buttons, increasing the response rate.

Households receive $30 a month to participate in the sample. Arbitron argues that even members of affluent households are willing to take the time to scan the UPC symbols on just-purchased items for that amount of money.

Arbitron began its experiment with a 600-household sample in the Denver market in April 1987. The cost was high—about three times as much as Arbitron's diary service—and only one station in the market used it. The others were

FIGURE 4-7 ScanAmerica. *(Used by permission of Arbitron Ratings Co.)*

unwilling to pay for both Nielsen's and Arbitron's people meter services. However, advertisers are very much interested in the additional demographic and consumer data that a single-source measurement service can provide. Arbitron expanded ScanAmerica to St. Louis, Sacramento, New York, Minneapolis, and Phoenix in 1990.[12]

Arbitron recently abandoned its plan to provide a full national sample of households.[13] The company still plans to convert each of its metered markets to ScanAmerica by 1995.[14]

Overnights Since the objective of programming is to attract and maintain audiences and deliver them to advertisers, it is crucial that programming meet this objective or advertiser support will decline and the profits of the electronic media outlet will suffer. Any new television series is an unknown quantity in spite of all of the care taken in selecting its cast and testing its appeal. The final judges are the viewers, who may or may not watch a program in sufficient numbers to justify its continuance. The sooner that has been determined, the more efficiently the rest of the production machinery can be operated. If the program is a hit, more episodes can be ordered. If a network has erred in its judgment, the decision to cancel a program and substitute another or to move a poorly performing show to another time period can be made quickly.

Arbitron and Nielsen each provide **overnight ratings** to stations, networks, producers, and advertisers to keep them apprised of the performance of programs. A computer-generated report of a **metered market** that is measured by a special sample of people meter households can be on the executive's desk the morning after a telecast.

Both Arbitron and Nielsen currently measure more than 25 television markets, with meters installed in a sample of households in each one.[15] Nielsen estimates that it is measuring over 45 percent of the nation's households with meters rather than diaries (Box 4-6).[16]

The overnight ratings are made available on a market-by-market basis as well as collectively to subscribers in other markets. They provide a quick evaluation of program performance before local ratings reports are issued. Although the sample is limited to the largest markets, the population's preferences are an indicator of what the more thorough market measurements will report.

QUALITATIVE RESEARCH

Advertisers have come to recognize that although one program may not deliver as large an audience as others do, it may contain a much higher concentration of target consumers. To the right advertisers, this audience is worth paying for. Who wins among electronic media operators? Several may, but for different reasons. The station or network with the largest audience

---

**BOX 4-6
RESEARCH SERVICES:
SUMMARY**

NIELSEN MEDIA RESEARCH

- Television market reports: diary
- National audience reports: people meter
- Metered market (overnight) reports: people meter

ARBITRON

- Television market reports: diary
- Radio market reports: diary
- Metered market (overnight) reports: people meter
- Single-source reports: ScanAmerica

may attract advertisers of general-consumption products such as soft drinks and antiperspirants. A program with a smaller but more demographically focused audience may actually be worth more to many advertisers because it allows them to reach their target consumers more efficiently. Advertisers have been willing to pay a premium to reach 18- to 34-year-old viewers on late-night shows such as *Arsenio Hall.* Even though *thirtysomething*'s low ranking of around 66th during the 1990–1991 season no doubt was the major factor in its cancellation, it ranked 26th among women age 18 to 49, a group highly desired by advertisers.

With the mass audience being fragmented by the many media services vying for its attention, most outlets must narrow their appeal to attract a portion or segment of the audience. At the same time, advertisers have become increasingly sensitive to the inefficiency of paying for **waste exposures,** or extraneous audience members. Because the cost of advertising on a program is usually based on its total audience size, an advertiser must pay for the whole audience even though many of those listeners or viewers are not part of the consumer group considered most likely to purchase a product. Products such as Nike athletic shoes and Levis 501 Blues jeans, for example, have been developed to appeal to men 18 to 24 years old. Their advertising messages, which are intended to appeal directly to that market segment, are placed in programs that deliver large numbers of these target consumers. Consequently, Nike and Levi ads appear on programs such as NBC's *Saturday Night Live* or on programs on the MTV network.

Still, the demographic characteristics of the audience, no matter how finely they may be defined, do not differentiate between types of people who happen to be of the same age and sex (Figure 4-8). Every one knows people who started out in the same hometown, attended the same high school, and even entered the same college but are radically different types of individuals. The quality of the audience can be identified through attributes such as occupation, income, lifestyle, and interests.

Much electronic media research is **quantitative research,** or a systematic tabulation of data in the categories of age and sex. Rather than simply counting categories such as age and sex, **qualitative research** identifies characteristics in an audience that indicate its likelihood of being customers for products ranging from blue jeans to luxury automobiles (Box 4-7).

Psychographic and Lifestyle Research

Audiences can be identified, or segmented, by age, sex, income, and other demographic attributes, but they can also be identified by their inner values, or **psychographics** (consumer mind-sets). Psychographics have been described as

a collection of marketing research procedures which seek to describe or explain consumer behavior using characteristics that go beyond demographic descriptions. The characteristics used generally include product attributes, lifestyle characteristics, and psychological characteristics such as self-concept, interests, and opinions.[18]

SRI International has developed a categorization system that it calls values and lifestyles (VALS). A number of behavioral and psychological attributes have been identified to segment consumers as "need-driven," "outer-directed," or "inner-directed." Among outer-directed consumers there is a subcategory of emulators, or upwardly mobile individuals who emulate the rich and successful. The buying style of emulators characterizes them as conspicuous consumers who will sacrifice comfort and utility for show; they are likely purchasers of flashy, expensive sports cars and other similar products. In contrast, inner-directed individuals include those in the experiential category, who prefer process to product and are interested in what the product does for them, not what it says about them.

Whereas psychographic research concentrates on the audience member's self-perception, **lifestyle** studies take a broader approach by focusing not only on the respondent's inner state

THE ONLY THINGS THESE PEOPLE HAVE IN COMMON ARE AGE AND SEX.

You'll never know who buys the stereos, drinks the beer or wears the tweed if all you're looking at is an age and sex demographic. You need a way to know who buys what in order to get the most out of television advertising. That's why Arbitron Ratings developed Product Target AID.℠ It's a powerful marketing tool that lets you pinpoint the buying habits of a television audience to a degree never before possible.

Product Target AID combines audience ratings with lifestyle information and product user profiles, so you can see what kinds of consumers a television program is reaching. Now you can generate ratings for stereo buffs or beer drinkers by pinpointing those viewers whose lifestyles make them good prospects for a specific product. That can mean better buys for advertisers and better sales for television stations.

Product Target AID works on your own IBM® XT personal computer. In minutes, it delivers more of the information you need to analyze avails, to find a station's strengths and to demonstrate how a program reaches the viewers who are most likely to buy the product or service an advertiser wants to sell.

Product Target AID. It brings a whole new focus to television advertising. Contact your Arbitron Ratings representative for more information. Arbitron Ratings (212) 887-1300.

ARBITRON RATINGS

⊖⊖ ARBITRON RATINGS COMPANY
a Control Data Company

© 1985 Arbitron Ratings

FIGURE 4-8   The only things these people have in common are age and sex. *(Used by permission of Arbitron Ratings Co.)*

**BOX 4-7
THE PROGRAM
ATTRACTING
SMALLER AUDIENCES
MAY ACTUALLY BE
THE MOST VALUABLE**

Given two stations with overall ratings . . . of 14.0 and 18.0 and similar CPMs [cost per thousand], one would expect the rational advertiser to pick the higher rated station. This would maximize reach [the number of different people who watch the program and thus see or hear an ad], and in a sense, would be the more efficient buy. But suppose the analysis of the audiences for these stations is extended. If the stations were compared on their ability to draw a particular audience segment, a different picture might emerge. For example, among the women, 18–34, married and upscale segment, the station with lower overall ratings may substantially out-deliver the "higher" rated station.[17]

That is, the lower-rated station actually reaches the desired (target) audience more effectively. If two stations attract similar-sized audiences and if their advertising rates result in a similar cost for reaching those viewers, the logical advertising buy would be the station with the higher rating, which allows one to reach more viewers at the same efficiency rate.

The analysis can be extended to consider how well the two stations attract a particular group desired by the advertiser as the most likely purchasers of a product. Even though one station has a lower overall rating, it may have a substantially higher rating among a more narrowly defined group, such as married women age 18 to 34, who are further classified by their income, area of residence, and occupation as upscale consumers.

If the advertiser is trying to sell Gucci handbags or similarly expensive goods, the lower-rated station may be the more efficient advertising buy.   ∎

---

of mind but on his or her activities, interests, and opinions. For instance, identifying groups such as "mature singles" and "double income, no children" can pinpoint the motivations that transcend the traditional quantitative segmentation of age and sex.

Geodemographic Research

Geodemographic research combines an analysis of demographic variables with the geographic locations of subjects. That is, certain attributes of audience members who reside in specific areas defined by ZIP codes are fairly consistent. But because there are fewer ZIP code areas in smaller markets, geodemographic research is not feasible except in large markets where there are enough ZIP code areas to allow a meaningful segmentation of the population.

One such geodemographic service is Cluster-Plus, offered by Simmons Market Research Bureau and Donnelley Marketing Information Services. It uses census data to identify over 1600 demographic clusters by ZIP code and create 47 distinct lifestyle clusters. Residential ZIP codes

are assigned to a cluster that describes a particular lifestyle. One such cluster could be labeled "top-income, well-educated professionals, prestige homes." Another cluster could be called "poorly educated, rural blue-collar families with children." As was discussed earlier, it should be apparent that these descriptions are much more meaningful than traditional demographic descriptors such as "women 18 to 34" and "men 55 to 64."

The Claritas Corporation's PRIZM is another lifestyle segmentation system based on consumer households identified by the U.S. Bureau of the Census. The measured attributes are marital status and family composition, ethnicity, language and national origin, education and school attendance, occupation, urbanization and household density, housing, rents and values, length of residency and mobility, and possession of cars, appliances, and household conveniences.

The result is 40 unique clusters of consumers identified by their ZIP codes. These clusters are given names such as "Blue Blood Estates," "Pools and Patios," "Bunker's Neighbors," and "Hard Scrabble," which suggest their socioeconomic status. These groups are assigned to broader "cluster groups" that have descriptive titles such as "Educated, Affluent, Elite White Families in Owner-Occupied, Green-Belt Suburbs" (consisting of the "Blue Blood Estates," "Furs & Station Wagons," "Two More Rungs," and "Pools and Patios" clusters). The four clusters in this group have high socioeconomic status, a college education, families with school-age and teenage children, owner-occupied housing, and conspicuous levels of consumption. They represent about 30 percent of households with an income of $50,000 or more.

With this detailing of consumer habits, socioeconomic status, and location of residence, predictions on purchasing habits can be made. The most likely buyers of high-cost lawn mowers, for example, reside in suburbs, not in urban areas where lawns are typically very small. Moreover, a certain level of affluence would be required to fit the profile of a likely customer.

The more a programmer knows about audience members' leisure-time activities, jobs, and ways of viewing themselves and the world, the greater the possibility of presenting programming that will appeal to them. If particular lifestyle or attitudinal traits can be pinpointed, and if programming can be developed that meets the needs of audience groups with these characteristics, there is a better possibility of attracting audiences. For example, it may be possible to identify a significant segment of people in the potential audience of a radio station who feel somewhat insecure in social situations, want to belong to an in-group, value being well informed on a variety of subjects, and want companionship. A radio program that includes discussions of interesting topics by the disc jockey or program personality, along with interviews with experts and calls from listeners, may attract this group of listeners.

SUMMARY

To do an effective job of attracting and keeping listeners or viewers so that they can be delivered to advertisers, a programmer must know the potential audience. Research provides objective, systematic information to aid in this process. Research is not a panacea but provides insight for making program decisions. It will not tell why people like or dislike programs, but it will identify which programs they will watch among those available to them.

Research projects should first state the problem, or what is to be studied. After the universe, or population to be studied, is defined, a sample can be drawn. A research study's results may be biased if groups of potential respondents are excluded from the sample. Probability sampling gives each subject in the population an equally likely chance of being selected. Moreover, probability sampling permits the researcher to deter-

mine the sampling error, or the precision of the results that are obtained.

Even when they are objectively drawn, samples provide only a limited estimate of the population's habits. The larger the sample size, the smaller the margin of sample error. However, research clients such as stations and networks are not willing to pay the high cost of the most accurate measurements. Thus, research in the electronic media includes compromises based on cost that affect or limit the information obtained.

A low in-tab raises questions about the representativeness of results that do not include the responses of sample subjects because these responses were not received or were unusable. Consequently, research firms attempt to obtain a high response rate and ensure that the responses they obtain are complete.

Survey research is the most important means

of observing audience habits. A survey implies a sample of respondents who represent the population. Survey research generally relies on probability sampling, in which an equally likely chance of being selected is given to every subject in the population.

The diary method is used to measure both television and radio audience patterns. TV viewers and radio listeners write down the programs and times they watched or listened.

The other important means of obtaining information about radio listeners is telephone recall surveys in which respondents are asked to account for their listening habits during the previous 24 hours. There are some advantages to both the diary method and the telephone recall method. A larger sample size can be contacted at lower cost with telephone interviews, but only one listening day can be reported. In the case of diaries, there is an opportunity to obtain more detailed information, but respondents may tire of filling out the reports or may record incorrect information.

Mall intercept studies contact large numbers of people in central locations, but there are some hazards in this technique. Unless field workers are carefully supervised, they may avoid contacting some types of people. Intercept studies can only approximate the demographic distribution of the population and therefore do not yield representative results.

Research companies have begun to replace TV diaries with people meters, devices that record which program is being watched when the set is on. The people meter was developed as a more reliable means of obtaining demographic information about television viewing. Respondents push a button to indicate when they are viewing. The data that are stored for each household set are gathered every day and processed in the overnight reports made available to stations, advertising agencies, and program producers. The speed with which the data can be reported is helpful in tracking program performance, and thus in formulating decisions about whether changes in programming should be made.

The increasing sophistication of research techniques has enabled clients to employ qualitative techniques in analyzing audiences. Psychographic research looks at the attitudinal characteristics of audiences. Lifestyle research combines the attitudinal and demographic attributes of audiences. Program outlets can identify the kinds of people who are inclined to purchase certain kinds of products and services and who also are attracted to certain kinds of programs. Even though some programs may not attract the largest audiences, the kinds of people who watch or listen to them may possess the specific attributes desired by certain advertisers. Thus, a lower-rated program may be a more efficient buy than a highly rated one that creates a large number of waste exposures for the advertiser.

SUGGESTED READINGS

Beville, Hugh Malcolm, Jr.: *Audience Ratings: Radio, Television, Cable,* rev. ed., Lawrence Erlbaum, Hillsdale, N.J., 1988.

This is the most comprehensive explanation of audience ratings, written by the dean of electronic media audience research. Following a career in research at NBC, Beville served as executive director of the Broadcast Rating Council (now the Electronic Media Research Council) for 10 years and remained a respected authority on broadcast research. The book includes a history of the development of broadcasting ratings research and describes the major commercial research companies and the nature of their services. Their methodologies are described in detail, and the strengths and shortcomings of each are objectively assessed.

Hartshorn, Gerald G., ed.: *Audience Research Sourcebook,* National Association of Broadcasters, Washington, D.C., 1991.

This is a clearly written, practical primer for people who lack a background in conducting broadcast audience research as well as more experienced practitioners who want to review procedures. In chapters written by prominent research and station consultants, the reader is given an overview of research concepts and purposes for conducting broadcast audience research. Survey research design is explained, and types of surveys are described, as are questionnaire design, sampling procedures, analyses of the data that are gathered, and applications of the findings.

Webster, James, and Lawrence Lichty: *Ratings Analysis: Theory and Practice,* Lawrence Erlbaum, Hillsdale, N.J., 1991.

Program ratings and their relationship to advertising and programming decisions are the thrust of this book, which emphasizes analytic applications. The discussion includes ratings analysis, a description of research services and methods, and explanations of the analytic techniques used in examining ratings data. The treatment of the subject in this book will help readers increase their knowledge about the use of audience research. In the competitive environment in which programmers operate, this can be a distinct advantage.

Buzzard, Karen S.: *Chains of Gold: Marketing the Ratings and Rating the Markets,* Scarecrow Press, Metuchen, N.J., 1990.

Buzzard offers a historical review of the development of television ratings services, with explanations of the influence of technological developments, business demands, and the competition between companies that have at times merged or gone out of business. This book is helpful in putting the ratings services in perspective and describing how they have changed over the years.

NOTES

1. Hugh Malcolm Beville, Jr., *Audience Ratings: Radio, Television, Cable,* Lawrence Erlbaum, Hillsdale, N.J., 1985, pp. 20–71.

2. "More Stations Opting for Just One Ratings Service," *Broadcasting,* Sept. 3, 1990, p. 52; "Stations Opting for Only One Ratings Service," *Broadcasting,* June 3, 1991, p. 9; Rod Granger, "Arbitron Cutting Back, Repositioning," *Electronic Media,* July 29, 1991, p. 17.

3. "NAB Offers Design for New TV Diary," *Broadcasting,* June 25, 1990, p. 24; "NAB Unveils New Personal Viewing Diary," *Broadcasting,* Dec. 3, 1990, p. 76; Laura Malt, "NAB Takes Aim at People Meters with New Ratings Diary," *Electronic Media,* Dec. 3, 1990, pp. 4, 62.

4. Beville, op. cit., pp. 109–112.

5. Ibid.

6. "Kids Aren't Pushing Buttons: People-Meter Study," *Multichannel News,* June 19, 1989, p. 6; "Silent Viewers: Difficulties Measuring Children," *Broadcasting,* March 25, 1991, pp. 77, 79; "Nielsen Kids' Measurements Questioned," *Broadcasting,* Dec. 9, 1991, p. 10.

7. Adam Buckman, "TV Research Chiefs Target Meter Flaws," *Electronic Media,* Dec. 18, 1989, pp. 3, 102; Bob Knight, "Webs Seek Changes from Nielsen," *Variety,* Dec. 20, 1989, pp. 37, 42; "Nielsen Peoplemeters Get Two-Year Network Review," *Broadcasting,* Dec. 18, 1989, pp. 68–70.

8. "Adjustments Are Not the Answer to Meter-Diary Gap, Says Arbitron," *Television/Radio Age,* June 27, 1988, p. 34.

9. Adam Buckman, "'Passive' Meter Plan Draws Active Approval," *Electronic Media,* June 5, 1989, pp. 2, 39; "Nielsen to Develop Passive Peoplemeter," *Broadcasting,* June 5, 1989, p. 31.

10. "Arbitron Close to Deal on Passive People Meter," *Television/Radio Age,* June 12, 1989, p. 18.

11. Buckman, "'Passive' Meter Plan Draws Active Approval"; "Nielsen to Develop Passive Peoplemeter."

12. "Five ADIs Go Single-Source," *Beyond the Ratings,* Aug. 1989, p. 19.

13. "ScanAmerica Signs CBS; CBS Signs Arbitron," *Broadcasting,* Nov. 4, 1991, pp. 65, 71; Wayne Walley, "Arbitron Axes National Ratings," *Electronic Media,* Sept. 7, 1992, pp. 3, 23.

14. Remarks by J. J. Aurichio, ScanAmerica Press Conference, June 21, 1988; see also John Dempsey, "Nielsen Competitors on the Warpath," *Variety,* June 20, 1990, p. 47; "ScanAmerica Delayed," *Broadcasting,* Dec. 3, 1990, p. 96.

15. Arbitron metered markets include New York, Los Angeles, Chicago, Washington, D.C., Philadelphia, Detroit, Boston, San Francisco, Dallas–Fort Worth, Houston, Miami, Cleveland, Atlanta, Denver, and Pittsburgh. See "Atlanta Is Signed Up," *Beyond the Ratings,* April 1989, p. 10; "Pittsburgh to Get Overnight Ratings," *Electronic Media,* Oct. 15, 1990, p. 8.

16. *Electronic Media,* July 17, 1989, p. 22; "Phoenix—Nielsen's Newest Metered Market," Nielsen Media Research *Media News,* April 1989, p. 1. Nielsen overnight markets include Portland, Phoenix, Milwaukee, St. Louis, Indianapolis, Cincinnati, Sacramento-Stockton, Miami–Fort Lauderdale, Minneapolis–St. Paul, Houston, Washington, D.C., Boston, Philadelphia, Los Angeles, Hartford–New Haven,

Denver, Seattle, Atlanta, New York, Chicago, Dallas–Fort Worth, San Francisco–Oakland, Charlotte, and San Diego. "Nielsen Expanding 'Overnights' to 20 Markets Now, 22 Cities Next Fall," NAB *TV Today,* April 24, 1989, p. 3; "Portland Latest Overnight Market for Nielsen," *Multichannel News,* July 10, 1989, p. 16; Rod Granger, "Detroit Loses Local Nielsen Meters," *Electronic Media,* Sept. 2, 1991, pp.

3, 23; "San Diego to Get Meter-Based Ratings," *Electronic Media,* Dec. 16, 1991, p. 40.

17. Richard V. Ducey, "Qualitative Audience Research: A New Tool for Marketing Your Station," *NAB Research Memorandum,* Dec. 1983, p. 2.

18. Bennett M. Griffin, "Psychographics . . . the Next Step," *NAB Research Memorandum,* Sept. 1984, p. 1.

CHAPTER 5

Audience Research Services

The electronic media deliver an audience to advertisers. Therefore there is a need for an objective way to ascertain and describe this entity. This information is important not only to the sales staff for selling advertising time but to the programmer, who must decide which audiences to target and which techniques to use in that quest.

In Chapter 3 it was noted that the most commonly applied audience research method is the audience survey. The ways in which the major audience research services—A.C. Nielsen and Arbitron—apply that method and the kinds of reports they give their clients are discussed later in this chapter. To understand how research results are used, it is important to first look at the basic components of electronic media audience measurement, including how markets are defined and where listeners and viewers are located.

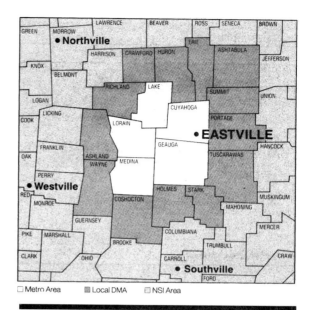

FIGURE 5-1   A Nielsen designated market area. *(From Nielsen Station Index: Your Guide to Reports, Services. Used by permission of Nielsen Media Research.)*

ELECTRONIC MEDIA MARKETS

The electronic media **market** is the geographic area that is served by an outlet. Each county in a state is assigned to a market by the audience research companies, based on the proportion of households (television) or persons (radio) who watch or listen to stations located there. State boundaries are not considered; many broadcast markets consist of counties in two or even three states.

Metro Area

Both figuratively and literally, the center of a radio or a TV market is the **metropolitan survey area,** or metro area. This area usually receives the best coverage by a station's signal since the stations in the market are licensed to a city located there. As Figure 5-1 shows, the metro area is the heart of the broadcast market. As the most densely populated part of the market, it is a prime retail area for many local advertisers.

A metropolitan survey area is defined by the U.S. Department of Commerce's Office of Feder-

al Statistical Policy and Standards as the county or counties lying within a **Metropolitan Statistical Area (MSA).** To be identified as an MSA, an area must include a city with a population of 50,000 or greater or an urban area of at least 50,000 residents within a total metropolitan area of at least 100,000 residents. This city or other identified population cluster serves as the focus of economic and cultural activity for an area. While people who live in communities surrounding this city may fill up their gas tanks at local convenience stores or auto service stations, they more often travel the few extra miles to the central or largest city in the MSA to make most of their major purchases. A reasonable density of population is thus necessary to support shopping centers, movie theaters, furniture stores, auto dealers, and other businesses, and the majority of such businesses are generally located in or near the largest cities in the area.

For example, Clearview lies in the center of an area designated as an MSA. It is a city of about 70,000 with an additional population of 50,000 in the surrounding small towns and rural area. Most of the people living there make most of their purchases in the Clearview area. As is typical of population centers, the two shopping malls serving the area are in Clearview. About 60 miles away is Steeltown, a city with a population of 500,000 and a surrounding suburban population of almost 1 million. Some Clearview residents travel to the larger MSA to shop, attracted by the mammoth shopping malls in Steeltown's suburbs. Nevertheless, most of the things that the majority of Clearview residents want to buy are available in stores and businesses conveniently located in the Clearview metro area. For people who live on the fringe of either MSA, though, the time required to travel to either Clearview or Steeltown is about the same. Like a stronger magnet, the larger MSA has a more powerful economic attraction to the people who live close to it.

In the largest radio and television markets, the metro area is defined as the **Consolidated Metropolitan Statistical Area (CMSA),** a designation given to areas with populations of more than 1 million. A CMSA consists of two or more contiguous MSAs. The individual statistical areas that constitute the CMSA are called Primary Metropolitan Statistical Areas (PMSAs). Thus, PMSAs consist of a large urbanized county or cluster of counties that have very strong internal economic and social links with and close ties to neighboring areas. CMSAs and PMSAs are the basic, or nonoverlapping, geographic areas.[1] This can be seen in Figure 5-2, which shows Arbitron's San Francisco radio market. Although San Francisco is the largest city in the market, other cities in the geographic area are designated as MSAs. Thus, the San Francisco metro area is an aggregate of several primary MSAs.

Television Markets

Nielsen designated market area The Nielsen local television market is called a **designated market area (DMA).** A DMA is a group of counties in which commercial stations licensed to a metro area achieve the largest audience share. As Figure 5-1 shows, the metro area (in white) is the central part of the DMA.

The counties that make up the total market, or DMA, are assigned on an annual basis. As Figure 5-3 shows, each county is assigned to a DMA because stations in each metro area receive the largest share of the viewers in that county.

Figure 5-4 shows the metro area and the local DMA for Indianapolis, Indiana. As the map of white and gray-shaded counties shows, the Indianapolis television market area is not circular even though television station signals generally radiate in a circular pattern. A market's shape is partly due to topography, which can inhibit signal coverage. Another influence on a market's shape is the attraction of TV signals from other markets. A close look at the map will explain the influence of competing markets. The two closest TV markets to the south of the Indianapolis metro area are Terre Haute, to the southwest and Louisville, to the southeast. Directly to the west is the Champaign-Urbana market. Directly to the east is the Dayton, Ohio, market, only a few miles east of the Indiana-Ohio state line. To the north is the Chicago, Illinois, market.

Like people across the country, people who reside in the counties in Indiana tend to watch the TV signals they receive with the greatest clarity. For instance, viewers in Putnam and Montgomery counties, east of the Terre Haute DMA, get better reception from Indianapolis's TV stations than they do from Terre Haute's. Viewers in Jay County, to the east, watch signals broadcast from Dayton, Ohio.

Nielsen reports a third area in addition to the metro area and the DMA. Household viewing is reported separately for the metro area, DMA, and station total area. Viewing data are reported for the DMA and station total area. The station total area adds all viewing done from locations outside the market, such as on cable systems, to each station's total audience.[2]

Arbitron ADI The **area of dominant influence (ADI)** is Arbitron's label for a television market. Like Nielsen, Arbitron assigns counties to ADIs

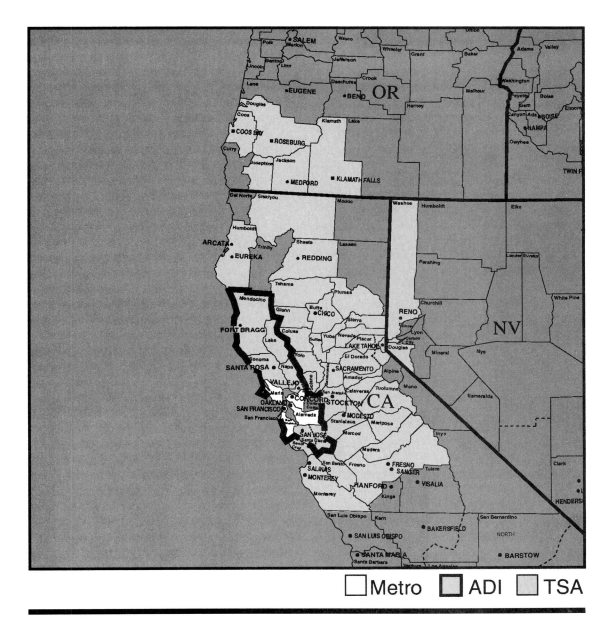

FIGURE 5-2   **San Francisco radio market map.** *(Used by permission of Arbitron Ratings Co.)*

on the basis of dominant viewing. The market with the largest share, or total percentage of viewing in a county, is considered the dominant influence in that county. Each ADI must have at least one commercial, nonsatellite home station (a **satellite station** rebroadcasts the signal of a station assigned to another market). As in the case of Nielsen television markets, each county in the contiguous United States is assigned exclusively to one ADI and there is no overlap.[3] Arbitron ADIs and Nielsen DMAs sometimes recognize TV markets served by a single

FIGURE 5-3 Nielsen designated market areas map. *(Used by permission of Nielsen Media Research.)*

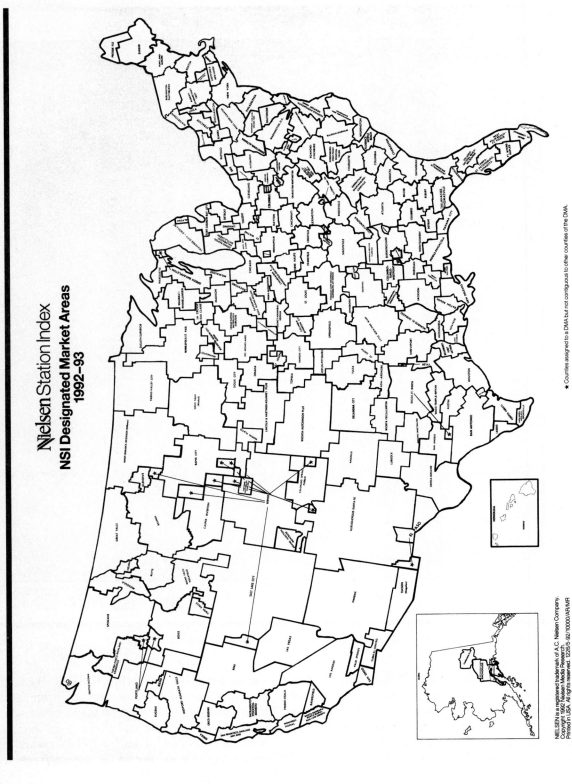

Nielsen Station Index
NSI Designated Market Areas
1992–93

★ Counties assigned to a DMA but not contiguous to other counties of the DMA.

NIELSEN is a registered trademark of A.C. Nielsen Company.
Copyright 1992 Nielsen Media Research.
Printed in USA. All rights reserved. 12205-92/10000/AR/MR

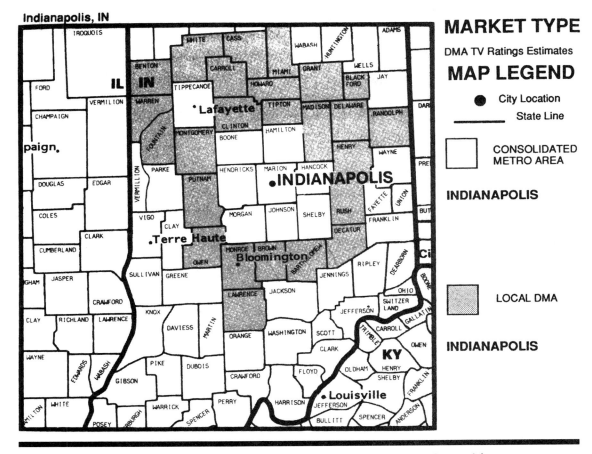

FIGURE 5-4   Indianapolis, Indiana, DMA map. *(Used by permission of Nielsen Media Research.)*

commercial station. For instance, Figure 5-4 shows the close proximity of Lafayette, Indiana, to Indianapolis. Nielsen includes Lafayette in the Indianapolis DMA, whereas Arbitron has determined that Lafayette is a separate market.

Arbitron reports three geographic areas in its television ratings reports, as shown in Figure 5-5. Arbitron reports viewing in the MSA. In addition to reporting viewing in the total market, or ADI, Arbitron also reports viewing in the **total survey area (TSA).** This geographic area includes all of a market's metro and ADI counties. In addition, the TSA includes the other counties that account for 98 percent of the viewing of that market's commercial home stations in its TSA measurement. Unlike MSAs and ADIs, a mar-

ket's TSA may include overlapping counties. Thus, the TSA permits the user of a ratings report to identify an even larger geographic area in which viewing of each station occurs. The TSA demonstrates TV stations' total geographic reach beyond the ADI.

Radio Listening in the ADI   For the 50 largest radio markets, Arbitron radio audience reports include listener estimates for the television market in which each radio market is located. Even though these estimates are of no particular use to most radio programmers, readers of this book who are unfamiliar with Arbitron's radio market reports may be confused when they notice that information. The purpose of reporting ADI lis-

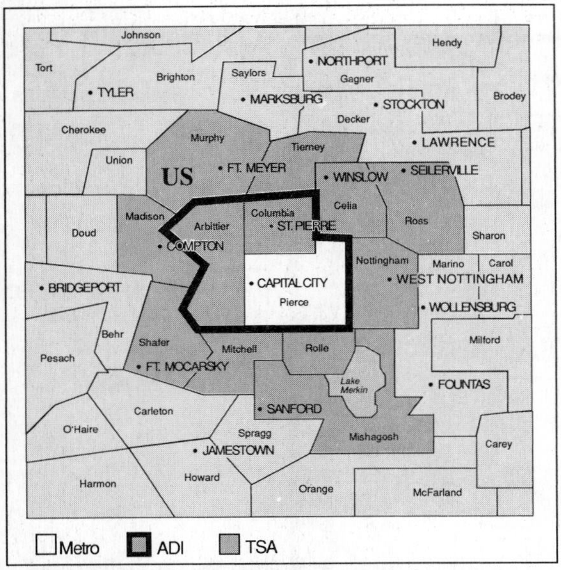

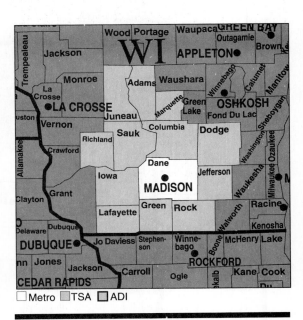

FIGURE 5-5   Capital City TV market map. (From How to Read Your Arbitron Television Market Report, *1989. Used by permission of Arbitron Ratings Co.)*

FIGURE 5-6   Madison, Wisconsin, radio market map. (Used by permission of Arbitron Ratings Co.)

tening is to give advertisers data with which to make comparisons on the efficiency of reaching target audiences through television or radio.

Radio Markets

Metro area   The core of the radio market is the MSA, as shown in Figure 5-6, where the metro area for the Madison, Wisconsin, radio market is designated by horizontal hatching. The white area identifies the other counties that constitute TSA. Since this is not a top-50 radio market, the Madison TV ADI is not reported.

The metro area is generally much more important for radio than for television because many radio signals do not cover as broad a geographic area as TV signals often do. Moreover, the highest concentration of listeners can be found in the metro area. Depending on the signal strength of the radio station and the appeal of its programming to listeners in the outlying areas of a market, the programmer of a radio station may decide to concentrate on the metro au-

dience rather than on the audience in the TSA. For instance, if the signal of a station does not effectively cover beyond the metro area, it is obvious that the potential for attracting listeners will be limited to the metro area. There is little incentive for a low-powered station in the San Francisco market (Figure 5-2) to include reports on freeway traffic conditions because the people who listen will not be able to receive the station clearly during their commute from the city out to the suburbs. Instead, such a station might concentrate on information and issues that have a direct bearing on the lives of its possible listeners in the urban area it can cover. In other words, the programmer should determine how the station can fulfill the needs and wants of the available audience in order to find its niche.

Total survey area   In addition to reporting on radio use in the MSA, Arbitron provides listener estimates for two additional larger geographic areas. We have already noted that Arbitron reports radio listening in the ADI. The more important geographic area is the total survey area, which is defined by counties. Unlike metro areas, TSA counties may overlap for adjacent markets. For a county to be included in a radio TSA, at least 10 survey respondents who live in the county must have indicated that they listen to stations licensed to a metro area and those mentions must account for at least 10 percent of the total station mentions from that county. Thus, the San Francisco TSA (Figure 5-2) includes many counties that lie far beyond the metro area because people in Redding, Chico, Sacramento, Stockton, Modesto, and other metro areas listen to stations licensed to San Francisco.

As Figure 5-2 indicates, stations that effectively cover the TSA can amass very large audiences among residents of the suburban areas of the market. Many San Francisco Bay area commuters drive into the city every day from their homes in the outlying TSA. Since a large number of people spend a long time in their cars going to and from work, TSA audience estimates are crucial. Thus, in a market such as San Francisco, programming strategies to attract commuting drivers during the morning and afternoon periods take on greater importance than they would in much smaller markets such as Madison, Wisconsin.

Cable Markets

Cable TV markets are defined on the basis of the number of households passed by the system. The unit affecting a cable system's size is the city in which the system operates. A franchise to operate a cable system is issued by the municipal government, usually the city council. The authority of the city to approve a cable operator is based on the fact that the coaxial cable must be strung on utility poles or buried underground in the municipal right-of-way.

If a city has 100,000 households, that is the size of the cable market. When a cable system also serves adjacent towns, the cable operator must seek a franchise from each city government even when a single cable system serves all the households in the different municipalities. Moreover, is possible to define a cable market more broadly when several cities are interconnected, even if they are not close to each other. In such a case, the operator of several cable franchises sends the same signals to channels carried on the different systems.

Whether the cable system consists of a single cable franchise or the interconnection of several, the objective is to connect the highest possible number of households. To achieve maximum household penetration in their franchise areas, cable operators must offer attractive services to their subscribers. As is discussed in detail in Chapter 20, cable operators are likely to include a network such as ESPN because it is a program service that many sports fans like to watch. Since teenagers "need their MTV," that service is often offered on systems as an incentive to subscribers. The children will pressure their parents to get cable because they want to have MTV on their TV sets.

Cable systems serving the largest cities must offer a wider range of services than small-town systems do. Unlike people who live in or near big cities, residents of remote communities often have a greater incentive to subscribe to cable just to get a full complement of broadcast network signals, particularly in areas where the off-air reception is poor or nonexistent. Since those subscribers' priorities are better reception and more channels than are possible off the air, operators of small-town cable systems often have less of an incentive to provide a wide range of channels and program services. In contrast, operators of systems in areas with good off-air TV reception must often agree to provide a larger array of channels to subscribers in order to get a franchise. However, they also do so voluntarily to provide greater benefits to potential subscribers.

RATINGS REPORT CONCEPTS

The discussion above dealt with the question, Where are listeners and viewers located? in defining the parameters of electronic media markets. The next question is, Who is in the radio or TV audience? The answer to this question requires a consideration of a number of concepts that are integral to the way in which radio and television audiences are measured.

Demographic Categories

Measurements of the audience are most frequently made by identifying the age and sex of listeners and viewers. While segmentation of audiences on the basis of these two attributes is not a wholly satisfactory or definitive descriptor of preferences, it defines the audiences that can be delivered to advertisers and thus affects programming decisions. For the purpose of reporting ratings estimates, audiences are broken down into specific age and sex groups, or basic audience segments (Table 5-1).

In television audience reports, the total audience is defined as "viewers 2+," which includes every viewer age 2 years or older. In radio audience reports, the total audience is defined as "listeners 12+." Measurement is not made of persons below age 12 since so few children are regular listeners.

As was discussed earlier, advertisers have varying audience needs. Thus, it is important to

understand that research companies report the numbers of men and women in the audience separately. A store that wants to sell sweater and skirt outfits needs to get its message to women, whereas a shoe store that wants to sell athletic shoes has to reach young men. Unless the audience is differentiated according to sex and by age, there is no way to know the extent to which a target consumer group is present. "Men 18–24" means something different from "women 18–24" or "men and women 18–24."

From the perspective of the programmer, the viewing and listening habits of men and women often differ and the kind of music or other program content that appeals to one sex may drive members of the opposite sex away. Young women, for instance, like soft ballads much more than do young men, whose tastes run to much harder rock music. Furthermore, some segments of the audience are available in greater or lesser proportions during different times of the day. During the evening hours, for instance, most broadcast network programs are designed to attract adult men and women since both groups are present in large numbers. In contrast, daytime programs such as soap operas are designed to appeal to adult women because that group predominates in the morning and early afternoon. However, programmers also monitor the success of their competition in targeting segments of the audience. Thus, an outlet may offer a program that targets a different segment if a competitor's program is especially successful in attracting a specific portion of the audience. During the 1900–1991 season, for example, the CBS Television Network scheduled programs that had great appeal to adult women, including *Murphy Brown, Designing Women,* and *The Trials of Rosie O'Neill,* as a demographic alternative to *ABC Monday Night Football*'s strong appeal to adult men.

Audience estimates are reported in distinct age categories for both men and women as a convenience to advertisers and programmers, who can use the data separately or combine them to suit their purposes. Candy products are

TABLE 5-1 Basic Audience Segments

Radio Demographics		TV Demographics	
Teens (12–17)		Children 2–5	
		Children 6–11	
		Teens (12–17)	
		Girls 12–17	
		Working women 18+	
Men	Women	Men	Women
18–24	18–24	18–24	18–24
25–34	25–34	25–34	25–34
35–44	35–44	35–49	35–49
45–54	45–54	50–54	50–54
55–64	55–64	55–64	55–64
65+	65+	65+	65+

targeted to children, and so an advertiser of bubble gum may need to reach older children (age 6 to 11) whereas MacDonalds or Burger King may target all children (age 2 to 11) in their campaigns describing the toys included in their Happy Meals or Kid's Club Meals.

Children are an important category in television audience measurement. In addition to having their own allowances to spend, they influence many adult purchasing decisions for products ranging from breakfast cereals, fast food, and candy to video games, dolls, and basketball shoes. It is easy to see how specifically both younger (2 to 5 years) and older (6 to 11) children are targeted by Saturday morning cartoons. Where *Muppet Babies* attracts younger children on Saturday mornings, those age 6 to 11 are more likely to watch *The Guys Next Door.* Similarly, *You Can't Do That on Television,* presented on Nickelodeon, and *Teenage Mutant Ninja Turtles,* broadcast by TV stations across the country, attract older children. Earlier in the day, cartoon series such as *The Noozles,* which appeal primarily to younger viewers, are scheduled. The younger children are available to watch, and the older children, who wouldn't like *The Noozles* anyway, are in school.

Basic Audience Report Definitions

One aspect of grasping the rules by which audiences are defined and reported is an understanding of the research nomenclature and the meanings behind those terms. This way, the reader will be able to readily apply the information provided by Nielsen Media Research and Arbitron.

Minimum listening or viewing The first consideration in achieving the largest possible audience is to know *how* a person is counted as a listener or viewer. Each research service requires that a person watch or listen for at least 5 continuous minutes in order to be included in the audience. When people rotate through the channels, watching snatches of different TV programs, or push buttons on their radio receivers after listening to a single song, they may be tuned in for only 1 or 2 minutes. This is hardly enough viewing or listening time for audience members to be the recipients of the advertising messages that accompany the program content. Consequently, the programmer must try not only to get people to sample the program but to entice them to stay tuned. As will be discussed in later chapters on programming strategy, the 5-minute rule is crucial in determining whether a program is credited with audience members.

Average quarter hour Another important criterion for audience measurements is that they be calculated in 15-minute increments. Measurements thus account for the audience as it comes and goes from, say, 7:00 to 7:15 a.m., then from 7:15 to 7:30 a.m., and so on throughout the day. Since audiences are measured every quarter hour, this means that the viewer or listener must remain in the audience for a full 5 minutes during each quarter hour if credit is to be received for that person during any given quarter-hour period. In other words, it won't do for a person to tune in at 7:12 and watch or listen until 7:19. As illustrated in Figure 5-7, that person was not in the audience during either quarter hour for the requisite 5 minutes in spite of the fact that his or her total listening exceeded that amount of time.

Ratings are reported on the basis of average audience size over the period of time being

FIGURE 5-7   Listening or viewing during two quarter-hour periods: 7 minutes that don't count.

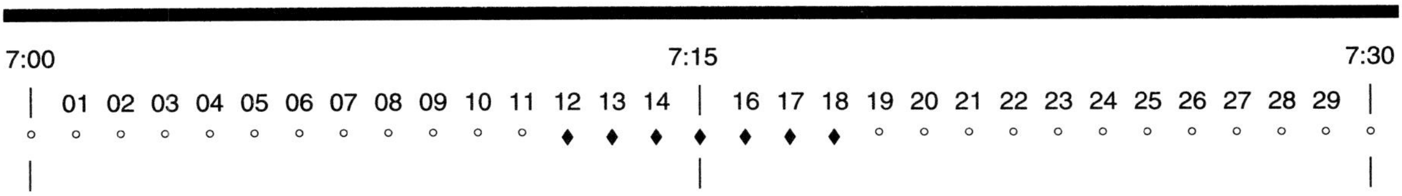

7:00   7:15   7:30

| 01 02 03 04 05 06 07 08 09 10 11 12 13 14 | 16 17 18 19 20 21 22 23 24 25 26 27 28 29 |

reported. **Average quarter hour (AQH)** estimates are calculated by dividing the number of people in the audience during each quarter hour by the number of quarter hours in the period:

$$AQH = \frac{total \ quarter\text{-}hour \ listeners}{number \ of \ quarter \ hours \ in \ the \ time \ period}$$

Imagine the station as a kind of net being lowered into a sea of potential listeners (the universe) every 15 minutes. Some listeners are caught in the net. In the ensuing period of time, some escape (tune out) and others enter (tune in). In each 15-minute period the audience is counted again. When the net containing listeners is again dropped into the sea of potential listeners, some of those in the net escape but some of the original audience members remain in the net and are joined by new listeners. Thus, as illustrated in Table 5-2, measurements are made in 15-minute increments. However, 15 minutes is a short period of time, and advertising messages are most often scheduled on the basis of broader periods of the day; therefore, averages are computed in order to better handle the information.

A quarter-hour measurement is made for all members of the audience (listeners 12 and over or viewers 2 and over) and for the other reported demographic segments. The broader the time period being reported (e.g., 6 a.m. to 10 a.m. versus 7 a.m. to 8 a.m.), the less useful the AQH figure can be as a specific indicator. This is the case because the average of all quarter hours does not indicate when the greatest number of listeners or viewers tune in during the time period. For instance, more listeners are tuned in at about 7:30 a.m. than at any other time of the day in most radio markets across the country. Thus, rather than looking at the average for all the quarter hours included in the period 6 a.m.–10 a.m., one should refer to the hour-to-hour estimates that are included in the standard reports provided by Arbitron.

Dayparts The broadcast day is broken into several time periods, or **dayparts** (Table 5-3). These time periods are linked to the habits of the radio and television audience. For example, the largest audience for radio is found in the 6 a.m.–10 a.m. daypart. In larger markets, where many people spend a long time in their cars commuting, this daypart has come to be called morning **drive time.** Similarly, the afternoon daypart from 3 p.m. to 7 p.m. is often referred to as afternoon drive time because so many people listen to their car radios on the way home after work.

Morning drive, between 6 a.m. and 10 a.m., is radio's **prime time,** when the largest and most diverse audience is tuned in. Television's prime time occurs between 8 p.m. and 11 p.m. (Eastern time), with the exception of Sunday, when prime time begins an hour earlier, at 7 p.m. These dayparts and others will be discussed throughout the remainder of the book.

Particularly as they are applied to radio, the standard dayparts can be arbitrary and lack sufficient specificity. In many markets, radio stations change their programming at 9 a.m. instead of 10 a.m. because the audience has settled into its work pattern for the day by that time. In markets where commuting and workdays begin earlier, stations program to the realities of their markets and may define their early-morning daypart as 5:30 a.m. to 9:00 a.m. Regardless, the ratings companies report listening by dayparts, but they report listening by the hour as well, except in reports on the smallest markets.

Cume The number of different listeners estimated to be in the audience during a specific period

TABLE 5-2   Average Quarter-Hour Listening for 7 a.m. to 8 a.m.

	QH1 7:00	QH2 7:15	QH3 7:30	QH4 7:45
QH listeners	300	350	500	400
Total listeners: 1550 ÷ 4 quarter-hour periods = 388 AQH listeners				

TABLE 5-3 Standard Dayparts

Radio	Television
Morning drive: 6 a.m.–10 a.m.	Morning: 7 a.m.–9 a.m.
Midday: 10 a.m.–3 p.m.	Daytime: 9 a.m.–4 p.m. (EST/PST) 9 a.m.–3 p.m. (CST/MST)
Afternoon drive: 3 p.m.–7 p.m.	Early fringe: 4 p.m.–7:30 p.m. (EST/PST) 3 p.m.–6:30 p.m. (CST/MST)
Evening: 7 p.m.–midnight	Prime-time access: 7:30–8 p.m., Mon.–Sat. (EST/PST) 6:30–7 p.m., Sun. 6:30–7 p.m., Mon.–Sat. (CST/MST) 5:30–6 p.m., Sun.
Overnight: Midnight– 6 a.m.	Prime time: 8–11 p.m., Mon.–Sat. (EST/PST) 7–11 p.m., Sun. 7–10 p.m., Mon.–Sat. (CST/MST) 6–10 p.m., Sun.
	Late news: 11–11:30 p.m., Mon.–Fri. (EST/PST) 10–10:30 p.m., Mon.–Fri. (CST/MST)
	Late fringe: 11:30 p.m.–1 a.m. (EST/PST) 10:30 p.m.–midnight (CST/MST)

of time is called the cumulative audience, or **cume.** Each member of the cume is unduplicated; that is, each is counted only once during the period of time being measured. As illustrated in Figure 5-8, new listeners tune in and some others leave the audience during each quarter hour. However, listeners who remain in the audience during several successive quarter hours are counted *only once* in the cume for the time period, which may be an hour or a whole daypart.

The cumulative audience of unduplicated listeners during the time period is a useful commodity for advertisers concerned with the **reach** of their message, that is, the number of different sets of ears or eyes estimated to have heard or watched it. From the standpoint of reach, someone who listened during all four quarter-hour periods of a particular hour does not count for any more than the individual who listened for only 5 minutes during the second quarter hour.

Rating A **rating** is the percentage of the potential audience, or universe, that is watching or lis-

tening to a program at a specific time. A rating of 2 equals 2 percent of the total possible audience. In television, such a rating means that 2 percent of households with working sets are watching TV at that particular time. In radio, a rating of 2, or 2 **ratings points,** means that 2 percent of all the listeners in the market were listening to a station. Ratings are also calculated for individual viewing or listening. A rating of 2 among women 25 to 54 indicates that 2 percent of all women age 25 to 54 were in the audience.

A rating is thus an indication of how well a program is attracting listeners or viewers among all who could potentially be gathered in the audience. Thus, ratings compare the effectiveness of different programs that are broadcast on different days or at different times. Since there are fluctuations in listening and viewing during the broadcast day, ratings are tied to the rise and fall in the available audience. The *Tonight* show, which begins its broadcast at 11:30 p.m., would be expected to have a lower rating than *Knot's Landing* or any other prime-time show

7:00-8:00 Cume*

QH1	QH2	QH3	QH4

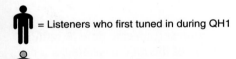

	QH1	QH2	QH3	QH4
QH Listeners:	300	350	500	400
New Tune-ins:	300	150	250	100
Cume Listeners:	300	450	700	800

Total QH Listeners: 1,550 ÷ 4 QH periods = 388 AQH listeners

Cume Listeners: 800 Cume Listeners

= Listeners who first tuned in during QH1

= Listeners who first tuned in during QH2

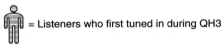 = Listeners who first tuned in during QH3

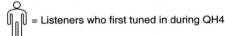 = Listeners who first tuned in during QH4

*Each symbol represents 50 listeners

FIGURE 5-8   The 7:00–8:00 a.m. cume.

because so many more people watch during prime time.

In reporting ratings, the decimal is dropped. Thus, 2 percent (0.02) of the potential audience would be reported as a rating of 2. Another convention in discussing ratings is that the "percent" designation usually is dropped. Instead of saying that a program attracted 0.285 (28.5 percent) of the potential audience, its rating would be reported as 28.5.

Share   A program **share** is the percentage of actual audience members listening or households watching at a given time. Whereas the rating is the percentage of those who *could be* listening or viewing, the share is the percentage of those who *are* listening or viewing. The share immediately indicates how well a program is doing against all the other programs presented during the same time period.

It may be helpful to think of share on the basis of a dollar. If each listener or each household in the audience is represented by a penny, the total of the shares is 100, or 100 percent. If four programs share equally in the audience, each one has 25 percent of the audience, or a 25 share. In another case, 500 people are listening to radio during the period being measured. If 250 of these listeners are in a particular station's audience, its share is 50. Just as in reporting ratings, although the figure is a percentage, that designation is not generally used. Thus, to refer to a 3.2 percent rating or a 28 percent share would be redundant.

Our earlier discussion of the *Tonight* show and *Knot's Landing* did not address the question of how well either show did against direct competition during its time period. A late-night show cannot expect to get a very high rating because the number of people who are watching TV is lower than it is during the earlier part of the day. Still, the show is in competition with other programs that are scheduled at the same time. This is where share figures are valuable. If the *Tonight* show gets a 5 rating and a 40 share, it may win its time period very handily and remain on the air, whereas *Knot's Landing* may get an 11 rating but only a 16 share and be canceled because it does not do very well against the other shows on at that time.

Households using television Households using television (HUT) is the percentage of households in the survey area with **sets in use** at the time of the audience measurement. HUT is calculated by dividing the number of households watching TV by the universe:

$$\text{HUT} = \frac{\text{households with sets on}}{\text{potential households (universe)}}$$

As Figure 5-9 shows, the television audience, reported as the percentage of households using TV, grows to its peak between 8:30 and 9:00 p.m. and then begins to rapidly decline as more and more viewers turn off their sets to go to bed.

HUT has a direct effect on audience ratings. Figure 5-10 shows an example where the HUT is 60; that is, 60 percent of the households in the universe are watching television. For the sake of clarity, we are pretending that there are only three choices available to the viewers in this market. Among the households that are

watching, 20 percent have tuned in the ABC affiliate. The CBS affiliate has a 30 share, and the NBC affiliate has the remaining half of the households, or a 50 share. The rating is easy to calculate, since it is based on the percentage of total households. The HUT of 60 means that 60 percent of all possible households are using TV, and so 60 rating points are shared by the stations.

Since half (50 percent) of the households are watching the NBC affiliate, that station has half the rating points available at that time. Consequently, the NBC station's program achieves a rating of 30. The CBS station's share of 30 translates into an 18 rating, which is 30 percent of the 60 possible ratings points. The ABC station garners the remaining 12 ratings points, which totals to an HUT of 60.

The total of the ratings can exceed HUT because the total sets in use in multiple-set households may cause share points to exceed the assumed 100 percent of HUT. Television has become a more individual medium because of the increasing number of multiple-set households.

Persons using television The confusion caused by HUT statistics will no doubt be alleviated in the future when the electronic media industry adopts a "persons viewing" measurement as its standard. **Persons using television (PUT)** is the number of individuals in an age or sex category divided by the total of that group in the universe.

Increasingly, advertisers are interested in spe-

FIGURE 5-9 Nielsen percentage of households using television. *(From What TV Ratings Really Mean. Used by permission of Nielsen Media Research.)*

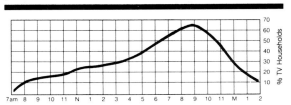

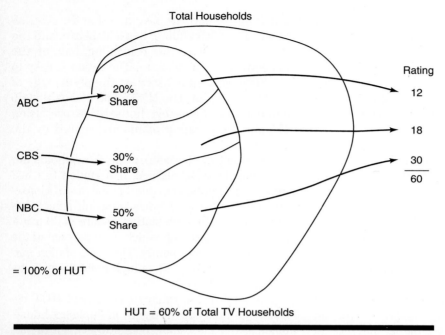

Total Households

FIGURE 5-10   Rating and share.

cific segments of the total audience. Moreover, the added competition for viewers from new cable services has led television programmers to target more narrow groups in the total audience. Consequently, the HUT figure will inevitably give way to PUT. As radio did before it, television is becoming an individualized medium as a result of a widening array of choices that appeal to increasingly narrow segments of the audience.

The range of demographic segments reported by Nielsen is shown in Figure 5-11. Demographic figures are reported in columns across the report page, with the programs in rows at the left. The numbers for specific age and sex categories are often referred to as **cells,** since they appear in the space that would be formed by the intersection of vertical lines on either side of a column with horizontal lines above and below the line on which each program appears on the page. Both Nielsen and Arbitron television audience reports break down the audience into standard age and sex categories. For instance, in column 20 in Figure 5-11, the rating for women

viewers 18 and over (18+) for each program in the time period is reported. Column 25 displays estimated viewing by working women, a valuable target audience to advertisers of microwave dinner entrees.

If the demographics presented in the published report have not been defined in the most useful way, the user can refer to the station totals (Nielsen) or TSA (Arbitron) figures that report on the actual number of viewers. If it is desirable to have a program rating for adults 18 to 34, for instance, all the programmer has to do is add the estimated number of men 18 to 34 and women 18 to 34 viewers together. This new demographic is then divided by the total adults 18 to 34 during the time period, a figure derived by adding the total number of men 18 to 34 and the total number of women 18 to 34.

Persons using radio Persons using radio (PUR) is the total estimated cume or AQH listenership in a given demographic. PUR figures are reported on the last line in columns in radio

EASTVILLE — TIME PERIOD

TUESDAY 11:00PM–11:30PM

WK1 1/31-2/06 WK2 2/07-2/13 WK3 2/14-2/20 WK4 2/21-2/27

Station	Program	METRO HH RTG (1)	METRO HH SHR (2)	DMA HOUSEHOLD RATINGS WEEKS 1 (3)	WEEKS 2 (4)	WEEKS 3 (5)	WEEKS 4 (6)	MULTI-WEEK AVG RTG (7)	MULTI-WEEK AVG SHR (8)	SHARE TREND NOV 'XX (11)	MAY 'XX (12)	FEB 'XX (13)
	R.S.E. THRESHOLDS 25+% (1 S.E.) 4 WK AVG 50+%	4 1		7 2	7 2	7 2	7 2	2 LT				
	11:00PM											
WAAA	JUDGE	<<		<<	<<	1	<<	<<				
WBBB	AVG. ALL WKS	14	26	13	11	11	11	11	23	23	24	24
	EYEWIT NWS 11	16	29	13				13	24			
	NWSCHNL 5 NW11	14	26		11	11	11	11	22			
WCCC	AVG. ALL WKS	21	39	18	19	18	20	19	37	33	38	35
	CBS TUE MOV	21	39	18				18	34			
	NWSCENTER 8-11	21	39		19	18	20	19	38			
WDDD	CH 3 NWS AT 11	7	14	8	7	7	4	6	13	23X	17	23
WEEE	AVG. ALL WKS	1	2	1	<<	2	<<	1	2	2	3	4
	WKRP IN CINN	1	1	1	<<		<<	1	1			
	CINEMA 19	1	2			2		2	4			
WFFF	COSBY SHOW II	4	7	3	3	1	2	2	5	2	5	2
WGGG	AVG. ALL WKS	<<		<<	<<	<<	<<	<<				
	T BROWNS JRNAL	<<		<<		<<	<<	<<				
	GRT PERFRMNCES	1	1		<<			<<				
	HUT/PUT/TOTALS*	55		52	54	47	48	50		40	46	47

DMA RATINGS

Station	Program	PERSONS 2+ (15)	18+ (16)	12-24 (17)	12-34 (18)	18-34 (19)	18-49 (20)	21-49 (21)	25-54 (22)	35+ (23)	35-64 (24)	50+ (25)	WOMEN 18+ (26)	12-24 (27)	18-34 (28)	18-49 (29)	25-49 (31)	25-54 (32)	WKG (34)	MEN 18+ (35)	18-34 (36)	18-49 (37)	21-49 (38)	25-49 (39)	25-54 (40)	TNS 12-17 (41)	CHILD 2-11 (42)	CHILD 6-11 (43)
	R.S.E. THRESHOLDS 25+% (1 S.E.) 4 WK AVG 50+%	2 LT	2 LT	6 2	4 1	4 1	3 1	3 1	2 1	2 1	3 1	3 1	2 1	9 3	7 2	3 1	4 1	3 1	4 1	2 1	7 2	4 1	4 1	4 1	4 1	11 3	8 2	10 3
	11:00PM																											
WAAA	JUDGE																											
WBBB	AVG. ALL WKS	5	7	1	2	2	6	7	8	9	10	8	7	2	4	8	9	9	7	6	1	5	5	6	6	1		1
	EYEWIT NWS 11	6	8	1	3	4	9	10	11	10	11	6	9	3	6	11	13	13	10	7	2	6	7	8	8			
	NWSCHNL 5 NW11	5	6	1	2	2	5	6	6	9	9	8	7	1	4	6	7	8	6	6		4	5	5	5	2		1
WCCC	AVG. ALL WKS	11	14	4	8	10	11	11	13	17	16	19	15	3	11	12	14	15	13	13	8	10	10	11	11	2		
	CBS TUE MOV	10	13	5	8	9	11	11	12	15	15	17	14	2	8	12	14	14	14	12	10	9	8	10	9	4		
	NWSCENTER 8-11	11	14	4	8	10	11	11	14	17	17	20	15	4	12	12	14	15	13	14	8	10	11	12	12	1		
WDDD	CH 3 NWS AT 11	3	5	1	1	2	2	2	3	6	5	9	5	1	2	2	2	3	5	4	1	2	3	2	3			
WEEE	AVG. ALL WKS		1				1	1	1	1	1	1	1		1	1	1	1	1									
	WKRP IN CINN		1							1	1	1	1		1	1	1	1										
	CINEMA 19	1	1				1	1	1	1	1	1	1			1	2	1	1		1		1	1	1			
WFFF	COSBY SHOW II	1	1	1	2	2	1	1	2	1	1	1	2	2	2	2	2	2	1	1	1	1	1	1	1	1		
WGGG	AVG. ALL WKS																											
	T BROWNS JRNAL																											
	GRT PERFRMNCES											1																
	HUT/PUT/TOTALS*	29	37	16	22	27	31	32	35	43	42	48	39	16	30	34	36	39	34	34	23	28	28	30	31	8	2	2

Application:
The Time Period Section contains audience estimates by half-hour segments during primetime and quarter-hour segments during other times. The Time Period section provides Monday–Friday and individual day averages so that the user of this section can look at TV audience estimates during specific time periods.

1 When more than one program is telecast during the same time period on a station, two lines are reported under the heading "Avg. All Wks" (Average All Weeks). In the example, the CBS Tuesday Movie and Newscenter 8 at 11 aired on WCCC during this time period. CBS Tuesday Movie received an 18 rating in week one; and Newscenter 8, which aired weeks 2, 3 and 4, garnered DMA household ratings of 19, 18 and 20 respectively.

2 As reported in the Program Averages section, users of this section will be able to track programs on an individual week basis. For example, on Tuesday at 11:00PM, WDDD had an 8% rating in week one, 7% in week two, 7% in week three and 4% in week four.

3 The multi-week average for Ch 3 News on WDDD was a 6 rating and a 13 share.

4 The share trend guide provides a tracking of programs for the three previous measurement periods. In this case, WCCC's current share increased 2 points from year-ago. This trend gives the user a quick overview of a station's past performance and seasonal variations, as well as changes in audience viewing.

5 The DMA ratings for key demographics are reported in over 20 columns. For example, 6% of Men 25–54 were watching WBBB during this time period.

FIGURE 5-11 Nielsen DMA ratings report. ***(Used by permission of Nielsen Media Research.)***

audience reports. PUR is reported for each time period and each demographic.

Sweep A sweep is the period during which an audience survey is conducted. Arbitron and Nielsen conduct four full sweeps a year (November, February, May, and July) in which all television markets are measured. The survey period is 4 weeks for television.

Arbitron radio sweeps are done over a 12-week period. Arbitron conducts one full radio sweep in the spring. Only the smallest markets are included in this full sweep; other markets are measured twice a year, and the largest are measured four times a year.

Ratings Efficiency: Cost per Thousand

The sale of advertising time is the major source of revenue for broadcast stations and cable services. In this and the previous chapters, a number of important research concepts were introduced that show how advertisers, sales representatives, and programmers calculate the efficiency of a program in reaching a target audience.

The measure of the efficiency of an advertising buy is the **cost per thousand (CPM)** for target audience members. Increments of 1000 listeners or viewers are used because the size of a mass audience with several thousand audience members makes that a logical unit of measurement.

Advertisers often have to determine which stations or programs are the most efficient at reaching target consumers. This can be done objectively on the basis of which reach the greatest number of viewers or listeners at the lowest unit cost. CPM is determined by dividing the cost of an advertising message, or spot, by the audience size. Most advertisers use a spot placement strategy in which they advertise in several programs, scheduled at different times and on different days, to reach the broadest possible audience. As opposed to sponsoring a show, which requires concentration of the advertising budget, spot placement permits the message to be placed in programs where different portions of the target audience can be reached.

As can be seen from the calculations in Table 5-4, Station B is the better advertising buy for two important reasons: It delivers twice the audience of Station A, and although the advertising rate is higher, Station B's CPM is much lower and thus more efficient in reaching the audience.

TABLE 5-4   Calculation and Comparison of Cost per Thousand*

	Station A	Station B
AQH audience	5,000	10,000
Spot rate	$35	$42
CPM	$7.00	$4.20

$$\frac{\$35}{5(000)} = \$7.00 \qquad \frac{\$42}{10(000)} = \$4.20$$

$$*\text{CPM} = \frac{\text{spot rate}}{\text{audience} \div 1000}$$

Most advertisers are interested in the CPM for target listeners or viewers rather than for the total audience or households. The same formula is used regardless of the specific demographic. Moreover, there is nothing sacrosanct about the practice of breaking the audience down into units of 1000.

As the mass audience has become more segmented, cable networks may calculate cost per hundred (CPH) or even cost per viewer (CPV) because audiences for individual cable programs are so small that the practice of breaking down the mass audience into units of 1000 is not meaningful. The formula remains the same, except that the unit of division is either total estimated audience members divided by 100 or, in the case of CPV, the total persons in the cell.

Audience Viewing and Listening Patterns

Television   Television audiences change with the weather. Figure 5-12 illustrates the dramatic decline in viewing levels during the warmest months of the year, when people spend more time outdoors participating in recreational activities and going to ball games. The annual change to daylight savings time during the summer months provides a longer period of light during the evening hours in most areas of the country. Furthermore, the majority of Americans take their vacations during the summer and are thus less available to watch TV; if they watch in hotels and motels, their viewing is not included in the audience estimates.

As Figure 5-12 shows, household viewing drops to its lowest levels in July, rising only slightly in August. In September and continuing through the fall and winter months, household viewing climbs, reaching its highest level in January.

Daytime viewing remains fairly consistent throughout the year (Figure 5-13). However, prime-time viewing, which reaches its highest level in February at about 65 percent, is much lower during the warmer months, particularly in July, when HUT drops to around 55 percent. There is virtually no seasonal change in late-night viewing.

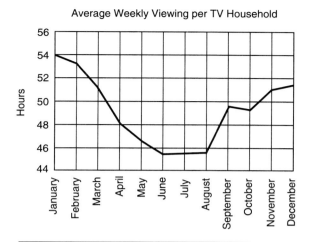

Average Weekly Viewing per TV Household

FIGURE 5-12 Average weekly viewing per TV household for each month. *(From* Electronic Media, *August 24, 1989. Copyright 1992 Crain Communications Inc. Reprinted from Electronic Media with permission.)*

There is a notable difference in viewing levels on different days of the week. Figure 5-14 shows that Sunday has the largest prime-time audience

of any day of the week. Considering the weekly routine of the typical viewer, that is not surprising. Most viewers must go to work or school on Monday, and so fewer of them elect to be away from home on Sunday evening, a day traditionally devoted to church and family activities. Since people do most of their socializing and dining out on the weekend, it is not surprising that Friday night is the least viewed evening, followed closely by Saturday. Even though programmers want more people to watch TV on these evenings, it is not likely that they will. Therefore, the rating that is possible on certain evenings may be a bit lower because fewer people are watching television.

Radio Unlike TV viewing, radio listening varies little from day to day during the week (Monday through Friday) or from season to season during the year. As Figure 5-15 illustrates, television and radio prime times are at the opposite ends of the broadcast day.

As can be seen in the listening pattern illustrated in Figure 5-15 and the figures shown in Box 5-1, weekday radio listening peaks early, at

FIGURE 5-13 Percentage of households using television. *(From* Report on Television. *Used by permission of Nielsen Media Research.)*

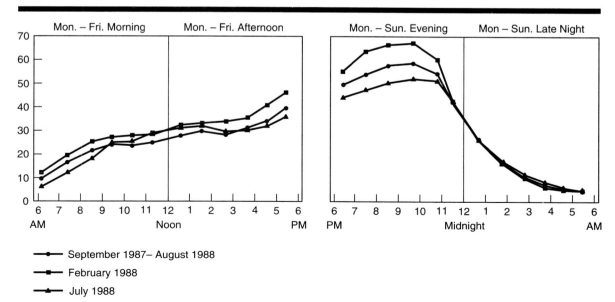

September 1987– August 1988
February 1988
July 1988

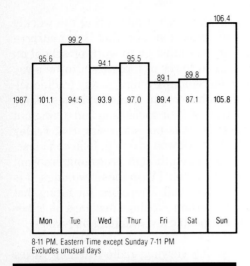

FIGURE 5-14 **Television viewing by night of the week.** *(From* **Report on Television.** *Used by permission of Nielsen Media Research.)*

about 7:30 a.m. The morning and early-afternoon periods have the greatest listening, particularly in larger markets, where the drive time commuting audience is of particular importance. During the day the audience levels off, but it swells again in the afternoon drive period. In smaller radio markets, the 7:30 a.m. peak is sharper and the midday audience is somewhat higher than it is in larger markets. Large-market listening levels remain high, whereas listening declines much more sharply after 5 p.m. in smaller markets. The differences may be attributed to the shorter commute time in smaller markets, especially in the afternoon drive period, because people can get home more quickly. Listening levels do not decline as sharply in large markets as in smaller markets since many people tend to arrive at work later in the morning, perhaps because of the long time needed to travel to work. In larger markets more people remain at work later in the day, and it takes these people much longer to travel home after work.

The listening pattern of the weekend radio audience is considerably different, with smaller audiences from 6 a.m. to 10 a.m. than in the comparable Monday through Friday daypart. Weekend midday and afternoon audiences, though,

FIGURE 5-15 **Patterns of radio and television use.** *[James G. Webster and Lawrence W. Lichty,* **Ratings Analysis: Theory and Practice** *(Hillsdale, NJ: Lawrence Erlbaum Associates, Inc., 1991). Copyright © 1991. Used by permission of Lawrence Erlbaum Associates, Inc., and Prof. James G. Webster.]*

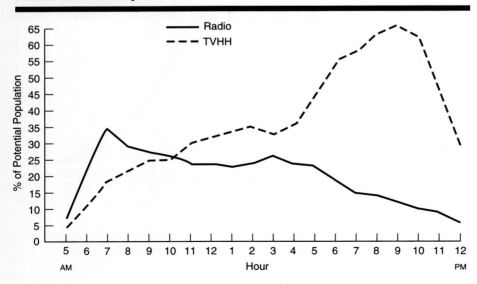

Daypart	PUR
Mon.–Fri., 6 a.m.–10 a.m.	23.7
Mon.–Fri., 10 a.m.–3 p.m.	22.8
Mon.–Fri., 3 p.m.–7 p.m.	20.3
Sat., 6 a.m.–10 a.m.	15.5
Sat., 10 a.m.–3 p.m.	22.3
Sat., 3 p.m.–7 p.m.	20.3

**BOX 5-1
PERSONS USING
RADIO BY DAYPART**

SOURCE: From Birch/Scarborough spring 1989 reports for 12+ listeners in 97 markets, as reported in Ed Cohen, "Saturday Audience Is Still Climbing," *NAB RadioWeek,* July 31, 1989, p. 8. © National Association of Broadcasters, 1989. Used with permission. ∎

are comparable in size to their Monday through Friday dayparts. Thus, as the figures in Box 5-1 report, these audiences are virtually as large as those on the weekdays but begin tuning in later.

The Saturday midday audience is especially strong, peaking at 11 a.m. The strength of weekend daytime listening suggests the utility of scheduling attractive programming at that time to take advantage of the large audience available. The strongest weekday radio personalities are generally those who are on the air in the morning on Monday through Friday. If these personalities are to be used on either Saturday or Sunday, the listening patterns indicate that they should be scheduled for midmorning to attract the largest number of potential listeners.

UNDERSTANDING RATINGS REPORTS

A published ratings report is a sea of numbers. Arbitron is fond of saying that a market report contains over 100,000 numbers. While each figure may be of value in understanding the audience in a market, the big picture can be overwhelming. It is better to take it in small pieces by screening out what is not of immediate concern. For instance, if the programmer is interested in a station's share of males 18 to 24 years old, other columns containing the figures for other demographics can be ignored, at least for the moment. As Figures 5-11 and 5-16 illustrate, the report page appears to be quite complicated at first glance, but if one deals with individual de-

mographics or time periods, its complexity can be reduced.

The Radio Report

As illustrated in Figure 5-16, each audience report page includes the following information: the market being reported, the survey period, the demographic groups, the daypart, and the stations. The measurement that is being reported, such as AQH, cume, share, or rating, is identified in the column headings. Estimates for the various audience segments are reported in columns displayed across the page. The stations in the market are listed on the left side of the page.

Stations Only estimates for commercial radio station audiences are reported by Arbitron. **Out-of-market stations,** which are licensed to serve other metro areas but are listened to by persons in the market, often garner substantive audiences. Such stations are reported below a broken line on each page. In many instances, these "below-the-line" stations perform better than do some of the local outlets.

Demographics Demographic categories for radio audiences are reported from the very broadest (persons 12 and above) to the very specific (men 18 to 24). Men, women, and teen segments are broken down separately in columns on the page. Totals (PUR) for each demographic category are reported at the bottom of the page.

It is possible to add across segments to create

Specific Audience
MONDAY-FRIDAY 6AM-10AM

	Persons 12+	Persons 18+	Men 18+	Men 18-24	Men 25-34	Men 35-44	Men 45-54	Men 55-64	Women 18+	Women 18-24	Women 25-34	Women 35-44	Women 45-54	Women 55-64	Teens 12-17
+WAAA WRRR															
MET AQH PERSONS	122	118	42		2	8	13	1	78	8	12	6	8	4	3
MET AQH RATING	.3	.3	.3		.1	.3	.6	.1	.5	.3	.3	.2	.3	.2	.1
MET AQH SHARE	1.5	1.1	1.2		.2	1.2	2.4	.2	1.8	1.4	1.1	.9	1.4	.7	.7
MET CUME PERSONS	547	542	166		21	73	42	15	353	33	57	60	33	20	23
MET CUME RATING	1.5	1.4	1.0		.5	2.4	1.7	.8	2.1	1.3	1.4	.9	1.3	.9	.6
TSA AQH PERSONS	122	120	41		2	8	13	1	77	7	12	7	7	4	3
TSA CUME PERSONS	547	542	166		21	73	41	15	357	32	57	60	32	20	23
WBBB															
MET AQH PERSONS	69	65	36		4	12	13	7	27	1	3	11	1		6
MET AQH RATING	.2	.2	.2		.1	.4	.6	.4	.2		.1	.3		.1	.2
MET AQH SHARE	.9	.8	1.0		.4	1.8	2.4	1.5	.7	.2	.6	1.5	.2	.3	1.5
MET CUME PERSONS	671	623	318		72	79	90	76	304	17	45	109	17	46	48
MET CUME RATING	1.8	2.0	2.1		1.9	2.6	4.1	4.1	1.8	.7	1.0	3.4	.7	2.2	1.3
TSA AQH PERSONS	72	65	37		4	12	13	9	28	1	3	11	1	2	7
TSA CUME PERSONS	701	653	341		72	79	90	101	312	17	45	109	17	46	48
WCCC															
MET AQH PERSONS	161	149	116	51	49	9	4	2	33	10	13	4	10		11
MET AQH RATING	.4	.5	.8	2.2	1.3	.3	.2	.1	.2	.4	.4	.1	.4		.2
MET AQH SHARE	2.1	1.9	3.3	9.4	5.3	1.3	.6	.5	.8	2.1	1.4	.5	2.1		2.9
MET CUME PERSONS	1750	1566	1042	364	442	176	20	21	526	206	201	96	206		187
MET CUME RATING	4.7	4.9	6.8	15.8	11.5	5.6	.9	1.1	3.1	8.9	5.1	3.0	8.9		4.6
TSA AQH PERSONS	206	192	141	54	70	10	4	4	51	14	22	10	14		13
TSA CUME PERSONS	2131	1908	1211	412	544	199	20	22	679	262	333	108	262	3	223
WDDD															
MET AQH PERSONS	68	65	40		24	12	4		23	3	9	8	3		3
MET AQH RATING	.2	.2	.3		.6	.4	.2		.5		.2	.2	.1		.1
MET AQH SHARE	.8	.8	1.2		2.6	1.8	.7		.6	.9	1.1	.6			.7
MET CUME PERSONS	648	632	301		137	150	14		331	38	172	83	38		17
MET CUME RATING	1.7	2.0	2.0		3.6	4.8	.6		2.0	1.6	4.4	2.6	1.6		.4
TSA AQH PERSONS	69	66	42		24	15	4		24	3	9	8	3		3
TSA CUME PERSONS	671	645	314		137	155	23		331	38	172	83	38		17
	707	699	334	5	35	59	62	91	365	4	3	49	4	92	8
	2.1	2.2	2.2	.2	.9	1.9	2.8	4.8	2.2	.2	.1	1.5	.2	4.4	.2
	8.8	9.1	9.4	.9	3.8	8.8	11.3	21.1	8.8	.9	.3	6.7	.9	16.1	2.0
	3453														78
	9.7														2.0
	733														73
	3657														1.9
	339														8
	1.1														73
	4.2														
	1730														1
	4.8														.2
	365														21
	1848														.5
															1
															21

SPECIFIC AUDIENCE

DEMOS   P12+,18+; TEENS (12-17); M&W 18+, 18-24, 25-34, 35-44, 45-54, 55-64

GEOGRAPHY   METRO AND TSA

ESTIMATES   METRO AQH PERSONS, AQH RATING, AQH SHARE, CUME PERSONS, CUME RATING, TSA AQH PERSONS, TSA CUME PERSONS

DAYPARTS   MON-SUN 6AM-MID; MON-FRI 6AM-10AM, 10AM-3PM, 3PM-7PM, 7PM-MID; SAT 6AM-10AM, 10AM-3PM, 3PM-7PM, 7PM-MID; SUN 6AM-10AM, 10AM-3PM, 3PM-7PM, 7PM-MID

Specific Audience:
Specific Audience presents a full range of demographic groups for each of 13 dayparts so you can thoroughly examine the sex/age listening characteristics for stations in a market. You can even combine various demographic groups to create estimates for selected sex/age breaks.

TOTALS															
MET AQH PERSONS	16169	8077	7576	3542	933	669	550	433	4123	466	1011	733	577	572	404
MET AQH RATING	11.5	22.6	23.1	24.3	23.4	22.9	25.0	22.8	24.2	19.7	25.4	22.4	24.5	27.1	10.3
MET CUME PERSONS	85395	26826	25666	11987	3014	2414	1847	1496	13601	1822	3231	2617	1960	1744	2229
MET CUME RATING	60.8	77.9	79.7	78.2	78.6	78.6	83.9	82.7	81.3	78.1	82.3	81.9	83.4	82.7	56.7

Footnote Symbols: * Audience estimates adjusted for actual broadcast schedule. + Station(s) changed call letters since the prior survey - see Page 5B. # Both of the previous footnotes apply.

RADIO MARKET, USA   ARBITRON   WINTER 1989
102

FIGURE 5-16   An Arbitron radio report sample page. (*Used by permisssion of Arbitron Ratings Co.*)

other demographics. For instance, adding the numbers for men 18 to 24, men 25 to 34, men 35 to 44, men 45 to 54, and men 55 to 64 gives the programmer the figure for men 18 and over that was reported for a particular station. Logical male and female demographic segments can be combined into a new category such as adults 18 to 34 if that is useful for a station's strategy.

Since these figures are estimates, numbers are rounded and reported in hundreds. To derive the figure representing the estimate of the actual number of listeners in a specific demographic category such as women 18 to 24, two zeros (00) should be added to the number in the column. For example, in Figure 5-16 at the right side it can be seen that for women 18 to 24, WBBB has an AQH of 22 in the metro area and an AQH of 24 in the TSA. Those figures represent an estimated 2200 women 18 to 24 in the MSA and an estimated 2400 women 18 to 24 in the TSA.

The daypart—in this case, Monday through Friday from 6 a.m. to 10 a.m.—is indicated at the top of the page. This particular page reports only AQH estimates, but it allows the reader to compare stations and demographic segments. The demographic groups for which information has been provided are labeled at the tops of their respective columns. The figures at the bottom of each column give the totals in each demographic segment being reported.

When people listen A wide variety of time periods are reported, beginning with the totality of the weekly broadcast schedule, Monday to Sunday from 6 a.m. to midnight. This is the most general reporting period, encompassing the broadcast day except for the period from midnight to 6 a.m. Most comparisons between stations begin with their overall ratings, but just as different demographic groups tend to predominate in different stations' audiences, particular dayparts attract various groups of listeners. Consequently, breaking down listening into the standard daypart estimates generates much more useful information for both programmers and advertisers. Reports for larger markets include hour-by-hour estimates which enable a programmer to track the performance of one station or all the stations in the market, identifying when the audience comes and goes throughout the day.

Arbitron subscribers are given estimates of listener duplication between dayparts. A finding that a large proportion of the audience in one daypart also listened during another suggests that the programmer should provide more variety between the programs or time periods to maintain the attractiveness of the content. By contrast, if listener duplication between time periods is low, much content can be repeated since it will be heard by different groups of listeners. Arbitron also reports the percentage of cume duplication between stations. With this information, the impact of competitors' promotion or new on-air personalities can be tracked. Such monitoring provides guidance on strategic times in which to counter such special efforts at building an audience.

Where people listen In addition to reporting *when* people listen, larger-market audience reports indicate *where* they are listening to the radio. Arbitron Radio reports "at home," "in-car," "other," and "at work" listening locations in its reports. Since the introduction of the "at work" location in 1988, Arbitron estimates of listening away from home have increased.[4] The location of listening of three demographic segments—persons 12 and over, men 18 and over, and women 18 and over—is reported for the standard dayparts.

As Figure 5-17 indicates, drive time can be a misnomer since the period of time during which large numbers of listeners are in their automobiles varies from market to market. In smaller markets the average commute time from home to workplace may be 20 minutes or less, while in larger markets many drivers may be in their cars for over an hour going to work. It should be apparent from the traffic patterns in the market how important it is to present programming content that appeals to listeners in cars.

As important as knowing the volume of traffic and the typical length of the morning and afternoon peak drive times is knowing which demo-

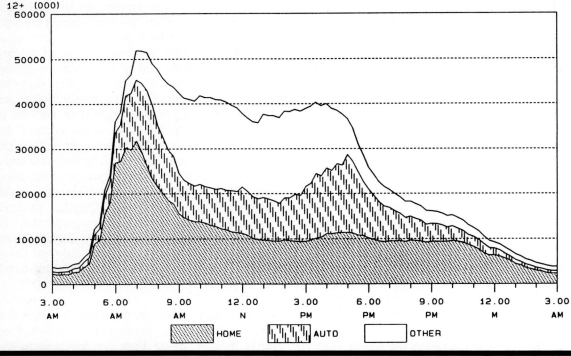

TOTAL PERSONS
12+ (000)

FIGURE 5-17 Location of radio audiences. *(RADAR ® 44, Fall 1991, © Copyright Statistical Research, Inc.)*

graphic segments predominate as audience members in listening locations. For example, many more adult males than women listen in cars. As the trend toward double-income households has continued, the number of working women who must commute to work has increased, but men still predominate as car listeners in the morning and afternoon drive periods.

The Television Report

Television ratings reports are more complicated than those for radio audiences because each TV outlet presents many distinctly different programs that are scheduled throughout its broadcast week, whereas radio audiences are measured only in terms of time periods. The weekly program estimates in printed reports for television are the most useful to programmers. These

are AQH estimates, but the increment of time used in reporting program viewing is the half hour since television programs are broadcast in units of 30 minutes. Even though a program may be 60 minutes in length, it is likely to be scheduled against half-hour programs on other stations or channels. The exception to this convention occurs during the time when local-market news programs are being broadcast, for example, 6 p.m. to 6:15 p.m.; 6:15 p.m. to 6:30 p.m., 11 p.m. to 11:15 p.m., and 11:15 p.m. to 11:30 p.m. Eastern time.

Stations In the weekly programming time period averages report shown in Figure 5-18, audience estimates are reported for half-hour periods. The program broadcast during each time increment is listed in the left column, below the call letters of each station.

The signal of the primary station is sometimes extended by a satellite station. The legend for the symbols that designate each such station is presented at the bottom of the report page. On a line directly after the parent station's separate ratings, the combined audience for parent and satellite station combinations is reported. This figure indicates the size of a program's audience in the entire market.

When different programs have been scheduled during the same time period, a 4-week average is presented. This line reports the station's average audience during the time period regardless of what was scheduled. For example, NBC's *Saturday Night Main Event,* a wrestling show, is telecast occasionally in the time period normally occupied by *Saturday Night Live,* and so the reader of a report will see that the 4-week average audience has been reported. This information is useful to advertisers who wish to buy time in both shows, but the programmer will be interested in how effectively the program itself attracts viewers.

Demographics Television demographic breakdowns are printed across the top of each page, as shown in Figure 5-18. Unlike radio, where few children are regular listeners, children watch television at a very early age. Thus, children's television viewing is reported in two demographic categories: ages 2 to 11 and 6 to 11. By subtracting, the programmer can also define a narrower demographic: children 2 to 5. In Arbitron TV market reports, the teen demographic (12 to 17) is reported as it is for radio audiences, but Nielsen television reports also break out teen girls. Again, the number of teen boys can be determined by subtracting teen girls from all teens. The adult demographic segments are like those broken out for radio reports.

Trend data A report reader should look at all the labels on the page to ascertain the market being reported, the date of the survey on which the report is based, and the day or days (e.g., Monday to Friday) represented by the figures.

The week-by-week rating for each of the 4 weeks included in the survey is reported for each program. The share and rating for the current reporting period are presented. Audience share trends for previous reporting periods are also displayed. These data permit the tracking of viewing patterns which may alert the programmer to influences on higher or lower viewing levels that have occurred from one measurement period to another. Assume that a station broadcasts a former network situation comedy at 11:30 p.m., after the local news. If the program's ratings have dropped over the 4-week period, the programmer should first determine whether the changes can be attributed to sampling error. It is also wise to see whether competing programs have pulled viewers away. If the comedy has been broadcast in that time period for several months, the audience may be getting tired of those familiar episodes and it may be time to replace the show with something fresh.

RATINGS SERVICES

The clients for audience research reports are networks, cable operators, stations, and advertising agencies. Advertisers need this information for making media buying decisions, while networks, stations, and cable operators use it in making programming decisions and selling advertising time. In many instances analyses of the data made available through a research report are shared with advertising clients to convince them that placing a message in a particular program will enable them to reach their target consumers. The following discussion describes the principal forms of such audience research information.

Nielsen Media Research

Most television viewers associate TV audience ratings and the Nielsens, but the typical lay viewer is unaware of the extent of the services provided by Nielsen Media Research. Consideration has periodically been given to reentering the

Time Period Estimates

This figure is a dense Arbitron television ratings table for New Orleans, Friday, November 1991 time period averages.

Column group headings:

- DAY AND TIME / STATION PROGRAM
- ADI TV HH RATINGS BY WEEKS (1 OCT 30, 2 NOV 06, 3 NOV 13, 4 NOV 20)
- RTG / SHR
- ADI TV HH (OCT 91, MAY 91, FEB 91, NOV 90)
- ADI TV HH SHARE/HUT TRENDS
- METRO TV HH (RTG / SHR)
- ADI RATINGS: PERSONS (2+, 18+, 12-24, 12-34, 18-34, 18-49, 21-49, 25-49, 25-54, 35+, 35-64, 50+); WOMEN (18+, 12-24, 18-34, 18-49, 21-49, 25-49, 25-54, W W); MEN (18+, 18-34, 18-49, 21-49, 25-49, 25-54)

RELATIVE STD-ERR THRESHOLDS (1σ): 25% / 50%

Programs listed by time period:

FRIDAY 6:30P–7:00P — WWL WHEEL OF FOR; WDSU CURRENT AFFR; WVUE MARRD CHLD-S; WGNO FULL HSE-S, E EDWRDS POL; WNOL CHEERS-S, EDWRDS GOVNR; WYES PTV; WLAE PTV; HUT/PVT/TOT

7:00P–7:30P — WWL RSCUE 911 SP, PRFCT CRIMES, SCRTS UNKNWN; WDSU MATLOCK, FRESH PRINCE; WVUE FMLY MATTERS; WGNO GERALDO, LSU BSKTBALL; WNOL AM MST WANTD; WYES PTV; WLAE PTV; HUT/PVT/TOT

7:30P–8:00P — WWL RSCUE 911 SP, PRFCT CRIMES, SCRTS UNKNWN; WDSU MATLOCK, NBC MV WK FR; WVUE STEP BY STP; WGNO GERALDO, LSU BSKTBALL; WNOL AM MST WANTD; WYES PTV; WLAE PTV; HUT/PVT/TOT

8:00P–8:30P — WWL C BURNETT SH; WDSU FLESH BLOOD, NBC MV WK FR; WVUE PRFCT STRNGR; WGNO 8 OCLOCK MOV, LSU BSKTBALL; WNOL ULTMT CHLNGE, BST OF WORST; WYES PTV; WLAE PTV; HUT/PVT/TOT

8:30P–9:00P — WWL C BURNETT SH; WDSU REAL LIFE SP, DEAR JOHN, NBC MV WK FR; WVUE BABY TALK; WGNO 8 OCLOCK MOV, LSU BSKTBALL; WNOL ULTMT CHLNGE, HIDDEN VIDEO; WYES PTV; WLAE PTV; HUT/PVT/TOT

9:00P–9:30P — WWL PALACE GUARD, FACE TO FACE, TRL ONEIL FR; WDSU RSNBL DOUBTS, NBC MV WK FR; WVUE 20/20; WGNO 8 OCLOCK MOV, GRT SPT LGND; WNOL STR TK NX PR; WYES PTV; WLAE PTV; HUT/PVT/TOT

NEW ORLEANS

Footnotes:
- * SAMPLE BELOW MINIMUM FOR WEEKLY REPORTING
- ** SHARE/HUT TRENDS NOT AVAILABLE
- – DID NOT ACHIEVE A REPORTABLE WEEKLY RATING
- ‡ TECHNICAL DIFFICULTY
- + COMBINED PARENT/SATELLITE
- ▲ SEE TABLE ON PAGE v

FIGURE 5-18 Arbitron TV report page: weekly programming time period averages. *(Used by permission of Arbitron Ratings Co.)*

Time Period Estimates

DAY AND TIME / STATION PROGRAM	TN 12-17	CHILD 2-11	CHILD 6-11	TV HH	PERS 18+	PERS 12-34	WOM 18+	WOM 18-34	WOM 18-49	WOM 25-49	WOM 25-54	WKG WOM	MEN 18+	MEN 18-34	MEN 18-49	MEN 25-49	MEN 25-54	TNS 12-17	CHILD 2-11	CHILD 6-11	ADI TV HH RTG	MET TV HH RTG	TSA TV HH	TSA WOM 18+	TSA MEN 18+
(col #)	36	37	38	39	42	41	45	46	47	48	49	50	51	52	53	54	55	56	57	58	5	8	39	45	51
RELATIVE STD-ERR 25%	15	13	17	12	18	19	14	15	14	13	13	13	14	16	14	13	13	17	27	21	2	3	12	14	14
THRESHOLDS (1σ) 50%	4	3	4	3	4	4	3	3	3	3	3	3	3	4	3	3	3	4	7	5	-	-	3	3	3
FRIDAY 6:30P-7:00P																									
WWL WHEEL OF FOR	7	9	7	132	190	33	113	14	43	39	48	28	77	8	29	27	36	11	27	14	22	22	136	112	79
WDSU CURRENT AFFR	6	2	2	101	127	55	73	22	44	39	43	18	53	24	33	28	30	10	6	4	13	15	82	59	45
WVUE MARRD CHLD-S	3	1	1	32	47	20	24	4	15	14	16	11	23	12	20	14	15	5	2	2	7	7	45	33	30
WGNO FULL HSE-S	7	13	18	43	49	35	34	15	28	22	23	6	15	7	13	10	10	12	37	30					
E EDWARDS POL				25	12	17	9		6		6								12						
--4 WK AVG--	8	11	16	38	40	30	28	12	23	18	19	6	12	5	10	8	8	13	31	26	6	7	37	26	13
WNOL CHEERS-S	2			22	29	17	14	8	12	5	5	3	15	6	11	7	8	4	1	1					
EDWRDS GOVNR				14	26	24	12			12			14		14			2							
--4 WK AVG--	1			20	29	19	14	9	12	7	7	4	15	7	12	6	7	3	1	1	3	3	22	18	12
WYES PTV	1			7	11	1	6		2	2	2	2	5	1	3	3	3		1		1	1	8	4	3
WLAE PTV	1			2	3	1	1						2	1	1	1		1					1		1
HUT/PVT/TOT	32	36	39	332	447	159	259	61	139	119	135	69	187	57	108	87	100	43	70	47	59	59	331	252	183
7:00P-7:30P																									
WWL RSCUE 911 SP	2	5	3	51	71	34	50	21	31	28	33	16	20	11	15	13	15	2	16	6					
PRFCT CRIMES				44	61	18	36		16		21		25		14		14								
SCRTS UNKNWN				62	119	41	56		33		28		63		49		39								
--4 WK AVG--	4	5	5	52	80	32	48	16	28	25	29	14	32	10	24	19	21	6	14	9	15	16	92	81	55
WDSU MATLOCK	2	4	3	112	153	21	93	8	29	27	32	15	60	7	24	24	26	6	11	6					
FRESH PRINCE				51	71	41	52				43				21		19	11	15						
--4 WK AVG--	2	3	3	97	132	26	83	15	33	25	29	15	49	7	20	20	23	4	6		15	17	99	77	51
WVUE FMLY MATTERS	25	27	28	122	172	116	102	43	75	60	65	39	70	34	53	40	43	40	78	49	12	14	77	63	47
WGNO GERALDO	1	1		29	37	8	21	4	11	11	11	6	16	3	6	6	9	1	2						
LSU BSKTBALL				37	66	27	26		19			22	39		36		26								
--4 WK AVG--	1	1	1	31	44	13	23	5	13	13	14	7	22	7	14	11	13	1	3	2	6	5	35	25	17
WNOL AM MST WANTD	5	3	3	35	45	22	24	9	14	9	12	4	21	5	10	8	10	8	8	5	4	4	27	18	17
WYES PTV	1			12	20	2	11	1	3	3	3	4	9	1	4	4	5		2		2	2	10	8	7
WLAE PTV				1	1	1	1						1					1					1		1
HUT/PVT/TOT	47	50	53	350	494	212	291	89	166	135	152	83	204	65	126	102	115	59	114	71	62	62	341	272	195
7:30P-8:00P																									
WWL RSCUE 911 SP		4		44	56	22	39	13	23	23	28	13	17	9	13	13	14		10	2					
PRFCT CRIMES				24	28	6	19		12		12				9		5								
SCRTS UNKNWN				48	62	46	30		26		26		32		30		15								
--4 WK AVG--	1	3	2	40	50	24	32	12	21	21	24	12	19	10	15	12	12	2	9	4	7	8	46	39	25
WDSU MATLOCK	2	3	3	118	160	25	97	11	30	26	33	16	63	9	27	27	30	4	8	5					
NBC MV WK FR				62	77	33	38		24		25		39		31		35								
--4 WK AVG--	2	4	4	104	140	27	82	12	28	25	31	16	57	10	28	28	31	5	10	6	15	17	100	83	53
WVUE STEP BY STP	21	22	24	104	137	92	89	36	65	51	56	33	48	23	33	25	28	33	65	42	18	21	113	96	58
WGNO GERALDO	1	1		31	39	9	22	4	11	11	11	7	17	5	7	7	9	4	2						
LSU BSKTBALL				35	60	30	23		15			19	38		34		22								
--4 WK AVG--	1	1		32	44	14	22	5	12	12	13	7	22	9	14	10	12	3	1		5	4	31	22	22
WNOL AM MST WANTD	6	4	4	39	50	26	25	10	16	12	14	6	24	7	12	10	13	9	11	6	6	7	37	24	23
WYES PTV				8	9	2	9		2	2	2	3	3	2	5	5	5		1	2	2	2	12	10	8
WLAE PTV				1	1	1	1						1		1		1	1					1		
HUT/PVT/TOT	41	44	46	331	439	186	259	75	144	123	140	77	179	62	108	90	101	49	101	60	63	64	340	274	190
8:00P-8:30P																									
WWL C BURNETT SH		4	3	81	111	23	74	15	29	26	35	18	37	7	17	17	17	1	10		10	12	61	53	28
WDSU FLESH BLOOD	1	2	2	44	54	10	33	6	16	15	15	5	21	2	11	11	11	2	4	3					
NBC MV WK FR				76	96	45	57		42		44		39		34		38								
--4 WK AVG--	3	3	3	52	64	19	39	10	23	21	23	12	25	4	17	17	18	5	7	5	12	13	78	61	41
WVUE PRFCT STRNGR	15	17	19	91	119	75	73	27	50	42	45	25	46	24	35	26	29	23	50	32	16	18	98	81	47
WGNO 8 OCLOCK MOV	4	6	7	51	61	33	33	12	25	20	22	11	28	13	19	12	14	7	16	12					
LSU BSKTBALL				41	75	25	34		26			30	42		34		28								
--4 WK AVG--	3	4	5	48	65	31	33	11	25	22	24	12	32	14	23	14	18	5	12	9	6	6	40	27	26
WNOL ULTMT CHLNGE				23	44	9	20		3		6		23		8		4								
BST OF WORST	2	2	1	15	15	11	8	4	5	4	7	2	7	3	5	5	6	4	4	2					
--4 WK AVG--	3	1	1	17	22	11	11	3	4	4	7	2	11	4	5	5	5	4	3		2	4	28	18	18
WYES PTV				11	17	2	8		2	2	2	3	9	2	5	5	5				2	2	11	8	8
WLAE PTV				2	1		2						1										1		1
HUT/PVT/TOT	35	37	41	301	400	161	239	66	133	117	137	73	161	55	102	83	92	38	82	52	61	63	317	249	169
8:30P-9:00P																									
WWL C BURNETT SH		3	2	78	105	19	69	12	25	21	31	13	36	6	13	13	13	1	7		13	15	79	72	37
WDSU REAL LIFE SP				20	32		18		6		7		14		9		9								
DEAR JOHN	4	1	1	56	61	26	33	10	15	13	13	6	28	10	18	16	16	6	3	2					
NBC MV WK FR				69	87	34	49		35		34		38		32		36								
--4 WK AVG--	3	2	2	50	60	22	33	9	18	15	17	10	27	7	19	18	19	5	6	3	7	8	51	36	26
WVUE BABY TALK	10	13	14	72	86	58	55	24	41	34	36	23	31	14	18	15	20	16	38	25	13	16	83	65	39
WGNO 8 OCLOCK MOV	4	6	7	51	64	35	34	14	26	20	22	11	31	14	21	14	16	7	16	12					
LSU BSKTBALL				39	74	25	32		25			28	42		34		28								
--4 WK AVG--	3	4	5	48	67	32	33	12	26	22	24	12	33	14	24	16	19	5	12	9	7	7	48	33	32
WNOL ULTMT CHLNGE				24	44	9	20		3		6		23		8		4								
HIDDEN VIDEO	2	3	3	18	26	11	11	7	7	6	8	1	9	6	7	7	8	4	8	5					
--4 WK AVG--	3	2	2	19	26	14	13	5	6	5	7	1	13	6	8	6	7	4	6	4	3	3	19	13	12
WYES PTV				11	15	2	7		2	2	3		13	8	2	4	4				2	2	12	7	9
WLAE PTV				2	3		2						1										2	1	1
HUT/PVT/TOT	33	33	37	280	362	147	212	62	118	99	118	62	149	53	93	75	82	31	69	44	59	60	294	227	156
9:00P-9:30P																									
WWL PALACE GUARD				16	21		17		5		5		4												
FACE TO FACE				36	46		34		10		18		12		5										
TRL ONE IL FR		2		59	69	6	49	6	25	25	29	9	19	2	2	4			5	3					
--4 WK AVG--		1		43	51	3	37	3	16	16	20	9	14	2	2	3			3	2	10	11	60	53	24
WDSU RSNBL DOUBTS	2			50	64	17	43	11	24	20	24	15	21	2	12	12	15	3	1						
NBC MV WK FR				61	74	30	41		29		32		33		28		32								
--4 WK AVG--	3	2	2	52	67	20	43	12	25	22	26	15	24	4	16	16	19	4	6	3	8	9	52	39	25
WVUE 20/20	7	5	8	113	165	61	104	30	55	46	56	34	61	21	38	29	34	10	15	12	15	18	91	78	45
WGNO 8 OCLOCK MOV	4	7	9	52	63	30	35	13	26	18	20	9	28	9	17	13	16	8	20	16					
GRT SPT LGND				35	26	10	15		12			11		7		8									
--4 WK AVG--	3	6	7	43	54	25	30	10	22	17	18	9	24	9	14	11	14	6	15	12	7	7	46	32	30
WNOL STR TK NX PR	1	2	2	23	37	26	18	11	15	13	13	6	18	13	15	8	8	2	5	3	4	4	22	16	16
WYES PTV				5	9		5			2	2		4	1	1	1					1	1	8	6	6
WLAE PTV				3	5	1	2						1										3	2	2
HUT/PVT/TOT	31	24	32	282	388	136	239	66	135	116	135	72	147	47	86	67	79	23	44	32	57	59	282	226	148
(col #)	36	37	38	39	42	41	45	46	47	48	49	50	51	52	53	54	55	56	57	58	5	8	39	45	51

Daily

radio measurement field, abandoned in 1964, but the decision has always been to remain exclusively in television audience measurement.[5]

Television is, in fact, only a small part of Nielsen's business, although it is the service that has garnered the greatest attention. The A.C. Nielsen Company, which merged with Dun & Bradstreet in 1984, has always specialized in marketing research, including reports on grocery store purchasing trends that are particularly useful to advertising agencies and consumer products companies.

Nielsen Television Index The most widely known of Nielsen's television audience measurements is the **Nielsen Television Index (NTI),** which reports on audiences for national sponsored network programs. People meters record viewing habits in a national sample of 4500 households.

Nielsen publishes a weekly report that summarizes household and personal viewing estimates for all sponsored network programs. Clients who want to have information from Nielsen's computer sent directly to a personal computer can obtain audience ratings for network programs on the day after a telecast. Such information is valuable not only to advertisers who want to know how effectively their message reached targeted consumers but to network programmers who must decide whether to keep shows on the air or cancel them if they are not competitive.

Local market report Nielsen's plans to eventually convert all of its local market measurement, which it calls the **Nielsen Station Index (NSI),** to people meters. Because of criticism of the accuracy of people meter measurement, that plan is being delayed until improvements in the technology are made. For now, most Nielsen markets are still measured by the diary method. Each market is measured at least four times a year, in November, February, May, and July. Larger markets are measured up to seven times a year.

Nielsen provides special research based on its NSI diaries and also conducts telephone coinci-

dental surveys when specific information is desired quickly by its clients.

Nielsen micro services All the major audience research firms supply ratings data to their clients in printed form. Increasingly, though, survey results are made available to stations and advertising agencies that use IBM-PC and compatible personal computers or microcomputers. In addition to services provided by third-party vendors, or companies that have developed computer software to analyze ratings data, Arbitron and Nielsen supply computerized services directly.

Nielsen's Audience Analyst software provides analytic tools for an electronic version of its ratings report. Users thus turn their computers into an "electronic ratings book" for determining how a program rates or ranks against other programs. Programmers can get access to Nielsen audience estimates more quickly in this manner. Equally important, the data can be used in the way most meaningful to the programmer for analyzing audience traits.

Metered market service Daily overnight reports on the previous day's viewing in metered markets are provided to station, agency, and network clients. Even though samples are not representative of the nation's viewing, metered measurements of viewing in many of the nation's largest markets provide a clear indication of how well a program will do before the NTI or local market report becomes available. Thus, programmers who want to quickly determine how well a new show is doing can consult the overnight ratings to anticipate whether to cancel a series or continue it because it attracts key demographics.

Report on Syndicated Programs Nielsen's Report on Syndicated Programs, issued four times a year, provides profiles of audiences, competitors, and lead-in programs for over 300 syndicated shows. Data from Nielsen's market reports are rearranged to show DMA summaries by market rank, summaries by daypart, and information on demographics, program types, and the number of episodes available.

Information on performance in other markets provides a basis for predicting the likely success of a show if it is scheduled in the programmer's market. Moreover, it provides some guidance on how successful that show may be in various dayparts. Even though a program has been successful during its network run, it may not attract viewers during other time periods, especially when their composition differs from that of the prime-time audience. Action/adventure series such as *Hunter* do not always fit the predominantly female audience's viewing tastes during the daytime. Consequently, that show and others with similar appeal may have the best chance of attracting a substantial share of viewers later in the day, when more men are available to watch. However, even some shows that appeal to daytime viewers seem to attract larger audiences during certain time periods. Therefore, if a programmer is considering a new talk show for the early fringe, a check of the ratings achieved by stations in other markets during the same time period is a good predictor of its potential. If stations that scheduled the show during early fringe did not enjoy the ratings success of stations that broadcast it in midmorning, the programmer will know that another program must be sought to fill the early fringe slot.

NSI Plus NSI Plus is a supplemental service that provides clients with studies of **audience flow,** or the movement of audiences from one program to the next in a station or network schedule. Programmers assume that audience members remained tuned to a channel, or flow into a succeeding program that has similar demographic appeals. Knowing how effectively a program's audience is thus delivered is valuable in determining which programs, in which order, can be most effective in attracting and maintaining audiences throughout a daypart.

NSI Plus also reports on program loyalty as indicated by audience **turnover,** an index of audience stability that is also known as tune-in and tune-out. If a large number of audience members sample a program but then tune out, the programmer will have an indication that many potential viewers are dissatisfied. This initial clue can be probed by conducting special audience studies to determine the reasons for such audience dissatisfaction.

The NSI Plus report on audience **recycling** (the same people in the audiences of different programs) provides programmers with an index of audience viewing of the same program from day to day or from time period to time period. For example, an "only-only-both study" can evaluate households and persons viewing only the early local news, only the late-evening local news, or both programs. With this information, the programmer can adjust the content of the newscasts. For instance, if an 11 p.m. news program repeated most of the stories included in the station's 6 p.m. broadcast, viewers might turn to a competing news program at 11 p.m. for variety. Knowing this, the station could try to make the late-evening newscast fresher by updating the stories, including new material, or even using different anchorpersons to convey that it was a different program from the one people saw earlier in the day.

Cassandra Nielsen offers a computer-generated report it calls Cassandra that reports on all programs—syndicated, network, and local—in all markets. This service allows clients to assess the effectiveness of a program in attracting viewers while taking into consideration the competing programs and the influence of the time period in which the program was scheduled, the size of the audience for the programs that preceded and followed it, and trend data for selected programs on a market-by-market basis.

These reports are tailored to clients' specifications. The programming department of Katz Communications Inc., a major station representative firm, uses the Cassandra data base to prepare its Comtrac syndicated programming reports, which it makes available on a fee basis to the stations it represents. This report provides a record of syndicated program performance according to daypart, market size, and network-affiliated versus independent station. In addition, program performance is summarized for the top-50, second-50, and top-100 markets. In this way, programmers can evaluate the success of specific syndicated programs in markets with characteristics similar to their own.

Homevideo Index   The impact of cable channels and videocassette rental on broadcast television is measured in Nielsen's **Homevideo Index (HVI).** This service, which is an extension of people meter measurement, offers Nielsen clients reports on the viewing of major satellite-distributed networks such as the USA Network, TNT, and ESPN as well as on local cable system viewing and the use of videocassette recorders and other new video formats.

Nielsen measures cable networks on the basis of *viewers per viewing household (VPVH)* in the DMA. Nielsen also reports local cable audience ratings, which are available for every TV market. The advantage of this service is that it reports only on households that are connected to cable systems; this can greatly increase a cable program's share since that program is available to all the households in the universe. The result is an index of cable viewing, which is computed by dividing the NSI diary cable household ratings in the cable system by the NSI diary cable network national household rating during the same daypart and then multiplying by 100.

Timeshifting is increasingly practiced in American television households. A number of timeshifting experiments have been tried in attempts to attract an audience. ABC TV once proposed sending programs on scrambled signals late at night that customers with descrambling devices could record by presetting the timers on their VCRs for daytime or evening playback. The Movie Channel currently offers an overnight service allowing subscribers to record movies late at night and then watch them at a convenient time. Through a special device attached to the home VCR that encodes a signal on tapes being recorded, the system can report whether viewers are watching or fast-forwarding over this ma-

terial. This signal is then recorded by the people meters installed in the metered markets. The Homevideo Index allows cable and broadcast television programmers to know when people are timeshifting programs so that they can be counted in the audience. In the future, it is probable that other program services will try to capitalize on the convenience of timeshifting since so many households have VCRs.

Advertisers are, of course, very much concerned about the number of people who watch their messages. The advertising industry generally assumes that "real-time" viewers are watching commercials, even though it is known that many people leave the audience during commercial breaks to use the bathroom or go to the kitchen for a snack. With recorded programs, viewers can fast-forward through the uninteresting parts of a program, including the commercials. Therefore, timeshifting as a viable programming strategy may be dependent on whether viewers watch or ignore the commercials. However, knowing where the lulls in viewer interest come in the program content can provide programmers and program producers with insights into how to improve the product to heighten audience interest and keep more people in the audience.

Nielsen has persuaded the major distributors of home video rentals to encode a signal on rental tapes. These codes can be read by 2500 of Nielsen's people meters, which recognize a particular video program when it is played back. Thus, the HVI also documents viewing patterns and demographics that were not known before. The measurable influence of video rentals on the television audience has put the networks in a position where they will have to counterprogram against this added competition for the TV audience.[6]

Arbitron Television

Local market report   Arbitron measures each ADI at least four times a year, during November, February, May, and July. Larger markets are measured as often as seven times a year because client stations and advertising agencies want additional information in the most competitive markets and are willing to pay for it. Additionally, a number of communities with television stations that lie within a dominant ADI are also reported four times a year. For example, Ann Arbor, Michigan, a large university town but a non-ADI market, is within 20 miles of downtown Detroit.

Arbitron TV microservices Arbitron's microcomputer software, called TV Maximiser, allows station sales representatives to quickly develop a schedule of spot placements in programs watched by specified demographic groups in order to meet the advertiser's budget in reaching target consumers. Even though advertising sales are not directly pertinent to programming objectives, TV Maximiser is useful to programmers as well. The software permits analyses of individual program performance and time periods, enabling a programmer to quickly assess the effectiveness of the entire program schedule.

Computers make possible the generation of other customized research reports. Through **Arbitrends** II, Arbitron TV clients can analyze local market ratings data on their own microcomputers. The reports can be customized to analyze competitive situations, trends, and other aspects of program performance. Clients can receive the data for the sweep period more quickly than they could if they waited for the printed report. With computer analysis, it is possible to isolate special broadcasts or movies and sports events and analyze their ratings performance. For radio clients, Arbitrends reports can be customized to the needs of the station because the data are received and held in the station's computer.

Metered market service Arbitron clients in metered markets can receive overnight household ratings on their personal computers and proceed with their analyses without having to wait for a printed report. Moreover, clients can track the performance of a program over many months; this enables programmers to identify trends in audience viewing and then decide whether to continue a program.

Target AID Programmers are increasingly able to turn to qualitative research in making programming decisions. Target AID is an on-line computer service that allows Arbitron's clients to profile audience lifestyle attributes. By specifying demographics that are selected from particular counties and ZIP codes, these reports identify the lifestyle characteristics of audience members who are clustered in groups such as "young, mobile, upscale families, children, new homes" and "less educated, downscale, rural families, children." The percentages of the audience that are in such qualitative clusters can be identified, and the programmer can use that information in making decisions about scheduling programs to attract the desired groups.

For example, a station that programmed *The Andy Griffith Show* was having trouble selling advertising. In spite of the program's high ratings, advertisers thought it would reach only downscale and less educated viewers, who were not the target consumers for their products. Target AID showed that the audience for *The Andy Griffith Show* was actually dominated by younger, more upscale audience clusters. Thus, the program could be demonstrated to be a good advertising buy.[7]

Arbitron Radio

Arbitron markets are categorized according to whether they receive continuous-measurement, standard, or condensed-measurement reports. About 80 markets receive **continuous measurement,** which means that diaries are kept by respondents in those markets for 48 of the 52 weeks of the year. These are among the largest radio markets in the country.

Each of Arbitron's radio sweeps is 12 weeks in length, corresponding to the four seasons of the year. The length of these sweeps has eliminated some of the problems associated with the use of special promotions and contests that can induce audiences to tune in a station to participate in contests conducted during a ratings sweep, only to go back to their normal listening habits after the contest. If a station uses contests or other promotions to increase its ratings, it must do so over a long period of time for the effect to be felt.

Standard-measurement markets are measured during the spring and fall and cover media buying decisions in the reported markets for the two halves of the year. The spring report is used more intensively in buying and selling advertisements.

Condensed market reports are provided for the smallest markets, which are measured only during the spring sweep. These reports provide limited information to the programmer since audience figures are reported only for dayparts, unlike the standard market report, which breaks out listening on an hour-by-hour basis. The lack of demographic detail provided in a condensed market report is also a drawback. Teen listeners are not reported, but the numbers can be broken down so that those figures can be determined. For instance, by subtracting cume adults 18 and over from cume listeners 12 and over, the programmer can determine the cume teen audience for a station. Daypart figures are broken out for persons 12 and over, for both men and women 18 and over, and for adults 18 and over. Other demographics reported include adults 18 to 34, 18 to 49, 25 to 54, and 35 and above. These demographics limit the usefulness of a condensed market report. In contrast, the standard market report provides a breakdown of all the standard age segments by sex, and this makes the definition of a station's audience much more precise.

Audience estimates for noncommercial stations are not reported in Arbitron radio reports. An independent consultant, Radio Research Consortium, has the license for Arbitron noncommercial station data and makes the data available to public stations for a fee. In addition, this company provides ratings consultation to its client stations.

Monthly reports With the introduction of continuous measurement in 1986, Arbitron began offering subscribers its Arbitrends service, which supplements the four regular quarterly market reports. Arbitrends provides stations with an interim *rolling average report* which combines data from the most recent month with information from the previous 2 months. The benefit is early warning about the direction of trends in a station's audience. Thus, a station can take appropriate action when it has observed a trend of audience loss that may be due to factors such as a change in call letters, a new format, or new on-air personalities.

AID Arbitron Information on Demand (AID) is a service that permits subscribers to create customized audience analyses directly from Arbitron's diary data base. The client can run AID on the station's computer by direct access, or Arbitron will perform the analysis. AID's Programmer's Package offers an analysis of the ratings that reveals more about listener behavior, including where, when, and how often listeners are tuning in, to assist in making programming decisions. The program will calculate how long people listen, whether audience members listen during more than one daypart, and whether audience members are listening exclusively to one station or are dividing their listening and also tracks tune-in and tune-out, showing trends for five quarterly reporting periods. Specific demographics and geographic data based on ZIP codes, can be pinpointed, making AID particularly attractive to programmers whose stations are in large, diverse markets.

AID's greatest disadvantage is its cost, which runs to 6 percent of a station's annual Arbitron subscription fee plus computer access time, which is charged in minutes. Since the data are not completely double checked, they may contain errors that affect estimates of listening.

Mechanical diary A much less costly alternative to AID is a **mechanical diary,** which is a printout of the information included in the diaries that mention the client station. This provides insight into who is in the audience and how the audience members responded in filling out diaries. The client station can order a station mechanical diary from Arbitron for analysis at the station. While relatively inexpensive, Arbitron's mechanical diary service is slow, since it is printed out for clients rather than being available on-line.

With the mechanical diary, a programmer can analyze where listeners live, how long they listen to the station, when they leave to tune in a competitor, time of listening, age and sex of listeners, and location of listening (at home, in a car, at work, or in another place). The mechanical diary is also a means of checking how appropriate the sampling was in the market.

Among the benefits of the mechanical diary are insights into ways to improve music scheduling, recycling of news and traffic information, and scheduling of promotions when the programmer knows the patterns of the station's audience. For example, if it is determined that many afternoon listeners also listen later in the evening, a programmer may consider providing a greater variety of music at night so that listeners won't tire of hearing the same music several times a day. Conversely, if a large number of respondents indicate that they listen only between 7 a.m. and 8 a.m., it may not be necessary to revise newscasts or other information for later broadcasts because the majority of those in the audience after 8 a.m. will not have heard the earlier material. Or it may be discovered that a majority of a station's listeners tune in between 7 a.m. and 8 a.m. With that information, the programmer may conclude that this period offers the best opportunity to schedule promotional announcements or run contests that can be won only during other time periods, encouraging morning listeners to tune in at other times of the day.

Arbitron also offers a *market mechanical diary,* a computer printout of the complete listening entries used to process the audience estimates for a market report. These "full-market mechanical diaries" can be analyzed only at an Arbitron sales office or at the Diary Review Center in Arbitron's Laurel, Maryland, headquarters. Without access to the market mechanical diary, though, the analysis will be incomplete, since the station mechanical contains only entries pertaining to the client station. The market mechanical diary gives the programmer access to information about competing stations to provide insights such as when audience members switch stations.

Diary reviews The only way to be sure the numbers that Arbitron reports are valid is to examine the actual diaries completed by survey respondents. Arbitron permits representatives of client stations to visit its headquarters to look over these books. A station visit is limited to a single day and to three people per visit. Thus, those making the trip may include the general manager, sales manager, and program director. If the station has a research director, that person is a logical individual to send instead of one of the other people. Some stations use the services of research consultants instead of examining and analyzing the diaries directly.

The trip to Laurel, Maryland, may help the client find Arbitron mistakes or errors by diary keepers that affect its ratings. Equally important, the opportunity to analyze the raw, original data provides the reviewer with insights that can be applied to improving the station's ratings in future sweeps. There's nothing like seeing the original unaltered entries to help programmers go beyond conventional wisdom (Figure 5-19). Thus, it may be discovered that errors by diary keepers negatively affected the credit the station received for listening. As was discussed in Chapter 2, many stations use identifiers such as Q-104, which may be confused by diary keepers with the identifiers used by other stations in the market. If, as Arbitron representatives assert, most respondents designate stations by call letters rather than slogans, this discovery will point to the utility of scheduling frequent presentations of the call letters to remind listeners which station they are listening to.

TUESDAY

	Time		Station			Place			
			Call letters or station name	Check (✓) one		Check (✓) one			
	Start	Stop	Don't know? Use program name or dial setting.	AM	FM	At Home	In a Car	At Work	Other Place
Early Morning (from 5 AM)	5:50	6:50	The FOX		✓	✓			
	8:30	8:45	ZBN		✓		✓		
	9:00		Eagle 102					✓	
Midday		12 N							
Late Afternoon	5:00	5:30	WMMQ				✓		
Night (to 5 AM Wednesday)									

If you didn't hear a radio today, please check here. ☐

FIGURE 5-19   A completed diary page. (Used by permission of Arbitron Ratings Co.)

Diary keepers' comments are invited on the last page of the diary (Figure 5-20). These comments can provide the programmer with information about how these respondents feel about a station personality, which, to judge from the volunteered comments in this case, is not very positive. The only way to retrieve such notations is by examining the original entries, since none of this potentially valuable information is encoded in Arbitron computer reports. If a pattern in the comments is observed, the programmer may not wish to discount them as the isolated reactions of overly critical listeners but consider them indications of problems in the programming.

An important part of the diary review visit is verification of the data printed in the mechanical diary. The only way to ascertain whether a station has received full credit for its listeners is to check the original entries against the data that have been entered in Arbitron's computer, since these data form the basis of the ratings report. When data entry errors are discovered and the station can back up its claim, it may be able to receive the additional listening credit that is due.

Arbitron diary changes Changes in Arbitron's radio diary have made a difference in the ratings of some stations. A new diary format, called the **soft format** because Arbitron does not place dividing lines between dayparts, was introduced in

Quick questions

1 **What is your age?**
_26_ years

2 **Are you male or female?**
☑ Male   ☐ Female
  1   2

3 **Where do you live?**
City _____
County _____
State _____
Zip _____

4 **Do you work away from home?**

☑ Yes   ☐ No
  1   2

If yes: How many hours per week do you usually work away from home? *Check (✓) one.*

Less than 20   20-29   30 or more
☐   ☐   ☑
  1   2   3

Your opinion counts

Use this space to make any comments you like about specific stations, announcers or programs.

John MacFee (McPhee?) On The
Eagle 102 is a total Dork his
jokes are lame.

FIGURE 5-20 Diary comments. *(Used by permission of Arbitron Ratings Co.)*

1987. This change was made because of concern over declining response rates.

The soft format (Figure 5-19) permits the respondent to draw a line down the page to indicate listening over a period of time. It was thought that this change would elicit the reporting of longer listening times since survey respondents can more easily indicate when they listen. Thus, some stations have altered their programming in an attempt to induce longer listening.

Another important change in the reporting format introduced in 1987 was the addition of a place in the diary to report listening at work in addition to at home, in the car, and in other places. This designation means that stations that make specific efforts to reach people who listen to the radio at their workplaces may be rewarded by an increase in their audiences. After discovering that respondent reporting of midday listening has increased as a result of the new diary category, some stations have redoubled their efforts at attracting office workers.

An additional change occurred in the language. Whereas Arbitron previously asked respondents to report on radio listening, respondents are now informed that listening means that they "hear a radio." Thus, some respondents may note listening that they did not report before, such as visits to stores where radios are played. Other respondents may report that a radio was on all day where they work even if they ignored it. In any case, the soft format diary has been found to benefit formats such as Adult Contemporary, Soft Rock, and Oldies and Classic Hits during the midday period, particularly in regard to **away-from-home listening**.[8] This indicates that more respondents are reporting workplace and out-of-home listening.

Differential survey treatment Programmers must know the research company's methodology to compete effectively. For example, the requirement that listeners be in the audience for 5 minutes during each quarter hour is a crucial "rule." Programmers who are aware of that rule develop strategies to keep listeners at least long

enough to receive credit for their listening. Many music-oriented radio stations start records near the end of a quarter hour so that they end after the new time period has begun, carrying audience members into the new quarter-hour period. To ensure that people who listened to the record will stay tuned for a few minutes longer— at least long enough to meet the stipulation of the 5-minute rule—another song is presented immediately. Commercial breaks and other interruptions in the entertainment that might prompt people to tune out are carefully placed at other times during the quarter-hour period.

Another illustration of a rule can be found in an Arbitron methodology change that caused controversy when it was initiated in 1982, although station disgruntlement over the possibility of a detrimental effect on ratings has since abated. Arbitron determined that a particular audience segment, black males 18 to 34, was underrepresented in its in-tab because this group was not returning diaries.

The solution, called **differential survey treatment (DST),** was to offer those persons a higher premium to complete and return their diaries. By increasing the premium from $1 to $5 and conducting follow-up reminder calls to respondents, Arbitron was able to improve the response rate of this group, making its survey results more representative of all black males age 18 to 34. Later, the DST was applied to Hispanic males 18 to 34 for the same reason.

Each of the markets in which an ethnic DST is applied has been identified as a **high-density black area (HDBA)** or **high-density Hispanic area (HDHA).** At least 25 percent of the population in the market must be black or be Hispanic before a DST is put into effect.

Not surprisingly, radio stations with Black Appeal and Urban Contemporary formats benefit from DST. Album-Oriented Rock formatted stations, which at that time appealed primarily to white males age 18 to 24, may lose rating points since pre-DST estimates may have overrepresented this group. The hue and cry, primarily from AOR formatted stations whose programmers thought their ratings were being hurt by this research method, died down, and stations have accepted DST. More recently, Arbitron extended DST to include nonethnic males 18 to 24 and took an extra step by offering the increased premium and follow-up reminders to all other diary keepers in households that include a male age 18 to 24. Industry observers expected that the ratings of AOR formatted stations would rise. Instead, stations with Adult Contemporary formats fared better; this has been attributed to the heightened attention that somewhat older listeners gave to completing their diaries when they were the recipients of the expanded DST.

Biases in Arbitron results There are some biases inherent in Arbitron's diary results. Audience members age 35 and above have been found to be more reliable in returning diaries. The best diary keepers tend to be married, white-collar, higher-income people. Since education correlates highly with these attributes, literacy is a

contributing factor in the completion rate. As was discussed earlier, men 18 to 24 have a poor diary return rate.

Arbitron's listening estimates may be influenced by the increased awareness that DST respondents surely have of their listening, since the incentive to report on it has clearly motivated a higher level of cooperation among the members of this group.

In Arbitron market studies, the benefit appears to go to stations featuring Easy-Listening, Middle-of-the-Road, Soft Rock, and Country music. Their formats attract older listeners, who respond more often in Arbitron surveys.

Industry leaders have not been able to resolve these potential limitations of methodology. Thus, programmers should take biases into account before assuming that the listening reported for a station using a particular format is significantly higher or lower than that for competitors using other formats.

SUMMARY

Audience measurement provides information to advertisers and programmers on the kinds and sizes of audiences attracted to electronic media programs. Measurement is usually focused on markets. The Metropolitan Statistical Area, also known as the metro survey area, is the geographic heart of radio and TV markets. This is where the greatest number of listeners or viewers are located and where the signal for each station in the market has the strongest reception. Arbitron radio reports include the metro area and a total survey area (TSA) that consists of surrounding counties from which listeners have indicated that they listen to stations licensed to the metro area.

In addition to metro survey area viewing estimates, Arbitron television reports include viewing in the area of dominant influence (ADI), which consists of counties assigned exclusively to a market. A third market area, the total survey area, includes counties in which significant viewing of the stations assigned to a market is report-

ed in surveys. Nielsen Media Research reports viewing for the metro area, the designated market area (DMA), and the station total area. The DMA consists of counties assigned exclusively to a market. The station total area includes all viewing of stations licensed to a market.

Ratings are reported for a variety of demographic categories. Radio listeners are defined as persons age 12 and older. Viewers 2 and above are measured in television audiences. The demographic breakdowns for radio and television audiences include teens; women and men 18 to 24, 25 to 34, 35 to 44, 45 to 54, and 55 and over; and other aggregates of these groups. Television audiences are also reported for children 2 to 5, children 5 to 11, and girls 12 to 17. If one subtracts an audience segment known to be in a broader group, two demographic segments can be identified. For example, to find teen boys, the analyst need only subtract girls 12 to 17 from the larger teens 12 to 17 figure.

Quarter-hour estimates are especially important in radio audience estimates. To be included in the audience, a person must report listening or viewing for at least 5 continuous minutes during a quarter-hour period. With this rule in mind, stations work out programming strategies that induce listeners to stay tuned for as many quarter-hour periods as possible.

Radio listening is reported in average quarter hour (AQH) estimates and in cume listening. AQH is an average of the number of persons who listened during each quarter hour in the period being measured. Cume is an estimate of the total number of different persons who listened during a given period.

A rating is the percentage of the total possible listeners or viewers in the universe that are listening or watching. A share is a program's percentage of those viewers or listeners actually watching or listening during that time period.

Although television audience ratings are measured in quarter-hour increments, they are reported for half-hour periods except for news programs, when 15-minute viewing increments are provided. The HUT (homes using television) level forms the basis for TV ratings. HUT is the percentage of total households in the market that are actually using their sets at any given time. Persons using television (PUT) refers to the percentage of individuals using TV among all those who could be viewing, taking into account multiple-set households.

The HUT level builds during the morning as more people join the television audience and peaks during the winter months at around 65 percent. In the summer, when people are on vacation and spending more time outdoors, HUT drops to around 55 percent. Programmers do not schedule their most appealing programs during the summer because advertisers are unwilling to pay premium rates for smaller audiences. HUT levels vary on different nights of the week as well. Friday has the lowest and Sunday has the highest prime-time viewing.

Radio audiences also vary, but their levels are not affected as drastically during the warm months as television audiences are. The peak in

radio listening comes at about 7:30 a.m., Monday through Friday. On Saturday and Sunday the highest listening occurs at about 11 a.m.

The efficiency of advertising is measured in cost per thousand (CPM) viewers or listeners. This is a measurement that programmers need to know to understand the value to advertisers of the audiences that are attracted to their programs. Cable networks may stress cost per hundred viewers because their audiences are so small compared to those of broadcast networks. CPM is calculated by dividing the cost of an advertising spot by units of 1000 listeners or viewers. Cost per hundred is done the same way except that the unit is 100 listeners or viewers.

Ratings estimates for radio are reported for each hour and for the standard dayparts: 6 a.m. to 10 a.m., 10 a.m. to 3 p.m., 3 p.m. to 7 p.m., and 7 p.m. to midnight. Ratings for television are reported for dayparts and for individual programs. In addition, both Nielsen and Arbitron provide overnight ratings reports for over 20 markets through their people meters. Nielsen provides the only measurement of network viewing through its Nielsen Television Index (NTI). The data for national viewing estimates are gathered through a sample of 4500 households equipped with people meters.

Estimates of the number of listeners are provided by Arbitron, where radio listening is measured through the diary method. Arbitron ratings tend to be higher for radio stations with formats that appeal to older (35 and over) listeners, creating a potential bias toward stations using formats that attract older listeners.

Although reports on listening and viewing are still provided to stations in printed form, that information is available more quickly in electronic form for analysis on microcomputers. Many electronic media outlets take advantage of this means of accessing listening and viewing estimates for their markets because it allows their sales and programming staffs to quickly perform more specific and extensive analyses of audience trends than is possible with the printed reports.

SUGGESTED READINGS

Description of Methodology: Arbitron Ratings Company Market Reports—Television, Arbitron Ratings Company, New York, 1989.

Description of Methodology: Arbitron Ratings Company Market Reports—Radio, Arbitron Ratings Company, New York, 1987.

Nielsen Station Index Reference Supplement 1990–91: NSI Methodology, Techniques and Data Interpretation, Nielsen Media Research, Northbrook, Ill., 1990.

Your Guide to Nielsen Reports and Services, Nielsen Media Research, Northbrook, Ill., 1987.

These reports explain the rules of the game as determined by Arbitron and Nielsen. Their contents describe exactly how each company defines the market, the length of a survey period, and other details that a programmer should keep in mind when trying to attract and maintain the largest possible audience. These sources allow programmers to interpret ratings data and capitalize on the rules in seeking a maximum audience response in ratings surveys.

Fletcher, James E.: *Profiting from Radio Ratings,* National Association of Broadcasters, Washington, D.C., 1989.

The key portion of the book—the first 92 pages—is a comprehensive explanation of the contents of printed radio ratings reports. Chapters review the accuracy of ratings along with the geography of ratings surveys and sampling procedures. A chapter is devoted to the use of ratings for sales, and another deals with the use of ratings to improve programming. The book features self-tests that enable readers to check their understanding of the concepts. Appendixes include copies of ratings reports.

NOTES

1. James E. Fletcher, *Broadcast Research Definitions,* National Association of Broadcasters, Washington, D.C., 1988, p. 51.

2. The station total area consists of the metro area, the DMA, and viewing outside the NSI area. (The NSI area consists of the metro area, the DMA, and any additional counties that are targeted to constitute about 95 percent of the average quarter-hour audiences for stations assigned to a market.) See *Nielsen Station Index Reference Supplement 1990–91: NSI Methodology, Techniques and Data Interpretation,* Nielsen Media Research, Northbrook, Ill., 1990, p. 3.

3. The formula used for that determination is discussed in *Description of Methodology: Arbitron Ratings Company Market Reports—Television,* Arbitron Ratings Company, New York, 1989, pp. 1–6.

4. "Arbitron Introduces New Radio Diary," *Broadcasting,* May 30, 1988, p. 48; "Radio Listening Is up in Prime Consumer Cells," *NAB RadioWeek,* May 1, 1989, p. 6.

5. Hugh Malcolm Beville, Jr., *Audience Ratings: Radio, Television, Cable,* Lawrence Erlbaum, Hillsdale, N.J., 1985, pp. 20–71.

6. Richard Katz, "Exploring Home Video," *Channels,* Sept. 1989, p. 26.

7. "Viacom Uses Target AID to Demonstrate Andy Griffith Show's Upscale Appeal," *Beyond the Ratings,* July 1986, pp. 5–6.

8. "Radio Listening Is up in Prime Consumer Cells"; "Hard Questions on Soft Diaries," *Broadcasting,* Sept. 25, 1989, p. 42.

Program Assessment:

Applying Research

Success in programming results from having an idea that works in a creative mix that includes the available audience, social trends, and personalities and program structures. Because television program development is so expensive and so few shows are successful regardless of their producers' creative energy and a careful assessment of their appeal, there is much concern with the high cost of producing programming that fails to attract or keep an audience. In both television and radio, research provides guidance to programmers for the selection of content that will appeal to targeted audiences.

In the preceding chapters we introduced the fundamentals of conducting research and described the kinds of services provided by audience research firms. This chapter will deal with the application of research information to program decision making. First, we discuss research that goes beyond the ratings reports. Whereas audience ratings measure *who* is listening or watching, other methods are used to determine *why* people watch different programs, that is, to identify the elements or features of a program that attract its audience. Later in the chapter we examine radio program performance based on information obtained in standard audience research reports. This is followed by a consideration of research that can aid radio programmers in the selection and scheduling of music. Then we look at some of the ways in which decision makers attempt to reduce the risk in developing television programs and schedules.

FOCUS GROUP RESEARCH

The ratings reports supplied by Arbitron and Nielsen provide information on who is listening, for how long, and to which programs or stations. These data do not explain audience motivations but simply report what the audience tuned in to watch or listen.

When a decline in the audience cannot be explained as a statistical error, it is wise to learn the reasons for that erosion. A "delving" method known as focus group interviewing can provide insight into how people perceive radio and television programs. A **focus group interview** is a controlled discussion led by a researcher who tries to draw out the opinions and feelings of participants that are typical of people in the target audience for a particular program. As consultant Ed Shane has described it, a focus group is "an intimate conversation between a carefully chosen group of 'informants' and a researcher called a 'facilitator.' This conversation 'focuses' on a topic or problem."[1]

The objective of focus group interviews is to get inside the heads of actual or potential audience members. That is not literally possible, but focus research is one of the best methods for approaching this goal. It is best thought of as an exploratory or diagnostic tool that provides its users with insight. As Fletcher and Wimmer have put it, focus group interviewing gives programmers the ability to interpret trends by "adding richness of human rationales to the cold facts of the rating report."[2]

It is not easy to understand why people like or dislike certain stations or programs. It is even more difficult for the people involved in producing a program to understand how things they take for granted could be listener or viewer **irritants;** that is, they grate on the nerves. For example, the morning personalities on a radio station may have a routine that includes badgering the female newsperson who works with them. While they feel that this is a humorous bit and the newsperson may help plan the exchanges, many people in the audience may perceive it as picking on someone who cannot defend herself or even as sexist. Focus group interviews may reveal that some people feel uncomfortable when they hear such exchanges. That knowledge in turn may explain why certain targeted listeners are avoiding the station.

Similar benefits can be obtained through focus group research for TV. A television producer who has worked on the conception of a series and has been responsible for developing the characters and the story line may be too close to the project to see some of the things that bother viewers. Suppose a station spent a considerable sum of money to create a set for its local morning show. The producer whose idea it was to create the set might have made some unwarranted assumptions about the closeness of his or her taste to viewers' perceptions. Thus, it may be determined through focus group interviews that the set appears to be cluttered and distracting to members of the audience.

Once such an insight has been gained, the challenge is to identify ways to change the program and alter audience perception. One success story centered on the former CBS series *Cagney and Lacey,* which originally starred Tyne Daly and Meg Foster. The concept had tested well, and Daly's audience appeal score was good. However, Producer Barney Rosenweig obtained focus group study results that indicated that viewers perceived a lesbianlike relationship between the two characters. The personas of both actors were perceived to be "mannish," and the plots called for them to be close friends. When Foster was replaced by the more feminine-appearing Sharon Gless, the series took off. In this case focus group research helped identify where the chemistry between the characters was wrong and allowed the development of a new approach toward audience identification and appeal.

Even when a program idea has been successful, nothing remains the same for very long. As David MacFarland has pointed out, the radio stations that continue to succeed are those which have never quit "fixing things" instead of following the adage "Don't fix it if it ain't broke."[3] Both radio and television programmers can profit from that admonition. If spotted early, negative audience trends can be dealt with to prevent a decline in the station's success (Box 6-1). Thus, an important use of focus group research is to fine-tune programming. For example, a TV series that has enjoyed a successful run may eventually become too predictable. Its writers may get into a rut where the situations in which they place characters are too similar from week to week. A solution might be to introduce new characters who enable the show to develop fresh story lines and enhance the roles of the original characters. For instance, if Michael J. Fox's character, Alex, on *Family Ties* is given a permanent romantic interest, how will the audience members react? Will they feel this is a reasonable or normal development that makes the show more interesting, or will they feel that the addition of a girlfriend distracts from the interplay between Alex and the members of his family and the other established characters?

Capabilities of Focus Group Interviews

Focus group research is of the greatest use in cases where it is important to know what people think or why they react as they do. Thus, this procedure can help define situations that cannot be quantified. Knowing that the audience for a program is steadily declining or that viewers leave the program in large numbers at particular times is not the same as knowing *why* these things occur. One might surmise that audience members do not like particular characters in a program or a particular anchor or disc jockey, but that supposition is dangerous. Speculation

---

BOX 6-1
PURPOSE OF FOCUS
GROUP INTERVIEWS

- Gain insight
- Help interpret other research data
- Elicit human rationales to embellish the facts in ratings reports
- Explain why
- Obtain audience perceptions that might otherwise never be known to the programmer
- Develop questions for representative survey research

can be put to rest by probing focus group participants. Nothing can be fixed until an objective assessment has been made.

Survey research has limitations, including the brief period of time during which respondents may be induced to answer questions over the telephone. While not cheap, the focus group technique serves as a quicker, less expensive alternative to a full-scale survey. Its usefulness is enhanced by the ability to probe and encourage participants to share their feelings and attitudes.

Focus group research does not yield statistically representative results. It can provide important insights with a reasonable likelihood that the pattern it reveals can be observed across the targeted audience if and only if the participants in the interview groups have been selected carefully. A programmer should avoid basing decisions entirely on focus group responses. Thus, the observations elicited in focus group sessions can be validated through a survey of a broad-based sample of the target audience.[4] For example, if focus sessions reveal that most participants share the perception that the station's newscasts are too long, a survey of listeners in the market can be conducted to determine whether that finding will hold up.

Focus Group Interview Procedures

Since focus research is nonrepresentative, the more carefully the participants are screened, the better. That is, only people fitting the profile of targeted audience members should be included in the sample. Otherwise, the research will cost much more because there will probably be many respondents in the sample who are not important to the programmer's objective. If a TV station is concerned about its local news programs and has determined that its target audience is men and women age 25 to 54, all the subjects should be screened to fit that demographic profile. For example, the Arts and Entertainment network has attempted to position itself as a service for well-educated affluent viewers. When such a network orders focus group research on one of its programs, its programmers specify the

kind of viewer they are interested in. Thus, the researcher will screen potential respondents by asking them whether they have a college degree before inviting them to participate in a focus group interview.

The number of groups to be used is often determined by how much the client is willing to spend to conduct the research. Although many clients settle for two groups, program research consultants recommend conducting four or even six interview sessions.[5]

Groups should be no larger than 10 members, with 8 being an ideal number, so that the discussion is not unwieldy.[6] When there are fewer than eight participants, the cost of the interviews is unnecessarily high. When there are more than 10 people, some individuals in the group may not be drawn into the conversation and their input will be lost.

Focus group participants must travel from their homes to the session and be willing to participate at night, since it is difficult to schedule people during the day, when they are at work. The people who are recruited are offered a specified fee ranging from $25 to $40 or even more in some cities. The amount paid depends on the size of the metropolitan area and other conditions, such as the cost of living, that affect people's willingness to spend time at such a session.

Focus group sessions may be conducted at the office of a research firm, but in many cases the interview site is a meeting room at a local motel or another central location. A facilitator starts the conversation and attempts to elicit points of view from all the participants. The discussion is guided by research objectives that have been determined by the client. For example, a station's management may be interested in finding out whether the interaction between the anchorman, the anchorwoman, and the weather reporter on a local TV news program is effective, or the news director may want to know whether viewers perceive a loss in anchor credibility when the anchorwoman laughs at comments made by the anchorman.

It is very beneficial to provide focus group members with a common frame of reference for the discussion. Thus, the researcher may play an excerpt from the program on a video monitor. Similarly, a tape recording of music or of disc jockeys may be played to give all the participants a common orientation. The participants are then asked to react to what they have heard or watched.

The client should not participate in the discussion because it is too easy to become involved or even defensive when people are critical of a program or station. Seasoned researchers tell of having to restrain angry program directors or program producers who wanted to march into the interview room to reply directly to a participant who was critical of the show. Needless to say, that kind of reaction does not encourage individuals to speak their minds.

The ideal focus group interview room has a one-way mirror so that the client can observe the proceedings unobtrusively. Clients may be given a videotape or audiotape recording of the sessions as an alternative to observing the actual proceedings (Box 6-2).

Individual Focus Sessions

A refinement of the focus group interview technique is the *individual focus session*. Its objectives are the same as those of focus group sessions, but the interviewees participate in a one-on-one session that lasts about 45 minutes.

This technique allows for more thorough probing of a person's thoughts than can be done

---

BOX 6-2
FOCUS GROUP
INTERVIEWS

- An outside moderator, not someone involved in the program or with the station, should be used to ensure objectivity.
- The moderator should administer a questionnaire early in the session to compare with the comments made during the discussion. Otherwise, there is no way to ascertain whether some participants' comments were influenced by those of other group members. Some people are easily intimidated, especially by participants who grandstand to impress others.
- The moderator should not influence the responses of the group by interjecting personal opinions.
- Group size should be limited to about 10 participants. Sessions should last about 90 minutes.
- The minimum number of groups is two. It is impossible to judge whether a single group is reasonably representative of the population. Also, one or two participants in a group may dominate or otherwise influence the outcome. Ideally, the number of groups should range between four and eight, depending on the nature of the questions and the audiences of whom they are being asked and the client's willingness to pay for the sessions.
- Sessions should be conducted at a neutral site to avoid influencing or biasing the responses.
- Nonviewers or nonlisteners should be recruited to participate in the group along with known audience members. It is important to learn why people don't listen or watch.
- The number of topics to be discussed should be limited.
- Follow-up survey research will ascertain the degree to which the principal perceptions identified in the focus groups are present in the general population.

SOURCES: Adapted from James E. Fletcher and Roger D. Wimmer, *Focus Group Interviews in Radio Research* (Washington, DC: National Association of Broadcasters, 1981) and Jhan Hiber, *Winning Radio Research: Turning Research into Ratings and Revenues* (NAB, 1987). © 1981, 1987 National Association of Broadcasters. Used with permission. ∎

in a group session. Moreover, the individual session removes the influence of group pressure, which may prevent a shy person from discussing the program.

The cost of conducting individual interviews is greater than that for group sessions, and researcher fatigue can affect the reliability of responses. However, such limitations are outweighed by the amount of detail that is gathered.[7]

PERCEPTUAL STUDIES

After individual or group focus interviews or other sources of insight have identified problems or raised further research questions, the programmer of an electronic media outlet may wish to conduct a perceptual, or "image," study to evaluate its position in the market. A **perceptual study** can encompass assessments of the various elements that constitute the format or the program, including music, information, personalities, advertising, and contests.

How does the station or program "fit" in the minds of potential audience members in the competitive environment, which may have changed during the last year? RKO Radio Research vice president Terry Danner has compared perceptual research to going to the doctor for an annual checkup. The early symptoms of a serious illness can be diagnosed and treated before the patient's condition becomes dangerous.[8] A change in the anchor personnel on one local TV news program may affect not only the audience of that program but audiences of local news broadcasts on competing stations as well. Or perhaps the audience feels that the format on the top-ranked radio station has become stale. The strong personalities who have kept the station at the top for the past several years may have become tiresome to listeners. For these and similar questions, a representative survey can help determine the perceptions that are held by the members of the target audience.

Perceptual studies are generally carried out through interviews of 300 or more persons. The sample size is determined by the number and specificity of the segments of the audience to be examined and the cost of conducting the research.

Under most circumstances, station personnel are poorly equipped to field their own studies without consulting firms or individuals skilled in survey procedures. The time involved and the lack of detachment can be important deterrents, as can the expense of mounting a poorly designed study that does not glean objective, valid data for analysis and decision making.

RADIO PROGRAM PERFORMANCE MEASURES

By identifying the efficiency of a program in attracting and keeping an audience, a programmer can compare the programs that are in direct competition for the same target audience. The programmer can also compare performance against the trends of the whole audience.

One of the principal differences between television and radio program research lies in the ways in which programs are constructed. Television programs are scheduled in increments of half hours or whole hours. In contrast, the majority of radio programs are designed to appeal to a continuous flow of listeners entering and leaving the audience after short periods of listening. Unlike television, most radio programs have no clear beginning or ending because listeners continually tune in and out.

Quarter-Hour Maintenance

Since electronic media audiences are measured in quarter-hour increments, programmers want to carry as many of these persons through as many quarter-hour periods as possible. If listeners are kept for just 5 minutes in a new quarter-hour period (a **quarter-hour audience**), the station's ratings will be higher. Even if the listeners have been absent for two-thirds of the time period, the rules of the ratings game have been followed. Consequently, many radio programmers schedule popular songs to start near the end of quarter-hour periods. Since the recordings finish playing during the next quarter-hour period, they carry listeners into that time period. This is known as **quarter-hour maintenance.**

Turnover

One measure of audience habit is the length of time its members stay tuned. One means of identifying this trait is **turnover,** an estimate of the number of times the audience is replaced by new viewers or listeners during a specified period. To calculate turnover for the time period under consideration, the cume is divided by the AQH:

$$\text{Turnover} = \frac{\text{cume persons}}{\text{AQH persons}}$$

As shown in Table 6-1, Station WCHR-FM has a 12+ audience cume of 1121(00) and an AQH of 165(00) during the period from 6 to 10 a.m. Thus, WCHR-FM's turnover during that daypart is 6.8, which means that the audience changes almost seven times during the time period from 6 a.m. to 10 a.m.:

$$\text{Turnover} = \frac{1121}{165} = 6.8$$

A low turnover indicates a long time spent listening (TSL); one measure mirrors the other. In most markets the average turnover is around 2.5, but that does not specifically reflect the format of a station and the inclinations of specific segments of its audience.

The figures in Table 6-1 are rounded off in the same manner in which figures are reported by Arbitron and Nielsen. Since these figures are estimates and to save space in the computer printouts, the numbers are rounded by hundreds (00) in radio reports and by thousands (000) in television reports. For example, Table 6-1 reports that WURB-FM had a cume audience of 75 for men 18 to 34 during the daypart from 6 a.m. to 10 a.m. If the user of that data wishes to report on the actual number of listeners, she or he simply adds (00) to that number to get 7500, the estimate of different persons listening during that period. The result will be the same whether the zeros are included or dropped.

Time Spent Listening

Time spent listening (TSL) is an estimate of the length of time, in quarter hours, during which audience members watch a program. The calculation for TSL is only slightly more complex than the turnover formula. The number of quarter hours in the time period being considered is multiplied by the station's AQH estimate, and this figure is divided by the station's cume for the time period:

TABLE 6-1   Ratings Data, Monday through Friday, Morning and Afternoon Dayparts

	6 a.m.–10 a.m.						3 a.m.–7 p.m.					
	Persons 12+		Men 18–34		Women 18–34		Persons 12+		Men 18–34		Women 18–34	
	AQH (00)	Cume (00)	AQH (00)	Cume (00)	AQH (00)	Cume (00)	AQH (00)	Cume (00)	AQH (00)	Cume (00)	AQH (00)	Cume (00)
WCHR-FM	165	1121	32	115	48	304	161	1242	41	344	44	325
WURB-FM	160	774	27	75	46	233	139	717	31	212	45	217
WWAC-FM	253	1129	39	98	79	345	182	1090	37	291	67	364
WCTR-FM	295	1313	36	160	52	220	174	1149	24	163	40	220

$$\text{TSL} = \frac{\text{no. quarter hours in time period} \times \text{AQH}}{\text{cume persons}}$$

Thus, to calculate the TSL for 6 a.m. to 10 a.m., we start with the fact that there are 16 quarter hours (4 quarter hours per hour × 4 hours in the daypart). Then we look up the AQH audience and cume audience estimates from the appropriate report. For example, the AQH for WCHR-FM is 165(00) and the cume is 1121(00), as we have ascertained from Table 6-1.

$$\text{TSL} = \frac{16 \times 165}{1121} = 2.36, \text{ rounded to } 2.4$$

TSL can be calculated on the basis of daily or weekly listening or viewing. There are 80 quarter hours in the daypart Monday through Friday, 6 a.m. to 10 a.m., for instance (16 quarter hours × 5 days = 80), and so 80 can be substituted for the 16 used above. In the following example, audience members of WCHR-FM listen on average for about 35 minutes a day, or just under 12 quarter hours a week:

$$\text{TSL} = \frac{80 \times 165}{1121} = 11.78 \text{ quarter hours per week}$$

The turnover and TSL for each of the stations reported in Table 6-1 are shown in Table 6-2. As those figures show, there are some clear differences among the stations and among the audience segments that listen to each station.

Because turnover and TSL are closely related to a station's format and to the attributes of the particular market, the best way to determine whether either index is typical is to compare indexes for the station's audience with the indexes for all listeners to the format. Similar comparisons can be made among all listeners in the target demographics and for the whole listening audience.

Television programmers may wish to track the turnover of program audiences to determine how effectively a program maintains the audience that was inherited from the previous program. For instance, if it is found that the audience for *Laverne and Shirley* turns over during the succeeding local news program, the programmer should consider whether the news program is in the right place in the schedule or if the preceding situation comedy is attracting the kind of audience that wants to watch the news. In other words, there may be a better sequence of programming for maintaining an audience throughout that period.

Cable TV networks such as CNN and the Weather Channel do not expect their audiences to watch for very long periods. As a consequence, two strategies prevail. One is to provide programming that accommodates the fairly brief time spent viewing by presenting a cycle of weather or news report on a predictable basis. Thus, viewers know they will be rewarded with the information they seek within a short time after tuning in either service. The other strategy is to devise ways to make the content so interest-

TABLE 6-2 Turnover and TSL: 6 a.m.–10 a.m., Monday–Friday

	Persons 12+			Men 18–34			Women 18–34		
	Turn-over	Daily TSL	Weekly TSL	Turn-over	Daily TSL	Weekly TSL	Turn-over	Daily TSL	Weekly TSL
WCHR-FM	6.8	2.36	11.78	3.6	4.45	22.26	6.3	2.53	12.63
WURB-FM	4.8	3.31	16.54	2.8	5.76	28.80	5.1	3.16	15.79
WWAC-FM	4.5	3.59	17.93	3.3	4.90	24.49	4.4	3.66	18.32
WCTR-FM	4.5	3.59	17.97	4.4	3.60	18.00	4.2	3.78	18.91

ing that viewers will want to stay tuned longer. Among these programming ploys are Weather Channel documentaries that explain how a hurricane or a tornado works. These longer reports on weather-related topics go beyond an explanation of the current weather to provide interested viewers with background. On CNN, an hour-long nightly news program, *The World Today,* not only competes with broadcast network nightly news programs but gives CNN viewers a reason to stay tuned longer. Similarly, CNNs *Moneyline* report on the financial world and the midday *Sonya Live* and the evening *Larry King* interview programs sustain viewer interest and encourage regular viewing.

The turnover and TSL indexes provide direct help to radio programmers in determining how much variety to include in a program. Popular music radio listeners are rewarded for tuning in by being able to hear their favorite songs. Consequently, most stations try to schedule the most popular songs as frequently as possible. The top-10 or top-20 tunes usually receive the most airplay, but few listeners want to hear the same song twice during the time when they are tuned in. Thus, a long TSL indicates that the top-20 songs should be interspersed with other songs to prevent repeating any of them during a given period. Moreover, radio programmers can be guided by TSL and turnover in determining the number of times they should schedule promotional announcements, contests, humorous sketches, and other program material. The frequency of scheduling these items may be reduced or increased, depending on whether listeners are likely to hear them more than once while they are in the audience. The general trends in TSL shown in Table 6-3 serve as a predictor for major formats.

Programmers of Contemporary Hit Radio (CHR) formatted stations typically develop a shorter list of songs that are played on a regular basis to accommodate the relatively brief time during which their listeners are tuned in. The most popular tunes are assigned to a fast (hot) **rotation,** or frequency of air play, since listeners

TABLE 6-3   Average Time Spent Listening per Week

Format	No. Quarter Hours
Talk	40
Beautiful/Easy	40
Album-Oriented Rock	36
Country	30
News	26
Middle of the Road	25
Contemporary Hit/Top 40	22

SOURCE: Arbitron Ratings Company.

tune in to these stations expecting to hear their favorite music. Programming consultant Ed Shane recommends considering the TSL when one is determining the rotation of records but cautions that slavish adherence to a formula can be a self-fulfilling prophecy: If the programmer reduces the hot rotation to, say, 60 minutes, this can guarantee a TSL of no longer than 60 minutes.[9]

The number of people who work in offices offers many stations a potential to build a large midday audience. The programmer of a station that is pursuing that strategy will schedule a greater variety of songs to minimize the possibility that listeners will hear the same tune while they are in the audience. Repetitions are noticeable despite the background nature of the format and should be avoided if possible.

Whereas the news department of a radio station with a high turnover (and thus a low TSL) may be able to repeat a newscast, stations with listeners who stay tuned longer should have a policy of freshening and updating the news stories with each newscast to prevent listeners from feeling that they are being given redundant information.

Audience Recycling

Along with other indexes of audience loyalty summarized in Box 6-3, an important calculation to aid in program decisions is *recycling.* For

---

BOX 6-3
INDEXES OF
PROGRAM LOYALTY

- *Turnover:* the total number of different groups that make up a station's audience
- *TSL:* an estimate of the number of quarter hours the average person spends listening or viewing during a specified time period
- *Recycling:* the portion of the audience in one daypart that also listens or watches in another daypart; a measure of audience flow from one daypart to another
- *Exclusive listeners:* the station's "franchise"—the proportion of persons who listen to a station exclusively   ■

---

radio, the most important occurrence of recycling comes between the morning and late-afternoon periods (6 a.m. to 10 a.m. and 3 p.m. to 7 p.m.). Audience members listen to their favorite station in the morning while getting ready for and traveling to work, and many tune in again in the afternoon as they return home.[10] For television, it is a question of how much of the audience for the early-evening local news also watches the late-evening newscast.

To calculate audience recycling, one must look up the cume of the combined dayparts, which is a separate measure of cume. This figure is found in the daypart combination section of audience reports and should be subtracted from the sum of the cumes for the two dayparts. That figure should be divided by the cume of one of the two dayparts:

$$\% \text{ Recycling} = \frac{\begin{array}{c}\text{cume daypart 1 + cume daypart 2}\\ - \text{ cume of combined dayparts}\end{array}}{\text{cume of one period}}$$

Typically, radio programmers are interested in recycling between morning drive and afternoon drive. Thus, the cume for 6 a.m. to 10 a.m. would be added to the cume for 3 p.m. to 7 p.m. minus the combined dayparts cume. This figure would then be divided by the cume for 6 a.m. to 10 a.m. to yield the percentage of the audience that was recycled from the earlier to the later period.

If a high proportion of the audience is recycled in the afternoon, it will probably be more effective to have a different configuration of program events scheduled during that period. For instance, if the music rotation pattern, program features, and contests presented on a radio station in the morning are repeated during the afternoon, they may seem redundant to those in the audience who heard this content earlier in the day.

As the figures comparing stations in Table 6-4 show, a comparatively low percentage (39.8 percent) of WWAC-FM's audience is recycled into

---

TABLE 6-4   Percent of Recycling in Morning and Afternoon Dayparts among Men Age 18 to 34 (00)

	Cume Monday–Friday 6–10 a.m.	+	Cume Monday–Friday 3–7 p.m.	–	Cume Combined Dayparts	÷	Cume Monday–Friday 6–10 a.m.	=	Recycling, %
WCHR-FM	115		344	= 459	398	= 61	÷ 115		= 53.0
WURB-FM	75		212	= 287	249	= 38	÷ 75		= 50.7
WWAC-FM	98		291	= 389	350	= 39	÷ 98		= 39.8
WCTR-FM	160		163	= 323	212	= 111	÷ 160		= 69.4

the afternoon daypart from the morning drive. Thus, as our example shows, WWAC-FM's audience of men 18 to 34 had the least loyalty between dayparts, while WCTR-FM's audience had the highest rate, with 69.4 percent recycling from the morning to afternoon dayparts.

It is especially important for WCTR-FM's programmer to schedule music, news, and other program content so that listeners don't feel they have heard it all before when they tune in again. WWAC-FM can be less concerned about giving its afternoon listeners a sense of redundancy, but that station could heavily promote its morning show during the afternoon and its afternoon programming during the morning to entice listeners to tune in during the other daypart. A tactic that may help accomplish this would be to run contests that require participants to listen during both dayparts.

Exclusive Listeners

If a programmer is contemplating a change in format, it is wise to first consider the number of **exclusive listeners,** or people who report listening to that station only:

$$\text{Exclusive listeners} = \frac{\text{exclusive cume}}{\text{total cume}}$$

This calculation tells the programmer the size of the program's most loyal audience and points to growth or stability in the audience. That is, a program's audience may be large, but as it matures, it will eventually decline if few new listeners or viewers sample that program.[11] When a programmer determines that the audience is stagnating, steps should be taken to revise the content to attract new viewers. Once they have been identified, such problems can be examined further through follow-up research, such as focus group interview sessions.

A decision to change formats is based on the assumption that a new audience can be attracted even though many currently loyal listeners may be alienated. The potential loss of audience, even if it is considered only a temporary setback

TABLE 6-5 Exclusive Listeners: Exclusive Weekly Cume Estimates for 12+ (00), Monday–Sunday, 6 a.m.–Midnight

	Exclusive Cume	Total Cume	Exclusive Listeners, %
WCHR-FM	577	2206	26
WURB-FM	247	1449	17
WWAC-FM	296	1658	18
WCTR-FM	641	2009	32

resulting from the change in the appeal of the program, can be understood by considering the percentage of exclusive listeners to the station. The figures reported in Table 6-5 indicate that a change in formats would hurt WURB-FM and WWAC-FM the least, since those stations' respective proportions of 17 percent and 18 percent of exclusive listeners are much smaller than those of WCHR-FM (26 percent) and WCTR-FM (32 percent). Although WURB-FM and WWAC-FM's cume audiences are smaller than those of the other two stations, they are not markedly so. Therefore, neither station would probably change formats solely because their audiences were not as loyal as those of other stations.

WCTR-FM's 32 percent exclusive listeners would caution against a change in format. Its cume audience is the second highest of the stations reported, and it has the highest exclusive listenership. Because a market or format leader must innovate to maintain that position, it seems especially important that WCTR-FM keep a high profile in the market to entice other stations' listeners to tune in. Without an influx of new listeners, the station's performance will eventually stagnate.

The other stations are not necessarily doing anything that suggests that they make major alterations in their formats even though they share a greater proportion of their audiences with competitors. It may be worth investigating why listeners sample other stations. By examining the Arbitron market mechanical diary, the programmer can identify the other stations that audience members are also listening to.

By targeting audience members shared with the competition, a station may be able to determine a strategy to expand its exclusive listenership. For instance, as we have already noted, WWAC-FM has a low portion of exclusive listeners. If it was discovered that this Adult Contemporary formatted station shared a high percentage of its audience with WCTR-FM, a Country station, WWAC-FM's programmer could consider adding a number of songs that were also aired on WCTR-FM. That way, WWAC-FM might fulfill the wishes of a larger number of listeners who satisfied their listening needs by tuning in WCTR-FM part of the time.

Efficiency of Target Audience

Another measure of the effectiveness of a station in reaching desired listeners is provided by a formula that calculates a program's **efficiency of target audience (ETA)** (Box 6-4):

$$ETA = \frac{\text{target audience TSL}}{\text{total audience TSL}}$$

The higher the ETA, the better the program is reaching its target audience. Thus, the ETA can help a station determine which demographic segments are being reached most efficiently. Moreover, the ETAs of different stations with similar target audiences can be compared to help determine whether the current programming strategy should be changed. Table 6-6 displays ETA figures for four stations that were calculated for two target demographic segments: men 18 to 34 and women 18 to 34. First, the TSL for each target demographic and for listeners 12 and over must be calculated (Table 6-2). Then, if

we divide the target audience TSL by the total audience TSL, the ETA for each station is determined (Table 6-6).

The ETA figures reported in Table 6-6 indicate that WCHR-FM is the most efficient of the four stations in reaching its target audience. Moreover, WCHR-FM is much more efficient in reaching men 18 to 34 than it is in reaching women 18 to 34. If the programmer of this CHR station wants to increase its efficiency in reaching targeted women, the programming should be changed somewhat. As Table 6-6 shows, WCHR's ETA of 1.07 for women 18 to 34 is considerably lower than the ETA of 1.89 for male listeners. Although the data do not indicate the nature of the music being played on WCHR, we can speculate that it includes a fairly heavy proportion of hard rock music, which men find more appealing than most women do. If this is the case, the programmer might consider "softening" the station's air sound. This could be accomplished by including more soft rock tunes and limiting the airplay of the harder rock music selections.

The similarity of the ETA for men and women 18 to 34 suggests that WCTR-FM has found a good formula for evenly appealing to its audience. By contrast, the 1.0 ETA for men 18 to 34 indicates that WCTR-FM is much less efficient than its competitors in reaching men although it holds its own in reaching women 18 to 34. This comparison points to the possibility that the age segment men 18 to 34 is not the appropriate target audience for this station. WCTR-FM's audience niche can be better determined by analyzing all the audience segments to ascertain where it has the highest ETA.

Three of the four stations whose ETAs are shown in Table 6-6 share a pattern in that they are much more efficient in reaching male than

---

**BOX 6-4
PURPOSE OF
EFFICIENCY OF
TARGET AUDIENCE**

- Identify the demographic segment that is most efficiently reached by a station
- Compare different dayparts to determine the time of greatest ETA
- Compare the ETAs of different stations with similar target audiences   ■

TABLE 6-6 Efficiency of Target Audience for Men 18–34 and Women 18–34, Monday–Friday, 6–10 a.m.

		TSL Target Audience	÷	TSL Persons 12+	=	ETA
WCHR-FM	Men 18–34	4.45		2.36		1.89
	Women 18–34	2.53		2.36		1.07
WURB-FM	Men 18–34	5.76		3.31		1.74
	Women 18–34	3.16		3.31		0.95
WWAC-FM	Men 18–34	4.90		3.59		1.36
	Women 18–34	3.66		3.59		1.02
WCTR-FM	Men 18–34	3.60		3.59		1.00
	Women 18–34	3.78		3.59		1.05

female listeners 18 to 34. If women 18 to 34 is a highly desired target demographic, a careful look at the program content would be in order, and perhaps the content should be altered. As was discussed in detail earlier in this chapter, focus group interviews can help identify why targeted audience groups aren't listening. In focus group sessions, persons in the target audience would be asked to explain why they like or dislike various aspects of the station's programming.

Location of Radio Listening

Arbitron reports radio listening at work in addition to listening at home, in the car, and in other places. This information helps stations determine adjustments to their formats during different dayparts so that they can base their appeal to listeners on what these people are doing while they listen.

Let us suppose that men 25 to 54 constitute a station's target audience (Table 6-7). The AQH estimates are drawn from the "location of listening" page in an audience ratings report for each station and for the total persons using radio (PUR). The percentage of AQH represented by each listening location for each station is also reported; it is calculated by dividing the AQH for the listening location by the sum of the AQH for the daypart.

It is important to program the daypart to accommodate listeners where they are. In the morning daypart, for instance, WCHR-FM will probably want to program to the high proportion of commuters listening in their cars (37 percent) and in the workplace (52 percent), because only 11 percent of its audience's listening occurs in the home during that time period. Since the station has a high proportion of listening in other places, that probably includes the workplace. The proportion of listening in other places rises even higher, to 72 percent, during the midday period from 10 a.m. to 3 p.m., further indicating listening in the workplace.

Again assuming a target audience of men 25 to 54, WCHR-FM's music director should carefully screen the music being aired during the morning and midday dayparts to minimize its obtrusiveness. Hard rock songs could be saved for later in the broadcast day since much of that kind of music is distracting to people in the workplace. If it is played, many of those who are listening at work may turn the station off. Similarly, WCHR-FM and other stations will probably instruct their disc jockeys to hold talking to a minimum, since for many listeners chatter is distracting and interrupts their work.

The programmer can calculate the time spent listening before deciding how rapidly the music should be rotated. Since many people are listening in the workplace, they probably stay tuned for long periods. Consequently, the programmer wants to avoid playing records so frequently that listeners hear them more than once while they are in the audience. Many stations not only have addressed this pattern of TSL but have capitalized on it by promoting "no-repeat workdays." This tactic positions the station as one that provides entertainment for people who are at work without annoying them by repeating overly familiar music.

In contrast to WCHR-FM, the programmers of WURB-FM will probably want to concentrate on providing program content directed at people listening in the home during the morning since the highest proportion of this station's listening (73 percent) occurs there. Therefore, WURB-FM could run contests that require listeners to call the station in order to participate, whereas the majority of WCHR-FM's listeners may not be able to become involved in that kind of contest because they cannot use a telephone at work or are not near one while in their cars.

During afternoon drive (3 p.m. to 7 p.m.), the proportion of WCHR-FM's audience that listens in other places declines from 72 percent to 43 percent while car listening almost doubles from 26 percent to 41 percent as workers make the trip home. A similar pattern can be seen for the other stations in the market. Consequently, the programmers of each station should consider scheduling the kind of information that commuters are interested in, including traffic conditions and weather reports. Moreover, since many of these listeners may not have had access to a radio during the day, they are interested in catching up on news and sports information so that they can feel they are in touch with the world.

RADIO MUSIC RESEARCH

Regardless of the format, the essential ingredient needed to attract and keep an audience is content that listeners want to hear. Since the

TABLE 6-7 Location of Listening

AQH Estimates (00) for Men 25–54								
	6–10 a.m.			10 a.m.–3 p.m.			3–7 p.m.		
	Home	Car	Other	Home	Car	Other	Home	Car	Other
WCHR-FM	5	17	24	1	15	42	7	19	20
WURB-FM	19	4	3	17	9	2	12	13	—
WWAC-FM	24	17	22	9	24	36	11	29	14
WCTR-FM	20	24	41	15	14	63	25	21	21
PUR	141	146	105	73	98	173	121	150	83

Percentage of AQH								
	6–10 a.m.			10 a.m.–3 p.m.			3–7 p.m.		
	Home	Car	Other	Home	Car	Other	Home	Car	Other
WCHR-FM	11	37	52	2	26	72	15	41	43
WURB-FM	73	15	12	61	32	7	48	52	—
WWAC-FM	38	27	35	13	35	52	20	54	26
WCTR-FM	24	28	48	16	15	68	37	31	31
PUR	36	37	27	21	28	50	34	42	23

predominant ingredient in most radio programming formulas is music, ongoing research on audience preferences has become very important. If they tire of a particular song or if a station plays too many tunes that lack appeal, listeners are likely to drift away and join a competitor's audience.

Call-Out Research

Call-out research monitors the popularity of the specific songs a station airs (Box 6-5). It is generally conducted in-house by members of the station's staff who survey listeners to keep abreast of their music preferences. The technique is especially useful in identifying the appeal of a song and its **burnout,** or the point at which listeners begin to tire of a recording. Thus, the objective of call-out research is to nurture the core audience or widen it by gaining a better understanding of the preferences of the target audience.

Most important is the insight this kind of research can provide programmers in their decisions to schedule particular recordings in the music mix. Knowing the kind of music that listeners especially like is invaluable. Equally important, the programmer may discover that certain popular songs are *irritants.* Many early-morning listeners, for instance, may not be ready for the jolt of a hard rock song because they like to start the day slowly. Similarly, adult listeners who do most of their listening during the morning may not like rap songs. Therefore, if a song is found to irritate segments of the audience who are heavy listeners during the early morning, a decision may be made not to play it during that daypart.

A secondary benefit of call-out interviews is the information they yield on the time of day when audience members begin listening, whether they have the station tuned in on a clock radio, and other listening behaviors. Call-out research can also help programmers market their stations by asking questions such as, "If you now listen to WBBB, who were you listening to before?" Such a question can help WBBB's programmer understand why certain groups of listeners have switched their allegiance from a competing station.

Sampling Since most programming strategies are based on the identification of a target audience, a random sampling and screening procedure should be used in call-out research to limit the survey sample to people who are part of a station's desired audience. At the least, they should be people who listen to the format or at least to the kind of music being programmed by that station. To obtain such a sample for a Country music formatted station, random-digit dialing techniques can be used to reach households, and the interviewer can ask to speak to a person who is between the ages of, say, 18 and 54. When a person who meets that qualification has been reached, he or she can be asked whether he or she listens to Country music. If the response is no, the interview will be terminated; if it is yes, that individual will become part of the sample.[12] The sample should be balanced so that the responses from people in the range of ages and the proportion of male and female respondents reflect the preferences of the target audience. Program consultants recommend that at least 100 respondents be interviewed to ensure statistical validity.[13]

Panel research There are two philosophies of defining the sample for call-out research. A station can select a new sample for each weekly or

---

**BOX 6-5
PURPOSE OF CALL-
OUT RESEARCH**

- Identify and track the familiarity of a song
- Obtain listeners' positive or negative reaction to a song
- Test the burnout tolerance of a recording

biweekly call-out study, but sample selection is a fairly costly process because of the necessity to screen respondents. A less expensive alternative is a **panel** study, which surveys the same respondents periodically over a span of time. In the case of call-out panels, sample members are asked about their music preferences, usually on a weekly basis.[14]

The length of time a respondent can be included in the sample is fairly brief, typically 4 to 6 weeks. Periodic replacement of panel members keeps the evaluation fresh by reducing the likelihood that participants will become "experts" on music.[15] Individuals who know they will be asked about the latest records being played on a station are more likely to listen attentively and may even begin reading articles about pop music and seeking information from other sources. This behavior would be detrimental to the **validity** of the research, or whether it actually is measuring what the researcher thinks it is measuring. The programmer needs to know the preferences of normal listeners who give little thought to what they hear on the radio.

Active and passive respondents **Active** samples consist of known listeners. These listeners can include persons who have participated in station contests or have called to request that songs be played. The advantage of using an active sample is that the preferences of the listeners whom the station wishes to keep in its audience can be monitored. The greatest disadvantage is that this group is already loyal. It will presumably be satisfied with the program content, and its preferences will not provide insight into how to attract others.

Furthermore, participation in contests and the phoning in of requests for songs require a commitment that many audience members do not have. Thus, the profile of contest participants or people who call on the request line may be very different from that of regular listeners. The procedure is described here not to recommend it but because it is used by various practitioners.

The more valid sampling technique for call-out research is random sampling of the potential listeners in the station's target audience. Thus, a **passive** sample consists of *possible* listeners. This sample is drawn by means of random selection and screening procedures, as described above.

Call-out procedure In a weekly system, respondents are called to solicit their responses to particular songs. A recording of the **hook,** or the most recognizable portion of a record, is played for the respondent over the telephone. Hooks need only be long enough (about 8 to 10 seconds) to enable the respondent to identify the song. Most research consultants recommend that a maximum of 25 to 30 music hooks be played during an interview to optimize respondent interest and participation.[16]

Each respondent is asked to indicate a preference for each song according to criteria like those shown in Box 6-6. In this way, a sizable sample of listeners can be contacted each week in a fairly short period.

BOX 6-6
CALL-OUT RESEARCH
RESPONSES

Rating	Interpretation
0	Never heard of it before
1	Would change stations if I heard that song
2	Don't like it but would listen to it
3	Used to like it but am burned out on it
4	Neutral
5	Like the song
6	One of my favorites

Interpretation of call-out research The value of call-out research lies in the perspective it gives its users. The popularity of records can be identified, and that information can be used to determine how frequently they should come up in the music rotation. Within 2 or 3 weeks a programmer can have an idea of whether a recording that has been added to the group being broadcast by the station is liked, lacks appeal, or is a listener irritant. Otherwise, unappealing music may continue to be aired until other information about its appeal, such as record sales, becomes available.

Like other forms of research, call-out research is subject to limitations and must be interpreted carefully. Researcher James E. Fletcher points out that familiarity is an essential ingredient in the appeal of popular music. When familiarity is low, respondents' rankings tend to fluctuate unpredictably, but as familiarity increases, "liking" scores tend to stabilize.[17] Thus, the call-out technique is least effective in testing new releases since listener familiarity is linked to the amount of airplay a record has received. It is most effective in identifying songs in the station's current rotation that should be placed in its "power" (most frequent) rotation category, those which should be aired less frequently because listeners are beginning to tire of them, and those which should be removed from airplay altogether.

Auditorium Music Testing

A related music research technique is **auditorium music testing,** in which groups of people in a station's target audience are gathered in one place to listen to hooks or entire recordings. As with call-out research, the purpose is to determine the relative appeal of music. A major differ-

ence, though, is that auditorium research is most often applied to making predictions on the appeal of records before they are added to a station's on-air library, whereas call-out research monitors the acceptance and appeal of songs currently being aired by a station (Box 6-7).

Auditorium testing is a useful way to identify oldies records that have high appeal to a station's target audience. Some oldies are so obscure that targeted listeners may not be familiar with them, and others may receive so much airplay that listeners are tired of hearing them.

Testing by program consultation companies is carried out for client stations in their markets, but stations in small markets that can't afford custom research can still obtain reports on auditorium tests. Although these tests are more general, the sample approximates the tastes of listeners in the target audience, and the station is able to use this kind of information to make better decisions about the music it should play.

Procedure In auditorium studies, a large number of songs—around 200 titles, although some consultants recommend 300 to 400—can be evaluated. Respondents rate the songs on a positive to negative scale, such as the one shown in Box 6-8, which is used by Paragon Research, a leading research consulting firm.[18]

The usual sample size for an auditorium music test is 100 or more persons, who should be chosen from a fairly narrow group that is representative of the station's target audience, say, 25- to 44-year-old men and women.

The most effective, although most expensive, sampling procedure for auditorium music testing is to screen target audience members through a random selection procedure. As in focus group research, the amount of money nec-

**BOX 6-7
PURPOSE OF
AUDITORIUM
RESEARCH**

- Identify music familiarity, burnout, and overall popularity among target audiences
- Determine the rotation of songs in a station's music library ■

**BOX 6-8
AUDITORIUM MUSIC
TEST RESPONSES**

- Favorite
- Like
- Dislike
- Hate
- Tiring (burnout)
- Unfamiliar

---

essary to make it worth a person's time to participate depends on the particular market.

Interpretation of auditorium research As with call-out research, auditorium research is best considered as a means of gaining insight. It does not provide definitive answers about program content. Some people don't feel comfortable in a large gathering, and those who are willing to express their opinions in a public setting are not considered to be representative of typical listeners.[19] Only with the most rigorous controls can an auditorium study provide statistically generalizable results. However, it can provide a programmer with a sense of direction and eliminate some of the guesswork involved in building a station's music library.[20]

Auditorium research results are helpful when a station is contemplating a switch in formats or an expansion of its format to broaden its demographic appeal. New music styles may be added to an existing format, or a new format may be created to position the station more effectively in the market. Before such steps are taken, auditorium testing of the appeal of specific recordings can point to whether they will work in the proposed format. Let's say a station uses a "traditional" Country format that features mostly older Country music and finds that its core audience is men and women 55 and over. To appeal to younger listeners, the station may test songs that are ranked on the current Country music charts along with variety of Top-40 and "gold" rock songs to determine how they will appeal to a new target audience such as men and women 25 to 54. It may be found, for example, that the targeted listeners like certain current Country songs as well as specific older rock tunes by such performers as the Allman Brothers, Jim Croce, and Kansas. It may even be found that songs by Paul Simon and Bette Midler are also liked by this group. With this information, the programmer can devise a music mix that will attract members of the target audience by giving the station a much more contemporary sound without the listener-perceived stigma of sounding Country.

TELEVISION PROGRAM RESEARCH

Just as call-out and music auditorium research are highly useful to radio because of the nature of that medium's program structure and audience usage, other research methods are advantageous in television program research. This section will look at determinants of the strength of the appeal of programs and performers, tests of program concepts that are carried out before producers go to the expense of actually producing a program, and research on the appeal of program pilots.

Program and Performer Popularity

The producer of a network variety **special,** a one-time-only program produced to be broadcast in place of a regularly scheduled program, is faced with the problem of choosing a personality to host the program and selecting others to be guests. If these performers are known and liked by the viewing public, there is a good chance that a large number of viewers will watch the program. But how does one objectively determine who is popular?

Marketing Evaluations/TvQ, Inc., offers a

qualitative research service based on the "favorite" concept. Its argument is that the more favorably disposed people are toward a television program, the more likely they are to tune in, pay attention, and watch the commercials in it.

TvQ TvQ is a measure of the degree of audience liking of programs and performers. A national mail panel of about 1600 persons evaluates programs and performers in accordance with the following criteria:

1 One of my favorites
2 Very good
3 Good
4 Fair
5 Poor
6 Program I have never seen (someone you have never seen or heard perform)

Three indexes, based on the responses to the scale shown in Box 6-8, are reported. The *familiarity score* is the percentage of respondents who expressed any opinion about the program, the *favorite score* is the percentage of the sample that said the program was "one of my favorites," and the *TvQ score* is derived from the percentage of respondents indicating that a program was "one of my favorites" divided by the percentage of those who indicated being familiar with the program. Thus,

$$TvQ = \frac{\% \text{ "one of my favorite performers"}}{\% \text{ have any opinion}}$$

TvQ data are used to indicate the potential of programs to reach target audiences and those viewers' probable involvement in the programs. Networks have decided not to cancel some programs because they received encouraging TvQ scores. Among the series that were saved by their TvQ scores are *CHiPs, All in the Family,* and *Hill Street Blues.* These shows and more recent ones such as *Tour of Duty* and *China Beach* were given a chance by their networks because tests indicated that even though they had low recognizability, people familiar with the shows liked them, giving them a high TvQ score.[21] If a

program scores a high TvQ among children, it may be moved to a time period where it will have the best chance to attract that audience. For example, if *The Simpsons* or *Cosby* received low scores among children, neither would be scheduled at the start of prime time (8 p.m.). The networks schedule programs with high appeal to children between 8 p.m. and 9 p.m. Eastern time because so many children are in the TV audience at that time and exert a considerable influence over which programs are tuned in.

Performer Q The other ranking service proved by Marketing Evaluations is the Performer Q. Respondents are asked to rank performers on a scale ranging from whether the person is "one of your favorites" (1) to "someone you have never seen or heard perform" (6):

$$Performer\ Q = \frac{\% \text{ "one of my favorite performers"}}{\% \text{ have any opinion}}$$

In addition to Performer Q, personalities are rated according to audience recognition and appeal. A listing of "high recognition–low appeal" and "low recognition–high appeal" performers is thus derived. For instance, exercise show host Richard Simmons has a high familiarity rating of 80 but a Performer Q of only 8. Bill Cosby, by contrast, has a recognizability score of 96 and a Performer Q of 57, the highest of any personality thus measured.[22]

Local station applications TvQ measurement of theatrical movies shown during prime time offers TV stations a way to identify demographic appeal when scheduling films. An independent station that offers a midmorning movie probably wants to avoid scheduling a film that has been found to have low appeal to women age 35 to 54 since the audience available during that period consists predominantly of older women.

TvQ representatives argue that even though many television shows attract only marginal audiences during a network run, they may appeal strongly to particular audience segments, making them successful when broadcast locally. By identifying these demographic groups, TvQ can help a programmer find "bargain" programs. That is, low-rated network series are generally cheaper than more successful network shows. If the broadcast rights can be obtained at a discount and the program attracts key demographic segments, the station's profits may be greater than they would if it scheduled a program that attracted a larger audience during a network run. The more successful a network program has been in attracting an audience, the more the postnetwork distributor will want to charge the station since it will be offered for sale with a "proven" ability to attract large audiences.

Concept Testing

ABC, CBS, and NBC all require between 20 and 30 new series each year, and the newer Fox Television Network also needs several as it expands its schedule. The network program departments each consider about 2000 program ideas during this process. One of the ways in which such decisions on can be made objectively is through **concept testing.**

Program development starts with the program **concept,** or a summary of the show's premise, followed by the commission of a script and its rewrites. A program concept is a brief statement of one or two paragraphs that describes the program idea. An example of a concept is shown in Box 6-9.

In concept testing, respondents are asked to rate the idea after hearing or reading the statement. Not surprisingly, many concepts do not test well, but some of the measures may identify attributes that elicit more or less favorable responses among potential viewers. Since the promotion and advertising of programs contribute mightily to their success, concept research may point to areas of emphasis. For example, potential viewers who may not be attracted to a program on the basis of its social message may watch because of the program's romantic interest or exotic locale.

Concept testing is important for "one-shot" programs, such as made-for-TV movies, where tune-in is greatly influenced by advertising and promotion. Testing can identify the conceptual statements that will work best in promoting a program.[23] Still, concept testing is only one factor in the development of a series; the casting of actors to play the characters and the execution of the premise are crucial to its success.

Pilot Testing

After a concept has been developed and an initial script has been written and revised, but before the program assembly line begins to turn out a

---

**BOX 6-9
CONCEPT
DESCRIPTION FOR
*THIRTYSOMETHING***

This prospect focuses on the emotional problems of a couple in their 30's as they face the transition from the easy freedom they knew when they were both single to the responsibilities now thrust upon them by marriage. It seemed so simple to Michael and Hope when life was nothing more than going to work in the daytime and having a date that night. But now there is a home of their own to maintain with mortgage payments to meet, a leak somewhere in the roof and a back hedge that always seems to need trimming. Above all, there is that crib in the bedroom and that brand-new baby. What about a reliable baby sitter? How do you find one? Simple questions are puzzling to Michael and Hope and they underscore the basic theme of this concept: a warm look at the life of a couple learning how to build a family unit step by step. They will get lots of advice from their acquaintances, from Hope's two best girlfriends, Ellyn and Melissa, who are still single, and above all from Nancy and Elliot who are married and have two children.

SOURCE: From *Leo Burnett 1987–1988 Television Program Report* (Chicago: Leo Burnett U.S.A., 1987), pp. 46–47. Reprinted courtesy of Leo Burnett Co., TV Programming Department. ■

series, a **pilot,** or prototype, program is produced to represent what the series will be like. Pilot testing is done by the four networks before episodes are ordered from their producers and a series is scheduled. Whether a program makes it on the air often depends on how well it scores in theater tests, cable system showings, and focus interview groups. This is not to say that every pilot tests well; every year a number of programs get on the air in spite of testing poorly. Some are put on for prestige reasons, such as ABC's *Twin Peaks,* or to fulfill contractual obligations. ABC's 5-year deal with producer Steven Bochco, whose earlier credits included two major hits for NBC, *Hill Street Blues* and *L.A. Law,* saw his low-testing *Cop Rock* make its debut in the 1990 fall season because ABC was obligated and wanted to keep him happy so that other hits would be forthcoming.[24]

Theater tests A long-lived method for testing how well the audience will accept a new program is referred to as **theater testing.** The best known site for such tests is ASI Market Research, Inc.'s, "Preview House" in Los Angeles. Four hundred persons recruited from shopping centers or through telephone contact gather to watch pilots for television series. While watching a program, each participant controls a dial with five positions ranging from "Very Good" to "Very Dull." As the participants watch, a computer records viewer responses to the characters, their relationships, believability, the plot, and subplots.

After the screening, participants complete a questionnaire and then are broken into small groups of about 10 to participate in focus interviews. These sessions can help identify reasons why audience members reacted positively or negatively during certain points in the programs they just watched.

Cable system tests Cable tests are considered by many program researchers to be the closest approximation of real-life TV viewing. These studies are conducted in various cities across the country by running a program on an unused cable channel. Viewers are recruited in advance and then interviewed the day after they watch the program.

In addition to testing pilots, NBC tests episodes of series; this can help identify the characters and plot lines that work best. For example, respondents in the test audience indicated that they did not like the jobs held by Larry and Balky on *Perfect Strangers,* and so the producers gave them new ones. Other shows have dropped characters who didn't test well.[25]

In-home tape placement With videotape player penetration in U.S. households at over 70 percent, researchers have an alternative to cable and theater testing. Pilot or program episode testing can be accomplished by sending participants a videotape recording of a program to watch at home. As compensation, the viewers are generally given cash and get to keep the videotape. In some studies, viewers are interviewed by telephone after they have seen the tape. In other studies, respondents are invited to participate in a focus group interview or an individual focus session.

In most cases it is counterproductive to take the time to show participants an hour-long program during a focus group session since this will eat up a great deal of the available interview time. If the researcher tries to push the length of the session beyond the usual 90 minutes, boredom or fatigue may lower the cooperation of group members. Consequently, an advantage of in-home tape placement is that cooperating respondents arrive at the focus group site with a common viewing experience. Moreover, since the respondents are likely to watch with greater attention, they should be prepared to discuss more details in the program, making the interview session more productive.

In-home tape placement is an expensive procedure, but it can elicit considerable detail on the program being studied, and viewers can be asked to watch tapes containing several programs. Furthermore, different executions of a program can be tested by distributing the various versions to different groups of respondents.

Program Maintenance

Because the failure rate is so high, the development of new TV series is a very risky financial venture. Producers and networks want to nurture successful programs and keep them on the air as long as possible. Research can identify the strengths and weaknesses of ongoing series, enabling producers to nurture these programs and keep them on the air.

A problem prevalent in ongoing series is that the plots or situations in which the principal characters are placed can become stale. Other characters may be introduced to the show, continuing characters may have to be written out because an actor wishes to leave the show, or supporting characters may be given more important roles. Under such circumstances, it is important to assess how viewers will react. Thus, a show such as CBS's *Knot's Landing* is tested monthly through focus group interviews, and the characters and the plot lines are adjusted as a result.

When actress Valerie Harper left her CBS TV show *Valerie* after a contract dispute, she was replaced by Sandy Duncan and the show was renamed *The Hogan Family*. But before it was decided to go ahead with the production, the new version of the show was tested, and it was determined that audiences would accept the change in one of the principal characters. The show enjoyed a successful run with Ms. Duncan in the cast, its life renewed by the knowledge that the risk of losing its audience as a result of the change was minimal.

At the local level, when a popular local TV news anchor leaves the market for an opportunity elsewhere, the station must find the right replacement. Many stations try to minimize the risk of introducing a news program personality in the market by testing audience reaction to candidates for the job. In some cases, talented anchorpeople have not been given a position because samples of local viewers indicated that they felt no rapport with the person, who came across as lacking interest in the community. In one such case, the anchorperson was perceived as being "too objective" and respondents could not identify with him. If a rapport cannot be established between the news anchor and the audience, a ratings decline is almost inevitable.

Program Schedule Analysis

Programmers at network-affiliated stations can avail themselves of the programming expertise of their **rep firms.** Major **station rep** companies such as Katz, Blair Television, and TeleRep sell local station advertising time to national advertisers. Since rep firms make their money from advertising commissions, a number of them have built up programming departments because the prices their client stations can charge for advertising is based on the size of the audience a program gathers. The rep firms conduct analyses of *syndicated programs,* which show how well such programs have performed in other markets. For instance, a TV programmer who is considering acquiring the rights to *Alf* or *Golden Girls* can analyze both series' ratings, including their success in different dayparts.

Also based on performance in other markets, audience flow studies can show how the placement of a syndicated program is likely to perform in a station's schedule. For example, a TV station in the 87th market could track the performance of *Who's the Boss?* in similar-sized markets. This assessment could include a look at the strength of the preceding program's audience, which would be expected to stay tuned for the next program, as well as the audience strength of the program that followed *Who's the Boss?* since it would be expected to receive much of that audience.

Research and the Creative Community

Many members of television's creative community do not like program research. Researchers argue that this is because the results may not support producers' decisions. Producers argue that instinct and experience provide better insight. Producer Bob Shanks's perspective typifies that of his peers:

Executives who are trained up through law, research, accounting, or sales generally rely more heavily on this so-called objective evidence; those who have come up through the creative ranks usually rely more on instinct, a sense of actually experiencing what audiences like by having exposed themselves to audiences.[26]

Despite producers' antipathy, research will continue to be an important factor in making programming decisions. It is the only means of reducing risk when so much is at stake financially.

SUMMARY

Research is a tool that helps a programmer identify programming that will be successful in attracting the desired audience, reducing the risk of failing to achieve that objective.

A number of measures are used to determine the efficiency of programs in attracting and maintaining audience members. Many programming techniques are built around attracting and keeping the largest quarter-hour audience possible. Turnover is an indicator of how often the audience changes during a specified time period, while time spent listening (TSL) reflects the average amount of time listeners are tuned in. The higher the turnover, the lower the TSL. In both radio and television, a greater variety of program content will be necessary if the program has a long TSL. Programmers of radio stations whose audiences have a high turnover may schedule fewer songs and play them in a rapid rotation so that listeners will hear some of the most popular music while they are tuned in. On stations with a low turnover, a longer playlist will slow down the rotation of music, and that will minimize repetition during the period of listening.

Recycling is the measurement of audience attendance in more than one daypart. It may be found that a large proportion of the audience for a local early-evening TV news program also watches that station's late-evening newscast. The producers of programs whose audiences recycle from one daypart to another will want to revise the content of the earlier program to minimize repetitious material in the second time period. If recycling is low, however, the programmer can reuse much material during other parts of the day without it seeming redundant to the audience.

The measurement of exclusive listeners or viewers reveals the size of a program's most loyal audience. This figure can be compared with the figure for competing programs, and the programmer can monitor their stagnation or growth.

The focus group interview is a diagnostic tool for identifying program attributes that listeners or viewers find appealing, irritating, or confusing. This kind of information is especially helpful since program producers tend to lose insight because they are so close to the production. Individual focus sessions serve the same purpose. The individual focus session technique is more expensive and time-consuming, but it can yield richer detail because the interviewer has time to probe each participant's responses thoroughly.

Market perceptual studies are conducted to determine the position a program or station occupies among members of the target audience. Perceptual studies provide an important follow-up by ascertaining whether perspectives discovered in focus group interviews are held by the whole audience.

The efficiency of target audience (ETA) measurement permits programmers to identify the demographic segments most effectively reached by a station. A programmer can compare different dayparts to determine when the target audience is most efficiently gathered, and the ETAs of different stations can be compared. If a targeted audience segment is not being reached as efficiently as the programmer believes it should, a change in strategy may be called for to increase the listening of that group.

Radio programmers can track the location of their audiences' listening. If a large number of target audience members listen in their cars, frequent updates on traffic and road conditions can be provided. Those who are listening at work probably want less talk and a greater emphasis on music.

One way radio station programmers can keep abreast of the popularity of the music they play is through call-out research, in which a panel of respondents is contacted each week and asked to rate the songs aired on a station. Although call-out is a better measure of the appeal of established songs, it is also a useful way to track the acceptance or rejection of newer songs. Thus, call-out research helps programmers determine if certain songs are disliked by listeners as well as identify when listeners tire of hearing established recordings.

Auditorium music testing is done by gathering respondents at a location where they listen to hooks of songs and indicate their popularity. This technique is also useful for determining whether specific songs will be accepted favorably by the target audience.

TvQ measures the audience appeal and audience familiarity of television programs and personalities. A program featuring a personality such as combative talk show host Morton Downey, Jr., may have high familiarity and low appeal, which could preclude its being scheduled by many stations. Stations can use TvQ to identify movies and program series that have high appeal to target demographic groups even though their familiarity is low. Such programs may be purchased at a lower cost and aired at greater profit than other shows with higher familiarity.

In developing programs, the networks test program concepts, which are summaries of the plot and character interaction, to help determine their likely acceptance by audiences. If a concept tests well, a script may be ordered, and if the

script passes muster, a prototype or pilot program is made. A pilot may be tested by networks in theater sites where respondents indicate how well they like the show and the characters. These screenings are often followed by focus group sessions. Cable testing is the most popular means of researching a pilot program's potential. Sample members agree to watch a program that is presented on an unused cable channel. The day after the program is aired, respondents are called and asked about the program. In-home tape placement provides researchers with another means of testing programs. The people who agree to watch a videotape in their homes are then contacted for a follow-up telephone interview. Alternatively, respondents may be asked to participate in a focus group or individual focus interview session.

Audience acceptance is crucial to the ongoing success of any program. Producers often guide their decisions by testing programs to determine how audiences will react to changes. Consequently, ongoing focus group sessions or panel surveys are conducted to monitor audience reaction to plot development and feelings about characters in the program.

SUGGESTED READINGS

Hiber, Jhan: *Winning Radio Research,* National Association of Broadcasters, Washington, D.C., 1987.

In this book, an industry insider explains many of the ins and outs of conducting audience research. Although his focus is on radio, many of the techniques Hiber discusses are equally applicable to television program research. With an emphasis on practical application, Hiber lists the pros and cons of focus group and individual focus interviews as well as those of telephone, face-to-face, and mail surveys. Music research, particularly call-out and auditorium music tests, is reviewed. Hiber, a former Arbitron staff member and a longtime radio programming consultant, compares Arbitron and Birch Radio methods, describes their advantages, and explains how a programmer can use this information to achieve better ratings. Even though Birch ceased operation on December 31, 1991, Hiber's description is still useful as a contrast to

Arbitron's methodology. All in all, the reader will gain a good feel for different research techniques and their limitations.

Fletcher, James E: *Music & Program Research,* National Association of Broadcasters, Washington, D.C., 1987.

This is another useful primer that has many applications to television programming research. The fundamentals of research are reviewed, including probability and nonprobability sampling procedures. Clear examples accompany a description of methods for conducting music research, but Fletcher goes beyond the general conventions followed by programmers to advocate better methods for obtaining insight into audience preferences. Focus group interviewing, surveys, and laboratory research are illustrated in discussions on music testing and studies of audience reaction to news and information programming, radio personalities, and station format and position. Examples of questionnaires and ranking schemes are provided as models. The reader is carried through the process of applying research with models that describe some of the author's own studies. An appendix reports on research and the reliability and validity of scales used to measure music popularity. It shows the utility of expanding the scale to include a "familiarity" measure. A second appendix reports on a telephone call-out survey, which serves as a model for programmers who wish to conduct research for their stations. Yet another appendix presents a model for conducting research on audience perception of a station's news and information program content.

NOTES

1. Ed Shane, "Put Your Focus on Local Research," *Broadcast Communications,* April 1982, p. 26.

2. James E. Fletcher and Roger D. Wimmer, *Focus Group Interviews in Radio Research,* National Association of Broadcasters, Washington, D.C., 1981, p. 3.

3. David T. MacFarland, *Contemporary Radio Programming Strategies,* Lawrence Erlbaum, Hillsdale, N.J., 1990, p. 68.

4. Jhan Hiber, *Winning Radio Research,* National Association of Broadcasters, Washington, D.C., 1987, pp. 21–22.

5. Hiber, op. cit., pp. 40–42; Harvey Kojan, "Roberts: Give Focus Groups a Break," *Radio & Records,* July 27, 1990, p. 52.

6. Fletcher & Wimmer, op. cit., p. 11.

7. Roger Wimmer and Joseph R. Dominick, *Mass Media Research,* Wadsworth, Belmont, Calif., 1987, p. 155; Hiber, op. cit., pp. 83–88.

8. Terry Danner, "Executive Guide to Custom Radio Research," *NAB Research & Planning Memorandum,* July/August 1988, p. 1.

9. Ed Shane, *Programming Dynamics: Radio's Management Guide,* Globecom, Overland Park, Kan., 1984, p. 36.

10. See James E. Fletcher, *Profiting from Radio Ratings,* National Association of Broadcasters, Washington, D.C., 1989, p. 52; *Programmers Guide to Birch Radio Research,* Birch/Scarborough Research Corporation, Coral Springs, Fla., 1990, p. 29.

11. *Programmers Guide to Birch Radio Research,* pp. 13–14.

12. James E. Fletcher, *Music & Program Research,* National Association of Broadcasters, Washington, D.C., 1987, pp. 44–46.

13. Lon Helton, "Getting Down to Research Basics," *Radio & Records,* June 16, 1989, p. 54; Jhan Hiber, "Your Research Questions Answered, Part II," *Radio & Records,* April 12, 1985, p. 48; Joel Denver, "Callout Research—a Primer," *Radio & Records,* Oct. 8, 1982, pp. 19, 22; Rob Balon, "Callout Dos and Don'ts," *Radio & Records,* Jan. 11, 1991, p. 48.

14. Bill Engel, "Callout Research: Focus on Details," *Radio & Records,* Oct. 19, 1990, p. 35.

15. Denver, op. cit., p. 22.

16. Ed Shane, "Callouts Provide Valuable Data," *Broadcast Communications,* May 1982, p. 46; Helton, op. cit.; Hiber, "Your Research Questions Answered"; Balon, op. cit.

17. Fletcher, op. cit., p. 55.

18. Harvey Kojan, "What's In a Name?" *Radio & Records,* March 3, 1989, p. 52

19. Fletcher, op. cit., p. 60.

20. Rob Balon, "Straight Talk on Auditorium Testing," *Radio & Records,* Feb. 3, 1989, p. 52.

21. Dan Hurley, "Those Hush-Hush Q Ratings—Fair or Foul?" *TV Guide,* Dec. 10, 1988, pp. 3–6.

22. Ibid.

23. William S. Rubens, "Program Research at NBC, or Type 1 Error as a Way of Life," *Journal of Advertising Research,* June/July 1985, p. 14.

24. Rick Marin, "Loved the Pilot, Hate the Show," *Channels,* Sept. 10, 1990, pp. 43–45.

25. Ibid., p. 45.

26. Bob Shanks, *The Cool Fire: How to Make It in Television,* Norton, New York, 1976, p. 256.

PART TWO

Radio

In Part 1 we described ways of learning about electronic media audiences. The chapters in Part 2 discuss how that information is applied, along with other considerations in programming radio stations.

Chapter 7, "Assessing the Radio Environment," reviews the organization of radio stations. The programmer does not function alone but works in concert with a number of individuals who are also attempting to achieve the station's objectives. Thus we review the responsibilities of the programmer and his or her interaction with the persons in charge of other aspects of station operation. Chapter 7 also presents a market profile that draws on audience data to assess the possible programming strategies an underperforming station can use.

In Chapter 8, "Radio Formats," the ingredients of formula radio are described, as are the attributes of the major formats used by modern radio stations. Important considerations in selecting a format are discussed.

The ingredients in executing a format are described in Chapter 9, "Radio Programming Concepts," in which the discussion applies research concepts that were dealt with in earlier chapters. Chapter 10, "Radio Program Suppliers," continues the discussion of practical considerations in the execution of the format and delves into the sources of program content.

CHAPTER 7

Assessing the Radio Environment

Most people listen to the radio at some time during the week and enjoy it without giving much thought to how the material in the broadcast is put together. However, there is more to programming a radio station than is apparent to the casual listener. If the combination of disc jockey and popular music works, it is due not only to the chemistry between the listener and the on-air personality but to the careful selection of music and other program content and the effectiveness of the program director and the other station staff members in working together to achieve the common goal of attracting and maintaining a target audience. The program director serves as a catalyst, connecting all the elements in the station's operation and helping them contribute to the harmony of the on-air sound.

This chapter looks at the role of the program director and the interaction she or he has with the station's general manager. After a review of the responsibilities carried out by most program directors, we will examine the relationship between programming and other important aspects of station operation, including advertising sales and commercial scheduling, news, and the technical operation of a station. Then we will turn our attention to a consideration of the competition that exists in a radio market and assess the attributes and potential of the stations that compete for the available audience.

THE PROGRAMMER'S ROLE IN THE STATION ENVIRONMENT

A program director (PD) is sometimes depicted as a knight riding into the market on a white horse, ready to work his or her magic to pull the station up in the ratings. In fact, the program director is expected to oversee strategies that will attract an audience that is salable to advertisers. It isn't just a matter of the PD's ability to program the music. The traits necessary for a successful program director include marketing savvy, people skills, research sophistication, and knowledge of the broadcasting industry.[1] However, the PD alone does not make the station a winner; that is achieved by working in tandem with the other members of the staff.

Every radio station creates a unique environment with a distinctive organizational structure. A small-market station that is operated by its owner will have a setup different from that of a larger-market station, which is typically managed by a delegate of its ownership or board of directors. Broadcasting companies have differing operating philosophies which dictate the various levels of management and assignments of responsibilities.

In spite of their variations, every station operates under some variation of the structure of responsibilities shown in Figure 7-1. As a rule of

FIGURE 7-1 Radio station organization.

thumb, the smaller the station operation and the smaller the market, the more likely that several functions will be performed by a single person. Generally speaking, the larger the market, the more complex the division of responsibilities and the greater the number of people who carry them out. Whether a station has a large staff with specialized responsibilities or is a smaller operation where the program director takes on many different duties, the PD should appreciate and understand all the areas of the station's operation.[2]

General Manager

While the functions described in the next section may be carried out by program directors, PDs normally work very closely with the general manager, who approves program policies. In many cases the program director's role is to suggest or implement policy. Regardless of the amount of autonomy a particular program director has, she or he is still accountable to the station manager and works closely with other staff members and department heads to accomplish the objectives that have been set for the station by its top management.

Program Director's Responsibilities

The program director is the individual charged with developing and directing a station's on-air sound. This is not a job that a single person can perform, although in many stations responsibilities overlap and the PD may assume specific duties.

Overseeing research for programming decisions Many stations in larger markets now have research directors who administer music and entertainment program research. In such cases the program director works with that staff person. In other cases research is coordinated by the PD, who either supervises its conduct in house or contracts with consultant firms for its execution. Regardless of input from a research director, the PD should understand the strengths

and limitations of Arbitron and other research companies' methodologies. After carefully reviewing their reports, the PD should provide an interpretation of the figures so that the other members of the team can better understand their roles and the purpose of the station in meeting ratings objectives. Moreover, the PD should have the insight and flexibility to recognize when the station should change its format or otherwise adjust to changing audience preferences.

Monitoring competing stations The program director should regularly monitor the other stations in the market as well as out-of-market signals that attract potential listeners. Anticipating competitors' moves enables the PD to act rather than react, which is an important aspect of effective positioning. Suppose another station in the market using the same format is set to begin a massive billboard promotional campaign. Working with other station staff members, the PD may counter the competitor's move with a billboard "sit-in." A disc jockey, posted on a platform attached to a billboard located in a prominent place in the community, will promise not to come down until the local United Way contribution goal is reached or a similar objective is achieved.

If a competitor is slowly altering its format in an attempt to appeal to the station's core audience, the PD can develop a promotional campaign to fend off that attack. Take the situation of the program director of an Adult Contemporary station featuring current softer rock hits in combination with a high proportion of oldies. A Beautiful-Music station in the market has been adjusting its music selection away from lush instrumental recordings to include more contemporary ballads and light rock music. This change indicates that the competition is attempting to appeal to listeners in the Adult Contemporary station's target audience. Since most Beautiful-Music formats feature unobtrusive "background" service, the Adult Contemporary station could promote its personalities and information service to reinforce the importance of the station in its listeners' lives. Moreover, the music offered by the Adult Contemporary station could be emphasized through such techniques as "10 in a row" and "no-request workdays" to help maintain its position as a source of relaxing contemporary music companionship during the day.

Fostering showmanship An effective PD has a sense of show business. After all, people listen all day long to be entertained and informed, and many listeners are entertained by information. Therefore, the program director not only must be creative but must foster creativity among the other staff members. For example, commercials aired by the station not only should have technical proficiency but should feature polished performances by the announcing talent. Many sound too much alike because announcer performance, music style, and copywriting adversely affect the station's air sound. Similarly, when a disc jockey is well prepared and has a polished, smoothly coordinated show but the newscaster stumbles over words during a newscast, the overall performance quality of the station is diminished.

The PD is usually heavily involved in the station's promotional efforts, helping to determine ways to make listening to the station more enjoyable and rewarding. Thus, promotional campaigns and contests can contribute to a station's goals. A listener doesn't have to compete in order to enjoy a contest, for instance. For many people, the fun is in playing along with the contest even if they never bother to call the station or stop at a participating merchant to pick up the clues. Thus, imagination and a sense of fun, along with polished performances, contribute to successful programming.

Supervising staff members The program director is a part of the station's management. As the supervisor of staff members, the PD is responsible for communicating station policy to those persons and ensuring their compliance. To illustrate, a format is designed and executed to help the station meet its goals. If a disc jockey decides to skip records she or he doesn't like, the

objectives of the station will be confounded. Similarly, if the station's management has specified that off-color humor is not to be used on the air, it is the PD's duty to oversee compliance with that policy.

As a manager, the program director is responsible for scheduling announcers for shifts on the air and dispatching station personalities to locations in the market to carry out promotional activities. The PD must be able to use the staff to full advantage without exceeding the budget or violating local, state, and federal wage-hour guidelines.

Adherence to business ethics and regulations Broadcasting is a regulated industry, and a full knowledge of pertinent FCC rules and regulations is important. In developing station contests, for instance, the program director must be aware of their potential for violating restrictions on lotteries. For a contest to be considered a lottery, three elements must be present: There must be a prize, which can be money, merchandise, or anything of value; there must be an element of chance (no skill or talent is involved in selection of the winner); and a consideration must be given by the participant (by purchasing something or giving something of value) to the organization or person giving the prize.[3]

The PD must be aware of the potential for *payola*. FCC penalties for payola include imprisonment, fines, and license revocation.[4] Payola is unlikely ever to go away because of the importance to record companies of getting airplay in order to promote the sale of their records. There have been allegations during recent years of bribing disc jockeys with prostitutes, drugs, and cash to get records played.

A similar temptation is *plugola*. While the illegality of this practice is not as clear as it is for payola, it constitutes an ethical dilemma. For instance, if a disc jockey has a financial arrangement with a concert promoter, she or he could mention the event occasionally as "service" to listeners. Such a scenario would present a conflict of interest, particularly since many stations sell advertising time to concert promoters (Box 7-1).

**BOX 7-1
THE BALANCE
BETWEEN
RESPONSIBILITY AND
PROFITABILITY**

Sections 317 and 507 of the Communications Act define payola as accepting, paying, or agreeing to pay any money, services, or other valuable consideration for including any matter in a broadcast without disclosing the fact to the program producer or the broadcaster prior to the broadcast.

Each licensee is required to "exercise reasonable diligence to obtain from its employees, and from other persons with whom it deals," information that will allow it to comply with sponsorship identification requirements of the Communications Act and FCC rules. The station licensee is held responsible for the conduct or misconduct of its employees. Thus, licensees would be wise to establish and enforce a comprehensive procedure for guarding against payola at all staff levels.

SOURCE: Bob Branson, NAB Legal Department, in "Payola: An Update on Diligence," *NAB RadioWeek,* July 4, 1988, p. 7. © 1988 National Association of Broadcasters. Reprinted with permission. ∎

Instances of plugola or payola mean that the station's control over programming is jeopardized. Responsibility for knowing what is being presented over its airwaves is a legal requirement of station licensees. From the practical standpoint, management wants to be sure that everything that goes over the air helps support the station's goals. No manager or programmer wants to unwittingly abdicate control over the implementation of its policy to an outside entity.

Managing the music   An important part of the typical radio program director's week is the time set aside to review new music to determine whether it is appropriate for the station's format. Decisions on whether to air specific songs the audience wants to hear are crucial in maintaining the station's position.

In some stations, the PD handles that responsibility, but with the complexity and importance of selecting the right music, this task is often delegated. Usually the **music director** is a member of the station's announcing staff, one of the "first-string" announcers who handle a daily air shift.

At stations whose formats rely on music as a primary appeal to listeners, the responsibilities of the music director are extensive. The music director's duties include reviewing music popularity charts in trade publications such as *Radio & Records,* maintaining contact with stations in other markets to learn about audience accep-

tance of particular records, updating information in the station's computerized music control system, talking with representatives of record companies, listening to new music in consideration of giving it airplay, and monitoring local market research on record popularity.[5]

Sales Manager and Sales Staff

Music decisions are important, but the sale of time to advertisers is the driving force in most broadcast stations. Station account executives, who make a living from sales commissions, may have little interest in program content. Their attention is generally focused on getting the sale and perhaps overseeing the quality of the commercial message to satisfy the advertising client. Thus, in some stations the impact of **commercial announcements (CAs)** on programming appeal is of secondary concern.

Spot load   Advertising messages are often perceived as listener *irritants.* Enough irritants may influence some audience members to turn off the radio or, worse, tune in a competitor. Thus, what resonates as "cash flow" to an account executive may sound like listeners changing the dial to the PD.

An increase in the number of commercial messages sold by the station will surely please the station's account executives, who will see it as an opportunity to increase their incomes. But such a policy may prompt members of the audience to abandon the station because they perceive that it is loaded with commercial clutter. This situation confronts the program director with at least two choices: One is to exercise skill in scheduling commercials so that they fit into the programming strategy and thus minimize the irritation to listeners; the alternative is to convince the general manager and the sales manager that the commercial load should be reduced.

The station's **spot rate,** or advertising fee, is based on a combination of factors. These factors include tradition, which has usually been established on the basis of perceived quality; demand, or the amount advertisers are willing to pay; ratings and demographics, which rely on cost per thousand; the competing rates charged by other media outlets; the value to advertisers of reaching certain audiences; and the effectiveness of the station's sales force.[6]

Thus, in many stations there is a maximum **spot load,** or number of minutes of commercial time per hour. Although such a policy seems to limit sales opportunities, the larger audiences that may be attracted by this programming tactic should lead to higher revenue. The pricing of advertising time on a station can be enhanced by the number of spots available. Many sales account executives effectively argue that fewer spots mean less clutter and thus greater attention by the audience to their clients' messages.

Commercial compatibility with the format While audiences more often tolerate than enjoy listening to commercials, there are notable exceptions, including messages using humor or those with memorable music that may prompt the listener to sing along. Not only must the production quality be equal to that of the other programming content, the messages themselves must be compatible with the format.

A station using a Beautiful-Music or Adult Contemporary format will probably not want to schedule loud raucous commercial productions replete with the heavy metal sounds of amplified guitars because they are likely to irritate listeners who tune in to hear more melodic content. If the production does not fit the format, it should be rejected or revised. Many national advertisers produce a variety of commercial announcements that are compatible with different radio formats. Thus a CHR station could air a spot with a rock beat, while the same commercial with a country sound would be scheduled to run on stations using a Country format.

Thus, commercial announcements can be dealt with in a way that does not hurt the air sound. The program director should strive to learn the aims and problems of the sales department and help acquaint the sales manager with the objectives of the programming area. When a sales representative proposes selling a client a series of spots that clash with other program content, it is up to the program director to intercede. If amateurish talent (perhaps the owner of a business) is used or if other production values in commercial announcements detract from the air sound, for instance, the PD can negotiate for quality control. However, the PD will be ineffective if a clear perspective on the objectives of programming and sales is not maintained. Without the revenue gathered by the sales staff, the station will cease to function, but without an appealing air sound, the station's commodity—the listeners whom advertisers want to reach—may turn elsewhere.

Traffic director The program director, working with the music director, creates a formula for presenting music during each hour of the broadcast day. Scheduling the myriad of other daily events is the responsibility of the station's **traffic director.** This person is responsible for scheduling **traffic,** or the commercial announcements and other events broadcast by the station, which are compiled on the station's program log.

The **program log** is the schedule of all programs, commercial announcements, and other program content for each day. It is up to the program director to protect the on-air sound by supervising the way those items are scheduled and are executed by the on-air staff in compliance with the objectives and policies of the station.

These logs must be reviewed and corrected daily.

In the typical station, the traffic director schedules CAs during a particular quarter-hour period. It is up to the programming staff to determine when and in which order they are to be played during that period. Commercials can be programmed for airplay in the same way that music is. Just as each song is categorized according to its appeal to various segments of the station's audience, every commercial can be categorized by such attributes as tempo, production values, and listener appeal. Other programming events—news, weather, sports, traffic information, album giveaways, and concert promotions—can also be scheduled so as to maximize the time spent listening. The program director can specify the times when these events are to be scheduled by working closely with the traffic department.

Production Director

As an important part of maintaining the on-air sound and serving the advertising objectives of the station, the program director works closely with the station's production director, who is directly responsible for the creation of promotional announcements, skits, and commercial messages. The quality of the production director's work determines whether many of the commercial messages and other material interspersed with the music content enhance or detract from the station's sound. Polished and imaginative local production makes a real contribution to the air sound, whereas lackadaisical production means that commercial announcements can sound very much alike and promotional announcements may seem mundane. If the performers in a dialogue commercial are merely reading a script or if the actors in a dramatization sound like radio announcers instead of the characters they are portraying, much of the fun of listening is denied to the listeners. In those cases, even the quality of the most popular recordings that follow the commercial announcements is diminished.

Station Marketing and Promotion

Working in conjunction with the general manager and marketing director, the PD helps develop the station's positioning strategy. It is up to the program director to ensure that this strategy is consistently applied by keeping announcers and other personalities mindful of this goal. For example, suppose a station's positioning goal is to occupy a place in the minds of men and women age 25 to 54 as "the adult alternative." In implementing this strategy, every disc jockey is supposed to project a friendly, relaxed manner and avoid discussing subjects that would normally interest only teenagers. Thus, the PD may have to remind a disc jockey that information about a forthcoming Poison concert or a description of the latest AC/DC album is of little or no interest to the target audience.

The promotion director oversees the development and reinforcement of a positive image of the station in the community. This is important for several reasons: Commercial advertisers tend to avoid outlets that they perceive have a negative image that could be associated with their product or service. Moreover, the station needs to maintain "top of the mind" awareness among core listeners, which is to say that they immediately think of this station as the one that fulfills their needs. Thus, continual promotion is essential in maintaining the station's position so that it continues to attract targeted listeners and, consequently, advertisers.

Such promotion is most effective when it is fully integrated into the on-air presentation. For instance, if a station promotes itself as the "Most Music Station," it should deliver on that promise. One way to do that is to schedule blocks of music uninterrupted by talk segments (news and commercials). Depending on how this strategy is conceived and executed, these blocks of music could be 10 minutes in length or as long as 50 minutes. Commercial breaks should be filled with spots that use music in their production to reinforce the perception of "more music." At the least, such commercials will be less obtrusive than straight voice productions.

News Director

Even though many popular music stations seem to treat news as an incidental part of the programming, it is as important as any other content and should be treated carefully. Newspeople are personalities, just as disc jockeys are. If their contributions are integrated into the format, news personalities appeal to listeners rather than distracting from the principal fare—the music. This is one reason why many stations feature banter between newscasters and disc jockeys. It is an especially prevalent practice during morning programs, since listeners preparing for the day or on their way to work want to know the important events of the day.

When it is handled properly, the transition to news from entertainment is virtually seamless. A number of stations, particularly those with formats such as Adult Contemporary and Country, that target somewhat older demographics feature newspersons who chat for a minute or so with the disc jockey before each newscast. That way, listeners acquire a familiarity with the newsperson, just as they become acquainted with the disc jockey. During the course of the conversation, which typically deals with a current news event, the newscast begins. The audience is much less likely to notice that the entertainment portion of the program has ceased and the information part has begun. This is a way to weave talk and information into the cloth of the program.

Just like commercial announcements and specific music recordings, news content must be meaningful to listeners or it may be a tune-out factor. This does not mean that a station has to debase the informational or journalistic integrity of its news programming. It simply means that emphasis is placed on news that is of greatest pertinence to the audience being served.

A good example of this orientation to the target audience are the news broadcasts on Black Appeal formatted stations that are affiliated with the Sheridan Broadcasting Network (SBN). There is little difference between SBN newscasts and those on the CBS Radio Network. The subtle distinctions lie in the kind of news that is usually presented first in the newscasts and in the personalities, who receive more attention than they might on other newscasts. On SBN newscasts, lead stories often pertain to news of great interest to the black community. Black newsmakers such as the Reverend Jesse Jackson and former Atlanta Mayor Andrew Young receive greater prominence in stories than they might in news broadcasts on other networks. Similarly, the newscasters on many stations that target younger listeners inject greater energy into their delivery and emphasize news that is of interest to their young audiences. Thus, these newscasts have an orientation toward the events and newsmakers of greatest pertinence to the target audience.

It is questionable whether the audiences of some popular music stations are being adequately served. If news content is selected for its popular appeal instead of on the basis of what the audience should know, some listeners may be woefully underinformed about community, national, and world events. The program director and other staff members are obliged to consider the station's role in serving its audience and its community. For instance, will providing a straightforward, thorough local newscast cost the station any more than presenting tongue-in-cheek news? Probably not. Will listeners tune out because they hear actual news instead of a presentation where the disc jockeys interrupt the newsperson with jokes? Again, it is unlikely.

Chief Engineer

Depending on the size of the station's operation and labor union restrictions, disc jockeys in many markets routinely take transmitter meter readings as a part of their air shift duties. Although station *operating logs*—the records of transmitter and technical monitor readings—are normally the responsibility of the chief engineer, the program director may oversee the corrections that have to be made by the on-air staff. This is another instance where the PD must interact closely with another area of the station's operation. Of primary concern to the program director, though, is the quality of the station's sound.

In an age of increasing awareness of the acoustical properties of popular music, where compact disc players have been widely adopted by stations and listeners, attention to the technical quality of the signal has become critical to audience gathering. Listeners have invested in radio receivers capable of reproducing high-quality sound and can discern poor separation of stereo signals and a lack of crispness and fidelity in the sound.

While it is the responsibility of the engineer to make the system work, the PD must be able to communicate the importance of on-air and production needs to the engineering staff and to management when necessary. The smooth operation of equipment is very important to the effectiveness of the announcer on duty. Since station engineers do not actually operate the equipment, they may not appreciate how it should be configured for optimum efficiency. When a compact disc player or a cartridge tape playback unit does not cue properly, for example, it affects the rhythm of the on-air sound. Similarly, if a piece of equipment is difficult to reach, the disc jockey is distracted from communicating with the listeners by the need to stand or stretch to operate the device.

ECONOMICS OF RADIO PROGRAMMING

An important part of the programmer's job is to analyze the status of his or her station (Who am I?) and that of the competition (Who am I competing against?). The assessment should include each station's frequency and power, but those factors remain relatively constant. The most frequent changes are made in formats, which can affect the primary audience and the secondary demographics each station attracts. Moreover, the size of the market can be crucial. For instance, there could be as much as a $20 million difference in market revenues depending on whether a market is ranked in the top 10.[7] These factors are the key to determining how the station can compete.

Cost of Programming

The cost of programming music formats is relatively equal if the station has used a format for a reasonably long period of time. A start-up operation or a station that has switched formats may have to invest in a library of recordings that are suitable to its programming plan, however, since it does not have a backlog of music received over several months or years. Similarly, a station that programs Oldies will have to purchase some, if not all, of its music because it is unavailable from the record companies as complimentary material. A station specializing in a less popular music genre such as Jazz or Classical is probably going to have to purchase most of its material as well. The only recordings that are distributed free of charge to stations are new releases that the music company hopes to expose to the record-buying public via station play.

Radio is a labor-intensive business, and the highest costs are almost always for personnel. In small markets programmers usually have to settle for less experienced or less talented on-air personnel because the economics of the marketplace do not permit higher salaries. Moreover, the less direct competition there is, the less incentive the station management has to pay higher salaries.

The cost of extensive news programming is prohibitive in some circumstances. A marginal operation in a smaller market may not be able to afford to employ a full-time newsperson because of the salary, insurance, and benefits. Moreover, many stations have reduced or eliminated their news departments in recent years. FCC pressure to provide news has been virtually eliminated, and these programmers have determined that most listeners are not that interested in news, especially since there are so many other sources that can keep interested people up to date.

Even in large markets, news operations have been scaled back. In many stations, the only local newscasts are scheduled during the morning drive period. Any news provided during other times of the day is typically read by the disc jockey, who assembles news copy fed by a news wire service.

An increasing number of marginally profitable stations have turned to tape or satellite-distributed programming as an alternative to "going dark." With the right electronic gear and a personal computer, a station operation that requires five or more people can be programmed and can operate virtually unattended while the remaining employees are out on the streets selling advertising time.

Differences in AM and FM Audiences

The fortunes of AM facilities in many markets have been bleak. The fact that AM is losing listeners is increasingly clear (Figure 7-2).

Younger listeners in particular prefer FM to AM. In fact, 75 percent of all radio listening has been estimated to be devoted to FM stations, whereas 10 years ago AM listeners were in the majority.[8] Today FM radio receives between 75 and 80 percent of the annual advertising revenue available to radio.[9]

As important or as dismal as those statistics may be, an AM operator needs to understand the trends in audience composition. As Figure 7-3 shows, age is an important factor in the composition of most AM station audiences.

There are some notable exceptions in the fortunes of AM radio, as evidenced by stations in some of the nation's largest markets. In one study AM stations held the top spot among listeners 12 and over in 5 of the 10 largest markets and took second place in 2 more markets. In most cases, their formats were news or talk or a combination of the two.[10]

Since listeners age 12 to 40 grew up listening to FM stations, their habits are entrenched. Thus, the current potential for AM lies in formats that appeal to listeners over age 40.[11] Unless AM broadcasters can find ways to attract younger audiences, they must program to older listeners who are not particularly concerned by the lower fidelity of the signal. AM frequencies are capable of transmitting frequencies of about 50 to 5000 hertz, or cycles per second, while FM signals can reproduce frequencies in a range of about 50 to 15,000 hertz. Furthermore, AM signals are much more susceptible to interference from electric motors, atmospheric disturbances, and other electromagnetic signals.

FIGURE 7-2   AM and FM listening trends. *(From NBA RadioWeek, January, 1990, p. 8. © 1990 National Association of Broadcasters. Used with permission.)*

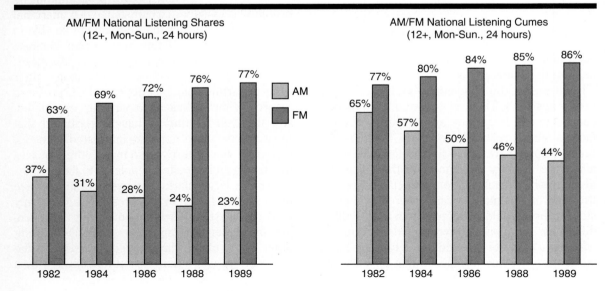

AM/FM National Listening Shares (12+, Mon-Sun., 24 hours)

AM/FM National Listening Cumes (12+, Mon-Sun., 24 hours)

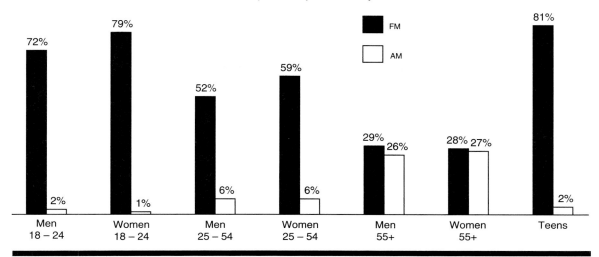

FIGURE 7-3 Radio weekly demographic reach on AM and FM stations. [*Used with permission of BROADCASTING Magazine (December 10, 1990). © 1990 by Cahners Publishing Company.*]

Analysis of Station Formats and Their Audiences

The following discussion analyzes a radio market. The stations operating there have achieved their positions on the basis of their facilities and the viability of their formats. The profile will serve as an illustration of many of the concepts that have been discussed throughout this book

and will enable the reader to project ahead to the discussions in subsequent chapters.

Table 7-1 identifies the stations that dominate the market in terms of total audience share. It is also easy to identify the audience segments that account for those shares. The top-ranked station among listeners 12 and over, WWAC has wide appeal to adult listeners 18 to 54 with its Adult

TABLE 7-1 Station Audience Shares in a Top-50 Market: Metro AQH Share, Monday–Sunday, 6 a.m.–Midnight

Station	Frequency	Power Day/Night	Format	Total 12+	18–34 Men	18–34 Women	25–54 Men	25–54 Women	35+ Men	35+ Women	Teens
WWAC	107.5 FM	100k	Adult Contemp.	13.8	19.0	20.0	21.3	18.7	13.2	9.0	6.8
WCTR	99.7 FM	100k	Country	13.5	11.6	10.9	13.8	15.4	19.1	15.6	3.4
WURB	102.3 FM	100k	Urban Contemp.	10.9	14.8	13.3	14.2	10.1	6.6	7.7	18.8
WCHR	101.5 FM	100k	CHR	10.0	12.7	15.4	8.4	8.4	5.1	2.9	25.6
WROK	96.9 FM	100k	CHR	9.8	18.0	11.2	5.9	7.3	3.5	4.0	25.6
WNWS	920 AM	5k/5k	News/Talk	5.6	3.7	1.1	2.5	3.6	8.6	9.8	—
WLIT	105.5 FM	100k	Adult/Lite	3.8	1.6	4.9	3.8	6.7	3.5	4.8	1.7
WREL	94.5 FM	100k	Religious	2.4	1.6	1.1	1.3	2.0	3.5	3.7	—
WOLD	1050 AM	5k/1k	Oldies	0.7	0.5	—	—	0.6	0.8	1.3	—
WWCW	860 AM	50k/1k	Country	0.6	0.5	—	2.1	0.3	1.6	1.3	—

Contemporary format. Table 7-1 also shows that in addition to attracting the largest share of both men 18 to 34 (19.0) and women 18 to 34 (20.0), WWAC also has the largest share of both men 25 to 54 (21.3) and women 25 to 54 (18.7). Among listeners 35 and over, WWAC has the second largest share of men (13.2) and the third largest share of women (9.0).

The Adult Contemporary station's strongest competition for audience share comes from the Country format FM station WCTR, which also has broad demographic appeal. Its core audience is men and women 25 to 54, particularly among the older listeners in this segment, since its shares of men 35 and over (19.1) and women 35 and over (15.6) are the highest of all stations. WCTR also has strong secondary strength among both men and women 18 to 34, with respective shares of 11.6 and 10.9. These shares illustrate WCTR's substantial appeal across a wide range of adult listeners, with the Adult Contemporary station skewing younger and the Country formatted station skewing toward older listeners.

Neither WCTR nor WWAC has much of an appeal to teen listeners. WWAC has a 6.8 share, and WCTR attracts only a 3.4 share of teenage listeners. In contrast, the third ranked station among listeners 12 and over, WURB, has a strong appeal to teens. This Urban Contemporary formatted station attracts an 18.8 share of teens as well as drawing well among men and women 18 to 34 with a 14.8 and a 13.3 share, respectively. WURB also draws strongly among listeners 25 to 54, with a men's share of 14.2 and a 10.1 share among women. Listening among older groups drops away, though, with a 6.6 share among men and a 7.7 share among women 35 and over.

The two CHR formatted stations in the market are in a virtual dead heat for shares of total audience. WCHR attracts a 10.0 share of listeners 12 and over, followed closely by WROK with a 9.8 share. Both WCHR and WROK appeal strongly to teen listeners, where they both achieve 25.6 shares. The clearest difference between the two stations lies in their appeal to different segments of the 18- to 34-year-old audience. WCHR's

strength is skewed toward women, with a 15.4 share, compared with only a 12.7 share of men 18 to 34. WROK, by contrast, garners an 18 share of men 18 to 34 but a much lower 11.2 share of women 18 to 34.

The strongest performing AM station in the market is WNWS, with a 5.6 share of the total audience. WNWS's showing can be attributed to listeners 35 and over, among whom the station attracts an 8.6 share of men and a 9.8 share of women with its News/Talk format. Among younger demographics, WNWS's shares are substantially lower, although its appeal is skewed toward male listeners. Among men 18 to 34, WNWS attracts a 3.7 share, compared with only a 1.1 share of women. In the segment age 25 to 54, the station has more even shares of 2.5 among men and 3.6 among women.

Two of the FM facilities attract much lower audience shares than the others do. WREL broadcasts a Religious format, and WLIT employs a "Lite Rock" format that features popular ballads and easy-listening rock music.

The owners of WREL may be satisfied with its 2.4 share of listeners 12 and over. Even though Religious formatted stations generally attract comparatively small audiences, these listeners are usually very loyal. Many of these stations rely on revenue from selling blocks of time to ministers who want to spread their message via radio. In disseminating their special message, religious broadcasters may have objectives different from those of the majority of commercial radio stations.

The most clearly underperforming FM station, then, is WLIT, with a 3.8 share of the total audience. WLIT's audience strength can be found in its women listeners. Although the station's demographic appeal holds fairly consistently across age segments, especially among women, its demographic shares are too low to be considered competitive in attracting a large audience compared with the other FM stations. The station attracts a 4.9 share of women 18 to 34, a 6.7 share of women 25 to 54, and a 4.8 share of women 35 and over. Except for WREL, these shares are far lower than those of any of the other FM stations serving the market, suggesting that the station may be able to to garner a larger share of listeners with a change in format.

Finally, two AM stations attract very low shares of the total audience. WOLD, an AM facility that uses an Oldies format, has its greatest strength among women 35 and over, but that is only a 1.3 share. WWCW, an AM station with a powerful daytime signal, manages only a 0.6 share of listeners 12 and over. Its Country format attracts a minimal share of younger listeners and has its greatest strength among older men and women. WWCW attracts a 2.1 share of men 25 to 54, but its core is among listeners 35 and over, with a 1.6 share of men 35 and over and a similar 1.3 share among women in that age segment.

Changes in Strategy

The stations most in need of change are those at the bottom of Table 7-1. FM stations dominate the market. One AM station, WNWS, has attracted a respectable 5.6 share of listeners 12 and over and holds third place among men 35 and over and second place among women 35 and over. WNWS seems to have established a niche with its News/Talk format, but the other AM stations can only hang on to their older audiences or hope to find a niche in the market by serving a more narrowly defined audience. Unless there is a cluster of potential listeners who are desired by advertisers, though, this station's prospects seem poor in comparison to those of the FM stations in the market.

If we discount the probability of WREL's owners' being willing to program more popular fare, the station with the greatest potential to attract a greater share of listeners is WLIT, because its signal is comparable to that of the other stations operating on the FM band. Where does the greatest potential lie for WLIT to reposition itself? Where should the programmer look for a target audience? Can the programming be changed without alienating the present core, or should the station start from scratch? What format should be adopted? How much consideration must be given to promotion?

Another look at Table 7-1 reveals where the potential exists for WLIT to establish a position as well as the audience segments where other stations seem to have an insurmountable hold on their positions. One such demographic is teens, where 80 percent of the audience has been captured by three stations: WCHR, WROK, and WURB. Thus, unless there is some reason to think that the programming of one of these stations has become stale or is dependent on past performance, WLIT's programmer should look elsewhere for better audience potential.

Among males 18 to 34, WWAC, the Adult Contemporary outlet, has a 19.0 share, which is followed most closely by WROK with an 18.0 share. WROK's stronger share of males 18 to 34 compared with its 11.2 share of women 18 to 34 indicates that its format tends toward harder rock music than the other CHR station, WCHR. Many of these men may be listening to WROK because no alternative station programs music more attuned to their interests.

Moreover, both WCHR and WROK attract only half the shares of men 25 to 54 compared with men 18 to 34. The only station programming oldies is WWAC, and it tends to play fairly light rock because of its Adult Contemporary format. Consequently, there may be a place for an AOR format in the market that could serve the musical tastes of many listeners to the Adult Contemporary and CHR formatted stations. With the right mix of oldies and a selective use of contemporary rock music, such a format could appeal to aging rock music listeners among men 18 to 54 as well as to some in the male segment 18 to 34 as an attractive alternative to the pop music typically featured on CHR formats. Furthermore, even though harder rock music seems to have its primary appeal to men, women listeners who are not satisfied with lighter rock or with the current pop music offered by the other stations could be attracted for the same reasons.

Still, male listeners seem to be less well served in the market among the existing formats than do females. The current WLIT Lite Rock format attracts a small share of women 18 to 34. Its core audience seems to be spread across women 18 to 54, but with small shares in every age segment. With the strength of WWAC and WCTR, it does not seem likely that the station will make further inroads into those stations' audiences with a Lite Rock format. Thus, if WLIT were to switch to a Classic Rock format, it would probably lose much of its core audience. But with careful promotion, it could attract a reasonable share of women 18 to 34 and, perhaps, a number of older women who would find their musical interests better served by something

other than the current offerings. Therefore, it seems possible that at least a comparable share of women could be attracted to make up for the loss of women who tuned in the Lite Rock format. The men in the WLIT audience would probably abandon it for something more like the station's present format, but as we have pointed out, there seems to be a large potential audience among men 18 to 34 who like harder rock music. It would appear that a change in the format would do no worse than retain a similar or larger share of total audience just by attracting a new core of men, with a secondary audience among women.

SUMMARY

Radio programming takes place in an environment that imposes certain limitations and expectations concerning how the programmer can do his or her job. The PD works closely with the general manager in most stations and is expected to help carry out the objectives that are set by the management.

A radio station is an environment that includes a number of operational units. A program director may be responsible for many of these functions, or they may be delegated to staff members who specialize in different aspects of the operation. In most stations the program director supervises the announcing staff. As a supervisor, the program director must oversee the preparation and development of the material that goes out over the air and monitor staff members to ensure that they comply with policies established to meet the objectives of the station. The PD works closely with the music director in selecting music that will appeal to the target audience.

The PD confers with a research director on audience listening and music preferences. Often in conjunction with the general manager, the PD is involved with the promotion director in creating ways to reinforce core audience loyalty and attract new listeners.

To support the station's objectives, it is important that sales and programming strategies coincide. This includes understanding the need to generate revenue through sales of advertising time and to broadcast commercial announcements that are compatible with the format. However, the PD is also concerned with scheduling commercial announcements in a way that minimizes their potential to alienate listeners. Therefore, while a close liaison with the traffic director is important, it may be up to the PD to schedule announcements that are placed in the commercial breaks for maximum effectiveness in the program format.

The PD works closely with the production director to achieve the highest quality in commercial production as well as in promotional and other spots that may be aired on the station. The recorded music aired by the station is of top production quality, and so the quality of local production must be compatible in order to maintain the quality of the air sound.

The engineering area of the station affects programming because the signal quality is important in attracting listeners. Moreover, when equipment does not function properly, on-air performance may suffer. Similarly, news is an element of programming that must be integrated with the other content to meet the objectives of the station. If news performance is not as good as that of the disc jockey's presentation, program quality will be diminished.

The chapters that follow will discuss specific aspects of programming that were only touched upon here. Some of the questions raised in our review of competition in the market described in Table 7-1 will be answered by readers who gain a better understanding of how to implement programming concepts.

SUGGESTED READINGS

Shane, Ed: *Programming Dynamics: Radio's Management Guide,* Globecom, Overland Park, Kans., 1984.

As a radio programming consultant, Shane advises programmers on how to improve their operation, which is a teaching function. Furthermore, Shane's advice in the many columns he has written for trade publications can be thought of as teaching. Backing up that trait, Shane Media Services supports a $3000 scholarship which is awarded annually through the Broadcast Education Association to a college student studying for a career in radio. In keeping with the author's proclivity to teach, the reader gets substantive advice, not the euphemisms that many program consultants present in their public pronouncements as a way to drum up business. While increasing his client base is an objective shared by Shane, the reader is taken through many substantive discussions on programming and music selection. The essays, written in clear, understandable prose, are useful to inexperienced and seasoned broadcasters alike. The ex-

amples remain as pertinent today as when they were written.

NOTES

1. Joy Dunlap, "Making the Programming-Management Transition," *NAB RadioWeek,* Dec. 12, 1988, p. 4.

2. See Steve Feinstein, "The Right Stuff," *Radio & Records,* April 27, 1984, pp. 78, 80, for a description of the qualities that general managers look for in hiring a program director; see Harvey Kojan, "The Ultimate PD," *Radio & Records,* Dec. 7, 1990, pp. 39–40, for a description of the program director's workday and the attributes needed to be effective.

3. Joseph Dominick, Barry L. Sherman, and Gary Copeland, *Broadcasting/Cable and Beyond,* McGraw-Hill, New York, 1990, p. 417.

4. Bob Branson, "Payola: An Update on Diligence," *NAB Radio Week,* July 4, 1988, p. 7.

5. Mike Kinosian, "MDs: More Than 'Music Librarians,'" *Radio & Records,* July 29, 1988, p. 70.

6. Charles Warner, *Broadcast and Cable Selling,* Wadsworth, Belmont, Calif., 1986, pp. 233–237.

7. "Miami May Break Radio Top Ten," *MediaViews,* Oct. 1991, p. 4.

8. Adam Buckman, "FM Listenership Continues to Rise," *Electronic Media,* June 20, 1988, p. 2; see also Ed Cohen, "Radio Listenership Holds, AM Slips," *NAB RadioWeek,* Jan. 2, 1989, p. 8.

9. "AM Radio Plays Hard to Be Heard Again as Audience Dwindles," *Insight,* July 4, 1988, p. 44.

10. "Winter Book Shows AM Healthy," *Broadcasting,* April 23, 1990, p. 41.

11. Gerry Boehme, "Answer on AM," *Broadcasting,* Feb. 12, 1990, p. 16.

Radio Formats

KEY TERMS AND CONCEPTS

Adult Contemporary (A/C)
Album-Oriented Rock (AOR)
Beautiful Music
Big-Band Music
Black Appeal
Block Programming
Christian Contemporary Music
Contemporary Hit Radio (CHR)
Country Music
Easy Listening
Format
Formatics (Format Execution)
Formula Radio
Full-Service Adult Radio
Hispanic Appeal

Middle of the Road (MOR)
New Age/New Adult
 Contemporary (NAC)
New Rock
News/Talk Format
Noncommercial Broadcasting
Nostalgia Format
Public Broadcasting
Public Radio
Religious Format
Soft Adult Contemporary
Top-40 Station
Underwriting
Urban Contemporary (UC)

Radio is a volatile medium in which little remains constant for long. The music, the information presented, and the personalities and their approach to communicating with listeners evolve as stations seek ways to attract a greater share of the audience. When a new wrinkle seems to work, it is quickly adopted by other stations. Innovations spread even more quickly when they are developed by programming consultants who advise stations in several markets. In previous chapters we pointed out the importance of understanding the characteristics of the individual market. That remains an important consideration, but many of the elements in programming work across formats and markets, keeping programmers and station consultants in steady work.

Personalities and styles can be copied, but the major constant among stations is their formats. The term "formula" is interchangeable with "format" and in some ways is a more apt label, for a radio **format** is a composition of program events, or ingredients, presented in the right mix to achieve the programmer's objective of appealing to an audience. Other terms, such as a station's "sound" or "image," sometimes mean the same thing as format.

This chapter takes a brief look at the development of the modern radio format and then describes the attributes of the major radio formats. An important characteristic of each format is its core audience. Another important consideration is a format's potential for generating revenue. The section on format selection considers advertiser demand and the economic potential of the various formats.

FORMAT INGREDIENTS

Target Audience

Chief among the considerations in choosing a format are the characteristics of the audience being sought. Regardless of how well a station is programmed, the format may not appeal to enough listeners to make it economically feasible. While an audience for most formats exists in virtually every market, that group of listeners may not be present in sufficient numbers to support some formats. As was emphasized in Chapter 2, the best approach is to identify the needs and interests of audience segments rather than attempt to "sell" a format to listeners. Even though a substantial audience may be present in the market, this does not guarantee that a station that adopts a format designed to attract it will be financially successful; the revenue potentials of different formats vary considerably.

Program Content

It is tempting to treat music as a separate format ingredient, but that would be misleading. While different music types typify radio formats, there are other alternatives, namely, news, sports, and talk, which includes interviews, opinion forums, and call-in programming, along with religious formats, fine arts, and other specialized ways to appeal to audiences.

Many people listen to stations to hear programming other than music. For many older listeners, news is as important a reason for tuning in as any other aspect of the program content. Most young listeners find news of value when it deals with subjects they can relate to; as they grow older, they tend to want greater detail and a broader range of subjects.

As audience members grow older, their musical tastes become more conservative. It is helpful for programmers to remember that popular music is the traditional province of the young. Indeed, a function of popular music has always been to be sufficiently offensive to adults that young people can safely call it their own. Few parents of today's teenagers understand or like rap music. In the mid-1980s parents found no redeeming value in punk rock and heavy metal music. When Elvis Presley came onto the national scene in 1954, teenagers immediately embraced his music but he horrified many adults. It's hard to believe now that ministers actually railed against "the king of rock 'n' roll" from their pulpits for leading the youth of America astray with his music and swiveling pelvis! Today many of the teenagers whose parents worried about the implications of Elvis's gyrations are parents and grandparents who cluck disapprovingly at what they see on MTV.

Regardless of the age group being targeted, music selection is a central ingredient in most radio formats. If a programmer is targeting listeners age 45 and above, she or he will probably limit current songs to soft rock and mix in older rock hits since many of the currently popular artists speak to a different generation. While older listeners generally don't like a lot in the current style, they still like the kind of music they grew up with.

News and Information

Some stations, seeking to offer an alternative to underserved audience segments, use an all-news format, while others specialize in presenting information on various subjects. However, virtually all formats include some news and also provide their listeners with varying kinds of information.

In some music-intensive formats, news is handled by eliminating it from the schedule. In other formats, long segments of time may be devoted to news. Furthermore, information is in the ear of the beholder. Young listeners find information about the availability of tickets to a concert by a currently hot recording group to be of particular value. Certain other listeners are much more interested in household hints or the latest trends in the stock market. In every case, the programmer must determine when to present this content and how much emphasis it should receive.

Commercial Announcements

Except for noncommercial stations, the bills are paid by selling time to advertisers and presenting their messages to the listeners. At the same time, commercials are not particularly appreciated by listeners.

Such a quandary can never be fully resolved,

but a programmer can placate listeners by overseeing how commercials are produced and where they are placed in the broadcast schedule. They can be placed in a way that provides a certain richness to the texture of the programming and thus minimizes their potential as irritants.

Other Nonmusical Events

In addition to news, information, and commercial announcements, many formats include material, such as promotions or contests, that may involve audience participation. Each event must be handled as a part of the format. If promotional announcements and contests are designed to appeal to the target audience, they will not be perceived as interruptions to the music or other content but as interesting and appealing. For instance, a recording of the excited reaction of a listener who has just won a cash prize can be integrated into the format so that it provides variety and excitement to the total sound, but if this reaction is drawn out or sounds flat, it may create a rough place in the station's sound. Polish, a sense of timing, and the building of excitement appropriate to the nature of the format and the temperament of the targeted audience must all work together.

Personalities

The people who present the content to the listeners are the catalysts that make the other ingredients come together. Two stations playing the same music can sound very different because of what is said and how it is conveyed.

As was explained in Chapter 6, the criteria for air checks performed by program directors are particularly important for making the format work. If the targeted audience is men and women 18 to 34, the disc jockey should have a personality that appeals to this group. If he or she sounds like a teenager or like a 40-year-old person, the appeal of the music will be a little flat. Disc jockeys who are ignorant of things that most listeners to the station know about may irritate many members of the audience. For example, many morning personalities read off a list of names of celebrities or other notable people who have birthdays that day. The listener who knows who Maria Callas and George McGovern are will feel at least mildly insulted on hearing a disc jockey profess his ignorance and lack of concern by making a comment such as "whoever *she* (or *he*) is." Thus, the disc jockey winds up appearing to be insensitive and dumb. The same sort of reaction will be elicited from a teenager who hears a disc jockey using slang in order to seem to be "with it" but getting it wrong.

Execution

Just as personality makes a difference in the success of a format, so does the way all the ingredients are presented. Of course, the personality of the individual who is on the air is integral to execution, but the programmer establishes the plan and dictates the pacing of the program by controlling the length of each event, the intensity of the music, and the quality of production. The programmer also determines the amount of time a disc jockey should devote to chatter between records and other events on the schedule. Moreover, the programmer decides on the optimum number of records to be included in a **music sweep,** or period of time during the program hour when several music selections are presented without interruption by commercials or other nonmusic events. Such an execution of the format is sometimes referred to as **formatics,** or format execution, by industry practitioners.

This chapter provides an overview of the development of formula radio and the attributes of the major formats. The modern radio formats examined on the following pages are constantly evolving and their descriptions change over time, but they all have roots in the 1950s.

DEVELOPMENT OF FORMULA RADIO

The concept of disc jockeys playing records for radio listeners was developed early in the history of radio. In 1932 Al Jarvis referred to his recorded music show in Los Angeles as the "world's largest make-believe ballroom." Later, Martin Block started his *Make Believe Ballroom* program on WNEW, New York, in 1935. And on WWL, New Orleans, *Poole's Paradise* was hosted by Bob Poole, who became the first big-name disc jockey in the south and midwest.[1]

Martin Block was the biggest name among the early disc jockeys. Starting at $25 a week, he eventually commanded a salary of $200,000 a year. Block's show was based on a formula of asking the audience to imagine a giant turntable stage that revolved to the different bands he introduced. Recordings of their best known tunes were interspersed with commercials. Block, who had a popular show in southern California before moving to New York, apparently got the idea for the title of his program from Al Jarvis.[2] His sincere, low-key presentation spawned hundreds of imitators.[3]

When the radio networks lifted their ban on playing recorded material in 1948, several attempts to provide disc jockey programming resulted. In 1954, for instance, Martin Block had an ABC radio program, and in 1955 NBC began its weekend *Monitor* program. The Mutual Radio Network broadcast imitations it called *Bits and Pieces, Mutual Morning, Matinee,* and *Evening.* Although they further legitimized disc jockey programs, such network broadcasts were short-lived because television overshadowed these full-service radio programming efforts.[4]

As television became established, the stars and most of the network programs radio stations had relied on were taken away. Pushed out of America's living rooms, radio had to create a new audience to survive doomsayers' predictions that TV would kill it. Thus came the change from a general, family-oriented service to a specialty medium. Formula radio, which included commercials, weather, time, contests, repetitions of the call letters, and popular music recordings interspersed with the comments of disc jockeys, really took off in the 1950s. Unlike the low-keyed, dignified presentations of radio personalities like Martin Block, however, the new disc jockeys were "screamers" who were part of a new brash, fast, hypnotic "sound."[5]

A number of other important developments contributed to the rise of formula radio. After World War II there was a population explosion— the baby boom of children born during the period from about 1945 to 1955. Along with the baby boom came a lowering of the median age. Ironically, today's aging baby boomers are influencing the current trend of radio and television programs that appeal to older listeners and viewers.[6]

The youth movement may be over, but back in the early 1950s the influx of teenagers in the potential audience coincided with urbanization and increasing affluence. Traditional large families raised on farms gave way to smaller families living in towns. Their teenage children had much more time and money on their hands. At the same time there was a shift of population to the suburbs, which created a nation on wheels. People living in outlying areas relied more on automobiles and increasingly commuted by car to work. The drive time audience was a natural for radio.

Technological advances also had a bearing on radio audiences. The development of the transistor by Bell Laboratories in 1947 made it possible to produce inexpensive radios no larger than a pack of cigarettes. The first transistorized radios were sold in 1953, and sales took off during the next several years. Equally important, a reduction in size and improvements in stability made automobile radios more reliable, and they began to be widely adopted. It is difficult to believe that only a generation ago many cars were sold without radio receivers.

Another important technological breakthrough came in 1946, when clock radios began to be marketed. This opened up a new radio audience that listens to its favorite radio stations the first thing each morning.

At about the same time, 33⅓-rpm long-playing and 45-rpm records were introduced. Record marketing took a dramatic turn from retailing in music stores to selling through "rack jobbers." Although music store remained plentiful, records and later tapes and **compact discs (CDs)** began to be sold in a wide variety of loca-

tions. Outlets included variety and department stores, where records were placed in display bins or racks that were replenished by distributors ("jobbers"). This not only gave records a wider distribution but made sales statistics more readily available as a means of monitoring popularity.

Perhaps none of these developments was as instrumental in the development of formula radio as the vacuum created by television. In the absence of full-service programming on the radio networks, many stations followed a standard or Middle-of-the-Road (MOR) format of music and news. They tried to program something for everyone, with particular emphasis on vocal and orchestral popular music. Other stations broadcast classical music, or "good music," consisting of orchestral recordings. Still others, mostly in rural areas, specialized in Country-and-Western music. In markets with substantial black populations, some stations programmed "Rhythm and Blues,"[7] one of the earliest specialty formats.

Fast-paced orchestral music and vocals were presented on stations that came to be known as formula or Top-40 stations. The key criterion was the *popularity* of the music. In the early 1950s, Top-40 formats included love ballads by established singers such as Nat King Cole, Teresa Brewer, Rosemary Clooney, Patti Page, and Tony Bennett, but as more young listeners tuned in, the music style changed.[8] Rock 'n' roll was emphasized by some radio stations as a means of putting something on the air that would attract an available audience, which was perceived to consist largely of teenagers.

Because the sound of one station was much the same as that of another, the personalities who introduced the records became paramount. Alan Freed, one of the early successful disc jockeys, labeled this new style of music "rock 'n' roll," which reflected its roots in black appeal Rhythm and Blues.[9] Another early disc jockey, Dick Clark, continues his remarkably successful career in radio and television today.

The fortuitous development of inexpensive, reliable portable radio receivers, an influx of young people in the population, a shift from urban to suburban living, and the emergence of rock 'n' roll converged when radio was searching for a new audience. Although pioneer disc jockey Martin Block had been playing the Top-30 hits since 1935, the concept really took off in the mid-1950s. Starting with "Sh-boom" by the Crew Cuts in 1954 and followed by Bill Haley's "Rock around the Clock" from the movie *Blackboard Jungle,*[10] radio programming began to be closely associated with popular music, which increasingly came to mean rock 'n' roll.

THE MAJOR FORMATS

In many ways the formats used by most of today's radio stations have their roots in formula radio, which is to say in a Top-40 format. Today's typical station targets a well-defined segment of the total listening audience. With a few exceptions—usually stations that serve smaller markets—most stations specialize in one type of music, news, and information to position themselves to attract an audience.

The major formats in current use are listed in Figure 8-1, but there are a great many other possibilities. In fact, there are often differences between stations that use the same format.

Figure 8-1 illustrates some of the commonalities and shades of difference in different formats which may share much of the music they broadcast. For instance, Contemporary Hit Radio (CHR), an outgrowth of Top-40 radio, generally targets younger listeners, usually men and women age 18 to 34. When some of the harder rock songs are removed and replaced by a few oldies and softer rock music, the CHR format edges closer to Adult Contemporary (A/C). When the CHR format ignores softer rock and ballads, it edges closer to Album-Oriented Rock (AOR), particularly when the programmer pays less attention to currently popular singles and gives album cuts some airplay. Another variation emphasizes music that has its primary or original appeal to black listeners but also attracts a strong secondary white audience. In such a

case, CHR moves closer to becoming Urban Contemporary (UC), a variation on the Black Appeal format. Depending on the ethnic composition of the market, the Urban Contemporary format may also include Latin or Hispanic music. For example, both Miami and Houston have large Hispanic and black populations, and so the music programmed on an Urban formatted station in either market will probably reflect those ethnic appeals.

In years past, distinctions between formats were much clearer. Middle of the Road meant light orchestral music, ballads, and show tunes, mostly by established artists such as Frank Sinatra, Jack Jones, Julie London, and Barbra Streisand. Top 40 meant rock 'n' roll. Country-and-Western (C & W) music, sometimes called "hillbilly music" or Country, featured the twangy steel guitar and fiddle music that backed up such artists as Hank Williams, Earnest Tubb, Kitty Wells, Faron Young, the Sons of the Pioneers, and Patsy Cline. Black Appeal radio stations played Rhythm and Blues by John Lee Hooker, B.B. King, and Hank Ballard and the Midnighters and Soul music by artists such as Marvin Gaye, James Brown and the Famous Flames, and the Temptations. Beautiful-Music/Easy-Listening stations broadcast lush instrumentals typified by Henry Mancini, Mantovani, and the Andre Kostelantez Orchestra and cheerful choral arrangements by the Mitch Miller Singers and the Ray Conniff Singers.

None of those distinctions seem apt today. As discussed below, refinements in formats embrace the music of different styles. Both the artists and their audiences have grown up listening to different styles of music and have incorporated those influences in their work and their tastes.

Top 40/Contemporary Hit Radio

The Top-40 format established a style that has evolved as the standard for modern radio programming. Its creators targeted a specific (in that case, young) audience and played a limited number of carefully researched hit songs. The

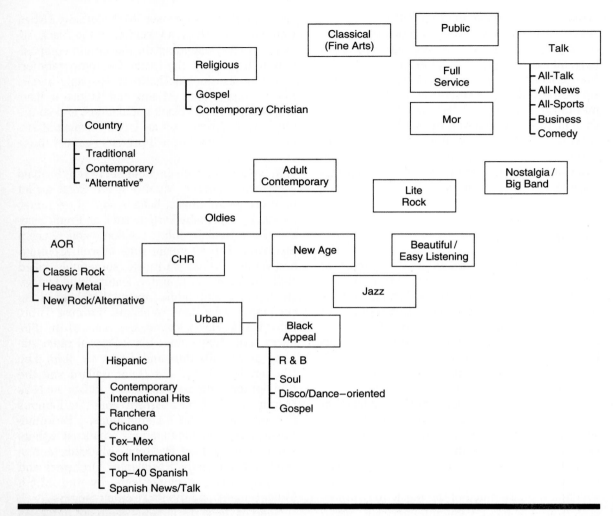

FIGURE 8-1   Radio formats.

story goes that format pioneer Todd Storz observed a waitress in a tavern using her own money to play the same songs that had been played repeatedly on the jukebox during the whole evening. Storz reasoned that people want to hear some songs over and over, and thus the Top-40 concept was born.[11]

The resulting format followed a number of important principles. First, programming was developed to fill a void by offering something different from and better than what was available in the market. Importantly, programming was given a status at least equal to that of selling advertising time. Programming decisions were made by appraising the tastes and desires of the audience. In the early days disc jockeys such as Alan Freed, Dick Clark, and Murray the K selected their own music, but in a number of cases management, not individual disc jockeys, determined the music to be played. As the format developed, strict policies for programming were established and there was careful monitoring and critiquing of on-air personalities to ensure compliance. A limited number of records were played, ensuring rapid rotation of the songs that listeners wanted to hear. Those criteria became the rule for Top-40 radio and most other formats.

Instead of trying to appeal to adult listeners, Top-40 stations deliberately drove them away with the energetic music and rapid-fire patter of the disc jockeys. These radio personalities became local celebrities among teenagers, who tuned in their programs for the music and the high energy level. For instance, teens living near the Mexican border in California tuned in XERB in Tijuana to listen to Wolfman Jack. The howls with which he punctuated the blues, rock 'n' roll, oldies, and novelty records he aired made him a legend even before he played himself in the 1973 movie *American Graffiti*.[12] Record hops hosted by popular disc jockeys were as well attended as dances featuring prominent area bands. In the early 1960s, for instance, appearances in central Indiana by Bouncin' Bill Baker, who "klipped along the kilocycles" on WIBC, Indianapolis, were major social events for teens.

The Top-40 stations of the 1950s and 1960s heightened audience interest through elaborate promotions, including such gimmicks as a contest by KILT, Houston, that gave the lucky winner a snowstorm on his or her front lawn in the middle of the summer.[13] Such zany promotions turned many advertisers off. They returned, however, when they recognized the efficiency of reaching a tight demographic group.

An important change in Top-40 radio came in the mid-1960s, when Bill Drake became program director of KHJ, Los Angeles. Drake, whose formula was widely imitated, shortened disc jockey chatter, curtailed the number of commercial announcements, and otherwise eliminated clutter to emphasize "much more music."[14] KHJ's "Boss Radio" format featured 33 songs, virtually all by established artists. The selections were made on the basis of each recording's "momentum," which meant national chart status and local record sales. KHJ's influence went beyond the Los Angeles market. The music "tip sheets" on which many programmers

based their decisions to put records on the air gave more emphasis to songs aired on KHJ than to those aired on most other stations. Since then, stations have alternated between emphasizing music over personalities and the reverse, but for younger audiences especially, the emphasis on music has been a major attraction.[15]

The Top-40 format embraced artists from virtually all musical styles. If a ballad was popular, it was included in a Top-40 playlist. Thus, Frank Sinatra's novelty song "High Hopes" and his ballad "Strangers in the Night" were played along with songs by Gladys Knight and the Pips and the Beach Boys. Instrumentals, while relatively rare, were aired on Top-40 formatted stations regardless of their acceptability in other formats.

An important conceptual change in the Top-40 format came in 1964, when the Federal Communications Commission enacted its AM-FM *nonduplication rule*. This required operators of AM/FM combination stations in the major markets to program their FM stations independently at least half the time. The rule was expanded to 75 percent of the time in 1979 and was applied to markets as small as 25,000 population. By that time, though, FM stations had begun to be profitable, and that provided enough of an incentive for their operators to program them separately.[16] The rise in the prominence of FM stations led to more specialized formats as a greater number of stations fought for a position in increasingly crowded radio markets.

Top 40 becomes CHR Today, Top 40 is a format with a stigma, which has caused it to give way to Contemporary Hit Radio. Top-40 radio became so narrowly identified that advertisers began to perceive it as a format that attracted only teenage listeners in spite of audience ratings that indicated the opposite. Moreover, the CHR label came into vogue at a time when stations were trying to reposition themselves as formats became more specialized.

A principal difference between the CHR and Top 40 formats is that a true Top-40 format appeals to a wide range of listeners, from teens through older adults, whereas CHR formatted stations tend to target listeners 18 to 34. CHR's primary core audience is men and women age 12 to 24, with a secondary audience among men and women 25 to 49. As the data in Figure 8-2 indicate, females 12 to 17 spend almost half their radio listening to CHR, compared with male teens, who spend 36 percent of their listening time with this format (many male teens are lured away by AOR formats). Males 18 to 24 devote about 20 percent of their listening to CHR, compared with 27 percent of women 18 to 24.[17]

Regardless of whether the format is called Top 40 or CHR, it is characterized by currently popular songs and a limited playlist. Established performers who receive heavy airplay on CHR stations include Madonna, Phil Collins, George Michael, Bon Jovi, Guns 'N Roses, John Cougar Mellencamp, Chicago, and Paula Abdul.[18] Since these artists have a string of hits, they are likely to be important for at least a few more years as others rise to prominence and fade into obscurity after only a hit recording or two.

Spinoff formats such as Adult Contemporary are refinements of the Top-40 concept that target other audience segments. Similarly, the Con-

temporary Country music format follows the principles that originated in Top-40 radio, including intensive music research and the placing of songs into popularity and demographic appeal categories to control the frequency with which and the times of the day when they will be aired. These concepts are applied in most music-intensive formats.

Country

Country music used to be considered a minor genre that was of interest only to listeners in the rural south, but its popularity began to grow steadily during the period commencing roughly with World War II, when many northern boys were introduced to the style while going through basic training in boot camps in southern states. Country music was all that played over loudspeakers in the barracks, and that caused many GIs from other regions of the country to acquire a taste for it.

During the war period many southerners migrated to work in factories in the midwest and elsewhere. These changes in the nation's de-

FIGURE 8-2 CHR format shares. *(From* Radio Year Round: The Medium for All Seasons. *Used by permission of Arbitron Ratings Co.)*

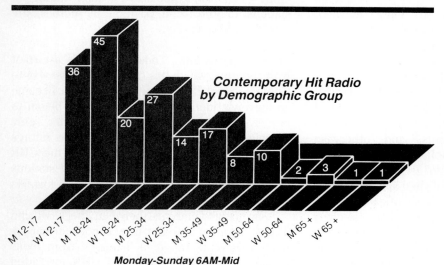

mography helped diffuse musical and cultural tastes. Today Country seems to occupy the same niche for many listeners that MOR radio once did. It is melodic, the words can be understood, it is usually appropriate for slow dancing, and many Country songs are romantic.

In the 1960s, WIRE, Indianapolis, was in the vanguard of major-market midwestern stations programming Country. By the 1970s other major-market stations had begun to program Country while applying the formula techniques used in other formats. Until then, playlists at many stations consisted of 60 or 70 records, but in 1975 WMAQ, Chicago, shortened its list to 35 songs.[19] The disc jockeys were not "down-home country" but had personalities that could have been heard in any other format. The greatest difference between their format and that of a Top-40 or CHR station was that most of the music aired was performed by mainstream Country artists.

The 1970s also saw the development of progressive Country music, including what has been called the Austin revolution. Texas-based artists such as Jerry Jeff Walker and Asleep at the Wheel emerged on the national music scene. This movement was bolstered by Willie Nelson, who moved back to Texas from Nashville, the "capital of Country music." He and a number of other "outlaw" artists, such as Waylon Jennings and Hank Williams, Jr., broke from the Nashville Country music establishment and its traditions. Their increased popularity also attracted a wider audience for the format.

Country music was also given a boost in popularity by the success of the movie *Urban Cowboy,* starring John Travolta.[20] In addition, crossover songs by performers such as the Australian singer Olivia Newton John and the pop folk artist John Denver were aired on Country stations. These changes helped give Country greater visibility and respectability in larger markets.

Regardless of the roots of currently popular Country songs, the Country format has become as sophisticated as any other, with on-air personalities who could easily move to stations that use

other formats. With few exceptions, disc jockeys who espouse the stereotyped "rustic" approach are found only in smaller markets.

Contemporary Country   Country music has steadily evolved as a mainstream format, and some of its roots are in rock 'n' roll. That is apparent in the music of entertainers who have been successful in releasing "cover records," or new versions, of songs such as Conway Twitty's version of "Slow Hand," originally made popular by the Pointer Sisters on Top-40 and Black Appeal formats and "The Rose," which had been an A/C and Top-40 hit for Bette Midler. Moreover, a number of major country stars started as rock 'n' roll performers. Jerry Lee Lewis, for instance, had great success during the 1950s with such songs as "Whole Lot of Shakin' Going On" and "Great Balls of Fire" before his popularity plummeted. He reemerged in Country music, where he found a wide audience. Conway Twitty's first big song, "It's Only Make Believe," was a Top-40 hit. Now he is one of Country music's major artists, continuing to record hit songs year after year.

Contemporary or "progressive" Country format stations do not limit their playlists to established Country artists but also air songs by other popular musicians who are not normally considered Country but appeal to listeners and fit within the context of the format. Even though it incensed traditionalists, Olivia Newton John, with her **crossover songs,** once won the Country Music Association's female vocalist of the year award. Even a major black pop group, the Pointer Sisters, has had a Country hit, and 1950s and 1960s rock 'n' roll hits have been recycled by Country artists. Although Elvis Presley was a Top-40 artist, he is as likely to be heard on a Country station as on a CHR or Adult Contemporary station today. Songs by major rock groups of the 1970s such as the Eagles, the Allman Brothers Band, and Jim Croce are often programmed by Country stations today. Many listeners to today's Country music formats cut their teeth on rock 'n' roll and still enjoy that kind of music.

As with other forms, Country music trends come and go. During the mid-1980s a resurgence of the traditional Country sound gave great success to such artists as Ricky Skaggs, whose forte is an amplified, more hard-driving version of traditional bluegrass music, and Randy Travis and George Strait, whose styles are reminiscent of those of 1950s artists. Other Country music artists whose records receive heavy airplay on Country stations include Lee Greenwood, Alabama, Randy Travis, Reba McEntire, the Judds, Merle Haggard, Ricky Van Shelton, Ronnie Millsap, and Shenandoah.[21]

Thus Country music, which owes allegiance to a variety of styles, including Texas Swing, Rhythm and Blues, Bluegrass, Gospel, and nineteenth-century Scotch, Irish, and English ballads, has changed over the years. Just as rock music has evolved since the 1950s, Contemporary Country has emerged from a traditional sound.

Traditional Country Traditional Country formats are most often broadcast in rural areas. These stations have often been characterized by their aversion to programming popular artists whose appeal "crosses over" to Country listeners, whereas the Contemporary Country format embraces a much wider variety of artists and styles.

It is difficult to categorize stations as either contemporary or traditional except for one overriding characteristic. Once Country music artists

are established, they tend to hang on to their popularity for much longer than do most popular music performers. The tradition of the Grand Old Opry, broadcast on WSM, Nashville, and now on The Nashville Network on cable, as the Mecca of Country music reinforces the stature of longtime stars such as Porter Wagoner and Roy Acuff, whose songs are still played even though they have not recorded a hit for years, and homage is still paid to long-dead performers such as Earnest Tubb, Hank Williams, Sr., and Cowboy Copas, who were stars in a bygone era.

Country music station programmers are concerned that their formats do not attract the most desirable demographics. Consequently, there has been a steady attempt to position the format to avoid losing out on the audience age 18 to 34. As Figure 8-3 shows, listeners to Country music are older and male-dominated. Country's primary core audience is men 35 to 64, with a secondary core among women 35 to 64.[22]

Alternative Country formats Figure 8-1 illustrates variations in radio formats that represent attempts by stations to position themselves in their markets. The Country format is no exception. There has been an important conceptual change from traditional listeners, who are loyal to the artist to listeners who are loyal to the song.[23] As KMTS, Seattle, program director Tim Murphy commented, "People don't sing artists, they sing songs."[24]

FIGURE 8-3 Country format shares. *(From* Radio Year Round: The Medium for All Seasons. *Used by permission of Arbitron Ratings Co.)*

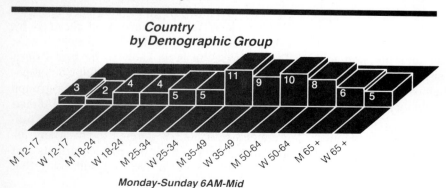

An alternative Country format that has been used successfully in southern markets mixes standard Country with southern rock music by such groups as the Kentucky Headhunters, Southern Pacific, and the Desert Rose Band. The format features up-tempo, hard-driving music and emphasizes current Country and Country Rock songs, along with AOR standards by such groups as Lynyrd Skynrd, the Marshall Tucker Band, Bob Seger, Little Feat, ZZ Top, and the Allman Brothers. The objective is to appeal "to the image and lifestyle of the 33-year-old male who likes music with energy, who thinks of himself as rowdy and raucous—even if he doesn't act that way."[25]

Another variation mixes songs by Contemporary Country artists such as Tanya Tucker, Randy Travis, and Eddie Rabbitt with such established Adult Contemporary artists as Jennifer Warnes, Bread, and Crosby, Stills, & Nash. Stations may not use the term "Country" on the air to avoid alienating potential Adult Contemporary and Classic Rock listeners.[26]

Album-Oriented Rock

The Album-Oriented Rock music format evolved after a few stations began featuring "Under- ground Rock" music during the 1960s as an alternative to the tightly controlled Top-40 sound that started with Bill Drake. Much of this material was counterculture, or "protest," music replete with a heavy rock beat and lyrics that espoused a way of life considered to be out of the mainstream. Underground Rock gave way in the 1970s to "Progressive Rock," a format that greatly restricted the disc jockeys and emphasized music with more commercial appeal.[27] In broadening the format to make it more attractive to a greater number of listeners, AOR programmers attempted to attract Top-40 listeners who liked only some of the music that was being aired. The key was artist familiarity, a change from the song title familiarity of Top-40 radio. Whereas a Top-40 station might play the two or three hit songs recorded by an artist, an AOR station would play 15 or 20 cuts by that artist.[28]

Artists who receive considerable air play on AOR formats include groups such as U2, Pink Floyd, Van Halen, Aerosmith, and ZZ Top. Other prominent AOR artists are John Cougar Mellencamp, Eric Clapton, Bruce Springsteen, and Tom Petty.[29] AOR's traditional audience base (Figure 8-4) is narrow, consisting primarily of teenage and young adult male listeners. The traditional core audience has been males 12 to 34,

FIGURE 8-4   AOR format shares. *(From* Radio Year Round: The Medium for All Seasons. *Used by permission of Arbitron Ratings Co.)*

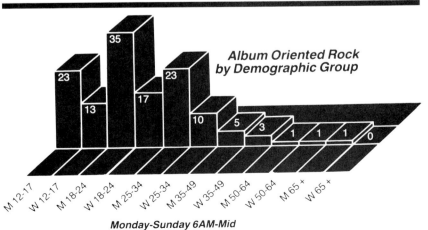

Album Oriented Rock by Demographic Group

M 12-17 W 12-17 M 18-24 W 18-24 M 25-34 W 25-34 M 35-49 W 35-49 M 50-64 W 50-64 M 65+ W 65+

Monday-Sunday 6AM-Mid

with males 18 to 24 spending 35 percent of their listening time with the AOR format.[30]

With the shrinking of the youth population and the rise in the average age of listeners, many stations have reoriented their formats to target an older audience (the "graying of AOR"). Some have called their adapted formats Classic Rock in an attempt to recapture listeners who grew up with that music. Reacting to demographic shifts in the population, most AOR programmers have targeted an older audience.[31]

Even with the predominance of an older AOR audience, programmers in some markets are being forced to choose between listeners 25 to 44 or 25 to 54 and an influx of younger listeners. Although advertisers are more interested in the older demographics, a new generation of listeners has grown up with an affinity for newer performers. Traditional AOR had its genesis in such artists as Cream, Led Zeppelin, Jimi Henderix, and the Rolling Stones. The addition of newer, younger-targeted bands such as Queensryche, Cinderella, and the Black Crowes has changed the mix. Some AOR stations may be able to maintain a delicate balance and appeal to a wide range of listeners. In other markets, though, the format will be fragmented as changes in audience and the appeal of other formats force programmers to decide whether to target younger or older listeners.[32]

New Rock/Alternative

Rock music has often been somewhat ahead, or at least off to the side, of mainstream tastes. Traditionally, rock 'n' roll was a young person's music; in fact, it is arguable that rock has always functioned in part to alienate adults. Regardless of the perennial test of wills between parents and their offspring, there are music fans who reject mainstream pop. In addition to many college stations operated by students, an Alternative Rock music format has been embraced by a number of full-fledged commercial operations.

The New Rock format appeals primarily to younger listeners, notably those in the 18- to 34-year-old age range. Although groups that receive airplay on CHR and AOR stations, such as the Talking Heads, INXS, Sting, David Bowie, U2, and Elvis Costello, are considered core artists, performers such as Chris Isaak, the Divinyls, and Jesus Jones are also played.

There is a heavy reliance on album cuts rather than singles. In fact, some stations that program New Rock consider this format a derivation of AOR.[33] A 2-hour morning alternative music program, *World Cafe,* features such core artists as Elvis Costello, Paul Simon, the Neville Brothers, and Shawn Colvin. It is aired on public radio stations, which receive it via satellite from American Public Radio.[34]

Beautiful Music/Easy Listening

Beautiful Music, also called Easy Listening, has been a mainstay of FM radio since the 1950s, when many AM operators acquired FM licenses as a hedge against the future. Programming lush instrumentals complemented by an occasional ballad was a safe and inexpensive way to fill the program day. For many years the FM radio medium was typified by an Easy-Listening, or background music, image. The action was on AM radio, where the Top-40 format reigned. Then, in the late 1960s, an increasing number of stations began programming popular music and FM eventually became the dominant radio medium.

One of the hallmarks of Beautiful Music has been the presentation of the format via automated broadcasting equipment. An electronic programming device triggers the start and stop of the music tape so that prerecorded commercials and other content can be played. Automation has worked especially well with this format. Listeners tend to stay tuned for a long time since the music serves as a background service. Announcers are low-key and unobtrusive, and so the absence of spontaneous live personalities is not a drawback. Importantly, automated equipment eliminates the need for live announcers, which holds down the station's operating costs. Most Beautiful-Music stations subscribe to syndicated services such as Bonneville Music and Kalamusic, which program the music and provide it on tape for their client stations.[35]

Beautiful Music seems to be largely a generational format. Those who came of age during or before World War II grew up in the big-band era, in the days before rock 'n' roll. Their children, the postwar generation, are now middle aged and comfortable with the rock music base of Adult Contemporary formats. Moreover, the children of the postwar baby boomers are now themselves teenagers and young adults. As they mature, their taste in music will soften, but its base will again be rock music, unlike the experience of their grandparents. Beautiful/Easy Listening's primary audience (Figure 8-5) is men and women 50 and over with a secondary core among men and women 35 and over. The format particularly appeals to females above age 35.[36]

In years past, standard instrumentals predominated in Beautiful-Music formats, accompanied by a few vocals performed by choral groups or crooners such as John Davidson and Perry Como. Today, as much as half the music in some dayparts may consist of vocals performed by currently popular artists such as Lionel Richie, Anne Murray, and George Winston.[37]

Anticipating a change in the audience, Group W Radio developed a new Easy-Listening format for its stations that it dubbed "Adult Spectrum Radio." Instead of playing Andy Williams, Tony Bennett, and Frank Sinatra—artists who appeal much more to 55 and above listeners—Group W programs to the audience age 35 to 54 by playing Roberta Flack, Stevie Wonder, Dan Fogelberg, and Billy Joel, along with Barbra Streisand, Johnny Mathis, and instrumental recordings, for a mix of music that includes Light Jazz, Soft Rock, New Age, Oldies, and modern Country.[38]

Adopting a similar positioning strategy, some stations have changed their identification from Beautiful Music to Easy Listening in an effort to get away from the perception that Beautiful Music is an old person's format. Such repositioning has continued as baby boomers have aged and have begun to lose their taste for hard rock. In attempting to dispel the notion that Beautiful Music is a background format, many of these stations run contests and have given increased emphasis to information and personality.[39]

Such developments blur the lines between formats. The Adult Contemporary format, which targets Beautiful Music's prime demographic, listeners 35 to 54, has posed a serious competitive threat.

Adult Contemporary

The progression from Top 40 to CHR was largely due to the perception that young people pre-

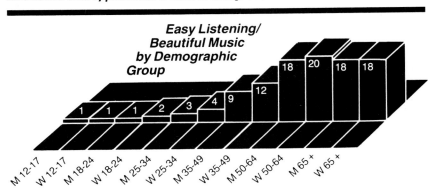

FIGURE 8-5   Beautiful-Music format shares. *(From* Radio Year Round: The Medium for All Seasons. *Used by permission of Arbitron Ratings Co.)*

dominated in the Top-40 audience. Similarly, the Adult Contemporary format represents one of the important format shifts toward audience segmentation. Recording artists in A/C formats include Phil Collins, Elton John, Chicago, Lionel Richie, Barbra Streisand, Whitney Houston, the Beatles, Anita Baker, Kenny G., and Billy Joel.[40]

While A/C formats include many of the songs programmed on CHR, their programmers limit their playlists to avoid irritating listeners between 25 and 54. Personalities sparkle, but without the level of outrageousness and high-decibel energy level some CHR and AOR station personalities affect. Listeners age 25 to 54 do not generally find the off-color humor and the harder rock music associated with those formats as appealing as younger audience segments do.

The Adult Contemporary audience (Figure 8-6) is predominantly female, with women 25 to 34 and 35 to 49 having the largest shares of listeners. Thus, the core demographics for A/C are women 25 to 49, with men and women 18 to 24 and men 25 and over as secondary core audiences.[41]

With many Beautiful/Easy-listening formatted stations attempting to reposition themselves to maintain an audience, Soft Adult Contemporary has emerged as an alternative format. Unlike the personality-oriented mainstream A/C format, Soft A/C is a song-driven format that targets men and women 35 and over.[42] Another variation in the shift from the aging demographics attracted to Beautiful Music to a format that targets younger listeners has been called Light (or "Lite") Rock because it features light-tempo rock music and popular ballads. Regardless of its label, and an advantage of the A/C format is that it can be played in offices during working hours without being obtrusive. However, this format maintains a contemporary feel because its musical selections are performed by established pop music artists such as Cher, Linda Ronstadt, and Michael Bolton.

Middle of the Road

The Middle-of-the-Road format dates back to the 1950s, when teens listened to Top-40 stations and adults tuned in MOR stations that typically featured personalities, news, weather, sports, and popular music but not rock.[43] Today's MOR station is still found on the AM dial and features a talk-intensive format often described as Full-Service or *Full-Service Adult* radio. Most of these stations are high-powered major-market AM facilities that have provided listeners with a full

FIGURE 8-6   FM Adult Contemporary format shares. *(From* Radio Year Round: The Medium for All Seasons. *Used by permission of Arbitron Ratings Co.)*

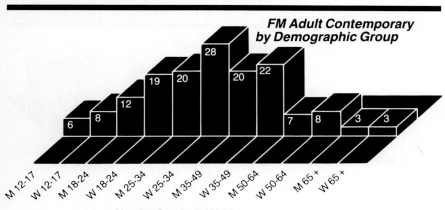

Monday-Sunday 6AM-Mid

range of news, weather, agriculture reports, and adult-oriented call-in programs for many years. The on-air personalities typically appeal to listeners over age 30.

Music on MOR/Full-Service stations is a secondary part of the programming strategy that is used to fill in between other program events. Even so, it often appeals to younger listeners. The typical MOR station plays current music only if it is listed on both the A/C and CHR charts. The idea is that although listeners 50 and over may not like Madonna or Bruce Springsteen, they are much more likely to tolerate that music than a 30-year-old is to stay tuned for artists whose pop tunes were popular in the 1950s, such as Patti Page and Frankie Lane.[44]

While MOR stations play music—typical artists include Carly Simon, Barbra Streisand, Bette Midler, and Peter Noone—they give much greater emphasis to talk programs and discussion. Listeners may be encouraged to call in to share their perspectives. The subjects and their targeted listeners may shift dramatically between dayparts going from issues of interest to women during midmorning to sports, politics, or civic affairs at night. Many successful Full-Service stations have a heavy schedule of sports broadcasts, carrying the area's professional baseball, basketball, hockey, and football games.

Although a wide range of listeners can be attracted to different programs, MOR core listeners are in the male and female age groups 35 and over (Figure 8-7).[45]

New Age

A purposively narrow-appeal audience segment format is New Age, also referred to as New Adult Contemporary (NAC). Created as an alternative to appeal to a subset of listeners of 25 to 54 years old, this format is labeled by some people as the opposite of rock 'n' roll and by others as Beautiful Music for yuppies.

Its originators have tapped the growing popularity of newer music styles that blend ethereal "space music" by such artists as George Winston and Andreas Vollenweider with "jazz fusion" performers such as Kenny G., Spyro Gyra, and Acoustic Alcemy, along with pop singers who include Sting, Steely Dan, Anita Baker, Paul Simon, and Sade. A record label closely associated with this concept is Windham Hill; others include American Gramaphone, Narada, and Global Pacific.[46]

The defining characteristic of this format is that it is uplifting, as if designed to calm the tensions of its listeners. It is subdued and uses minimal talk. New Age could be described as an environment for listeners, an aural sea of tranquility in which the listener can be immersed as a shield against the stresses of the fast-paced urban lifestyle. The positioning liners used by

FIGURE 8-7 **AM Adult Contemporary format shares.** *(From* Radio Year Round: The Medium for All Seasons. *Used by permission of Arbitron Ratings Co.)*

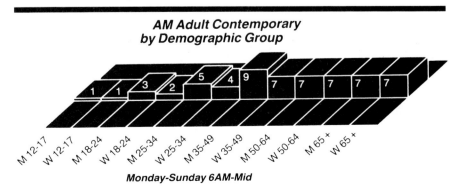

one New Age formatted station exemplify this concept: "a fresh new sound," "unique by design," and "an oasis in the desert of sound."[47]

Nostalgia and Big Band

The difference between the Big-Band and Nostalgia formats may be largely a matter of musical emphasis. A Nostalgia format can include music from any era and may feature contemporary artists. This format includes nonrock hits from the 1960s, 1970s, and 1980s, whereas an authentic Big-Band format features original recordings by Tommy Dorsey's Orchestra, Glenn Miller, Glen Grey and the Casa Loma Orchestra, and others from the heyday of the big bands, principally the 1940s and early 1950s. In either case, the positioning strategy is to offer the popular music of a bygone era. Most stations that use this format rely on a syndicated service such as Al Ham's *Music of your Life,* or Satellite Music Network's *Stardust.*

The format definitely appeals to older listeners (Figure 8-8). The core audience for Nostalgia/Big Band is concentrated among listeners ages 50 and over, with slight dominance among males.[48]

Nostalgia and Big-Band formats have been widely used on AM stations whose market shares have eroded as a result of competition from FM. Big Band is a natural format for AM stations since the recording techniques available during that era were not sophisticated and none of the music of that era was released in stereo. Thus fans of this music have been accustomed to listening to lower-fidelity monaural sound. Moreover, the hearing of the older audience, to whom Big-Band and Nostalgia most appeal, tends to decline with age. Consequently, fewer of the format's core listeners are able to recognize the range in sound that can be reproduced with modern recording and playback techniques. Equally important, this is the age group most accustomed to listening to AM radio, whereas younger listeners largely ignore that medium.

Black Appeal

The Black format is one of the oldest specialty radio formats, getting its start in 1947 on WDIA, Memphis, and soon thereafter at WVON ("Voice of Negro Radio"), Chicago,[49] playing Rhythm and Blues, Blues, and "race records" for black audiences.

Black Appeal stations, which emerged in the south and spread to northern markets, have traditionally specialized in playing music performed

FIGURE 8-8 Nostalgia/Big-Band format shares. *(From* Radio Year Round: The Medium for All Seasons. *Used by permission of Arbitron Ratings Co.)*

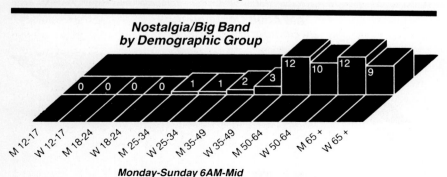

by black artists and emphasize news and events of particular interest to the black community. The Black format has always been a Full-Service radio format, appealing to a wide age range. It has traditionally included religious programming and black gospel music.[50]

Because music trends wax and wane, many Black Appeal programmers have found themselves beleaguered by the wider popularity of many artists traditionally featured on their stations. Black Appeal formats have always had a substantial minority white audience, but competing stations have given some black artists greater airplay, luring some of those listeners.

A number of CHR formatted stations, adapting to the competitive conditions in their markets, have developed something akin to Urban Contemporary which includes many dance songs and performances by black artists. Their objective is to reclaim the white listeners who are attracted to Black Appeal formats and to increase their black audiences.

Many Black Appeal formatted stations feel a need to position themselves as something other than Black Appeal or Urban Contemporary. As the data in Table 8-3 (p. 218) show, these formats have been stigmatized by advertisers, who think that they cannot reach the prime consumer segments that will purchase their goods and services.

A number of stations that use a traditional Black format do not have the technical resources to compete for wider audiences because they operate at a signal strength lower than that of their competitors. Some have attempted to define their positions by "blackening" their music programming by playing more Blues, Jazz, and other music that the CHR stations will not air.[51] A number of AM stations have found success by programming black music from the late 1950s through the present. For instance, the *Heart and Soul* service from the Satellite Music Network includes a heavy mix of Rhythm and Blues, Soul, black pop, ballads, dance music, and even white artists such as Hall and Oates, the Doobie Brothers, and Dr. John. The AM stations target older listeners for whom the rap recordings and

scratch records so prominent in current black pop music lack appeal.

An important ingredient in some Black Appeal formats is rap, a music form that entered the mainstream in the late 1980s.[52] Some stations, seeing their audiences drift away to formats that have added black performers to their rotations, have fought back by emphasizing rap artists such as Run-D.M.C., Ice-T, and LL Cool-J.[53] But Amos Brown of WTLC, Indianapolis, contends that rap has polarized black audiences.[54] Most programmers feel that black adults are as likely to be driven away by rap music aired on Black Appeal stations as white adults are to be alienated by loud "current-based" youth-appeal music.

Urban Contemporary

Urban Contemporary evolved from the traditional Black Appeal formula by presenting a mixture of music that appeals to a more ethnically diverse audience. Although the base for the UC format is Black Appeal, music by Latin artists and other music reflecting the more eclectic taste of major-market listeners has been included. The precise mix of music varies with the market. For example, Latin music is much more likely to be a predominant music form on a Miami UC station than on a station in Detroit.

Little differentiation is made between Black Appeal and Urban Contemporary by the general radio industry, with the latter name often being used to describe the format. Regardless, it is noteworthy that yet another format has evolved, with some stations leading the way in a further definition of what they offer listeners.

As Figure 8-9 shows, Urban Contemporary/ Black formats have their strongest appeal among younger listeners, particularly teenagers. A strong secondary core is found among male and female listeners age 18 to 49.[55]

Core Urban Contemporary artists include Luther Vandross, Anita Baker, Michael Jackson, New Edition, Levert, Prince, and Freddie Jackson.[56] The format has proved especially successful in large cities because it attracts a wide spectrum of listeners. Older people tune in because it

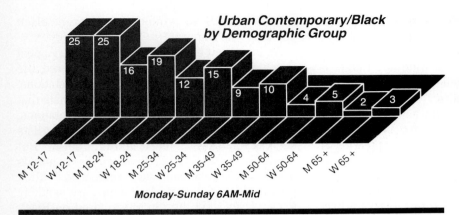

Urban Contemporary/Black by Demographic Group

Monday-Sunday 6AM-Mid

FIGURE 8-9 Urban/Black Appeal format shares. *(From* Radio Year Round: The Medium for All Seasons. *Used by permission of Arbitron Ratings Co.)*

Oldies

The future of the Oldies format is secure since every currently popular song can eventually be added to the repertoire. However, stations that program Oldies exclusively face the dilemma of keeping their formats fresh, since there is a limited number of songs available from the 1950s, 1960s, 1970s, and 1980s.

A strong incentive for programmers to consider adopting an Oldies format or include a heavy mix of Oldies in the present format's rotation is the burgeoning segment of the radio audience age 25 to 54 that has been swelled by aging baby boomers. Oldies can attract listeners who do not find current music appealing. Furthermore, the Oldies format is one that local advertisers can identify with. For this reason, some advertisers are inclined to buy advertising time on Oldies stations regardless of where they are in the overall audience competition.[57] Still, a consideration for a programmer contemplating a "pure" Oldies format must be the considerable competition from Adult Contemporary stations that program a heavy mix of Oldies. Such stations constitute one of the greatest threats since both the A/C

is often the only strong choice for Black Appeal music. Younger listeners who seek a sound different from CHR are also attracted.

and Oldies formats have to strong appeal to listeners 25 to 54.[58]

Regardless of whether a station programs all Oldies or mixes them with contemporary songs, music research is crucial in avoiding burnout and identifying the tunes that will have audience recognition and appeal. Some programmers identify two eras in Oldies music: pre-Beatles and the period starting with the "British invasion." With the coming of the Beatles, the Rolling Stones, the Dave Clark Five, and other British rock groups in the early 1960s, rock experienced a dramatic change in its style. Therefore, many Oldies stations do not play music from the 1950s.

Hispanic

The potential for Hispanic radio formats is greatest in the southwest and California, where the largest proportion of Hispanic people live. The format has also been successful in large markets, such as Miami, that have become magnets for significant clusters of Hispanics. The six largest Hispanic radio markets in order of population size are Los Angeles, New York, San Antonio, Miami, San Francisco, and Chicago.[59]

There are some distinct cultural differences among the groups in the broad Hispanic audience. Listeners in Miami have a socioeconomic status and a cultural orientation different from those of Hispanics in California, who differ from Hispanics in Texas. Similarly, the large Puerto Rican population on the East Coast has tastes and interests that are unique. It is important to recognize that these radio listeners have their cultural origins in different countries: The largest Hispanic audience is Mexican, followed by Puerto Rican, Cuban, Dominican, Columbian, and Central American—which includes El Salvador, Guatemala, and Nicaragua—followed by smaller populations from Venezuela, Argentina, and Spain.[60]

As the Hispanic population has grown, it has taken on new economic and political importance. Advertisers have become increasingly interested in tapping this market, and there has been an increase in the number of stations programming to Hispanics. With increased competition for this audience segment, Spanish-language stations have adopted modern programming techniques and have employed a wide variety of formats (Table 8-1).

The most popular Hispanic appeal format is Contemporary International Hits, currently programmed on 41 percent of all Hispanic stations. Ranchera (equivalent to Country) Contemporary Spanish Hits is programmed on 18 percent of Hispanic stations.[61]

As young Hispanics move into the mainstream of American culture, many are attracted to rock music formatted stations that promote music

TABLE 8-1   Hispanic Radio Formats

Format	Primary Audience
Contemporary International Hits	AM: 25–44 FM: 18–34
Ranchera/Contemporary Spanish Hits	AM: 25–44 FM: 18–44
Ranchera	AM: 25–34 and 55–64
Chicano	AM: 18–34 FM: 25–34 and 55–64
Tex-Mex	AM: 25–44
Soft International Hits	AM: 45–64
Top-40 Spanish	AM: 25–54 FM 18–44
Spanish News/Talk	AM: 45 and over

SOURCE: From *NAB RadioWeek,* May 22, 1989, p. 2. © National Association of Broadcasters, 1989. Used with permission.

sweeps and feature less talk. Thus, the language and the music are key to the position of any station targeting a Hispanic audience. But with greater competition, stations must be programmed to attract and maintain a more specific segment of the Hispanic audience than was necessary in the past.[62]

Figure 8-10 shows that Spanish-language

FIGURE 8-10   Hispanic format shares. *(From* Radio Year Round: The Medium for All Seasons. *Used by permission of Arbitron Ratings Co.)*

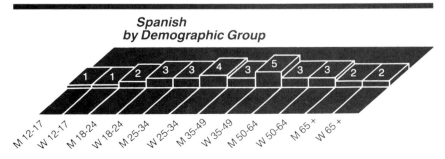

Spanish
by Demographic Group

M 12-17 W 12-17 M 18-24 W 18-24 M 25-34 W 25-34 M 35-49 W 35-49 M 50-64 W 50-64 M 65+ W 65+

Monday-Sunday 6AM-Mid

radio has a larger share of female than male listeners, with dominant age groups of 25 to 64. The secondary core audience is men and women 18 and over.[63]

Religious

With some exceptions, the Religious format is dominated by a conservative form of Protestant Christianity. One approach to Religious programming is evangelical broadcasting, which attempts to spread the word into the world. The other approach is to minister to the body of believers by providing entertainment as well as enlightenment and urging adherence to the faith.[64] Religious programmers choose between these objectives, although in reality many attempt to provide blocks of time for both.

Religious stations may program music or avoid it altogether. Religious stations that do not program music concentrate on Christian or religious features. Many of these stations sell blocks of time to ministers who rely on donations from their listeners.[65] Some stations generate considerable revenue from such block programming.

Christian Contemporary music Christian formatted stations have difficulty selling national advertising, but their growth is predicted to remain steady. With increasing competition for financial support, some stations have turned to music as a way to differentiate themselves into their markets.[66]

Increasingly, contemporary music styles are being used by performers who espouse a religious message. A number of stations program Christian Contemporary music that features artists such as Stryper, Petra, and Crystalvox, whose performances are based on current rock music. They feature announcers whose styles are like those on "secular" radio.

As Figure 8-11 shows, the primary core audience for Religious radio is women 25 and above, with a secondary core of men 25 and over.[67]

A number of satellite-distributed religious networks provide 24-hour programming in a variety of formats. These include Adult Contemporary Christian, Country Gospel, Lite Adult Contemporary/MOR Sacred Music, and Instrumental and Vocal Beautiful Sacred Music.[68]

Classical Music

Classical Music formats, sometimes called Fine Arts, are predominantly found on noncommercial or public stations. Commercial Classical stations are found only in large markets, but their owners seem to be solidly committed to the format. The country's first commercial Classical radio station, WQXR-FM, New York, recently moved into new state-of-the-art studios.[69]

FIGURE 8-11 Religious format shares. *(From* Radio Year Round: The Medium for All Seasons. *Used by permission of Arbitron Ratings Co.)*

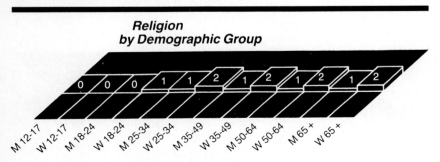

Religion by Demographic Group

0 0 0 1 1 2 1 2 1 2 1 2

M 12-17 W 12-17 M 18-24 W 18-24 M 25-34 W 25-34 M 35-49 W 35-49 M 50-64 W 50-64 M 65+ W 65+

Monday-Sunday 6AM-Mid

Another of the best known commercial Classical Music stations is WFMT in Chicago. Like other stations using this format, WFMT is especially concerned with the quality of its signal since many Classical Music listeners place a high priority on the purity of the sound. To enhance that quality, WFMT's commercials are all broadcast live. The only exceptions are recorded political advertisements.[70]

The primary core audience for Classical Music stations is men and women 35 and over, with men constituting a slightly stronger listening group.[71] Commercial Classical programmers acknowledge that they are attracting a small proportion of the total audience. Regardless, this audience is highly desired by some advertisers since these people tend to be among the best-educated, highest-income listeners in the market.[72]

Changes in musical tastes and new ownership of some Classical Music stations have influenced changes in programming. To broaden their appeal, programmers have reduced the amount of talk and increased the proportion of instrumental music. The music is selected with the objective of keeping listeners tuned for longer periods, and this represents a shift away from playing long selections. Thus, the emphasis is on entertaining listeners, not educating them.[73]

Although programmers at Classical stations generally are not concerned about the tempo of the music they air, they avoid playing downtempo music during the drive time periods. Furthermore, shorter pieces are programmed during the morning and afternoon dayparts to accommodate the commercial schedule.[74]

Many Classical Music stations also program Folk and Jazz segments, often on weekends or during the late-evening hours. WQXR-FM programs Jazz, Classical, and New Age within the same 2-hour time period, for instance. Other stations block out time segments for Jazz and Folk music on a weekly basis.[75]

Information

The decline of AM stations that formerly dominated their markets has prompted adjustments to changed market conditions as FM stations have become the principal outlets for music formats. The alternative of News or Talk is available to virtually every station, but these formats usually succeed only in the largest markets. The power of most smaller-market AM stations is relatively low, and none operate on class 1-A clear-channel frequency assignments. Thus the problem of limited signal coverage during the daytime is compounded by the sparser population reached by these signals. Even though nighttime AM signals travel farther, only the strongest have much chance of reaching a large audience.

In smaller markets the likelihood of attracting an audience large enough to be of interest to most national advertisers is diminished. Furthermore, most small-market listeners spend less time in automobiles. The majority of the population can satisfy its demand for news more easily than can those who live in large, sprawling metropolitan areas. Moreover, the necessity of attracting a sufficiently large mass of listeners normally can be met only in larger markets. This is further complicated by the high cost of the format, which requires a larger staff than does a music-intensive format to operate effectively. Thus, the higher cost requires a larger potential audience for the format to be financially feasible.

News and Talk formats have their strongest appeal among older listeners (50 and over) (Figure 8-12). A secondary core audience consists of men 35 to 49. Among listeners under age 50, males are heavier listeners.[76]

News The 1991 Persian Gulf war gave News radio a boost. Whereas many music formatted stations provided little information, news-oriented stations provided listeners with extensive audio coverage. Although the majority of Americans watched the war on TV, about 18 percent of the American public found out about the war through radio. When the news broke, radio listening doubled during the evening period. In the major markets, the shares for All-News stations went up about 66 percent, and stations with a News/Talk format in those markets increased

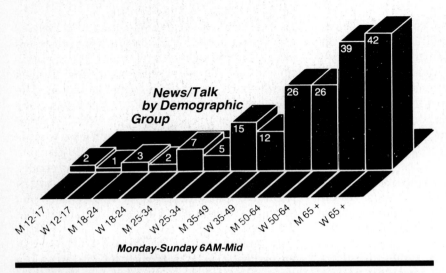

News/Talk by Demographic Group

M 12-17	W 12-17	M 18-24	W 18-24	M 25-34	W 25-34	M 35-49	W 35-49	M 50-64	W 50-64	M 65+	W 65+
2	1	3	2	7	5	15	12	26	26	39	42

Monday-Sunday 6AM-Mid

FIGURE 8-12   News/Talk format shares. *(From* Radio Year Round: The Medium for All Seasons. *Used by permission of Arbitron Ratings Co.)*

their shares by about 36 percent as radio audience members adjusted their listening from their usual stations.[77]

Most stations do not rely exclusively on News but feature a combination of News and Talk programming. The News format is generally broadcast during the morning and afternoon dayparts, when listeners are going to and from work.

Talk   Talk radio programming can include interviews, discussions, and informative talks, but most stations using this format try to involve their listeners. The most direct and effective way to get such listener participation is through call-in programs.

The Larry King Show, broadcast on the Mutual Radio Network, has attracted a large national following. ABC Talk Programing has countered with Tom Snyder and Deborah Norville, the former *Today* cohost. In addition to Rush Limbaugh, alternative talk program services are available to stations on a 24-hour basis.[78] A testament to the potential listener interest in News/Talk has come in the satellite distribution of the signals of KOA, Denver, and the Minneapolis stations WCCO and KSJN to cable sys-

tems. These AM signals are converted to FM frequencies for cablecasting and will eventually be available to over 1 million subscribers.[79]

A number of AM radio stations have signed on with satellite-delivered Talk radio networks as an alternative to shutting down their stations. These stations can receive as much as 24 hours of programming a day on a bartered basis in which 4 minutes of commercial time an hour is given to the network.[80]

Sports   The launching of WFAN, New York, as an All-Sports format illustrates the potential for that direction in Talk radio. The concept, similar to that of All-News radio, includes a variety of sports features. WFAN's broadcasts of sports events at night fill many hours.

WIP, Philadelphia, is another major-market station that has adopted an All-Sports format. The station carries Philadelphia Flyers NHL hockey, Eagles NFL football, and 76ers NBA basketball, along with major college basketball from local schools. The station airs programs featuring coaches in the city and has daily shows featuring sportswriters from both local papers. More recently, WSCR-AM, "The Score," made its debut in Chicago in October 1991, billing itself as having a local Talk/Personality format. Following on WFAN's success in New York, a Minneapolis AM station has adopted the call letters KFAN and has embraced an All-Sports format, as have stations in San Diego and Denver.[81]

Other Narrowcasting Formats

In their search for a market niche, AM stations have embraced a number of nontraditional formats. From 1985 to 1989 a Little Rock, Arkansas, station, KPAL, programmed an All-Children's format that featured storytelling and children's music. The format included a joke call-in program and had a news staff consisting of local elementary school teachers.[82]

A Houston station tried an All-Beatles format, and a Cincinnati market AM station operating at 500 watts launched an All-Elvis format but abandoned the idea after a year. In spite of initial advertiser interest, sales dropped off when the station could not attract an audience large enough to appear in the market's rating book. After an attempt to attract listeners with Elvis's music, the station switched to an All-Business format.[83]

Other stations have adopted All-Business formats, and several networks (Chapter 9) have been created to supply them. In Los Angeles, KMNY, an AM facility, has launched a financial news operation, and the Business Radio Network of Colorado Springs has been able to sell programming to some stations.[84] In a related effort, several AM stations have adopted a Motivational format that features talks by business consultants such as Zig Ziglar, Tom Peters, and Dr. Leo Buscaglia, who offer advice on how to improve personal business and sales productivity skills. Three- to 5-minute segments from motivational cassettes are interspersed with stock market updates, news, business reports, and lifestyle news.[85]

Other AM stations have tried Comedy formats. Although others have failed, a Ventura County, California, AM station, KMDY, has been using this format successfully since 1984. The station, which targets automobile listeners, features cuts from comedy albums during the daytime. At night it runs old-time radio comedy shows such as those starring Jack Benny.[86]

The use of such narrowly defined formats represents an attempt to find a niche in the audience and to attract advertisers, but specialty formats can work only in markets where the audience is large enough to attract advertisers. If a format runs its course, the station's management must be able to recognize the need to abandon it and try something else.

Public Radio

Public radio (noncommercial radio) operates with motivations different from those of commercial broadcasting and has historically offered an alternative to commercial fare. Most **noncommercial broadcasting** stations rely on a host institution for at least some of their financial support. The licensees of many **public broadcasting** stations are universities, although libraries, public school systems, independent civic boards, and religious groups also operate stations. The licensee must either provide all the money for the operation or permit the station to solicit support from businesses in the listening area and seek donations and station memberships from individual listeners.

Although public radio stations are noncommercial, their programming must be carefully selected if they are to receive listener donations and underwriting support. Consequently, public station programmers and "development directors," or fund-raisers, have become increasingly active users of demographic and psychographic research that can identify the attributes of their listeners. They use this knowledge to solicit financial support. Thus, at an increasing number of public radio stations the programming is intended to appeal to an audience willing to contribute to keep such programming on the air.

Contributions from individual listeners provide important support for the operation of many public stations, whose staffs devote considerable time and attention to fund-raising drives. Still, this source generally provides less operating revenue than most stations need to sustain their operation, and so many stations also seek money through other solicitations.

The FCC permits public stations to obtain **underwriting,** or financial support to cover the costs of presenting programming. Stations are permitted to announce the names and brief descriptions of their underwriters' locations and services. The most likely program underwriters are corporate donors that value the enhancement to their images that an association with high-quality programming can bring. These underwriters are often attracted to public radio because they can reach listeners who are considered "opinion leaders" whose goodwill may be beneficial. For example, Texaco Oil has supported broadcasts of symphony concerts for many years. Of course, prototypical Classical Music listeners are highly educated, are among the highest paid segments in the population, and include a disproportionate number of corporate heads.

Three formats—Classical Music, News, and Jazz—take up almost three-fourths of most public radio stations' broadcast time. The three most predominant sources of programming are local-origination programming, most of which is Classical Music and Jazz; National Public Radio (NPR), which supplies morning and afternoon news magazine programs and some cultural programming; and American Public Radio (APR), which supplies a variety of music and cultural programs.[87]

Unlike commercial stations, many public stations rely on network sources for important programming, including *Morning Edition* and *All Things Considered* from NPR. These morning and afternoon news/magazine programs feature long reports on news events, public affairs issues, and cultural topics. These and other services of NPR and APR are discussed in detail in Chapter 9.

In spite of this heavy reliance on network programs, most public radio stations have a distinctly local sound that reflects the interests of listeners in the service area. Whereas stations in the northeast, the southwest, and other locations may give emphasis to the concerns of Native Americans, stations in the Appalachian region may program a considerable amount of music that reflects that heritage.

Most public stations use **block programming,** with the heaviest scheduling of news in the mornings and afternoons, Classical Music during the middle of the day and evenings, and Jazz later at night. The weekends are usually programmed differently from the schedule that is aired Monday through Friday, with specialty programs including folk music and various half-hour or hour programs. A variety of public stations and other sources are sources for such offbeat programs as *My Word,* a linguistic game show from the British Broadcasting Corporation (BBC). A widely distributed program is *Radio Reader,* a daily half-hour reading from a current best-selling book syndicated by Michigan State University.

The typical program director on public radio must oversee a staff that is knowledgeable about Classical Music, its composers, and its performers. Stations that present Jazz programming must employ announcers who are able to identify categories of music and artists in order to present an appealing mixture to an audience that knows and appreciates the music. Depending on the philosophy of the station, the programming strategy may be to appeal to knowledgeable Classical or Jazz Music lovers or to help the uninitiated develop an appreciation for the material.

Still, noncommercial radio does not necessarily mean cultural programming, even though the majority of these stations emphasize Classical Music and, to a lesser extent, Jazz. At least one station in the south programs Beautiful Music throughout its broadcast day, with wide acceptance in its broadcast community. Furthermore, there are scores of noncommercial licensees whose objectives differ from those of typical NPR-affiliated public stations. Some stations are operated by high schools and colleges as training vehicles for students. Others broadcast classroom instruction, while still others are operated by student governments and serve their student constituencies with Progressive music and campus-oriented material. Moreover, about 25 percent of Religious formatted stations are noncommercial.

FORMAT POPULARITY

The popularity of the major radio formats is an indicator of their success, yet a relative lack of popularity may also point to the potential for a format if its uniqueness could position a station in its market. As was discussed above, New Age and Classical, although not widely used commercial formats, have proved successful in some markets because they fulfill the needs of a select segment of the audience.

National Appeal

As the audience has grown older, its preferences in radio listening have been reflected in the formats that stations offer. Figure 8-13 illustrates the Country format's continued popularity during recent years. Most of this format's recent growth has come from FM stations that have adopted it. It is important to note that the adoption of a format by an FM station is an indication that its greatest audience potential will

FIGURE 8-13 Radio format popularity. *(Used with permission of* BROADCASTING *Magazine.* © *by Cahners Publishing Company.)*

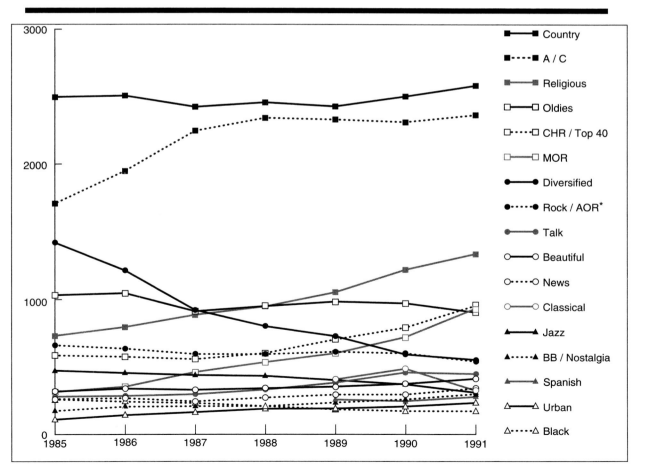

be reached, since AM audiences have been dwindling across the nation and many AM stations have "gone dark," or ceased operation, as a result.

The growth of the second most widely used format, Adult Contemporary, can also be attributed to its adoption by FM stations. Another reason for the 1991 increase in A/C stations is the change to "Hot Adult Contemporary" and "Mix" formats by some former CHR stations. A number of stations moved to some variation of the Adult Contemporary format when they concluded that their listeners did not like the youth-oriented music emphasized on CHR formats. MOR and Full-Service stations are also in decline as more stations seek a niche format and as AM stations, where MOR has been most heavily represented, have declined.

Strong growth has been experienced by Religious/Gospel formats on both AM and FM stations. The News format, which is often coupled with Talk, has also increased. Its growth is also split between AM and FM stations.

The number of stations using Rock/AOR formats was fairly consistent between 1985 and 1987, but there was an increase during the period 1988–1991. Much of this growth can be attributed to Classic Rock and Oldies, which grew at a faster rate than did other formats. The number of stations using a Beautiful-Music/Easy-Listening format have declined as formats appealing to younger listeners have been adopted.

Spanish stations have increased in number, while there has been only a slight increase in the number of stations programming Black Appeal formats. Part of the decrease in Black format stations is attributable to the rise of Urban Contemporary stations. In many instances Urban Contemporary has supplanted the traditional Black Appeal format with one of broader demographic appeal.[88]

Regional Appeal

Programmer's awareness of national trends of format popularity is helpful, but another facet of determining the appropriateness of a format is its potential in a specific situation. Clearly, the potential of a format is determined on a market-by-market basis, but some guidance can often be found in regional format penetration.

A programmer seeking a new station format should give consideration to the relative strength of the major formats within the region before coming to a decision. Adult Contemporary is not as strong in the southern region of the country as it is in the east and midwest. AOR also has less reach in the south than in the other regions, while Country and Urban Contemporary are particularly strong in the south.

The above trends should not lead the reader to conclude that formats that are less popular cannot work. Format popularity is information that can be used in conjunction with other facts to develop a programming strategy. One such consideration is the economic potential offered by a format in a particular market. This is perhaps the most important criterion for format selection.

FORMAT SELECTION

Three principal factors influence the selection of a format. One is whether a station is thought to be attracting a sufficiently large audience. The second factor is the format's potential to generate revenue. A third consideration is the demographic composition of the audience in the market. A station may build a loyal audience, but if it is not of sufficient size, advertisers will not be attracted. To illustrate, KLSK, Santa Fe–Albuquerque, which was programmed by its owner, well-known programming consultant John Sebastian, switched from New Age because advertisers would not support that format, but advertisers were found within a few weeks of the change to a Classic Rock format.[89]

The potential for a format's success increases greatly when the needs of a group of listeners are not being adequately met by another station in the market. The decision to change formats may be made because a station is languishing at or near the bottom in the ratings and something must be done to increase its revenue potential. Or a station may be given a new format because its programmer feels that a competitor has become vulnerable and that some of its audience can be taken away. In either case, the programmer should reexamine the research and the decisions that led to the establishment of the station's current format. Did conditions in the market change, leading to the demise of the station's position or that of a competitor? Were other factors involved, such as a change in station personnel?

The programmer may be able to identify the causes that have led to the station's current unfavorable status. For instance, if the station personnel have become complacent or if the most talented on-air personnel have departed, could revitalization of the staff or the hiring of new talent begin to turn the station around? If the station's facilities are a limitation, another format may be appropriate. Many AM programmers concluded that the only hope for survival was a switch in formats after the majority of potential audience members switched their allegiance to FM. Similarly, some FM station programmers may conclude that the potential for attracting an audience is affected by transmitter power, antenna height, or antenna location, which limits the geographic area that a station's signal can cover.

Splitting the Format Audience

If a single station is dominating the format audience, a competing programmer may feel that his or her station can offer those listeners an attractive alternative. First, though, it must be determined that the existing station's format has shortcomings that could make at least some of its audience willing to seek out an alternative. For instance, that station may be vulnerable if its staff has taken the audience for granted, if the execution of the format has become stale, or if the format appeals to a narrow segment of the potential audience, whether younger or older listeners. Second, the potential listener segments that constitute the station's target audience must

be present in the market in sufficiently large numbers.

Thus, as was discussed in Chapter 2, it may be possible to challenge the leading station and at least obtain a workable market share. A station does not have to be the market or format leader to deliver a salable audience because many national advertisers use two or more stations in a market to reach their target demographics. Moreover, as was noted in Chapter 6, the effectiveness of a station's sales staff and the standing of that station in its market can be important influences on sales of advertising time.

Sometimes format choice is less a matter of art than of mathematics. If, for example, two A/C formatted stations are splitting a 15 audience share and another station needs only a 5 share to be profitable, it could adopt an A/C format. The third station might anticipate drawing enough of an audience from the other two A/C stations to establish itself. Station loyalty is fleeting, and the new player could establish itself within two audience reporting periods. Still, if the A/C format leaders are well established, a third station may end up far down in the ratings rankings and consequently out of the running for advertising dollars.

For a station considering a format change, a better alternative may be to consider improving the present format. In the long run this may be far more profitable. A programmer who decides to switch formats is faced with the possibility of losing the station's core audience. Moreover, the station will incur considerable expense in promoting the new format, conducting market research, designing new logos, and hiring new personnel. Furthermore, the station's cash flow will be diminished as it builds a new audience. Economic considerations often dictate programming decisions.

Advertiser Demand

At this writing, the highest demand among national advertisers is for listeners in the demographic age 25 to 54 with the segment 18 to 44/ 18 to 49 in second place. As shown in Table 8-2,

TABLE 8-2 Advertiser Demand for Demographic Groups

Demographic Group	National Spot Contracts, %
25–54	35
18–49/18–44	19
Other/no demographic	16
25–49/25–44	11
18–34	6

SOURCE: From *NAB RadioWeek*, September 26, 1988, p. 1. © National Association of Broadcasters, 1988. Used with permission.

those in the age group from 18 to 34 are less in demand. This younger segment spends considerably less on costly or high-ticket consumer goods than do those in the broader, somewhat older groups. For specific products such as jeans, sneakers, and certain automobile models, though, the segment 18 to 34 is the most desired by advertisers.

It is not surprising, given the advertiser demand for the segment age 25 to 54, that so many stations across the nation use Adult Contemporary and Country formats (Figure 8-13). These formats deliver those desirable demographics in large numbers.

Revenue Potential

The single-most important criterion in evaluating the potential of a radio format is its likelihood of generating advertising revenues. James H. Duncan, Jr., who compiles radio audience data for the industry, has developed a useful statistical indication of the success of a format in terms of a ratio of market revenue share divided by the audience share of stations using that format (Table 8-3).

The figures in Table 8-3 report revenue share as a percentage of audience share for the major radio formats. The proportions were calculated by dividing each station's "adjusted audience

TABLE 8-3 Revenue Share as a Percentage of Audience Share

Format	Major Markets*	Medium Markets	Small Markets	Very Small Markets	All Markets
Adult Contemporary	134.1	144.1	138.1	125.8	136.3
News and Talk					126.1
MOR/Full Service	143.0	117.8	109.5		122.2
Oldies/Gold	129.7	114.2	112.6		120.9
AOR	122.5	127.4	108.1		119.0
Classic AOR	122.5	98.6			113.7
Country	106.8	118.6	119.5	107.3	112.9
Jazz/New Age					104.1
Hispanic					103.3
CHR/Top 40	97.8	101.1	105.1	94.2	99.5
Soft A/C and Easy Listening	88.3	84.4	83.1		85.6
Classical					84.6
Black/Urban					68.7
Nostalgia/Big Band					60.2

*Major markets = Arbitron markets 1 through 40; medium markets = Arbitron markets 41 through 80; small markets = Arbitron markets 82 through 120; very small markets = Arbitron markets 121 and above.
Note: Figures show revenue share as a percentage of audience share. The means reported are the average of the results for all stations in the format in the specified market size. For some formats, there were not enough stations to allow a breakdown for each specific market size.
SOURCE: James H. Duncan, Jr., *The Relationship Between Radio Audience Shares and Revenue Shares* (Indianapolis: Duncan's American Radio, Inc., March 1991). © 1991. Used by permission.

share" into its revenue share (the percentage of the market's total gross revenue that is controlled by a particular station). An adjusted audience share was determined by subtracting listening to stations outside the market and to "nonlisted" stations such as college stations, NPR affiliates, and noncommercial Religious stations. These stations are noncommercial and consequently are not reported by Arbitron. The remaining share of audience listening to stations in the market was divided into each station's individual share. This yields a share that is adjusted to the immediate competition among stations in the market.[90]

While MOR/Full-Service stations do very well, many programmers are unable to successfully adopt this format. As was discussed earlier in this chapter, the typical large-market MOR station has been long established in the format; this may explain the high revenue share as a percentage of audience share reported in Table 8-3. The revenue potential drops considerably, however, from large to medium markets and from medium to small markets.

News and Talk formats are also potentially very profitable, but their prospects are mostly limited to major and medium markets where large cume audiences can be gathered. Thus, unless a small-market programmer can figure a way to increase time spent listening, this format will continue to be relegated to the largest markets. Moreover, Duncan points out that News and News/Talk formats do much better (mean = 149.3) than Talk and Talk/News formats (mean = 101.1).

The data in Table 8-3 show that for some formats, revenue and audience shares decrease as market size declines. In addition to MOR/Full-Service stations, this pattern is characteristic of stations using an AOR or Oldies format. In the case of AOR, revenue share as a percentage of audience share drops about 19 points from medium to small markets. Similarly, Classic AOR drops almost 24 points from major to medium markets. In the case of Oldies, the drop is not as drastic but is nevertheless sharp, with about a 15 point difference between major and medium

markets. These differences are a general indication of the lower potential for these formats in smaller markets.

Black Appeal stations do best in the largest markets, but Duncan's data show that they do not do nearly as well as stations using other formats. As was discussed earlier, most Black Appeal stations do not receive a share of revenue commensurate with their audience shares. Similarly, Beautiful-Music/Easy-Listening and Nostalgia/Big-Band formats do not achieve revenue in proportion to their audience shares.

Some formats do better in smaller markets than in larger markets. The ratio of revenue to audience share for Country formatted stations is somewhat better in medium and small markets than in the largest markets, although some well-established Country stations in major markets perform exceptionally well.

The Adult Contemporary format does well in all markets because it attracts such a high percentage of listeners age 25 to 54. Since so many stations have already adopted this format, there may not be room for another station in a particular market to position itself with a variation of A/C. The value of trying that format may depend on whether another station using the same format is vulnerable to competition. Still, the buzzword for the 1990s is niche formatting, in which some stations try a narrow approach to standard formats with variations such as Oldies-oriented A/C and Adult-oriented CHR.[91]

Commercial Classical Music stations are located in the largest markets. Their small but affluent audiences make these stations an appealing advertising buy for purveyors of expensive luxury items and services. As was pointed out earlier in this chapter, Classical or Fine Arts stations often attract a high proportion of well-educated, affluent listeners who are prized by some advertisers.

New Age formatted stations rank higher than Classical stations in their ratio of revenue share to audience share. These niche formatted stations, mostly located in major markets, do especially well in attracting age 25 to 54 listeners. Based on surveys of active listeners to their affiliated stations, Progressive Music Network, which distributes *The Breeze* New Age programming service by satellite, says its audience is predominantly college-educated, with a high income and other indications of being an upscale audience.[92]

CHR formatted stations tend to have younger audiences with less purchasing power and do not rank high in revenue/audience potential. Niche broadcasting is a factor here as well, as the CHR formats that do best economically have a sizable core of listeners age 25 to 54. Stations whose dominant core is teens do not generate as much revenue. Thus, a programmer who is attempting to help his or her station generate as much revenue as possible should program music and features that will position the station as an adult-oriented CHR rather than target younger CHR listeners. Once again, this approach skirts Adult Contemporary and further illustrates the attractiveness of A/C as a radio format.

Duncan's data suggest that at least one Hispanic formatted station and perhaps two can do very well in markets with large Hispanic populations. In several markets, Duncan's data indicate considerably less revenue potential for a second or third station to compete.

A comparable estimate of revenue potential for radio formats has been compiled by Miller, Kaplan, Arase & Co. Their "power ratio trends" (Table 8-4) are similar to Duncan's format economic indicators. Both sets of data were compiled by dividing each stations' percentage of market revenue by its share of the market's audience.

There is some variation between the Duncan rankings and the Miller, Kaplan, Arase & Co. rankings of the revenue potential of formats. Some of that is due to differences in the methodologies used by the two sources, including how they differentiate or combine formats. Nevertheless, the general pattern is similar between the data in Table 8-3 and the data in Table 8-4. Where Miller, Kaplan, Arase ranked A/C, News/Talk, Country, Oldies, and MOR/Full Service as the top revenue-producing formats, Duncan had A/C, News/Talk, MOR/Full Service, Oldies, AOR, and Classic Rock. Country seems to be the only format for which there was a lot of disagreement in revenue potential. This format, which ranked in the middle of the formats in the Duncan scheme, was ranked closer to the top in Table 8-4. Equally important, there was agreement at the bottom, where CHR, Urban, Nostal-

TABLE 8-4 Market Ad Revenue by Audience Share

Format	1990	1989	1988	1987	1986
Adult Contemporary	1.46	1.31	1.41	1.34	1.38
News/Talk	1.44	1.42	1.43	1.44	1.47
Country	1.39	1.34	1.49	1.38	1.42
Oldies	1.39	1.28	1.12	.93	.83
Full-Service AM	1.33	1.38	1.40	1.28	1.16
Classic Rock	1.25	1.04	1.13	1.14	1.06
AOR	1.23	1.07	1.13	1.14	1.04
Soft/Lite A/C	1.22	1.36	1.24	1.18	1.26
Spanish	1.21	1.26	1.27	1.32	1.24
Classical	1.04	1.28	1.26	1.30	1.35
CHR	1.03	1.00	1.07	1.08	1.07
Urban Contemporary	.76	.72	.75	.76	.83
Nostalgia/Big Band	.75	.71	.83	.75	.71
Easy Listening	.69	.60	.85	.82	.83

SOURCE: Adapted with permission of BROADCASTING Magazine (April 1, 1991). © 1991 by Cahners Publishing Company.

gia/Big-Band and Beautiful-Music/Easy-Listening formats had the lowest ratios of revenue to audience share.

The data in Table 8-4 show revenue potential for these formats over a 5-year period. The top three formats—AC, News/Talk, and Country—have remained fairly consistent over that period. The Oldies format, however, has come on strong as a revenue generator during more recent years, which indicates revitalized potential and, not surprisingly, increased adoption of that format. Similarly, the revenue potential for AOR has increased during this period, and that has been reflected in a revitalized interest in this format among stations across the country.

The ratio of revenue to market share for stations using the Classical format has dropped. Some of that revenue may have been picked up by stations that have adopted the New Age format. Finally, the revenue potential for the Easy-Listening/Beautiful-Music format is trending downward. Since a number of stations have

abandoned or modified their formats to become Light A/C, it is likely that those stations have picked up some of the revenue potential that seems to be slipping away from Easy-Listening/Beautiful-Music stations.

As these data suggest, the most prominent commercial formats, as identified in Tables 8-3 and 8-4, are also among the most popular, as was shown in Figure 8-13. Careful programmers will examine the format popularity and the potential for revenue as part of their consideration of what may work most effectively in a particular market. Regardless of these considerations, the competition in the market is ultimately a decided influence on format selection. For example, even though CHR is not among the formats with the highest revenue potential, many CHR stations have established themselves in their markets. Moreover, effective sales staffs can enable a station to achieve financial success regardless of what the averages reported above may predict.

SUMMARY

A radio station is identified by its format, a term that describes the parameters of its programming content and indicates its potential audience. A format is executed through a formula in which program events such as music, news, and information segments are presented in a prescribed order during the broadcast day.

When television took over the living rooms of American households, radio was left bereft of program material as the networks concentrated their resources on the newer medium. Radio lost its place, and some programmers turned to recorded music. Top-40 innovators concentrated on playing carefully researched music that was selected to appeal to a youthful audience. From its beginnings, format radio targeted an audience rather than attempting to appeal to all listeners. Modern formats have evolved and have become more narrowly focused, but their origins are in Top-40 radio.

The rise of Top-40 and later formats paralleled the increasing sophistication of advertisers who began to segment the market on the basis of product appeal. Thus, format radio and advertising trends were a marriage of convenience.

There are always exceptions, but the demographics attracted to various radio formats are consistent. CHR, for example, attracts a younger audience, while Adult Contemporary appeals to older listeners. As more stations went on the air, competition for listeners increased, and so stations began to refine their formats to appeal to even narrower segments of the audience. Thus, variations on CHR, Country, and A/C formats, among others, tend to attract younger or older audiences, depending on how they are executed.

The CHR format emphasizes currently popular rock-based music that appeals to listeners 18 to 34 or sometimes 12 to 24 years old. Because older audience segments are targeted by many advertisers, Adult Contemporary has become one of the most popular formats. By emphasizing currently popular music, but without the hard rock edge sometimes associated with CHR, or by including Oldies in the music mix, Adult Contemporary can appeal to listeners age 25 to 54.

The most popular format, Country, is also effective in attracting listeners age 25 to 54. Contemporary Country stations are programmed very much like CHR and Adult Contemporary stations in that they use a formula for rotating music based on its popularity. Country on-air personalities rarely sound "Country," but could be at home in most other formats. Traditional Country formats emphasize the traditional style of Country music, whereas Contemporary Country stations often cross over to play some of the rock music their listeners grew up with.

Album-Oriented Rock has undergone a change in its emphasis on youth as its core audience has aged. Classic Rock formatted stations attempt to appeal to listeners 25 to 54 who grew up enjoying the hard rock music of the 1970s and 1980s. With the arrival of a new generation of listeners, though, some AOR stations may target a younger audience, leaving their competitors to play older rock music.

The Urban Contemporary format has taken over for many of the Black Appeal stations. Depending on the market, UC stations program a variety of music that appeals to diverse ethnic interests. In a market with a large Hispanic population, for instance, some of the music will have a Latin appeal.

Spanish formats are as diverse as all the others that have been discussed in this chapter. As the Hispanic population has grown, its economic clout has been felt and more stations are attempting to target a portion of it with formats that emphasize variations ranging from Country music called Ranchera, to International Hits, to Tex-Mex, depending on the location, competition, and available audience.

Selection of a format should be based on the availability of audience segments and how effectively they are being served by the other stations in the market. In addition to demographic considerations, the programmer should take into account the potential for generating advertising revenue. Some formats generate a much greater ratio of market revenue to audience share than do others. In large markets, News and Talk formats perform well, as do MOR/Full-Service stations. Adult Contemporary formats are at the top of the list because they attract the demographics desired by the biggest advertisers. The formats that have the lowest ratios of revenue share to audience share are Beautiful-Music/Easy-Listening, Nostalgia/Big-Band, and Black Appeal.

Another consideration in identifying a format's potential for success is its geographic appeal. Country formats, for example, are most popular in the southern regions of the country, while AOR has its strongest following in the eastern states.

Programmers considering format changes should be mindful of the difficulty of taking away audience share from format leaders. In those situations, a station may be financially better off by keeping its current format and improving on it. In other cases, the programmer may decide that his or her station can compete effectively for a sufficient share of the audience and make money without being the format leader.

This chapter has concentrated on describing the attributes of the major formats and the audiences that are typically attracted to them. Chapter 9 will describe the techniques used to execute formats to attract and maintain the largest possible audience.

SUGGESTED READINGS

Duncan, James H., Jr.: *American Radio: Tenth Anniversary Issue 1976–1986,* Duncan's American Radio, Inc., Kalamazoo, Mich., 1986.
James H. Duncan, Jr., provides a singular service by compiling statistics on radio broadcasting. Although his tenth anniversary issue is now somewhat dated, it is the only source for summaries of historical data on national trends and station performance in individual markets. Readers should look for new summary issues as they are released. In his tenth anniversary issue, Duncan reviews changes in the radio

industry between 1976 and 1986 and summarizes audience data for various radio formats. A major portion of the book is devoted to market-by-market summaries of stations' audience shares and cume ratings, along with format shares and revenue and ownership data for the years 1975–1986. Another large section of the book is devoted to essays by industry practitioners who comment on the major formats. This is a unique compilation of data on radio. The reader can keep up to date with Duncan's *American Radio* reports, issued quarterly, which summarize radio programming and ratings information for each market. National ratings are included in the spring and fall editions.

Duncan, James H., Jr.: *The Relationship between Radio Audience Shares and Revenue Shares,* Duncan's American Radio, Inc., Indianapolis, March 1991.

This assessment of the relationship between stations' audience shares and revenue shares in their markets is issued each April. As with other Duncan publications, these are somewhat costly for individual purchasers, but stations and college libraries should acquire them. In addition to the summary data discussed in this chapter, this annual report breaks out station performance in market size for each of the reported formats. Thus, the programmer can delve into comparisons of markets similar to his or her own in assessing the feasibility of adopting a format. It is a valuable aid in making informed programming decisions.

Keith, Michael C.: *Radio Programming: Consultancy and Formatics,* Focal Press, Boston, 1987.

Keith provides a useful summary of the development of formula radio and the role of consultants who advise stations on their formats. The book provides an overview of the attributes of the major formats interwoven with commentary from various station programmers and consultants as Keith describes how various stations approach the programming of a particular format. "Hot clocks" illustrate how the programming concepts for each format are carried out, and each of the chapters describing a format concludes with a consultant's critique of a station using that format. This book is especially useful for acquainting readers with the distinctions between and the similarities in formats. The astute reader will also learn much about the expectations for executing the various formats from the consultants' critiques.

NOTES

1. Edward Jay Whetmore, *The Magic Medium: An Introduction to Radio in America,* Wadsworth, Belmont, Calif., 1981, pp. 43–44.

2. Sydney W. Head with Christopher H. Sterling, *Broadcasting in America,* 4th ed., Houghton Mifflin, Boston, 1982, p. 156; Lawrence W. Lichty and Malachi C. Topping (eds.), *American Broadcasting: A Source Book on the History of Radio and Television,* Hastings House, New York, 1975, p. 309.

3. David T. MacFarland, "Up from Middle America: The Development of Top 40," in Lichty and Topping, op. cit., p. 400.

4. David T. MacFarland, "The Development of the Top 40 Radio Format," Ph.D. dissertation, University of Wisconsin–Madison, 1972.

5. Sydney W. Head, *Broadcasting in America,* 2d ed., Houghton Mifflin, Boston, 1972, pp. 221–222.

6. Dychtwald: 'Boomers' Next Will Swell Ranks of Middle Age, Mature Markets," *Television/Radio Age,* May 29, 1989, p. 19; "Study Shows Power of 50 + Consumer," *NAB Radio Week,* Dec. 12, 1988, p. 1; Stuart Naar, "Seeing Gold in the Gray," *Radio & Records,* July 14, 1989, p. 37; Cynthia Price, "Radio in the 1990s: A 'Baby Boom or Bust' Scenario," *NAB Radio Week,* Nov. 27, 1989, p. 4.

7. Christopher H. Sterling and John M. Kittross, *Stay Tuned: A Concise History of American Broadcasting,* 2d ed. Wadsworth, Belmont, Calif., 1990, p. 338.

8. Whetmore, op. cit., pp. 50–51.

9. Michael C. Keith, *Radio Programming: Consultancy and Formatics,* Focal Press, Boston, 1987, p. 2; Sterling and Kittross, op. cit., pp. 339–341.

10. Mike Joseph, "CHR Radio," in James H. Duncan, Jr. (ed.), *American Radio: Tenth Anniversary Issue,* Duncan's American Radio, Kalamazoo, Mich., 1986, pp. B-49–B-50.

11. MacFarland, "The Development of the Top 40 Radio Format"; see also Keith, op. cit., pp. 2–3.

12. Whetmore, op. cit., pp. 54–55.

13. Joseph S. Johnson and Kenneth K. Jones, *Modern Radio Station Practices,* 2d ed., Wadsworth, Belmont, Calif., 1978, p. 253.

14. Whetmore, op. cit., pp. 57–61.

15. R. Serge Denisoff, *Solid Gold: The Popular Record Industry,* Transaction, New Brunswick, N.J., 1975, pp. 236–241.

16. Head and Sterling, op. cit., pp. 153–154.

17. Arbitron, *Radio Year-Round: The Medium for All Seasons,* Arbitron Ratings, New York, 1987, p. 17.

18. Joel Denver, "CHR Chooses Its Core Artists," *Radio & Records,* May 26, 1989, p. 40.

19. Lon Helton, "1973–88: Growth, Success, Respect," *Radio & Records,* Oct. 7, 1988, p. 68.

20. Ibid.

21. Lon Helton, "Everybody Loves Alabama," *Radio & Records,* May 6, 1989, pp. 53–54; Lon Helton, "Paragon's Hits . . . and Misses," *Radio & Records,* June 29, 1990, p. 54.

22. Arbitron, op. cit., p. 20.

23. Tom Cassety and Gregg Lindahl, "The Country Music Format," in Duncan, op. cit., p. B-74.

24. "Country Radio Looks to Fragment as Choices Expand," *Variety,* July 4, 1990, p. 44.

25. Lon Helton, "WTDR Thunders After WSOC's Flank," *Radio & Records,* April 20, 1990, p. 60.

26. Lon Helton, "KQOL: Seeking Hybrid Success," *Radio & Records,* April 27, 1990, p. 62.

27. Whetmore, op. cit., pp. 64–65.

28. Burkhart/Abrams/Douglas/Eliot, "The AOR Format," in Duncan, op. cit., pp. B-58–B-59.

29. Harvey Kojan, "Drafting AOR's Heavy Hitters," *Radio & Records,* May 26, 1989, p. 48.

30. Arbitron, op. cit., p. 18.

31. "AOR Audience Continues to Age, Says Katz Analysis," *Television/Radio Age,* July 24, 1989, p. 20; John Parikhal and David Oakes, *Programming Radio to Win in the New America,* National Association of Broadcasters, Washington, D.C., 1989, p. 52.

32. "AOR Radio Experiencing 'Generation Gap,'" *Broadcasting,* April 15, 1991, pp. 72–74.

33. "Coming of Age," *Radio & Records,* April 2, 1991, p. 66.

34. "World Airways," *Broadcasting,* Oct. 7, 1991, pp. 47–48.

35. Ed Cohen, "Easy Listening Radio: A Survey of Programmers," *NAB Info-Pak,* Feb. 1988, p. 1.

36. Arbitron, op. cit., p. 18.

37. Steven Trivers, "The EZ Listening Format," in Duncan, op. cit., p. B-86.

38. Adam Buckman, "Group W Installs New Easy Listening Format," *Electronic Media,* May 22, 1989, p. 39; Bruce Ingram, "Group W Revamps Easy-Listening to Woo Aging Baby Boomers," *Variety,* May 24, 1989, p. 56.

39. Donna Halper, "What Do the '90s Hold for Beautiful Music?" *NAB RadioWeek,* May 14, 1990, p. 4; Cohen, op. cit., pp. 1–3.

40. Mike Kinosian, "Collins, Whitney, Basia Flex Format Muscle," *Radio & Records,* May 26, 1989, p. 51.

41. Arbitron, op. cit., p. 19.

42. Mike Kinosian, "Ex-B/EZs Invading AC's Territory," *Radio & Records,* May 25, 1990, p. 53; "More B/EZs Migrate to AC," *Radio & Records,* Dec. 21, 1990, p. 43.

43. Randy Michaels, "MOR/Full Service Radio," in Duncan, op. cit., p. B-66.

44. Ibid., p. B-67.

45. Arbitron, op. cit., p. 19.

46. Bill Holdship and Adam White, "A New Age Primer: The Experts Speak," *Radio & Records New Music,* Spring 1988, pp. 3–8.

47. Mike Kinosian, "NAC's Ratings Oasis," *Radio & Records,* Dec. 6, 1989, p. 43.

48. Arbitron, op. cit., p. 21.

49. Keith, op. cit., p. 166.

50. Amos Brown, "Black Radio—Adapting to a Changing Radio World," in Duncan, op. cit., pp. B-79–B-83.

51. James T. Jones IV, "Black Radio Stations Lose Listeners, Dollars," *USA Today,* June 2, 1988, Sec. D, p. 4.

52. Janice C. Simpson, "Yo! Rap Gets on the Map," *Time,* Feb. 5, 1990, pp. 60–62.

53. "For Some, Rap Is a Solution," *USA Today,* June 2, 1988, Sec. D, p. 4.

54. Brown, op. cit., p. B-83.

55. Arbitron, op. cit., p. 20.

56. Walt Love, "Lining Up UC's All-Stars," *Radio & Records,* May 26, 1989, p. 45.

57. "CBS Radio Believes Golden Oldies Are a Foolproof Investment," *Variety,* Aug. 16, 1989, pp. 49, 53; "Radio Lures 'Boomers' with Oldies," *NAB Broadcast Marketing & Technology News,* June 4, 1990, pp. 33–34.

58. "Study Shows Oldies Most Popular Format," *Broadcasting,* Dec. 3, 1990, p. 57.

59. "Special Report: Targeting the Hispanic Market," *NAB Broadcast Marketing & Technology News,* Dec. 1988, p. 7.

60. Herb Levin, "A Look at Spanish Radio," in Duncan, op. cit., p. B-99.

61. "'International Hits' Is Top Hispanic Format, Says Katz," *NAB RadioWeek,* May 22, 1989, p. 2.

62. Robert Marking, "The Coming of Age of Spanish Radio," *NAB RadioWeek,* Aug. 8, 1988, p. 4.

63. Arbitron, op. cit., p. 22.

64. Paul Baker, "Gospel Radio Plunges into the Mainstream," *Christian Citizen Newsmagazine,* Oct. 1981, p. 26.

65. Keith, op. cit., pp. 172–174.

66. Baker, op. cit., p. 25.

67. Arbitron, op. cit., p. 22.

68. Bob Andelman, "Twenty-Four-Hour Syndicated Programming," *The Pulse of Radio,* Aug. 27, 1990, pp. 23, 29.

69. "WQXR, Upbeat on Its Classical Format, Strives for Prestige Demographic," *Variety,* June 28, 1989, p. 46.

70. "WFMT Is Interwoven in Chi Woof and Warp," *Variety,* Nov. 18, 1987, p. 74.

71. Arbitron, op. cit., p. 21.

72. "WQXR, Upbeat," p. 46; "WFMT Listeners May Be Few and Far between, but Demos Are Choice," *Variety,* Nov. 18, 1987, p. 78.

73. "'Yuppie' Approach Becoming Common at Classical Stations," *Television/Radio Age,* May 30, 1988, pp. A2–A11.

74. Keith, op. cit., pp. 113–117.

75. "WQXR, Upbeat," p. 46; Keith, op. cit., p. 118; "'Yuppie' Approach," p. A3.

76. Arbitron, op. cit., p. 17.

77. Birch Scarborough Research, *How America Found Out about the Gulf War,* Birch Scarborough Research, Coral Springs, Fla., 1991.

78. "Talk Networks Pursue Role of AM 'White Knight,'" *Broadcasting,* Aug. 27, 1990, pp. 40–42.

79. Tim McGovern, "Jones Subsidiary to Uplink AM Radio Stations," *Multichannel News,* Oct. 31, 1988.

80. "American Radio Networks Keeps AM's Talking," *Broadcasting,* March 19, 1990, p. 55.

81. Jim O'Donnell, "All-Sports Radio to Hit Chicago in October," *Electronic Media,* Sept. 30, 1991, pp. 8, 24; "New All-Sports AM Set for Chicago Debut," *Broadcasting,* Oct. 14, 1991, p. 39; "Listening to Two Guys Sitting in a Bar," *Broadcasting,* July 29, 1991, p. 61.

82. Bruce Ingram, "Little Rock Radio Format Proves a Hit for Preteens, Parents Too," *Variety,* Oct. 5, 1988, p. 132; Adam Buchman, "Radio Station De-

signed with Kids in Mind," *Electronic Media,* June 27, 1988, p. 27; "Imagine That," *Broadcasting,* Aug. 20, 1990, p. 14; "Radio Is Kid's Stuff," *Broadcasting,* March 12, 1990, pp. 51–52.

83. "WCVG Debuts 'All Elvis,'" *Radio & Records,* Aug. 5, 1988, p. 4; "Elvis Everywhere," *Broadcasting,* Oct. 24, 1988, p. 8; Larry Nager, "'The King' Lives 24 Hours a Day on Cincinnati AM," *Electronic Media,* Aug. 22, 1988, p. 8; Larry Nager, "AM Station Puts Elvis Format to Rest," *Electronic Media,* Sept. 4, 1989, p. 8.

84. Andrea Adelson, "A Push for All-Business Radio," *New York Times,* Nov. 27, 1987, p. 29.

85. Adam Buckman, "Motivation Is New Strategy for AM," *Electronic Media,* Nov. 21, 1988, p. 3.

86. Bruce Ingram, "4½-Yr.-Old Comedy Format for California AMer Still a Hit," *Variety,* Aug. 31, 1988, p. 67.

87. "Public Radio Programming Report Fiscal Year 1986: Highlights," *NPR Research & Evaluation,* June 1988, p. 1.

88. "Following the Formats," *Broadcasting,* June 12, 1989, pp. 38–39; "'Baby Boomer Formats' Growth Increasing," *Broadcasting,* April 15, 1991, p. 75.

89. "Putting the Dream on Hold," *Radio & Records,* Feb. 22, 1991, p. 36.

90. James H. Duncan, Jr., *The Relationship between Radio Audience Shares and Revenue Shares,* Duncan's American Radio, Indianapolis, 1991.

91. Jeff Pollack, "Format Search: The Seven Deadly Sins," *Radio & Records,* Aug. 10, 1990, p. 40; Cynthia Price, "Radio in the '90s: 'Niche' versus Mix," *NAB RadioWeek,* Dec. 4, 1989, p. 8; New York Times News Service, "Struggling Stations Seek Niche," *Tuscaloosa News,* May 20, 1990, sec. E, pp. 1, 5; Rob Balon, "Finding Your Niche: Making Marketing Magic in the '90s," *Radio & Records,* Oct. 20, 1989, p. 40.

92. "Expanding Breeze Format Targets 25–54 Upscales," *Television/Radio Age,* June 2, 1989, pp. 30–31.

CHAPTER 9

Radio Programming Concepts

PROGRAMMING AND TIME PERIODS
   Quarter-Hour Maintenance
   Dayparting

EVENT SCHEDULING
   The Playlist
   Music Values
   News, Sports, and Weather
   Commercials
   Liners

PROGRAMMING CONSIDERATIONS FOR SMALL-MARKET RADIO

SUMMARY

SUGGESTED READINGS

NOTES

KEY TERMS AND CONCEPTS
Artist Separation
Beats per Minute (BPM)
Billboarding
Burnout
Dayparting
Events
Front Loading and Back Loading
Horizontal Separation
Hot Clock
Linear Clock and Chain Programming
Liner
Music Intensity
Music Rotation
Music Sequencing
Music Sweep
Music Tempo
Music Texturing
Playlist
Production Values
Promoting
Quarter-Hour Maintenance Strategy
Recurrents
Rewarding Listeners
Spot Set
Stop Set
Teasing
Vertical Separation

Demographic statistics, knowledge of the marketplace, and awareness of the options for using various formats are important instruments in the programmer's tool kit. The rules of the game in the competition for radio audiences have been largely defined by Arbitron. Programmers base their strategies on the need to induce audience members to report their listening so that their stations will show to their best advantage in the audience ratings reports and therefore become more salable.

This chapter extends our earlier discussion of audience measurement by considering how audiences can be attracted and kept. As was shown in Chapter 8, most stations use a music-intensive format. Therefore, music programming is emphasized throughout this chapter. We begin by looking at ways to keep listeners in the audience for as long as possible. Another consideration is the audiences that are available during different dayparts. Thus, keeping listeners for as long as possible and orienting the programming to the demographic groups that predominate during different time periods influence the placement of and in some instances the extent to which different categories of music and other programming elements, including commercial messages and news, are presented during the broadcast day.

Although current popularity is the principal criterion for deciding which songs will be presented on the air, other aspects of music can be taken into account so that music can be presented in the most appealing sequence for listeners. Similarly, we shall discuss strategies that can minimize the potential of commercial messages to irritate and possibly drive listeners away. Later in the chapter we consider small-market radio stations, whose audiences and coverage areas often differ from those of stations serving larger populations.

PROGRAMMING AND TIME PERIODS

Quarter-Hour Maintenance

One challenge to the programmer is to attract new listeners; a second challenge is to get them to listen more. As was discussed in Chapter 6, a person must listen for 5 continuous minutes to be counted in the audience for a given quarter hour. Even if a person tunes out after 5 minutes, the station is credited with that audience member. Consequently, a *quarter-hour maintenance strategy,* or an attempt to keep listeners tuned in for as many quarter hours as possible, is usually implemented. There is a lot at stake. If an audience that listens for an average of 45 minutes a day can be induced to stay tuned for just one more quarter hour, the station can realize a 33 percent gain in ratings.

A number of techniques have become standard in audience maintenance, but this does not mean that other ideas cannot work. In fact, anyone who figures out a new way to attract and maintain audiences will probably be lionized by his or her peers.

Rewarding listeners A strategy that is fundamental to effective radio programming deals with listener **reward** for staying tuned to a station. A listener expects to hear his or her favorite song or expects to be relaxed, stimulated, or informed. A listener may tune in a station specifically to find out the time or temperature or to learn whether there are any traffic conditions that may impede his or her commute to work. If those expectations are met, the listener is rewarded for his or her effort.

It should be apparent, though, that if a station attempted to reward specific listeners instantly, it would devote far more effort to overly specific aspects of the programming than would be warranted in its attempt to attract a large audience with broad interests. Nevertheless, typical listeners are willing to wait only a short time if they feel that a reward is forthcoming.

A programmer's strategy may be affected by the relative impatience of the targeted listeners and by how important some things are during different dayparts. For instance, teenagers may not be willing to wait through a long series of commercial announcements to hear one of their favorite songs, whereas adult listeners may, as may commuters who wish to know whether they should take an alternative route to work as they back out of the driveway in the morning. During the middle of the day, though, the same listeners may consider such content a distraction if they listen to the station at work.

Programming consultant Rick Sklar observed that the listening public of the 1990s wants instant gratification. While listeners want to be informed, he said, they don't want to wait through a long newscast before being presented with a song they instantly recognize and enjoy. Sklar advocated dropping in headlines, which satisfy listeners' desire for information, and then quickly getting back to the music.[1] Whether such impatience is true of all audiences is not the point. Identifying the thing that listeners want, whether it is "songs that I like," news headlines, or details on the stock market, and rewarding them with it is a fundamental strategy for keeping listeners.

Teasing Teases offer listeners an incentive to stay tuned in for the next quarter hour or more. The tease comes through announcing that a hit song or a chance to win the "hundred-dollar cash jackpot" is coming up in a few minutes. For many listeners, hearing a featured song or having the opportunity to participate in a contest is a reward for staying tuned through an interruption such as the news or a commercial announcement.

An example of teasing occurs when the disc jockey **billboards,** or lists, one or more of the most desirable songs and artists to be featured during the forthcoming period with an announcement such as "We'll be back with Def Leppard's latest after the news." The announcer should not give a specific time for such a song because that will lessen the anticipation of a listener who desires to hear it. Once that song has been aired, an incentive to stay tuned has been fulfilled. A more effective approach is to delay airing a promoted song until two or more others have played. The program director should nevertheless remain mindful of the possibility of alienating listeners. The objective is to build anticipation without delaying the reward for so long that audience members feel they have been conned.

The first quarter hour of each clock hour is the most important, because that is when the most tune-ins occur. When a contest or other program feature is teased during the first, second, or even third quarter hour, some listeners may be enticed to stay tuned longer than they otherwise would.

Promoting The purpose of promoting is to attract listeners, whereas teasing is done to retain them. Consequently, programming should provide an extension of the campaign for attracting and maintaining listeners.

Listener interest can be solicited through the promotion of station contests, news, weather, or other features and activities. Such *outside promotion,* carried out on TV or billboards and occasionally in newspapers and other media, will be less effective if it is not tied in with what is presented on the air. The attributes of the station's format should have a thematic consistency so that listeners can immediately relate the impression they gained from seeing a billboard or reading a newspaper ad to what they hear on the air. Suppose a station attempts to position itself as the place on the dial where "you know the traffic conditions in the morning." If listeners tune in and aren't given that information within a few minutes, the positioning statement will lose credibility. By contrast, if traffic reports are presented too often, many people in the audience will be irritated by the redundancy. Among the ways to get around that dilemma and still reinforce outside promotion by rewarding listeners is to tease full reports with a one- or two-line summary of conditions on a specific road or in a specific part of the metropolitan area. Thus, the morning personalities could announce between records and other program events that conditions are normal on specific roads. This information, while brief, is continually changing, and it lets listeners know that they can count on learning about any traffic situation that may affect their commute.

Similarly, carefully selected recorded positioning statements can be used to repeat a theme such as "Good Rockin' on WZZZ, 95-point seven FM" that was promoted in television ads and on billboards. Such a statement can be aired within the first 5 minutes of the start of each quarter hour to reinforce the identity and position of the station. It is important that the concept be carried out through the music and other aspects of the format. The recordings must be tested to ensure that they fit the targeted audience's perception of what is in the realm of "Good Rockin'" music.

Music sweeps Many stations feature *music sweeps* in which several songs are played without commercial interruption. The purpose is to increase listening across several quarter hours. Thus, if a station uses a 40-minute sweep, listeners can conceivably be kept across all four quarter hours.

A benefit of music sweeps is that they help establish and reinforce a "more music" image for the station. The primary benefit, however, is the increase in quarter-hour listening that should result. Another advantage of a long music sweep is that while the competitors are airing commercials, the station using the sweep approach is presenting music. If the format includes longer album cuts, that music can be accommodated more easily than is the case when time deadlines must be met more frequently.

There are disadvantages to long periods of music, though. Most prominent among them is that commercials must be presented within a shorter listening period, which entails running long clusters of spots. In the case of a 40-minute sweep, the entire hourly commercial load is presented within the remaining 20 minutes of the hour. Unless the station decides to reduce its commercial load, listeners who tune in during this period will be inundated with these messages and may form a negative impression that results in tuning out.[2] Moreover, advertisers whose messages may be lost in the potential clutter of commercials aired during the last 20 minutes of the hour may wonder whether listeners are receiving their messages. Such apprehension may cause some prospective clients to decide not to place their advertising on stations using this format.

Dayparting

The strategy of **dayparting** involves adjusting program content so that it appeals to the demographic composition of the audience that is available and caters to its needs and desires at the time. Although a station does not have to program according to the standard time periods, most find it practical to do so, since Arbitron breaks down the broadcast day into dayparts.

The one daypart in which music sweeps are generally not done is the morning period, usually defined as 6 a.m. to 10 a.m., because of the nature and habits of that demographically diversified audience. The emphasis during morning drive is usually on personality, with frequent doses of topical humor. The music scheduled for airplay from 6 a.m. to 10 a.m. is almost always familiar. Few stations air new recordings during this period because audience members are distracted by the need to prepare for and get to work. They want information to help them start the day. For many listeners, the humorous material they hear gives them something to talk about with their friends and coworkers: "Did you hear what Bill Weber said this morning on WXXX?"

Although many younger adults and teens are in the audience during the early morning, older adults dominate during that time period (Figure 9-1). Midday listening is dominated by adults, as teens are in school, but younger listeners are also likely to be in the audience. The size of the audience has dropped from the morning period, and stations emphasize music over personality. In many markets there is a substantially greater proportion of women in the audience, and programming reflects this by presenting softer, slower-tempo music. Since many listeners are in their workplaces, the programming must be unobtrusive if the station wants to attract the increasingly large segment of those who can listen at work.

The audience during afternoon drive time from 3 p.m. to 7 p.m. is also diversified, with many adults listening as they commute from work. Most stations pick up the tempo during the after-

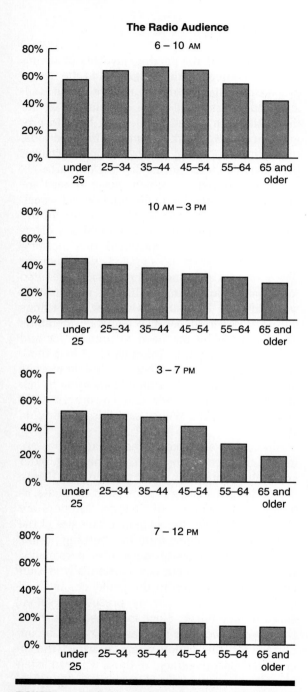

The Radio Audience

FIGURE 9-1   The radio audience. *(From* InfoPack/December 1989–January 1990. © *National Association of Broadcasters, 1990. Used with permission.)*

noon period, but not to the extent of the morning pace. There is usually an increase in newscasts and information on traffic and road conditions. At most stations, afternoon format personalities are not as important as the music because their listeners are winding down the day.

During the evening hours most people over age 25 abandon radio in favor of television. Pop music radio is largely the province of younger listeners, especially teenagers, after 7 p.m. Whereas reports on popular musicians and rock trivia do not interest the majority of the listeners during the morning, such content is programmed for the younger audience at night. Popular music disc jockeys tend to be more raucous, appealing to adolescents. Many adult-oriented formats switch to talk, call-in, and interview programs that proceed at a relatively slow pace since their listeners are able to stay tuned for a longer period.

Some stations employ a daypart program strategy by featuring a Jazz or other less popular format during the evening hours. Since the number of listeners at night is much smaller, these stations attempt to attract a different audience to their nighttime programming. A danger in dayparting is that listeners may think that the format they hear at night is used during the daytime as well, and this can result in a loss of listeners during the more important dayparts. Still, if the choice is clear and does not result in a misconception of what the station offers during the daytime hours, dayparting can be successful in expanding the station's total audience.[3]

Most public radio stations daypart by using a block programming strategy in which periods of time are devoted to different programs or musical types. Programmers at public stations rely on the interest and knowledge of listeners who will tune in specific programs much as television viewers do. In fact, many of these stations publish monthly or quarterly program guides that describe works to be performed in concerts, give details about operas, and include summary previews of the regularly scheduled programs on the schedule.

EVENT SCHEDULING

The typical commercial radio program is a stream of **events;** every record, commercial announcement, station promotion, jingle, and newscast is part of the flow. Music is the staple for the majority of the radio stations in the United States, but the other events are just as important regardless of the format or the target audience. Whether a station's air sound is smooth or choppy, rapid or slow, or consistent or jarring is largely dependent on how events are scheduled.

Radio programming thus entails the placement of program events in a particular order and at strategic times during the clock hour to maintain the audience. For instance, the placement of program events may cause some listeners to delay showering or arrive at work a few minutes later because of something they wanted to listen to. If the station is going to air an exclusive interview with a major recording artist who is visiting town or is going to announce a clue in a contest, well-placed teases may lure listeners to stay tuned just a little longer so that they won't miss the event.

Content consistency is essential in attracting and maintaining audiences. Listeners tune in regularly because they think they will hear information and entertainment they appreciate at any time of the day. It is the programmer's job to reinforce this perception.

To make the content appealing and consistent from hour to hour, daypart to daypart, and day to day, the program director devises a *formula* in which events are scheduled in a pattern to maintain consistency. The number of **stop sets** (clusters of commercial announcements and other nonmusical material) and where they are to be placed and the number of hit tunes and oldies and where they are to be presented during the hour are specified. If the program director relinquished this decision to the individual announcers, she or he would leave to chance whether listeners will find the content appealing when they tune in or even whether they will recognize and thus stay with the station.

To keep the audience, the program director attempts to eliminate content that may prompt listeners to turn off the radio or tune in another station. Playing too much music that is unfamiliar and overdoing music the audience is tired of hearing can be potential irritants. For example, some PDs advocate placing the most researched records (those which have been aired for a long time but still retain high audience popularity) at the ends of quarter hours. These records might be followed up by a very popular oldie selection, which also can be recognized immediately by most listeners. The idea here is to schedule an event such as a record with very strong appeal near the end of the quarter hour to keep listeners through the next quarter hour. To ensure that they remain in the audience for at least 5 minutes, the first event in the quarter hour should be another strong song that compels listeners to remain in the audience. Scheduling a song to begin on or before the start of a quarter hour can bridge the two time periods, keeping listeners in the audience. Similarly, announcing a "two-in-a-row" feature can help maintain the audience through the crucial 5-minute period in the new quarter hour.

The Playlist

The station **playlist** is an internal station document that lists the specific records that are assigned to various categories of music that will be aired during the reporting period. As the playlist in Table 9-1 shows, the rise and fall in recordings can thus be tracked by the station.

Music assigned to various categories, such as the top 10, are played in accordance with a predetermined frequency or **rotation.** For example, to ensure that listeners have an opportunity to hear the most popular records when they tune in, the station's format may call for records in the top-10 category to be played at specified intervals during every hour. Other categories may be scheduled less often, and some are aired only during specified dayparts. A song that has been on the list for a long time normally receives less

TABLE 9-1   WZZZ Playlist for March 1, 1991

2 Weeks Ago	Last Week	This Week	Title	Artist	Label	Category
2	1	1	"Coming Out of . . ."	Gloria Estefan	Epic	Top 10
6	5	2	"You're in Love"	Wilson Phillips	SBK	Top 10
3	3	3	"Show Me the Way"	Styx	A&M	Top 10
12	10	4	"Night and Day"	Bette Midler	Atlantic	Top 10
4	6	5	"Don't Hold Back"	Daryl Hall and John Oates	Arista	Top 10
5	2	6	"All the Man I Need"	Whitney Houston	Arista	Top 10
1	4	7	"All This Time"	Sting	A&M	Top 10
16	7	8	"Chasin' the Wind"	Chicago	Full Moon/Rep	Top 10
7	9	9	"Forever's as Far as I Go"	Alabama	RCA	Top 10
8	8	10	"Mercy Mercy Me"	Robert Palmer	EMI	Top 10
22	14	11	"Waiting for That Day"	George Michael	Columbia	11–20 riser
15	13	12	"I Will Be Here"	Steve Winwood	Virgin	11–20 riser
29	23	13	"Baby, Baby"	Amy Grant	A&M	11–20 riser
17	16	14	"Rhythm of My Heart"	Rod Stewart	Warner Bros	11–20 riser
29	20	15	"New York Minute"	Don Henley	Geffen	11–20 riser
9	18	16	"You Gotta Love Someone"	Elton John	MCA	11–20 decliner
18	19	17	"The Shoop Shoop Song"	Cher	Geffen	11–20 riser
13	17	18	"Crazy in Love"	Kenny Rogers	Reprise	11–20 decliner
29	22	19	"Fairy Tales"	Anita Baker	Elektra	11–20 riser
11	11	20	"Real Real Gone"	Van Morrison	Mercury	11–20 decliner
10	15	21	"Someday"	Mariah Carey	Columbia	Recurrent
14	12	22	"Rumor Has It"	Reba McEntire	MCA	Recurrent
19	25	23	"Love Will Never Do"	Janet Jackson	A&M	Recurrent
30	28	24	"Miracle"	Jon Bon Jovi	Mercury	Recurrent
	30	25	"Promise Me You'll Remember"	Harry Conick Jr.	Columbia	New addition
20	21	26	"Love Can Build a Bridge"	The Judds	Curb/RCA	Recurrent
	29	27	"I'll Give All My Love"	Keith Sweat	Vinertainment	New addition
21	26	28	"I'll Be Your Baby Tonight"	Whitney Houston	Arista	Recurrent
26	27	29	"Way You Do/Thing You Do"	UB40	Virgin	Recurrent
		30	"Love Will Survive"	Donny Osmond	Capitol	New addition
			"We've Got It Made"	Lee Greenwood	Capitol	New addition
			"Here Comes The Sun"	Beatles	Capitol	Gold
			"Sailing"	Christopher Cross		Gold
			"Three Times a Lady"	Commodores		Gold
			"Every Breath You Take"	Police		Gold
			"Dust in the Wind"	Kansas		Gold
			"Maggie May"	Rod Stewart		Gold

airplay than does one that has been introduced recently and has not been available long enough to establish its popularity before listeners begin to tire of hearing it. Such a formula is carried out by having the station's on-air personnel follow a "hot clock," as discussed later in this chapter.

Deciding what to include   Radio is still a prime means of stimulating sales of recordings, although MTV and the other television music video outlets have grown in importance. Major-market stations are inundated with new music from record promoters who know that their sales success is heavily dependent on receiving airplay to gain exposure. Thus, former WLS, Chicago, program director Art Roberts once described the process of selecting the music for his station not as a matter of deciding what to play but as a matter of deciding what *not* to include. Many music directors schedule a day each week on which they accept calls from promoters who describe their new releases, hoping to gain airplay.

It is easy to point to why a record should be played on a station after it has become popular. It is another thing to judge when and whether a new release should make its debut on a station's playlist of records. Such decisions often depend on the attitude of the programmer. Some programmers, particularly those who work for market or format leaders, adopt a very conservative stance in which they will not take chances by adding records from new performers until these records have demonstrated their popularity. In such cases programmers can monitor the success of new recordings from untested artists that are played on other stations, usually in smaller markets. Regardless of the market size or the status of a station in the market, the objective is to present the most appealing program content to the target audience.

Independent indicators of music popularity are superior to the personal tastes and preferences of the individuals who select the content. Since most people like certain songs and artists more than they like others, it can be difficult to remain detached when one is deciding whether to exclude or add selections. Record popularity can be determined more objectively by conducting call-out and auditorium research. Another objective measure of music preference can be achieved by tracking local purchases of records, compact discs, and tapes. The PD or music director can establish a liaison with record distributors who service local outlets to ascertain the volume of record sales in the market area. It is helpful to solicit the cooperation of music chains because their record keeping is generally good.

A company called SoundScan compiles point-of-purchase data on U.S. record sales from about 7500 retail outlets. The information is read into a computer from the Universal Price Code labels on the packages. This sales information is made available to the record industry and is also used in compiling national record popularity charts. Stations can get this information through the ABC Radio Networks, which distribute sales reports on the 50 top-selling singles and albums.[4]

Many stations keep a log of the music requests they receive. This information should be used with caution, though, because the respondents are self-selected and have some motivation for calling in. Still, research that involves **active respondents** can be helpful, particularly in getting an early fix on the audience's interest in new additions to the station's playlist.

In addition to record sales and local audience preference research, music requests received by the station, assessments by the station's staff, and indicators provided by the national trade publications and tip sheets can be used in a ranking formula. With this information, a programmer can track the ascent and decline of each record that is included in the playlist.

An astute music director also monitors other markets with a similar demographic composition to spot acceptance of new releases for the playlist. Ideally, the music director has direct contact with other music directors at stations using the same format in other markets. At the least, though, the music director is responsible for reading trade publications and tip sheets such as *Billboard, Radio & Records, Cashbox,* and *The Gavin Report* (Box 9-1) to glean information on new music and reports on airplay by stations in various markets. The program or music directors at many stations maintain regular contact with the trade publications and try to become regular reporters to heighten their stations' visibility among record distributors.

Most of the current music charts found in the "trades" use record sales as an index of popularity, although some base their reports on station airplay. In either case, the basis for the ranking goes back to record sales, since that is one of the few objective means of ascertaining whether people really like a record and determining how

**BOX 9-1
TRADE PUBLICATIONS
FOR RADIO**

Aspiring professionals can become familiar with the following trade publications and utilize that information in their decision making.

Billboard

Sean Ross, Radio Editor, (212) 764-7300. Charts A/C, albums, Black, Country, Dance, Hot 100.

Breneman Review

Betty Breneman, Publisher, John Leonard, General Manager, (818) 348-3162. Charts Top 40 and Hot A/C. Reviews new releases and provides demographic appeal, daypart, and rotation information based on reporting stations.

CashBox

George Albert, President and Publisher, (212) 586-2640. Reviews records and charts albums, Black, Latin, Country, Top 100.

Gavin Report

Ron Fell, Managing Editor, (414) 382-7750. Charts A/C, albums, Country, Jazz, New Age, Top 40, Urban.

Hits

Lenny Beer, Editor in Chief, (818) 507-7900. Charts CHR.

Bobby Poe's Pop Music Survey

Bobby Poe, Publisher, (301) 951-1215. A weekly personalized record tip sheet that charts "Hot–40" CHR based on 200 reporting stations; sponsors an annual Top-40 programmer's convention.

Radio & Records

Ken Barnes, Editor, (213) 203-9763. Charts AC, AOR, CHR, Country, Jazz, New Age, and Urban; includes columns dealing with audience research, format programming trends, tips on management.

Radio Only

Articles on broadcast sales and programming; includes numerous tips on programming from consultants and PDs.

■

long it remains popular among a large number of consumers.

Figure 9-2 shows the "Hot 100 Singles" chart published in *Billboard* magazine. The circled ranking numbers indicate records with the greatest airplay and sales for the week. The "New" records on the chart give the programmer an indication of how quickly these records are being accepted by the record-buying public.

Billboard's chart tracks music that is typically included in CHR station playlists. Much of the same music may appear on other music charts reported in this weekly publication, including Country, Adult Contemporary, and Black Appeal.

Music programming is partly a science and partly an art. Decisions should be made objectively, but chances must be taken, relying on the intuition and experience of the music programmer and his or her staff. A wrong decision can be rectified if the station follows careful monitoring procedures, including call-out research, to track the acceptance of the music included in the playlist.

Music categories As will be described later in this chapter, each of the categories of music included in the playlist is scheduled in a certain pattern to ensure that the disc jockeys on duty execute the format in accordance with a prescribed formula. Music categories not only must be understandable, they must be mutually exclusive. That is, either a song is in a category or it is in another category. If the categories are defined too loosely, misunderstanding and poor execution of the format will result.

Billboard® HOT 100® SINGLES™

FOR WEEK ENDING MAY 2, 1992

COMPILED FROM A NATIONAL SAMPLE OF TOP 40 RADIO AIRPLAY MONITORED BY BROADCAST DATA SYSTEMS, TOP 40 RADIO PLAYLISTS, AND RETAIL AND RACK SINGLES SALES COLLECTED, COMPILED, AND PROVIDED BY SoundScan

THIS WEEK	LAST WEEK	2 WKS AGO	WKS. ON CHART	TITLE — PRODUCER (SONGWRITER)	ARTIST — LABEL & NUMBER/DISTRIBUTING LABEL
1	1	3	5	★★★ No. 1 ★★★ (2 weeks at No. 1) **JUMP▲** — J.DUPRI (J.DUPRI)	◆ KRIS KROSS — (C) (T) (V) RUFFHOUSE 74197/COLUMBIA
2	2	1	14	**SAVE THE BEST FOR LAST ●** — K.THOMAS (W.WALDMAN,J.LIND,P.GALDSTON)	◆ VANESSA WILLIAMS — (C) (CD) (V) WING 865 136/MERCURY
3	3	2	13	**TEARS IN HEAVEN▲** — R.TITELMAN (E.CLAPTON,W.JENNINGS)	◆ ERIC CLAPTON — (C) (V) REPRISE 19038
4	4	4	31	**BOHEMIAN RHAPSODY** — R.T.BAKER,QUEEN (F.MERCURY)	◆ QUEEN — (C) HOLLYWOOD 64794
5	5	8	7	**MY LOVIN' (YOU'RE NEVER GONNA GET IT)** — T.MCELROY,D.FOSTER (T.MCELROY,D.FOSTER)	◆ EN VOGUE — (C) (M) (T) ATCO EASTWEST 98586
6	6	7	11	**AIN'T 2 PROUD 2 BEG ●** — D.AUSTIN (D.AUSTIN,L.LOPES)	◆ TLC — (C) (M) (T) LAFACE 2-4008/ARISTA
7	7	6	11	**MAKE IT HAPPEN** — D.COLE,R.CLIVILLES,M.CAREY (M.CAREY,D.COLE,R.CLIVILLES)	◆ MARIAH CAREY — (C) (CD) (M) (T) (V) COLUMBIA 74239
8	10	14	8	**LIVE AND LEARN** — L.JOB,JOE PUBLIC (CARTER,SAYLES,SCOTT,WYATT,SAYLES,BROWN,BYRD,LENHOFF)	◆ JOE PUBLIC — (C) (T) COLUMBIA 74012
9	15	52	5	**EVERYTHING ABOUT YOU** — R.DORN,UGLY KID JOE (K.EICHSTADT,W.CRANE)	◆ UGLY KID JOE — (C) (V) STARDOG 866 632/MERCURY
10	9	12	12	**HAZARD** — R.MARX (R.MARX)	◆ RICHARD MARX — (C) (CD) CAPITOL 44796
11	8	5	14	**MASTERPIECE** — D.E.LEWIS,W.I.LEWIS (K.NOLAN)	◆ ATLANTIC STARR — (C) (V) REPRISE 19076
12	24	35	5	**UNDER THE BRIDGE** — R.RUBIN (A.KIEDIS,FLEA,J.FRUSCIANTE,C.SMITH)	◆ RED HOT CHILI PEPPERS — (C) WARNER BROS. 18978
13	13	19	8	**ONE** — D.LANOIS,B.ENO (BONO,U2)	◆ U2 — (C) (CD) (T) ISLAND 866 533/PLG
14	12	9	16	**BEAUTY AND THE BEAST** — W.AFANASIEFF (A.MENKEN,H.ASHMAN)	◆ CELINE DION AND PEABO BRYSON — (C) (V) EPIC 74090
15	11	10	18	**BREAKIN' MY HEART (PRETTY BROWN EYES)** — J.JOHNSON,MINT CONDITION (L.WADDELL,STOKLEY,J.ALLEN)	◆ MINT CONDITION — (C) PERSPECTIVE 0004/A&M
16	14	15	11	**EVERYTHING CHANGES** — R.WAKE (D.WARREN)	◆ KATHY TROCCOLI — (C) (T) (V) REUNION 19118/GEFFEN
17	19	24	8	**THOUGHT I'D DIED AND GONE TO HEAVEN** — R.J.LANGE,B.ADAMS (B.ADAMS,R.J.LANGE)	◆ BRYAN ADAMS — (C) A&M 1592
18	26	27	4	**LET'S GET ROCKED** — M.SHIPLEY,DEF LEPPARD (COLLEN,ELLIOTT,LANGE,SAVAGE)	◆ DEF LEPPARD — (C) (V) MERCURY 866 568
19	17	13	14	**I CAN'T DANCE** — GENESIS,N.DAVIS (T.BANKS,P.COLLINS,M.RUTHERFORD)	◆ GENESIS — (C) (CD) (V) ATLANTIC 87532
20	18	16	7	**HUMAN TOUCH/BETTER DAYS** — B.SPRINGSTEEN,J.LANDAU,C.PLOTKIN,R.BITTAN (B.SPRINGSTEEN)	◆ BRUCE SPRINGSTEEN — (C) (CD) (V) COLUMBIA 74273
21	25	31	5	**WILL YOU MARRY ME?** — V.J.SMITH,P.LORD (P.LORD,S.ST.VICTOR,V.J.SMITH,P.ABDUL)	◆ PAULA ABDUL — (C) (V) CAPTIVE 98584/VIRGIN
22	22	23	9	**I'M THE ONE YOU NEED** — D.MORALES (J.WATLEY,D.MORALES,A.SHANTZIS)	◆ JODY WATLEY — (C) (M) (T) MCA 54276
23	16	11	15	**REMEMBER THE TIME ●** — T.RILEY,M.JACKSON (T.RILEY,M.JACKSON,B.BELLE)	◆ MICHAEL JACKSON — (C) (CD) (M) (T) (V) EPIC 74200
24	21	20	14	**WE GOT A LOVE THANG** — S.HURLEY (E.MILLER,J.MCALLISTER,C.SAVAGE)	◆ CECE PENISTON — (C) (CD) (T) (V) A&M 1594
25	23	17	20	**I'M TOO SEXY▲** — TOMMY D. (F.FAIRBRASS,R.FAIRBRASS,R.MANZOLI)	◆ RIGHT SAID FRED — (C) (CD) (T) (V) CHARISMA 98671
26	46	—	2	★★★ POWER PICK/AIRPLAY ★★★ **IN THE CLOSET** — T.RILEY,M.JACKSON (M.JACKSON,T.RILEY)	◆ MICHAEL JACKSON — (C) (CD) (M) (T) (V) EPIC 74266
27	20	18	20	**TO BE WITH YOU ●** — K.ELSON (E.MARTIN,D.GRAHAME)	◆ MR. BIG — (C) (V) ATLANTIC 87580
28	31	33	6	**MONEY DON'T MATTER 2 NIGHT** — PRINCE,NEW POWER GENERATION (PRINCE,NEW POWER GENERATION)	◆ PRINCE AND THE N.P.G. — (C) (V) PAISLEY PARK 19020/WARNER BROS
29	27	21	16	**GOOD FOR ME** — K.THOMAS (T.SNOW,J.GRUSKA,A.GRANT,W.KIRKPATRICK)	◆ AMY GRANT — (C) (T) A&M 1573
30	32	39	8	**TAKE TIME** — N.MARTINELLI (C.WALKER)	◆ CHRIS WALKER — (C) PENDULUM 64813/ELEKTRA
31	43	65	4	**BABY GOT BACK** — SIR MIX-A-LOT (SIR MIX-A-LOT)	◆ SIR MIX-A-LOT — (C) (CD) (M) (T) DEF AMERICAN 18947/REPRISE
32	34	37	7	**COME AS YOU ARE** — B.VIG,NIRVANA (K.COBAIN,NIRVANA)	◆ NIRVANA — (C) (V) DGC 19120
33	37	41	10	**NU NU** — L.TOWNSELL (HULA,K.FINGERS,L.TOWNSELL,SILK E.)	◆ LIDELL TOWNSELL — (C) (CD) (M) (T) MERCURY 866 445
34	36	43	6	**NOTHING ELSE MATTERS** — B.ROCK (HETFIELD,ULRICH)	◆ METALLICA — (C) ELEKTRA 64770
35	28	25	14	**THINKIN' BACK** — R.BAYYAN,H.LEE (COLOR ME BADD,H.LEE,T.TAYLOR)	◆ COLOR ME BADD — (C) (V) GIANT 19074
36	30	26	24	**I LOVE YOUR SMILE** — N.M.WALDEN (N.M.WALDEN,S.WILSON,S.JACKSON,J.BAKER)	◆ SHANICE — (C) (V) MOTOWN 2093
37	58	76	3	**DAMN I WISH I WAS YOUR LOVER** — R.CHERTOFF,R.SCHUCKETT (S.B.HAWKINS)	◆ SOPHIE B. HAWKINS — (C) COLUMBIA 74164
38	29	22	14	**JUSTIFIED AND ANCIENT** — THE KLF (J.CAUTY,W.DRUMMOND,R.LYTE)	◆ THE KLF FEATURING TAMMY WYNETTE — (C) (CD) (M) (T) (V) ARISTA 1-2401
39	53	73	4	**TENNESSEE** — SPEECH (ARRESTED DEVELOPMENT)	◆ ARRESTED DEVELOPMENT — (C) (T) CHRYSALIS 23829/ERG
40	33	28	12	**MAMA, I'M COMING HOME** — D.BARON,J.PURDELL (O.OSBOURNE,Z.WYLDE,L.KILMISTER)	◆ OZZY OSBOURNE — (C) (V) EPIC ASSOCIATED 74093/EPIC
41	60	74	4	**JUST TAKE MY HEART** — K.ELSON (E.MARTIN,A.PESSIS,A.CALL)	◆ MR. BIG — (C) (CD) (V) ATLANTIC 87509
42	45	47	5	**HIGH** — D.M.ALLEN,THE CURE (SMITH,GALLUP,THOMPSON,WILLIAMS,BAMONTE)	◆ THE CURE — (C) (CD) FICTION 64766/ELEKTRA
43	39	36	26	**ALL 4 LOVE ●** — H.TEE (COLOR ME BADD,H.THOMPSON)	◆ COLOR ME BADD — (C) (V) GIANT 19236
44	35	29	15	**MISSING YOU NOW** — W.AFANASIEFF,M.BOLTON (M.BOLTON,W.AFANASIEFF,D.WARREN)	◆ MICHAEL BOLTON — (C) (V) COLUMBIA 74184
45	95	—	2	★★★ POWER PICK/SALES ★★★ **SMELLS LIKE NIRVANA** — A.YANKOVIC (K.COBAIN,NIRVANA,A.YANKOVIC)	◆ "WEIRD AL" YANKOVIC — (C) SCOTTI BROS. 75314
46	54	63	10	**YOU THINK YOU KNOW HER** — S.ROWLEY (ROWLEY)	◆ CAUSE & EFFECT — (C) SRC 14025/ZOO
47	44	61	8	**DON'T BE AFRAID** — H.SHOCKLEE,G.G-WIZ (H.SHOCKLEE,G.G-WIZ,F.F.FISHER,A.HALL)	◆ AARON HALL — (C) (CD) (T) SOUL 54330/MCA
48	55	71	5	**COME & TALK TO ME** — D.SWING,AL B.SURE! (D.SWING)	◆ JODECI — (C) (M) (T) (V) UPTOWN 54175/MCA
49	52	58	5	**PLEASE DON'T GO** — D.AUSTIN (N.MORRIS)	BOYZ II MEN — (C) (V) MOTOWN 2155
50	42	42	32	**FINALLY ●** — F.DELGADO (C.PENISTON,F.DELGADO,E.L.LINNEAR,R.K.JACKSON)	◆ CECE PENISTON — (C) (M) (T) (V) A&M 1586
51	47	48	15	**WHAT GOES AROUND COMES AROUND** — C.JIMENEZ (C.JIMENEZ)	GIGGLES — (CD) (M) (T) CUTTING 256*
52	62	68	6	**3-2-1 PUMP** — D.GUPPY,J.MANN (D.GUPPY,M.WHITE,W.VAUGHN)	◆ REDHEAD KINGPIN & THE F.B.I. — (C) VIRGIN 98592
53	80	—	2	**IF YOU ASKED ME TO** — G.ROCHE (D.WARREN)	◆ CELINE DION — (C) EPIC 74277
54	40	32	16	**OOCHIE COOCHIE** — R.ANDERSON (S.DAVIS,M.BIVINS,C.ANDERSON,K.WALES,T.YOUNG)	◆ M.C. BRAINS — (C) (T) MOTOWN 2146
55	57	55	13	**EVERYTHING'S GONNA BE ALRIGHT** — NAUGHTY BY NATURE (V.BROWN,K.GIST,A.CRISS,B.MARLEY)	◆ NAUGHTY BY NATURE — (CD) (M) (T) TOMMY BOY 999*
56	48	51	6	**LOVE ME** — F.BROWN,T.ROBINSON (F.BROWN,T.ROBINSON)	◆ TRACIE SPENCER — (C) CAPITOL 44820
57	56	56	9	**ALL WOMAN** — I.DEVANEY,A.MORRIS (L.STANSFIELD,I.DEVANEY,A.MORRIS)	◆ LISA STANSFIELD — (C) (T) (V) ARISTA 1-2398
58	63	59	10	**THE CHOICE IS YOURS** — W.MCLEAN,A.TITUS (W.MCLEAN,A.TITUS)	◆ BLACK SHEEP — (C) (M) (T) MERCURY 866 086
59	69	77	4	**LIFT ME UP** — R.CULLUM,H.JONES (H.JONES,R.CULLUM)	◆ HOWARD JONES — (C) ELEKTRA 64779
60	38	30	11	**ROMEO & JULIET** — O.LEIBER (O.LEIBER)	◆ STACY EARL (FEATURING THE WILD PAIR) — (C) (V) RCA 62192
61	75	85	3	**NOT THE ONLY ONE** — D.WAS,B.RAITT (P.BRADY)	◆ BONNIE RAITT — (C) (CD) CAPITOL 44764
62	68	70	8	**IT'S OVER NOW** — M.J.JACKSON (M.CRIPPS,T.GUNS,P.LEWIS,K.NICKELS,S.RILEY,J.VALLANCE)	◆ L.A. GUNS — (C) (CD) POLYDOR 865 494/PLG
63	59	64	8	**SHE'S GOT THAT VIBE** — R.KELLY (R.KELLY,B.HANKERSON)	◆ R. KELLY & PUBLIC ANNOUNCEMENT — (C) (T) JIVE 42026/RCA
64	70	81	4	**WHY ME BABY?** — K.SWEAT (J.TODD,T.RILEY,K.SWEAT)	◆ KEITH SWEAT — (C) (M) ELEKTRA 64777
65	65	44	11	**IF YOU GO AWAY** — W.AFANASIEFF (W.AFANASIEFF,J.BETTIS,L.SMITH III)	NKOTB — (C) (V) COLUMBIA 74225
66	83	—	2	**I WILL REMEMBER YOU** — M.OMARTIAN (A.GRANT,G.CHAPMAN,K.THOMAS)	◆ AMY GRANT — (C) A&M 1600
67	61	49	13	**TOO MUCH PASSION** — E.STASIUM (P.DINIZIO)	◆ THE SMITHEREENS — (C) (CD) CAPITOL 44784
68	66	53	12	**BABY HOLD ON TO ME** — G.LEVERT,E.NICHOLAS (G.LEVERT,E.NICHOLAS)	◆ GERALD LEVERT (DUET WITH EDDIE LEVERT) — (C) ATCO EASTWEST 98639
69	67	50	13	**CAN'T CRY HARD ENOUGH** — D.KERSHENBAUM (D.WILLIAMS,M.ETZIONI)	◆ THE WILLIAMS BROTHERS — (C) (V) WARNER BROS. 19326
70	64	54	14	**YOU SHOWED ME** — EXCALIBUR & THE INVINCIBLES (R.MCGUINN,G.CLARK)	◆ SALT-N-PEPA — (CD) (M) (T) NEXT PLATEAU 50165*
71	87	99	3	**JUST ANOTHER DAY** — E.ESTEFAN,JR.,J.CASAS,C.OSTWALD (J.SECADA,M.A.MOREJON)	◆ JON SECADA — (C) (CD) SBK 07383/ERG
72	81	—	2	**SILENT PRAYER** — N.M.WALDEN (N.M.WALDEN,J.COHEN)	SHANICE — (C) MOTOWN 2165
73	77	75	7	**I WANNA ROCK** — K.TERRY (L.CAMPBELL)	◆ LUKE — (C) (M) (T) LUKE 98619/ATLANTIC
74	89	84	5	**IF YOU WANT IT** — DJ QUIK (D.BARNETT,K.MCDONALD,D.BLAKE)	◆ 2ND II NONE — (C) (T) PROFILE 5361
75	72	69	20	**I'LL GET BY** — K.OLSEN,E.MONEY (A.ARMATO,A.HILL,E.MONEY)	◆ EDDIE MONEY — (C) COLUMBIA 74109
76	76	66	13	**BOOM! I GOT YOUR BOYFRIEND** — DANNY D,D.J. WHIZ,S.TEMPO (D.SPOON,J.ALBELO,S.BLOUNT,R.MCCALL)	◆ M.C. LUSCIOUS — (C) (CD) (M) (T) AVENUE 7203
77	51	38	10	**CHURCH OF YOUR HEART** — C.OFWERMAN (P.GESSLE)	◆ ROXETTE — (C) (CD) (V) EMI 50380/ERG
78	71	72	6	**THIS IS THE LAST TIME** — M.P.DESANTIS,J.MELILLO (M.P.DESANTIS,J.MELILLO,M.FACHINNI)	LAURA ENEA — (M) (T) NEXT PLATEAU 50172*
79	NEW ▶		1	★★★ HOT SHOT DEBUT ★★★ **HOLD ON MY HEART** — GENESIS,N.DAVIS (T.BANKS,P.COLLINS,M.RUTHERFORD)	◆ GENESIS — (C) (V) ATLANTIC 87481
80	78	79	7	**IT'S NOT A LOVE THING** — P.GLENISTER (G.WILLIAMS,M.JONES,S.STIRLING,P.GLENISTER)	◆ GEOFFREY WILLIAMS — (C) GIANT 19029
81	82	88	3	**DON'T TALK JUST KISS** — TOMMY D. (F.FAIRBRASS,R.FAIRBRASS,R.MONZOLI)	◆ RIGHT SAID FRED — (C) (CD) (T) CHARISMA 98595
82	85	90	3	**HELLUVA** — A.ACRE,D.MICHERY (E.BRIGATI,F.CAVALIERE,S.MCDUFFIE)	◆ BROTHERHOOD CREED — (C) (M) (T) GASOLINE ALLEY 54350/MCA
83	73	60	16	**UNTIL YOUR LOVE COMES BACK AROUND** — C.LORD-ALGE (MAES)	◆ RTZ — (C) (V) GIANT 19051
84	86	—	2	**LOVE YOU ALL MY LIFETIME** — D.GAMSON (I.KLARMANN,F.WEBER)	◆ CHAKA KHAN — (C) (CD) (T) WARNER BROS. 18987
85	88	91	5	**MARIA** — J.GARDNER,KAYEL (KAYEL,J.GARDNER)	TKA — (M) (T) TOMMY BOY 520*
86	91	94	3	**WHAT YOU GIVE** — S.THOMPSON,M.BARBIERO,TESLA (J.KEITH,F.HANNON)	◆ TESLA — (C) GEFFEN 19117
87	92	—	2	**YOUR SONG** — T.HORN (E.JOHN,B.TAUPIN)	ROD STEWART — (C) POLYDOR 865 944/PLG
88	74	62	14	**WHAT BECOMES OF THE BROKENHEARTED** — A.BAKER,T.FARAGHER (J.DEAN,P.RISER,W.WEATHERSPOON)	PAUL YOUNG — (C) (V) MCA 54331
89	79	67	18	**STAY** — D.SWING,AL B.SURE! (D.SWING)	◆ JODECI — (C) (M) (T) UPTOWN 54285/MCA
90	84	80	17	**A DEEPER LOVE/PRIDE (IN THE NAME OF LOVE)** — R.CLIVILLES,D.COLE (R.CLIVILLES,D.COLE,U2)	◆ CLIVILLES & COLE — (C) (CD) (M) (T) COLUMBIA 74136
91	93	87	4	**GOODBYE** — AL B.SURE!,K.WEST (AL B.SURE!,K.WEST)	◆ TEVIN CAMPBELL — (C) QWEST 19008/WARNER BROS.
92	100	—	3	**JAMES BROWN IS DEAD** — D.SLEMMING (D.SLEMMING)	L.A. STYLE — (CD) (M) (T) ARISTA 1-2387*
93	NEW ▶		1	**WHITE MEN CAN'T JUMP** — D.AUSTIN (D.AUSTIN,R.RAN)	◆ RIFF — (C) SBK 07384/ERG
94	NEW ▶		1	**ANYTHING AT ALL** — A.PAYSON (M.MALLOY,M.RIBLER)	◆ MITCH MALLOY — (C) (V) RCA 62196
95	NEW ▶		1	**DO IT TO ME** — S.LEVINE,L.RICHIE (L.RICHIE)	LIONEL RICHIE — (C) (CD) MOTOWN 2160
96	99	95	3	**NO SUNSHINE** — MR.MIXX,FROST (A.MOLINA, JR.,B.WITHERS)	◆ KID FROST — (C) VIRGIN 98583
97	94	89	8	**DO NOT PASS ME BY** — HAMMER,F.C.PILATE II (HAMMER,F.C.PILATE II)	◆ HAMMER — (C) (CD) (T) CAPITOL 44797
98	98	—	2	**THE LIFE OF RILEY** — I.BROUDIE,S.RODGERS (I.BROUDIE)	◆ THE LIGHTNING SEEDS — (C) (CD) MCA 54195
99	90	78	13	**RIGHT NOW** — A.JOHNS,T.TEMPLEMAN,VAN HALEN (S.HAGAR,E.VAN HALEN,M.ANTHONY,A.VAN HALEN)	◆ VAN HALEN — (C) WARNER BROS. 19059
100	NEW ▶		1	**INNOCENT CHILD** — P.RADFORD,B.MITCHELL (B.MITCHELL,P.RADFORD)	◆ COLOURHAUS — (C) INTERSCOPE 98613

◯ Records with the greatest airplay and sales gains this week. ◆Videoclip availability. ● Recording Industry Assn. Of America (RIAA) certification for sales of 500,000 units. ▲ RIAA certification for sales of 1 million units, with additional million indicated by a numeral following the symbol. Catalog number is for cassette single. *Asterisk indicates catalog number is for cassette maxi-single; regular cassette single unavailable. (C) Cassette single availability. (CD) Compact disk single availability. (M) Cassette maxi-single availability. (T) 12-inch vinyl single availability. (V) 7-inch vinyl single availability. © 1992, Billboard/BPI Communications.

90 BILLBOARD MAY 2, 1992

FIGURE 9-2 Hot 100 Singles chart. *(© 1992 BPI Communications. Used with permission of Billboard.)*

The information given below avoids using terms that require extensive definitions, especially since such terms may not be widely used anyway. The discussion that follows is meant to provide a simple overview of categorizing recordings for airplay. As described later in the chapter, that process can become complex.

Top 10 While a station may want to use another configuration (e.g., top 5, top 15), a generally accepted music category includes the most popular songs on the station's playlist. In this case, we mean the 10 most popular or important songs for the playlist period.

These would be considered the most important songs the station airs because listener interest is continuing. Normally this category would be placed in a faster rotation, or more frequent play schedule, under the assumption that listeners want to hear the most popular songs.

11–20 A song either is in this category or it is not. For instance, if a CHR formatted station relied exclusively on *Billboard* magazine's Hot 100 top songs as its guide to programming, all songs ranked 11 through 20 on that weekly chart would be included here.

Risers and Decliners There is a difference in listener appeal between songs that have peaked in popularity and those which are continuing to gain interest. Consequently, many stations have developed subcategories such as 11–20 risers and 11–20 decliners. These subcategories differentiate between newer songs that are rising in popularity, which listeners presumably most want to hear, and more familiar records that have been on the playlist for a longer time.

Currents Recordings ranked in the top 10 or from 11 through 20 are often called *currents* by programmers. Other programmers may refer to the most popular recordings as being in their *power rotation,* meaning that these songs receive the greatest amount of airplay.

21–30 In our system, these are records ranked between 21 and 30 according to the station's

scheme for determining record popularity. Again, programmers may categorize these records as risers or decliners in order to control their rotation. Placing the decliners in a slower rotation will minimize their *burnout.*

Recurrents The term **recurrents** is widely used in radio programming to refer to songs that have peaked in popularity but still retain much listener appeal. Depending on how a particular station defines this category, it may mean songs that have dropped out of the top 30 currently most popular records but have not declined so much that listeners are altogether tired of hearing them.

Many stations have rested these songs for a while by removing them from their playlists before placing them back in the recurrent category. Thus, the burnout factor is reduced and listeners enjoy hearing these records again, but not as often as they once did. In most formats recurrents do not come up in rotation as frequently as do the current top-10 or top-20 records.

Depending on the format, a recurrent may be from about 6 months to a year old. In CHR formats, which usually emphasize currently popular songs, a recurrent may be from 3 to 9 months old. In any case, the songs in this category are proven favorites with the audience that have been given reduced airplay to minimize their burnout.

New Additions New releases are not the same as new additions to the playlist. New releases are often held in abeyance until their prospects for building popularity have been evaluated. The larger the market, the less likely that a programmer will add a song that has just been released unless it is an anticipated release by a major performer. Because the largest stations have much to lose if they alienate listeners by playing untested music, they tend to be more conservative than are stations in smaller markets, where the competition is usually not as fierce.

Unless a programmer is prepared to take a chance on whether a new record will appeal to listeners, he or she may prefer to wait until there is some indication of listener acceptance before adding new music. Programmers at larger-market stations monitor the progress of regional and smaller market "breakouts" and add those records to the rotation when it is apparent that they have appeal to listeners. Record companies often get the best exposure for their new, unestablished recording artists on college radio stations, where these artists are given an opportunity to build a following. Two such groups are the B-52s and the Indigo Girls, who developed a following on campuses long before their records were added to mainstream playlists. In addition, some stations subject new releases to auditorium testing before adding them and then carefully monitor their acceptance by tracking telephone call-ins and doing listener call-out research in anticipation of removing them from the playlist if they do not catch on.

Gold One listener's fond memory may be tedious to another listener. For some stations, gold is as recent as a top-10 record from a year or two ago. For others, it means a classic hit that has certified sales of at least 1 million copies. If the programmer merely wants to identify the greatest hits from a specific year, there are reference works that list, according to specified format or music type, the top songs on *Billboard*'s Hot 100 from the 1950s through the 1980s.[5]

Although they are useful, these music guides do not tell programmers how appealing a specific song may be to listeners in their markets. Therefore, many stations contract for auditorium research in which as many as 700 to 800 records are tested two or more times a year to determine their burnout among target listeners.

Although custom research may be prohibitively expensive, smaller-market stations can obtain national auditorium testing to help determine the appropriate oldies for inclusion in the rotation. Of course, such a service has limitations. The most notable shortcoming is that a national study does not accommodate the particular preferences of the audience in a specific market. But this information, even though it lacks market specificity, may be a small-market programmer's only access to this kind of objective assessment. Paragon Research of Denver, Colorado, for in-

stance, conducts auditorium tests of music throughout the year for its clients. Thus, programmers can identify the most popular established songs among audiences whose preferences should be similar to those of the audiences of their own stations.

Album Cut The number of album cuts that may be included—if they are programmed at all—depends on the format. Since AOR and New Age programmers attempt to position their stations in ways that make them distinct from Adult Contemporary and CHR stations, their formats may go two or even three deep in an album by including one or more songs beyond the most popular cut in the rotation. This is one way AOR can appeal to listeners who identify with popular artists without sounding like the CHR stations they compete with. Similarly, a New Age station can position itself against an Adult Contemporary station.

Other Variations The disadvantage of the top-10, 11–20, 21–30 category scheme is that it does not differentiate between records that are rising and those which are declining in popularity. This is why many stations use some other means of categorizing records, such as assigning alphabetical designations to identify records that are relatively new and rising in popularity (which will probably be programmed more frequently) and those in decline (which will probably be programmed less often). For instance, some programmers may designate records in the 11–20 category that are moving up as A records and those which are moving down in listener popularity as B cuts to differentiate them.

Some programmers further categorize records according to their demographic or daypart appeal. Thus, a C record may designate a subcategory such as top-10, hard rock that is programmed less frequently than other music groups. Such songs may be limited to airplay only after 7 p.m., when the audience consists mostly of teens. They would not be programmed during morning or afternoon dayparts because of the possibility of irritating adults who tune in during the day.

There are advantages to assigning alphabetical letters or color codes to designate music categories, and many stations do that. A term often used in categorizing songs is "power," as in "power gold" or "power release," to indicate a recent addition to the playlist that is rising very rapidly in popularity. There are probably as many music categorization schemes as there are stations, and many buzzwords, nicknames, and slang terms are used in describing these categories. If a programmer devises music categories described by a color code and it works, good; but the more complex the scheme, the greater the risk of confusing the on-air personnel who must follow it. Category labels such as "power red" and "yellow superstash" should be avoided unless every staff member understands exactly what those terms mean and can apply them properly in the program formula.

Executing the format: the hot clock   A programmer who relies on the astuteness of disc jockeys to make decisions leaves a great deal to chance. Too often, the personal preferences of on-air personnel are interjected into the selection process. Moreover, under the pressure of live on-air performance, announcers can easily overlook such concepts as rewarding listeners and maintaining proper pacing in the presentation of program events unless they are given clear guidelines.

Consistency must be maintained over all the events presented on the air so that what is heard appeals to the audience available to listen at that time. As was discussed earlier in this chapter, even though some listeners' musical preferences may not be accommodated during some dayparts, the station's air sound should be consistent so that they will recognize "their" station regardless of when they tune in. Otherwise, there is a great chance for confusion and thus a loss of the audience.

A directive for executing the format is provided by the **hot clock,** also referred to as a format wheel, which visualizes where format events are scheduled for specified times during the hour. The clock is laid out in quarters, according to the minutes in the hour, making it easy to follow.

A copy is typically posted prominently in the control room for constant reference by the on-air personalities. The variations in the programming formula intended to appeal to the audiences available during different times of the day are controlled by using a different clock for each daypart. Figure 9-3 shows that the morning drive clock includes newscasts and **liners** (preproduced comedy sketches, informational bits, and other non-news events) which are not included in the 10 a.m.–3 p.m. clock. Moreover, record category Z, which designates songs that test well among teens and men and women 18 to 24 but hold little appeal to listeners over age 35, are not included on the daytime clocks, and so they air only during the daypart from 7 p.m. to midnight.

As Figure 9-3 shows, specific events such as commercials are scheduled for airing during specified quarter-hour periods. While some events, particularly records, are not of consistent length, most will fit within the scheduled quarter hour. When they won't, the announcer can adjust by skipping a designated event such as a second "gold" selection in order to stay on schedule.

In most music formats, records are carefully placed to reward listeners for staying with the station through stop sets and other breaks in the music. Instead of leaving it to chance whether the disc jockey will remember to play the appropriate recording, the program director may, for instance, dictate via the hot clock that a top-10 record be scheduled immediately after a stop set. Thus, listeners who "endured" the commercial messages are rewarded with a song that has been determined by the programming staff to be among the currently most popular recordings.

The music aired during the morning daypart on the typical Adult Contemporary station is up-tempo and cheerful. This can be controlled by the station's morning daypart clock, which may restrict the airplay of records whose tempos are considered too languid or dreamy, such as love ballads and instrumentals. During the middle of the day, between 10 a.m. and 3 p.m., though, the tempo may be slowed down to be less obtrusive in order to create a greater appeal to people who

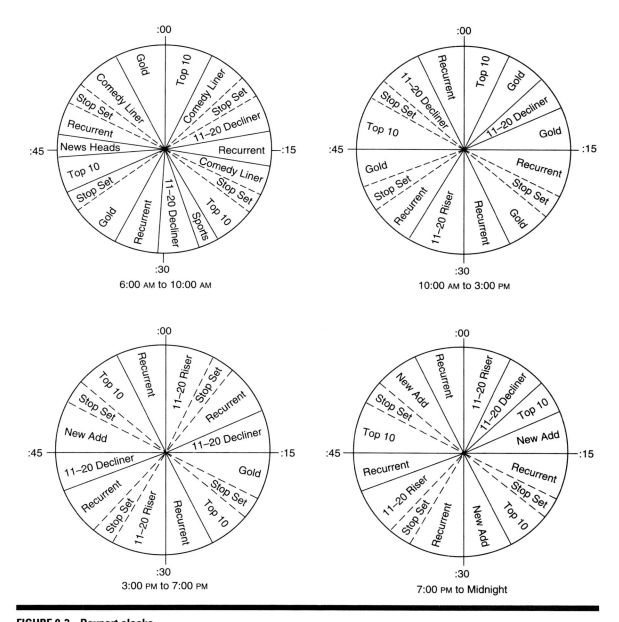

FIGURE 9-3 Daypart clocks.

are at work in offices and other locations. During either daypart, the music mix can be controlled by the categories that appear and the frequency with which they come up on the daypart clock.

Because many adults are in the daytime audience, gold records are often given a heavy rota-

tion on the daytime clocks of many stations regardless of format. However, because adults abandon radio for television during the evening, categories designating current material predominate in the 7 p.m.–midnight clock. If a CHR station, for example, has a more extensive clock system, perhaps the 7 p.m.–8 p.m. clock will prescribe one hard rock song during the hour while two or more may be scheduled during the 8 p.m. –9 p.m. hour. That way, the station can make the transition more gradually from one audience period into another. The potentially irritating program content can be avoided or minimized until a fairly large number of older listeners have left the audience.

An alternative: the linear clock Some programmers prefer to use a sequential programming scheme instead of a hot clock. These "chains" or **linear clocks** have the advantage over the hot clock that their sequence of events is played out regardless of the clock time, whereas a disc jockey who is following a hot clock begins again at the top of each hour. Thus, a linear clock may be more spontaneous since the listener can't detect where the "hottest" recordings will come up during an hour.[6] Proponents of the linear clock argue that its execution avoids airing the same categories at the same time and thus avoids burning out records in the station's rotation. Furthermore, the linear clock (Table 9-2) makes it very difficult for competitors who monitor the station to figure out its rotation and then program against it.[7]

TABLE 9-2 Linear Clock

Event	Category
1	Top 10
2	Recurrent
3	New addition
4	Liner
5	Top 10
6	Stop set
7	Recurrent
8	Gold
9	11–20
10	Recurrent
11	Top 10
12	Liner
13	11–20
14	Gold
15	New addition

There is a distinctive disadvantage to the linear clock, though. If the sequence is at its weakest event during the most important quarter hours, its execution may drive away some listeners. For example, if the sequence is followed, a stop set may come up during the first 5 minutes of the first quarter-hour period, which is when the greatest number of new listeners tune in. As was discussed earlier, this is not the kind of program event with which a programmer wants to greet audience members.

Music Values

The single most important way to categorize music for airplay is in accordance with its popularity. Thus, as described above, music is included on a station's hot clock on the assumption that listeners will want to hear certain songs when they tune in and that these songs should be in a frequent, or hot, rotation. In addition, subcategories are created to reflect the appeal some songs have to certain demographic groups which may be present in large numbers during some dayparts. Although the criteria of popularity and demographic appeal usually dictate the music rotation, recordings can also be programmed in accordance with the attributes of the songs. Thus, music values constitute an important way to optimize the appeal of the air sound a station dispenses to its listeners.

Sylvia Clark of Burns Media Consultants, Inc., has described "the earpearance of sound resulting from the woven arrangement of vocals, instrumentation, and harmonies."[8] The "fabric" achieved in programming music depends on how records of varying textures, intensity, and tempo are sequenced.

Music texturing **Music texturing** takes into account all the aspects of what the listener hears, including the timbre of a singer's voice. It would be difficult to consider a Rod Stewart, Bruce Springsteen, or John Cougar Mellencamp vocal as "thin" in texture, but songs by Michael Jackson, Phil Collins, and Dolly Parton might qualify. Even though a singer's voice could fairly be considered "thin," it is the recording that people listen to. Thus, the singer is only an instrument, coupled with others, that contributes to the effect of the production. Even though Michael Jackson's voice is high and thin, the electronically amplified guitars, drums, and synthesizers that back it up can contribute to a full-textured recording.

Music can be categorized according to three basic textures: thin, medium, and full. The programmer can break these textures down further (e.g., thin, medium-thin, medium, medium-full, and full). This is a subjective process, and great care must be taken to maintain consistency.

Full-textured music is typically loud, busy, and driving. Because it requires a lot of attention, it appeals to younger listeners. Older listeners find songs with thinner textures more appealing because they do not wish to devote as much attention to the music. Michael Bolton's "Time, Love and Tenderness," for example, has a powerful, driving arrangement with lots of intensity. In a format that emphasized hard rock this song might be considered of medium texture, but in an Adult Contemporary format it would probably be classified as a full-textured song. Music with a thinner texture creates a more tranquil atmosphere. Christopher Cross's "Sailing" is an example of a song that most programmers would probably classify as having a thin texture. Simon and Garfunkel's "Bridge over Troubled Water" has a decidedly thin texture when the song begins, but it builds in intensity. Again, it depends on the context in which a recording is played whether the programmer will categorize it as having a thin or a medium texture.

Tempo Music can be categorized as fast, medium-fast, medium, medium-slow, slow, and very slow (sometimes described as "dead" or "dirge"). The rhythm of the tune, which is typically measured by the number of **beats per minute (BPM)**, indicates its tempo. Many programmers use BPM as a factor in scheduling songs.[9]

The faster pacing usually sought in the morning and afternoon dayparts can be achieved by avoiding slow or very slow songs. Many programmers eliminate songs in their two lowest BPM categories during the morning period and do not play songs in the lowest category during the afternoon drive. In any daypart, the programmer should refrain from scheduling two songs in a row from the same tempo category.

Intensity Music intensity transcends tempo and texture and can be described as the degree of loudness. One might visualize an artist whose performance has high intensity as exerting so much energy that the blood vessels stand out on his or her temples because the singer is giving it all he or she's got. For example, the typical Barry Manilow song is full in texture and slow in tempo but builds to a high level of intensity. Most Phil Collins and Genesis songs are very high in intensity. Similarly, Lee Greenwood's lyric "I'm proud to be an American" in his song "God Bless the U.S.A.," which received much exposure during and after the 1991 Gulf war against Iraq, seems thin in texture, medium in tempo, and very high in intensity.

If songs can be categorized as high in intensity (some would describe these recordings as "high scream"), they should be scheduled as "islands," separated by other songs that are of less intensity. AOR and youth-intensive CHR are probably the only formats in which it is logical to program two high-intensity selections back to back.

Music sequencing To use the subtle music classification schemes of texture, tempo, and intensity, the programmer should devise a procedure that is as objective and consistent as possible for classifying each song on the playlist. Program consultant Ed Shane has suggested a five-step scaled system ranging from slow to fast: -2, -1, 0, $+1$, $+2$. In stations where he consults, the disc jockeys may not play two songs with the same number or move more than two units on the scale. His system allows for a flow of tempo, moving from lower to higher intensity and tempo without the jarring effect of a very slow record following a very fast one.[10]

A traditional consideration in scheduling music is to avoid playing female artists or male-female duets back to back. Relatively few songs of either type appear on most playlists, and the variety these selections can contribute to the format is minimized when they are clustered. Another concern is that many female artists perform at a higher pitch which can become dominant when such artists are clustered. With separation, both their appeal and variety in the format can be enhanced.

Yet another consideration for music scheduling is the utility of **artist separation** in scheduling the play of recordings made by performers in various stages of their careers. For instance, some time should elapse between the airing of a solo by Paul McCartney and the airing of a record by the Beatles or Wings of which he was a member or a duet with another artist such as Stevie Wonder ("Ebony and Ivory") except when the station is specifically promoting a music set that features two songs by an artist.

Because listeners generally tune in at the same times each day, programmers must keep their formats from becoming stagnant. Few attributes are as noticeable and irritating as hearing the same song or other event at about the same time on successive days. To prevent such a pattern, astute program directors establish **daypart separation,** in which a song is not played in the same daypart on successive days. If a song is at the height of its popularity, daypart separation is probably not much of an issue. The song may be played twice during the same daypart, and it may be desirable to repeat it on successive days as well. However, when a song is being rotated less frequently, it does not warrant that level of exposure. It is much better not to present that material to the same listeners too often.

Programmers may also use **horizontal separation,** in which a song has at least an hour of separation on consecutive days. Thus, a song that was played on Monday at 7:15 a.m. would not air again until after 8 a.m. on Tuesday and not until after 9 a.m. on Wednesday. Then it could return to the 7 a.m. hour on Thursday. This is another way to minimize the possibility that a listener will hear songs being played at about the same time every day.

Some stations practice **vertical separation** by separating the plays of a song by a specified period of time. In stations where the announcers maintain a log of music played during their shifts, a disc jockey who is preparing for a shift is often required to review his or her predecessor's music log to avoid playing any song within 1 or 2 hours of its previous airing. A variation of vertical separation is **quarter separation,** where plays of a song rotate to different quarters of an hour.

Programming music by separation categories requires a lot more effort from both the programmer and the disc jockeys who execute the format. If the system is clear and the PD educates those who select the music, a station can present a more balanced and controlled service to its listeners.

Following Play Rules As the description above illustrates, music sequencing can be complex and thus difficult to control. Many stations now program music with the aid of computer software such as MusicScan, Columbine, and Play List II. Without close supervision of personnel and added technical support, greater reliance must be placed on the on-air personnel to follow programming policies and make decisions when the occasion warrants.

This software makes it possible to schedule recordings according to all the criteria discussed in this chapter. Thus, a top-10 song that has high intensity or high BPM, for instance, will automatically be excluded from play during any daypart the programmer designates. Furthermore, songs can be programmed to accommodate vertical, horizontal, or quarter-hour separation. The disc jockey is given a printed list of the order of the particular songs that should be aired at particular times during the air shift. Thus, the computer program permits much more sophisticated control over the music than would be possible if one attempted to keep track of all its attributes by hand.

In the absence of a computerized music sequencing system that is programmed to follow the station's play rules, the disc jockey normally works from the front to the back in each category, literally placing the music that has been aired at the back of the group to maintain the rotation. There are exceptions to this rule, depending on the station's policy. If the song being played is a slow ballad and the first tune in next category also has a slow tempo, the announcer may be permitted to skip over the slow song for the next selection in the category, a fast, up-tempo tune, to achieve a better music balance. The program and music directors need to be sure that announcers do not avoid songs they don't like to play. After all, the music has been researched and selected for well-conceived reasons. If individual announcers are permitted to use their discretion about what is to be aired, the program concept can be destroyed.

News, Sports, and Weather

Although the news has been a secondary programming service on the majority of radio stations over the years, virtually all radio stations have traditionally provided at least one newscast during most hours in the broadcast day. While some stations make a greater effort to provide true local news coverage by hiring news staffs and covering local events, other stations limit their news effort to "rip 'n' read," which means that the disc jockey clears the Associated Press or United Press International news wire. After the continuous paper that is fed into the printer has been scanned, the portions where the selected stories are printed are separated or "ripped" apart. The on-air personality thus hastily assembles a collection of news items and, if she or he is sufficiently professional, at least reads them aloud in rehearsal before presenting them on the air. The stories usually pertain to the state or nation. Little news, if any, deals with the area directly covered by the station's signal. Rip 'n' read is far less expensive than hiring newscasters, who not only use the wire service with greater discrimination and rehearsal but also have some time to cover local news. In spite of the cost,

many stations employ a news staff to provide a better-quality broadcast.

After 1981, when the FCC removed its rule requiring news and public affairs as a program service, some radio stations, mostly those in larger markets, gutted their news operations or reduced the size of their staffs. In small and medium markets, though, deregulation has had little effect on news practices.[11] Many smaller-market stations provide more general programming, and the local news may be an important aspect of their service, especially in markets that are not served by a daily local newspaper.

The removal of the requirement for newscasts encouraged programmers in markets where other stations offered strong radio news services to give less emphasis to news or abandon it altogether because their managements felt that listeners who wanted that service would find it elsewhere. When this occurs, stations may offer an abbreviated news service that is targeted to their audiences.[12]

A concurrent influence on the decision to program radio news is its expense. At some stations the fate of local news may hinge on the perception by the station management that a state radio news network or one of the satellite-delivered services is a less expensive substitute for local news organizations. To operate a good news department even in a small market, two or more people are needed to cover the important local events. These individuals represent a significant operational expense. If three entry-level newspeople were put on the payroll at $14,000 apiece, the station's budget would increase by $42,000, plus employee benefits, immediately. Consequently, news has been given a secondary role in many radio operations.

A station's format is often instrumental in influencing the emphasis it gives to news. Popular music stations have found that news and most other nonmusic or talk programs are tune-out factors and have given up their network affiliations because of the interruption of music programming by newscasts. On many such stations the news service, such as it is, ends with the morning drive. AOR and CHR formatted stations in particular tend to position their morning newscasters as "sidekicks" of the morning personalities, acting as chorus members who laugh and cut up. The programmers of these stations perceive their target audiences as being uninterested in news and have developed comedy and feature shows for the morning period.

This has brought about a greater integration of the personalities and events that make up the morning programming on some stations. In "zoo" formats, where zany, sometimes outrageous antics, jokes, and comments prevail, the straightforward, detached approach of traditional newspersons may seem out of place. Some of these stations present parodies of the news that are heavy on soft news or feature stories, with an occasional standard breaking news story as events warrant. Much flippancy is incorporated in the delivery.

The downside to the trend toward creating news personalities is that the integrity of news is depreciated. Even in more staid formats, news personnel are often confined to the studio to bolster the personality aspects of the air sound. Many programmers want the newscasters to engage in banter and discussions with the disc jockeys, integrating the news more fully into the on-air sound. Consequently, fewer radio reporters are out on the street to gather news and interpret information of potential value to their audiences.

Which approach is proper and which is most likely to win out? In an era of marketplace-driven programming decisions where regulatory requirements are at best a secondary concern, the commercial interests of the station are most likely to prevail. However, the pendulum has a way of swinging back, and trends die. Stations with formats targeted to younger listeners have always considered news as a tune-out factor, but not every programmer believes that it is necessary to treat newscasters as entertainment personalities to increase listening.

There is a middle ground. Many stations consider news an important part of their appeal. The fact that an on-air reporter has a sense of humor and can engage in conversation with the disc jockey does not necessarily diminish journalistic credibility. In fact, one study has shown that when a newscast is straightforward, there does not seem to be a negative effect if the newscaster jokes with the disc jockey before or after the newscast, although a high level of joking can cause the newscaster to be less appealing to the audience, resulting in listener tune-out.[13] This requires maturity and good judgment on the part of the program director, the disc jockey, and the newsperson.

Newscast placement The traditional time for scheduling radio news and sports was on the hour or 5 minutes before, but listeners became aware of that practice and in some cases began to tune out when news programs were presented. Youth appeal stations began placing the news at 20 minutes before or 20 minutes past the hour. The "20–20" news concept was intended to minimize listener awareness of the times for news. Tune-out was lessened during the important first quarter hour, keeping listeners tuned through at least the first 5 minutes of the second quarter-hour period. Since most listeners use the beginning of the hour and half past the hour as traditional points of reference, newscasts came at times that were not in their perceptual clock. Thus, 20–20 news did not automatically trigger the impulse to tune out and seek a station playing music. Moreover, news scheduled at 20 minutes past or 20 minutes before the hour permits 5 minutes of sampling in the second quarter hour and 10 minutes of sampling during the third quarter hour. As an alternative, news scheduled at 50 minutes past the hour allows the listener to sample music for 5 minutes before the potential tune-out event is presented. Each of these strategies is designed to elicit that all-important 5 minutes of listening during the quarter hour to maximize the ratings.

The frequency of newscasts depends on their importance to the target audience. For older listeners, the value of news and other such information is normally higher. Full-service stations that carry network news as well as extensive local coverage may schedule local news immediately after the network news feed, but if music is

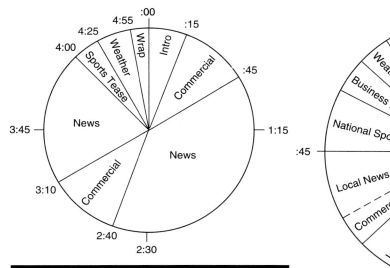

FIGURE 9-4 Five-minute news program clock.

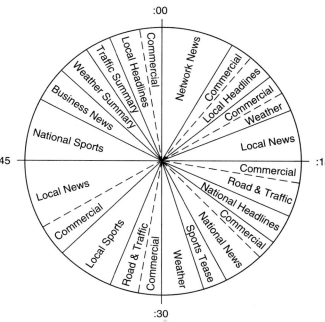

FIGURE 9-5 News format hour clock.

the most important appeal in the format, there should be a break between news programs.

Newscast length The traditional newscast length for radio was 5 minutes, including commercial messages (Figure 9-4). For music-intensive formats, this has been shortened on many stations to $2^1/_2$ minutes or less. While some programmers have concluded that news is a listener irritant, listener perception can be altered by the way an event is programmed.

If two separate newscasts of 2 minutes and 30 seconds in length were presented during the hour—one at 20 past and the second at 10 minutes before the hour, for instance—more actual news might be conveyed than in a single broadcast of 5 minutes that included commercial announcements.

All-News format The format of an All-News station is much like that of a station using a music format. The morning and afternoon dayparts include a sequence of local news, weather, traffic conditions, perhaps an editorial or commentary, sports, headlines, and network news. At other times of the day features on money, politics, sex,

and health are scheduled. If these latter segments are short enough, they may also be included during drive time.

News formats are usually designed not to attract the largest AQH audience during a daypart but to compete on the basis of cume listeners. Since most people tune in to catch up on the latest news, formats are designed to provide what listeners want, much in the same fashion that music format listeners are induced to tune in to hear their favorite songs. Twenty-minute news blocks which include local, regional, and world news are fairly standard.[14]

The typical All-News station's schedule (Figure 9-5) may include a network news feed at the top of the hour followed by local headlines, weather, local news, business news, sports, and brief national headlines to serve as a tease for the full network feed to follow at the top of the next hour. Traffic and road conditions are interspersed on a scheduled basis.

WBBM Newsradio in Chicago has identified three groups of news listeners: The largest consists of listeners who tune in for brief periods to get quick updates one or more times a day. The second group listens for an average of an hour or more. The third group tunes in to get details on a disaster or on breaking news it has heard about through another source. All-News formats attract high cume audiences, and so the second group of listeners is being targeted to increase WBBM's AQH listening by reducing repetition. When a story is used again, it is updated by rewriting it and using a different **sound bite,** or excerpt from an interview.[15]

Talk programming Call-in shows must be as carefully produced as any other kind of format. Programs in larger markets have producers who screen calls to keep cranks and frequent callers off the air. Equally important, the producer permits only callers who can contribute to the subjects being discussed to get on the air.

The producer plays an important role in the preparation of the programming as well. In addition to extensive reading of newspapers and magazines to keep abreast of topical material, the producer contacts and lines up guests to appear on the show.

Talk programming content varies according to daypart. For example, subjects such as divorce and the family are emphasized during the midday period. During the evening hours, political and sports topics dominate.

Typical News/Talk radio formats present news and information during the morning and afternoon drive times and fill the other dayparts with discussion and call-in programs. One mid-sized-market station, for example, devoted an hour during its midmorning period to interviewing the director of a juvenile offender facility and discussing juvenile delinquency. The topics and guests one day on WWRC, Washington D.C., included a congressman who talked about the constitutionality of proposed federal antidrug legislation, a new book on parents' problems in dealing with adolescents, and erotic telephone services.[16]

Talk programming is also carried on many stations that feature music and other content as their primary programming. They often broadcast "party line" programs, which may be scheduled for an hour or so during midmorning. Typically, listeners call in to ask for advice on refinishing furniture or household problems like stain removal or to announce they have an item for sale. In other cases a guest may respond to calls from listeners.

In larger markets, "opinion radio" programs elicit points of view from callers as well as providing a forum for their hosts to espouse their own perspectives. Listeners to these programs are more interested in opinion than in fact, which is capitalized on by such talk-show personalities as Rush Limbaugh, whose show is distributed nationally via satellite. Other versions of this approach are represented by many local broadcasts where "hot line" call-in programs permit listeners to discuss subjects that may be limited to a single topic or may range across all the subjects on callers' minds.

Some News/Talk format stations schedule sports discussion programs at night in which current issues such as drug use and academic cheating are the main topics, along with the performance of various players or teams in recent contests. Since there is wide interest in sports, call-in programs that discuss current sports events can attract a substantial nighttime audience. Furthermore, coverage of sports events is staple for many talk formatted stations, which carry college and professional football, basketball, and baseball throughout their seasons.

Sports Research on the times to present separate sports reports on most stations regardless of format has shown that 25 minutes past the hour is a popular time. Many stations combine news and sports, with the sports report taking up the last minute or so of the hourly newscast. In music-intensive formats, particularly those which target younger listeners, sports information is often limited to the scores of important games. On such stations there may not be a formal sports report, but the information may be presented as a drop-in event. This allows the flexibility of providing the information that many listeners want without interrupting the flow of music programming.

Weather Weather is another category of information that is often tagged on at the end of newscasts. Regardless of its status as news, the weather affects all listeners, and a majority want to know the current conditions and the forecast. Consequently, some programmers schedule weather information at least once during each quarter hour, particularly during the morning drive period, when listeners want to know how their day will shape up. During other dayparts, weather information may be given less frequently. With this flexibility, the programmer can easily increase the number of reports during times of volatile weather conditions. This rewards listeners with information they want. Careful handling enhances a station's position among its listeners as the place they can tune to satisfy their needs and wants.

Commercials

Commercials present a programming quandary. They are the classic listener irritant, but without them the station's purpose for being would be compromised. This section discusses ways in which commercial messages can be programmed not only to minimize their potential to alienate listeners but to weave them into the fabric of the format. Thus, **spots,** which are so named because of the placement of commercial messages in various programs and dayparts, can add an element of entertainment or at least reduce the potential for listener irritation.

Stop sets Most radio programmers schedule commercial announcements in strategically placed clusters. This practice emerged in the 1960s, when FM broadcasters attempted to capitalize on the greatest advantage they had at the time: no commercial clutter. Whereas their AM competitors were presenting up to 18 minutes of commercial matter during each hour, FM stations, which attracted much smaller audiences, were sometimes lucky to sell any commercial

time at all. Programmers emphasized a "more music" positioning strategy and announced a policy of limiting the number of commercial interruptions per hour.

Thus, programmers discovered an effective way to minimize the irritation of commercials. Spots were scheduled in groups, or sets, to eliminate the clutter and distraction they caused among the records and other program events. **Spot sets** are groupings of commercials, whereas stop sets include commercial announcements and other program announcements such as station promotions and public service announcements (PSAs), aired at no cost to an agency such as the American Cancer Society. In either case, the sets are scheduled at specified times during the hour. Seldom, if ever, can an audience member distinguish between a PSA and a commercial. Similarly, station promotions may be considered commercial announcements by audience members, and listeners may perceive announcer talk about unrelated subjects as commercials regardless of how those events are categorized in the program log. A perceptual study of the station's programming may help discover this kind of listener impression. It may then be necessary to reconfigure the station's commercial programming policies.

Scheduling stop sets Some programmers feel it is best to schedule stop sets in the middle of the quarter hour to avoid losing listeners at the beginning of the time period, but programmers also analyze their competitors' clocks and attempt to program against them. Thus, if other stations run stop sets at 20 minutes past and 20 minutes before the hour, a countering move might be to schedule music to air during that time and air stop sets 2 or 3 minutes earlier or later. That way, the station can pick up listeners who are tuning around the dial during times when most of the competitors are airing commercials.

Yet another consideration is the length of a stop set. An advantage of scheduling spots in 2-minute blocks of time is that fewer stop sets are needed in each hour, but tune-out may occur because of their length. However, scheduling shorter but more frequent sets may give listeners the impression that the format is cluttered and that more commercials are being scheduled than is the case.

When a station's research shows that listeners perceive commercial breaks to be overly long, a programmer may be able to justify limiting the length or number of spots in a set. The station must maintain a delicate balance between generating revenue and minimizing the irritant factor of commercials.

If, for instance, the station is scheduling 10 minutes of commercial announcements an hour during a daypart, it may be best to use a schedule with a light **front load** and a heavier **back load.** That is, the PD may schedule 4 minutes of commercials during the first two quarter hours and 6 minutes during the second half of the hour. This will minimize irritants for listeners who tune in during the first two quarter hours.

The greatest number of listeners tune in during the first quarter hour, followed by the third quarter hour. Since most people regulate their lives by the clock, they usually set their radio alarms to come on at 6 or 6:30 a.m., for instance, and most people schedule appointments to begin on the hour or half hour. Therefore, since more listeners join the radio audience in the first and third quarter-hour periods, tune-out due to commercials aired during the second or fourth quarter hour will cause less damage to the cume or AQH audience estimates. But with incentives such as contests and special features, there is a likelihood that the audiences for the first and third quarter hours will be enticed to stay tuned during the next quarter hour.

Commercials as irritants Virtually every market has a "Crazy Lenny" local advertiser who likes to yell at listeners or whose communication is otherwise so inept that the presentation taints the station's air sound. Most programmers are reluctant to schedule this kind of spot because it compounds the problem of listener irritation.

Some stations have a commercial acceptance policy. A Beautiful-Music/Easy-Listening station, for instance, probably will not accept a spot

that includes intense loud music and a shouting announcer because it will destroy the tranquil sound created by subdued announcers and low-intensity music. Research into the influence of irritating commercials on radio listening has found that listeners younger than 49 are more likely to be irritated by commercials than older listeners are. The research also pointed to some evidence that rock station programmers have little need to single out irritating commercials because many listeners to those formats are inclined to change stations upon hearing any commercials. By contrast, audiences for Easy-Listening formats change stations during irritating commercials more than others do. Country music listeners are the least likely to change stations during irritating commercials but are also less likely to shop at an advertiser whose commercials irritate them.[17]

Thus, programmers of formats that target younger demographics may need to be more sensitive to ways to minimize potential tune-out. More important, young people make changes in station listening more frequently, and males change more than females do. For example, CHR station programmers, especially when they target male listeners, need to be more concerned with diminishing the negative effect of spot sets than do programmers of some other formats. While Country music programmers may not have to be as concerned as others about losing listeners, they may be able to make a better case to advertisers to avoid irritating commercials.

Program consultant Ed Shane recommends that when airing an offending message is inevitable, program the commercial. This can be accomplished by minimizing the number of irritating commercials that will be included in any stop set. Another possibility is to schedule the irritating message as the last one in the stop set and immediately reward the listener with a highly desirable song. Another way to minimize the damage is to instruct the disc jockey to "presell" or tease a listener reward that will follow the commercial. Finally, Shane suggests that an irritating spot can be run by itself to get past its potential harmful effect quickly. In no case, though, should the on-air personality call attention to the commercial by talking about it.[18]

Commercial production values Most commercial announcements (CAs) are neither grating nor enormously appealing but lie somewhere between those extremes. These messages can have listener appeal because of their production values, or the inclusion of such elements as music, interesting voices, dialogue, sound effects, and compelling dramatic situations—the things that make any program more or less interesting.

A **straight-voice commercial** usually has the lowest production values or listener interest, although a notable exception is spots in which unique and skilled voices are used. Many commercials are produced with a **music bed,** which is music in the background, under the announcer's voice. This should heighten interest, assuming the music is appropriate to the format or is especially appealing in conjunction with the message. Commercials that include dialogue or feature character voices may have higher production values, as may spots that include sound effects. Messages that incorporate a **jingle** can attract interest and attention and give the listeners enjoyment. The widespread use of multitrack recorders, voice synthesizers, and other electronic marvels makes very sophisticated commercials with high production values readily available.

Sound effects, multivoice dialogue, and music can all be handled ineptly or skillfully. Deciding whether a spot is an irritant or is an asset because it is high in production values in comparison to others is a judgment call, but it can and must be made.

Programming within stop sets Aside from a consideration of how to handle particularly irritating spots, there are at least three philosophies on how to program commercial announcements. One is to begin the stop set with the announcement with the lowest production values (say, a straight-voice commercial) and build through

the set to end with the CA that has the highest production values. The second approach is to do the opposite: begin the set with the spot with the greatest interest, entertainment, and production values and descend to the final announcement, which has the lowest production values. A third approach is to start with a commercial with high production values, descend to the middle spot, which has the lowest values of the ads in the set, and then ascend to the final spot, which has production values comparable to those of the announcement that began the set.[19]

Some stations schedule 60-second spots first during their stop sets and end with spots that are 30 seconds or shorter. They follow a pattern of beginning with a spot containing high production values and placing "dry" spots in the middle so that they can end the set with an upbeat spot.

There is no "correct" philosophy. It is important, though, for the program director to justify an approach and communicate it to all the persons concerned with carrying out station policy. If the traffic director can schedule spots according to their production value, that leaves one less element to chance and the attentiveness of the announcer on duty.

Liners

The definition may vary from station to station, but a **liner** generally is any program event other than music, commercial announcements/PSAs, or news and sports, although some stations consider news and sports to be liners. Typical liners include comedy sketches and syndicated features such as *Dr. Dean Edell Medical Minutes* and Paul Harvey's *The Rest of the Story.*

Regardless of the specific definition, a liner is an event that provides nonmusic content. It should be an event that rewards listeners for tuning in. Thus, liners, such as comedy sketches, that are incorporated into the format should be scheduled to capitalize on their impact as listener appeals.

The *Chickenman* syndicated comedy series[20] provides a good example. One station carried the same episode at about 9 a.m. and again at around 2:30 p.m. The episode could be repeated since few morning listeners were recycled in the early afternoon. Importantly, there was some flexibility in scheduling the episode from day to day. In order not to miss that day's segment, *Chickenman* fans had to tune in somewhat early and might be required to listen to the station for about 20 minutes before being rewarded. While such a strategy attracts listeners for more than one quarter hour, it also rewards them within a fairly short time. Without such a payoff, listeners may not feel the effort is worthwhile.

PROGRAMMING CONSIDERATIONS FOR SMALL-MARKET RADIO

Large markets are most frequently held up as examples, and there is utility in illustrating concepts by pointing to the most competitive situations. However, most readers of this book are currently employed or will begin their careers in small markets, and so the realities of small markets should be understood. Thus, the kind of programming a station does may be a key to its financial success. A small-market station that programs farm market reports, weather information, and county agent programs is much more likely to sell advertising time to agricultural products distributors and farm service suppliers even though competing stations may reach many more people. The point is to program to the interests and needs of those in the listening area and to heed the needs of the advertisers who want to reach those listeners.

In many small markets the only local news outlet other than the radio station is a weekly newspaper. Thus, radio news can provide an essential service to the community. Because peo-

ple rely on community stations to keep them informed, sponsorships of news programs can be sold more easily.

Generally, the programmer of a small-market station must select general-appeal content. Although an audience for AOR no doubt exists just about everywhere, the number of actual listeners in a small market will be few, and even fewer potential advertisers are likely to be among them. Keep in mind Duncan's data, discussed in Chapter 8, which show that stations using Country formats have a higher revenue share as a percentage of audience share in smaller markets than in larger ones. Similarly, Adult Contemporary formatted stations do better in medium and small markets than in the largest markets. These two formats, which have great appeal to older, more conservative audiences, are more appealing to advertising clients who base their decisions on what they think their customers listen to.

In attempting to appeal to more groups of listeners, small-market stations may have more positioning flexibility than do their counterparts in larger, more competitive markets. By dayparting, a full-service small-market station can accommodate available listeners during different times of the day. A mixture of news, farm reports, and popular music may work during the early-morning period, followed by easy-listening or light rock music along with issues of the day, interviews with public officials, or "swap shop" call-in programs during the midmorning period. A greater emphasis on news and sports in the afternoon period interspersed with light rock music could be followed in the evening daypart by much harder rock music. Such a format may work if there are few choices for listeners either in the market or from out-of-market stations.

SUMMARY

Since a station's success is determined by whether it attracts targeted listeners, many programming procedures are related to audience

measurement. Quarter-hour maintenance techniques are designed to keep listeners from one-time period through the next. Thus, billboarding and teasing present listeners with reasons for staying tuned. Carefully programmed stations reward listeners who stay tuned in spite of potential irritants such as commercials.

Radio formats are executed by placing program events in a sequence intended to have the greatest possible appeal to the target audience. To illustrate, a person must listen for at least 5 minutes to be counted in the audience during any quarter-hour period. Since programmers know that listeners who tune out at the end of a quarter hour will not be counted in the next period, they often use songs with high appeal to bridge the two periods, carrying listeners over the time threshold. Furthermore, commercials are often scheduled to be aired during the quarter hours when any tune-out they cause will do the least harm.

The composition of the audience changes throughout the day, and so stations often alter their programming to reflect the activities listeners are engaged in, such as commuting or working in an office. Similarly, programmers appeal to the demographic segments that predominate during different time periods. Teenagers, for instance, constitute a large proportion of the listening audience during the period from 7 p.m. to midnight. Dayparting can mean scheduling different program content to appeal to a specific group that may not listen during other times of the day, or it can be applied through the addition or deletion of events such as news. Similarly, some categories of music may be excluded or given greater emphasis during certain periods in the broadcast day.

The station's playlist is used in executing the format by categorizing recordings that are played on the air on the basis of their popularity and thus their presumed appeal to the target audience. By specifying the rotation, or frequency of the play, of each category, the programmer can ensure that the most desired music is made available to listeners while avoiding the overexposure of songs.

Music popularity is only one factor in presenting records on the air. Music values, including music texture (thin, medium, or full), and tempo

(usually measured in beats per minute), along with production intensity, should be taken into account to control the ebb and flow of the stream of music presented to listeners. Moreover, repetition can be controlled so that listeners who routinely tune in at the same time each day are provided with variety instead of hearing the same selections every time they tune in.

Events in a format are controlled by the station's hot clock, which represents the time placement for the various categories of music, commercial announcements, liners, and other events. Daypart clocks are oriented to the different audience segments and the activities they engage in during different times of the day.

News is scheduled on a station's hot clock in accordance with the programmer's perception of its importance to listeners. Whereas a Country or Adult Contemporary formatted station may present news on the hour, a CHR format hot clock may have news scheduled at 20 minutes past and 20 minutes before the hour. In these and other formats, the programmer may decide that a song from the top-10 category on the station's playlist will be scheduled immediately after the news to reward listeners who tuned in to hear music. The hot clock also shows the on-air personalities where spot sets should be aired. Commercial clusters are placed at times that will minimize tune-out and have the smallest effect on AQH listening.

As important as the placement of stop sets during the hour is the sequence of commercials that are placed in the sets. One method is to build to a peak, or climax, by beginning the stop set with the spot that has the lowest production values and ending with the message that has the highest production values. An alternative is to begin with the most interesting and end with the least interesting commercial. Yet another approach is to begin the set with a spot with high production values and dip to the "driest" spot in the set before building up to a final spot with production values comparable to those of the first spot.

Small-market stations have a different set of programming challenges. Large-market stations usually must focus their formats in order to find a niche in a very crowded competitive environment. Because there are not enough people in any specific segment in a small market to support a station, these stations usually have to be more general in their appeals to a wider segment of the population. This means that small-market news programming plays a much more important role, since the station may provide the only daily news service to its listeners.

Audience ratings are not used to a great extent in most small markets. Thus, subjective impressions of the service of a station often influence the decision on whether to buy advertising. Therefore, the programming must fit the advertiser's conception of what his or her customers will listen to if the station is to be successful. Although there may be the same proportion of people in the small market who want to listen to an AOR format, their number is smaller, and many local merchants may not think of that format as one their customers like because they do not like it themselves.

SUGGESTED READINGS

MacFarland, David T.: *Contemporary Radio Programming Strategies,* Lawrence Erlbaum, Hillsdale, N.J., 1990.

One of the dangers in learning the conventions for any endeavor, including radio programming, is that the initiate limits himself or herself to the restrictions of conventional thinking. That is why we recommend that serious programmers get a copy of this book and look beyond the standard approach. The author uses communication and human behavior theory to develop models of listening behavior. Programmers should be intrigued, for example, by MacFarland's proposition that audience needs may be driven by a biological clock that dictates moods. The music that is programmed can be selected and scheduled with this in mind. Moreover, MacFarland points out that listeners often tune in to change their moods, not to sustain them. Thus, his argument leads to a "mood-evoking music progression" concept for programming, a real departure from the conventions of the industry. Mac-Farland's book should be considered an advanced course in programming. As he acknowledges, the ap-

proach is not to describe radio programming as it currently exists but to provide an exploration into probable but not guaranteed outcomes. The future belongs to the imaginative, and this book challenges its readers to think not only about how to attract and maintain listeners but about how to test approaches that may prove more effective in achieving that goal.

May, Michael: *Building with the Basics: Radio Personality Development,* Michael May Enterprises, Billings, Mont., 1979.

This little book published by a Montana radio personality who runs a broadcasting school offers a wide range of practical information on program format execution. It offers a clear definition and explanation of radio programming nomenclature and how it is applied. At the least, the attentive reader should be better able to understand and use the language of radio broadcasting, which can only contribute to a better on-air performance and understanding of programming principles regardless of the differences in stations where this knowledge may be applied.

NOTES

1. Rick Sklar, "The No-Wait '90s," *Radio & Records,* Aug. 17, 1990, p. 36.

2. Harvey Kojan, "To Sweep or Not to Sweep," *Radio & Records,* April 7, 1990, pp. 56–57.

3. Cynthia Price, "Dayparting: Temporary Stopgap or Format Alternative?" *NAB RadioWeek,* Jan. 2, 1989, p. 4.

4. "ABC, SoundScan Sign Deal for Distribution," *Broadcasting,* Oct. 7, 1991, p. 47.

5. One such source is "The Music Director" Programming Service, Box 103, Indian Orchard, MA 01151, which offers services such as "Safest Oldies on Tape" and "Safest Oldies Lists" for specific formats. The company also publishes books listing top songs according to *Billboard* charts for various music categories.

6. Ed Shane, "Systematic Programming Basics," in Ed Shane, *Programming Dynamics: Radio's Management Guide,* Globecom, Overland Park, Kan., 1984, pp. 39–40.

7. Joel Denver, "How Hot Is Your Clock: Aligning Formatic Elements," *Radio & Records,* Feb. 16, 1990, p. 56.

8. Sylvia Clark, "How to Win the Ear-pearance Game," *Broadcast Communications,* July 1982, p. 30.

9. Disco Beats, Inc., offers a "BPM Books" service to stations in which BPM listings are provided for records.

10. Shane, op. cit., pp. 38-40.

11. Vernon A. Stone, "Deregulation Felt Mainly in Large-Market Radio and Independent TV," *RTNDA Communicator,* April 1987, pp. 9–12.

12. Eric Zorn, "The Specialized Signals of Radio News: Giving Listeners What They Want," *Washington Journalism Review,* June 1986, pp. 31–33.

13. Brad Messer, "Rating Jock-to-News Handoffs," *Radio & Records,* June 24, 1988, p. 36; "Is Newscaster/Disc Jockey Interaction Desirable?" *RTNDA Communicator,* March 1989, p. 28.

14. Michael C. Keith, *Radio Programming: Consultancy and Formatics,* Focal Press, Boston, 1987, p. 100.

15. George Swisshelm, "All-News Stations: Are They Dispensing in Smaller Doses?" *Television/Radio Age,* Oct. 31, 1988, p. 46.

16. Ibid.

17. Jack Crowley and Jim Pokrywcznski, "The Influence of Irritating Commercials on Radio Listening," *NAB News,* Sept. 24, 1990, pp. 28–32.

18. Ed Shane, "Develop Commercial Sensitivity," in Ed Shane, *Programming Dynamics: Radio's Management Guide,* Globecom, Overland Park, Kan., 1984, pp. 15–17.

19. Michael May, *Building with the Basics: Radio Personality Development,* Michael May Enterprises, Billings, Mont., 1979, pp. 118–121.

20. *Chicken Man* is syndicated by the Chicago Radio Syndicate, 1134 North La Brea, Los Angeles, CA 90038. This daily adventure/comedy series was created by Dick Orkin as a spoof of the *Batman* and *Get Smart* television series.

CHAPTER 10

Radio Program Suppliers

RECORD DISTRIBUTORS
    Obtaining Promotional Recordings
    Song Libraries
    Copyright Fees

RADIO FORMAT SUPPORT SERVICES
    Jingles and Station IDs
    Show Preparation Services

RECORDED PROGRAM SERVICES
    Broadcast Programming, Inc.
    Bonneville

SATELLITE-DISTRIBUTED PROGRAM SERVICES
    Satellite Music Network
    Unistar
    Drake Chenault/Jones
    The Nashville Network Radio
    Westwood One
    Business Networks
    Talk Radio Networks
    Radio News Services

TRADITIONAL RADIO NETWORKS
    ABC Radio Networks
    CBS Radio Networks
    Cadena Radio Centro
    CBN
    CNN
    ESPN
    Mutual

    NBC
    National Public Radio
    American Public Radio
    Spanish Information Service
    Sheridan Broadcasting Networks
    USA Today Spanish News Service

SUMMARY

SUGGESTED READINGS

NOTES

KEY TERMS AND CONCEPTS
ASCAP
Automated Systems
Barter
BMI
Live Assist
Satellite Network
SESAC
Traditional Radio Network

A radio station is physically made up of studios, with microphones, turntables, CD players, and cart machines among the sources of signals that are transmitted to listeners. However, those devices represent only a small portion of the investment it takes to attract and maintain an audience. The personalities and the programming talent who use the equipment necessitate a considerable financial commitment on the part of a station's management. Moreover, this investment may vary with the nature of the broadcast service the station offers. The targeted audiences of some formats desire certain information that can be originated at the station level even though a higher-quality product could be obtained elsewhere at a lower cost. For instance, because small-market stations usually can't afford to pay the salaries that the most effective air personalities command in larger markets, they often have to settle for less experienced personnel. Consequently, if the cost of originating content at the local level is prohibitive or if the desired level of quality is unavailable at the station, programmers can look elsewhere for product to feed the transmitter.

This chapter examines outside sources of programming that enable stations to present content that is attractive to their target audiences. Because the stock in trade for so many stations is music, we look first at recorded music as a program product. Then we examine a number of the major sources that provide recorded music directly to stations or provide music format services by satellite. Satellites also deliver news, information, and talk programming to client stations. Finally, we will look at the traditional radio networks and the services they provide.

RECORD DISTRIBUTORS

Recorded music is the programming staple of the vast majority of stations. Deciding what to do with music in a format is only one consideration. First, the programmer must acquire it.

Obtaining Promotional Recordings

No station wants to find itself without the hot new release that its competitors are playing, a situation that can happen to many smaller-market stations because their audiences can also receive the signals of larger-market stations. The problem is that record promoters are less willing to provide promotional copies to stations in the small markets. In addition to the cost of the promotional copies, packaging and mailing expenses add up quickly. There is a much lower potential return on the investment required for blanketing small-market stations with promotional copies than can be recouped in the resulting record sales.

Obtaining the latest records is not a problem for stations in the largest markets. Record companies depend on radio exposure to develop demand for their product. Large-market stations are prime targets for promotional efforts since airplay on these stations can mean the difference between a hit record and a financial flop. The smaller the market, the harder music and program directors must work to receive recognition and maintain record service.

Regardless of market size, the music director needs to build a list of local or regional distributors and promotional representatives of record labels and keep in constant contact with them. The development of a weekly or biweekly playlist that is sent to these individuals, along with periodic telephone contact, can work wonders in obtaining promotional record service. Record promoters do review playlists. Their feedback often includes returning playlists on which they have circled the songs distributed on their labels.

Even though promotional copies are free to the station, obtaining a music service requires spending for long-distance calls, playlist printing, and postage. Moreover, music and program directors must have perseverance. Most record promoters will eventually send a station new material if it provides consistent and professional communication that demonstrates that a particular label is being played.

This process involves identifying the promotion person (they change jobs as frequently as disc jockeys do) and keeping up a businesslike contact. Even a beginning music or program director can build a list of contacts quickly by reading publications such as *Billboard* and *Radio & Records* to learn who's who in the record industry. *Radio & Records* lists telephone numbers and addresses for record companies and their national promotion representatives in its biannual *Ratings Report and Directory,* which comes as a special supplement to subscribers.

In markets that are large enough, music directors can become reporters to the trade publications and music tip sheets that were described in Chapter 8. These stations provide weekly information to a particular publication on record rankings and new additions to and deletions from their playlists. Being a reporter gives a station and its music director status in the industry. At the least, it helps firm up the service from record distributors and helps the individual get his or her name known by others in the field. For stations reporting to the most influential publications, record promoters often facilitate station promotions, such as opportunities to interview recording artists and do tie-ins with their concerts and to obtain concert tickets and record albums that can be used in station giveaways.[1]

Song Libraries

Although record promoters may provide copies of their newest releases, this will not help a station build its library of current or past hits. This can be a special problem when a station decides to change its format. Suppose the programmer of a station using a Country format decides to switch to CHR. Suddenly, the programmer faces the problem of obtaining not only the current CHR hits but a library of gold and recurrent songs as well. All those hits by Madonna and other artists that have never been considered for inclusion on the Country playlist are now very important. The music director must be successful in obtaining authorization from the station's management to purchase copies of older records appropriate to the format. A variety of firms in *Radio & Records' Ratings Report and Directory* provide stations with current or oldies recordings on *analog* tape, *digital* audio tape (DAT), and compact disc (CD).

Subscription services are also helpful to stations in small markets that cannot obtain promotional copies from record companies. For a moderate fee, the station can obtain the releases in a programming category that listeners may be hearing on other stations. Although this is less desirable than obtaining free promotional copies, it is better than going without songs or buying them at a record shop.

Copyright Fees

Although the majority of radio stations do not pay for the recordings they play on the air, this use is not free. Both commercial and noncommercial stations must pay copyright fees to the composers through their licensing agents. Stations obtain the rights to play copyrighted music compositions under blanket licensing agreements with performance rights representative organizations. A blanket license authorizes a station to perform publicly any licensed composition as many times as it desires during the license period, which is typically 1 year. Whereas noncommercial stations pay a flat license fee, commercial stations pay fees of under 2 percent of their gross income to a licensing agency.[2] Noncommercial stations either negotiate an annual fee with the licensing agent or pay a fee set by the Copyright Tribunal. The industry average for commercial radio stations is about $15,000 a year, and stations in large markets can pay up to $75,000 a year for music rights.[3]

The **American Society of Composers, Artists and Performers (ASCAP)** is one of the two major music licensing groups. **Broadcast Music, Incorporated (BMI),** is the other major licensing organization. A third company is **SESAC.**[4] SESAC originally represented European publishers, but soon after its founding in 1930 it began affiliating American publishers. Its repertory is now primarily American, although it still represents some foreign works.

ASCAP tallies the performances of its members' works on radio stations by monitoring broadcasts across the nation. Auditors in ASCAP's offices listen to tape recordings of these broadcasts. Royalty payments are issued to the writers and publishers whose works are credited with performances during the sample period. BMI tabulates performance credits by examining records of works that have been broadcast that are submitted by a representative sample of stations. BMI royalty payments are based on the number of performances a work has had during the survey period as well as its past performance history.[5] SESAC royalty payments for radio station airplay are determined by monitoring stations, and reviewing playlists, *Billboard* Information Network, *Radio & Records,* and other data bases. Radio stations pay SESAC a license fee based on their market size and spot advertising rate.[6]

RADIO FORMAT SUPPORT SERVICES

Jingles and Station IDs

Jingles and station identification productions can add greatly to the polish of a station's air sound, enhancing the image of most formats beyond what can be accomplished through local production. Firms such as Jam Productions, Pams Jingles, and TM Century, Inc., specialize in these services, providing customized and market-exclusive packages to stations. For a reasonable cost, smaller-market stations can obtain many versions of these packages that were created originally for a large market.

Show Preparation Services

Many of the humorous liners broadcast on stations across the country are prepared by firms that distribute scripts to subscriber stations. Some are joke services, while others provide scripts for skits and humorous fake commercials or produce such material on tape.

Stations affiliated with some of the radio networks can receive a daily satellite feed of offbeat actualities and topical happenings to aid in the preparation of the morning show. A variety of "show prep" services are listed in the *Radio & Records* special supplement *Ratings Report and Directory.*

RECORDED PROGRAM SERVICES

The differences between traditional radio networks, program syndicators, and a host of newer radio program services have blurred in recent years. Newer technologies have combined desktop computer programs with equipment capable of reading signals sent from Dallas or Los Angeles or programming 20 or more CD players to start and stop. About 20 percent of all radio stations in the United States program part or all of their broadcast days with material from services on reel-to-reel tape, CDs, DAT, or satellite. **Automated systems,** where the music, prerecorded commercial announcements, and other program material are programmed for playback, have made it possible for radio operators to provide programming services that are heavy on music, which is what many listeners want.[7]

Detractors point out that automated systems cannot duplicate the spontaneity of local live broadcasting. Furthermore, the more general syndicated program content may not meet the particular interests of the listeners in a market. The personalities that appear in the programming are detached rather than being directly aware of and reacting to the lives of the listeners residing in the market.

Some of these problems can be circumvented since automated program material can be used in **live assist,** a system where an announcer at the station can interject live comments or read commercials between songs. Depending on the station's needs, this service can be used in an automated facility. In addition to music, synchronized "chatter tracks" that introduce or back announce music, news, commercials, and other content can be programmed by computer.

Especially for stations in small markets, the problems involved in attracting and keeping talented announcers and obtaining and programming music product have made syndicated programming services attractive. The resources for researching music appeal, maintaining contact with record promoters, and supplying the appropriate music for the station's format are available from the companies that provide these services.

Most syndicated program services are paid for in cash or sometimes a combination of cash and **barter,** in which a certain number of commercial spots are presold by the syndicator for airing on stations that carry the program service. The advantage of a barter arrangement is that a station can obtain the program service at a lower initial cost. The drawback is that less commercial time is available to sell locally.

There are many services available to stations. The following descriptions highlight a few as examples of the variety of programming that can be obtained.

Broadcast Programming, Inc.

Broadcast Programming, Inc. (BPI), is the largest tape-distributed radio format producer, with a variety of formats offered. These include several variations of the Adult Contemporary, Easy-Listening and Beautiful-Music, Country, CHR, Rock Classics, Oldies, Nostalgia and Big-Band, Christian, Gospel, and New Age formats.

After its acquisition of several tape syndicators, including Kalamusic in 1990, BPI became a prominent syndicator that provided over 40 stations with its Easy-Listening format. The company served over 30 stations with its Big-Band format, a Country format, and a variety of Adult Contemporary and Easy-Listening formats. BPI has retained the Kala Easy Contemporary and Big Band–Jon Holliday's Swing Era format identities.

BPI's position was capped by the acquisition of Drake-Chenault in 1991. This company was formed by legendary Top-40 programmer Bill Drake and station owner Gene Chenault. Drake-Chenault provided 300 or more stations with a variety of formats, including Country, Stereo Rock, Adult Contemporary, Lite Hits, Easy Listening, Lite Jazz, and Gold, on tape or VHS hi-fi.[8]

One of Drake-Chenault's selling points is that the music is researched before being included in the clients' tapes. In addition to its syndicated format service, the company offers its clients Playlist Plus, a weekly computer-generated music list designed for the individual station, perceptual research to determine audience desires, and auditorium research.

Drake-Chenault also offers library service, songs recorded on tape, and special syndicated features such as a 52-hour *History of Rock and Roll* and *The History of Country Music,* and Christmas programs.

Bonneville

Bonneville Broadcasting System is the leading supplier of Easy-Listening or Beautiful-Music programming, with about 150 stations using its Ultra service. The Ultra format, which appeals primarily to listeners age 35 and over, is an upbeat easy-listening sound that features instrumental versions of popular and standard tunes. Ultra Plus is an instrumental version of adult contemporary hits aimed at listeners 35 and over. Bonneville also offers four Adult Contemporary formats, including Soft Adult Contemporary, Lite Rock, Adult Contemporary Mix, and Classic Hits.

Unlike its direct format competitors, Bonneville distributes its service on audiotape and compact discs. With the product on CD, client stations can customize the format, fine-tuning it to the needs of the market.

Bonneville's Beautiful-Music CD system uses about 22 CD players per station that are tied to a personal computer. Its Adult Contemporary format typically uses about 12 CD players. The CDs are packaged and coded by Bonneville so that operators never handle the discs.[9] At this writing, there are no plans to distribute the service by satellite.

SATELLITE-DISTRIBUTED PROGRAM SERVICES

Where once only a few networks served stations via land lines rented from telephone companies, there are now about 100 nationally distributed live services available. These "new networks" are hybrids of the traditional network services and music program syndicators. By distributing live programming via satellites, these suppliers can offer high-quality program content tailored to the needs of stations trying to position themselves with unique news, information, and entertainment appeal.

Almost all commercial radio stations have at least one satellite dish, and more than half have two or more. The proliferation of this technology has made network service an attractive alternative to producing local programming. Not only is the signal quality often an improvement over locally originated programming, the equipment necessary for reception can be installed for $3000 or less.[10] With modern cuing technology, stations can achieve a local sound even though the music and personalities are originating from hundreds or thousands of miles away.

Each satellite network has programmed "windows" for the insertion by local stations of advertising, news, or talk. In most cases the station has the option of breaking in or continuing with satellite-fed programming. Inaudible signals fed by the satellite program service can be set to trigger the station's automated system reel-to-reel or cartridge tapes, which are preloaded with commercials or other locally produced content that has been timed for each designated break. Alternatively, live assist allows the station to have an operator at the console who can manually turn off the satellite program audio and start local spots. This permits the station to provide some local imagery for its listeners.

For many stations, the traditional network services of customized news, sports, and features permit the delivery of a broader service to the local audience. Some stations use a satellite program service during the overnight part of the broadcast day, which, for many, is the least prof-

itable period. Such stations retain local personalities during the prime parts of the day. Some affiliates take the network feed, while others break away to insert local newscasts and other program content during network breaks.

As with syndicated services, broadcasters are attracted to satellite networks because of the high cost of developing and maintaining quality programming. Of particular concern in smaller markets is the cost of training and keeping talented personnel. By taking on a satellite-distributed network program service, stations can reduce the number of people required for operation while obtaining major market-caliber personalities and programming.

Networked program services are not the answer to all problems. One problem is that nothing the network announcer says can be completely localized. For instance, she or he can only be as specific as "it's 25 minutes past the hour" since the signal is being fed across the country. Furthermore, the personalities featured in this programming cannot be regularly promoted in the market because they are not there. Other disadvantages include the contrast between the voices of their much more polished and professional personalities and those of the local announcers used in station-produced station breaks and commercials. If the station is willing to pay the fee, network announcers may record local commercials, but that does not alleviate the problem of expense, consumption of time, and the possibility of mispronouncing local names.

Still, for many stations these limitations are balanced by the advantages of receiving better-quality programming than they can produce locally. The resources of the program supplier can offer client stations researched music selections as well as consultation about the market.

A new kind of programming skill is in the offing. With this system, while the music selection is taken care of by the network, local breaks for commercials and other inserts must be scheduled; this requires an approach different from the one used in "live jock" radio formats.

Most satellite networks have a barter and cash arrangement with their affiliates, although some operate a strictly on cash basis. In small and medium-size markets the cost to a station can be about $1000 to $1200 a month or more, depending on factors such as market size and the relative attractiveness of the service.

As satellite time has become more plentiful and less expensive, network services have proliferated. Today it is possible to find a format variation that is designed for a very wide range of demographic segments and for specialized appeals within many of those segments.[11] The following discussion highlights a few of the major services as examples of the variety that can be obtained.

Satellite Music Network

Owned through a buyout by Capital Cities/ABC Inc., Satellite Music Network (SMN) provides live 24-hour formats that incorporate music, news, features, and specials. SMN has a variety of formats, including an upbeat modern Country format targeted to listeners 25 to 54; a traditional Country format that targets listeners 25 to 64; a CHR format, "The Heat," targeting 12- to 24-year-olds; soft AOR, "The Wave," which includes New Age artists and targets 25- to 59-year-olds; "Z-Rock," a Hard Rock format targeting 12- to 34-year-old males; and Oldies, Adult Contemporary, and Nostalgia formats that serve more than 1000 stations.

SMN provides newscasts that are integrated into the format on a 24-hour basis. Regular weekly features on several of these formats offer countdown programs or Oldies shows.

Unistar

Unistar offers eight music formats to stations. Its services include Unistar Country, which targets listeners 25 to 54; an Adult Contemporary service, A/C II, that targets listeners 25 to 44; and The Oldies Channel, which targets listeners 35 to 44 with an emphasis on males. Format 41 targets listeners age 32 to 49, hence its median tar-

get age of 41. This service programs softer contemporary artists such as Neil Diamond, Lionel Richie, and Simon and Garfunkel. As Figure 10-1 shows, the station operator knows when commercial breaks are scheduled and where options are available for locally produced program content. As was mentioned above, the network sends inaudible cue tones that trigger the switches to start and stop local playback equipment.

Unistar's AM Only targets listeners age 40 to 54 who grew up with music from the 1950s and 1960s, including such artists as Frank Sinatra, Dionne Warwick, and the Kingston Trio. Although the service is not limited to AM stations, a majority of the subscribers are AM broadcasters. Niche 29 targets listeners age 21 to 36 who like rock 'n' roll but not AOR, which has a harder rock edge. Seventy-five percent of the music is from the 1980s, including such artists as Genesis, the Police, and Huey Lewis. These artists are supplemented with music by groups from earlier years, such as the Eagles, the Beatles, and the Moody Blues.

Special Blend is an Easy-Listening format targeted to listeners age 35 to 54 while holding on to listeners 55 and over. The format is a mix of soft, easy vocals by the original artists such as Dionne Warwick, Tony Bennett, the Carpenters, and Anne Murray, with a few instrumentals. Special Blend is designed to supplant the traditional Beautiful-Music format, which has been losing audience share.

In addition to its 24-hour program services, Unistar syndicates a number of weekly "countdown" programs for various formats, including *Dick Clark's Rock Roll & Remember* and *Countdown America,* which is designed for Adult Contemporary formatted stations; nostalgia programs such as *Motor City Beat,* a 3-hour review of 1960s music; and *The Weekly Country Music Countdown.* A weekly 4-hour program with Houston morning radio personality John Lander features a toll-free number that lets listeners call in. Another Unistar program, *The Great Sounds,* is a 4-hour review of music of the 1940s and 1950s.

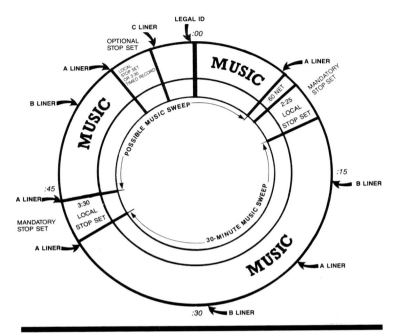

FIGURE 10-1   **Format 41 hour clock. *(Used by permission of Unistar Radio Network.)***

Daily programs include *The Daily Country Special,* a 1-hour *Solid Gold Country* special offered five times and a week, *Country Datebook,* a daily 2¹/₂-minute profile of a Country music artist that is offered each day. CHR formatted stations are served with a daily hour program featuring Los Angeles disc jockey Rick Dees.

Drake Chenault/Jones

Drake Chenault/Jones Satellite Services supplies about 300 affiliates with 24-hour live programming in five different formats. These include Great American Country, which targets listeners age 25 to 54; Adult Contemporary, targeting listeners 18 to 44; Prime Demo, which features light music from the 1960s to the present that is between Adult Contemporary and

Easy Listening/Beautiful Music and targets listeners age 3 to 49; Goldies; and E-Z, an Easy-Listening format.

The Nashville Network Radio

A spinoff from cable television's The Nashville Network, The Nashville Network Radio (TNNR) is a Country service that is distributed by satellite in stereo, 24 hours a day live, from Nashville. Music programs are hosted by veteran Country music personalities. This service features live interviews, record countdowns, concerts, record reviews, and entertainment news. Through an agreement with Associated Press Radio, TNNR provides 5-minute hourly newscasts.

Among TNNR's featured programs is the *Wolfman Jack Show,* which is presented from 10 p.m. to 1 a.m. Monday through Friday. A weekly feature is *Yesteryear with Bill Anderson,* a Country nostalgia show.

Westwood One

The parent company of Mutual Radio and the NBC Radio Network and the publisher of the trade paper *Radio & Records* syndicates music, entertainment, features, interviews, comedy, and concerts for various formats, particularly pop music. One of the major programs is *Casey's Top 40 with Casey Kasem,* a weekly countdown of the Top-40 hits; another is *Scott Shannon's Rockin' America Top-30 Countdown.*

In addition to its regularly scheduled programming services, Westwood One has produced rock concerts around the world, including Madonna's "Blonde Ambition" concert from Nice, France, and David Bowie's "Sound + Vision" concert, which came live via satellite from Great Britain.

Westwood also has a number of rock history shows, such as *Psychedelic Psnack,* which reviews the music of the 1965–1969 period. Another service is the *Dr. Demento Show,* which features "off-the-wall" artists such as Weird Al Yankovic and Monty Python, satirists such as Tom Lehrer, and Spike Jones, whose crazy orchestrations were famous in the 1940s and 1950s. In addition to pop music and youth-oriented programming, Westwood offers programs that appeal to Spanish-language audiences, black listeners, and listeners who like Country music.

As radio station formats have fragmented, Westwood One has adapted by offering different versions of some of its programming. For example, three versions of Westwood's *In Concert* series are offered: the original mainstream AOR version, a "new rock" version, and a "high-voltage" version.[12]

Business Networks

A resurgence in interest in financial news and declining audiences on AM radio stations, the traditional users of Talk formats, converged in the late 1980s when business networks were started. Business radio formats are much like those of All-News stations, with constant updates of national news. The programming includes interviews with analysts and brokers, along with international economic reports. Affiliates are provided with time to broadcast local news and weather.[13]

There are two traditional 24-hour business networks. One is Money Radio, which provides news, call-in talk programs, and stock market updates to its affiliates 24 hours a day. Like the other services, Money Radio targets older retired investors and baby boomers at the peak of their earning potential. The network publishes *Personal Investing* magazine, which is circulated to 25,000 paying members and various investment conventions.

Financial Broadcast Network, another 24-hour service, programs its primary service around a "business day" that runs from 6 a.m. to 6 p.m. and publishes a newspaper supplement, *Money Weekly,* that is inserted in the major newspapers in the markets of affiliated stations. Other times and weekends are devoted to talk programming on various financial subjects.

Yet another 24-hour service is Business Radio Network, which offers its listeners less technical business programs along with a schedule of sports and weather forecasts, dining and travel shows, and national and world news. On weekends the network's programming is devoted almost entirely to money-management shows. Many of these shows take calls from listeners.

Radio Amex offers daily stock market reports, while *Amex Business Talk* is a weekly 15-minute business feature geared to a general audience. Topics include choosing a broker, the airline industry, and the business of baseball.

The *Wall Street Journal Report* is a 3-minute report on economic and financial news broadcast each hour during every business day. The *Dow Jones Report* is a 1-minute breaking news briefing on business and financial news with a consumer slant which is broadcast hourly from 6 a.m. to 8 p.m., with reports also scheduled on weekends. This service has been designed to be used with music formats.

Talk Radio Networks

Talk programming has always been a staple on AM radio, and its resurgence has come as more AM stations have sought low-cost programming that can help them reestablish a niche in their markets. Talk radio has emerged as the most popular of the "AM Savior" formats.[14] In addition to the services provided by the traditional network, a variety of new satellite-delivered network talk services have emerged.

The American Radio Network, operating out of Albany, New York, devoted much time to Roseanne Barr's controversial rendition of the national anthem in which she made a vulgar gesture to the audience members after they booed her screeching performance before a San Diego Padres baseball game. The Iraqi invasion of Kuwait was discussed extensively.[15] ARN's talk service runs in 4-hour blocks, featuring "'intelligent' conversation that is 'exciting' and, at the same time, 'simple and civil.'"[16] Topics featured include sports, daily headlines, nutrition and health, entertainment news, business news, and financial news. ARN is available to its affiliates on a bartered basis in which the station must relinquish 4 minutes an hour to the network.[17]

The Sun Radio Network, based in Tampa, Florida, offers a 24-hour schedule of shows on astrology, business, sports, and real estate and a farm/consumer hour. Sun Radio stays away from controversial political topics and does not permit its hosts to get carried away with a cause.[18]

Other networks are not as reluctant to broach controversy. One such service, EFM Media, distributes the controversial *Rush Limbaugh Show*, which is presented daily for 2 hours. Limbaugh, who espouses a strongly conservative philosophy, deals mostly in opinion on such topics as the Middle East, obscenity, the environment, and animal rights.[19]

Radio News Services

Associate Press Radio serves over 1000 affiliates with commercial-free 5-minute news on the hour and $2^1/_2$-minute newscasts on the half hour 24 hours a day. A wide variety of features and interviews, business reports, and a news insert service are also offered.

The UPI Radio Network, a division of United Press International, serves 200 affiliates 24 hours a day with 5-minute newscasts on the hour, headline news on the half hour, and sports reports, business reports, and feature feeds throughout the day.

The UPI Spanish-language service, UPI Radio Noticias, provides 7-minute newscasts Monday through Friday from early morning until night. Each report provides 2 minutes of national and international news and 2 minutes of news focusing on Mexico as well as 2 minutes of eastern regional news that focuses on the Caribbean, Puerto Rico, and Cuba. Each affiliate is required to broadcast at least the first 3 minutes of each newscast.

TRADITIONAL RADIO NETWORKS

The traditional radio networks offer compensation to their affiliates in return for carrying the network feeds. The networks, although unhappy with the cost, still provide incentives to keep their outlets. This amount can range up to $1 million for the most valuable affiliates to virtually none for small markets. Thus, for some stations, the compensation may barely justify the cost of receiving the service. Since a station can sell commercial time adjacent to the network feed, though, it may make money by carrying the service. However, even if it does not actually generate revenue from its network broadcasts, a station is still able to offer its listeners a national news service which has the ability to cover major breaking stories. This capacity was proved to be especially effective during major national or international stories such as the Persian Gulf war, where ratings increased, particularly for All-News formatted stations.[20]

Satellite distribution has increased the initial cost of affiliation, as the station must pay for the installation of a satellite receiver dish and the related electronic equipment in order to receive the signal. In spite of the expense, a station can at least avoid the monthly telephone company line charges that were required for linking with the network.

As was discussed above, a plethora of nationally distributed services are available to radio stations today. Just a few years ago there were only four separately owned national networks: ABC, CBS, NBC, and Mutual. Now NBC and Mutual are owned by the same company. This sort of expansion has occurred at CBS and ABC as well, where a variety of services are offered to stations.

ABC Radio Networks

In 1967 ABC Radio pioneered the concept of multiple network services when, with special FCC approval, it began offering four networks: Contemporary, Entertainment, Information, and FM. From 1967 to 1973 ABC increased from about 300 affiliates to more than 1200.[21] Thus, ABC's networks could serve up to four stations in a single market. The services each network featured were oriented to the needs of specialized formats. The feeds for each network were scheduled at different times during the hour on a shared land line. Newscasts were delivered by the same network personnel, but their length, style, and story emphasis were structured to fit different formats. The Entertainment Network newscasts, for instance, were briefer, and the stories were oriented toward the younger audience that tuned in Top-40 or other contemporary music-intensive stations. Thus, ABC was able to draw on its central resources to offer different services to a greater number of stations at no added cost for distribution.

In 1982 ABC initiated a new concept in radio networking with Superradio, which offered a 24-hour satellite-distributed contemporary music format featuring established air personalities that targeted 21- to 49-year-olds.[22] The Satellite Music Network preceded ABC's venture and succeeded, whereas Superradio failed almost immediately. The vanquished later purchased the victor when ABC acquired and began operating SMN.

ABC Contemporary This ABC network service is provided to 250 CHR and Urban Contemporary formatted stations. Affiliates can choose 60-second "News-in-Briefs" or the contemporary newscasts, which run at 3:30.

ABC has an arrangement with *USA Today* in which it sends lifestyle, health, business, and feature items to affiliates via satellite at 5 a.m., before the paper is published. In addition to this morning show aid, ABC feeds its affiliates a Morning Prep service of produced topical comedy bits, along with comedy and rock oldies feeds.[23] ABC News also feeds morning correspondent reports and features of interest to targeted listeners.

ABC Direction Four hundred fifty stations are affiliated with ABC Direction, which targets listeners age 25 to 54 who are being served by music-intensive formats. Four-minute newscasts are offered at 50 minutes past the hour, as are 1-minute "newsbriefs." Brief sports reports and features are also provided.

ABC Entertainment ABC Entertainment is designed for listeners 25 to 54. Four-minute newscasts are presented at the top of each hour, and a 2-minute news update is scheduled at 3 minutes before the hour. Sports reports are regularly scheduled. ABC Entertainment is the base network for *American Country Countdown,* a 4-hour weekly broadcast that makes 6 minutes an hour available for local sale.

ABC-FM The ABC-FM Network, with 150 affiliates, is targeted to listeners age 18 to 34 and is designed to be compatible with the music formats of its FM affiliates. Two-minute newscasts are offered at 45 minutes past the hour 20 times a day, and an *FM Newsminute* is scheduled 15 times a day to stand on its own or be incorporated into the affiliate's newscast. In addition to sports and special coverage, ABC-FM feeds *Young Adult Newscalls,* which include sound bites and correspondent reports oriented to the target audience.

ABC Information The ABC Information Network serves 600 stations whose programming emphasizes news and information. The service includes 5-minute newscasts on the hour and headlines at 27 minutes past the hour. Sportscasts, business reports, and commentary programs are also scheduled regularly. Weekend programming includes a 24-minute *World News This Week* and a half-hour *This Week with David Brinkley.*

ABC Rock Radio This network for young adults, with a 15- to 24-year-old target audience, serves 125 affiliates. The service is designed for AOR formatted stations, with 2-minute newscasts that begin at 45 minutes past the hour. Other network features include *Young Adult Newscall* and *Backstage with the ABC Rock Network.*

ABC Talkradio As a barter service of ABC, talk personalities Deborah Norville and Tom Snyder are featured in daily 3-hour programs that are offered at staggered times to serve stations located in the Eastern and Pacific time zones. Norville is a former cohost of the NBC *Today* show. Snyder was an NBC News correspondent and hosted a late-night NBC interview program earlier in his career.

ABC also syndicates *Paul Harvey News.* A number of weekly popular music countdown programs are also syndicated by ABC, including *American Top 40* with Shadoe Stevens, *American Country Countdown* with Bob Kingsley, and *The Musicmakers* with Bob Kingsley.

CBS Radio Networks

One of the two oldest traditional radio networks, CBS Radio offers a wide range of news and sports programs to 450 stations. In addition to hourly 6-minute newscasts, sports reports are fed several times a day.

The network offers its affiliates 19 daily news feeds beginning at 3 a.m. These consist of cuts and bits and interviews from which the station can select what it wants to use in its locally originated newscasts. CBS also provides *The Morning Circus,* a comedy service consisting of vignettes, features, and bits that range between 3 and 90 seconds in length. The *Circus* is intended for use by morning teams who incorporate items from it into their shows. CBS also provides its stations with advance synopses of articles that will appear in Time, Inc., magazines, including *People, Money, Time, Fortune,* and *Sports Illustrated.* These commercial-free bits are fed daily to stations at no charge.

CBS Radio offers its affiliates baseball and NFL football as well as coverage of golf and tennis tournaments, college football bowl games, and NCAA basketball championship tournaments. Several regular programs feature the best known CBS news and sports personalities, such as Charles Osgood, Dan Rather, and Susan Spencer.

Another CBS network, CBS Spectrum, serves 150 affiliates by targeting audience members age 25 to 54. Stations receive 15- to 20-second news wraps and material geared to specific formats. Features include an environment program, *Down to Earth,* with Harry Smith and *The Parent Factor,* which is anchored by Paula Zahn. Smith and Zahn are the CBS morning news coanchors. Spectrum affiliates also receive packages of hard news actualities as well as entertainment and music news.

The CBS Hispanic Radio Network broadcasts baseball and football games in Spanish and is contemplating Spanish-language newscasts.

Cadena Radio Centro

A Spanish-language satellite network, Cadena offers 24-hour music, news, and features. Newscasts are offered on the hour, along with sportscasts, long-form concerts, and feature programs. Over 20 stations whose signals reach about 75 percent of the Hispanic population are affiliated.

CBN

The CBN Radio Network, the radio broadcast arm of the Christian Broadcasting Network, which serves cable television systems, features Christian music, news, and talk shows. CBN offers its 84 affiliates a 5-minute newscast every hour of the day, with an optional 90-second breakaway which gives the affiliate the option of resuming locally originated programming if it does not want to carry the full newscast. The CBN format clock is shown in Figure 10-2.

CBN News Today, a 30-minute news analysis program, is broadcast at 5 p.m. Eastern time, Monday through Friday. Although CBN is produced by a religious-based organization, the service is not restricted to religious format stations.

CNN

CNN Radio, a spinoff of Ted Turner's television Cable News Network (CNN), is fed by the Unistar satellite network to 140 affiliates. CNN Radio is a 24-hour service that offers 5-minute newscasts at the top of the hour and $2^1/_2$-minute news at half past the hour. Headlines are fed at 5 minutes before the hour and a 2- to 4-minute business report is fed at a quarter past. At a quarter before the hour sports is scheduled (Figure 10-3). CNN also offers live coverage of major events and features such as *Hollywood Minute, Celebrity Watch,* and *Business Interview.*

ESPN

ABC Radio Networks and cable TV's ESPN network joined forces to introduce the ESPN Radio Network in 1992. The service started as a weekend evening service, feeding its affiliates on Saturday and Sunday from 6 p.m. to 1 a.m. While ABC handles network sales and affiliate recruitment, ESPN provides the programming, including the use of ESPN Television Network on-air personnel. The programming includes sports news, game reports, guest interviews, and features excerpted from ESPN's cable service.

Mutual

The star of the Mutual Broadcasting System is the *Larry King Show,* a nightly talk/call-in program. In addition to regular feature programs such as *Business Beat* and *Human Side of the News,* Mutual provides coverage of major college football and basketball and college football bowl game coverage as well as news on the hour and half hour. Mutual is owned by Westwood One, as is the NBC Radio Network.

NBC

The oldest American radio network was bought by Westwood One in 1987. NBC provides its 389 affiliates with 5-minute newscasts on the hour and news updates at 25 minutes past the hour. Sports programming is also scheduled on a regular basis, along with business and consumer reports, features on religion, and college bowl games.

In addition to its traditional network, NBC also serves 120 affiliates with The Source, a young-adult network that targets listeners 18 to 34. One of the services offered to affiliates allows celebrities to make live-via-satellite promotional visits to stations. Guests such as comedian Howie Mandel, actors Elliot Gould and Tim Conway, and celebrities such as Robin Leach are featured on stations' morning shows through feeds from The Source's New York or Los Angeles studios.

NBC Talknet is a nighttime talk service that has 287 affiliates. It provides nighttime programming in which listeners can call in for discussion and advice. The programming starts at 7 p.m. Eastern time and continues through 4 a.m. Weekend programming includes a husband-and-wife team who dispense advice on personal finance. Another weekend advice program is hosted by a psychiatrist. Listeners can call Talknet on a toll-free 800 number.

National Public Radio

NPR, a noncommercial network that serves 425 public radio stations, is funded by contributions

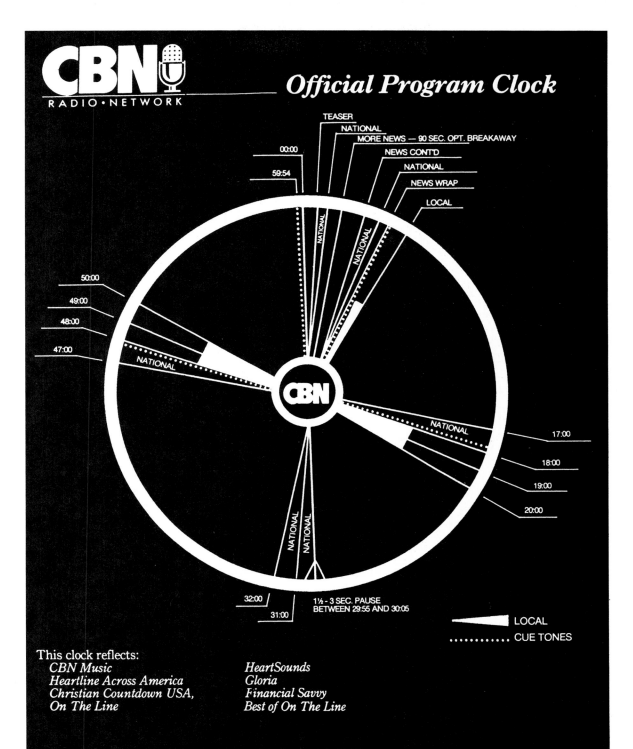

FIGURE 10-2   CBN Radio Network program clock. *(Courtesy of CBN Radio.)*

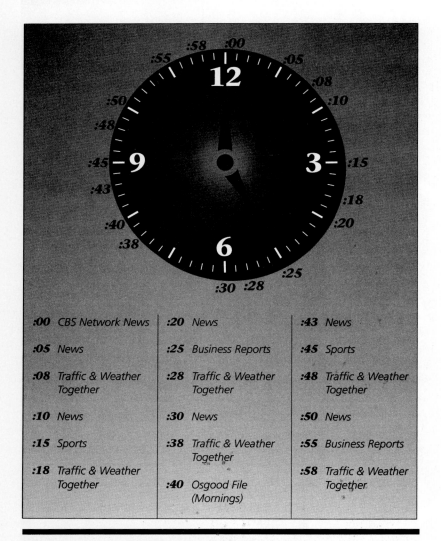

:00 CBS Network News	**:20** News	**:43** News
:05 News	**:25** Business Reports	**:45** Sports
:08 Traffic & Weather Together	**:28** Traffic & Weather Together	**:48** Traffic & Weather Together
:10 News	**:30** News	**:50** News
:15 Sports	**:38** Traffic & Weather Together	**:55** Business Reports
:18 Traffic & Weather Together	**:40** Osgood File (Mornings)	**:58** Traffic & Weather Together

FIGURE 10-3   Local radio news format clock. (WCBS NEWSRADIO 88, New York.)

from its member stations and by grants and underwriting from corporations, foundations, associations, and individuals.

NPR's principal news programs are *All Things Considered, Morning Edition,* and *Weekend Edition,* to which stations specifically subscribe. These are news-magazine formats that feature extensive coverage of world and national affairs as well as science and the arts. Press briefings,

congressional hearings, presidential speeches, and other live events are available to stations that subscribe to the morning and/or afternoon news services. NPR members must purchase the service for an hourly 5-minute newscast.

A large number of cultural programs are offered to affiliates through NPR's Arts and Performance Service, for which stations pay a flat fee. Among these NPR shows are *Performance*

Today, an arts program fed for 2 hours on Monday through Friday that features performances mixed with reviews, commentary, and interviews dealing with classical music. It has a low-key, cohesive format of events. *Bob & Bill* is a weekday classical music service that features the historical and cultural stories behind the music.

Other popular programs are a weekly humor and car repair call-in show, *Car Talk.* In her daily interview program *Fresh Air,* Terry Gross features guests from the popular arts, politics, and public life. NPR has developed a number of entertainment programs, including *BluesStage* and *Afropop Worldwide,* that broaden the diversity of its offerings.

American Public Radio

Another service to noncommercial or public radio stations is offered by American Public Radio, which distributes programming developed by stations and independent producers. In addition to an APR membership fee, stations pay a fee for some shows that is based on their market size. For instance, *Marketplace,* a daily half-hour stock market and business news magazine, requires a quarterly fee that ranges from nearly $3000 in the largest markets to around $700 for stations in markets with a population below 25,000.

One of APR's most popular programs was *A Prairie Home Companion* with author and humorist Garrison Keillor, which brought the network to national prominence. Keillor eventually left the show but has returned to host APR's *American Radio Company of the Air.* Another of APR's humor shows is *Whad'ya Know,* an interview-quiz format that features the humorous barbs of sharp-witted host Michael Feldman. American Public Radio also offers its affiliates a variety of cultural and music programs, including *The Los Angeles Philharmonic* and *Saint Paul Sunday Morning,* in which classical musicians

perform and are interviewed about their technique, and *Mountain Stage,* which features contemporary acoustic music.

Spanish Information Service

This Dallas-based network with over 40 affiliates feeds 5-minute newscasts on the hour, Monday through Friday, from 7 a.m. to 10 p.m. and sports three times a day. On weekends, newscasts on the hour are fed from 1 p.m. to 8 p.m. The emphasis is on South America and Mexico. Coverage of major sports events from Latin America is provided in addition to regular sportscasts.

Sheridan Broadcasting Networks

Sheridan, which merged with the National Black Network in 1991, provides its affiliates with black-oriented news, feature programming, interviews, and talk. Hourly news and sports reports are provided along with other daily sports programs and seasonal sports features.

Sheridan's STRZ Entertainment Network provides syndicated entertainment, sports, and special feature radio programs. Among them is *Top 30 USA,* a weekly 3-hour urban music countdown and music magazine program. *Jazzmasters* and *Cameos of Black Women* are 60-second programs structured to include local and network commercials. *Major League Baseball Notebook* is a 5-minute program with station and network spot times.

USA Today Spanish News Service

The Gannett service features 5-minute newscasts on the hour via satellite. The broadcasts originate out of Gannett's Washington headquarters with stories edited for Hispanics living in the United States.

SUMMARY

A wide variety of program support and full-fledged programming services are available to radio stations. For programmers who wish to control all aspects of their stations' programming, music can be obtained directly from distributors and record company promotion representatives. Some stations, especially those in small markets, do not have the resources to cultivate these sources. They may not receive promotional copies but can obtain the product if they are willing to pay for it by subscribing to a music library service.

The operators of many stations find syndicated program services attractive because they are inexpensive and offer more consistent programming than local personnel may be able to provide. The supplier provides music that has been researched and sequenced for immediate airplay, lessening or even eliminating reliance on local programmers' skills.

A proliferation of networks that provide full-time programming services for a wide variety of formats has resulted from satellite communication. Again, the cost of these services may be lower than the cost of generating similar locally originated program content. Equally important, satellite networks offer their client stations flexibility in their use of the services as well as consistently high programming quality. A station can rely completely on a network or can select portions of its service to include in its program day. The variety of services available gives the programmer many options for providing locally originated content.

Traditional networks all distribute their services by satellite. There are network services available to fit virtually all formats and target audiences. A programmer can select a service that has lengthy news and information programs or very brief newscasts and sportscasts. There are national networks that serve stations targeting ethnic audiences and other specialized networks that provide business news throughout the day.

SUGGESTED READINGS

The growth and diversification of radio syndication services, hybrid satellite-delivered program services, and radio networks has been so rapid that it is likely that the information in this chapter will soon be dated. This is not a subject that remains consistent for very long. Readers who wish to keep up with the changing services and status of networks and syndicated services as sources of radio programming should regularly read "the trades," including *Broadcasting* and *Radio & Records*. *The Pulse of Radio* provides a summary of the offerings of many networks, and the National Association of Broadcasters publishes periodic updated summaries as well.

NOTES

1. Donna L. Halper, *Radio Music Directing,* Focal Press, Boston, 1991, pp. 81–91.

2. Bruce Wendell Mims, "The Licensing of Music for Broadcast Performance: An Assessment of Alternative Licensing Procedures," unpublished master's thesis, University of Alabama at Tuscaloosa, 1986, pp. 46–48.

3. Barry L. Sherman, *Telecommunications Management: The Broadcast & Cable Industries,* McGraw-Hill, New York, 1987, p. 291.

4. SESAC legally changed its name from the Society of European Stage Authors and Composers in the 1930s.

5. Mims, op. cit., pp. 48–50.

6. Gary Voorhies, SESAC, Inc., Nashville, Tenn., personal correspondence, June 24, 1991.

7. Bob Andelman, "24-Hour Syndicated Programming," *The Pulse of Radio,* Aug. 27, 1990, p. 14.

8. "BPI Buys Drake-Chenault," *Broadcasting,* March 11, 1991, pp. 38–39.

9. Andelman, op. cit., pp. 14–15.

10. Scott Chase, "Radio and Satellites: New Networks, New Opportunities," *NAB Research & Planning Memo,* April/May 1989, p. 4.

11. "Radio and Satellites: New Networks, New Opportunities," *NAB Info-Pak,* April/May 1989; "Satellite-

Delivered Formats: Local Programming from the Sky," *Broadcasting,* Aug. 6, 1990, pp. 47–48; "Radio Satellite Programming Update," *NAB RadioWeek,* Jan. 7, 1991, pp. 7–8.

12. "Pushing the Right Buttons in Radio Syndication," *Broadcasting,* June 24, 1991, p. 32.

13. "AM Radio Looks to Business Programming for a Niche," *Broadcasting,* Feb. 19, 1990, p. 45.

14. "Talk Networks Pursue Role of AM 'White Knight,'" *Broadcasting,* Aug. 27, 1990, p. 40.

15. Ibid.

16. "More Voices Join Satellite-Delivered Talk Format," *Broadcasting,* Feb. 20, 1989, p. 46.

17. "American Radio Networks Keep AM's Talking," *Broadcasting,* March 19, 1990, p. 55.

18. Ibid., p. 42.

19. "Limbaugh: The Host's the Thing," *Broadcasting,* Aug. 27, 1990, p. 43.

20. "Birch Research Shows Big Increase for News Stations," *Radio & Records,* Feb. 22, 1991, p. 1.

21. Lawrence W. Lichty and Malachi C. Topping, *American Broadcasting: A Source Book on the History of Radio and Television,* Hastings House, New York, 1975, p. 162.

22. Phillip Keirstead, "Satellites Bringing Renaissance to Radio Networking," *Broadcast Communication,* October 1981, pp. 58–62; "Full-Format Satellite Net Orbits into Radio Market, *Broadcast Management/Engineering,* May 1982, pp. 3–4.

23. "The Expanding Universe of Radio Networks," *Broadcasting,* Feb. 19, 1990, p. 40.

PART THREE

Television

Television is the most widely used form of entertainment in the United States, providing something for virtually every interest from comedy to the latest news of the nation and the world. The chapters in Part 3 discuss the ways in which programmers attempt to attract and maintain broadcast television audiences.

Chapter 11, "Assessing the Television Environment," describes TV viewing according to demographic preferences and by time of day and the concept of program modularity as it affects the way in which programs are structured to accommodate viewers at different times during the day. In Chapter 12, "Basic Television Programming Strategies," the habits of viewers are translated into basic strategies for attracting audiences. Chapter 13, "The Syndicated Marketplace," discusses programs that are sold to individual stations, usually on an exclusive basis. Financial considerations in acquiring rights to programs are discussed in detail because profitability is a crucial aspect of television programming.

While most television stations can rely on the network to supply the bulk of their programming, independent stations go it alone. Chapter 14, "Programing the Independent Station," discusses considerations in programming the independent station in order to attract at least some of the audience. The advantages of not being affiliated with a network do not

override the problems of competition in the television market. Chapter 15, "Programming the Network Affiliate," describes the strategies used by affiliated stations in programming throughout the day.

A principal concern of affiliated stations is the effectiveness of their networks' schedules. In Chapter 16, "Broadcast Networks," we discuss program development, which starts with ideas that are developed into shows that can be put on the air. Strategies for scheduling programs during different times of the day also take into account pressures from affiliates to attract large audiences. Program development is therefore crucial, as the failure rate for network programs means that new ones must continually be prepared as replacements.

The majority of Americans get most of their information from television. Thus, broadcast news has increased in volume, presence, and power over the past three decades. Chapter 17, "Television News," chronicles the growth and current condition of broadcast news.

Public television has been a "little engine that could" for 25 years. However, like the engine in the story, it has had to expend every bit of its energy to meet its goal, which in this case is survival. Chapter 18, "Public Television," examines public television from 1967 through its dark days of the 1980s and its ray of hope in the 1990s.

CHAPTER 11

The Television Environment

KEY TERMS AND CONCEPTS *(Cont.)*

Modularity
National Association of Television Programming
    Executives (NATPE)
Owned and Operated Stations
Prime-Time Access Rule (PTAR)
Representative Firms
Syndicated Exclusivity (Syndex)
Syndicators
Television Dayparts
Zapping
Zipping

Very few people would tell doctors how to diagnose patients or instruct plumbers on how to fix leaky sinks, but people seem comfortable making programming suggestions. The members of the post–World War II generation have grown up with television, and so, viewers do know something about television's workings. They understand the structures of TV, when commercials are coming, and when they are supposed to laugh or cry. If they don't know what's funny, the laugh track prompts them to respond.

TV viewing is an effortless activity, allowing its users to be passive much of the time. Most people do not think about how the programs they watch get on the air and why. It is for this reason that everyone becomes a self-appointed programmer: Programming looks so effortless that most viewers believe that it is easy. However, there are principles that successful professional programmers follow and practices that have proved reliable in guiding programming decisions. Once they have been learned, a programmer can break these rules selectively for special purposes, just as a classically trained musician learns to improvise.

A continuing viewer trend is the practice of watching television instead of particular shows.[1] Ask yourself, How often do I turn on the set just to see what's on and choose from what is available, and how often do I tune in for a specific show? The answer is probably that you turn on the TV, go around the dial, and stop when something interests you.

Over two decades ago the head programmer at NBC, Paul Klein, developed the least objectionable program (LOP) theory of television viewing. He postulated that viewers look over the available choices on the tube and stick with the one which offends them the least. Thus, he argued, programs should be as inoffensive as possible even if that means developing bland programs.[2]

This chapter is concerned with the basics of television viewing, the organization of the television industry, major factors which dictate programming decisions, and important forces in the television environment. The programmer's job, the acquisition of programs, the departments of a typical station, and important industry powers will be examined.

TELEVISION AUDIENCES

Television audiences are potentially very large, as 98 percent of American households have one or more televisions.[3] This large audience is often broken down by demographic characteristics for the purposes of analysis and program selection and placement. As was discussed in Chapter 6, specific demographic groups are important to programmers. However, the groupings used in television are a bit different from those used in radio, because radio stations are more specialized and reach highly fragmented audiences. Television, by contrast, still reaches for wider demographic groups. Therefore, this discussion will deviate from the pattern of radio demographic groups laid out in Chapter 6.

The primary demographics reported in television ratings books are age and sex. Demographic characteristics such as income, race, and education are sometimes used as well. This discussion will focus primarily on age and sex demographics.

Women and men are categorized in television ratings books and surveys in the age categories 2 to 11, 12 to 17, 18 to 24, 18 to 34, 18 to 49, 18 to 54, 25 to 34, 25 to 49, 25 to 54, 35 to 49, 35 to 54, and 55 and over. Each category has a use for some product advertisers and programs. For example, an advertiser of cosmetic products targeted to young women will be interested in the viewing habits of women age 18 to 24 or 18 to 34. A manufacturer of denture adhesive will be more inclined to look at people 55 and above of both sexes. Makers of products such as cleaners will be interested in women 18 to 54 years old, while a marketer of fur coats will want a slightly older audience with more money to spend on clothing, perhaps women 35 to 54.

The teen category includes 12- to 17-year-olds of both sexes and can be broken out by sex but not by age. This group shares an interest in general products such as foods, entertainment products such as movies and records, and skin care products associated with the teen years. Sex grouping is used to focus on products such as clothing and toiletries.

The ages 2 to 11 are used to classify children. Sex differences are evident in advertisements for dolls and action figures. Age breakdowns occur in the groups age 2 to 5 and 6 to 11. The younger segment is targeted for such products as coloring materials, preschool clothing, and some toys, while the older segment is introduced to athletic wear, more sophisticated toys, and electronic gadgets. The entire group age 2

to 11 gets attention from cereal, gum, and fast-food purveyors.

For our purposes, we will stay with the four basic categories: women 18 and over, men 18 and over, teens 12 to 17, and children 2 to 11. However, there will be times when we focus on more narrow segments within those groups.

Weekly Viewing by Demographic Groups

Women watch more television than men in all segments of the day and all days of the week.[4] In Figure 11-2 the trend is most pronounced in the daytime, when the audience is overwhelmingly female. Adult women watch 3 to 4 hours more a week than men watch. Among teens, however, the story is different: Boys watch about an hour more per week than girls. Overall, women watch from 10 to 20 percent more television than men do. Combined with the tendency of women to be responsible for the majority of shopping, this frequency of viewing makes women the target for the bulk of commercials and the focus of many programs. While there are exceptions, especially sports, most programs depend on a sizable base of women viewers for success.

Younger children (age 2 to 5) watch TV nearly

FIGURE 11-1   *Calvin and Hobbes © 1990 Watterson. Dist. by Universal Press Syndicate. Reprinted with permission. All rights reserved.*

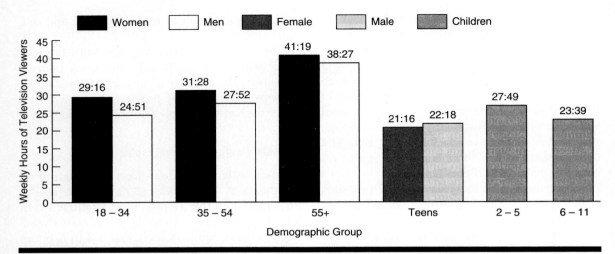

FIGURE 11-2   Viewing by demographic groups: television viewing per week in hours. (*Used by permission of Nielsen Media Research.*)

28 hours a week, but this falls to approximately 23½ hours for the group age 6 to 11. As school and outside activities become more important, television viewing falls off. That trend continues through the teen years, where viewing drops to about 22 hours a week for males and 21 hours a week for females.

At age 18, the drop in viewing is reversed and a steady increase in viewing begins. This culminates in more than 38 hours of television viewing a week for men 55 and over and more than 41 hours a week for women 55 and over.

These figures show how pervasive television viewing is. The group that views television the least—teens—still averages over 3 hours a day. The oldest viewers average between 5 and 6 hours of television viewing a day.

Household Viewing

Much TV viewing is shared with clusters of family members and friends. Television can be a social activity, and this is illustrated by the figures for household viewing. The average household has a television on 7 hours a day, almost half of its waking time. This makes television the most pervasive entertainment and leisure activity of Americans.

People have changed their use of free time more because of television than because of any other technology. The automobile changed travel behaviors, and people who own cars travel farther than do those without cars. However, both groups spend about the same amount of time traveling whether in privately owned cars or on public transportation. By contrast, television takes time from reading, listening to the radio, listening to records, socializing, gardening, and playing with pets. People who own televisions even sleep 15 minutes less a night than do persons who do not own televisions.[5]

Television viewing increases with household size (Figure 11-3). This is not surprising, as the addition of persons adds individuals who choose to watch shows, thus increasing the household average.

Household income, however, is inversely related to television viewing. The lowest-income households have the highest level of viewing per week, while the highest-income households have the lowest. Differences between adjacent income categories are not substantial, but the difference between households earning $30,000

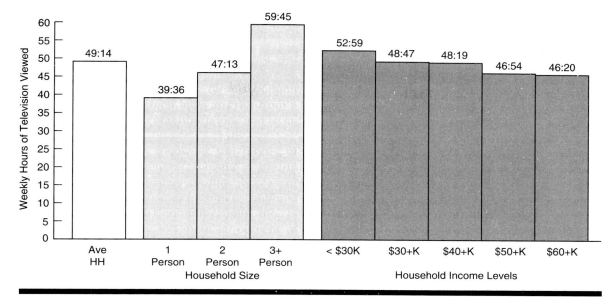

FIGURE 11-3   Household viewing, viewing by household size, and viewing by household income: television viewing per week in hours. (*Used by permission of Nielsen Media Research.*)

and above and those earnings $60,000 and above is well over 2 hours a week.

AUDIENCE VIEWING TENDENCIES IN THE TELEVISION ENVIRONMENT

Viewing by Time of Day and Season of the Year

Television viewing fluctuates by time of day. In the early morning at 6 a.m. the television is on in only about 10 percent of homes (Figure 11-4). Slowly that figure rises to about 25 percent at noon, a time when schoolchildren and most men and working women are not available to watch. Starting at about 4 p.m., as people begin arriving home from school and work, viewing levels begin to rise sharply. By 6 p.m. about half of all homes have the television turned on, and by 9 p.m. that figure has risen to about 60 percent. After that, viewing declines rapidly and stands at about 32 percent at midnight. By 2:30 a.m. only 10 percent of homes are tuned in, falling to a low of about 5 percent at 5 a.m.

Figure 11-4 also illustrates the seasonal nature of television viewing. The highest viewing rates in the afternoon and evening occur in February, when the weather is at its worst and the sun goes down early. The lowest viewing rates in the afternoon and evening occur in July, when the weather is more pleasant and the days are longer.

There are about 93 million television homes. Peak viewing of 65 percent in February represents about 60 million homes, and peak viewing of 50 percent in July represents about 46 million homes. The difference of 14 million homes is substantial, representing a decline in viewing of about 25 percent.

Viewing by Sex and Time of Day

As one would expect, the movement of people out of the home for school, work, and other activities causes fluctuations in television watching. Figure 11-5 shows that viewing by women in the daytime is about twice that by men. With an audience that is two-thirds female during

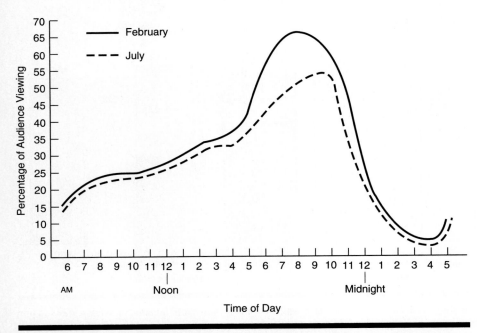

FIGURE 11-4 Viewing by time of day and season of the year: percentage of potential audience viewing television. (*Used by permission of Nielsen Media Research.*)

FIGURE 11-5 Viewing by sex and time of day: television viewing per week in hours. (*Used by permission of Nielsen Media Research.*)

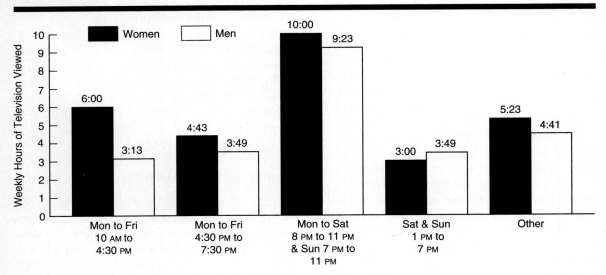

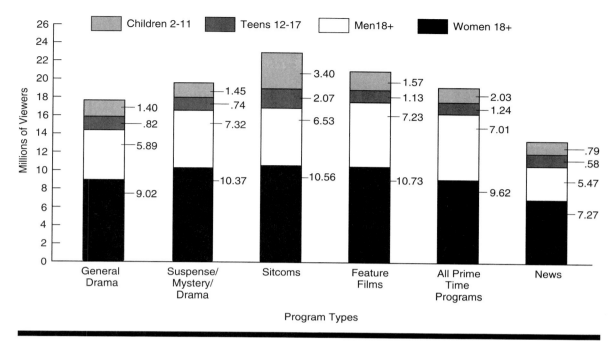

FIGURE 11-6 Viewing of program types: television viewing per week by audience segments (millions). (*Used by permission of Nielsen Media Research.*)

the day, programmers and advertisers have a clear focus on audience composition. Daytime programs and advertisements are aimed at women.

In the hours between 4:30 p.m. and 8 p.m. women outnumber men in the audience by a much smaller margin. Thus, programs in this daypart tend to be aimed at both women and men.

During the prime-time hours from 8 p.m. to 11 p.m. (7 p.m. to 11 p.m. on Sunday) Eastern time, the audience is about equally split between women and men. Thus, programmers place a variety of program types on the air to attract all viewers at one time or another. (Rather than repeatedly refer to Eastern time, we will assume that Eastern and Pacific schedules are the same except for live events. Television schedules in the Central and Mountain time zones run 1 hour earlier except for live events. Thus a program seen at 8 p.m. Eastern and Pacific times is seen

at 7 p.m. Central and Mountain times. All times given will be Eastern/Pacific with the assumption that Central and Mountain times are 1 hour earlier unless otherwise specified.)

Viewing of Program Types

Looking at the basic types of programs—general drama, suspense/mystery/drama, situation comedy, and feature film—in Figure 11-6, we see that all viewers taken together lean toward comedy programs. It is important to note, however, that the teen preference for comedies over feature films is almost two to one and that children's preference for comedy over feature films is more than two to one. This youth audience provides the margin for overall comedy preference over feature films because both men and women are more drawn, although only slightly, to feature films. Suspense/mystery/drama finishes third, and general drama comes in fourth.

TABLE 11-1   Programs Preferred by Different Demographic Groups: Top Five Programs for Women, Men, Teens, and Children

Women 18+	Men 18+	Teens 12–17	Children 2–11
1. *Roseanne*	*Monday Night Football*	*Different World*	*Cosby*
2. *Cosby*	*60 Minutes*	*Cosby*	*Different World*
3. *Golden Girls*	*Cheers*	*Wonder Years*	*Full House*
4. *Empty Nest*	*Sunday Football*	*Roseanne*	*Roseanne*
5. *Murder She Wrote*	*Roseanne*	*Who's The Boss?*	*Wonder Years*

In the area of informational programming between 6 p.m. and 7 p.m., women outnumber men in the audience. In the past men were the primary audience for news, but that has changed.

Top Five Programs by Demographic Group

A way to understand the variability of tastes in programs between demographic groups is to chart what each group watches the most. In Table 11-1 the top five programs are listed for women, men, teens, and children. Each group has a different number one. For women, it is *Roseanne;* for men, *Monday Night Football;* for teens, *A Different World;* and for children, *The Cosby Show.* The top four choices for women are all comedies, while two of the top three for men are sports programs. Teens have all comedies in the top 5; in fact, the top 15 shows (not shown) in teen rankings are all comedies. The same is true of children in their top five rankings—all comedies. Children also have all comedies in their top 10.

Viewing by Day of the Week

As was mentioned in Chapter 4, viewing shifts by day of the week. In Figure 11-7 Sunday stands out as the most viewed evening. The so-called family night is characterized by family-oriented programs including *Life Goes On, America's Funniest Home Videos, America's Funniest People,* and *ROC.* There are also many programs for adults, including *60 Minutes, Murder She Wrote,* and *Married . . . with Children.* ABC,

NBC, and CBS also program movies on that night, a programming form that draws substantial audiences.

Monday and Thursday are second and third in terms of viewership. This may be attributable to the strong CBS lineup on Monday and the strong NBC and FOX lineups on Thursday.

At the bottom of viewing is Friday. This is a night when people go out and many of those who stay home watch tapes on the VCR. The same is true of Saturday, which is next to last in television viewing. Saturday is the largest tape

FIGURE 11-7   Prime-time viewing by day of the week: viewing of prime-time television by average numbers of persons (millions). (*Used by permission of Nielsen Media Research.*)

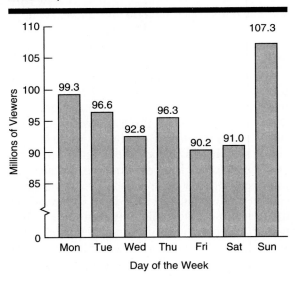

rental day of the week, followed by Friday.[6] Thus, when traditional viewership of television is down, rental activity and alternative uses of the home television are up.

Channels Viewed

Even though some homes receive 54 channels, the average person watches approximately 8 television channels in a given week.[7] Of course, those crucial eight television channels vary for members of different groups. If the viewer is 12 years old and has access to cable, one of the eight is probably MTV. If the viewer is a man over age 25, one of the eight is likely to be ESPN.

Cable is not needed to give viewers a large selection of station choices. In major cities there are many affiliated and independent broadcast stations. In New York City noncable households can receive more than 15 over-the-air stations. However, the typical cable home can receive 30 or more broadcast stations and cable networks. Members of cable households can watch many cable services that are highly specialized for particular tastes, such as MTV, ESPN, CNN, Lifetime, and the Weather Channel.

When older cable systems upgrade from 12 to 25 or more channels, much sampling of the new services occurs. The average number of channels viewed jumps from 8 to 12 or even 15 for a while, but after a few months the average viewer settles into a more limited group of regular choices. The new eight-channel field may represent some changes, but the overall number stays fairly static.

The television environment offers a variety of choices, giving viewers many options. This choice-rich landscape creates problems for programmers. Each has many more competitors and a more fragmented audience to consider, and any given audience member may watch many other channels on a regular basis.

The implications of this are substantial. If people continue to watch relatively few channels and if the number of available channels continues to escalate as new cable networks and inde-

pendent stations go on, the share of the audience available for any given service will decrease. At some point there will be a winnowing of program services unless people expand the number of channels they watch. Even then, their expansion of channels viewed will lessen the amount of time devoted to any one channel, resulting in the same lowering of relative shares.

Relative Passivity of Television Viewing

Viewers are relatively passive in their interactions with television. In reading a book, a person must pay attention to the physical act of reading itself as the reader's eyes must move across the lines of the book. Then the reader has to use his or her mind to supply the imagery the author is trying to transmit. That makes the act of reading a book an active affair.

Radio calls for less effort than does reading, but it still requires the listener to invent mental images. Most of the time listeners use radio as agreeable background noise, and so most listeners do not care whether the disc jockey is tall and has a mustache; they are just listening to music. Listeners do develop some kind of imagery when the station catches their attention with a new song or a creative commercial. The funny characters that many morning personalities create are seen in the listener's mind. Television, however, does all these things for its audiences by providing the sound and the picture. All the viewer has to do is look.

All this passive viewing can become boring after a while, and so television has become more **interactive,** giving viewers more to do. New shows try to involve viewers by asking questions about current issues and requesting that they telephone to register their points of view. Shows such as *Larry King Live* on CNN, *Oprah Winfrey,* and *Donahue* invite viewers to call in and speak with the guests.

In the late 1980s the children's show *Captain Power* took this process a step further. Children could use a "power jet" to shoot at targets on the screen, targets that shot back. The score for each child registered on the jet, which could be temporarily disabled by the bad guys shooting from the screen. Although the show was discontinued because of low ratings, the technology of interactive viewing had been tested and proved.

Viewers of *Wheel of Fortune* can use a similar device to play the game at home and compete with the regular contestants. This interactive format may represent the wave of the future as television offers viewers more alternatives to passive viewing.

TECHNOLOGICAL INFLUENCES ON THE TELEVISION ENVIRONMENT

Remote Control

The rise of the **remote control,** now in about 77 percent of homes,[8] has led to a phenomenon called grazing. **Grazing** is the practice of using the remote control to wander through many channels in search of something to watch. Grazers usually go through channels to see what is on because they are bored or fear they may be missing something good on another channel. This practice has changed the landscape of television because grazers are notoriously restless and are quick on the trigger when it comes to changing the channel. Long expositions, slow-moving scenes, and individual characters they do not like can drive them away.

A variation of grazing is zapping, which refers to changing channels when a commercial comes on. During a zapping period typical viewers go to another channel and then return after a period of time. However, they do not always come back. This has forced the creators of advertisements to work especially hard to be entertaining, particularly in the first 5 seconds of the ad, to dissuade or at least slow down the zapper.

An outgrowth of zapping and grazing, especially among younger viewers, is the creation of new program hybrids by viewers. By watching two or more shows simultaneously—jumping from one to another—the viewer takes bits and snatches from each show, creating a television mosaic.[9] A variation of this is viewing two sporting events by flipping back and forth between them. Men report increasing use of remote controls to monitor several events simultaneously.

The time for such switches often corresponds to the appearance of a commercial on the screen. Viewers zap the commercial breaks to watch other content. When the new channel goes to a commercial, the viewer zaps again.

Videocassette Recorders

VCRs are currently in over 70 percent of American homes. The VCR allows for control of time, a form of control that viewers did not have in the past. Programmers controlled time before the advent of VCRs. If one wanted to see a favorite show, it was necessary to make arrangements to watch it. That was convenient for advertisers, who could place time-specific messages in programs. For example, Burger King might place an ad at 10:30 p.m. or 1 a.m. asking, Aren't you hungry? At those times many people are. However, if a tape of the program is being viewed the next day just after dinner, the ad loses its timeliness and effectiveness. Controlling time frees the viewer from any schedule rigidity that programmers may impose, but it is a negative factor for advertisers who depend on the timing of original viewing to spark some kind of action.

The second practice of viewers with VCRs that is of concern to advertisers is zipping, or using the search and fast-forward buttons to "zip" through commercials when playing back pro-

---

**BOX 11-1
COLLEGE
STUDENTS' AD
ZAPPING GAME**

College students have turned zapping into a game in which each person takes a turn jumping from station to station with the remote control. When the contestant hits a commercial, he or she is "zonked" and turns the control over to the next player. The player who amasses the greatest total time without encountering a commercial wins.   ∎

gram tapes. In most VCRs this eliminates all commercial sound, and if the search speed is 10 times normal, a 30-second ad moves by silently in 3 seconds. No advertiser could be heartened by such a practice. As one might expect, advertisers are studying zapping and zipping to see how widespread these practices are.

PROGRAMMING TO THE VIEWING ENVIRONMENT

The Television Program Director's Changing Responsibilities

The title of the television programmer varies by station and system. The most common title used at stations is program director (PD). At the network level, PDs are often called vice presidents or president of the division of programming or entertainment. At affiliated and independent stations and in cable systems, other duties may be added and the title may be changed. A popular title is program manager. For convenience, we will use the title program director.

Whatever the title, as in radio, the program director's goal is to help the station, network, or cable system succeed. To accomplish this goal, the program director must evaluate, acquire, and schedule programs in order to maximize revenues.

That is easy to say and difficult to do. Competing stations and programmers have the same goals. Each is after the same few "good" programs for similar time slots. Furthermore, there is considerable risk: A particular show may or may not be successful in attracting the desired audience. For example, all networks would benefit from having shows such as *The Simpsons* and *Doogie Howser, M.D.,* but only one network gets any given show. Most stations want to have *Oprah Winfrey* and *Jeopardy,* but only one station in each market gets to play each program at any one time. Several cable networks could benefit from showing reruns of *Murder She Wrote,* but only one can. The trouble is that there is no way for a broadcast network, station, or cable network to know how a program will perform be-

fore putting it on. It is often the programmer's judgment about a show and its potential for success that leads to its acquisition; thus, the PD is praised if the program succeeds but blamed if it fails.

The television program director's tasks and skills As was discussed in earlier chapters, selling advertising time during programs is a station, broadcast network, or cable network's only or major source of revenue. To sell advertising time at the highest rates, a station or network generally must promise to attract the best possible audiences to convince advertisers that their money will be well spent. Increasingly, an audience can be sold to advertisers if it contains a demographic group that advertisers want to reach. The most sought after groups are women age 18 to 49 and 25 to 54 because they control product purchase decisions and account for the spending of the most dollars.[10]

Other demographic groups are also of interest to advertisers and programmers. Men, for example, are the targets for a series of products. A look at the commercials in team sports events such as football and baseball will reveal a number of ads for beer and automotive products. Teens must be attracted too. Many advertisers, including soft drink and fast-food companies and athletic shoe manufacturers, derive substantial income from the teen market, and scheduling occasional programs that appeal to teens allows the programmer to make clients of those advertisers. Children have increasing economic clout in the marketplace, and a number of products are designed for their use. Toy, cereal, and snack product advertisers need to reach these consumers, and so the careful programmer includes programs for children.

Generally, different audience segments are most available to the programmer at specific times of the day or on particular days of the week. Women, for example, are available as the predominant members of the audience during weekday daytimes. Men tend to cluster during weekend afternoons. Teens view TV on late Saturday mornings, and children tend to watch most heavily on weekday afternoons and Saturday mornings. Thus, a programmer can build schedules that reach the most available demographic groups by noting when those persons tend to watch television in the largest numbers.

As was outlined in earlier chapters, a programmer must be conversant with ratings and the uses of research. Measurement of audience size and demographic composition is crucial to the development of schedules. Ratings data also provide information about strong and weak areas in a station's performance. Studying ratings data helps programmers discover what programming problems may exist and expedites moves to solve them. A documented weakness in children's viewing, for example, may lead to the acquisition of a program that appeals strongly to children.

Central to the programmer's skills is knowing how and where to acquire syndicated programs, or those which are purchased for local airing from the companies that own the rights to them. These include movies, action programs, comedies, dramas, sports, and children's programs. Knowing where to find programs is not sufficient; the programmer also negotiates the prices to be paid for them. A programmer who pays too much becomes a liability to the station or network because the profits are negatively affected.

Having backup plans is necessary for programmers as they try to purchase the best programs. No programmer is going to get all the first choices, and so programmers must be flexible and adapt to complex, competitive situations characterized by many competitors attempting to acquire the same programs.

Programmers need to know how to place programs together within dayparts to maximize the ratings and control the flow of audience from program to program. If a PD uses the audience of one program to provide the foundation for the audience of the next program, scheduling effectiveness is enhanced. For example, on Monday night CBS appeals strongly to women with *Murphy Brown,* which is followed by *Love and War* and *Northern Exposure.* The effective programmer knows how to use all program types, including comedy, sports, and drama, to the best advantage at specified times of the day and/or days of the week.

To determine whether a program will be profitable, a programmer must be able to estimate how much income it can generate as well as how much it costs. This assessment allows the programmer to negotiate program prices with the goal of making a profit in each time slot. Judicious scheduling of programs in time slots that take maximum advantage of available audiences, thus attracting advertisers, creates greater revenues for the station.

Another important issue for the programmer is community relations. Programs affect people both positively and negatively. Programmers need to monitor public opinion to note when programs may harm the station's image. Programs containing strong language, explicit sex scenes, and/or violence galvanize a negative community response. A programmer should be sensitive to viewer attitudes and mores and be ready to formulate responses to any crises that arise. Knowing how to respond to organized groups is an invaluable tool when one is dealing with people's responses to programs they find offensive.

Economic pressures on stations and systems In the past 10 years, as more television stations have come on the air, cable networks have grown in number and variety, and broadcast stations, networks, and cable systems have been sold, economic pressures have mounted. Whether a debt results from the purchase price for a station or network or is part of the start-up cost of a new enterprise, it places pressure on programmers to find audiences that advertisers want to reach. Programmers have a smaller margin for error than they did in less debt-driven times, and a miscalculation of a program's anticipated success can be catastrophic. Programmers are increasingly concerned with the bottom line and with avoiding mistakes that could place the station in jeopardy.

One outgrowth of economic pressure is increasing input from general managers of stations and systems about programming decisions. In some stations and systems, the programmer's job has been eliminated altogether and programming tasks have been taken over by general managers.[11] A variation of that practice is "team" decision making, in which program acquisition decisions may be made by a committee consisting of the general manager, the program director, the sales director, and others whom the general manager considers knowledgeable.

Organization of Stations and Cable Systems

Stations Most broadcast television stations have the following departments: programming, sales, general administrative, production, technical/engineering, news, and community affairs (sometimes called public affairs).

The programming department determines the content broadcast by the station. It is there that decisions are made concerning which product to acquire (programs are generally referred to as **product** in the industry), which programs to produce, and when to schedule those shows. Programming departments spend vast sums of money but do not directly generate revenue for the station. They are charged with drawing large audiences with their programming; the sales department then sells those audiences to advertisers. The ability to deliver audiences to advertisers lies at the heart of the programming process since advertising revenue is the only source of income for stations and broadcast networks and constitutes a large portion of a cable network's income. That makes for a close relationship between the programming and sales departments.

The sales department takes the audience figures for each of the station's shows to advertisers and tries to sell commercial spots. This is the only department in the station that directly generates revenue. Consequently, salespeople tend to be the highest paid workers at a station; they work on commission, and their earning potential is limited only by their creative abilities and the station's ratings. They take the audiences that programmers and news directors attract and offer them to advertisers, turning audiences into income.

The general administrative wing of the station includes the internal management, or those charged with financial record keeping (accountants and bookkeepers), office personnel, and service personnel. Contained within this wing is the business department, which is concerned with personnel, security, maintenance, and management information systems. Other managers, such as program directors, sales managers, and community relations managers, are usually considered parts of their respective departments rather than being included with the general administrative section.

Feedback from this department to the programmer tends to concern money. Charged with the responsibility of managing the financial affairs of the station, persons in general administration tend to be very well informed about how individual programs are performing and which ones are earning the highest profits. The relationship between general administration and programming is an advisory one. Profit-and-loss statements and financial reports contain information about and recommendations for programming.

The production department produces all programs originated by the station. The bulk of local production consists of news programs, which may account for as much as 3 hours a day of finished product, but other kinds of programs are produced as well. Talk shows focusing on local issues and interview programs featuring celebrities who are passing through town are often hosted by a local newsperson. These programs have increased in number and popularity. Public affairs programs and local sports programs are also created.

The engineering/technical department is responsible for keeping the station on the air, maintaining the equipment, and maintaining a good signal. Its relationship to the programming department is also advisory. Programmers need to know how far the signal reaches and how good the signal is when it gets there. Are viewers getting a good picture? If a poor signal in outlying areas can be improved through technology, more viewers will be reached and that will translate, through increased advertising rates, to additional revenue.

News departments are large, complex organisms that grind out substantial amounts of local programming on a daily basis. Of great interest to the programmer is the fact that news programs are the most extensively viewed local shows. Some stations place news under the control of the programming department with the view that news is programming. This consolidates decision making by making one person responsible for everything the station airs. In a station with this kind of organization, the news director may report to the PD rather than to the general manager; this does not occur when the news department is separate.

The community affairs department checks the pulse of the community and tries to position the station as part of the community and as a good corporate citizen. This is done through public relations campaigns, promotions, and involvement in and sponsorship of events and charities. This department is called the promotion department in some stations. It is useful to the programmer, who may be able to combine community campaigns with programming efforts to enhance the image of the station in the community.

Cable systems The departments of cable television systems include programming, administration, technical, sales, and sometimes production. Not all cable systems have advertising sales departments, though all have subscriber sales departments, and some systems do not have a production department because they do not originate programs.

Cable programming is not much like station programming. Cable systems simply carry cable networks, and the choice of which cable networks to carry is based on viewer demand and channel capacity. For example, most subscribers want at least one of the following: CNN, ESPN, MTV, USA, Lifetime, HBO, and Nickelodeon. The programmer of a cable system acts like a traffic cop, making sure that cable networks are assigned to channels on the system.

There is another consideration in placing cable networks on the system: payment. Most basic cable networks charge local cable systems for their carriage. These payments range from 5 cents to 35 cents per subscriber per month. Thus, the cost of a channel is a factor in its placement. Popular networks such as ESPN and CNN are carried despite being among the most costly, but marginal and unproven cable networks have more difficulty getting onto systems.

The sales department at a cable system does not have the close relationship to the programming department that is the norm at stations. This is the case because cable sales departments usually focus on subscriber sales—bringing in more paying customers. Because the system's economic base is monthly subscriber fees, the connection to specific programs is much less direct. However, many cable systems have begun to sell advertising time on their own channels on which they originate local programming and on cable networks such as ESPN, CNN, CNN2, USA, MTV, and Lifetime. The networks make some advertising time available for cable systems to sell locally as a partial inducement to carry the networks. In these cases programming is related to sales a bit more directly. Still, since programmers do not make decisions about the product on cable networks, the relationship between the departments is not as interdependent.

Administrative departments at cable systems perform the same functions as do those at stations: accounting, bookkeeping, clerical, and support functions. As with stations, the administrative department shares economic reports with the programming department, along with occasional advisories to carry or drop networks.

The technical department of a cable system performs some complex tasks. It is responsible for bringing in all the satellite signals of the cable networks and for capturing broadcast signals from local stations and placing them onto channels for transmission to the subscribers. The relationship of the technical department to the programming department in cable is similar to the departmental relationships in broadcasting. If people have trouble with their reception, no level of programming quality will solve that problem. However, the technical quality of what shows up on the customer's screen is more controllable in cable because the system literally brings all the signals right into the home. In broadcasting, the station's signal can be foiled if the consumer has an inadequate antenna. Even if the signal is good, poor equipment can make it look bad. By contrast, in cable, the antenna is supplied by the cable company in the form of the individual line connected directly to the customer's television. This helps the cable company control signal quality and assures programmers that their materials will arrive at customers' homes in good condition.

The existence of a production department means that the cable system produces some of its own programming. Not all cable systems do this, but systems that produce programs create a wide variety of them, ranging from local school board and city council meetings to sports and talk shows featuring local personalities. Sometimes the cable system turns over time each week to individuals and groups to create their own programs.

The relationship between programming and production is very close. Since whatever is produced will help define what people think of the cable system, programmers are interested in that content. They want to know that programs will enhance the cable system's reputation, not harm it. In many systems, the production department is part of the programming department. In others, it is organizationally independent but the programmer is in continual contact.

THE INFLUENCE OF DAYPARTS ON PROGRAMMING DECISIONS

Programming strategy is based on three fundamental questions which affect the selection or creation of programming: What time is it? Who's out there (in the audience)? and What are they doing? By answering these questions, the programmer can develop effective strategies to capture and hold audiences. These questions seem simple, but the issues and complications they raise are complex.

What time is it? refers to dayparts. Radio dayparts were discussed in Chapter 4, but television dayparts are different. Who's out there? gets into audience composition by sex, age, and any other demographic characteristic deemed important. We will concern ourselves with sex and age for now. What are they doing? deals with audience activities, and those change with the time of day.

Television Dayparts

Television dayparts differ from radio dayparts in terms of how and when the two media are used. Radio is often played in cars and is most often used as a background medium while the listener does other things. The listener doesn't have to look at the radio or pay close attention to plot developments. Television, however, generally cannot be viewed in cars and requires some attention to what is happening. Hence, radio usage is highest when people are in their cars during the morning and afternoon drive times, and television usage is highest when people are near their televisions and can pay attention during prime time and the hours just preceding it.

Television's dayparts are early morning (EM), 7 a.m. to 9 a.m.; daytime (DAY), 9 a.m. to 4 p.m.; early fringe (EF), 4 p.m. to 8 p.m.; prime time (PT), 8 p.m. to 11 p.m. (except for Sunday, when it is 7 p.m. to 11 p.m.); late fringe (LF), 11 p.m. to 1 a.m.; and overnight (ON), 1 a.m. to 6 a.m. These vary slightly from the list of dayparts presented in Chapter 4 in that prime access from 7:30 p.m. to 8 p.m. is included within early fringe and late news from 11 p.m. to 11:30 p.m. is included within late fringe. These are Eastern and Pacific times; Central and Mountain schedules run 1 hour earlier. Thus, in the Central and Mountain time zones, early fringe is 3 p.m. to 7 p.m. and prime time is 7 p.m. to 10 p.m. Of course, live events such as sporting events run on real time in each time zone. A Super Bowl that begins at 6 p.m. Eastern time starts at 5 p.m. Central, 4 p.m. Mountain, and 3 p.m. Pacific.

The potential audience for television changes by time of day, day of the week, and season of the year. In this section we look at fluctuations in audience composition by time of day. The HUT level, as outlined in Chapter 4, rises from early morning to evening, after which it declines, but the demographic composition of the audience changes as well.

Early Morning

In general, children and adults who awake early make up the audience for the **early morning.** Network affiliates appeal to the adults with news shows that start as early as 6 a.m. Other services offered include business news, farm reports, and weather information. Independent stations target children by programming cartoons until it is time for school. Cable networks, which are typically more specialized, program their normal fare.

Activities center on getting ready for the day. Showering, shaving, dressing, and planning for the day create a busy and sometimes hectic atmosphere. This is one of the busier times of the day for many people.

Daytime

Men leave the home in large numbers from 7 a.m. to 9 a.m., and many children leave for school at this time. By 9 a.m. the available audience is primarily women who do not work outside the home. There are other viewers available: the elderly, the unemployed, shift workers, the very young, and the ill. However, none of these groups constitutes an appealing primary demographic for delivery to advertisers. Thus during the **daytime** hours of 9 a.m. to about 4 p.m. programmers vie for the female audience.

While it is nowhere near as large as it is during prime time, the audience during the daytime is a favorite of advertisers. Women make most point-of-purchase decisions, buying household products, clothes, food, and almost everything else. Men purchase beer, cars, tires, and toiletries. However, that pattern is breaking down. In the latter part of the 1980s Michelin Tires began aiming its ads at the female as well as the male audience, and women now purchase nearly 50 percent of automobiles.

Advertisers can connect with the exact demographic they want during the daytime. Women are typically available in large numbers during this daypart. The increase in the number of women who work outside the home has affected the daytime audience's demographic composition by removing some of the most desirable consumers, but the core audience is still primarily women, and that appeals to both advertisers and programmers.

The activity level varies within the daypart. Earlier in the daypart activities include shopping, errands, bill paying, housework, and assorted family and household matters. Labor-saving devices make it possible to dispense with the more time-consuming tasks in the first half of the daypart. The second phase, from about noon on, is characterized by seat work such as letter writing and hobbies.

Early Fringe

At about 3 p.m. a change begins. Children begin arriving home from school, and the audience becomes more mixed. During the next 3 hours men and working women enter the audience. First come blue-collar and other shift workers, followed by white-collar workers and professionals. The local road system and the resultant commuting time affect specific arrival patterns, but by about 6 p.m. the audience is totally mixed and will remain so until the children start going to bed.

The primary activity in **early fringe** is dinner: planning, preparation, serving, eating, and cleanup work. Most family members are involved in part of this work. There are also household chores, errands, family meetings, and homework to do. As with early morning, this is a relatively active time.

Prime Time

Who's out there in prime time? Everybody, and that is very good news for programmers. With dinner, cleanup, and errands out of the way, the family can settle down for television viewing. Children begin to go to bed at around 8:30 p.m., and that makes the audience increasingly adult as the hours pass. By 10 p.m. most children are out of the audience.

Activity levels are low during this time. The more heightened pace associated with after-school and after-work activities, preparations for the evening, and household duties is finished. The primary evening activity in most homes is watching television.

Late Fringe

The audience changes again during this period. As people go to bed, the audience shrinks and is dominated by more specific demographic groups. Generally speaking, people with jobs go to bed earlier because they have to get up early. Those who do not have jobs or who are students can stay up later. College students, for example, are in the audience because they have some control over their class schedules and sleeping late is one of their options. **Late fringe** audiences tend to be younger than those for other day-parts, and that helps explain the success of programs such as *Late Night With David Letterman* and *Arsenio Hall.*

People begin preparations for bed and for the coming day. That gives them things to do for anywhere from a few minutes to an hour, depending on their hygienic habits and level of organization. They watch television with less concentration and less attention as they go about their tasks.

Program Modularity

Who's out there, and what are they doing? is a central question because it influences how viewers use TV at any given time. **Modularity** refers to the use of short stand-alone pieces within shows or to a show's tendency to be broken into individually viewable pieces. The length of the pieces, or *modules,* determines the pace of the show. Modularity is an outgrowth of the two primary areas: available audience and activities. More than anything else, however, modularity is dependent on the activity levels of viewers.

The modules on the *Today* show rarely exceed 4 minutes, and most are much shorter. An interview with an author may last 3 minutes, and a movie review 1 minute. Such a show is considered highly modular because it is broken into so many short, unconnected bits. A viewer can watch one module, such as Willard Scott's weather, and then ignore the following modules. There is no relationship between the program segments, and so long-term viewing commitments are not necessary. If a viewer with tooth-brush in hand stops in front of the TV to watch an interview with a current rock star, the commitment is only for a couple of minutes. The next piece, on a subject of no interest, will provide the chance to continue getting ready for the day.

There is a natural relationship between modularity and the time of day. When peoples' activities do not permit careful viewing, as in the early morning, shows must be highly modular to attract viewers. Consequently, movies, soap operas, and other plot-intensive programs don't appear at that time.

Shows that require a high level of viewer attention do not work especially well in the early morning, but those which accommodate short bursts of attention do better. Morning shows such as *Today* and *Good Morning America* do not require steady viewing; they function like "video radio." Cartoons provide a similar service; children who are beginning their day can watch in bursts while getting ready for school.

By 9 a.m., a change in the activity level allows for slightly more intensive viewing. The hectic activity level which characterizes the beginning of the day has passed. Different kinds of household and personal tasks, including cleaning, errands, and bill paying, come to the fore.

During this time period semimodular shows are usually scheduled. Talk shows such as *Oprah Winfrey* and *Donahue* are modular in construction, with talk segments, audience segments, and phone segments. Unlike the early-morning programs, however, each broadcast is wrapped around a single theme. Still, this kind of semimodular structure allows viewers who are completing chores to use the show in ways similar to the use of early-morning TV. They can do some work, watch a module, and then return to a task.

Game shows fit into the semimodular category because they can be joined at any point. One can begin watching *Wheel of Fortune* in midpuzzle or *Jeopardy* in the middle of Double Jeopardy without being oriented to what has gone on beforehand.

Similarly, comedies that revolve around gags and slapstick, such as *Alf* and *Gilligan's Island,* can be watched in modular terms because plot is not of the essence. Viewers are not likely to delve into the recesses of the skipper's psyche or examine the reasons for Thurston Howell's acquisitiveness. Instead, they see sight gags and hear puns. Comedies such as *Cheers* and *M*A*S*H,* however, which take their humor from situations and context, are less modular. The viewer may study a character's motivation, making the episode more plot-intensive. A case in point is a *Cheers* episode in which the shy Cliff is placed in a relationship with a woman, but because it is Halloween and they are masked, they do not see each other's faces. The audience must wait for the climactic meeting face-to-face to see how the characters relate to each other without their disguises. The humor is poignant, based on character and plot development. One doesn't get the joke without the context. Such comedies must be placed in time slots where more careful viewing is possible. Early daytime typically requires more modularity than comedies of this sort can provide.

By 12:30 p.m., when most tasks have been completed, relaxed total viewing is more the norm. The activity level has dropped dramatically by the start of the soap operas, permitting a different kind of interaction with the television set. "Sitting activities" such as correspondence and hobby work can be done while one is keeping track of a television program.

Soap operas and movies require more careful attention to plot twists and multiple story lines. Soap operas can have eight or more ongoing stories and deal with four or more in a given episode, and so the faithful viewer has to watch closely. There is some modularity in that multiple stories (modules) are in progress. True, they are redundant and contain conversational "summaries" for the viewers' benefit, but these conventions are a help to viewers who miss occasional episodes and need to catch up.

Theoretically, a viewer could be interested in one module (story) but not the others. Thus he or she could watch for developments in that module and then go off to run errands. However, this kind of reaction is as uncommon as watching parts of a movie (subplot modules) while ignoring others.

At about 3 or 4 p.m. the programming changes not only because people come into the house but because household activities change. In addition to the customs associated with arrival, the preparing, serving, and eating of dinner and the cleaning up afterward will be a central focus. That occupies members of the family until 7 p.m. or later, and then another round of relaxed viewing occurs during prime time.

Moderate modularity returns in the early fringe as family members return and as preparations for dinner and evening obligations begin. This is also a time for some chores to be done by various members of the family. Television programs must be more modular during this period to reflect increased activity levels and spotty viewing. Talk shows, game shows, and sitcoms predominate. Of course, news is the ultimately modular program.

Moderate modularity remains in force until prime time, when longer programs begin to return. Programs aired from 8 p.m. to 9 p.m. still have some modularity since children are in the audience (but they are being shuttled off to bed). At 9 p.m. modularity requirements drop sharply. Hour-long shows and 2-hour movies are ideal for audiences who can sit back and be entertained.

Activity levels usually continue to drop until bedtime, allowing for viewing with very little interruption. At 11 p.m., adults begin preparations for bed and fairly high modularity returns. The news is highly modular, as are the sitcoms that stations run in this period. The Leno and Letterman shows are also highly modular and are just right for people with a TV in the bedroom and a timer or remote control to turn it off. If they like a module, they can watch. If they don't, they can close their eyes and wait for the next module or turn off the set for the night.

Depending on the time of day and the day of the week, different modularity principles are at work. The important thing for programmers to remember is the level of audience activity and the modularity level that is appropriate to that activity.

Set Control

Who controls the set? used to be a more important question than it is now. When one set was shared by the whole family, who made the decision about what to watch made a difference to programmers. Currently, however, two-thirds of homes have more than one television set. This means that if children and parents or husband and wife want to watch something different, they can, and the VCR allows anyone who is left out to record a choice for later viewing. Still, a third of homes have only one set, and so a discussion of set control still has relevance.

Who controls the set varies depending on the time of day and the day of the week. In the early morning adults control the set. Unless the father is a real television viewer, the mother will probably decide what will be watched. However, her choices are limited by the similarity of programming content. Children usually control the second set.

During the day control falls to women, since little competition exists. That is why daytime programming is so uniform in its demographic appeals. However, a struggle for control starts at about 3 p.m. Women vie with children for control; women may want to watch but may be too busy to compete for set control.

Finally, larger numbers of men enter the mix

starting at about 4 p.m. For the most part they watch whatever women and children have chosen until 6 p.m. At that point, adults make a point of tuning in the news and children have less of a say.

During the prime-time access and prime-time periods, the family decides how a shared TV is to be used. Adults make the final decision, but children exert whatever influence they have. After 9 p.m. TV program fare becomes much more adult in orientation as adults take uncontested control of the set.

Fridays are different in the prime-time hours. Many adults go out, leaving the children with baby-sitters, and control of the set falls into the hands of young people. Children make more television demands on Friday because they can stay up later to watch. Thus Friday night network schedules over the years have featured *The Incredible Hulk, The Dukes of Hazzard, Knight Rider, Full House, Family Matters,* and other youth-oriented programs.

Many parents sleep late on Saturday morning, and so children, who tend to get up early, have control of the set. Thus, children's shows predominate on Saturday morning.

On Sunday morning few people are watching, and so old movies may be scheduled. Some stations schedule children's programming along the lines of a typical Saturday morning schedule. On many stations the time is sold to religious broadcasters. In recent years more network-affiliated stations have moved away from religious and children's programming in favor of *CBS Sunday Morning* and *Sunday Today.*

Because men tend to enjoy sports, they exert set control on Saturday and Sunday afternoons. These time periods have become a haven for sports programming.

In sum, who is watching, what they are doing, modularity, and to some extent who controls the set determine the nature of the programming at any given time. While there are fluctuations of taste in different markets and variations by time zone, the general principles of programming can be applied to these times of day.

IMPORTANT FORCES IN THE TELEVISION ENVIRONMENT

The television environment is greatly influenced by organizations, groups, companies, and policies. They are an integral part of the environment because they define its landscape and evolution. This section examines programming distribution systems and outlets, program syndicators, ownership trends, outside companies that provide programming advice, and regulation.

Programming Distribution Systems

Broadcast networks The four broadcast networks are CBS, ABC, NBC, and Fox. While Fox is not technically a network, it functions like one and therefore will be discussed here.

Networks purchase the rights for two airings of most entertainment programming from production companies. After the original airplay and one rerun, the rights to an episode of a show revert to the producers. Because they have been restrained by the Federal Communications Commission from producing more than a few programs of their own, the networks do not produce much entertainment programming. Still, most viewers in prime time view one of the networks; the combined network share of audience for the traditional networks (ABC, NBC, CBS) in prime time is approximately 62 percent.[12] Thus what the networks choose to put on the air is very influential. Networks do produce sports and public affairs programs such as NFL Football, *Meet the Press,* and *20/20;* usually these programs have little repeat value.

Networks are largely distribution systems. They purchase temporary program rights from producers and then make those programs available to about 200 stations around the country. Some of those stations are owned by the network; they are called **owned and operated stations (O and O's),** but that accounts for only five to eight stations each. The rest are **affiliates** which have agreements with a network to carry programs in exchange for advertising time. For example, NBC sends free programs such as *Empty Nest* and *L.A. Law* to affiliates but retains most of the advertising time in these programs, which it sells. The network can sell the audience for each affiliated station to advertisers as part of a national package. That is how a network makes money to pay for program rights, employees' salaries, and business costs.

Networks also produce news and public affairs programs such as *The CBS Evening News, Good Morning America, 60 Minutes, This Week with David Brinkley,* and *Nightline.* The arrangement with affiliated stations is much the same, as programs are exchanged for advertising time. What varies is the amount of time retained by the network.

Cable networks There are technological differences between broadcast networks and cable networks. Broadcast networks' programs are distributed through free over-the-air television stations, and the consumer must have an antenna to receive them in their over-the-air form. Cable networks distribute programs through cable systems, and the consumer must subscribe to the local cable system to receive those programs. Cable systems, though, do carry affiliated and independent stations, and that provides a second way for consumers to receive broadcast programming without an antenna. However, if a subscriber has the cable removed, broadcast signals can be picked up by installing an antenna, although the cable signals will be lost.

An economic difference exists as well. Rather than providing programming free, a cable network usually charges local cable systems for the privilege of carrying the network. Thus, cable operators pay ESPN, CNN, and other cable networks a monthly fee for each subscriber in exchange for carrying that network. The cable network generates additional income by selling advertising time in the programs it airs. That gives a cable network two sources of revenue compared with a broadcast network's one.

Cable networks acquire programming much as broadcast networks do: They pay producers or organizations fees for the rights to carry events. ESPN, for example, carries college and professional football, a right for which it pays. CNN produces most of its own programming, the cost of which is recovered through fees to cable systems and advertising revenues.

Program Syndicators

Syndicators hold rights to programs and sell them to stations which want to air those shows. For example, after *Growing Pains* accumulated enough episodes, the series was offered for sale to one station or cable network in each television market. In a syndication purchase, a station or cable system gets the sole rights to a specified number of airings of each episode (often six) over a number of years (most often 3 years). When the rights expire, the syndicator can resell them in the market either to the station that has been running the series (the **incumbent station**) or to a competitor if the incumbent is not interested in renewal.

Syndication is essentially an exchange of program rights for money. A local network-affiliated station, for example, does not receive all its programs from the network, and so it must look elsewhere to fill the gaps in its schedule. Independent stations do not have a network to supply programs to them and look to syndicators for nearly everything. Most cable networks do not produce all their programs; they look to syndicators too.

Syndicators are production companies or their representatives. They hold the rights to programs and arrange to sell them to anyone who wants to buy. Thinking back to the sections on broadcast and cable networks, where do the airplay rights of programs go when the networks have exhausted the plays for which they have paid? They revert to the producers, who are now free to sell them to other buyers. If you produce *A Different World,* you can sell episodes after the two network plays of each episode have finished. In some cases the production company has its own syndication division to handle the business of selling to stations and cable networks. Sometimes it hires a syndication company to manage that task. In the case of *A Different World,*

Carsey-Warner Productions uses Viacom, a large syndication company, to arrange all sales.

National Association of Television Programming Executives The National Association of Television Programming Executives (NATPE) is an organization that brings together programmers and syndicators. Once a year NATPE holds a national conference and program fair at which syndicators show their wares. Station management and cable network representatives negotiate the rights to the shows they want to acquire. Of course, much buying and selling goes on before and afterward, but the conference allows thousands of people in the same business to come together and get a feel for what the others are doing. Held in January or early February each year, it gives programmers time to create ideas for the fall schedule and make the purchases they need. In 1991 over 8000 people attended the meeting in New Orleans.[13]

Independent Television Association The Independent Television Association (ITVA) serves the needs of independent, non-network-affiliated television stations. One of its functions is to hold a programming fair for its members each year. Like the NATPE conference, it brings syndicators and stations together, but in this case fewer stations. Syndicators who are interested in sales to affiliated stations can go just to NATPE, but those who are interested in serving independent stations go to ITVA also. It is held about a week or two before NATPE each year. In 1993 the two conventions were combined.

Programming Distribution Outlets

Affiliated stations As was mentioned in the section on broadcast networks, affiliated stations distribute programs for networks. Trading away time for programs works to the benefit of the affiliate as well as the network because the local station can present a strong lineup of popular shows. That makes the advertising time that the network allocates to the affiliate more valuable. Selling more time in a less popular program may not produce as much revenue as selling less time at a much higher rate in a more popular show.

Affiliates have many time periods of their own to program. Sometimes they use syndicated programs, and occasionally they produce their own shows. One program that almost all affiliates produce is local news. Partly because of the strength of their network lineups, the rest of the programs tend to do well also, making them a formidable force in local station economics.

Independent stations Independent stations have no network from which to receive programs; they must build their own schedules. This means that they have to buy programs in the syndication marketplace and produce whatever programs they can. A disadvantage of independence is the lack of free, highly popular shows around which to build a reputation with viewers. A related disadvantage is that all programs have to be supported through advertising revenues, and those advertising spots have to be sold against competition from affiliated stations which typically have strong lineups.

The syndication marketplace gives independents access to strong programs that were formerly on networks, such as *Cheers* and *Family Matters*. After its network run, no show is tied to its original network. Thus, independents can build attractive schedules through the purchase of these programs. Other programs that are not played on networks exist as well. Aimed directly at the syndication market and not the networks, programs such as *Star Trek: The Next Generation* and *Deep Space 9* are available to all buyers, including independents. Whereas an affiliated station is primarily an outlet for network programs, an independent is an outlet for syndicated programs.

Cable systems Like local stations, local cable systems are an outlet for programs from national sources and create some shows of their own. Cable networks develop their own schedules and then make the whole package available to the cable system. Unlike an affiliate, which receives most of its schedule from a network, and an independent, which purchases each piece of its schedule, a cable system does not put schedules together before airing them. Instead, it bundles a collection of nationally and regionally distributed cable networks for presentation to subscribers. Cable systems are almost pure outlets.

Cable systems can also produce programs, and many systems do. Local political events and meetings, sports events, parades, fairs, and entertainment ranging from rock bands to interviews can be produced. How much production a system chooses to do depends on local interest and taste as well as equipment, personnel, and facilities.

Ownership Trends

Perhaps the most important trend in ownership is that toward fewer owners owning more outlets. The big three broadcast networks—CBS, ABC, and NBC—were all purchased in the 1980s, as were more than half of stations in the 50 largest television markets. Fewer companies now own a greater number of stations. These larger companies have the advantage of clout and specialization. The problem with such growth is that with fewer companies owning more media outlets, the potential for reduced competition and diversity exists. However, this trend is not limited to stations. Cable owners have become larger and fewer as well. One company, Tele-Communications, Inc., (TCI) accounts for about 20 percent of all cable subscribers.[14]

Group owners in broadcasting The trend toward **group ownership** (ownership of several stations) by one corporate or individual owner has led to changes in television programming as well as corporate structures. As in other industries, the move to group ownership in the mass media was affected by the potential economic advantage it offered. A group owner can practice economies of scale in most areas of business operations. For example, purchases of items from office supplies to equipment can be carried out by a single purchasing department, which can receive lower prices from sellers by buying in bulk. Functions such as accounting and inventory can also be centralized to avoid redundant tasks at each station. That lowers the per-station operating costs for the group.

Group owners often purchase syndicated programming for many stations at one time. While this practice allows for discounts through volume purchases, it does not always work to the best advantage of each station. This system sometimes imposes a show that may not be entirely appropriate on a station. *The Dukes of Hazzard,* for example, plays better in rural than in urban areas. A group owner with some stations that have a predominantly urban viewership and some that have a large rural audience may impose a conflict on some of the outlets by forcing a show appropriate for one type of station onto the other type. More important, group ownership tends to centralize programming decisions at corporate headquarters instead of at local stations. Since the central administration thinks more in group terms than individual terms, programming decisions may become less locally oriented while the local stations lose some of their local identity.

Another effect of group ownership is the use of the collective economic resources of the group to develop programming. Some station groups have created programs to be shared by all their stations. A program that an individual station cannot afford to produce can be produced by splitting the costs 10 or 12 ways. Shows such as *Entertainment Tonight* (produced by Paramount, Cox Communications, Group W, and Telerep) were developed because these groups wanted a particular kind of show for a particular slot, in this case the access period. Instead of assigning the job to an outside producer, a group can exercise more control over content by doing it in-house. If the show succeeds, the producer's profit accrues directly to the group.

Program cooperatives work in a similar fashion. Several groups may come together to produce a program that will be shared by the members of all the groups involved. One of the players in the cooperative may be a rep firm, agency, or syndication company that wants to create a salable product. *Entertainment Tonight* is a cooperative production.

Cable multiple system operators Broadcast ownership is restricted by law so that no single company can own more than 12 television stations or own stations that cover more than 25 percent of U.S. television households.[15] No such rule exists in the cable industry, and so cable is characterized by bigness. Through direct ownership or partnerships, TCI controls about 9.5 million subscriptions out of approximately 50 million nationwide.

This creates the same economies of scale associated with group ownership. Goods and services are bought in bulk, and so everything is purchased more inexpensively. Perhaps more important, MSOs can diversity their holdings. TCI, for example, owns portions of Turner Broadcasting, Black Entertainment Television, and American Movie Classics, all suppliers of cable networks carried on TCI's more than 100 systems.[16] That gives the company extraordinary control over the networks which seek to be carried on its systems. Without TCI carriage, it would be very difficult to develop a new cable network.

Outside Companies That Provide Programming Advice

Rep firms National station representative companies, or rep firms, have become more of a force in local station programming over the last few years. Their primary function is to represent local stations to national advertisers. Stations usually do not sell all their commercial time locally, and so commercial minutes are left over. Thus, rep firms take over the responsibility for selling the spots that are still available.

Rep firms bring stations with time to sell together with national advertisers that wish to buy time. Through their contacts with advertisers and advertising agencies, rep firms know who is looking for advertising time. They keep computerized spot inventories of the stations they represent and bring those stations to the potential advertiser. The advertiser gets time, the station sells its available time, and the rep firm profits from handling the transaction.

In the competitive field of television, rep firms become fairly well informed about programming issues as they interact with stations all over the country. They see that some stations are programmed better than others are. Such stations draw more viewers and can therefore charge higher rates. Since rep firms' commissions are greater when their client stations get higher ratings, they pass along programming suggestions to weaker stations in hopes of raising audience levels and, consequently, ad rates.

What began as informal suggestions to stations worked well, and it became apparent that more money could be made by both rep firms and stations if stations' ad rates could be increased. Rep firms therefore developed in-house programming departments for their client stations.

Programmers within rep firms examine programs in syndication to determine their potential, keep track of the rights to broadcast programs in each market, and develop specific suggestions and strategies for their client stations. This information helps client stations develop programming strategies and acquire needed programs. Some rep firms provide on-site help by sending a staff member to the station to give advice about the development of programming schedules that will be successful. All the major rep firms provide these kinds of services.

Katz Communications, one of the largest rep firms, provides a multitude of services to its clients. After each sweep period Katz sends its client stations a summary of syndicated programs and their ratings performance around the country. Included in the mailing is a book on comparative schedules for each television market, along with the ratings earned by each program. A programmer may examine how particular shows do against other specific programs in other markets; this can be helpful in formulating strategies for the future.

Katz also sends an analysis of the programs that are coming into syndication for the coming year and a complete listing of all the programs available in the syndication market. This quick reference guide helps the programmer locate specific programs and their suppliers.

Advertising agencies Advertising agencies are positioned between stations and advertisers, but their clients are advertisers rather than stations. Product manufacturers hire an agency to design and distribute advertising. In placing television advertising, agencies examine research reports on the overall viewing of the stations in the market as well as the viewing of particular shows. They try to match the demographic group targeted by a client with stations and shows in the market. Thus, they take the initiative in contacting stations on behalf of their clients—advertisers—whereas rep firms contact advertisers on behalf of their clients—broadcast stations. Both function as middlemen.

Regulation

Regulation is a complicated and cluttered area, but there are three pieces of regulation that have a substantial impact on programming: syndicated exclusivity (syndex), financial interest and syndication (fin-syn), and the prime-time access rule (PTAR). Syndex has an impact on broadcast stations and cable systems, fin-syn is aimed at broadcast networks, and PTAR affects broadcast networks and stations.

Syndex When a local station buys the rights to a program, it expects to be the only station in the market running that program: It has purchased an "exclusive." Syndicators and stations had little trouble with that notion until cable came into many homes. How could the rights to *Family Ties* be exclusive to a station in Detroit or Los Angeles when it was coming into half the homes in those cities on WGN TV, Chicago, via cable? Local broadcasters were upset about having to compete with another outlet for the viewing of a show for which they had expected exclusivity. In 1988 the FCC reinstated **syndicated exclusivity (syndex)** which had been in effect before 1980. Syndex meant that local stations could have their exclusive rights and cable systems bringing in programs conflicting with local rights would have to black out those programs. This rule took effect in 1990.

Fin-syn   The big three networks were very powerful entities in the first decades of television, and they still are. But in early 1971 the FCC adopted the **financial interest and syndication rules (fin-syn),** which prevented the networks from owning the programs they aired. News, sports, and public affairs were exempted because they have little or no syndication value. Networks eventually were allowed fin-syn interest in 3½ hours a week of entertainment programming if they wanted.[17]

At that time, the big three were the most powerful players in the television field and the FCC was concerned that control over programming would give them creative, distribution, and syndication control over virtually all programs. By creating fin-syn, the commission hoped to expand the production community, make it more independent of network influence, and keep networks from controlling programs after those programs left network air.

The rules worked. Production companies expanded, and the syndication market grew in size and importance. Networks purchased the rights to programs from independent producers, and then those program rights reverted to the producers for later syndication. A profitable arm of the business had been lost by the networks, but the production industry had been expanded.

With the growth of cable, home video, and increased numbers of independent stations, net-

work power and viewership dwindled. In 1979 the combined network share of audience of the big three in prime time was 91 percent; by 1991 it had fallen to 62 percent. The networks asked that the rules, scheduled to run out in 1992, be rescinded because networks no longer offered the monopolistic threat they once had and needed the profit center that syndication could offer. They did not get exactly what they wanted from the FCC. While fin-syn rules were relaxed, they were not abolished. Networks could negotiate with producers and participate in syndication in 40 percent of their prime-time schedules. This was a step forward but one that left many questions about the form of their participation in financial interest.

Prime-time access rule   The **prime-time access rule (PTAR)** was designed to give back time that networks had been programming prior to 1971 to local station control. In those days, network schedules began at 7:30 p.m. As with fin-syn, the FCC wanted to prevent the networks from having too much power, in this case over local stations. PTAR limited the networks to 3 hours of prime-time programming daily, except for Sunday, when 4 hours was allowed. The hour from 7 p.m. to 8 p.m. was given back to the stations. Another portion of the rule kept any network programs, including those in syndication, from running on affiliated stations in the 50 largest markets. This was meant to ensure that networks would not get into local schedules through the back door.

The hour before prime time is the most viewed hour outside of prime time and is therefore valuable. The FCC hoped to spur diversity of programming—either local or produced for syndication—with this rule. While not much local production was spurred, the goal of keeping networks out of the access hour was achieved. Happily for independent stations in the 50 largest markets, syndicated network programs were very attractive to viewers; because they could run them when affiliates could not, the independents became more competitive.

SUMMARY

The television audience is large, heterogeneous, and committed. The average household has the television set on 7 hours a day, and the average viewer watches for more than 3 hours a day. Among the basic demographic groups of women 18 and over, men 18 and over, teens, and children, women watch the most television in all age groups except teens. Generally, older people watch the most television and teens watch the least. Another group that watches less television is the upper-income group; income is inversely related to television viewing.

Viewing fluctuates by the time of day. The highest viewing levels are in prime time, and the lowest are in the overnight period. Women constitute two-thirds of the daytime audience, and programs in that daypart are aimed at them. Viewing also varies by time of the year, with higher viewing in the winter and lower viewing in the summer. The size of the television audience changes by the day of the week. Sunday, Monday, and Thursday prime-time programs are heavily viewed. Saturday and Friday prime-time programs are the least viewed.

Among program types there is an overall preference for comedies and movies. Teens and children are strongly drawn to comedies. This is evident in lists of favorite programs for different demographic groups. Women like comedies and dramas, and men like sports.

Viewers tend to spend most of their viewing time with about eight channels. Viewing is passive but promises to become more active as interactive programs draw viewers into various forms of participation ranging from 900 call-in numbers to electronic devices.

Remote control and the VCR have had an effect on viewing habits. Grazing is on the rise, and zapping commercials is part of that phenomenon. VCRs have allowed people to control television schedules and watch programs when it's most convenient for them. For some people part of the tape-viewing process is the practice of zipping through advertisements.

Television programming is a complex art that requires flexibility. A TV programmer needs to be well versed in research methods and interpretation, audiences and their habits, station economics, program acquisition and placement, technical considerations, and community affairs. In some stations the power of the program director has been reduced as general managers have taken a more active role in programming decisions. In some cases there is no PD.

While typical station and cable system organization into departments may create the illusion that each department is separate, these departments are interdependent. The programmer needs to have a sound understanding of the operation of each department.

The basic elements that must be considered in television programming include the makeup of the available audience, what audiences are doing (activities), modularity, and set control. By determining each factor during a given period of time in the programming day, a wise programmer can make better decisions.

An important element in the programming mix is modularity. The audience's desire for modularity waxes and wanes throughout the day. A programmer needs to look at modularity as one of the central elements in scheduling. If modularity is misused, it becomes much harder to attract audiences.

Some of the important forces in television include broadcast networks, cable networks, syndicators, affiliated stations, independent stations, cable systems, broadcast group owners, cable MSOs, rep firms, and advertising agencies. Organizations such as NATPE and ITVA help stations find programming by holding syndicated programming fairs.

Regulation is a factor in the current environment because it is likely to change in the near future. Fin-syn, which has kept networks from producing most of their entertainment programs, is under attack and may be eliminated. Syndex is now in place, and cable systems have to black out programs that interfere with local syndication rights. The prime-time access rule is keeping network programs out of the access hour for now. With lobbying by broadcast and cable forces, these rules may be changed as the FCC reinterprets the state of the television environment.

SUGGESTED READINGS

Compaine, Benjamin M. (ed.): *Anatomy of the Communications Industry: Who Owns the Media?* Knowledge Industry Publications, White Plains, N.Y., 1982.

This book predates much of the merger mania that characterized the 1980s and led to the growth of broadcast station groups and multiple system operators on cable. Its premises are that concentration of ownership in fewer hands stifles creativity and diversity and that big-money control stifles initiative and leads to reduced competition and higher prices for products and services. If anything, these trends have become more pronounced.

Head, Sydney W., and Christopher Sterling: *Broadcasting in America: A Survey of Television and Radio,* 6th ed., Houghton Mifflin, Boston, 1989.

This has been the standard introductory text on electronic media for years. While devoting only one chapter specifically to programming, it lays the groundwork for all electronic media study, including programming. Its bibliography, arranged according to categories, remains one of the best.

Broadcasting

Long the primary industry trade publication, *Broadcasting* has grown to encompass cable and new technologies. It has also expanded its coverage of programming to the point where information relative to broadcast and cable programming can be found weekly.

Electronic Media

A weekly tabloid-sized trade publication, this magazine serves as a competitor to *Broadcasting*. It tends to run briefer stories and assumes less inside knowledge on the part of the reader. It is often recommended to students who are beginning their study of the media, while *Broadcasting* is recommended for the more sophisticated.

Multi-Channel News

This smaller tabloid-style trade publication is the source of choice on cable issues. Its articles are incisive, insightful, and, most important, understandable. It deals with important questions in programming, management, and policy that do not appear often in the general trade publications.

Television Quarterly

TVQ is something like a trade publication and remotely like an academic journal. The subject matter of the articles is timely and is oriented to the real world, unlike most academic journals. However, the articles are longer and more thought out than is typical of the more glib trade press. It provides a way for professionals to expand their reading beyond the weekly trades.

NOTES

1. Kathleen McCarthy, "TV Addicts Not Lured to Shows, but Medium," *American Psychological Association Monitor,* November 1990, p. 42.

2. Paul Klein, "When Men Who Run TV Aren't That Stupid," *New York,* Jan. 25, 1971, pp. 20–29.

3. *Nielsen Report on Television, 1990,* New York, 1991, p. 3.

4. Ibid., p. 8.

5. John P. Robinson, "I Love My TV," *NAB News,* Dec. 3, 1990, p. 17.

6. "Tape Rental Activity," *Video Store,* January 1991, p. 4.

7. Peter Ainslie, "Confronting a Nation of Grazers," *Channels,* September 1988, p. 54.

8. "On the Trail of the Elusive 90's Viewer," *Nielsen Newscast,* Spring 1990, p. 2.

9. Janice Caster, "View from the Ivy Tower," *Channels,* September 1988, p. 61.

10. Stuart Elliott, "Changing Times for Ads," *USA Today,* Aug. 7, 1989, p. 5B.

11. "PD: Almost Extinct?" *Extra/Extra,* Jan. 18, 1990, p. 1; see also "New Careers on Horizon in Programming: But PD's Especially Vulnerable to Changing Roles," *Extra/Extra,* Jan. 16, 1991, p. 38; President Rick Reeves of NATPE sent a letter to general managers on April 15, 1991, allowing them to designate the GM as the voting member of NATPE rather than the program director, as reported in "Power to the GM's," *Broadcasting,* April 22, 1991, p. 8.

12. "NBC Primed to Recapture Prime Time Sweeps," *Broadcasting,* May 13, 1991, p. 27.

13. "NATPE Attendance Down," *Television Digest,* Jan. 14, 1991, p. 6.

14. "Looking for New Sources of Income," *Television Business International,* February 1991, p. 32.

15. Joseph Dominick, Barry Sherman, and Gary Copeland, *Broadcasting/Cable and Beyond,* McGraw-Hill, New York, 1991, p. 405.

16. "The Basic Cable Programming Universe," *Broadcasting,* Jan. 7, 1991, pp. 94–95.

17. "FCC Plots to End Fin-Syn in Three Years," *Broadcasting,* Feb. 25, 1991, p. 19.

CHAPTER 12

Basic Television Programming Strategies

While some of the strategies TV programmers use to attract and hold audiences are similar to those employed in radio, most are specific to television. This chapter will look at some of the basic strategies of programming, particularly audience flow, hammocking, tentpoling, and blocking.

Dayparts and time slots (time periods) and the people who tend to be viewing during those times are also important to programmers. A programmer must take into consideration the characteristics of the slot, including modularity, the type and size of the demographic audiences that are available for each slot, and the kinds of programs that fit most comfortably in each period. Moreover, programmers need to understand the types of viewer appeals that are at work within programs and the ways in which different viewers can be reached.

BASIC STRATEGIES

Flow

Programming strategies revolve around the principle of audience flow or, more simply, flow—the delivery of an audience from one show to the next. Ideally, the viewers of one show should be willing to view the following program if it has a similar appeal.[1] Thus programs with similar styles and appeals tend to be scheduled in groups. For example, *Murphy Brown* flows well into *Love and War* because both are comedies that feature strong female characters, ensemble casts, and literate scripts. They thus tend to appeal to the same kinds of viewers.

Before the widespread adoption of remote control devices, **tuning inertia**—the tendency to stay with a channel when a viewer is already tuned to it—kept many viewers tuned to one channel because it was too much trouble to get up and change stations.[2] Such inertia has been greatly reduced since most viewers today need only press a remote control button to change channels. As a consequence, the reliability of audience flow has been reduced. Still, it is important in scheduling because people are creatures

of habit even when they have access to a remote control.

The strategy in building a daypart schedule is for the first show in the daypart to capture the audience and then flow it to subsequent offerings. Shows aired at 8 p.m., such as *Full House, Fresh Prince of Bel-Air,* and *The Simpsons,* are expected to gather the audience for the evening and deliver as much of it as possible to subsequent programs.

While simple in concept, flow can be difficult to achieve in practice. There are several channels competing for the attention of viewers, along with video games and rented movies for the VCR. Therefore, many strategies are employed to support the goal of flow.

Blocking

Scheduling similar shows during a time period is known as blocking. A block of similar shows[3] can include two to four comedies, filling 1 to 2 hours, or as many as three action/adventure programs (3 hours) (Table 12-1). In 1989, CBS experimented with a full evening schedule (3 hours) of comedy programs during prime time. Six shows—*Major Dad, City, Murphy Brown, Designing Women, Newhart,* and *Doctor, Doctor*—were in the lineup. If the audience likes one show, the programmer assumes that it will like more of the same. Later *City, Newhart,* and *Doctor, Doctor* were canceled, and *The Trials of Rosie O'Neill* (later *Northern Exposure*) was placed at 10 p.m. in a return to more traditional blocking. However, the precedent had been established, and NBC would pick up on the pattern on Saturday nights with the half-hour shows *Carol and Company* and *American Dreamer* from 10 to 11 p.m. Later, Carol Burnett moved to an hour program at CBS and *American Dreamer* was canceled. In the fall of 1992, Fox went a step further by scheduling eight half-hour comedies during Sunday prime time.

Sometimes flow is enhanced by competing schedules. For years *Roseanne* delivered the bulk of its audience to *Coach.* The audience flows forward to later programs not necessarily

TABLE 12-1   Thursday Network Prime-Time Schedule, Winter 1992

Time	ABC	CBS	NBC	Fox
8:00	*Pros and Cons*	*Top Cops*	*Different World*	*Simpsons*
8:30			*Rhythm and Blues*	*Babes*
9:00	*FBI: Untold Stories*	*48 Hours*	*Cheers*	*Beverly Hills 90210*
9:30			*Wings*	
10:00	*Prime Time Live*	*Knot's Landing*	*L.A. Law*	Local

because of *Coach*'s wide appeal but because the other two networks most often program hour shows in the Tuesday time period from 9 p.m. to 10 p.m. and *Coach* does not alienate the audience it has received.

Since tuning in during the middle of an hour show can be disorienting, viewers often watch the next half-hour show in a block because they can see it from the beginning. Thus, competitive decisions by the other networks have been part of the success of *Coach*. A similar event occurred on Thursdays with NBC's lineup (Table 12-1).

Because *Cheers* wins in its time slot, a similar benefit accrues to *Wings,* which sits in the 9:30 slot, where it is opposed by the second halves of the hour shows on the competing networks. ABC flows a mystery into a drama/adventure and then into a seminews program. The demographic is more consistently male than that of any of the other three networks. CBS, by comparison, starts with a show that draws men, moves to a similarly male-oriented program at 9 p.m., and then moves to a specifically female-oriented show at 10 p.m. Fox stays with a broad-based set of shows (as does NBC) with programs that do well with all audiences.

Hammocking

Hammocking is a strategy for bracketing a weaker show between two stronger shows which are called **posts.**[4] Just as a hammock is tied to two strong trees, hammocked shows are supported on both ends by strong programming. *Rhythm and Blues* for example, is hammocked by *A Different World* and *Cheers.* These posts are

the shows that draw tune-in audiences and encourage an audience for the first program to stay tuned for the second by watching the show in between. For half-hour shows, the posts of the hammock are on the hour and the hammocked show is in the weak slot on the half hour. Shows are placed in hammocks because they are perceived as not being sufficiently strong to draw large audiences on their own.

Some hammocked shows become strong enough to be taken out of the hammock and scheduled as posts elsewhere. This was the case with *Perfect Strangers,* which originally was hammocked after *Who's the Boss?* on Tuesday night. It was moved out of the Tuesday night hammock to bring new life to a sagging ABC Friday schedule. After placing additional strong shows in the Friday night lineup, especially *Full House,* ABC dramatically improved its ratings there. *Full House* subsequently moved to lead off ABC's strong Tuesday night lineup, and *A Different World* was moved out of the 8:30 hammock to the 8 post.

While many shows cannot withstand a schedule change because such a change requires audience members to change their viewing habits, *Perfect Strangers* did so without incident. After providing a lead-in for the Friday night schedule at 8 p.m., it was moved to 9 p.m. as a support for the middle of the lineup, while *Full House* was moved into the 8 p.m. slot. Shows are typically scheduled in hammocks at the beginning and the end of their network runs. It is difficult to break viewers' habits and get them to sample new offerings by giving them a trial viewing. Without an established audience, a show must find a way to get viewers' attention. If viewers sample and like what they watch, a show can survive. Otherwise, most shows that receive low audience ratings are canceled. *Chicken Soup,* a comedy on ABC, was scheduled on Tuesday nights after *Roseanne.* Although *Chicken Soup*'s ratings were comparatively high for a hammocked show, it was canceled because it did not hold its lead-in audience or deliver it to the 10 p.m. show.

Coach was moved into the 9:30 p.m. slot and remained there because it delivered its audience to the 10 p.m. post more effectively. Shows can coast in the hammock with somewhat lowered expectations, but when they are perceived as damaging the posts which hold them up instead of simply using them for support, they are removed.

Lead-Ins and Lead-Outs

Lead-ins and **lead-outs** refer to shows that come before and after the show being examined.[5] Typically, the more important show is the lead-in. As we have already noted, *Cosby* served as a very strong lead-in for *A Different World.* It also served for many years as the general lead-in for NBC's Thursday prime-time lineup. A strong show that leads a daypart, usually prime time, is called the **anchor show.**

Lead-ins can make or break a show, and weak lead-ins and anchors can ruin a whole night. When the posts go down, there is no support for the shows in the hammock, but with a lead like *Funniest Home Videos* (for *America's Funniest People*) or *Roseanne* (for *Coach*), weaker shows can survive and even prosper.

Lead-outs are important, but less so than lead-ins. They tend to be more important when normal blocking is being broken, as with early fringe news programs which are usually fronted with comedy and game blocks. In this situation, a lead-out show is used to regather lost audiences. For example, 6 p.m. (5 p.m. in many markets) is typically a news curtain time. A **curtain time** is any time when a viewing change is natural, usually between dayparts but occasionally within a daypart. The news curtain time disrupts the nonmale and younger viewing patterns in early fringe. Women drawn through comedies and afternoon talk shows may be more difficult to draw into news. Children will certainly abandon the newscast despite their viewing of lead-in programs. Thus, the lead-out scheduled in the 7:30 p.m. **access** slot is important because it functions as a magnet to pull lost audience segments back to the station. Having *Wheel of Fortune* in access helps its station regroup lost audience segments after the adult-oriented, upscale news. As news draws off more affluent viewers from the audience, many other viewers switch to alternative comedies on independent stations and cable. A show like *Wheel of Fortune* (often a lead-out for news) helps draw those nonnews viewers back to the station.

Tentpoling

Tentpoling is a strategy through which a very strong show raises the ratings for all the shows near it.[6] If the show is a sufficiently strong draw, people will tune in early to make sure they don't miss it and will be counted in the ratings for the preceding show. Perhaps people will watch that channel as much as an hour earlier to make sure they do not miss their favorite program. Presumably, the audience will flow into the following programs as well, perhaps as many as two shows removed. In the earlier discussion of *Perfect Strangers,* the program was moved to 9 p.m. in part to function as a tentpole rather than as an anchor until other programs could gain strength.

Another example is *Roseanne.* It was tentpoled by ABC at 9 p.m. on Tuesday nights, and this helped the ratings for its lead-in, *The Wonder Years,* and for *Coach* and *thirtysomething,* which followed. *The Wonder Years* gained sufficient strength that it was eventually moved to Wednesday at 8 p.m. to anchor the lineup and improve ABC's Wednesday ratings. *Roseanne* had been a force in the success of *The Wonder Years* by serving as a tentpole for the evening.

A show with that level of success can greatly

influence the prime-time ratings of a network. Later, in syndication, it should have a similar impact during early fringe for a station. *Roseanne* has already helped ABC's Tuesday night lineup, and many stations buying the syndicated rights hope it will work similar wonders during their early fringe periods. Whether a station uses it to lead into news or to compete against news programs on other stations, the show is considered as one that functions effectively as a tentpole.

Counterprogramming

Stations and networks also use the strategy of **counterprogramming,** or scheduling an alternative to the kind of programs the competition is offering.[7] Often counterprogramming involves targeting a secondary demographic group that is not being served by competing stations in a particular time period. While the predominant available demographic group that is in demand by advertisers, such as women age 18 to 54, tends to dictate the programming in a given slot, it is sometimes worthwhile to target an unserved secondary audience segment as long as it is sufficiently large to justify the strategy.

An example of targeting a secondary audience segment occurs in the Saturday and Sunday sports block. The availability of male viewers and their desire to watch sports programming lead all three networks to cater to that demographic group. However, just because male viewers are dominant, that doesn't mean women are not watching TV. While affiliate stations air sports programs aimed at men, independents often run comedies and movies aimed at women and at men who do not like sports. Since the secondary demographic of women is substantial, important, and unserved, counterprogramming in this situation makes sense.

Another example of counterprogramming occurs in early morning and early fringe. The networks go after the primary adult audience with news/magazine programs in the morning and soaps in the afternoon, but there is a sizable secondary audience composed of children. Since

the affiliated stations seem to have a lock on adults and there is no other broadcast competition for this unserved demographic group, independents counterprogram with cartoons and other children's fare. Similarly, during early fringe news blocks on affiliates, independents counterprogram with comedies to draw off younger viewers and adults less interested in news.

Stunting

Stunting, as the name suggests, involves doing something highly unusual. In the case of television, it refers to a special or spectacular program designed to draw audiences away from successful competitors.[8] Since so much of a highly rated program's success depends on habitual viewing, breaking viewers' habits can weaken the power of that juggernaut. Thus, a network will gain the rights to a blockbuster movie or popular rock concert and place it opposite the successful competing program. Audiences are faced with a dilemma: Should they watch this wonderful one-time program or stick with their favorite? Often they go with the stunt because they feel they can always see their favorite program at another time. It will return the next week, or they can watch it in reruns. Of course, the stunting network tries to line up another stunt the following week. After a while it may be able to weaken viewer loyalty to its successful competitor.

However, this success in disrupting loyalty and flow in a competitor comes at a price. Stunts ruin the stunting station's flow as well as that of the competitor. While a network, station, or cable network is stunting, no continuity exists for it in that time period. Thus, it is a destructive tactic designed to hurt a competitor, but it does no good for the stunting organization. The only loyalty this station has bought from the audience is specific to each program. Still, a considerable amount of stunting occurs when (1) a network or station has a very weak program, (2) the competition is especially strong, and/or (3) it is a sweep period and overall ratings are more important than usual.

Stripping

Running the same show in the same slot every weekday is called **stripping**.[9] While stripping is usually associated with weekdays, programs can be stripped 6 or 7 days a week. *Wheel of Fortune* and *Jeopardy* run on Saturday as well as on weekdays. News is stripped all 7 days, while most early fringe programs are stripped on weekdays. Stripping allows people to quickly know what shows are going to be on during a period of time because of the day-to-day consistency of the schedule.

While stripping is a great convenience for viewers, there is a problem for the programmer when failing shows become associated with a time slot. It takes a lot of promotion to get viewers used to a new show in that slot.

Checkerboarding

Checkerboarding is the practice of placing a different show in the same slot each day.[10] A station may broadcast *WKRP in Cincinnati* and *Three's Company* on alternate days during the time period from 11:30 to midnight every day, for instance. Checkerboarding was used in the late-night period by CBS when that network ran action programs including *Sweating Bullets, Dark Justice,* and *Scene of the Crime.*

In 1987 several NBC-owned stations experimented with a checkerboarding strategy during the prime-time access period. Many independents, imitating the larger affiliated stations, did the same. The presumption was that viewers would like the variety of different shows each day at 7:30, just as they liked the daily changes in prime-time shows.

Five comedy shows had been selected for the experiment and were produced in **first-run syndication;** such shows are not intended for a network run but go straight to local stations for airing for the occasion. Although the plan made sense, it was a failure. After a short time, all the cooperating stations resumed stripping game shows and comedies.

STRATEGIES FOR SPECIAL SLOTS

Some times within dayparts are important for special reasons. Access is one of these dayparts. To stem the tide of network control over program content, the FCC implemented the prime-time access rule (PTAR), which limited affiliate stations serving the 50 largest markets to 3 hours of network-originated programming during prime time. Because the networks were programming the period from 7:30 p.m. to 8 p.m. Eastern time, the result was that a half-hour period (7:30 to 8 p.m.) was given back to the affiliates. Since, according to PTAR, stations in the 50 largest markets are not permitted to use network reruns during this period, this rule has allowed a number of independent producers to supply them with first-run syndicated product.

This time period is especially valuable as it attracts more viewers than any daypart except prime time. Because of economic considerations, it was most efficient for stations to fill this period with syndicated programming.

The Access Slot and First-Run Syndication

Programs created for the access slot include *Wheel of Fortune, Entertainment Tonight,* and *A Current Affair.* These slickly produced shows provide local stations with attractive programming at affordable prices and satisfy the letter of PTAR. Independent and affiliated stations outside the 50 largest television markets are not restricted by this rule and can use off-network syndicated programs in access.

Since access has such great economic potential, it is one of the special slots where programming decisions are most important. Competition runs high in this slot because the shows that attract the largest proportion of a large available audience stand to make considerable profits. Since affiliates are barred from using attractive off-network shows in this time period in the 50 largest markets, independents can be much more competitive because of their exemption from PTAR.

News Slots

Since news attracts an upscale audience, advertisers are willing to pay more money to reach those viewers. However, the news slots of noon, 6 p.m., and 11 p.m. are also important for independent stations even though most indies do not program news. These **op-news slots,** so called because independent stations are competing opposite affiliates' news programs, particularly the 6 p.m. and 11 p.m. periods, can be very important in independent stations' programming strategies. The counterprogramming of attractive alternatives to news can hurt an affiliate's news ratings and help an independent's ratings. Since most independents cannot afford to mount major newscasts, competing effectively without such expense is especially attractive. For independent stations, op-news is almost as important as access during the early fringe daypart since HUT is generally high during the news hour.

Strong Slots, Weak Slots

Generally speaking, time periods on the hour are **strong slots** and are central in reaching and holding audiences. With few exceptions, these periods are filled with the best programs, shows capable of attracting viewers and holding them. What an independent or affiliated station programs at 7 p.m. is important because the audience is likely to stay for the 7:30 p.m. offering. It is crucial to have a good 8 p.m. show to lead the prime-time schedule.

There are exceptions to this rule. While hourlong programs should usually be started in strong slots on the hour, the rule can be violated at 11:30 p.m. At that time the audience is in transition and will accept a show that follows the news even though it is an odd length for the slot. It is a time of rapidly decreasing audience, and the normal procedures of programming do not always apply. Late-night talk shows usually schedule the most appealing guests or segments (modules) near the beginning of the broadcast. CBS failed in an attempt to violate this rule in

1990 by placing the 1-hour program *The Flash* in an 8:30 p.m. slot on Thursday evenings. The network quickly returned to a more traditional scheduling strategy later that year.

Weak slots occur on the half hour during most of the programming day. These shows generally depend on the strength of shows in the strong slots to sustain them. The rule holds outside of prime time as well. In early fringe, stations put their best comedies or game shows in strong slots and schedule weaker fare in weak slots. However, the access slot at 7:30 p.m. is a notable exception.

Since the 7:30 slot represents the greatest level of TV viewing outside of prime time, if the programmer has two shows of nearly equal audience appeal, the stronger one will go in access (7:30) and the weaker one at 7 p.m., assuming that there is no network newscast there. This is one of the rare times when the half hour constitutes the stronger slot.

Curtain Times

Curtain times usually start dayparts. As was mentioned earlier, a curtain time simply means that some shift in audience composition or viewing pattern occurs. Each daypart begins with a curtain time and, usually, a new type of programming. These are times when blocking strategies can be changed because audience members are making active decisions about what to watch.

The 4 p.m. slot is such a time. Affiliated stations are completing their soap opera blocks and making the switch to talk and comedy. Thus, at 4 p.m. the programmer doesn't have to be as concerned with the flow of audience from one show to the next. The change from daytime to early fringe represents an audience and modularity shift.

Prime time begins with a curtain time at 8 p.m. Eastern time. This is a daily decision time, not one where viewers stay with the channel they have just viewed. Although curtain times generally coincide with the beginning of a daypart, there is also one within prime time at 10 p.m. It usually signals the end of a comedy block (such as *Cosby* through *Wings,* as illustrated in Table 12-1), which allows for a change to drama, such as *L.A. Law* in NBC's Thursday lineup and *Northern Exposure* on CBS on Mondays.

Independents take advantage of this curtain time in some markets in the Eastern and Pacific time zones by placing newscasts there. Since prime time in those time zones ends at the relatively late hour of 11 p.m., many viewers may choose to get their news an hour earlier, at the 10 curtain time, by watching the news on an independent station. In Atlanta, the independent WGNX TV uses the slogan "All the news you need at a time you really want" to draw attention to the advantages of having one's information needs met early, allowing viewers to get to bed a little sooner. Opposing action/adventure and drama with weakly flowed leads is less difficult than going against more strongly flowed comedies.

APPEALS AND PROGRAMMING

Program appeals represent another set of variables that are used in selecting and scheduling programs. They can be used as part of an overall strategy to promote flow. If the appeals in a given block of programs are consistent, the audience drawn to those programs will be more consistent. Understanding the audience appeal of a program is critical in program promotion. When the tastes of the audience the show reaches are known, more focused promotions can be devised.

Appeals to Specific Demographic Groups

In years past, when the broadcast networks controlled the viewing choices of more than 90 percent of the available audience on any given evening, each show tried to gather as big a share of that audience as possible. As cable networks have matured, home video has spread, and independents have increased in number, the combined broadcast network audience has shrunk to 62 percent. When cable channels such as CNN and ESPN began laying claim to specific audience segments, such as men, the networks followed suit and began to offer shows tailored to the tastes of special groups.

Appeals to upscale viewers The groups most desired by advertisers are the upscale consumers age 18 to 49 and 25 to 54, and many network shows are designed to appeal to that aggregation. For example, Fox's *90210,* about the travails of life for young people, found a niche among the affluent young who identified with the characters and their problems. They felt the show's situations paralleled circumstances in their own lives. Not surprisingly, the show succeeded in reaching its intended audience.

In a similar vein, *The Wonder Years* is a reenactment of the youth of today's baby boom generation. Ask a consistent viewer of the show what he or she thinks is good about it and you are likely to hear how the show reminds that person of a warm time years back; this is exactly what the show is intended to do.

Appeals to downscale viewers There are other demographic groups to be targeted as well. Stations try to appeal to everyone in the audience with at least one program during the week. This defines the station's total viewer reach, which is important to national advertisers looking for programs with wide appeal. An important point to remember is that **downscale audiences** watch TV more than anyone else does.

Wrestling, for example, consistently draws large audiences, as the many *Wrestlemania* events have shown. There are several wrestling shows to choose from almost every day. Action/adventure programs attract younger, less educated, and less affluent viewers too.

Many game shows, such as *Wheel of Fortune,* also reach an audience that is older, more downscale, and female. That's acceptable to advertisers because of the size of the audience. All things being equal, shows aimed at upscale audiences can get by with somewhat smaller audiences because the profile of the audience is so appealing to advertisers. Downscale shows need relatively larger audiences to survive. Whereas the people at Mercedes-Benz like the specificity of the upscale audience for a golf tournament, downscale product representatives are drawn to wrestling and auto racing, where the desired audiences tend to appear in efficient clusters. It's all a matter of matching the audience to the product through the vehicle of the show (Box 12-1).

THE DEMAND FOR MORE PROGRAMS

The trend in the early 1990s is toward more stations and cable services and longer programming days. The amount of programming required by the television industry becomes a mathematical problem: How many hours of programming does it take to supply all these stations for a year? The result is that almost everything will be showing somewhere. Movies from the 1930s still grace the screen, and Beaver Cleaver will forever be 9 years old.

Cable Networks

Cable services have increased the pressure on available product, particularly when they have adopted daypart strategies that are similar to those of broadcast stations in many respects.

Lifetime, USA, and other cable networks run hours of off-network and other syndicated programming. Shows such as *The Days and Nights of Molly Dodd,* canceled by the networks, are sometimes revived by cable channels in need of fresh product. Cable networks have been aggressively seeking syndicated product and have gathered *Moonlighting, Cagney and Lacey, Murder She Wrote, Miami Vice,* and *L.A. Law.*

Repetition of Programs

There is a lot of repetition of shows on broadcast and cable channels and an increasing demand for television product. Shows with only a handful of episodes, such as *Bosom Buddies* and *Private Benjamin,* show up on broadcast stations' schedules, if only for a few months. Arts and Entertainment picked up *Buffalo Bill* despite its relatively few episodes. Very little product is considered "not good enough." Programmers must get maximum mileage out of the programs they have because it is becoming increasingly difficult to acquire the desired product.

The parsimony principle   This repetition gives rise to the **parsimony principle,** which holds that everything must be used as effectively and efficiently as possible.

**BOX 12-1
APPEALS TO
DEMOGRAPHIC
GROUPS**

TEENS PREFER SITCOMS

A 1988 study of the viewing habits of teenagers by Teenage Research Unlimited revealed some specific trends. Primarily, teens prefer to laugh. Of the top 10 shows among teens, 9 were comedies. The tenth, *Moonlighting,* has a distinct comic flair. Of the top 10 shows, NBC aired 7 and ABC aired 3. CBS had none in the top 10, which indicates that network's older demographic.

The 10 shows were: *Cosby, Family Ties, Moonlighting, Growing Pains, Who's the Boss?, Cheers, Facts of Life, Golden Girls, Night Court,* and *Alf.* Offbeat shows such as *Late Night with David Letterman* and *Saturday Night Live* also scored well with teenagers.

Action/adventure shows received negative responses, and soap operas received the least positive results. Interestingly, television ranked third behind radio listening and compact disc listening as a preferred form of media entertainment.

SOURCE: Teenage Research Unlimited, *1989 Survey of Television Viewing.*   ■

We see that principle applied in some portions of shows, such as the opening segment that is used in each episode to present the characters, program title, and introductory credits. These segments are created once and then run forever. It is not economically sound to create a new opening each week when that minute of content can be repeated weekly. In fact, openings generally run for years with only modest changes.

Of course, reruns are used until the show burns out, but even then, after a few months' (or years') "rest," the show can come back for another round of viewing. Audiences forget some of the material after episodes have been rested for a while and will return to watch subsequent showings, and new groups of people have grown into the program's target demographic, making it new for them. That has happened with older shows such as *The Honeymooners* and *George Burns and Gracie Allen.* Syndicators know that shows can be rested for a period of time and brought back later for another series of plays. Thus, programs from *The Partridge Family* to *One Day at a Time* are resurrected in cycles and replayed.

Programming Needs of Specialized Audiences

The television audience used to be characterized as large and heterogeneous, but that notion is breaking down. Advertisers are seeking more clearly defined audiences made up of persons who are potential consumers of their products. Thus, it is more efficient to reach these people without paying for others who are much less likely to purchase a product. Advertising messages for household cleaners reach their intended audiences more efficiently during the day when the predominant audience is women because that audience makes the most purchases of such products. While these products could be advertised in prime time, when working women can be more effectively reached, the viewership would include many men. Some of the desired audience would be contacted, but the advertiser would be paying for exposures of the advertisement to people who do not or cannot use the product (waste exposures).

Narrowcasting   Advertising, then, has been a contributor to the growing specialization of television. Cable executives quickly learned that specialized channels, like format radio, attract specific audiences that can be sold to advertisers. This phenomenon has been labeled narrowcasting. This concept, when carried out through such program services as the Science Fiction Channel (cable), has been called **slivercasting.** The only question involved in the move to narrowcasting is, How far can it go?

Cable networks such as ESPN have carved out a narrowcasting niche and delivered a salable audience to advertisers. CNN, Nickelodeon, and many others have done the same. As the narrowcasting trend has grown among cable services, it has started to affect network television. Programs such as *The Golden Girls* and *Murder She Wrote* had primary appeals to more specific audiences than did most network shows. Their success led to other programs aimed at smaller audience segments, such as *48 Hours* and *Doogie Howser, M.D.*

Narrowcasting may have had its origin at the network level at ABC. In the 1960s, ABC, running third in the ratings, began consciously courting the youth audience by promoting it to advertisers and offering programs tailored to its tastes.

The limits of narrowcasting   Television is an expensive medium. The cost of equipment and satellite time is the same whether the buyer is a network or a mom-and-pop operation. There is a limit to how much money can be generated by a narrow audience. That figure must square with the cost of being on the air. Overly fragmented services run the risk of trying to pay off multi-million-dollar investments with the lower revenues that can be generated through narrowcasting's advertising rates.

Regardless, the advent of narrowly defined program services has given viewers much more content diversity. The positive audience response suggests that the trend will continue as long as the economics and advertiser support are sufficient. The *Smithsonian* magazine will be advertised on the Discovery Channel but not on *Growing Pains.*

SUMMARY

Many strategies are applied to scheduling programs, but most of them revolve around flow. If audiences cannot be effectively delivered from one program to the next, the station or network loses a vital opportunity to bring viewers to subsequent shows. The primary strategies used to promote flow include blocking, hammocking, posting, lead-ins and lead-outs, tentpoling, counterprogramming, stunting, and stripping.

Some important time periods are programmed in particular ways. Strong slots occur on the hour and tend to hold post shows and tentpoles. Weak slots usually occur on the half hours and contain hammocked programs. There are special time slots which have to be programmed very carefully, including access, op-news, and curtain times.

The parsimony principle is important in television. With so much pressure on product, it is necessary to get the maximum use out of each piece of programming that is available. Thus, repeating programs for as long as audiences will watch is standard procedure.

As the competition for audiences has increased, programmers have begun to target more specific audiences, particularly those most desired by advertisers. Thus, programs can survive and succeed without huge audiences as long as they deliver targeted audiences. While most noticeable on cable, this kind of audience targeting has been showing up on the broadcast networks in shows such as *The Wonder Years*.

SUGGESTED READINGS

Goodhardt, G. J., A. C. Ehrenberg, and M. A. Collins: *The Television Audience,* Saxon House, Lexington, Mass., 1975.
This is the definitive work about scheduling strategies and the ways in which audiences react to them. Flow is well explained, along with techniques derived from flow, such as lead-ins and lead-outs. While it places more attention on tuning inertia effects than is relevant in today's remote control environment, it is still the first book to read on the subject of programming strategies.

Rose, Brian G. (ed.): *TV Genres: A Handbook and Reference Guide,* Greenwood Press, Westport, Conn., 1985.
Rose covers all the genres that have ever been used on television, giving the reader information about them and about their roots (often in film) as well.

Variety
This trade publication is known among members of the public for its concentration on the film industry, but some of the best day-to-day coverage of the television industry and its practices is printed in its pages. Essays on television are also first rate.

The Journal of Popular Film and Television
While considered a more academic journal, *JPFT* also covers issues related to programming television. The articles are well written and edited, deal with topics of general interest, and are understandable to the casual reader.

NOTES

1. Sydney W. Head and Christopher H. Sterling, *Broadcasting in America,* 5th ed., Houghton Mifflin, Boston, 1987, p. 303.

2. Ibid., p. 392.

3. Ibid., p. 303.

4. Ibid.

5. Ibid.

6. Richard Weiner, *Webster's New World Dictionary of Media and Communications,* Webster's New World, New York, 1990, p. 484.

7. Head, op. cit., p. 303.

8. Ibid.

9. Ibid.

10. Weiner, op. cit., p. 87.

CHAPTER 13

The Syndication Marketplace

KEY TERMS AND CONCEPTS

Amortization
Barter
Block Booking
Cash Syndication
Cash plus Barter
Colorization
Cooperative Productions
Exclusivity
First-Run Syndication
Foreign Production
Incumbents

Off-Network
  Syndication
Station Group
  Production
Stripping
Syndication
Warehousing
Weeklies

An independent station with no network to supply content for most of its air time is always on the alert for new product. A network affiliate also needs to fill time in the morning, in early fringe, and late at night. Exacerbating the competition for programs, cable networks such as Lifetime and USA have become increasingly aggressive players in the syndication market, searching for product with everyone else. This chapter will look at the types of syndication, how product is acquired, how programs are selected with specific goals in mind, and how negotiations are carried out with syndicators. It will also examine financial practices and show how profit and loss can be projected and measured for each show.

Acquiring the rights to a product does not mean physical ownership; it is more analogous to renting. The buyer (station, broadcast network, or cable network) pays for the right to air programs a certain number of times over a specified period. For example, a station or cable network buys the rights to *America's Funniest Home Videos* for 3 years and can run each episode a negotiated number of times during that period. When the rights run out because 3 years have passed or because the plays have been used up, the contract ends. The station or network has in effect rented the use of the program and returned it as promised. If another run is desired, a new price must be negotiated and the process starts again.

TYPES OF SYNDICATED PROGRAMS

Syndicated series, movies, and specials come from a variety of sources. The two most common program sources are off-network syndication and first-run syndication. Other forms of syndication include local, station group productions, cooperative, and foreign.

Off-Network Syndication

As the name implies, **off-network syndication** involves shows that were first aired on one of the broadcast networks. Increasingly, this product is also generated by cable networks as their original productions expand. Off-network syndication represents the greatest amount of available product because it goes back to the early days of television. Shows such as *Burns and Allen* and *I Love Lucy* from the 1950s still play on television sets across the country.

The good side of off-network product is its quantity; the bad side is that much of it has been burned out over the years. Just as hit songs burn out with repeated play, so do television programs. While older shows have nostalgic value to older viewers and offer novelty appeal to younger ones, they do not generally attract large audiences. Still, the right program, appealing to the right audience and available at the right price, can prove profitable. Much of this product does not air on stations but is carried on cable networks. Nickelodeon, for instance, carries the 1960s series *Get Smart* and *Dragnet*. The Arts and Entertainment Network has carried the 1950s CBS documentary series *World War I* and the former CBS News series *The 20th Century*. Most of the off-network product in which stations are interested, however, is more recent.

Shows have shorter life spans now than they did in past years. There may never be another *Gunsmoke* with a 20-year backlog of shows or even another *M*A*S*H* with 260 episodes. The smaller inventory of episodes in many recent off-network series causes them to burn out faster in syndication because each episode is repeated more frequently.

Packaging off-network shows for syndication The available episodes of off-network series are sold as a package to a station or cable network in each television market. The ideal off-network show has 130 episodes. Since there are 260 weekdays in a year, a show that is stripped 5 days a week requires exactly two runs to get through a year. Since many contracts call for six runs within 3 years, the math works nicely. Reality intervenes, however, and gaps are created. Many shows have only 90 or 100 episodes. Thus, stripping them means that filler is required for a certain number of weeks every year. The station can, of course, move straight through the runs and end the contract early, but programmers are increasingly reluctant to show first-rate product for which they have paid high rates in the summer, when audiences are down by up to a third and advertising rates fall accordingly.

Series with more than 130 episodes, an increasingly rare breed, allow a certain number of options to stations or cable networks that plan to run them out over the usual 3 years. For example, extra episodes can be placed where needed either as filler or to achieve a specific goal. One such goal might be to save the episodes of a very popular show by pulling it during the summer and substituting the extra episodes of a less attractive program during that time, when audiences are smaller and less advertising revenue is possible.

Usually a series needs to have 100 episodes or more to be placed on the market so that the episodes do not have to be repeated so frequently, but there are exceptions to this standard. Although only 79 episodes are available, *Star Trek* is in a class of its own in regard to continuing popularity. In the case of *Bosom Buddies,* both stars, Tom Hanks and Peter Scolari, have gone on to other successes, Hanks in films and Scolari in *Newhart* and other television projects. The show has been well received by viewers even though its network run consisted of only 36 episodes, and it has enjoyed some success in syndication. Of course, it requires frequent repeating since there are enough episodes to cover just over 7 weeks if it is stripped, and so it burns out quickly. Such programs with relatively few episodes and therefore less promising syndication prospects are called **short runs.** Still, many of these shows are used to fill in scheduling holes, especially in the summer, when viewing is down and stations do not want to use up the rights to their most attractive and expensive syndicated product.

Cable networks have been purchasing short-run product and using it with some success. The Arts and Entertainment Network has purchased the rights to two Dabney Coleman series, *The Slap Maxwell Story* and *Buffalo Bill.*

First-Run Syndication

Some series are not produced with network runs in mind; their producers offer the original episodes to stations. First-run syndication refers to a product that appears for the first time in syndication. This creates economic advantages and disadvantages for both syndicators and purchasers.

A network show such as *Empty Nest* typically costs about $500,000 per episode to produce, and the network pays about $350,000 in license fees for its two runs of each episode. Before syndication, then, the producers have a debt of $150,000 for each episode produced; that debt is wiped out when the program is sold in syndication. But what if there was no network run with the accompanying network financial backing to offset production costs? To make a profit, the producer would have to operate without that network capital of $350,000 per episode and the show would have to be produced for about $150,000 per episode, a figure that would allow profitability in first-run syndication.

Can an episodic show be produced for $150,000 an episode? Yes. Can first-rate, slick network-level programming be produced for that price? No. The stars of first-run comedies, for example, are not at the peaks of their careers, as is typical of network series. Often they are secondary players on other network programs. The professionals needed for the production, from directors to lighting coordinators, aren't from among those working on the top network shows. The sets and writing are not usually of network quality. Such concessions are made in the interest of keeping costs down, and they tend to show in the final product.

Usually less is expected of a first-run episodic product because its quality is perceived as being lower, and first-run ratings consistently lag behind off-network ratings, especially for comedy programs. Therefore, off-network shows are usually placed in the critical positions: news lead, opposite the news, and access. A first-run comedy is placed in the less important periods; *Out of this World* and *Small Wonder* are examples.

Some first-run programs are very successful and find their way to the better time slots in station schedules. These programs tend not to be comedies but game and "reality" shows. In the case of game shows, *Wheel of Fortune* and *Jeopardy* have been at the top of syndicated ratings lists for years, and they are first-run shows. First-run reality shows such as *A Current Affair* have performed well in early fringe slots.[1]

Game shows   Game shows require only one set and very few paid performers. The prizes given away are often donated; in fact, some manufacturers pay for on-air product mention in addition to donating their products. Thus, the show can be produced more inexpensively. This means that stations can acquire it for a lower price so that the program does not have to win high ratings to be profitable. When high ratings are achieved, the show is even more profitable for the station and the distributor. This has been the case with *Wheel of Fortune* and *Jeopardy,* in which inexpensive production has been married to high ratings.

Talk shows   Other first-run economic successes have occurred with talk and reality programming. Oprah Winfrey, Phil Donahue, and Geraldo Rivera have been able to parlay likable personalities and discussions of provocative subjects into substantial audiences, especially in the morning and early afternoon. Again, ratings expectations are lower in these time slots because of the smaller available audiences, and talk shows are very inexpensive to produce. All that is needed is one set, a studio audience, and a host. Production is simple, and the host is the only talent cost factor. As with game shows, if the host is well received and large numbers of people watch, the profits can be astronomical. Savings in talent and other personnel allow for spending on high-quality graphics and other production elements which give the finished show a better look.

Reality programs   Reality programs—shows that are based on real people and situations but have an entertainment appeal at least equal to their information value—have caught on in recent years. Shows such as *A Current Affair* and *People's Court* have found increasingly large audiences and have spurred imitators. Because they often use file footage and reenactments, they can be put together inexpensively. Like first-run game and talk shows, they can make sizable profits while allowing resources to be allocated to elements that enhance the show's look.[2]

For the buyer, then, first-run product offers some advantages. These shows can succeed with smaller audiences, and if the audiences grow, so does profitability. The risks are smaller as a result of lower budgets, and the profit potential can be considerable.

HOW SYNDICATION IS ORGANIZED

Most contracts for off-network television programs stipulate six runs of each episode over a period of 3 years. When a series does not have the requisite 130 episodes to allow two runs in a 260-weekday year, it is usually rested for the necessary number of days to make the contract come out right in terms of runs and years. Stations tend to rest their first-rate shows during the summer months.

Repeatability

First-run syndication game and reality shows are rarely repeated. Viewers want fresh episodes of game shows such as *Wheel of Fortune* and *Jeopardy,* whereas episodes of talk shows such as *Donahue* and *Oprah Winfrey* bear some repeating outside of sweeps and during the summer. Consequently, most deals for episodes call for one play with an occasional rerun. That way, the station knows its cost for each run and can determine the profitability of the show on a day-by-day basis by comparing cost to ad revenues without having to figure in the less predictable viewership projections based on second and third airings of episodes.

This practice is specific to program type, though. Episodic first-run programs repeat in the same ways off-network shows do. When the first-run comedy *Small Wonder* built up a sufficient number of episodes, it was made available for stripping. The same happened with *Star Trek: The Next Generation.* The stations which carried the first runs got the first option to air the strips.

Strong Shows to Strong Stations

Financial realities lead to some predictable station-syndicator relationships. For one thing, strong shows go to strong stations. Since the best product commands the highest prices and since strong stations are in the best position to pay higher prices, the most successful stations tend to end up with the best shows.

The exception, especially with an off-network product, occurs when an independent station purposely takes a loss in acquiring an attractive series. In this case the station is required to pay more for a show than it can realize in ad revenues. This is done to establish the station as a serious player and enhance its image with viewers. This practice has been especially prevalent in acquiring the rights to broadcast *The Cosby Show* and *Cheers,* two series that had especially strong potential when they were first offered in syndication.

First-run shows to affiliates The most successful first-run shows run almost exclusively on affiliated stations. The syndicator has to find the best station for the product to enhance profits and because new contracts are negotiated on a year-to-year basis. If the show is successful, the syndicator can reap the rewards more quickly. Thus, for shows such as *A Current Affair* and *Jeopardy,* the most desirable buyer is a strong affiliated station that can charge high ad rates and pay high license fees. When *Geraldo* was first being offered in syndication, the representatives did not seek out independent stations. Therefore, most of the show's **clearances** (the space cleared for a show on a station's schedule) were made by affil-

iates. Of course, with a less successful or less promising show, a wider range of stations can gain access to the program.

Short runs In the case of less successful shows, the syndicator helps the station by providing **back end distribution.** This means that the syndicator will allow more runs of each episode than normal to allow the station to fill gaps in the summer schedule or unexpected spaces created by cancellations of sporting events. Syndicators who are peddling series, such as *Greatest American Hero* or *Private Benjamin,* that have few episodes can enhance their salability by giving up more plays of each episode than the station would normally get.

Time Slot

Another factor in a syndication deal is the time period in which the show will run. Syndicators press for the best time slots for their shows when they make deals with stations. Naturally, they are more interested in a station that wants to run a show in early fringe (higher ad rates and thus greater license fees) than in one that has targeted late night for the product. Increasingly, deals are written with time slots or general dayparts specified.[3]

Tier deals Syndicators and stations are signing **tier deals** with greater frequency. Under this arrangement, the time slot is not set in the deal but a number of time slots are specified, each with a price which reflects the value of that slot. If one of the slots is the access period, the figure associated with that slot is higher; for late night, the rate is lower. As many as five time slots may be written into the deal. For example, in a tier deal for *Entertainment Tonight,* a station may pay $1000 a day for 4 p.m., $1500 a day for 6 p.m., $2000 for access, $1500 for 11 p.m., and $750 for 1 a.m. Obviously, the syndicator prefers the access slot and, depending on the program's ratings success, may be able to force the issue. Since a program that performs better also works to the advantage of the station, better programs end up in better time positions. The problem for the buyer is that no one can be sure how a program will perform and no one wants to be locked into access with a weak program. Thus, the tier deal works to the programmer's advantage because it allows an examination of the program and then a move to a better slot.[4]

This allows the programmer maximum flexibility because he or she can wait until the last minute before deciding where the show will best serve the station's programming needs. It is, however, a nightmare for the syndicator, who cannot estimate how much revenue a show will generate until each station has decided on that program's placement. Naturally, such deals are far more popular with stations than with syndicators, but they help syndicators complete sales that might not otherwise be made. By allowing stations flexibility, they make for a certain sale, even if at a potentially lower price.

Exclusivity

Exclusivity means that only one station in any market has the right to air a program or movie. In earlier days some cable systems imported distant signals through a microwave link. One such station was WTCG TV, later WTBS, Atlanta, the first independent station to have its signal distributed nationally by satellite, but the mixing of programs with markets was minimal. This practice of importing distant signals was not a major problem until the days of broadcast satellites, which allowed any signal to be imported from anywhere. With superstations and multitudinous cable networks that program much as local stations do, one might see *Family Ties,* which the local station bought in good faith, come into the market on a distant signal to compete against the local station. With 60 percent of American homes wired for cable, the potential problems were enormous.

If, hypothetically, the syndicator that sold *Family Ties* to the station also sold it to superstation WGN TV, Chicago, which is carried on cable systems in the market, the local station would have to compete against its own show.

Viewers don't care which channel brings them the show of their choice. Therefore, when there is no exclusivity in the market, the local station suffers the economic consequences associated with having viewers watch the show on another outlet; this translates to a ratings loss that lowers advertising rates.

A move to correct this problem began in 1988 and became a reality in 1990 with the introduction of syndex. When an out-of-market station carried on a local cable system runs a show, the cable operator is required to black out its presentation on the cable channel. Of course, this complicates the operation of cable companies and inconveniences viewers, who are unable to tune to programs listed in the local television listings, but it does protect exclusivity in the local market.

Rather than live with blank screens, cable operators looked for inexpensive programming, such as old black-and-white comedies, that could be substituted for programs blacked out because of exclusivity. At the same time, superstation WTBS was looking for "syndex-proof" programming, something that would not be duplicated in the local market. Much of the problem was obviated by original programming such as sports and by movie packages not available to local stations. Since WTBS had purchased MGM movies, it was able to make itself nearly syndex-proof.

FORMS OF SYNDICATION ACQUISITION

There are three ways to acquire product: cash, barter, and cash plus barter. All product can be obtained through one of these means.

Cash

A **cash deal** is the most straightforward means of product acquisition. The syndicator offers for sale the exclusive rights for airing a show to one station in each market. A deal is struck by placing a price on each episode in the package of the available episodes of the show.

Once the syndicator and the station agree on a price, the cost per episode is multiplied by the number of episodes in the package to arrive at a contract price. If a station agrees to pay $10,000 per episode for *Hunter* and gets 120 episodes, the contract price is $10,000 × 120, or $1.2 million. While this is a lot of money, the station gets six plays of each episode over a period of 3 years. This provides about 12 minutes of advertising time in each of the six plays of each episode, for a total of 72 minutes of ads per episode, or 144 30-second ad slots. If these slots were sold for an average price of $250, the station or cable network would realize 144 × $125, or $18,000 in revenues per episode, far more than the $10,000 it paid. If the program director manages to get such a show at a good price, it may start to return a profit in the second run. Sometimes it takes longer to reach profitability. If a station pays too much or the show is not well received, the station may end up taking a loss.

In making cash deals, programmers are betting that the sales staff can sell the ad slots at a high enough rate to ensure a profit over the number of runs being purchased. The programmer wants the show for as little money as possible in order to maximize profits, and syndicators want to sell it for the highest rates possible for the same reason. Consequently, these deals are characterized by negotiation and compromise.

Example of a cash deal Let's use *Who's the Boss?* as a hypothetical example of a cash deal. The syndicator delivers 130 episodes of the show at six plays per episode with 6^1/$_2$ minutes of ad time, or thirteen 30-second spots, per episode. For our purposes, we will count on selling 10 of the 13 spots in each episode during each play. The first play of each episode, when the show is fresh, will draw the best audiences and allow the placing of the program in one of the better time slots, allowing the station to charge the highest advertising rates (Table 13-1). As each episode is repeated again and again over time, viewers will be less inclined to watch and the value of the show will decrease.

That is called show burnout. Shows burn out at different rates, and those rates cannot be predicted accurately. It is reasonable to assume, though, that the sixth play will be seen by the smallest audience. The programmer must therefore be sure that a profit can be made as early as possible, preferably before the fourth play.

Projecting ads and audiences The programmer must determine the number of ads that can be sold during the time slot planned for a show, the size of the projected audience, and the projected ad revenues. These calculations will yield the potential income for the first run of each episode.

Next, the programmer must assume a falloff

TABLE 13-1 A Typical Cash Deal: *Who's the Boss?* at $10,000 per Episode for 6 Plays with 10 Spots Sold per Play

Run	Cost, $	Rating	Spot Rate, $	Income, $	+/−, $
1	4,000 (40%)	4.4	300	3,000	−1,000
2	3,000 (30%)	4.0	275	2,750	− 250
3	2,000 (20%)	3.6	250	2,500	+ 500
4	500 (5%)	3.2	225	2,250	+1,750
5	500 (5%)	2.8	200	2,000	+1,500
6	0	2.4	175	1,750	+1,750
	Total 10,000			**14,250**	**+4,250**

Profit = $14,250 (income) − $10,000 (cost) = $4250 per episode in audience of 10 to 20 percent for the second run and recompute the revenues. The combined revenue estimates for the first and second runs often constitute the figure used in a purchase offer for each episode of the show. The revenue from the last four runs can be projected as profit, while that from the first two runs covers the purchase price.

Such a luxury is not always possible. Returning to the example of *Who's the Boss?*, we see that the total revenues for the first two runs were $3000 plus $2750. By this reckoning, the programmer should have offered $5750 per episode for the program, but its popularity forced the station to spend more money than it would have liked. Even so, the station was able to earn more in ad revenues than it paid for the episodes.

Choosing slots A popular off-network show such as *Who's the Boss?* may command high prices, forcing placement in early fringe to generate the best revenues. However, the show may burn out more quickly than expected, and by the end of its second run it may actually be hurting the rest of the early fringe schedule because of audience drop-off. At that point it can be moved to early morning or late night. Those times have smaller audiences and produce lower revenues.

A programmer who has overpaid for a show by projecting six runs at early fringe rates has made a serious miscalculation. The most conservative stations try to offer only the revenues of the first run as the buying price as a hedge against such an occurrence. Of course, syndicators also know what advertising rates their customers can charge in the various dayparts and can calculate a show's true value to a station or cable network.

Program environment Another factor in determining a purchase price is the program environment: What other shows will surround this product? The surrounding programs' strengths and weaknesses will affect the new program's chances of success. Leading *Who's the Boss?*

with *Doogie Howser, M.D.* will help it to generate better ratings than would be the case if it were led by a lesser program.

Selling the program The track record of a station's sales staff is another important issue. If they have not sold out shows in the past, it would not be prudent to suppose that they can sell out *Who's the Boss?* just because it's a big title. In a less successful station, the programmer will have to project lower sales than in the 10 spots we used in order to be protected from financial calamity.

Cash, then, is the straight acquisition of the rights to a series of episodes to be played a set number of times each. At the end of the typical contract, the program rights return to the syndicator and can be resold in the market. The station which ran the show first, the incumbent, will almost always be contacted first for renewal. If a price for the second set of runs can be agreed on, the show will stay on that station. If the incumbent station does not want the product or won't pay what the syndicator asks, the show will be offered to other stations.

Barter

Barter, as the name implies, involves a trade. In a barter deal, the syndicator trades episodes of a show for a specified number of local advertising spots in each episode. The syndicator then sells those spots to national advertisers, agencies, or other interested parties. In this case, the syndicator has set up a kind of **ad hoc network** made up of the stations running the show.[5]

Barter deals are generally based on about 6½ minutes of advertising per half hour, although starting in about 1990, 7 minutes per half hour appeared. If the show is especially appealing, the split may be 3 minutes national (the syndicator's spots) and 3½ minutes local (the station's spots).

In industry shorthand, that would be 3N/3½L. If the show is less appealing and the syndicator has more trouble sparking interest, the deal may be 2N/4½L. That will keep more spots (called inventory or **avails** for availabilities until sold) under the station's control and allow for more revenue production through sales.

Advantages of barter

Low Risk Why would a station give up its inventory to a syndicator? First, there is no financial risk to the station. Since the show is free, all the spots that are sold represent above-cost revenue. If the station is having trouble competing with stronger stations for the better cash shows, barter can be very attractive. Also, if the station is new, is low on cash, or has a less effective sales force, barter can be an attractive alternative. Even a stronger affiliate may be interested in some barter product for weak times (late mornings on weekends and late at night) because sales may lag there.

Advertiser Potential As the number of stations and competition for advertising revenue from cable increase, more competitors are trying to corral the same local advertisers. Only so much ad revenue can be found in any market. At the same time, the networks tend to sell out much of their inventory to national companies with large advertising budgets. That leaves some advertisers looking for national advertising time on television with limited options for finding it at the traditional network level.[6] That's where barter can bring the two interested groups—national advertisers and local stations—together. Syndicators are in touch with the big advertising agencies or deal with third-party companies which are. Thus, they have more contact with national advertisers than do local stations and can sell avails that a local station may have a problem moving. Often a syndication company has no sales division. In this case it turns the job over, for a fee, to a company that specializes in selling barter spots.

The barter program may simply be the best program available to fit the needs of a station or cable network that is seeking a product. Increasing numbers of high-quality programs are going to barter distribution, a trend that hit its stride in

1991, when *Designing Women* was released in barter.

Network factors in barter There is another reason for the rise of barter: the decline of network ratings. Networks have not delivered the level of ratings for blockbuster events that they did in the past. The 1988 Summer Olympics fell short of expectations as did the $100 million epic miniseries *War and Remembrance.* As network ratings have declined, sponsors have become increasingly reluctant to depend on network viewer delivery. In barter syndication, they usually find a deal in which they can cover most of the country and get some guarantee on audience size that is tied to spot cost.

Barter content Companies are understandably concerned about the themes of the shows in which their ads appear. While Geraldo Rivera's 1988 special about Satanism drew huge audiences, not all the advertising spots were sold. The material was graphic, and both Rivera and NBC came under fire for presenting sensationalistic material. Also, sexual scenes on daytime soap operas have become increasingly explicit and the language has become more coarse.

Some advertisers have become more sensitive to content and look for shows which they feel provide an attractive context for their messages. Since prime-time and daytime ad opportunities are finite and not all shows are considered appropriate, some advertisers have turned to the barter syndication market. A barter spot on the *Wonder Years* or *Full House* will not sully an advertiser's image, as might one placed in a program with sensationalistic content.

Disadvantages of barter The downside of barter is that it removes inventory control from the station. This is especially vexing for more successful stations. Stations that consistently sell out their spots feel that giving away sellable time to barter actually constitutes paying higher prices in that a sale of the spots for six episodes in a cash deal could be more profitable. As more shows have moved into barter, these concerns have escalated because barter syndicators are asking for increasing numbers of minutes per half hour in these deals.

Another disadvantage is that the station or cable network taking the show is contractually obligated to air the national spots that come with the program even if the show fails and the station or cable network removes it from the air. Thus, after the failed show is removed from the schedule, its barter ads will have to run. Where? In the replacement show, so sellable spaces in the replacement show will be lost to the old show's commitment. Therefore, the buyer needs to choose programming that has a good chance of staying on the air long enough to honor the commitment to air national spots.

The future of barter   Barter is likely to continue to grow because of the advantages it offers. In an increasingly competitive environment, stations are not sufficiently cash-rich to pay the high prices that used to go to *Cosby* and *Who's the Boss?* At the start of the 1990s they resisted higher prices for *Golden Girls* and *Alf*. Thus, if a station cannot pay the cost up front, the barter option becomes attractive. If the right stations can be lined up nationwide and enough barter minutes can be delivered, the syndicator can actually achieve a greater return than is possible through straight cash deals.[7]

Cash plus barter   Cash plus barter (C+) involves the trading of cash and a smaller number of ad spots for programs. Cash plus barter has become increasingly popular because it deals with the concerns of stations and syndicators alike. On the one hand, it gives syndicators spots in attractive shows to sell to national advertisers. On the other hand, it reduces the amount of inventory a station must give up in order to get a show. In a C+ deal, there is usually a cash price, and one 30-second avail is given to the syndicator in exchange for a negotiated number of runs of each episode. C++ is similar but designates two 30-second spots in addition to the cash. As one might expect, the amount of cash given to the syndicator in a C+ agreement is smaller than that given in a straight cash deal. The amount of cash is further reduced in a C++ deal.

This device keeps 5½ to 6 minutes of inventory in the hands of the station. That is sufficient for a successful station. The salespeople still have ample spot avails to sell, and that makes them happy because they usually make their living entirely on commissions.

At the same time, advertisers who want to advertise in early fringe can still get into the shows of their choice by dealing with the barter syndicator or the syndicator's designated agent rather than taking the trouble to contact all the stations separately. Many shows new to syndication, especially the more successful comedies aimed at early fringe, are coming out in C+ or C++ form because that makes them more attractive to successful affiliate stations.

AMORTIZATION OF PROGRAM COST

To know what to buy, a programmer has to develop a way to determine the actual costs for each run of each program and compare those figures to estimates of how much income can be generated per run. The procedure of determining the cost per run is called **amortization.** Amortizing the cost for a six-run contract is a matter of calculating how much of the cost per episode is allocated to each run.

Accelerated Amortization

When a show comes into syndication for the first time, the first play of each episode attracts the largest audience. Thus, the station can charge the highest rates for ads in that run. But what of the second and the third runs? After three runs of each episode the show may no longer have sufficient appeal to hold its own against competition in early fringe. In that case, it will be moved to later in the night or perhaps earlier in the morning. Since each play declines in value to the station, shows tend to be valued for each run through the process of accelerated amortization.

In *accelerated amortization,* the first run in a six-run contract is valued at 40 percent of the cost per episode. The second run is valued at 30 percent of the cost per episode, the third at 20 percent, and fourth and fifth at 5 percent each; the sixth run counts as zero. Such a schedule gives the programmer a realistic picture of what can be expected from the show. If the last three runs are valued at near zero, the show can be placed in a less productive slot and will not have to register high ratings to produce a profit for that run. Since it is known that a show's value lies primarily in the first plays of each episode, one can place the most pressure to succeed there.

An example of accelerated amortization If a station buys *Who's the Boss?* for $10,000 an episode, how should it schedule the costs for each play? For tax purposes, the programming must be assigned a value. If the station is sold, a potential buyer must know what the station is worth. A large portion of the station's value may lie in its program inventory. If a show is in its fifth run of six, it will be hard to convince a knowledgeable buyer that the show is worth one-sixth of what was paid for it. In our earlier example (Table 13-1), 40 percent of the price for each episode of *Who's the Boss?* 0.40 × $10,000, equals $4000 to be charged against each episode's cost in the first run. Thirty percent of the episode cost— 0.30 × $10,000, or $3000—will be charged against each episode in the second run. Finally, by the sixth run no cost will be charged.

Straight-Line Amortization

The other form of amortization is *straight-line amortization,* meaning that the number of runs is divided into 100 percent to yield a cost per run. In a six-run contract, that would be about 17 percent of the episode cost per run (100/6 = 16.67, rounded to 17). That is simply not representative of the real value of shows except in the case of children's programs. Children will watch the sixth run of a program with the same relish as they watch the first. They have what is called high **repeat tolerance,** and their programs can be amortized on a straight-line basis. There is also a continuous supply of new children coming into the age group each year, and this translates to a constantly renewing resource. This is the only category so amortized.

Income against Amortized Cost

Now that we have figured cost, what about income? If the station has 6½ minutes of ad time per half hour to sell, spot rates for the time period can be used to calculate projected revenues. Assume that the station plans to charge $300 per spot based on projected ratings and a reasonable cost per thousand charge. With the 6½ minutes, it will have 13 spots to sell at $300 each, for a total of $3900. That will yield a near break-even situation in the first run.

However, certain realities prevail. It is unlikely that any station will sell all 13 avails, and even if the sales staff is that effective, some of those spots will be used to promote other shows on the station. What better time could a programmer choose to attract attention to other scheduled shows than during one of the most popular programs?

Then there is the matter of **make-goods,** which are given to advertisers to replace mistakes made in placing or playing spots. Sometimes an ad has a picture but no sound or the reverse. Sometimes the wrong spot is played, and the station must "make good" on the error by giving the advertiser a spot.

To take make-goods and promotional spots into consideration, the station never assumes that it will sell more than 80 percent of the available spots. In the 13-spot example, that comes to 10.4 spots, rounded to 10 because of the programmer's desire to make maximum promotional use of a strong show.

Multiplying a spot cost of $300 by 10 yields a revenue of $3000 during the first run. That means a loss of $1000 per day because the cost factor of the first run of each episode is valued at $4000. However, each subsequent run will "cost" less, while ad revenues will not fall that fast.

Since ad rates tend to climb a bit each year and since the station can charge more for some shows because they meet advertisers' content specifications, the station may be able to charge $275 per ad in the second run. The second run's cost is valued at 30 percent, or 0.30 × $10,000, yielding a cost of $3000. That amounts to a cost of $3000 and income of $2750, or a loss of $250 a day.

The station now has losses totaling $1250 per episode. In the third run it charges $250 per ad (10 spots) for a revenue total of $2500. The cost is 20 percent of $10,000, or $2000. Income then is $2500, and cost is $2000. Thus, the profit is $500 per day. Against the accumulated loss of $1250, that $500 profit still leaves a running deficit of $650 per episode. The fourth and fifth runs will be costed out at 5 percent, or $500 per play. Revenues projected for these two runs will more than exceed the deficit, and the station will make a profit on the show. The bottom line is a profit of $4250 per episode.

In this example the show does not turn a profit until the fourth run. Most programmers like to make a profit by the second run and no later than the third, but to get this premium show it may be necessary to spend more money than usual.

Accelerated amortization is a way to realistically determine the cost of each run in a multi-run contract rather than looking at the episode's cost as a lump sum split by the number of plays. If the station is sold in the interim, the percentage value attached to each run will give an accurate picture of the worth of the program inventory. If one compares the amortized cost of each run with the potential revenues, profits and losses can be predicted for each run and a figure can be arrived at for the total contract.

ADDITIONAL PROGRAM SOURCES

The bulk of programming comes to stations and cable networks via off-network and first-run syndication. There are, however, other sources of product, and those sources are growing in number and importance.

Local productions have occasionally found their way to the national level. *The Oprah Winfrey Show,* for example, was a local Chicago production before it was distributed nationally, and WCVB's *Chronicles* was picked up by the Arts and Entertainment Network on cable. For the most part, though, such local successes tend to be limited to major-market stations. Thus, only a small amount of programming comes from local sources. However, as demand for product continues to grow with the expansion of cable, local shows may be syndicated to other markets with greater frequency.

Cooperative Programs

Sometimes many stations get together to produce a program that can be shared by all the contributors. One of the first was *PM Magazine,* a show produced by Group W, Westinghouse Broadcasting. This format is still followed by programs that are based on the cooperative formula. There were local hosts who introduced each story, usually with a local hook. Then stories from all over the country were presented. Each cooperating station needed to produce stories only on an occasional basis to contribute to the pool of stories. The basic production expense was for the male and female hosts and some simple shooting of their introductions and banter. Such **cooperative productions** are cost-effective, but the quality of the stories may be uneven and the stations may feel that they have insufficient control over the content. While *PM Magazine* was eventually discontinued, the idea of cooperative production has remained.

Station group programming Some of the problems of cooperative programming can be overcome through **station group production.** A station group is a collection of different stations owned by the same company. Since the group is administered and usually programmed centrally, content control and quality control are more easily accomplished. The programs that are created can be shared by all the stations, making the group analogous to a network, but unlike a network, the group owns the show. Thus, its stations can have as many plays of each episode as are profitable.

There is an additional advantage to group production: first-run or subsequent syndication. *The Phil Donahue Show,* for example, is a Multimedia Company production. Since it has gained attention and interest outside Multimedia stations, it has been syndicated at great profit to other stations around the country. Another group-produced program, *Entertainment Tonight* (Cox Communications and others), has been similarly successful.

Foreign productions   At the 1992 meeting of the National Association of Television Programming Executives (NATPE), a record quantity of foreign programming was offered to American stations. In the past, American programmers had little faith in foreign productions despite the success of British programs on public television. Many Americans do not seem to accept foreign product as readily as citizens of other countries accept American programs. While many American shows are highly rated in other countries, foreign-made programs perform modestly on American television.[8]

Still, some foreign programs find their way onto American television. *The Benny Hill Show,* produced in Great Britain, has been syndicated with some success, as has the *Paul Hogan Show* from Australia, especially in light of Hogan's success with the Crocodile Dundee movies. Of course, the British dramatic shows included in the PBS series *Masterpiece Theatre* have played for years on American public television. More recently, they have been sought by cable networks on the lookout for quality product, but those shows tend to appeal to small audiences.

Economic necessity may have an influence on the future of television production. In 1992 the European Community (EC) was formed, and trade agreements were part of a package designed to make a united Europe a more potent economic force in the world market. One element of the EC was the encouragement of homegrown television programming and a cutting back on solely American product. Thus, to hold on to European distribution, American producers had to enter into joint ventures with European production concerns. The fruits of those ventures could be distributed in European countries as locally originated and distributed in North America as coproductions. The efficiency of getting two markets out of one product will bring more foreign content to American and Canadian television screens.

Several examples are relevant. In 1989 Paramount bought 49 percent of Britain's Zenith Productions. CBS and NBC have joint ventures with British companies, while ABC has minority stakes in French, German, and Spanish production companies.

An especially ambitious project in France was the production of a soap opera titled *Riviera,* which featured actors from many countries. Produced in English, it was dubbed into a variety of languages, including Basque and Catalan. When the show was distributed to a host of countries, its production costs could be covered. Then it was sold on the American market for a fraction of what a major production would cost, in part because lower production costs were combined with so much distribution potential.

Showtime has a deal with Great Britain's Yorkshire Television to produce made-for-television movies. A second deal with the BBC and Tiger TV will result in a series of comedy programs called *Funny Business.* Hanna-Barbara, Cinar (Montreal), and France Animation are combining to produce an animated series titled *Young Robin Hood.* Omnisphere Productions of New York has joined with Falcon Productions of France to produce a miniseries about World War I fliers. Worldwide television may be just around the corner.

CHOOSING AN OFF-NETWORK PROGRAM

Nobody knows for sure what makes a show a hit on a network or in syndication. Otherwise, syndication failures could be avoided.

Notable syndication failures include shows

that ran well in prime time but not in other slots. *The Waltons* serves as an example. There was nothing wrong with the quality of the show; it simply fit better in prime time than anywhere else. Its content and modularity were not appropriate for early fringe, and it was not strong enough to compete against more modular late-night programming such as the *Tonight* show. The lesson *The Waltons* teaches is that the programming of syndicated shows is as much an art as a science. While one can talk about the factors that must be taken into account when choosing shows, there is always an unknown element that can lead a sure hit to disaster and an obscure show to success.

Track Record

Just as scouts for professional sports teams ask where a player went to school and what quality of competition he or she played against, programmers look at original network performance and competing shows when considering the acquisition of an off-network property.

What kind of ratings did a show have, and against what kind of competition? It was fairly easy to predict the success of *M*A*S*H* in syndication. It had performed well on Monday night over many years against formidable competition including *Monday Night Football.* Programmers liked the show's **track record** (its ratings history) and bought accordingly.

Other shows have had a more questionable network performance. *Family Ties,* for instance, was on the verge of being canceled after its first season on NBC. Being placed after *Cosby* revitalized the show and helped it gain number two status in the ratings, but were these ratings to be trusted? On its own, it had failed to find an audience, and in the weak slot at 8:30 p.m. Thursday, behind the juggernaut of *Cosby,* it might have been the beneficiary of audience flow. Some had suggested that any show would do a 40 share behind *Cosby,* and so the track record of *Family Ties* could not be taken at face value. To some extent the question of its ability to hold its own was answered when the show was moved to

Sunday night during its last network season and survived. Its success on Sunday, although with lower relative ratings, sold *Family Ties* to stations as a good syndication investment.

Program buyers had similar questions about *Cheers,* perhaps another creature of flow, benefiting from the *Cosby* lead as *Family Ties* did, but the circumstances were a bit different. *Family Ties* was in a weak slot, and the other two networks had run hour shows against the *Cosby/Family Ties* block for most of *Family Ties'* Thursday network run. That meant that most viewers would be available to watch *Family Ties* because they would not be likely to switch to the second half of an hour show.

Cheers, though, had to compete on the hour. With remote controls in the hands of viewers, it had to make its own way. Thus, *Cheers* should have carried a positive track record into syndication, and it did. Still, each show has to be analyzed in terms of its placement and flow.

A Different World held second place in the ratings but got lukewarm reviews. As with *Family Ties,* many people thought its success was due to *Cosby* flow and predicted that it would die outside its protected time slot. Thus, it seemed at the time to be a questionable choice for syndication. Those questions were answered when the show went into syndication successfully.

Along similar lines, *Night Court* was thought to be a product of the success of the two post shows for its weak slot at 9:30 p.m., where it was hammocked between *Cheers* and *Hill Street Blues* or *L.A. Law.* Thus, many stations passed on *Night Court* in syndication, fearing that it could not hold its own against stronger competitors. A move to Wednesday night late in its network run was successful and helped create confidence in the program's syndication potential.

Another example with different considerations was *Silver Spoons.* During its network run, NBC paired it on Sunday night with *Punky Brewster* in the slot from 7 p.m. to 8 p.m. Neither show was a ratings success, but *Silver Spoons* was believed to be a show that would do better in syndication than in a network run. For one thing, the juxtaposition with *Punky Brewster* was cited as a factor in the show's lack of success. For another, many consultants pointed to the bankability of two stars, Ricky Schroeder and Erin Grey. The show's strongest supporters pointed to its themes, which revolved around family and love. The show was largely free of risqué content and profanity, and things always turned out happily. Many people thought these qualities were necessary for success in early fringe, and *Silver Spoons* was touted as the perfect fringe show. With a stronger program environment and lowered expectations in early fringe compared to prime time, the show should have been a hit, but it was not. The network track record had been the right predictor of the program's syndication success.

Demographic Appeals

Demographic appeals refer to the target demographic group or groups for a show. Some shows that run beautifully in a 10 p.m. network time slot prove to be "too male" in demographic appeal for early fringe. This is true of most action/adventure shows since they have insufficient appeal to women to run during this earlier time period.

The *A-Team,* while successful in its network run, especially in the earlier years, didn't do as well in syndication as had been hoped. Its appeal may have been too male in orientation for a non-prime-time slot.

There was concern about *Gimme a Break* when it became available for syndication. During its network run, the black audience embraced the show but whites did not. A report on network show preferences by race showed that blacks ranked *Gimme a Break* seventh among all shows but whites placed it fifty-third. That meant that the show was risky in markets where the black population was low.[9]

The syndicator fought back by selling the show on the basis of "Nellographics" (so named for the star, Nell Carter), saying that she crossed racial lines better than the ratings indicated. Their faith in the show was upheld. *Gimme a Break* ran well in syndication even in predominantly white markets such as Phoenix.

Conventional wisdom is not always reliable, but it is right much of the time. One should always examine the demographics of a show. If they do not match the market and the time period, the ratings may suffer.

A cable network in search of off-network product does not face the same problem. The audience for a cable network is national and thus more diverse than the audience in any one city or region. That makes it possible to place less emphasis on local demographic considerations. However, time slot considerations remain constant. Inappropriate modularity or content, especially in early fringe, can spell disaster for a station or cable network's syndicated acquisition.

Some shows deal with themes that do not fit the daypart. In early fringe, for example, heavy dramas and shows with violent or sexy themes do not work well. That is why hour shows tend to fail. The audience is dominated by younger viewers, and many parents do not want adult themes to be presented to 8-year-olds. That may militate against sexier sitcoms in early fringe, but show with themes too racy for an early daypart may do well at 11 or 11:30 p.m.

Time Period Needs

Perhaps the most important variable in choosing a show is the most obvious: choosing a time slot for the show or, more to the point, choosing programs for the time period. While this is the most obvious factor to consider, it is the most frequently ignored factor. As a rule, the programmer should not think about programs until he or she knows exactly where to place them. If the early fringe lineup is set for the next 2 years, a programmer is ill advised to buy a new product no matter how appealing it may seem. Getting into a bidding war for programs that the station does not need means putting a proven moneymaker on the shelf to make room for the new series.

CHOOSING A FIRST-RUN PROGRAM

The rules for choosing first-run programs are similar to those for choosing off-network product, but there are a few important differences. Chief among them is that first-run shows have no track record, leaving the programmer with a difficult decision.

Slot Requirements

As with off-network selection, the first thing to consider is the slot that needs to be filled. The news lead-in slot usually requires something more upscale and adult in appeal to flow well into the news. If it is opposite the news, the latitude is greater because upscale and downscale shows will all have an available audience from which to draw.

Program Costs and Quality

Once the important business of examining slots and demographic audience makeup has been completed, it's time to examine the show itself. While high cost does not guarantee success or quality, there tends to be a positive relationship between program resources and quality of production. As was mentioned earlier, without network license fees to help defray production costs, those costs must be kept relatively low. However, the image the station or cable outlet conveys to its potential audience is associated with the quality of its program product. Buying too cheaply can be detrimental in attracting an audience accustomed to watching high-quality fare.

Demographics and Themes

When one is looking at a program, one must ask what kind of demographic following it is trying to achieve. A show such as *Superboy* is aimed at a younger audience and may play best on Saturdays during the late morning. Since it is a low-budget production that does not feature known stars, it cannot be expected to compete effectively against high-powered programs in the better time slots.

Generally speaking, comedies in first run are weeklies, run one episode per week, and can be placed in only a few slots. *Out of This World* and *Small Wonder,* however, have family themes and more generalized demographic appeals that can work in weekend early fringe.

Networks run sports packages during weekend daytime, and independents tend to counter with movies—long forms that can fill large blocks of time. By evening, modularity is such that comedies fit in naturally.

Q-Ratings and Star Value

Another aid in deciding on both first-run and off-network programs is **Q-ratings** (see Chapter 4). These measures of personal popularity show how well known and liked a given star or program is. Certainly this measure favors well-known performers such as Bob Hope and Bill Cosby (two of the highest scorers), but it also can help determine whether a new show has a chance of gathering viewers.

The notion of star value can be used in place of Q-ratings. "What show was the star in before," and how well was he or she received? In *Family Feud,* for example, Richard Dawson was very well received as the host and the show did well in the ratings, but the ratings dropped for a new version with a new host. Measures of personal popularity can help determine how a show will fare.

Game Shows

The toughest prediction of success to make is for game shows. On paper, *Wheel of Fortune* did not look like a winner. The game was too simple, the set was too drab, and the host and hostess were unknown. Those apparent limitations were compounded by the fact that the prizes were small and unexciting. *$1,000,000 Chance of a Lifetime,* by contrast, seemed to be the perfect game show: The prize potential was great, the set glitzy, and the game fast-paced. However, it was eclipsed by *Wheel of Fortune,* a show that worked wonders because people liked the simplicity. Viewers solved the puzzles before the contestants could, making them feel good about themselves.

The best thing to do in a situation of this sort is to look at an episode of the show being considered to see what qualities it has before buying it. In such cases the programmer has to trust his or her instincts and experience.

Talk Shows

Talk shows are stripped during mornings and early fringe. Since the host personalities are usually known and the topics are easy to predict, the placement decision is not difficult. Most talk shows deal with adult issues and can be safely placed in the morning after 9 a.m., when children are in school. Talk shows also work well in early fringe, when women still predominate in the audience.

MEETING PROGRAMMING NEEDS

Weeklies and Strips

Shows are offered in syndication to meet different programming needs. Weekly shows such as *Star Search* are designed for weekend late morning, early afternoon, and late night, when the variety format offers a competitive alternative to science fiction, animation, and talk. Often off-network short runs, such as *Greatest American Hero,* that have fewer episodes run better as **weeklies** because they do not burn out as fast.

Most syndicated programs end up as strips. Virtually all of early fringe is stripped, and independents tend to strip against affiliates' soap operas, morning news shows, and early game shows. In effect, the entire weekday lineup is stripped for an independent and much of the lineup for an affiliate is stripped. Thus, there is considerable demand for programs that can be

stripped, especially comedies for daytime, early fringe, and morning.

A typical weekday schedule is shown in Table 13-2. Note that all programs are stripped on both affiliates and independents.

Increased Product Competition and Rising Prices

Since the average life span of a network show is declining, fewer shows are coming into syndication with large numbers of episodes. The demand is rising, and the supply is falling. This has led to infighting for product in markets that have many television outlets.

The best shows command huge—some people think ruinously high—license fees. Shows such as *Cosby* and *Who's the Boss?* have garnered prices previously unheard of in the marketplace. Shows such as *Golden Girls* and *Alf,* offered for sale after *Cosby* and *Who's the Boss?,* met with resistance in the marketplace. Stations argued that they had spent so much money on *Cosby* and *Who's the Boss?* that they could not come up with the money for *Golden Girls* and *Alf.*

The syndicators sensed a revolt, a form of collusion designed to bring product prices down. They argued that they offered quality programs—proven winners—and that stations were offering mediocre prices. Eventually the programs sold, but for prices below what syndicators wanted.

Whatever the outcomes of syndicator-station struggles, the main point is that product competition will increase as more programmers vie to acquire fewer high-quality shows. At the same time, those competitors cannot afford prices which will put them out of business.

HUT and Share

In projecting the ratings and shares for a given slot, there is a temptation to think that a change from *Three's Company* to *Full House* will double the audience, but that is not so. The number of persons watching television at any given time tends to remain fairly static. The introduction of a new show will not raise

TABLE 13-2 Sample Weekday Schedules for Affiliates and Two Independents

Time	ABC	CBS	NBC	IND 1	IND 2
7:00 a.m.	*Good Morning*	*CBS Morn*	*Today*	*Dennis the Menace*	*GI Joe*
7:30	*America*	"	"	*Muppet Babies*	*Jetsons*
8:00	"	"	"	*Disney*	*Widget*
8:30	"	"	"	"	*He-Man*
9:00	*Sally Jessy*	*Regis & Lee*	*Joan Rivers*	*Romper Room*	*Trapper John*
9:30	*Raphael*	"	"	*Kenneth Copeland*	"
10:00	*Donahue*	*Geraldo*	*Montel Williams*	*TJ Hooker*	*Police Story*
10:30	"	"	"	"	"
11:00	*Maury Povich*	*Price Is*	*Santa Barbara*	*Jenny Jones*	*Hill St Blues*
11:30	"	*Right*	"		"
12:00	News	News	News	*Love Connection*	*Matlock*
12:30 p.m.	*Loving*	*Young and*	News	*$100K Pyramid*	"
1:00	*All My*	"	*Days of Our Lives*	*Family Ties*	*Simon & Simon*
1:30	*Children*	*Bold and*	"	*Silver Spoons*	"
2:00	*One Life*	*As World T*	*Another World*	*Webster*	*Facts of Life*
2:30	*To Live*	"	"	*Peter Pan*	*Dudley Doright*
3:00	*General H*	*Guiding L*	*Love Stories*	*Chipmunks*	*Ducktales*
3:30	"	"	*One-on-One*	*Merrie Melodies*	*Chip & Dale*
4:00	*Oprah Winfrey*	*Inside Ed.*	*Cosby*	*Beetlejuice*	*Talespin*
4:30	"	*Current Af*	*Golden Girls*	*Bond Jr*	*Darkwing Duck*
5:00	News *(Local)*	News *(Local)*	News *(Local)*	*Ninja Turtles*	*Tiny Toons*
5:30	*People's Court*	News *(Local)*	*Now It Can Be Told*	*Saved by the Bell*	*Charles in Charge*
6:00	News *(Local)*	News *(Local)*	News *(Local)*	*Growing Pains*	*Different World*
6:30	News *(Local)*	CBS News	News *(Local)*	*Night Court*	*Full House*
7:00	ABC News	*Wheel of*	NBC News	*Cheers*	*Star Trek: Next Generation*
7:30	*Ent. Tonight*	*Jeopardy*	*Fam Feud*	*Married W/Children*	"

the number of households or viewers as much as it will tend to redistribute them. One must examine the number of viewers in the television audience and determine how many of them can be attracted to the station's new show. The wise programmer is conservative in estimating how much to offer for a show. If the estimate is overly optimistic, the station will lose money on the show and the programmer's decision will be listed as the primary reason for the shortfall.

Dealing with Syndicators

Buying programs is like buying a used car. A salesperson who has a high-quality product knows it and will force the buyer to pay a high price. However, if that salesperson has a less

than premium product or needs a sale, the buyer is in the driver's seat.

Often the scales tip in favor of the syndicator, but not always. *Alf* suffered in the marketplace because it was released on the heels of *Cosby* and *Who's the Boss?,* two comedies which had brought top prices from stations. Usually, though, when a "can't-miss" off-network show is in the offing, no concessions will be made at the bargaining table.

Minimum bids When offering big-name shows, especially comedies, syndicators generally set threshold figures with mandatory increments in the bidding process. This means that a price will be set for each market based on its prevailing advertising rates and what stations can afford to pay. That price will be considered the minimum bid.

In the New York market, where station ad rates are the highest in the country, the price may be $200,000 per half-hour episode. In a smaller market, the price may be only $1000 per episode.

If no stations bid the minimum, the product will be withdrawn from the market and a new round of bidding will begin. In Tampa, for example, no stations met the minimum bid for *Cosby* in the first round of syndication, and so the show was taken out and reintroduced later.

The threshold is a *minimum* bid. Usually all bids must be in increments of 5 percent over that minimum. In the case of a $200,000 minimum, bids will be in increments of $10,000: $200,000, $210,000, $220,000, and so on. In a sealed bid situation, no one knows what the others are bidding, and so each station must guess what its competitors plan to bid. Then they must try to overbid in 5 percent increments. Like the networks' efforts to secure the broadcast rights to the Olympic Games, the bidding on syndicated product can get out of hand, with the so-called winner gaining a product at a ruinous price. Still, stations must do what is necessary to compete. At times, that includes overpaying for a product.

Our previous illustration describes the process for acquiring the best shows. Only a few programs can command such prices or procedures. Most shows are sold in open bidding situations where all the outlets in the market have a chance to compare their bids and stop when they have reached their limit. Syndicators will tell stations what the others have bid. As in many auctions, stations may stay longer than they should, but at least the process is open.

Bargaining for programs Many older shows still have audience appeal but are not at the top of most stations' acquisition lists. A station can find an occasional bargain among these shows. There are also first-run shows, often bartered, for which there are few takers. Since value is determined by salability, if no one in the market wants a show, it has no worth. Worth is simply what someone is willing to pay, and a station thus may be able to acquire a real bargain.

Assume that no station wants the rights to an older comedy that has run several times. If no station in the market holds the rights, the syndicator is not making a dime on the product. By asking what price is desired, the programmer can start the bargaining process. Assume that the syndicator says the show is worth $1000 an episode. If it has not run in the market for more than a year, the market has determined that the product has no significant appeal, and so it is up to the programmer to determine a price. If offered $100 per episode, the syndicator must decide whether to wait for a better offer or take what is offered. By holding out for a better offer, the distributor may make nothing. If the syndicator accepts the offer, it can make a few dollars. Usually the syndicator will counter with another price that is still too high, such as $500.

The programmer must be careful not to make syndicators into antagonists, because they will have good product later. If they feel they have been abused, they will enjoy the opportunity to get even later. The programmer can make a low offer but qualify it by saying that he or she doesn't really need the product but that it could fill a nonessential slot in the schedule. The programmer will point out that the syndicator can make a modest amount of money on the deal, which is better than nothing. If there has been an ongoing relationship between the syndicator and the programmer, the programmer can point out the mutual benefits of that relationship and note that in this case the syndicator can afford to make less because in the past or future more dollars have been made or may be made. This soothes ruffled feathers and allows the deal to go through without bruised egos.

It is possible to secure programs for a fraction of their asking price without hurting anyone's feelings. As in buying a used car, the program purchaser shouldn't even look at sticker prices; they are irrelevant.

First-run offers The same scenario holds true for some first-run product as well as for occasional inserts such as 30-second health tips, comedy bits, and recipes. If the syndicator cannot clear the market, he or she may take a low offer in order to get the product sold. In such situations the programmer may be able to get the product rights for only a short time. Generally, the more successful it is on a station, the more interest a series will spark in the market. If finances are tight, the station may not be able to hold on to it but can try to close a deal on another show.

Hour program offers Less interest is currently being expressed in hour-long program series even though they too can sometimes be had for very little money.[10] A good tactic is to look over the rights lists for the market and identify hour shows that do not appear there. If the programmer identifies a show that would be of use in the schedule, a low offer can be made for it. The syndicator may be happy to get some value out of the show.

Some enterprising programmers have been buying up hour programs and blocking them like movies in prime time. Because of the lowered demand for hour shows, this is often more cost-effective than movie purchases are. An additional benefit is that these programs have been repeated fewer times than have most movies. Moreover, they retain the advantage of having been created for television. As long as hour prices remain depressed, this represents a possible strategy for filling prime-time film slots.

Copying owned and operated stations Owned and operated (O and O) stations are big-budget, complicated operations in the largest cities. Often, local stations wait to see what the O and O stations are buying on the theory that these stations, with their high-powered programming departments, know what's best. This is not necessarily so. They may know what is best for them, but that may not be what is best for other stations.

Sometimes, in fact, they do not always know what is best for themselves. For example, in 1987 the NBC O and O's decided to checkerboard in access. The idea seemed interesting—placing a different first-run comedy in the access slot each night. They bought shows such as

Marblehead Manor, She's the Sheriff, and *We've Got It Maid.* The fact that checkerboarding was neither new nor successful in earlier experiments (it had flopped in the 1960s) did not faze anyone. NBC's decision was followed by some local stations, and everyone lost. The shows did not warrant access placement and finished out their runs in late night. The important thing to remember is that an O and O can survive a $10 million mistake but a smaller station usually cannot.

On a more positive note, CBS introduced its "Crime Time after Prime Time" in 1991 with some success. It was a checkerboard scheme in which a different crime drama was offered on different nights of the week after the local late news.

Warehousing

Warehousing is the practice of buying up programs to keep them out of the hands of competitors. Stations will sometimes shelve such a program, not run it at all, or run it in a throwaway slot such as overnight. Such a strategy treats the first run as if it were the sixth because of its low-revenue time slot placement. Of course, such a program cannot produce the revenue normally expected. In any event, stations do not do this much anymore because it is too expensive.

Block Booking

Block booking is the practice of buying a weaker show in order to get a stronger one. Syndicators tie buyers to a weak product in return for the right to buy a strong one. The best advice is not to play this game. For one thing, it's illegal because buyers cannot be coerced into buying items they don't want in exchange for the right to buy items that they do. For another, it saddles the station with an inferior product. Some reputable syndicators do not block book. Some avoid the word if not the practice. Still others are block bookers and are open about it. In the long run the practice works to the detriment of the station.

Colorization and Syndication Value

Many programmers have lamented, "If only those old *Burns and Allen, Leave It to Beaver, My Three Sons,* and other programs were completely in color, they would still be usable today." Now the technology exists to make that a reality. The backlog of older programs is so great that programming shortages could be eliminated overnight through the use of colorization. **Colorization** is a computer-based process in which black-and-white movies and television shows are converted to color.

Since the rise of color television and the earlier move in film from black and white to color, audiences have become less accepting of black-and-white content. The young son of one of the authors said during a viewing of an old *I Love Lucy,* "Hey, Dad, turn it on in color, okay?" Younger viewers complain that black and white does not seem "real," while older viewers prefer to see vistas in color even though they understand the technological limitations of earlier black-and-white productions. Regardless of its genesis, this sentiment runs sufficiently deep that programmers try not to use black and white in any of the more important dayparts such as early fringe. The occasional show, such as *Twilight Zone,* that runs well despite its lack of color is still relegated to 11 p.m. or later.

SUMMARY

There are two primary types of syndicated programming: off network and first run. Off-network syndication refers to programs that have had a network run. They have a track record and are designed for repeat viewing. First-run programs cost less to produce, have no network track record, and often are not designed for repeat showing. Each form has its advantages and utility in different places on the schedule.

The term of a syndication deal is typically six runs of an episode over 3 years for an off-network product and some negotiated fee per run for a first-run product. In both cases the station wants to make more money selling advertising time than it has paid for the program that day.

Figuring those costs involves amortization, or the practice of attaching a price to any particular play of a program. That allows stations to accurately place a value on their inventory for tax and resale purposes.

Programs can come from sources besides off-network and first-run syndication. These include local production, cooperative programming, station group productions, and foreign productions.

In choosing a syndicated program, a programmer needs to examine its track record (if there is one), the demographic appeals of the show, its themes, and the time period needs of the station. Shows must be carefully matched with scheduling slots.

SUGGESTED READINGS

Variety

This industry periodical chronicles the economic ebb and flow of the entertainment industry. All major syndication deals, regulations, and trends are reported on in great depth. While not limited to broadcasting and cablecasting, *Variety* remains the organ of record for every form of deal making. When hour programs began to migrate to cable in syndication, it was here that the trend was first reported and analyzed. When stations and cable networks responded to ruinously high syndication, *Variety* was there with analysis and insight.

Broadcasting

This weekly is recommended at the end of many chapters in this book. It is the finest publication in the business. Despite its name, it treats cable issues at great length and with sharp insight. While other publications cover the dollar issues, this one tries to explain why things are happening and who is involved. *Broadcasting* was one of the first publications to detail tier deals and the shifts in power from syndicators to buyers and back. It takes the pulse of the industry and is read and believed by most industry professionals.

NOTES

1. "Freeze Frames: Syndication Scorecard," *Broadcasting,* March 4, 1991, p. 51.

2. "Yak, Yak, Yak: Talk Shows Proliferate," *Video Age International,* January 1991, p. 30; see also, "Freeze Frames," op. cit.

3. "Dick Robertson: Surveying the Supply Side," *Broadcasting,* Jan. 14, 1991, p. 63.

4. Debra Goldman, "Praying for Time," *Adweek,* Jan. 14, 1991, pp. 2–3.

5. "Changes in the Cash/Barter Mix," *Advertiser Syndicated Television Association Newsletter,* January 1991, p. 4.

6. "Syndication Outpaces Ad Spending," *Extra/ Extra,* Jan. 15, 1991, p. 18.

7. "In Tough Market, It's 'No Cash and Carry,'" *Broadcasting,* Dec. 31, 1990, p. 47.

8. "'Diversification, Not Uniformity' Key to Successful International TV," *Broadcasting,* March 4, 1991, p. 68.

9. "Television Viewing among Blacks," *Nielsen Newscast,* Vol. 2, 1987, p. 10.

10. Steve Brennan, "NATPE Sellers Slashing Prices of Hourlong Shows," *Hollywood Reporter,* Jan. 14, 1991, p. 1.

Programming the Independent Station

Independents are stations that are not affiliated with a network. As such, they do not have the benefit of network news programs, sports packages, prime-time comedies, and dramas with big-name stars and new episodes each week. No one supplies them with 60 to 70 percent of their programming. How do they get along?

Independents have to find programs to fill up to 24 hours a day. Without a consistent supplier, that search to fill the yawning programming "hole" can become frantic. This chapter will show how independents (indies) break the day into blocks and program it accordingly. Specific program acquisition and placement strategies will also be examined. First, let us delve into the disadvantages and advantages of independence.

THE PROBLEMS OF INDEPENDENCE

The Coverage Problem—VHF/UHF

Perhaps the greatest disadvantage for independent stations is their placement on the dial. Most are on the UHF channels in the television spectrum, channels 14 to 69.[1] Generally speaking, the lower its channel number, the farther a television station's signal can travel. The lowest channel position, channel 2, is the easiest to deliver to distant receivers; the highest, channel 69, requires much more power to get its signal out to viewers. In the early days of broadcasting, applicants for a broadcast license received lower-numbered, more desirable channels. Early television was designed for VHF transmission, and televisions were designed for VHF reception only. Since television was new and no one knew its future, the 12 available channels (channels 2 through 13) seemed to be sufficient to blanket the country. Most of the VHF allocations were assigned by the end of the 1950s, and the future growth of television would have to occur in the UHF band, channels 14 to 69. However, those channels' signals were much more difficult to send out and receive.

Burdens Placed on UHF

Early independent broadcasters had to operate in the UHF band with its signal problems. Unfortunately, television manufacturers and the FCC increased that burden. The manufacturers put only VHF tuners on their sets. When pressed by UHF station owners, they claimed that there were so few UHF stations that the expense of including UHF tuners was not justified. The argument was logical at the time. Cost-conscious manufacturers were reluctant to include all-channel tuners because that would raise the price of sets. Frustrated by the manufacturers, UHF broadcasters approached the FCC and lobbied for UHF tuners to be made mandatory on all new television sets. The FCC finally made such a ruling in 1964.[2] However, the commission did not set technical guidelines for the quality of UHF tuners, and manufacturers kept down their costs by installing tuners that worked like a radio dial instead of the familiar "click stop" tuners associated with VHF. The UHF signal reception tended to change when a person moved away from the set after tuning, causing considerable frustration. As a result, UHF stations remained unwatched in many households.

UHF broadcasters again approached the FCC, and in 1974 click stop tuners were mandated for all channels.[3] The battle had been won, but the war was already over for stations that had gone out of business. Since 1974, all new sets, whether using click stop tuners or the new quartz lock tuners, have had VHF and UHF tuners of equal facility of use. However, UHF stations still have image problems caused by the old radio-style tuners, and some viewers still are reluctant to tune in UHF stations.

Network Formation and UHF

Another manifestation of the UHF/VHF problem can be seen in the affiliated stations gathered by the first four television networks: CBS, NBC, ABC, and DuMont. CBS and NBC were extensions of the original radio networks of the 1920s and had developed a strong group of affiliates as well as great broadcasting expertise. They immediately signed up the VHF stations and thus had the stronger affiliates. The younger ABC made do with a mixture of VHF and some UHF stations. In larger markets ABC could find VHF stations to become affiliates, but in smaller markets mostly UHF stations were left after CBS and NBC had captured the VHFs. That made ABC stronger in urban areas but weaker in rural areas until UHF signals and viewer acceptance of them improved. The Du-Mont Network consisted mostly of UHF stations and went out of business in 1956. Interestingly, the current Fox Network is based on the core of stations that originally constituted DuMont.

Independent Station Economics

What makes independents' operation most difficult is their lack of a network source of fresh programming. Worse, they have to compete with affiliates that get a continuous supply of new shows from their networks. Independents, unlike affiliates, cannot make a profit simply by delivering network programs. Although competition between broadcast stations, both network-affiliated and independent, and cable networks is increasingly fierce, the big three affiliates still finish one, two, three in the ratings in most dayparts. Therefore, independents must generate most of their revenue in dayparts where they can compete on even terms with affiliates and where there are enough viewers to make a victory over affiliated stations highly profitable. Early fringe is the only such daypart in most markets because affiliated stations receive no programs for that period from their networks except for a half-hour newscast and must, like independents, fill their own schedules. Thus, independents spend large portions of their resources in that daypart.

Selling Advertising Time

There are some important economic facts of life for independents. First, they have to sell all their advertising inventory. An affiliate gets its programming free but gives up ad slots to the net-

work. Although the starting inventory of advertising spots for an affiliate is smaller, it is more attractive because of the network programming, making it easier for affiliated stations to sell commercial time. Independents have more ad inventory and have to sell it without the benefit of a network that gives them attractive, highly salable programs.

Second, independents operate at a disadvantage in their sales efforts because their programs tend to be older and more shopworn than those on the competing affiliates. It's tougher to sell the eighth play of *Family Ties* than it is to sell the first play of *Full House*.

Independent Counterprogramming

Affiliates' programs tend to grab the primary available demographic groups. If there is a desirable demographic group available, the networks will offer a show to appeal to it. Thus, independents live on leftovers. They survive by adapting to a tough environment and attacking the competition when they can. They do not program so much as they counterprogram. When affiliates run news, independents often run comedies. When affiliates program sports, independents may program movies.

Independent programmers are among the best and smartest because they have to be. They have no network programs, have more inventory to sell, and have up to 24 hours a day of programming time to fill. Independents get a little help in the competitive marketplace from exceptions to PTAR since they are exempt from restrictions on off-network programs during access. All that counterprogramming practice prepares independent programmers for battles with affiliates that occur on even terms, such as early fringe.

THE ADVANTAGES OF INDEPENDENCE

Flexibility

Although independents do not have the advantages of affiliation, they also do not have the disadvantages, such as rigid schedules.

Freedom in scheduling allows independents to do things that affiliates cannot do. **Festivals,** for example, may consist of a whole day of a particular show, and local viewers can be made part of the process. During one Super Bowl day, an independent ran 12 straight hours of *Star Trek* episodes. As part of the promotion, viewers were invited to vote on which 12 episodes should be selected. Prizes were given away, and fan interviews were aired during the festival.

Such festivals can be organized around any theme, and ancillary activities can be used to make the programming more interactive. Festivals do not have to be organized around events such as the Super Bowl or World Series but can be done at any time. New Year's Day, Labor Day, and other holidays when large audiences are available offer the same potential. It is, however, worth noting that several Super Bowls have been one-sided affairs in which the outcome was evident by halftime. That helps festivals as Super Bowl viewers look around the dial for something else.

The Importance of Positioning

How a station is perceived by the audience can make a big difference in terms of viewing. An independent needs to position itself in viewers' minds in special ways so that they come to associate that station with something special. One such approach is localism.

While radio stations are known for community orientation which inspires a local following, this is no longer the case for television stations. Most affiliates are now group-owned, and that has led to a reduction in local orientation. As was mentioned in Chapter 10, group ownership has transferred some programming decisions from the local level to corporate headquarters. Although affiliated stations have the powerful appeal of local news as a local tie and news is a program form that most independents still lack, these programs have increased their emphasis on regional, national, and even international news in recent years.

Indies thus can function like local radio stations by focusing on local events; producing shows about people and issues of local interest; sponsoring fairs, parades, and picnics; and participating in the community in a host of other ways. That positions the independent as a terrific corporate citizen in people's minds.

Positioning slogans As was noted in Chapter 2, a slogan does not fulfill a consumer's need but helps create a place in the consumer's mind so that the product or service, in this case programs, can have a greater impact. Some positioning slogans include "Your Family Television Station," "the Quality Station," and "Your Station for Wrestling." The slogan can be illustrated with clips from programs to help define a station's image. The point of positioning is to take a station's resources and, through carefully orchestrated promotion, fulfill a special need for viewers. For an independent station, the key to building an audience is **sampling,** or getting people to watch the station once so that they will tune in again. The right image can encourage that curiosity. Once they have been brought into a station's audience, viewers can be enticed by promotions about other programs on the schedule to tune in again.

In regard to positioning, independents can take a cue from radio. The promotions and giveaways that radio stations run help build sampling and eventually listenership. Independents can also make arrangements with local businesses to give away items, host community events, and get involved in local charities. These activities can stimulate sampling and support a positioning strategy by raising a station's visibility.

Positioning with movies Some independents bill themselves as "Your Free Movie Channel" as a way of taking advantage of the current popularity of pay-movie services and video rentals and the general appeal that movies have always had as television content. Since independents run a great quantity of movies, it is worth promoting movies effectively and getting the greatest possible positioning value out of them.

Theme weeks help independents use movies to the best advantage. Promotions focused on popular actors—John Wayne Week, Sylvester Stallone Week, Clint Eastwood Week, Meryl Streep Week—can be very effective. The movies can be promoted as a block as well as individually, and themes can be content-focused as well. Disaster Week can include *The Towering Inferno* and *The Poseidon Adventure,* while Love Week can feature *Love Story* and *The Goodbye Girl.* *Steel Magnolias* and *Beaches* could anchor Tearjerker Week.

USING MOVIES EFFECTIVELY

Movies are at the heart of an independent's schedule but not necessarily that of an affiliate. An NBC affiliate, for example, can get through a 20-hour programming day without running a locally purchased syndicated movie. Movies can't run during the morning news or *Today,* and they cannot preempt the soaps. As was discussed in Chapter 11, few affiliated or independent programmers run movies in early fringe. Prime-time movies are supplied by the network for its affiliates. With the *Tonight* show, *Late Night,* and *Later with Bob Costas,* there is no need for movies until after 1:30 a.m., at which time the station can simply sign off. The other networks provide similar programming in most dayparts. ABC and CBS do not provide as much late-night fare, but they supply some. An affiliate of those networks can also get through a programming day without airing a movie.

In the morning, after 9 a.m., affiliates have the best game shows and some network comedy feeds. They also get first crack at talk shows such as *Donahue, Geraldo,* and *Oprah Winfrey* because they can pay more money for them. Independents sometimes counterprogram with movies. While not the best content as far as modularity is concerned, movies are occasionally the best available option.

Similarly, there is no effective way to compete directly with network soap operas in the afternoon. In most markets there is no substantive secondary audience until children get out of school, and so a movie can be programmed at noon or 1 p.m. as an alternative to soaps and as a stopgap until children enter the audience.

In prime time, movies are critical to an independent because they fill large blocks of time and have good internal flow. Even when put up against superior network programs that recruit larger audiences, movies tend to hold the viewers they attract. In the absence of network-fed late-night shows, movies are useful and effective in that time period as well. Since modularity is not as much of an issue late at night, a movie is a cost-effective way of filling time.

The selection, placement, and promotion of movies are critical to an independent. A programmer who can perform these three tasks well is on the way to successfully filling the biggest hole in an independent's schedule.

Affiliates use some films, however, especially when no sports programming is available during weekend afternoons. Many use late shows on weekends and/or air an occasional feature during the summer, when the networks are delivering reruns of failed series. Therefore, the strategies described here for acquiring movies may be more important for independents because of the number of movies they run, but these strategies can be used by affiliates as well.

Movie Selection

First tier, or A-quality, movies Movies are purchased, like other program product, in packages. Just as a station buys 120 episodes of *Roseanne,* it may buy a movie package of 25 to 100 films. Like episodes of a sitcom, they can be repeated for a specified number of times over a specified period. Contracts for movie packages usually allow three to eight runs depending on the recency and value of the films. In any event, the better packages cost more, and such films are placed in slots where they can make the most money.

Movies fall roughly into three categories of quality and price, which we will call tiers 1, 2, and 3 depending on the time slot for which they are purchased. The word "tier" can be confusing because it is used to define time slots in syndication deals and sets of cable channels selected by cable subscribers. Here we will use the term as an indicator of quality in movie packages. The first **tier** is composed of the best movies and is directed toward prime time. Movies are purchased for this time slot because the greatest number of viewers is available and the best opportunity for profitability through movies exists there. Therefore, the most recent packages with the best titles are purchased for this time period. Movies such as *Home Alone 2, Dances with Wolves, City Slickers, Terminator 2,* and *Sister Act* fit into this category.

Second-tier movies Daytime and weekend afternoon audiences are smaller than those in prime time, but there is an audience for films at these times. Thus, a second tier of movies needs to be purchased. These titles are more worn and less recent, but they are good films and have utility. Movies such as *Terms of Endearment, Crimes of the Heart, Ghost,* and *Cocoon* fall into such packages. While less spectacular, these movies have bankable stars and solid track records and should gather an audience. Their themes play well with female audiences, making them appropriate for the daytime. Women who do not like soaps, men trying to avoid soaps, and channel switchers looking for something interesting may tune in.

These movies also play well on weekends, when the network lineups are dominated by sports. Women have reduced options for viewing as football, baseball, and basketball fill the screen. Many independents program Saturday and Sunday afternoons for women and for men who are not interested in sports. This counterprogramming makes movies useful for these slots.

Third-tier movies Third-tier movies fill the weekend morning and late-night slots. While a station needs to fill the time, it cannot spend much money doing so if it is to make a profit on time periods characterized by smaller available audiences. Third-tier movies are often either very old or very bad. Japanese sci-fi movies fit into the category, along with martial arts films. Horror

movies help fill out this classification. Very old movies, which have more limited audience appeal, are included. Many old black-and-white movies (except for "classics") are included. These titles run the gamut from *Godzilla versus the Smog Monster,* to *Enter the Dragon,* to *Fright Night,* to *I Was a Werewolf for the FBI.*

In general, science-fiction and kung fu movies play best on Saturday morning, appealing to younger viewers who are outgrowing cartoons and looking for something different. They are inexpensive, the available audience is small, and they fit the available demographic.

Slasher or horror films play best late at night, usually on Friday and Saturday. A "Chiller Theater" can be developed around these titles. Some sci-fi films can play here too.

Mainstream but older titles make the best late movies. The audience is more adult and may like the novelty of watching older films. Cable networks such as American Movie Classics, Encore, and the Nostalgia Channel are enjoying some success with these films.

It is important for a programmer to keep in mind the slot for which a movie package is intended. If the current prime-time movie lineup is working well and there is a backlog of good films to be run, there is no need to buy additional first-tier films even if the packagers offer tempting titles. Only the inventory needed for the immediate future (1 to 3 years) should be bought. If it's Saturday morning fare that the station needs, the programmer should not allow himself or herself to be induced to buy "wonderful old classics." What is needed for that time period is westerns, martial arts, and science-fiction films which can be acquired in packages at attractive prices.

Matching Movies with Audiences

As always, a programmer should examine the available audience to answer the question, Who's out there? Once the available audience has been defined for each of the station's intended movie slots, purchasing with firm objectives can begin.

The potential purchaser should examine all the titles in the package carefully before striking a deal. Some packages are mixed bags, with films aimed at different demographic groups. Perhaps several are aimed at women, a similar number at men, and a few at children. Can such a package be used? If it is a tier 1 package, the answer is usually no. Generally speaking, children are not available in an independent's prime movie slot of 9 to 11 p.m. If top dollar is spent on child-oriented movies, the money may be wasted as the primary play options for tier 1 lie outside children's normal viewing times. Children's movies are most effectively scheduled on Friday night, Saturday night, and weekend afternoons.

However, each of these times has disadvantages. The evenings are still problematic for children who go to bed before 11 p.m. Parents may not want to let younger children stay up that late. On the weekends, men assert more control over sets and watch sports. Thus, those slots are not going to justify a big price tag for a movie. Therefore, tier 1 movie packages should contain adult titles, with children's titles being relegated to tier 2.

The best packages appeal to a particular demographic group and contain titles of consistent quality and orientation so that each title can make a contribution to the lineup. Action, comedy, and drama packages allow the programmer to promote efficiently and schedule coherently in each tier. While theoretically desirable, such packages are rare at the tier 1 level. They tend to be more readily available at tiers 2 and 3.

Distributors have only a few solid winners and more than a few "clunkers" in most packages. In order to sell the less desirable films, the distributor makes them part of a package so that the buyer must take the lesser titles to get the better ones. That is why the programmer has to look at the potential of each movie in the package (Table 14-1).

Price has to be compared to projected ratings (and thus earnings) for each movie. If too many clunkers will make the overall contract unprofitable, it is wise to pass on the deal and examine other packages. Of course, the distributors know about the lesser titles they are trying to

TABLE 14-1 A Sample Movie Package: Action Pak 1 from Imperial Entertainment

Chains
Bloodfight
Ghosthouse
China O'Brien
Metamorphosis
The Mines of Kilimanjaro
Operation Nam
The Overthrow
Prisoner of Rio
The Shaman
Stay Tuned for Murder
Thunder Warrior III

Note: These 12 titles constitute a demographically focused package that serves the programmer's need for consistency. Because action themes and male-appeal movies are clustered, the buyer has predictability in the package.

SOURCE: *Extra Extra*, Jan. 23, 1992, p. 21.

sell along with the hits and may entertain a lower offer in order to move the merchandise. In that case, the package's potential for profitability rises. It's all in the negotiation.

Inevitable Decline of Tier 1 Movies' Ratings

There is one more important point to make about placement: Tier 1 movies decline in appeal with exposure and must eventually be moved to other slots. This must be figured into a movie's potential to make money.

The audience is largest for any syndicated show during the first play of each episode; with each succeeding play, the audience size goes down. That is not surprising. People simply say, "I saw that one," and look for another show to watch. Sometimes they say, "This is a good one; I'll watch it again." But what of the third play and the fourth, fifth, and sixth? Eventually audiences tire of the overly familiar.

So it goes with movies. When people watch a movie on TV, many times they have already seen it once, perhaps during its theatrical release, as a rental, on HBO or Showtime, or on a broadcast network. By the time movies get to stations, most have been through

- At least one theater release
- A pay-per-view showing
- Home video sale/rental release
- A pay-cable release
- A pay-cable "encore" release
- A network showing

These **release windows,** or different forms of exposure to public viewing, detract from a film's ability to draw at the local level because of pre-exposure. Add to that the cable pay-per-view release of many films which occurs between the theatrical release and the home video release, and the value of the film declines.

The only alternative is to shift the movie to the second tier: day or weekend. Thus, tier 1 movies run in prime time for only two or three plays. For the rest of the contract they tend to be scheduled in tier 2 slots. It is not unusual for a tier 1 movie to fall to late night (tier 3) for its last one or two runs.

The same decline affects tier 2 movies. After runs on the weekend and in the daytime, they begin to wear and are often moved to tier 3, which is late night (unless the title is an action, sci-fi, or horror film, in which case it moves to the weekend or Chiller Theater). Thus, in computing the movie's potential earnings for six plays, the programmer must factor in shifts downward in tier and burnout. Paying for tier 1 movies by estimating six plays in that tier's typical prime-time slots would probably be disastrous.

Because so few films hold up for six plays in the first tier, it is necessary to buy more tier 1 packages but negotiate their price to take the inevitable slippage into lower tiers into account. Purchases for tiers 2 and 3 can be adjusted accordingly, because these films will draw some plays from higher tiers. Recently, however, distributors have been negotiating three-run contracts for their best product as a result of increased demand from cable services and increasing numbers of independent stations. Still, the film buyer must assume that even three runs will not all occur in prime time.

The Need to Edit Theatrically Released Films

A problem with theatrical films is that they often have to be edited before they can be aired. Since they are not created for television's usual 2-hour time block, many feature films have to be cut or padded, and film fans may become agitated when stations and networks do that.

Another form of necessary editing involves cutting out violence, sex, and objectionable language. That makes for awkward plot lines because of missing scenes and unintentionally humorous voiceovers in which words do not sound like the actor's voice and do not match the actor's mouth movements. Movies such as *Blazing Saddles* and *Goodfellas* have been the most difficult in this regard. A few movies are so raw that they cannot be shown on television at all.

Made-for-Television Movie Packages

An important category of movies not always at the top of the programmer's consideration list consists of made-for-television movies. At first these films may seem to be of lower quality because they have lesser stars, smaller budgets, and lower-quality production, but made-for-television movies (known in the trade as made-fors) have some very good qualities.

Advantages of made-fors Freshness is one advantage. These movies have been through only a single exposure window, the network run, which includes only two plays. These films haven't been rented, haven't appeared on pay cable (unless they are cable made-fors), haven't been in theaters, and haven't been on pay-per-view. That counts for a lot in an age when movies are nearly worn out before they reach TV stations.

Another advantage of made-fors is that they are written for the "8-minute cliff-hanger" format of television. Because commercial breaks tempt viewers to stray to other channels, shows usually go to commercial breaks after some event of import has occurred; viewers then have to come back for the resolution. Another little cliff-hanger is built into the plot before the next commercial break, and so on.

Theatrical films are not written in this way. The audience is in the theater and unlikely to leave. Thus, long periods can be spent on one topic (a span of time that encompasses several commercial breaks in a television airing), and that will not necessarily hold television viewers over the break. One way television surmounts this problem in made-fors is to insert a tease scene at the start of the break to entice viewers to return for the exciting scenes to follow. Every 8 minutes or so an event occurs that requires resolution, but that resolution is not provided until after the commercial break.

Made-fors tend to feature television stars instead of film stars. Loni Anderson and Jaclyn Smith, who are usually associated with television, have enjoyed success in made-fors, while some prominent film stars have not fared well on television. The TV audience is familiar with its stars and seems to like seeing them. Many television viewers are not large consumers of movies; thus, their knowledge of and familiarity with television personalities are greater and their loyalties can run deeper. Moreover, TV and cinema attract different core audiences. Television's primary audience is age 25 and above, while 70 percent of all movie theater tickets are sold to people under 30 years of age.[4]

Promoting Movies

After a film has been selected and placed in a station's schedule, it must be promoted. On-air promotion is extremely useful, but it takes up valuable time that could be sold to advertisers. Consequently, it is impractical to promote each movie on a large scale.

A more efficient form of promotion involves featuring several films in a 30-second spot, which brings us back to theme weeks. The theme can be the focus of the promo, and the films can be listed within the theme. This helps alert viewers that the same type of movie will be on in the same time slot every day. Such promotions build consistency and habit and permit a more general promotion of the station, channel, or network.

A form of theme promotion was invented by Fred Silverman, the only individual to have programmed CBS, ABC, and NBC. Early in his career, while he was the programming director at WGN TV in Chicago, Silverman had a collection of old movies in his film inventory. They weren't particularly notable, just old. Attracting viewers to watch each title required an inordinate amount of promotion time. To overcome that inefficiency, Silverman came up with the title Family Classics.[5]

A distinguished-looking host appeared on a set that looked like an upper-class den to introduce each film. The host could also comment on the film as a way of filling time, thus saving on editing. Promotion of individual movies in the series was cut considerably, and the time was given over to promoting the format. The strategy worked because it conveyed a clear message. People knew that a movie suitable for the whole family would appear in that slot every day. The titles could be announced as part of a daily set of promos.

An updated variation on Silverman's principle was practiced by Cassandra Peterson, who acquired the rights to a collection of B-grade movies, covered her blond hair with a black wig, and presented the movies in syndication as Elvira, mistress of the night. She introduced each movie while reclining on a couch, dressed in a slinky black dress and looking for all the world like a sexy vampire. Audiences were attracted in great numbers to her camp escapades. Although the movies were hardly top drawer, people tuned in for Elvira's running commentaries, which were replete with double entendres. The promos were run for her rather than for the titles, and promotion time could thus be minimized.

In addition to promoting themes, options include solicitation of viewers' votes for titles, themes developed with the help of viewers, and unusual promotional schemes that get viewers involved. One example is a promotion in which viewers participate in a contest, after which the winner appears on the air during the broadcast of the film to make comments on it.

SPORTS PROGRAMMING

Independents have the flexibility of scheduling sports events on short notice without encountering the problems that an affiliate would have in dealing with preemption or delay of the network program schedule. It is important to appeal to all demographic groups at some time in the schedule so that all potential viewers watch the station. If they watch one thing on the station, they are more likely to watch something else. Sports packages help bring in male viewers, an important demographic group.

Independents cannot compete effectively against the amount or variety of sports programs offered by networks that have contracts for major sports. Much of the time, the independent must counterprogram against network sports. There are several options, though.

Cincinnati Reds baseball was brought into the Greenville-Spartanburg, South Carolina, market on an independent station. While there is no local tie to the Reds, there is no strong tie to any other baseball team either (the closest professional team in the region is the Atlanta Braves). Besides, baseball fans enjoy watching the different major league teams that play the Reds, and many fans follow the fortunes of teams that are long distances from where they live. Consequently, Reds baseball gave male viewers in that market the chance to watch major league baseball and follow one team closely.

This kind of decision must be made on the basis of local characteristics. While it worked in this instance, it would not work in all cases. It probably would not be wise, for example, to bring Reds games into California because of the many teams that play there.

Ad Hoc Sports Networks

Another sports programming opportunity comes from the ad hoc network, a collection of stations put together to air a particular event. Networks such as JP Sports (Jefferson-Pilot) and Raycom get the rights to various sporting events, often college contests. They then seek stations in all television markets to air them in exchange for cash or ad minutes. These broadcasts give stations an opportunity to make an impression on male viewers. Even if the ratings for the event are not high, goodwill and sampling are gained as men realize that the station is programming to their interests.

Contracts for college basketball and football have been expanded to include many more games and stations. Thus an independent that wants to get in on a sports package usually can find one. In the area of the Atlantic Coast Conference, for example (Virginia through Georgia), college basketball has always been extremely popular and games carried on television have achieved good ratings. Increased competition from national and regional cable sports channels such as SportsChannel America has made such acquisitions a bit more difficult in recent years, however.

Local Sports

Another option is local sports. Carriage of these contests has less prestige and is more difficult because local production is involved, but it buys goodwill for a station. A station can cover high school football, basketball, and other sports for later broadcast so as not to interfere with the live gate, using a relatively small crew. Small colleges in the area may be glad to receive coverage because their teams otherwise get very little television attention. By covering local sports, the station can establish a presence even if it is shut out of more desirable high-profile packages.

Wrestling

Most affiliates do not carry wrestling, partly because the network supplies so many hours of sports and partly because their managers fear that such carriage can sully a station's image. Regardless of its lack of mainstream respectability, wrestling draws audiences. Because of its popularity, many wrestling programs are available. This means that a station can lose out in its bid to purchase the rights to one version and pick up another, or the programmer can acquire two or more wrestling shows and run them as a block.

Another advantage of wrestling programs is that they are not tied to a time frame. Since wrestling is more entertainment than sport, the outcome is less important than the contest. Yet another important attribute of wrestling is its appeal to female viewers.

CHILDREN'S PROGRAMMING

Children are an important demographic segment for independents. While their discretionary income is low, their **nag factor**—the practice of badgering parents for particular products until they give in—is quite effective. Children are much more loyal to particular brands of products than adults are, and this translates into indirect purchasing power. There is no shortage of candy, cereal, and toy companies that advertise to children. Scheduling popular kidvid programs in otherwise unfocused time slots can be quite profitable. Of course, the fourth quarter of the selling year, which includes Christmas, is especially profitable.

The networks seldom cater to children except on Saturday mornings, when children are the primary demographic. At virtually all other times adults are primary, and affiliates go after primary audiences. Children constitute a substantial secondary demographic in other time periods, though, and independents can capitalize on this opportunity.

The second largest demographic group between 2:30 and 5:30 p.m. is children. Without a network station to serve their programming needs and desires, they are available for independents. Cartoon blocks that run from as early as 2:30 p.m. to as late as 5:30 p.m. are common, and independents tend to own the children's audience during these times.

Early Morning

Another opportunity to gather an audience of children exists during early morning, from 6 a.m. until about 8:30 a.m. Children are available to watch television then since getting ready for school may not take all their morning time.

The increase of second and third sets in the home has allowed children to watch cartoons while adults are watching the morning news. Moreover, many children have television sets in their rooms or beat their parents to the family set because they begin stirring around the house earlier than do other members of the family.

FIGURE 14-1 *Calvin and Hobbes © 1991 Watterson. Dist. by Universal Press Syndicate. Reprinted with permission. All rights reserved.*

Sunday Morning

While Sunday morning is something of a programming graveyard, as little viewing occurs, independents that do not have access to religious programs may find some success by running children's programming during this time period. Among all the possible demographic groups, children are the most likely to watch if something is provided for them. In this slot, they may also bring adults along. Traditional cartoon characters that are popular with adults as well as children—Daffy Duck, Bugs Bunny, and Woody Woodpecker—can do especially well.

Children's Game Shows

Another change has been the rise of children's game shows. This started with *Double Dare* and spread to *Fun House* and other shows. While parents were sometimes shocked to see how messy contestants got as they jumped into pools of whipped cream and crawled through butterscotch tunnels, children in the studio and at home were enthusiastic. The ratings were so high that *Double Dare* moved from its original cable home (Nickelodeon) to broadcast TV for wider distribution. The usual hysteria of game shows and their appeal to greed are magnified when children take part. Perhaps because of their lack of inhibitions, children do things adults will not do, and viewers are drawn to the zaniness.

INDEPENDENT SCHEDULING STRATEGIES

Scheduling strategies vary according to the environment in which each station operates. The number and strength of affiliates, the number of other independents, the percentage of homes using cable, and VHF/UHF allocations in the market all enter into the formulation of strategies. Here we discuss some general strategies for dayparts; the programmer must adapt them to the situation in a specific market.

Early Morning

The primary early-morning demographic—adults—is well served by affiliated stations' news blocks and is unlikely to watch other kinds of programs. The best bet for an independent is to target the strongest secondary demographic, which is children. Highly modular cartoons are the best fare because, like adults, children are preparing for the day. Live action and plot-intensive shows do not work as well. Children's tolerance for repeats makes it possible to rerun episodes more often or to run the same program in both the morning and the afternoon.

Daytime

Daytime is usually dominated by affiliates, but there are some windows of opportunity for an enterprising independent. The hour from 9 a.m. to 10 a.m. still belongs mainly to *Donahue* and other such talk/interview shows, but if each of the affiliates has scheduled such a program, an independent can counter with sitcoms and/or games. These shows should be fairly modular so that viewers who are occupied with other pursuits can still tune in and enjoy them without having to devote their full attention to the TV.

Game shows   From 10 a.m. until noon the affiliates broadcast a substantial number of game shows and an occasional sitcom fed by the network. If all the affiliates are programming games, sitcoms can constitute effective counterprogramming. Conversely, if two of the affiliates are doing comedies, a game may work well. It depends on the relative strength of each offering. *The Price Is Right* has run strongly for many years, but most other morning games do not have that show's drawing power.

Midday news   As the affiliates move through a short news block toward the soaps, it is time for the independent programmer to make a decision. The affiliates are vulnerable at noon because of the newscast, which is not as appealing to the primary demographic (women) as is what comes before or after. Thus, it can be counter-programmed effectively with comedy or even drama. The third option—a movie—is risky. Women may leave the affiliated station for the duration of the newscast but will usually return for the soaps. At 12:30 or 1 p.m. the affiliates' vulnerability ends. Women may not invest their time in a movie since they know they cannot see it through.

A good strategy for an independent station at noon may be to program two comedies, two game shows, or a 1-hour drama. Women can be drawn from the network affiliates for half an hour or an hour depending on when each network starts its soap opera schedule. Since the noon news is informational and the soaps are dramatic, comedies may be the best bet because they provide counterpoint, but their appeal depends on the specific shows the independent has available.

The soap opera block During the soaps, an independent has little opportunity to compete effectively for the primary demographic of women. Counterprogramming the soaps is difficult, and no substantial secondary demographic is available at that time.

One strategy is to run a movie from 1 p.m. to 3 p.m. and wait for the children to come home. A theme can help maximize whatever audience can be found, but this is not a time period when affiliates are vulnerable. Scheduling a movie simply constitutes a holding action.

A more aggressive strategy is to schedule comedies and dramas during that time period. In an increasingly mobile society, modular comedies can be very useful. Highly modular programs allow for both close and sporadic viewing, whereas low-modularity programs cannot be watched as easily in spurts. Another programming option—syndicated drama programs—takes advantage of the fact that off-network dramas, produced originally for prime time, have much a higher production quality than do daytime soap operas. One might pit syndicated episodes of *Dynasty* against daytime soaps.

From 3 p.m. to 4 p.m. the affiliates are still presenting soaps, but independents usually program a block of children's shows. This children's block can start as early as 2:30 p.m. If a comedy precedes children's programming, 2:30 is a transition time and a show that appeals to women and children and to available men is the wisest choice. Otherwise, 3 p.m. is considered a curtain time when an independent abruptly changes its programming appeals from women to children. Shows such as *Silver Spoons, The Brady Bunch,* and *Gilligan's Island* fill the bill. While they are older shows, overall television viewing levels are not suffficiently high to justify programming a higher-priced product.

Men in the daytime audience Most of the foregoing information ignores the presence of men in the daytime audience. While they are not a primary demographic group toward which to target programs in this daypart, men do constitute a secondary demographic segment. In very competitive markets with several independent stations, a station occasionally programs partly to this group for some portion of the daypart. Action shows and westerns shown in the daytime are examples. However, while men are important to advertisers, the number of women in the daypart tends to eclipse the men who are viewing.

Competing with affiliates in daytime In the example shown in Table 14-2, the first independent goes after a secondary demographic of males at noon with *Cannon,* an action show. The other independent uses an action show with a strong women's theme and presence in *Police Woman.* Both try to cut off the early soaps on CBS and ABC by programming hours that run through the 12:30 p.m. slot. Known as **front-ending** or **bridging,** this strategy centers on holding an audience with a longer program that begins earlier so that viewers miss the beginning or all of a competing program which starts later.

At 1 p.m. the independents go in different directions, with the first scheduling a drama, *Highway to Heaven,* and the second using the comedy *McHale's Navy.* The second independent

TABLE 14-2 Typical Afternoon Affiliate and Independent Schedules

	WNNN (NBC)	WCCC (CBS)	WAAA (ABC)	WIII (IND-1)	WJJJ (IND-2)
12:00	News	News	News	Cannon	Police Woman
12:30	News	Young/Restless	Loving		
1:00	Days of Our Lives		All My Children	Highway to Heaven	McHale's Navy
1:30		Bold/Beautiful			McHale's Navy
2:00	Another World	As World Turns	One Life to Live	One Day at a Time	Porky Pig
2:30				Favorite Martian	Ghostbusters
3:00	Santa Barbara	Guiding Light	General Hospital	Dennis the Menace	Thundercats
3:30				Smurfs	Chip 'N Dale

goes after children very early with *Porky Pig* at 2 p.m. That is a problem because many children are not yet home from school. A transitional show which appeals to both children and adults would be more appropriate for this slot. During the summer that would not be a problem since children are available to watch, unlike during the school year. Without the availability of children during the summer, the scheduling would effect a bumpy transition from the leading sitcom since *McHale's Navy* and *Porky Pig* do not figure to share demographic groups. If the station had programmed a show such as *The Brady Bunch,* it could have made a much smoother transition to children, as younger viewers would have more to identify with in *The Brady Bunch* than in *McHale's Navy.* Also, older viewers would respond more positively to *The Brady Bunch* than to *Porky Pig. Porky Pig* does lead effectively into the rest of the schedule, which is animation product.

The first independent still tries for some adults with the sitcoms *My Favorite Martian* and *Dennis the Menace* before moving to animation. Its use of *One Day at a Time* is appropriate at 2 p.m. because children are not yet in the audience. The transitional show at 2:30, *My Favorite Martian,* can appeal to both adult and younger audiences. Thus, it is effective in changing the focus from adults to children more gradually than the other independent station is able to do.

Both independents are counterprogramming the affiliated stations as well as each other. After

the adventure shows at noon, they do not run similar content again until 3:30 p.m. In the block from noon to 3:30, they offer alternatives to each other as well as to the networks. At 3:30 they provide a similar alternative to the networks and compete head to head for the same group—children. In the earlier period, between noon and 3:30, when women are the primary demographic, the independents have to try to attract some of this audience and pull viewers away from the affiliated stations' programs.

Generally speaking, affiliates compete against other affiliates while independents compete against both affiliates and other independents. But in the daytime period, when women are the only substantial demographic group, all stations are in direct competition. During early fringe, when affiliates program without network contributions, the competition opens up to all stations.

Early Fringe

Once into the children's block, the independents pretty much own that demographic group for the duration of early fringe. Soap operas end at 4 p.m., but women viewers generally are not drawn to the children's shows in progress on independent stations. They will probably stay with the affiliates and watch talk shows, court shows, game shows, and comedies. An independent can generally succeed by appealing to children until about 5 p.m.

The prenews hours   Five p.m. is a crucial time for both independents and affiliates. During the early fringe hours, affiliates get no programming except a half hour of news from the network. That means that all stations compete on much more even terms.

Most independents concede the adult demographic from 4 to 5 p.m. in order to keep control of the children's group. However, most affiliates move to news at 6 p.m., and their schedules become even more adult-oriented. Their scheduled comedies are more pithy, with fewer shows like *Happy Days* and more like *Cheers*.

It is here that an independent can begin the process of using an op-news (opposite the news) strategy to attract women, men, and children. This is a sizable group which can translate to high ratings, but the op-news show has to be strong and must be led properly because news is a powerful draw for adults.

Aging the audience   The 5 p.m. time slot for the independent requires another transitional show. But with higher viewing levels (HUT), more recent programs—which generally are more expensive to acquire—should be used. Shows such as *The Fresh Prince of Bel-Air* and *Growing Pains* can smooth the transition from animated kidvid to programs aimed at a wider audience. Both of these shows do very well with young viewers; they are also acceptable to adults and can constitute compromise shows for families in which there is a struggle for set control. The key is to provide an acceptable choice on which women, men, and children can all agree. That will also be the situation at 5:30 p.m. A show of the same type should be placed in this slot to enhance the likelihood that the audience will flow into the next time period with the independent rather than defecting to the news programs offered by the affiliates.

The op-news slot   This scenario assumes an affiliate newscast at 6 p.m. Not all markets follow that pattern, and so adjustments must be made for each market's news scheduling.

The op-news show itself must be very strong if it is to compete effectively with news. A good choice is a program that has ratings strength and is acceptable to all groups, even if it is expensive. Programs such as *Roseanne, The Simpsons,* and *A Different World* appeal to diverse audiences and have good ratings track records.

It is important to keep in mind that a major consideration for independents must be finances. Generally, independents do not have a programming budget comparable to that of affiliates. Thus, a quest to acquire many expensive programs can be financially ruinous. Moreover, since a growing number of independents are in competition for the best product, particularly in major markets, an already difficult situation has been exacerbated.

When an ideal show is not available and one of the three principal viewing groups cannot be targeted during the op-news time slot, the group that can most readily be given up is children. If the strongest available op-news show is *Dear John,* that is the program to schedule. The point is to flow as much of the 5 p.m. audience as possible into the op-news slot and hold it there.

The 6:30 p.m. weak slot   The weak slot at 6:30 p.m. is a little less important. If the audience has flowed through op-news, it is reasonably likely to stay through the rest of the hour without defecting to news. Affiliates normally air network news (the weakest draw in the news block) or are in the second half hour of a local newscast. Consequently, a contemporary comedy that runs well with the op-news show should work effectively.

The access hour   In many markets the affiliates finish their news block at 7 p.m. and compete more directly with what the independents have to offer. Most of the best products, including *Jeopardy, Wheel of Fortune, Entertainment Tonight, A Current Affair,* and other slickly produced shows, are almost exclusively the province of affiliated stations.

Since independents are exempt from the prime-time access rule, it may be helpful to schedule *Murphy Brown* or the best available program during the 7:30 access slot. The question for *Murphy Brown* owners is, Do we want to control the news block or the access slot? Obviously, doing both is most desirable.

Putting *Roseanne* in at 6 p.m. with *Murphy Brown* at 7:30 could constitute an effective one-two punch. Scheduling the two programs in the reverse order would also be potent.

Since 7:30 p.m. is one of the rare times where the half hour is the strong slot, the 7 p.m. show is less important as a lead-in than is normally the case. The best available comedy, even an aging one such as *Golden Girls,* can be placed at 7 p.m. Of course, outside of 7:30 and prime time, 7 p.m. has the highest HUT level.

Sex and violence in early fringe   The only don'ts in early fringe involve scheduling product with a heavy emphasis on sex or violence. All demographic segments are watching, including children, and such programs may draw the ire of parents.

Shows scheduled during early fringe have to be modular to accommodate the activities of preparing the evening meal, eating, and cleaning up. Besides being violent, action/adventure shows are typically plot-intensive. As such, they are not right for this daypart and tend to get poor ratings.

Many stations have tried hour-long drama or action programs in early fringe, but these programs don't generally work. All the promotion in the world will not save a program that is not right for the time period. For example, in the late 1980s *Magnum P.I.* was tried during early fringe. Promotional spots were targeted at women and younger girls, focusing on lead actor Tom Selleck's more comedic and "cute" scenes rather than on action. While they were very professional and effective promos, the content of the program did not meet the expectations generated by the announcements, and viewership declined. Most stations played out their runs in late night.

Hour shows are designed for 9 p.m. and 10 p.m. because the requirement for modularity is low at those times. Viewers will pay attention to the plot, and themes can be more adult, with

sex and violence liberally sprinkled into the content. The problem is that such shows don't play very well outside these time periods because the programming needs in other dayparts are different.

Prime-time soap operas replayed in early fringe   An independent programmer who buys the rights to an off-network nighttime soap opera such as *Dallas* with the intention of running the episodes in early fringe may be making a serious mistake. Soap operas, both daytime and nighttime, have little repeat value. Even during their network runs, prime-time soap repeats generate small audiences. Daytime soaps are not rerun. What a soap has to offer is suspense. Once the plot line has been unraveled, it loses its primary appeal.

The other problem with scheduling soaps in early fringe is their plot-intensiveness. They have little modularity and are therefore inappropriate for that daypart. An independent should not as a rule acquire soaps for early fringe. Affiliates can find more potential use for a syndicated prime-time soap as an early fringe lead because it can flow more naturally out of the afternoon soap block.

The programs that are scheduled during access are largely chosen on the basis of local considerations: Who owns the rights to what? Whatever the case, access is the time of day when an independent programs with maximum strength. Because the increasing quantity of news increases saturation, early fringe is a time when the affiliates are most vulnerable. An opportunity like this rarely arises for an independent.

In the example shown in Table 14-3, the first independent begins to age its demographic targeting at 5 p.m. with *Alf,* a program that reaches beyond children and teens, and again at 5:30 with *Silver Spoons,* which can appeal to adults as well as children. That makes for good flow into 6 p.m. and *Greatest American Hero.* Under other circumstances, this program would be considered too weak to carry the op-news hour, but the affiliates' newscasts do not start at the same time or follow the same pattern. Thus, the "traditional" formula that was outlined earlier

TABLE 14-3 Early Fringe Schedules for Affiliates and Two Independents

	WNNN (NBC)	WCCC (CBS)	WAAA (ABC)	WIII (Ind-1)	WJJJ (Ind-2)
4:00	Knot's Landing	Jeffersons	Oprah Winfrey	Woody Woodpecker	Jetsons
4:30		Current Affair		Ducktales	Real Ghostbusters
5:00	Jeopardy	Local News	Local News	Alf	Tale Spin
5:30	Local News		People's Court	Silver Spoons	Tiny Toon Adventures
6:00		Local News	Local News	Greatest American Hero	Gimme a Break
6:30		CBS News			Three's Company
7:00	NBC News	Family Feud	ABC News	Family Ties	Different Strokes
7:30	Wheel of Fortune	Inside Edition	Entertainment Tonight	Cheers	Roseanne

cannot be readily applied. The programmer must be flexible and responsive. This station has saved its strongest program for the access hour.

The second independent has a much smaller programming budget but has purchased one front-line show: *Roseanne.* The station stays with animation longer and has a bumpy transition between the animated *Tiny Toon Adventures* and *Gimme a Break,* a sitcom. The population in this market is 36 percent black, and so the 6 p.m. and 7 p.m. posts of *Gimme a Break* and *Different Strokes* are understandable. The weaker *Three's Company* lies in the hammock. Still, *Gimme a Break* is a weaker post than most programmers would like in view of the very low white viewership for the show (*Different Strokes* does well with white audiences). The posts could be switched to place the stronger program in the earlier post, but that would place the weaker program in a higher HUT slot. Such difficult decisions are common. Like WIII, the first independent, WJJJ saves its strongest programming for the access hour.

Affiliates' news decisions affect independents Much of the scheduling strategy in this market has grown out of affiliates' decisions to increase the length of newscasts. Initially, 1-hour newscasts ran at 6 p.m. During those times, the independents programmed more aggressively at 6 p.m., but a decline in the ratings of proven news-

lead series such as *M*A*S*H* led the affiliates to lead news with news. Confronted with a hodgepodge of starting times and blocking patterns from the affiliates, independents found it more difficult to know just how to counterprogram in these slots. Consequently, the independents countered with stronger access lineups and less expensive alternatives opposite the news shows.

Prime Time

Prime time is still controlled by the networks. The usual strategy for an independent is to run an hour of wide-appeal programming at 8 p.m., followed by a movie from 9 p.m. to 11 p.m. The programming from 8 to 9 p.m. can include comedy, drama, or action/adventure. Since it is early in the evening, the content should not be overly violent, as that may distress parents. Within that restriction, almost any other syndicated content may be workable.

Some stations turn this scheduling convention on its head by running a movie from 8 to 10 and an hour program from 10 to 11 p.m. This may not always be a wise strategy. First, the movie's content may be inappropriate for children. Second, the need for modularity is much lower at 9 than at 8 p.m. Third, flowing an audience to 10 p.m. gets it off the hook and possibly into an affiliate's hands an hour too early. The 10 p.m. hour is tough to program because of mass defections in the audience as many viewers begin preparations for bed. Scheduling a movie to end at 10 p.m. thus negates its advantage of a natural flow of viewers through the hour from 10 to 11 p.m. However, some independents have developed 10 p.m. news programs which are attractive and modular and offer a prime-time news alternative to the affiliates' 11 p.m. newscasts. In these cases, the movie scheduled from 8 p.m. to 10 p.m. is necessary.

Late Fringe

At 11 p.m. the affiliates largely repeat their 6 p.m. newscasts and thus make themselves vulnerable to competition even more than during their earlier news blocks. One big advantage they have is audience flow into their newscasts, which did not exist in early fringe.

As with the 6 p.m. newscast, a good counter to the news at 11 p.m. is comedy, which is highly modular and offers a strong alternative to news.

Programming the 11:30 p.m. slot is a matter of judgment. The half hour from 11 to 11:30 p.m. is the most heavily viewed in late fringe. Thus the 11 p.m. choice is important, and each half hour afterward becomes less important since the audience is rapidly departing for the night. For an independent that holds the rights to an old action/adventure show or comedy, this may be a good place to run the show out. However, if the independent broadcasts 24 hours, that strategy should be put off until after 2 a.m. because a reasonably large viewership is available until that time despite the migration of many people to bed.

The 11:30 slot can be filled with a movie that runs through to the sign-off. Modularity is high in this time period, but so is sleepiness. Decisions thus are somewhat less consequential. Although a highly modular program such as the *Tonight* show lets people fall asleep after watching a few portions of the broadcast, a low-modularity movie does much the same thing because people are generally lying down.

SUMMARY

Being an independent station has advantages and disadvantages. On the negative side, most independents are on UHF channels, which are difficult for many viewers to receive. A major drawback is the lack of network programming going to the station. An independent has a large hole to fill with programming and needs to sell large quantities of advertising time to stay afloat.

There are positives to independent existence. Flexibility and the ability to program nearly anything at nearly any time are pluses. Decisions can be made and implemented almost immediately. Independent programmers are among the best because they have to work in a difficult competitive environment. They are expert counterprogrammers, adept at surveying the competition and finding a way to offer viewers an alternative.

Among the program forms, movies, sports, and children's programming stand out here. Indepen-

dents use great quantities of movies and have to learn to evaluate movie packages and schedule them to the greatest advantage. Sports programming is different from most network packages but is important all the same. Independents participate in syndicated sports events and packages as well as local sports. Wrestling has provided many independents with an opportunity to score ratings points with programs usually not aired by affiliates. With children's programming all but gone from affiliates except on Saturday morning, independents provide hours of children's programs daily. By seeking out underserved demographic groups, independent programmers find ways to give them programming they enjoy.

Independents cannot dictate strategies to the stronger affiliated stations but must counterprogram and take advantage of their opportunities. One such opportunity exists during the early fringe period, where the prime-time access rule limits the affiliates in the 50 largest markets to first-run product or news programs. An independent can gather the best ratings of the day during early fringe, and so its best programs are placed there. Late fringe is another area of opportunity. While network programming helps the affiliates, an affiliated station generally leads the daypart with a newscast that is susceptible to counterprogramming.

Independents build much of their programming around what the affiliates are doing. By scheduling their best events opposite affiliates' weaker programs, independents can maximize the utility of their product. By placing children's fare in the afternoon, for example, they can control the youth demographic, which is attracted to their programs placed opposite the affiliates' adult-oriented shows.

With careful positioning and counterprogramming, independent stations can carve a niche in a market and in specific demographic groups. Their success during the 1980s and early 1990s is a testament to their ability to compete under difficult circumstances.

SUGGESTED READINGS

Marill, Alvin H.: *Movies Made for Television,* Zoetrope, New York, 1984.

This is a somewhat dated but very useful handbook of television movies for the independent programmer.

It supplies information about plot, length, and ratings performance for made-fors through 1983. Because independents use so many movies, reference works that supply important data on films are vital. Because made-fors have advantages over theatrical releases, tapping into this important resource is vital to the independent.

Brotman, Stuart N.: *Broadcasters Can Negotiate Anything,* National Association of Broadcasters, Washington, D.C., 1988.

This is must reading for every programmer in broadcasting or cable. While it is aimed at the sales department as much as at the programmer, dealing with syndicators for product is well covered. Brotman supplies tips and information about how syndicators operate and how to close the best possible deal on programs. As a guide for a "soldier" entering the "syndication wars," this book is without parallel.

NOTES

1. *Broadcasting and Cable Yearbook,* p. F-4.

2. Sydney Head and Christopher Sterling, *Broadcasting in America,* 5th ed., Houghton Mifflin, Boston, 1987, p. 88.

3. Ibid.

4. Joseph Dominick, *Dynamics of Mass Communication,* 3d ed., Random House, New York, 1990, p. 162.

5. Sally Bedell, *Up the Tube: Prime Time Television and the Silverman Years,* Viking, New York, 1981, p. 185.

CHAPTER 15

Programming the Network Affiliate

Programming a network-affiliated station—one which regularly transmits programs from NBC, ABC, CBS, or Fox—would seem to be much easier than programming an independent station, but that is only partly true. The increasing number of independent stations on the air, combined with the increasing success of cable networks, has made the task of a programmer at an affiliated station much more challenging. At one time an affiliate license was described as a license to print money, but those days are gone.

The acquisition of product for important dayparts, such as early fringe, has been complicated by the increased number of players in the game. Cable networks and superstations have become more aggressive in pursuing the most attractive off-network shows. In the past, cable mostly took hour programs which were not on most stations' wish lists. Eventually, though, cable went after the better half-hour shows, a process which caused uncertainty in prices and complicated the quest for top-quality programs.

The challenge in programming a commercial station is to maximize profit through competitive selection, acquisition, and placement of shows. The focus of this chapter is on the achievement of this goal at network-affiliated outlets. The chapter starts by describing the advantages of affiliation with a network and then moves to the economic aspects of affiliation. Next we describe the relationship, both contractual and procedural, between affiliates and their networks; in this area, there are some thorny issues brewing in the 1990s. Last, as with our discussion of independents in Chapter 14, we examine programming strategies as they are employed in each daypart. Affiliation has been called a gravy train, but often the ride is a bumpy one.

ADVANTAGES OF AFFILIATION

There are important advantages in programming an affiliated station. Consider the following:

1 Up to 70 percent of the typical affiliate's program schedule is supplied by the network at no cost to the affiliated station.

2 Network programming generally consists of the highest-quality programs.

3 When HUTs are the highest, the networks usually supply the programming; thus, an affiliate is almost guaranteed high ratings when they really count.

4 The diversity of network offerings is wondrous, including everything from sports to soap operas to world events.

5 The only *major* daypart an affiliate must program itself is early fringe, and even that period carries a news program supplied by the network. In addition to early fringe, affiliates generally are responsible for 9 a.m. to 11 a.m. and overnight.

6 Most syndicated programs are first offered for sale to affiliates because affiliates can pay the highest prices and produce the highest ratings.

7 Most, if not all, of the best access shows are developed specifically for affiliated stations by independent producers; in fact, all syndicated programs are offered to affiliates first.

8 The majority of affiliated stations broadcast on VHF channels, as most were among the first stations licensed. VHF signals have many advantages.

9 Affiliated stations get the best channel assignments on cable TV systems. Even with increasing competition, affiliates are still the dominant force in television markets.

10 Most stations get paid by their networks for carrying programs; they also get local spots with those shows and can sell the spots for the highest prices.

In the main, it is not feasible for stations to produce programming of the quality provided by the networks. The costs of hiring performing and production talent are prohibitive. Consequently, affiliated stations function as a conduit for network shows and profit from this arrangement by selling some of the available advertising time.

Another advantage is that the networks employ programming experts who have the contacts, the financial backing, and the scheduling expertise that stations do not have. If the networks fail to deliver on their stations' expectations, the affiliates are free to criticize their performance.

Trading Advertising Time for Programs

In exchange for supplying programs to affiliated stations, the network takes the lion's share of the available advertising spots within these shows. In prime time, the network takes all or most of the in-show spots and sells them to national advertisers.

In morning shows, the advertising time split is 50-50, with the network taking all the availabilities in two of the half hours and the affiliate taking the availabilities in the other two half hours. Other shows fed from the network vary in terms of spot division but fall somewhere between these two extremes.

Although the advertising inventory that an affiliate has to sell is limited, that is not necessarily a disadvantage. While an independent must sell most of its spots to cover the cost of the show, the affiliate has no "up-front" cost to cover. The affiliate gets free programming and can sell the spots allotted to it by the network. Because network programs attract large audiences, the selling process is less difficult and the revenues are high.

Adjacencies

Although the networks take the in-show spots in prime-time programs and sell them to national advertisers, the local affiliate gets to sell the **adjacencies**—the spots that appear between shows on the hour and half hour—to a combination of local and national advertisers. In the case of programs of an hour or longer, affiliates get some avails during the half-hour and hour breaks. These avails are sold at the rate of the higher-priced of the two programs between which they appear. For example, there is a large audience for an adjacent spot between *Roseanne* and *Coach,* making that adjacency valuable to the affiliate which gets it. This inventory of spots made available to the affiliated station amounts to about 2½ minutes an hour in prime time. While five 30-second spots per hour may not sound like much compared with an independent's 24 spots, the high ratings that come with network shows help those spots sell at high prices. With only five spots to sell and advertisers lined up to buy them, the sales process is less frenetic.

Network Compensation

An additional economic benefit to affiliated stations comes in the form of **network compensation,** which is money paid by networks to their affiliates to encourage them to carry network programs as scheduled. Compensation amounts to about 8 percent of ad revenues on the average, with larger-market stations getting more and smaller-market stations getting less. The amount and percentages vary by how badly the network needs to keep that station or market and can amount to a tidy sum over time.

It may seem silly for networks to pay compensation to affiliates at all. Since the programs given to affiliates are first-rate and the advertising spaces are profitable, one would think that was more than enough, but compensation has grown from historical roots. In the beginning, the networks competed for the best VHF stations. Network pioneers already knew the value of good local affiliates from their experiences in radio. One way to woo affiliates was to add something to the delivery of good shows, some icing on the cake. That was compensation. It can be thought of as an inducement or even a bribe, but compensation became a staple of the network-affiliate relationship. Later, after the relationships were established, compensation was a tool in spurring affiliation changes. If a strong network had a weak affiliate, it might approach a successful station in the same market and offer its strong lineup as a reason for switching affiliation. That was rarely enough reason, though, and attractive compensation rates were thrown into the bargain. Eventually local stations began to run occasional local shows instead of the network's offering, and that hurt the size of the network's national audience for that show, adversely affecting network advertising rates. Compensation was used as a bribe to encourage local stations to nearly always carry the network's programs. No compensation was paid for network shows that were not carried.

Now, after it may have outlived most of its usefulness, the networks are trying to cut back on compensation if not eliminate it entirely. Not surprisingly, stations have dug in their heels and fought any attempts to reduce compensation. However, compensation is already gone in some markets, and in a few others it never existed. The smallest markets have the least impact on national audience size. They are the most expendable and are not paid compensation because it is not necessary to buy their loyalty. The delivery of good shows and ad spaces is considered a blessing for them. This is one of the reasons why compensation may disappear by being phased out in the smaller markets and then in increasingly larger ones. With local competition being what it is, networks are in a better position to remind affiliates how good life is to them. Life as an independent would be infinitely more difficult.

THE NETWORK-AFFILIATE RELATIONSHIP

Affiliate Boards

The relationship between networks and their affiliates hinges on money and freedom. Affiliates give up freedom in order to make money, and networks pay money to hold affiliates in line for national sales purposes. The negotiations on those fronts are continuous. Each of the networks has an **affiliate board** made up of a group of general managers who represent the network's affiliated stations around the country. The affiliate board brings grievances to the network, and the meetings can be feisty. When CBS slipped to third place in the ratings in 1988, the cry from its affiliates was loud. The same noises had been made in earlier years by ABC and then by NBC stations.

Generally speaking, affiliates are most concerned when programs fail to produce audiences, and they lobby the network to replace those which are performing poorly. Network decisions to run documentary and other public service shows can draw fire from the boards since such shows almost always generate low ratings.

The boards also negotiate compensation. Networks want to cut compensation on the grounds that they should not have to pay affiliates to carry profitable shows. Since the affiliates are making money, the network argues, they need no further inducement to carry programs. If they wanted to make up their own lineups, they could become independents.

Not surprisingly, affiliate boards take a dim view of this philosophy. They point out how important the affiliates are to a network and how each station helps make high national ad rates possible.

Clearance and Preemption

What the networks encourage with station compensation is clearance, which means that the affiliate clears the time on its schedule and broadcasts the network's offering. That way, the network knows approximately what the size of the audience will be for a given episode of a show and can set advertising prices accordingly. Stations usually clear slots 2 weeks in advance. Thus an ABC affiliate clears space for *Full House, Roseanne, 20/20,* and the rest. CBS affiliates clear *Rescue 911* and *60 Minutes,* while NBC affiliates clear *Blossom* and *Unsolved Mysteries.*

Nonclearance Nonclearance is the refusal to clear space for a show. That hurts the network because it drains the national audience by the number of potential households represented in the markets of the uncooperative affiliates. Rejection is often based on a station's belief that the episode, special, or movie may draw negative reactions from local viewers.

In the 1970s some CBS affiliates objected to certain episodes of *All in the Family* and *Maude.*

In an episode that received low clearance, *Maude* had an abortion. Generally, though, affiliates clear shows because it is to their advantage to do so. They are not likely on their own to acquire programming capable of attracting audiences of the size that network offerings bring in. The popularity of network shows and their audience loyalty can translate to negative viewer response when an affiliate chooses to keep programs from the audience through nonclearance.

Preemption Another option for a local station is preemption. This does not denote a negative reaction to the show the network is feeding but occurs when a station acquires a program it wants to put in a good place in the schedule.

Locally produced programs generally garner smaller ratings but provide a community service or local focus. Stations will create and air them in prime slots to demonstrate their community involvement. Sometimes stations buy the rights to a big-budget, high-quality program that deserves a good slot. This is yet another circumstance in which a station will preempt. *Sadat,* the special detailing the life of the late Egyptian president Anwar Sadat, was such a show. While the station bears the network no ill will in a preemption situation, the loss of audience is felt at the network just the same. Continued preemptions make for friction in the network-affiliate relationship.

Generally speaking, nonclearance is a station's way of rejecting a network's offering. If a station believes that an episode of a show is too sexually explicit, for example, it will not clear it. Now, of course, it will have to scramble to find a program to replace it in the space it didn't clear. In a preemption situation the station already has a show and wants a place to air it. If it is a tribute to the city's Super Bowl or World Series winner, the station will kick something out of the schedule to make room for the sports heroes. The station is not angry with the network and is not out to prove any point. It just wants some time for this special program.

Since the net outcomes of nonclearance and preemption are the same—no network pro-

gram—networks and viewers perceive them as the same. Even some local stations have begun to use the terms interchangeably.

The economics of nonclearance Perhaps the most important factor in nonclearances and preemptions is money. When a station runs its own program, all the ad spots are available for sale by that station. Thus, a show can get only a third of the ratings of the show it has displaced and still make a profit. That assumes that all those spots can be sold in a local program that lacks the pizzazz of a typical network offering. If the station *can* sell those spots, though, and hold half the normal network audience, the profit will be greater still.

Preemptions tend to occur during a network's weakest shows because they are the most expendable. When the Billy Graham Crusade sets the TV schedule for its revival broadcasts, it tries to get an hour on the strongest station in each of the markets it buys. Because stations receive cash for the hour, they will preempt network shows that have weak audiences. This practice is a source of frustration to viewers who want to tune in a documentary program or cultural special being fed by the network, since this is where preemptions often occur. Documentaries are sometimes broadcast as **sustaining programs**—programs without commercials—because commercials cannot be sold. Just about as bad, the avails are sold at very low prices to advertisers because the audience is almost always very small, and so the station compensation is low. Consequently, the station can make much more money by preempting for the religious broadcast.

Looking at it economically, if there were 9½ minutes, or nineteen 30-second spots, available for network and affiliate sale in a 1-hour weak program, the affiliate would receive about 2½ minutes (five spots) to sell locally, plus it would receive some network compensation. When the program is preempted and the time is sold to the religious broadcaster, revenues will be received for all 19 spot avails in the hour. The religious broadcaster will pay for the time according to

TABLE 15-1 The Economics of Preemption

Program	Source	No. Spots for Local Station	Income per Spot, $	Total Income, $	Program Cost, $	Profit, $
Bulwark	CBS	5	3000	15,000	0	15,000
Lincoln	Syndicator	19	1500	28,500	6000	22,500
Crusade	Church	19*	2000*	38,000	0	38,000

*Spots do not run in the show. Instead, the church pays for the equivalent value of the spots that would have run in that time period.

Note: In this example, 9½ minutes per hour of advertising is assumed. Those minutes are further broken out as nineteen 30-second spots. Program cost is estimated on the basis of typical syndicator prices.

    The hypothetical network program *Bulwark* actually delivers the lowest profit to the local station. Religious programming, because of its lack of acquisition cost, is the most profitable.

how many spot positions are contained in it, including those which would normally go to the network. In this example, the station's gain is great because it does not have to pay either production costs or syndication fees for the preempting program, all avails are "sold," and the only lost revenue is the compensation, which was small anyway. Under normal circumstances, though, the station has to factor in considerably more money as either production costs for a local special or syndication costs for a special or movie. That makes the economic equation tilt toward the network and away from preemption (Table 15-1).

Affiliates' Displays of Independence

Because of their VHF dial positions and locations in large markets, some affiliates display surprising independence. For example, in the late 1980s WCVB TV, Boston, an ABC affiliate, purchased the rights to *Star Trek: The Next Generation* and preempted two ABC Friday primetime comedy series. That defection was frightening to the network. It was losing that time period in a major market not on a one-time basis but week after week. Worse, other stations saw the success of WCVB's action and were emboldened to make similar moves. Luckily for the networks, no other syndicated shows available to date have the strength to perform competitively in prime time, but a new era in network-affiliate relations seems to have begun (Box 15-1).

Affiliate Contracts

In accordance with FCC rules, network-station affiliation contracts may be made for periods of 2 years and then are subject to renewal. Either side can withdraw from the relationship rather than renew the contract. Stations can make much more money as affiliates than as independents, and so they value their relationships with the network. Still, like the example of WCVB cited earlier, they like to have some freedom of action. That flexibility is tied to market size and the configuration of the market.

Strains on Network-Station Relationships

The reciprocal station-network relationship can be strained if the network feels that an affiliate is not keeping up its end. A review of a hypothetical market, Midtown, illustrates how the players in the relationship can change.

    The Midtown market has six stations:

    WAAA, ABC (channel 2)
    WCCC, CBS (channel 7)
    WNNN, NBC (channel 4)
    WIII, independent (channel 13)
    WFFF, independent (channel 22)
    WPPP, PBS (channel 9)

Frequent preemptions The CBS affiliate, WCCC, is unhappy with CBS prime-time program rat-

**BOX 15-1
THE STRUGGLE FOR
CONTROL OF TIME**

There's an old saying, "Be careful what you wish for; you might get it." Stations have wanted their networks to provide programming, but they have often preempted that programming with impunity. They have also resisted networks' attempts to program additional time slots. At the May 1988 ABC affiliates meeting, the network made a surprising proposal to its affiliates: It offered to return an hour of prime time to affiliate control—the heavy VCR use hour between 8 and 9 p.m. on Saturday. This caught the affiliates by surprise because they had fought network hegemony in prime time and access for years. Now, confronted with the option of programming the hour themselves, they overwhelmingly turned it down, but a landmark had been established. If the affiliates were going to hound networks about certain slots and preempt the attempts that the networks made, the ball might end up back in the affiliates' court. In the future, any preempting in that time slot will constitute a message to the network that affiliates may want to control their own destiny in that slot, but that is a message they would rather not send.

SOURCE: "To Give or Take an Hour," *Electronic Media,* June 20, 1988, p. 12.   ■

---

ings and frequently preempts network offerings. It has gone so far as to buy the rights to *The Eliminators of Vulcan* and is running it on Tuesday from 8 to 9 p.m., to the expressed dismay of the CBS Television Network's affiliate relations office.

The network's options   CBS will first look over the market to see if it has any options for changing affiliates when the agreement with WCCC runs out. WAAA and WNNN are strong stations, but feelers are rebuffed since both are happy with their networks. CBS then calls WIII because it broadcasts on a VHF signal and might become a good affiliate. WIII is very much interested and says that as an affiliate it would almost never preempt network shows. While that promise is not legally binding, given the nature of affiliation agreements, verbal assurance has some impact. CBS now has an option: It can renew its affiliation with WCCC or change to WIII when the affiliation agreement with WCCC expires. The management of WCCC figures out that the network is unhappy, and so it too must make a decision.

Usually the network will give a station one more chance with the understanding that certain practices must be followed. The station makes the requisite promises and the contract is renewed for 2 years, but everyone knows that

WCCC is on probation. WIII will happily call CBS every time WCCC steps out of line with hopes of prying the two parties apart so that it can capitalize on an opportunity to markedly increase its market value by becoming an affiliate.

In markets with only three VHF assignments, the affiliates that hold those allocations have tremendous freedom of action. They know that their networks will be unlikely to turn away from them to affiliate with a UHF station, and so they can preempt with impunity.

Changing Networks

In this example, the market configuration gave the network an option, which rarely happens. In markets with fewer than three VHF channel assignments, there are not enough VHF stations to accommodate the networks, and so one network ends up with a UHF affiliate. If a VHF station in the market is aligned with the third-place network and a UHF station has the first-place network, a call usually ensues. The first-place network calls the VHF station and inquires whether that station would like the advantage—increased ratings—of association with number one. If the answer is yes and the contracts expire at the same time, the VHF station may change to a new network. That will leave the UHF station without a network and the last-place network without an affiliate in that market. Thus, out of necessity, they will get together. This happens with some frequency. In this form of "television Darwinism," the weakest network is usually affiliated with the UHF station while the VHFs can change to take advantage of a network's rising fortunes.

Such switches occurred during the middle to late 1980s, when the NBC Television Network moved from third place to first place. A benefit of NBC's success was that it attracted more VHF affiliates. Their wider coverage areas and larger audiences enhanced NBC's prospects for remaining the first-place network, and this was the case for some years.

Adding Channels to a Market

Occasionally a market with one or two VHF affiliates and one or two UHF affiliates is assigned a newly allocated channel. Let's say VHF 2 is CBS, VHF 7 is NBC, UHF 19 is ABC, and UHF 62 is Fox. After being advised that there are no technological barriers to doing so, the FCC adds a new signal to the market—channel 5. Most likely channel 5 will function as an independent until the end of UHF 19's affiliation contract, when channel 5 will become the ABC affiliate. As soon as the new channel allocation is announced, UHF 19 begins preparation for life as an independent. However, Fox, which has been on channel 62, will probably express an interest in channel 19.

Affiliation Agreements

The affiliation agreement is simple in that the station is obligated to do very little. The primary points are as follows:

1 Stations agree to air network programs unless they provide notice (usually 2 weeks) that they will not. If the affiliate does not clear, the network can air the program on another station in the market. What this boils down to is that the affiliate has the right of first refusal on a show.

2 The network will pay a negotiated amount in compensation, except in small markets, where none is paid.
3 The agreement expires in 2 years and then must be renegotiated.

Specific additional points can be written into the contract, but the basics are straightforward. The network is not allowed to dictate advertising rates, force clearance, or otherwise intimidate the affiliate. In reality, though, affiliates that anger their networks are vulnerable to being abandoned and forced to seek another network affiliation or deal with the difficulties of independent status.

AFFILIATE PROGRAMMING STRATEGIES

Dayparting

Strategies within dayparts have been developed over the years through analyzing audiences and determining their wants and needs according to the time of day. Thus, the term *dayparting* is applied to the process of developing shows that flow within dayparts if not necessarily between them.

All stations daypart their schedules to reflect audience changes by time of day. Shows must be tailored to audience composition and activities. For affiliate stations, most of the more difficult slots are filled by the network.

Early morning In early morning, the networks provide newscasts (starting at 6 a.m.) that eventually lead into the information shows that run from 7 to 9 p.m.: *Good Morning America, CBS Morning Show,* and *Today.* As was described in Chapter 11, these shows are highly modular and reflect the activities of audience members and their limited attention potential.

Morning Limited morning times have to be filled between the network news and game blocks. Affiliates schedule the period from 9 to 11 a.m. themselves, but they get help. A number of well-received talk shows are geared to this hour and center on issues of interest to women. They are moderately modular, matching the requirements of the time period. The primary clients are affiliates, which tend to be the stronger stations in their markets. Thus affiliates get the first shot at *Donahue, Geraldo, Oprah, Sally Jessy Raphael,* and *Joan Rivers.*

There are so many talk shows available that some stations buy 2 hours' worth and use one of them in the afternoon. Another option is to run talk shows for the 2 hours and lead them into network game shows. An hour of talk can also be supplemented with an hour of games or comedy. As long as modularity is maintained, both approaches lead well to the network games at 11 a.m.

At 11 a.m. the networks feed game shows such as *The Price Is Right* and the morning version of *Wheel of Fortune.* These shows are modular in structure, as the viewing audience is involved in chores, errands, and related activities. These programs lead into the affiliates' noon news shows, which are followed by the soap opera block.

Early fringe   At 4 p.m. affiliates must again begin to program their own schedules. The audience is in transition while the last soap opera is running; children are coming into the audience in substantial numbers. Affiliates know that most independents will be targeting children at 4 p.m., when the soaps end. This means that the primary demographic—adults—is still available. There are many options here. The primary available audience is still women, as substantial numbers of men will not begin to enter the available audience for another hour or so. Children form a secondary demographic segment, but they can be ignored and left to the independents.

Most affiliated stations choose comedies, talk shows, court shows and games for this time period. Program modularity is on the rise to accommodate changes in activities in the home. Thus, comedies need to be more joke-centered and less plot-intensive. A comedy such as *Family Ties* would fit more comfortably than would *Cheers.*

Other stations choose semimodular talk shows for the 4 p.m. slot. *Oprah Winfrey* has proved to be successful in that period. As the show is modular and sometimes oriented to lighter issues, it can flow to court shows, comedies, or games. The affiliate's strategy is to build a schedule that will provide a good lead-in to the local news at 6 p.m. Affiliates which schedule news at 5 p.m. have enjoyed success with *Oprah Winfrey* as a news lead.

Leading the News   At 5 p.m. the station has to start shifting the demographic appeals of its programming to allow for men and working women entering the audience without unnecessarily losing any of the established audience. These transitional shows include more adult sitcoms, such as *Cheers,* which focus on situations, relationships, and plots. The 5 p.m. show is also important because it must flow to the 5:30 show, which functions as the news lead in many markets.

The news lead can make the difference between first place and third place in a highly competitive market. Unfortunately, there are not enough shows that function as effective news leads. *M*A*S*H* used to be effective because of

FIGURE 15-1   *Reprinted with permission of* **BROADCAST-ING** Magazine *(January 14, 1991).* © *1991 by Cahners Publishing Company.*

Drawn for BROADCASTING by Jack Schmidt

"Look on the bright side. Your ski report was our highest-rated show of the season."

its upscale adult demographics, but it has been played many times and has finally burned out. The same thing has happened to *Barney Miller* and *Taxi*. They can do sufficiently well in late fringe but are no longer strong enough to lead the news.

This paucity of available product has led to some interesting solutions. One option is to use *Oprah Winfrey* at 5 p.m. The same issue orientation that makes it useful at 4 p.m. also makes it workable at 5 p.m. It can be fronted with comedies or court shows as well as games.

A second solution is to lead news with news. In a futile search for the perfect news lead, many stations have decided to extend the early news show and lead news with a softer, feature story–oriented newscast at 5:30. This makes good sense. If there is no comedy or other material that blends in well with news and preserves flow, news provides a solution. It is relatively inexpensive to produce an expanded show when the news staff is already in place, and the use of consumer, health, and nutrition reports has proved successful with female-dominated earlier audiences.

This tactic makes the 5 p.m. comedy or court program the news lead-in. In a world characterized by competition for programs, that makes one less show that the affiliate station must acquire.

The main consideration in the expansion of news to 5:30 or even 5 p.m. is that its content should be tailored to the available audience. As an earlier newscast it should appeal to women more than the 6 p.m. version does. Furthermore, it is being led by a show with a reasonably sized women's audience. This has led to the rise of feature news in early fringe newscasts.

The model already exists in the noon newscast. Because it is directed more toward women than is any other newscast in the schedule, it contains more human interest and feature stories. Adapting that model to 5:30 p.m. or earlier has not proved particularly difficult. Stations have added consumer reporters, health reporters, nutrition reporters, and family issues reporters.

One popular addition has been a consumer reporter who functions as an advocate in many markets. This reporter follows up on consumer complaints, arriving at the recalcitrant business complete with a video crew. This high-profile approach very often works with the business in question, enhancing the station's image with its viewers. The trend toward more news has been so successful that in some major markets, such as Los Angeles, stations run 3-hour local newscasts. Of course, if syndicated product is scarce, as it is in any market with many competing stations, additional news is cost-efficient. It can be produced for less money than some syndicated products, and it leads itself well. Even if the news gets a lower rating, it can generate more profit because of the rising cost of syndicated programs and because premium rates can be charged to advertisers who like the quality of the news audience.

After the local news comes the network newscast. In some markets in the Central and Mountain time zones, where all dayparts are moved up an hour, the network newscast often runs first, during the slot with a lower HUT level. In either case, the local and network news shows run back to back. When the news block ends at 7 p.m. (6 p.m. Central and Mountain), a decision must be made. How should the station move into access? As it is with an independent station, the 7:30 p.m. access slot is the more important of these two half hours.

Access and Affiliates Access is not as much of a problem for affiliates as it is for independents. Many shows have been created specifically for affiliates, including *Wheel of Fortune, Entertainment Tonight, A Current Affair,* and *Jeopardy.* Depending on what the affiliate has chosen to air during access, the 7 p.m. show can then be selected.

Since game shows flow well with other game shows and since they are a current force in access, stations scheduling a game show at 7:30 p.m. sometimes precede it with another such show at 7 p.m. This strategy makes for a somewhat bumpy transition following the news. Still, news doesn't flow especially well with anything else (at least naturally), and HUTs are rising, which means that new viewers are joining the available audience. Thus, a semicurtain time exists at 7 p.m. in many markets. Many shows are usable at this time, including *Jeopardy* (especially for a station that runs *Wheel of Fortune* at 7:30) and *Family Feud.*

Some shows fail, such as *Win, Lose, or Draw.* This show lost viewers rapidly and was canceled, leaving the affiliates that had purchased rights to it with a programming problem. With the prime-time access rule preventing affiliates from using off-network product, the options are limited.

This void has been filled by reality shows (sometimes called tabloid shows) such as *Inside Edition* and *A Current Affair.* These programs are highly modular, are aimed at adults, and are just titillating enough to stimulate more interest than protests. They fit well with news as well as with entertainment programs, which gives them flow flexibility. With their modularity and mix of information and entertainment, they can be scheduled with nearly any kind of programming.

Prime Time

Prime time is the domain of the networks. The predominant strategy is to have family shows of low to moderate modularity in the time period from 8 p.m. to 9 p.m. Since no activities will be pressing until bedtime at around 11 p.m., program modularity is low and flow within the daypart is reasonably consistent.

Late Fringe

Leno, Hall, Letterman, and Koppel rule in late fringe. Many ABC affiliates delay Ted Koppel's *Nightline* until midnight in order to run a profitable syndicated comedy after the news. This delay is costly to the network, but not as costly as nonclearance.

Late fringe can be scheduled by the station, or the station can simply accept the network feeds. Some CBS affiliates will not clear the network's late fringe action programs but substitute their own stable of comedies, action shows, and movies. In that way, they can control the advertising inventory and make more profit. Clearance is not quite as important at midnight as it is in prime time. Again, this is not a difficult period to schedule. A strategy for CBS affiliates is to follow the newscast with a reasonably modular comedy and then follow that with an hour show or a movie.

NBC affiliates are set for late fringe with *The Tonight Show with Jay Leno, Late Night with David Letterman,* and *Later with Bob Costas.* Some affiliates repeat the late newscast in the 1:30 a.m. slot before *Later* or at 2:30 a.m. as a service to shift workers.

A number of affiliates and independent stations have acquired *The Arsenio Hall Show,* which has proved to be an effective competitor against network late-night talk shows.

Overnight Overnight, from 2 to 6 a.m., is locally programmed by some stations although all the big three networks provide a news, issues, and interview program from 2 to 6 a.m. If the station is a 24-hour operation, that daypart provides a kind of elephants' graveyard for shows that have burned out or failed but whose local rights are owned by the station. The phrase "use them or lose them" applies here since rights run out over time even if the episodes do not air. This is a favored time for shows such as *Real People* and *Rhoda.* The first was not a syndication success; the second burned out.

Local Production

The cost of syndicated product has been rising for over 10 years. Occasionally syndicated product is ruinously expensive. Several buyers of *The Cosby Show* in syndication have actually sold off their rights to other stations to stem their losses.[1] The point has been reached where it is possible to create local shows that make a profit. If they are popular, they are available for unlimited replays in the future.

Consequently, more and more affiliates, particularly in larger markets, are rediscovering local production in the 1990s. With expanded news shows and large news crews already in place, marketplace factors have combined to make local production an attractive option.

These productions usually center on items of local interest. They tend to be upbeat and sometimes humorous because that draws audiences best. The poor conditions of roads may be of interest but probably would be boring to viewers. However, new rides at the local theme park can make for a viewable production. Local landmarks and events also make good subjects. Sometimes stations send crews to other cities to offer a form of travelogue for viewers. Celebrity interview shows modeled after the Barbara Walters specials have proliferated, with local anchors or entertainment reporters doing light interviews with personalities who are passing through town. These interviews can be compiled and run as half hours or hours depending on how many interviews can be secured. If the celebrity remains in the public spotlight, the program has good repeat value.

These productions are not difficult to mount because the news crews are accustomed to shooting footage and are becoming more adept at shooting feature footage and using creative angles and techniques to make that footage more visually interesting. As a result, these crews are better prepared than ever before to create feature programs.

Importantly, locally produced shows can raise the market profile of a station. These productions can help position the station as more locally focused in an era when local production has been in decline.[2]

For profit-making purposes, locally produced interesting programs can be run in prime time. As was outlined earlier, weak network programs can be temporarily replaced by a potentially profitable product.

Affiliates and Cable

Cable has helped affiliates in many cases. In areas at the fringe of the ADI, cable systems that carry affiliates' signals have often made them clearer for viewers. Thus, the station's signal is improved and reaches more households.

Cable system operators still tend to treat affiliates with more deference than they show independents. Since network programs still account for the largest block of all viewing, subscribers want to get affiliates' signals on their cable systems and don't want any confusion about where to find the network channels. Therefore, affiliates are more likely to get their normal channel numbers on cable.[3] In some cases a VHF affiliate is assigned a UHF channel on the local cable system, and this causes problems for viewers who become confused about the locations of their favorite stations. In this case the affiliate can respond by placing both its broadcast and its cable channel numbers on its logo to help its viewers.

SUMMARY

There are many advantages to network affiliation. An affiliate receives high-quality programming from the network in exchange for advertising time. By relying on the network for as much as 70 percent of its program day, the affiliate finds itself under much less of an acquisition burden.

The better early fringe and access programs are created with affiliates in mind. These affili-

ates are usually approached first by syndicators.

Most affiliates, at least for now, receive network compensation for carrying network programs. Stations sell the advertising adjacencies between prime-time shows.

The relationship between affiliates and networks is not always smooth. Affiliate boards are set up to give stations a vehicle for talking back to the networks. Problems with ratings for some programs make for unhappy affiliates. Still, in the main, stations prefer affiliation to independent status.

Affiliates daypart their schedules in an effort to present the appropriate programming to the largest available demographic groups. Since they can acquire most of the best programming, affiliates are in a position to consistently seek out the largest, most attractive demographic group available in each daypart.

SUGGESTED READINGS

Broadcasting

Interestingly, there are no great books dealing with local affiliated stations. The people who run stations and those who are in charge of affiliate relations at the networks do not write books about their work. This is an industry segment that has developed through doing without much written literature, but the information void is filled by the trade publications. Chief among these, when it comes to affiliates, is *Broadcast-*

ing. Each week the programming section of this magazine looks into current practices in network relations, scheduling, competing and cooperating with cable, program acquisition and development, and economics. Thus, the place for students of affiliated programming to study current events is the trade magazines.

Electronic Media

Like *Broadcasting, Electronic Media* devotes large portions of its space to programming considerations. It also looks at affiliate relations, economics, programming and scheduling practices, and program development.

NOTES

1. "KMOV-TV Sells 'Cosby' to Indie," *Broadcasting,* May 21, 1990, p. 33.

2. Arthur Kern, "Local TV Programming: The Long-Term Advantage," *Variety,* Jan. 9, 1985, pp. 82, 154.

3. Personal communication with W. B. Wood, operations manager, TCI Cable of Athens, Georgia, May 1991.

Broadcast Networks

For decades the big three television networks—ABC, CBS, and NBC—dominated prime time. On any given night they accounted for over 90 percent of all television viewing, with the little that remained being shared by public and independent stations. These kinds of stations were not considered worthy competitors, and cable was seen only as a service that enabled people in remote areas with poor reception to get network signals from the nearest major city.

Things have changed: The total network share of viewing in prime time has dropped to near 60 percent and may drop further.[1] What happened? The answer is fourfold. First, cable developed from a minor player in the early seventies to its current 60 percent penetration in an extraordinarily short time. Improved technology gave cable systems the capacity to deliver 36, 54, or more channels to subscribers. Many of those services were specifically designed to cut into the networks' audiences by targeting men (ESPN), women (Lifetime), or children (Nickelodeon). As cable penetration has increased, network audience shares have declined.

Pay services such as HBO have provided a steady diet of one of television's most successful program forms: movies. To make matters worse for the networks, the movies shown on pay cable include the most desirable recent titles that in an earlier era would have made their first appearances after theatrical distribution on network television.

Second, independent television caught on. Even with the problems of UHF signals, modern televisions had better tuners, and indies got a boost in audience potential when they were carried on cable systems, something that improved their signals and carried them farther. Thus, more independents stayed in business, and many became aggressive program buyers in their markets.

Third, VCR penetration and usage increased dramatically. From 2.5 percent penetration of American households in 1982, VCRs jumped to over 70 percent of homes in 1992. This diffusion of home video recorders gave rise to a whole new video industry, with rentals and sales on one side and home video camera productions on the other.

Fourth, the Fox Network became a serious competitor in 1991. After a modest Sunday night start with *Married . . . with Children, The Simpsons,* and *Totally Hidden Video,* Fox systematically expanded to other days. In 1990 *The Simpsons* was moved opposite *The Cosby Show* and survived.

With so many alternatives available, the traditional big three networks lost viewers to other outlets, but this is not the time to count them out. Like other media entities before them, the networks have evolved to meet the competitive challenge and now do some things differently. Regardless of their diminished stature, they are still the big three, the inventors of most program forms and the developers of most programming and scheduling strategies.

This chapter will look at how networks work with independent producers to develop programs. Next, network programming strategies will be examined. The chapter ends with a discussion of the programming problems that the big three traditional broadcast networks have been experiencing in the last few years.

NEW PROGRAM DEVELOPMENT

Networks commission programs from independent producers and hope those programs will draw audiences and generate revenue. As shows are constantly aging and dying off, replacements are in constant demand. Since there is always a last-place network, there is always a network in search of goodly numbers of programs.

Commissioning Programs

Three basic kinds of programs are carried on networks: network-owned entertainment programs, independent productions, and news/public affairs programs. Networks are limited in the number of shows they are allowed to produce by the restrictions of the financial interest and syndication rule (fin-syn). With the exception of news, public affairs, and sports shows, this rule generally limits networks to 40 percent of the prime-time entertainment product in which they can own a share of syndication rights. Therefore, they must commission most of their programs from independent producers who are free to sell them for broadcast again after they have completed their two network plays (see Chapter 13). Still, from the networks' perspective, the 40 percent rule is preferable to the original fin-syn rules that existed before 1991. Under the original rules, networks were limited to about 3½ hours of programming a week in prime time in which they could have a financial interest or participate in syndication revenues.

In news and sports and public affairs programs, which have little or no replay or syndication value, the networks have been free to produce, repeat, and retain rights, although those rights are of very little value after the initial play. Because the FCC wanted to limit the domination of the networks over television programming, the original fin-syn spurred the independent production industry. A network could make money on a nonowned show's network run by selling advertising time in the episodes it had "rented," but the production company owned all ancillary rights, such as overseas distribution and domestic syndication. After the 1980s, the networks were not the powerhouses they had been in the 1960s and 1970s and the rules were relaxed. By allowing networks to participate in the ownership and syndication of programs, the FCC helped them withstand increasing competition from cable, big production companies, and home video.

Networks develop programs in-house in ways similar to the way in which they help develop programs through independent producers. For our purposes, we will use the independent production model, which still accounts for the majority of prime-time programming and allows a more comprehensive look at the creative and economic processes involved.

Literally hundreds of ideas are pitched by would-be producers to the networks. Some of these notions are dismissed out of hand. The ones that seem to have possibilities are subjected to several levels of scrutiny, starting with a script.

Commissioning a Script

In many cases the producer and writer are the same person. The television industry is known for what it calls hyphens—producer-writers such as Stephen Cannell *(21 Jump Street, Wiseguy, Hunter)* and Linda Bloodworth Thomason *(Designing Women, Evening Shade)*—who write many of their own scripts. A script development process requires the services of writers and editors, and its costs run into the thousands of dollars. The network pays for script development with no promise of accepting the final product.

After a script has been developed, it is brought back to the network for consideration, and the winnowing process continues. Ideas that still seem promising can be subjected to concept testing, or a pilot can be commissioned by the network.

Concept Testing

Concept testing (see Chapter 4) is based on asking people to respond to a capsule form of the show's premise or a story line from the show. Here is an example:

A couple, having grown up in the liberal college atmosphere of the sixties, faces the trials and tribulations of raising their more acquisitive and conservative offspring in the 1980s. The clash of values centers on the oldest child, a Reagan Republican who operates in stark contrast to his more liberal parents.

This is, of course, an outline for *Family Ties*. While cheap and quick, concept test results often bear no resemblance to viewer reaction to a show that gets on the air. Some shows test well and fail after being introduced in a network's lineup, while others that test poorly succeed when they are produced. For example, would you be interested in the following show?

A New England innkeeper and his wife face life with a quirky handyman, a snooty and rather useless maid, and a trio of brothers from nearby who seem to have no social sense of any kind. He supplements his income by writing how-to books and hosting a pedantic talk show on a small local television station.

While this captures the essential features of *Newhart,* it captures none of the show's spirit, wit, and warmth. This concept might have tested terribly, but the show itself was an unqualified success.

Concept testing may not be the best way to test programs, but it is the least expensive. It would be prohibitively expensive to give all potential shows a full script and pilot test treatment. Many more concepts can be tested on paper at very little cost before more money is invested in the further development of the most promising ideas. Concept testing trades accuracy for savings.

The Pilot Test

Concepts and scripts that seem to have the greatest promise lead to the commission of a pilot. A pilot can be thought of as a prototype, custom-built and one-of-a-kind, that demonstrates to audiences the nature of the series that will eventually be produced. This production of an actual episode of the proposed series can be screened by programming executives to develop a better evaluation of the execution of the ideas that were presented earlier in scripted form. The pilot can also be shown to test audiences to obtain their reaction to it (Chapter 4).

A frequently used variation of the pilot episode is the made-for-television movie. That treatment allows for more substantial promotion than is possible with a single episode of an unknown series and permits the development of characters in more depth. Since the movie has some ancillary distribution possibilities, failure to gain a spot on the network schedule for the series being evaluated is not as costly to the producers. One episode of a show has no sales value, but a movie can be included with other movies in a package.

As in the earlier stages of development, the

poor prospects are weeded out after evaluation. Each network will continue its investment in the development of the potential series that seem most promising. The result may be an order for 4 to 13 episodes of the proposed show. The network has not committed itself to anything beyond the commissioned episodes; no guarantee is made that the episodes that were ordered will even run. Still, the producer now has what he or she has sought: a real tryout with the viewing public. If the show succeeds in the ratings, the network will order more episodes. If it fails, it will be canceled.

Network programmers have become more conservative in the program development process as corporate control of the networks has changed, forcing more attention to be paid to the bottom line. The cost-consciousness of the new owners has been demonstrated by mass layoffs, reduced perquisites, and fat trimming. This has narrowed the opportunities for producers. Network executives are more cautious in deciding on the new series they will introduce to the lineup because failure is increasingly expensive. Thus, producers with established records of success are much more likely to get shows on the air.

Spinoffs

Like a series of biblical "begats," a series can have several **spinoffs.** *Happy Days,* for example, gave birth to *Laverne and Shirley, Mork and Mindy,* and *Joanie Loves Chachie.*

This process is not limited to American programs. *All in the Family* came from the BBC's *Till Death Do Us Part,* and *Three's Company* came from the British show *Man about the House.*

Sometimes spinoffs do not work. The character Flo from *Alice* was given her own spinoff show, but her singular line "Kiss my grits" could not carry a half hour even though it had been successful in 1-minute segments. The same happened with *The Ropers,* a show about a one-joke couple that was spun off from *Three's Company.*

Still, successful spinoffs are more common than failures, and since they are dealing with known quantities—characters who have demonstrated their appeal to viewers—that is enough to recommend them to producers even though the failure rate for new shows runs to 75 percent. A spinoff allows the use of characters already in place from the original show, and this saves on development time. It is even possible to use writers from the original program because of their familiarity with the characters.

Licensing Agreements

Networks and producers arrive at licensing agreements on how much the network will pay for the use of an episode of a show. The standard agreement gives the network two plays of each episode. The payment is determined by the length of the show and the time period in which it will play. In almost all cases the **license fee** (the amount paid for each episode) does not cover the cost of producing a show. Although the average half-hour comedy costs about $600,000 an episode to produce and the average hour costs over $1 million, the network pays only a portion of the cost, around $350,000 to $400,000 for half hours and about $800,000 to $900,000 for hours.

This sharing of the risk between the network and the producer has advantages for both sides. If a show is successful, the network will keep it on the air, helping the producer build up episodes for sale in syndication even though that sale will not usually benefit the network. However, since license fees do not cover the cost of production, the producer can build up multi-million-dollar deficits for each season in production. That deficit *may* be erased in syndication. By contrast, the network that has nurtured the program for years gets nothing at the end except another slot to fill. On the other side of the coin, the network may be paying for a program that cannot seem to find an audience. If the network pays $900,000 per episode and cannot get that back in advertising sales because of viewer and advertiser rejection, it is left with a deficit of its own. It is in both parties' interest, then, to build winning programs. Networks can profit from the

advertising sales of a hit, and producers can profit from the syndication sale.

NETWORK PROGRAMMING STRATEGIES

Flow

Flow is a natural strategy for networks, which invented the concept of blocking, or placing programs of similar type together (see Chapter 12). Basically, a network runs programs of similar kinds as long as the audience will allow. Then it switches at curtain times (especially 10 p.m.) to give viewers some variety. In prime time, for example, because of viewer inertia, audiences tend to accept the 10 p.m. switch to a different kind of program. Thus, the otherwise bumpy ride from *Cheers* and *Wings* to *L.A. Law* is feasible. Within blocks, networks look for demographic similarity and consistency of content.

In the daytime, soap operas work the same way. While each has its own characters and story lines, these shows share modularity and structural characteristics. Despite what fans of specific programs may say, soap operas are interchangeable.

There are times of the day when networks do not counterprogram at all. In the early morning the news and information shows are essentially similar, and in the afternoon the soaps are of one form. Network newscasts have strong resemblances to one another. It is primarily in prime time and late fringe that networks counterprogram each other. On weekend afternoons programming and counterprogramming are seasonal, based on which sports are available and which network has a contract with which league. Still, in that time period network programming revolves around sports. We will use examples mostly from prime time and late fringe when discussing counterprogramming by networks.

Counterprogramming

If one network has a good product—a comedy, movie, or drama—the competition will counterprogram by length, type, or target audience appeal. Since stripping is not practiced by the broadcast networks in prime time, individual counterprograms are scheduled. When ABC succeeded in attracting a younger audience with *Full House* on Tuesday, CBS countered with *Rescue 911,* which appeals to a slightly older audience. That is a way in which each network can carve out a slice of the audience.

Network counterprogramming is a useful tactic. Sometimes the opposition has something so good that the other networks are forced to find a way to keep from being blown out. For example, some miniseries have the power to pull inordinate numbers of viewers when they are scheduled during sweeps. However, since counterprogramming a multiple-episode series with special programs is prohibitively expensive, it is easiest to counterprogram against the first episode of a miniseries with a very attractive movie or special that features stars who appeal to a wide audience. If one can keep viewers from getting involved in a miniseries in the first place, one can blunt the overall success of that miniseries.

Counterprogramming sports events such as the Super Bowl, the World Series, and the Olympics is a bit easier. The first two events appeal most strongly to men. To counterprogram effectively, one needs to find content with a strong female appeal. Since Olympic coverage spans so many days, it is wise to examine each daypart of coverage. Some sports appeal more strongly to men, while gymnastics and skating have high appeal to women. This makes counterprogramming more difficult.

Daytime With all the importance placed on prime time, one would think it the most important time of day for the networks. It is and it isn't. In the competition for recognition and prestige, prime time is the number one daypart, but it is not the most profitable daypart; that distinction belongs to daytime.

Because their tight demographics of women age 18 to 49 and 18 to 54 are infinitely more appealing to many advertisers than the more heterogeneous group found in the evening, soap operas are the best profit centers for networks. The benefit of low production costs and desirable audiences makes for soap success. Viewers are less concerned with the quality of sets, expensive chase scenes and car crashes, and big-name actors. They want stories, and that is what the soaps deliver. Close inspection will reveal cost-cutting efforts in every area of production, but that matters to the audience not a bit.

Table 16-1 shows some strategic moves made by the various networks in the soap blocks. Both ABC *(Loving)* and CBS *(The Young and the Restless)* begin their schedules at 12:30 p.m., after their affiliates' noon newscasts. That gives both a head start on the NBC lineup, which starts at 1 p.m. with *Days of Our Lives.* This front-ending strategy is especially useful to CBS as it uses the odd tactic of beginning an hour show on the half hour. The net effect is that it counters the beginning of both *All My Children* on ABC and *Days of Our Lives* on NBC. By front-ending both programs, CBS ensures that any viewers of *The Young and the Restless* will almost certainly be delivered to *The Bold and the Beautiful* at 1:30.

TABLE 16-1 Network Soap Opera Schedules

Time	ABC	CBS	NBC
12:30	Loving	Young and Restless	
1:00	All My Children		Days of Our Lives
1:30		Bold and Beautiful	
2:00	One Life to Live	As the World Turns	Another World
2:30			
3:00	General Hospital	Guiding Light	Santa Barbara

By starting with a popular offering that intrudes on its rivals, CBS begins the block from a position of strength. At 2 p.m. all the networks begin new programs, and the competition takes place on a level playing field.

Stunting

Sometimes one network carves out a large slice of the audience, severely hurting its competitors. *Stunting* is the practice of placing powerhouse specials or special showings of big-name movies against successful programs. If a competitor is doing well in a slot, the last-place network has to weaken the effect of that competitor's show. Stunting is even more effective when done on short notice, making it more difficult for the competitor to respond.

During sweeps, when audiences are measured, the last-place show in a slot may be pulled for a series of specials that can draw the audience from number one. A Bob Hope special will draw general audiences because of Hope's ability to sign guest stars ranging from Madonna to George Burns. During the same time period the next week the network may schedule a rock concert. During the week after that the programmer may schedule a special in which a performer recreates a Las Vegas musical act.

This strategy has the capacity to disrupt the flow of the competitor and, people being habitual, may hurt the opponent's show in the longer term. However, there is a downside in that it also ruins the stunting network's flow. That's why stunting is best practiced by the network in last place in a slot. That network sacrifices its own show to hurt the competitor. If the stronger program can be softened up, it may become vulnerable to a new series in the same time period that has been used for the stunt.

Dayparting

As with flow, the networks invented dayparting. Realizing that viewer activities would determine just how television would be used, Sylvester "Pat" Weaver, program head at NBC in the 1950s, invented two landmark shows: *Today* for early morning and *Tonight* for late night. These pioneering program concepts not only served audiences already inclined to watch but widened viewing by supplying interesting programming during periods that previously had been largely ignored. Each program was made up of modules, which would further shorten over time, that accommodated viewer activities during its daypart.

Over the years networks expanded beyond prime time to control the early-morning and daytime hours. They made early inroads into late fringe with *Tonight* but did not follow up that success until the relatively recent *Late Night, Later,* and *Nightline.* Competition between the networks has intensified during the late-night period, but network affiliates sometimes exercise their own judgment by stripping off-network sitcoms or the syndicated *Arsenio Hall Show.* These alternatives have weakened the network offerings by removing stations from the networks' national audiences.

The networks have responded to audience trends during the dayparts. Among the early news shows, for example, ABC's *Good Morning America* was the first to place an entertainer, David Hartman, on the air as the primary anchor. Viewers so liked the new direction—easy folksiness as opposed to tight-lipped news—that *Good Morning America* moved into first place in just a few years.

This was not lost on NBC, and when newsman Tom Brokaw left the *Today* show, later to anchor the *NBC Nightly News,* he was replaced by sportscaster Bryant Gumbel, who was teamed with Jane Pauley and later with Katie Couric. *Today* later won back the top spot among morning shows. The one holdout for the old-fashioned news approach—CBS—was consistently drubbed in the ratings. Finally it gave in to the trend and developed more of a "feel-good" approach to early-morning television with the likable team of Paula Zahn and Harry Smith.

Similar trends have been followed in late night. For example, modules have been shortened on the *Tonight* show. Although contract negotiations with Johnny Carson in the 1980s led to the cutting back of the show from 90 to 60 minutes, the effect was an improved pace as well as increased ratings for *Late Night with David Letterman,* which received the benefit of the earlier starting time. ABC's *Nightline,* which is news-oriented, is also modular. More discussants are added as the show moves along, and this gives the show both continuity and style. CBS essentially counterprograms these offerings with "Crime Time after Prime Time," a collection of action hours quite different from the news and talk programs with which it competes. Fox has stayed out of the late-night wars since the disasters of an earlier *Joan Rivers* show and *The Wilton North Report.*

Second Seasons

In bygone days a new season lasting 39 weeks made sense because it guaranteed fresh episodes through the May sweeps. The best 13 episodes could be selected for replay during the summer. Several factors made this both possible and logical.

There was never much need for fresh product in the summer since HUT levels drop drastically during that period. There was and is a July rating sweep, but it has never been a very important measurement. Advertising rates for the fall were based on the ratings from the May sweep. Because of the drop-off in summer viewing, July was not an appropriate sweep for setting ad rates.

Equally important, there was less competition for product. With only three networks and no fin-syn, producers were happy to get the work, and charges for license fees were more than reasonable for the networks.

That all changed with increased competition, increased television use, and the rise in the salaries of stars. Furthermore, production crews developed a strong union structure and demanded a larger share of the profits.

What developed out of economic forces and increased costs was a shorter season that fell to 32 weeks and eventually to 26, or for some

shows, 22 weeks. Increased costs dictated the need for a more efficient use of product (more repeats) and thus for the shorter season. This was cost-effective for the networks in that it allowed for the maximum use of each episode. All episodes were played twice. Series that did not have 26 episodes left space for sports, specials, and miniseries. For example, a show with 22 episodes would fill its time slot for 44 weeks of the year with one original play and one rerun of each episode. That would leave the slot open eight times during the year for special programming from blockbuster movies to the World Series.

The drawback, though, was that the May sweeps were filled with reruns. Without fresh episodes, the fall ad rates were being set by repeats on all networks, and that encouraged the tuning out of the networks and the viewing of one of the many alternatives that had sprung up.

With a 22-week season, the affiliates were left high and dry in May, and in the mid-1980s they began to voice complaints to the networks about the May situation. It was one thing for the networks to be philosophical in weighing the cost of additional episodes against somewhat higher ratings in May, but the process was hurting their affiliates' local ad rates for both spring and summer, and they wanted a solution.

One way toward a compromise was led by *The Cosby Show.* In the 1986–1987 season the show was running so strongly that in an off-sweep experiment (in January, when local ratings would not be affected), a rerun of *Cosby* was scheduled. The repeat episode did as well as the original, even against fresh opposition programs. Thus, *Cosby* producers were able to selectively repeat episodes during January, March, and April while saving up four new episodes for the May sweep.

In the May 1987 ratings period, *Cosby* clobbered the hapless competition by bringing out new episodes to run against repeats. NBC's affiliates were more than happy. A successful show was doing better than ever in the all-important spring sweep and helped set higher rates for the coming months. That has provided an example for lesser shows and has given affiliates and their networks a way to solve the May problem.

The shorter season has also led to a shorter time before the cancellation of faltering new shows. Whereas new entries in the networks' schedules were usually assured of a 13-week trial period, it is now normal to cancel shows after as few as four episodes. Overnight ratings results have given programmers a forecast of the acceptance of new shows much more quickly than was possible in earlier years.

So-called slow build shows that took a while to find an audience, such as *Cheers, Hill Street Blues,* and *St. Elsewhere,* have become less tolerated because networks do not give them time to catch on. By the fourth week affiliates are demanding substitutes for weak programs. In the early 1990s only NBC, then at the top of the heap, could afford to let shows develop more slowly. The other networks, playing catch up, tended to have the hook ready in less than a month.

Preparing for the Second Season

The networks know that many shows will fail, and so they routinely prepare for that contingency. With the hindsight provided by history, network programmers can usually predict fairly accurately how many shows will not make it even if they cannot be sure which specific shows will be included in that number.

The tendency toward quick cancellation has given rise to a *second season* that begins in January or February. Similar to the debut of the fall season, the second season is characterized by the premieres of replacement shows and the shuffling of schedules. There is enough change that it constitutes its own start-up period. In fact, shows that do not make the fall schedule are specifically listed as midseason replacements, and a certain number of episodes are ordered for each one.

The second season is ballyhooed for advertisers and viewers just as the fall season is. Promotional campaigns are rolled out for the new shows and new time slots are established for others to entice viewers to watch the new choices.

The hook need not be as quick for shows introduced in the second season because the two most important sweeps—November and February—have been completed. Consequently, these shows can be nurtured a bit longer to see if they can find an audience.

Specialization

Their shrinking share makes it mandatory for broadcast networks to court more specialized audiences. When they were cutting up a pie that consisted of more than 90 percent of all viewers, a show that received less than a 30 share was not considered a complete success. By contrast, a network show that attracts a 22 share is now considered competitive. In the case of Fox, the yardstick is different. Since Fox is available to about 80 percent of viewers and since most of its affiliates are UHF stations, its ratings and shares almost always run behind those of the big three. Therefore, a 14 share is more in line for a Fox program. These percentages can be realized through specialization.

The big three networks have specialized in some dayparts for a long time. Soaps are a form of specialization, targeting a particular segment. However, a single demographic group predominates in the daytime, and so targeting a slice of the available audience is not an unusual approach: The networks still want to reach *all* the available women in the potential audience.

In the late-night period talk and news programs constitute specialization via program type and modularity. But networks are still trying, especially with their talk shows, to capture the entire available audience by featuring a variety of guests who will appeal to everyone.

Attempts by the networks to target a specialized rather than general audience had rarely occurred during prime time. The historical example is ABC's *Monday Night Football.* However, increasing numbers of shows have been aimed at a narrower demographic group. One such series is *The Wonder Years* on ABC. Not a show for everyone, it is aimed at younger, more trendy viewers who don't mind the mixing of program forms, in this case drama and comedy, which creates the hybrid "dramedy." Another specialized ABC show, *thirtysomething,* was unabashedly aimed at young adults with young children. The show developed an extremely loyal core audience which just happened to constitute the most desirable selling demographic in mass media: adults age 25 to 49.

At NBC this trend toward specialization was begun with such shows as *Hill Street Blues* and *St. Elsewhere,* which attracted a younger, more upscale audience that could be sold to advertisers despite NBC's third-place position at the time. Other more demographically targeted shows on NBC have included *The Fresh Prince of Bel-Air* and *The Golden Girls.*

CBS brought us *All in the Family, Maude,* and *The Jeffersons.* Later it added shows such as *Murphy Brown, Designing Women, Northern Exposure,* and *Top Cops.* Because the CBS audience has traditionally been older and because CBS hit shows such as *60 Minutes* and *Murder She Wrote* attract older demographics, network officials have been able to tout their age advantage during an era when the average age of the population is rising.

Fox has aggressively courted specialized audiences, especially the younger audience, with great success. Shows such as *The Simpsons, Married . . . with Children, Beverly Hills 90210,* and *In Living Color* have delivered younger audiences as well as minority audiences. Fox's chief scheduler, Sandy Grushow, highlighted that network's philosophy when he pointed out that the Fox move of placing *The Simpsons* against *The Cosby Show* was successful because Fox attracted the core audiences of teenagers, 18- to 34-year-olds, and 18- to 49-year-olds. *Cosby* won the battle on a household basis and held a large edge in the demographic age 55 and over, but according to Grushow, "that's a demographic that means virtually nothing to Fox."[2] This is

even more evident in *Beverly Hills 90210.* One of the few shows successfully aimed at the teen audience, it has become Fox's most popular show. With its 58 share of adolescents, it pushes the highly rated *Cheers* for overall audience. Through clever promotion, astute strategy, and solid writing, Fox has created a counterprogramming hit. As a result of cast appearances at malls, the stars were made to seem more approachable. In reaching for its audience, Fox rolled out new episodes of the show during the July and August rerun season in 1991 and 1992. The move succeeded. Producers and writers were brought in from such shows as *Northern Exposure* to create good, realistic stories. Teens identify with the powerfully played stories about AIDS, alcohol, drugs, divorce, and sex.

Of course, with costs being what they are, broadcast networks cannot define their audiences too narrowly. They are not about to become specialists like MTV, CNN, ESPN, and the Disney Channel. Still, those specialized cable networks have shown how an audience position can be staked out, a demographic served, and the process made profitable. Thus, the networks have joined the move to specialization, which is bound to continue as cable entities siphon off demographic groups for portions of the broadcast day and Fox continues its success with niche programming.

Conceding the Time Period

A network can sometimes so dominate a time slot that competing shows cannot succeed there. The most recent example involves *The Cosby Show.* During the 1986–1987 season, that series averaged a 53 share. Considering the number of viewers with access to 30 or more channels, it is phenomenal that a single show could command half the viewers watching TV at the time. What could the other networks do? ABC had a very good answer in *Our World,* a compilation of old news footage with commentary by long-established newspersons Ray Gandolf and Linda Ellerbee. Scheduling *Our World* was a good strategy because it counterprogrammed a strong comedy with a show that had as part of its core a news theme. The show appealed to upscale viewers who enjoyed a weekly trip down memory lane. Since there were only two hosts, talent costs were minimal, and the use of file footage owned by the network kept the content cost very low. Thus, the network could put on a show each week that had the lowest production cost on television. Even if it won only a 12 to 15 share, ad spots could be sold in the show because of its demographics. If the ad spots sold, they would more than equal the low costs. Even against such formidable competition as *Cosby,* a profit could be made.

The essential strategy here is to concede the primary audience to the dominant show and look for a counterprogramming niche that costs as little as possible. Eventually the dominant show will weaken; such shows always do. Then the competing network can bring on a strong contender to finish off the older show. In the case of *Cosby, The Simpsons* undercut the youth audience. Then ABC's *Columbo* and CBS's *Top Cops* effectively siphoned audiences across many demographic groups.

Delivering the Final Blow to a Competitor

As popular shows age, they become vulnerable to competition that is fresh and strong. When a series's ratings start to slip, it becomes vulnerable to attack from competitors. It's a sort of television Darwinism, the law of the jungle as practiced by people in suits. Knocking off a competitor's show disrupts its audience flow in the daypart and allows the aggressor network to attract many displaced viewers.

In the 1983–1984 season NBC's *The A-Team* put an aging ABC program, *Happy Days,* out of commission and changed the Tuesday night balance of power. After ABC's long domination, NBC came to rule the Tuesday roost. Later ABC would reclaim Tuesday with *Full House* and *Roseanne.* Similarly, *Remington Steele* provided a lethal blow to *Three's Company,* and *Alf* delivered the death blow to *Kate and Allie.* The

Simpsons hastened the ratings decline of *The Cosby Show.*

PROGRAMMING PROBLEMS

Declining Audiences

Despite programmers' best efforts, network audiences are down. Since 1976, the combined network share of the prime-time audience has fallen from over 90 percent to 60 percent. With the resulting fall in revenue potential, the problem has become a serious one.

Audience declines that used to be mild are now accelerating. An example of this occurs in the summer, when network audiences fall by a third and spot rates do the same.[3] The networks are in a difficult position: Should they spend large sums of money to create fresh programming for a season when people are occupied by vacations and outdoor activities? Or is it safe to allow cable and independents to gather larger segments of the available audience while networks air reruns of failed programs and pilots? It constitutes a Hobson's choice that the big three began to address in 1990.

Summer programs In the summer of 1990 the major networks made some new inroads into the summer audience. Pushed by gains made during the summer rerun season by cable networks and by the upstart Fox, the traditional broadcast networks tried some daring experiments.

CBS programmed new series during the summer, particularly *Northern Exposure, Top Cops,* and *Manhattan Nights.*[4] While initial sampling was low, word of mouth slowly turned *Northern Exposure* into a popular program. Because of the summer start, the network was much more patient than usual, allowing the show to find its audience slowly. The patience paid off by mid-1991, when it was routinely winning its time slot. *Top Cops* was placed opposite *The Simpsons* and *The Cosby Show.* This was hardly a choice slot, but the show earned respectable ratings and stayed on the schedule. These moves signaled a change in the philosophy of networks toward summer programming. They had learned that audiences could be drawn back from cable with interesting programs and that hits could be planted in the summer and grow to success later.

NBC brought out *Seinfeld* and *Singer and Son* in the summer of 1990 as well, and *Seinfeld* became a regular on the following season's schedule. Like CBS, NBC learned that the summer could be used for more than burning out the rights to already rejected programs.

ABC dealt with the summer problem in a slightly different and novel way. The network joined Nickelodeon in a joint venture called *Hi Honey, I'm Home.* The comedy episodes would first run on ABC and then would be repeated later in the week on Nickelodeon. This symbiotic arrangement extended to cross-promotions in which the ABC airing was promoted on Nickelodeon and the Nickelodeon run was promoted on ABC.

Fox, which had been airing new episodes of several shows in the summer of 1990, took an additional step in the summer and fall of 1991. Citing the fall release season as overly crowded and artificial, the network moved to year-round program premieres. Thus, about two shows a month would begin a new "season" or a new program would be rolled out. The idea was to move large numbers of Fox shows out of the clutter of fall, where as many as 30 new network shows vie for attention, and give them some development time. In an additional commitment to spring and summer schedules, some programs, including *Married . . . with Children* and *In Living Color,* were given 30-episode contracts instead of the usual 22 or 26. Again, more fresh product would be available for times normally given over to repeats, allowing Fox to compete more effectively with the big three.[5]

Hourlong Programs

Hour programs have been ignored in the syndication market. As an example, the highly popular *Miami Vice* could not be sold to stations because there were not enough takers. Instead, it went directly to basic cable. *Wiseguy* languished for months without buyers. The story has been the same for *St. Elsewhere, Hill Street Blues,* and *Cagney and Lacey.* Prime-time soaps such as *Dallas, Dynasty,* and *Falcon Crest* have enjoyed only limited distribution because local stations have become much more sophisticated about what to run in specific slots. Nighttime soaps are a bit risqué for early fringe, and because they depend so much on suspense, which has little repeat value, and because they are too low in modularity for early fringe, prime-time soaps do not have much utility in syndication.

Finding a space in the lineup for a crime/detective series such as *Spenser: For Hire* is also difficult. It cannot run in early fringe because it is too violent and is so low in modularity. It cannot run in the morning because its content and strong male orientation make it inappropriate for the predominately female audience that watches then. The most feasible slot for the show on an affiliated station is 11:30 p.m., after the late news. An independent could perhaps run it as the prime lead at 8 p.m., but the content may be a bit rough for that. Of course, with typical movie scheduling on an independent, it cannot be aired at 9 or 10 p.m. Thus, like many other off-network hours, the program was sold to a basic cable network.

To solve the problem of deficits in hour programs and shrinking syndication possibilities, two producers—Stephen Cannell *(21 Jump Street, Wiseguy, Hunter)* and Steven Bochco *(Hill Street Blues, L.A. Law, Doogie Howser)*—have signed unusual contracts with ABC and NBC. In exchange for their widely acknowledged creative genius in the hour format (which is still quite useful at 9 p.m. and 10 p.m. for networks, if not for independent stations), the networks have agreed to pay license fees that cover the entire cost of production. By removing the pressure of deficit production that has typified hour shows over the last decade, the producer can greatly reduce the uncertainty of making a profit. Whatever money is made after the network run, whether from foreign distribution or domestic syndication, will be profit.

The networks are not making such deals for the good of the producers but for their own self-preservation. The hour drama and adventure forms have a long tradition and are extremely popular. They practically fill the slot from 10 p.m. to 11 p.m., and many are shown earlier as well. If there were no future for the form, producers might stop making these shows as a matter of basic survival. By rewarding those who have the best track records in the form by guaranteeing them profitability, the networks may well have saved the beleaguered hours.

Shortened Life Spans of Shows

Series wear out faster than they used to because viewers have more choices. Television as an entity is less inherently fascinating than it was when it was new and people wanted to watch even the test patterns. Since people watch television more than they watch specific shows, it is harder to build loyal audiences, making series more vulnerable to competition. *Kate and Allie,* for instance, controlled the 8 p.m. time slot on Monday for CBS, but within a year of its debut in the same time period, *Alf* took over first place in that time slot as *Kate and Allie* viewers moved over in large numbers. By the end of the 1987–1988 season, *Kate and Allie* had been moved to 8:30 and then back to 8 p.m. Finally, the show was listed as a possible midseason replacement for the 1988–1989 season. It had been shuffled into the wings and was subsequently canceled.

That scenario is not unusual these days. Contracts with creative participants in shows (such as stars and producers) are set up for 7-year runs, and some are structured for 5. Even if the series is very successful, many actors don't want to be tied up for such a long stretch. With so many new channels offering programming, even if much of it consists of off-network reruns, audiences have more choices and become more easily bored. A 9-year network program life span would be considered extraordinarily long today.

This complicates the lives of network programmers. To keep older but successful shows on the air, increased license fees and pay raises for the stars are the norm. Keeping *Cheers* on the air for a tenth season was a good move because of its keystone position in NBC's Thursday night lineup and because even in its advanced years it was the number one show for the 1990–1991 season. Similarly, *The Cosby Show* was signed for an extra 2 years, at great expense, because of its top-10 standing. However, these are unusual examples. Even shows that burn brightly for a time may be off in less than 5 years. Included in that number are *Alf, thirtysomething,* and *China Beach.* When there are 30 or more channels in the environment, it is increasingly difficult to hold the average viewer's attention over time.

Standards and Practices

The department of standards and practices at each network is responsible for overseeing content. This is the censorship department, although the people who work there cringe at the word "censor."

The censor's job is a thankless one. He or she is charged with seeing that program content is kept clean (reducing sexual content) and free of ethnic and gender stereotypes and that violence is kept to a minimal level.

Much as Mae West managed to get in her famous line "Are you carrying a gun or are you just glad to see me?" in the film *My Little Chickadee,* producers try to outfox censors. One strategy is to load the script with so many zingers that some are bound to get through. This "volume approach" was practiced in the show *Soap,* where the weekly script meeting with the censors called for several discussions per page. Terms such as "fruit" and "bimbo" were sprinkled between the "hells" and "damns," and double entendres were frequent. The censors had to decide how far to go.

Other producers fight qualitatively for content. Scripts are written with a few offending passages, and producers fight hard to keep them in. The fights are less frequent but more intense, and so the meetings last just as long.

Censors exist because broadcast television has always been considered a guest in the home. The consumer must choose to go to a theater or a video rental store to be exposed to a movie. She or he chooses and must purchase the reading materials that get into the house. But broadcast television and radio come into the home uninvited. Children can turn them on and use them as easily as adults can. Even cable is bought; it's invited. Thus, the broadcast networks are especially careful about what they send out because the criticism of them is much more visible and vitriolic than anything leveled at films and cable.

Competition between Networks

Management's increased concerns over return on investment, shrinking network shares, and added competition have combined to make network operations more pressured, but the means of competition remain much the same. The networks invented most of the standard programming strategies, from dayparting to audience flow, and still practice those techniques today. However, in the 1990s strategies are not enough. Money is of the essence.

Less expensive programs The "reality boom" represented by programs such as *Prime Time Live, 48 Hours, 20/20, 60 Minutes, Top Cops, Rescue 911, Unsolved Mysteries, America's Most Wanted, Cops,* and blooper shows has proved to be a godsend for the networks. These are programs that draw sizable audiences but are inexpensive to produce for the most part. As relatives of *Our World,* they make use of available footage, dramatizations, and available personnel.

The ultimate program of this sort may be *America's Funniest Home Videos.* The content of this program is created by unpaid amateurs who happily pay their own postage to send tapes in for broadcast. With a host, a set, and prizes for the best pieces, a show was born. Soon afterward, *America's Funniest People* was born and followed in its parent's footsteps.

NBC carried things a bit further in the 1990–1991 season with a show called *Sunday Best,* a compilation of the programming of the week presented immediately prior to their airing. As all the footage was already in the archive, all that was required was some editing and someone to provide transitions from one clip to the next. This might have been the ultimate in cheap programming.[6]

Another advantage of these programs was that they had no license fees. As public affairs and news shows, they were exempt from fin-syn. Thus the networks could air and repeat a program which they owned at very little cost.[7] It is no wonder that *Real Life with Jane Pauley, Exposé,* and *True Detectives* all found their way onto network schedules.[8]

Fox

The growing appeal of the Fox Network is making it more of a factor in the competitive marketplace. While it only recently began to offer programs every night of the week, and if not for the full number of prime-time hours, its schedule is expanding and earning better ratings. Thus, the big three are quickly becoming the big four, but for now the traditional networks offer the strongest competition.

One problem Fox had in the past was too few affiliates to cover the country. Even by 1990 the network was available only to 80 percent of viewers, compared with 99 percent for each of the big three. Fox developed a creative deal with TCI, the cable giant, in which cable systems would carry Fox programming in areas not served by a Fox affiliate. In a short time Fox was able to expand its coverage to most of the country. At the same time, an inroad was made into cable for the newest network, giving it the potential to develop a basic cable channel in the future.

The combination of innovative programming, success with important demographic groups—especially the young—and growing success with advertisers has made Fox a major player in the network universe of the 1990s. Its creative roll-out schedules for new programs and fresh

FIGURE 16-1 © *1990 Washington Post Writers Group. Reprinted with permission.*

episodes of existing series have forced the competitive issue with the traditional networks.

Fox has been the beneficiary of certain regulations. First, Fox is not defined as a network. While it walks and talks like a duck, it is not considered a duck: It has affiliates to which it sends programs, it takes most of the in-show ads for itself and gives affiliates mostly adjacencies, and it has an affiliate board and a structure like that of any other network. However, as a new enterprise which offers diversity to consumers, it has drawn favorable assistance from the FCC. In 1991 the FCC defined a network, in part, as an entity that provides in excess of 15 hours of prime-time programming per week to affiliates. The big three provided 22 hours per week of prime-time programming; Fox provided 14. As a nonnetwork, Fox was exempt from several regulations. For one thing, it could produce and own its own programs. It was thus syndex-proof. That meant that when *Married . . . with Children* went into syndication, it could occupy choice access periods even on affiliates. Thus, Fox has had advantages that have allowed it to explore new programming ideas such as *The Simpsons, Beverly Hills 90210,* and *In Living Color* while traditional networks have been reluctant to do the same.

The flip side is that the networks could theoretically solve all their syndex problems by downsizing some of their operations. Assume, for example, that the big three offered only 2 hours of programming each evening Monday through Saturday and 3 hours on Sunday. That would come to 15 hours a week, and the networks could own their own programs. Another benefit would be that the difficult 10 p.m. time period could be avoided. The problems with hour programs would be moot for the most part, and affiliates could begin newscasts at 10

rather than 11 p.m., taking advantage of larger audiences. Late-night programming on both coasts would move to 10:30, again taking advantage of larger audiences. Still, such restructuring would be drastic and might foster new regulations to halt it. While it may have possibilities, don't look for the big three to try this soon.

SUMMARY

The days of domination by the big three broadcast networks are over. The rise of cable, independents, VCRs, and the Fox Network has seen to that. The viewing audience now has many more choices.

Network systems for getting shows on the air have changed little over the decades. Shows are still pitched and commissioned when they seem promising.

Program concepts may be tested to sample potential viewer reaction to the idea for a show. When a script is ordered, the process of deciding whether a show will be placed on the network schedule continues until a pilot episode is prepared and tested. Then the network may order episodes of the program. Sometimes this order is made for the fall season, and sometimes for the second season.

In exchange for two plays of each program episode, the network pays a license fee. Most shows are deficit-financed; that is, they cost more to produce than the license fee covers. However, a few producers with successful track records are starting to negotiate 100 percent license fee contracts in which all production costs are covered by the network.

In a conservative programming environment where losses and failures are many, spinoffs remain an important programming option. Because they offer a track record and a known relationship between audiences and characters, they constitute a lower risk.

A shorter television season has sprung from economic necessity. As programs have become increasingly expensive to create and license, fewer can be ordered each season. The shortening of the season from 39 to 22 episodes has created a problem in the May sweeps, where repeats are being shown during a time when fall ad rates are being set. Affiliates are not happy with this circumstance.

In the late 1980s the networks began their first forays into prime-time specialization. While they have served specialized audiences on weekends and weekdays for years, specialization in prime time is something new. The specialization success of cable networks may give one an idea of what is to come in network television.

There are continuing areas of concern for the networks. One is the fate of the hourlong program. Because of its decline in syndication value, the hour has become less profitable for its producers. To keep their most important 10 p.m. form, the networks will have to reward hour producers to keep the product coming.

Shows do not last as long as they used to. With shortened life spans for shows, the pressure on programmers to revise schedules is almost constant. Pressure from cable, independents, and home video does not allow any time for rest in the continuing struggle to attract audiences.

Costs are increasingly a concern for programmers. While reality programs are inexpensive to produce and are popular, there is no guarantee that they will remain so. Television is a cyclical medium, and the appeal of reality shows is sure to wane at some point, spurred no doubt by the production of so many of them. The question for networks is, What will be the next trend, and will it be affordable?

Finally, Fox has come into its own as a network. Through clever demographic targeting, fresh and innovative programming, and creative scheduling, Fox has started to make its mark in the television landscape. One can only wonder if Fox's success will encourage the development of a fifth network.

clusion. In either case he always interjected a personal touch into the programming process.

Blum, Richard, and Richard Lindheim: *Primetime Network Television Programming,* Focal Press, Boston, 1987.

This is an excellent account of network programming strategy as practiced at the big three broadcast networks (CBS, NBC, and ABC). The book is especially strong in explaining scheduling strategies with explanations of how each network moved to counter the others. Like a big chess game, each network constantly maneuvers for position and power. The authors are also thorough in their description of how the networks are organized and how that organization drives programming decisions.

SUGGESTED READINGS

Bedell, Sally: *Up the Tube: Prime Time Television and the Silverman Years,* Viking Press, New York, 1981.

This is an insider's account of how network programming decisions are made. Known for his "golden gut"—an uncanny ability to anticipate what viewers will like—Fred Silverman used a variety of methods for arriving at programming decisions. The only person to be programming director at all three networks, he shaped the programming landscape during his career. What is most interesting in Bedell's account is how Silverman arrived at his decisions. With the resources of world-class research departments, he often ignored advice and went with his feelings. Other times he pored over charts and graphs, using research data to arrive at a more information-based con-

NOTES

1. "Networks Suffer Record Ratings Doldrums," *Broadcasting,* July 15, 1991, p. 20.

2. "Prime Time Network Schedulers," *Broadcasting,* April 1, 1991, p. 41.

3. William Mahoney, "Trying to Lure Summer Viewers," *Electronic Media,* June 20, 1988, pp. 1, 16.

4. Debra Goldman, "The Eternal Season," *Adweek,* June 11, 1990, pp. 8–14.

5. "'New' Is the Word for the New Season," *Broadcasting,* May 27, 1991, pp. 27–28.

6. Bill Carter, "Networks Seek Viewers on the Cheap," *New York Times,* Dec. 3, 1990, pp. B1, B6.

7. Ibid.

8. Nancy McAlister, "Reality Programming versus Prime Time Reruns," *TV Week,* July 20, 1991, p. 2.

Television News

For most network-affiliated television stations, news programming constitutes an important profit center.[1] Moreover, programmers consider news the key to a TV station's position in its market. Because off-network programs can be seen on other stations in syndication and increasingly on cable networks (e.g., *Cagney and Lacey* and *LA Law* on Lifetime and *Murder She Wrote* and *Miami Vice* on USA), a station's identity is highly dependent on its local news programming.[2]

This chapter discusses strategies for obtaining optimum audiences for TV news programs, including their placement and the scheduling of other programs that may affect their audiences. Even though the news director handles the operation of the news department, including hiring personnel and determining the content of news programs, it is advantageous for the programmer to understand story placement and other principles of news program construction. Furthermore, although TV stations originate local news programs, much of the material used in those broadcasts is obtained from sources outside their markets. After a description of the sources of material available from syndicators, we discuss the news coverage available from across the nation and the world via satellite cooperatives. Then we turn to cable news and information networks, which have become an alternative to broadcast news programming. The fragmentation of television audiences by cable news networks was particularly evident during the Persian Gulf war. Finally, we discuss the role of news consultants, who are used extensively by stations seeking the largest possible audience for their news programs.

NEWS PROGRAM SCHEDULING

Expansion of TV News

The extent of a station's local news programming is usually related to its market size, since news-gathering resources and the variety of news topics are greater in the larger markets. Another important consideration is the time period during which new viewers join the audience. The larger the market, the longer the time required for commuting from work to home in the afternoon. Thus, great numbers of blue-collar workers arrive home early from shift work, while those who work in professional occupations and other office jobs some distance from their homes join the audience later. An important consideration in deciding whether to schedule longer local newscasts is the cost of news programming. In comparison to the high cost of acquiring other programming product, a television station may be able to expand its local news programming by recycling material. Most stations repeat much of the news content from one time period to the next, updating stories where appropriate, and this helps make news programming cost-effective.

News programming does not have to achieve the highest audience ratings during its time period to be profitable. First, the cost of acquiring the rights to syndicated program product is increasing, particularly when a program has established its ratings success. Second, advertising agencies are targeting audiences that may not be delivered by entertainment programs and are available at a better CPM in news programs. Thus, a station may make more money by airing the number two program than by winning its time period.[3]

Daypart Scheduling

The trend in scheduling television news is to emphasize the station's news "presence" in the market on a 24-hour basis. Consequently, an increasing number of stations offer a brief news summary every hour. Furthermore, many stations are scheduling full half-hour newscasts during the early morning hours, at 2 and 3 a.m. In some cases these are taped repeats of the 11 p.m. newscast, presented to an audience that is unlikely to have been in the audience during its original presentation. Such audiences include not only insomniacs but night shift workers who were on the job during the late fringe period. These repeats thus serve the available audience during a time period of low HUT without incurring any program cost.

Stations have also increased their news programming during time periods when much larger audiences are available. More than 500 network affiliates now broadcast a half-hour or 60-minute news program between 6 a.m. and 7 a.m. on weekdays.[4] With the increase in the number of working wives, more people get up earlier. Many of the stories produced for the previous day's newscasts can be recycled, and since morning news shows require fewer people to put the newscast together, they are relatively cheap to produce.[5] For instance, a Salt Lake City station added five staff members to produce a news program from 6 to 7 a.m. In Denver, the ABC affiliate had to add only three staff members to create the hour show that follows *Good Morning America.*[6]

In addition to a network news program, most network affiliates in the largest markets program 90 minutes or more of news during the early fringe period of 4 to 7:30 p.m.[7] Overall, 42 percent of network affiliates broadcast 1 hour or more of local news during early fringe.[8]

Many stations emphasize lighter, feature-oriented material in the first afternoon newscast, particularly if a station is located in a large enough market to begin at 4 or 4:30 p.m. Often this early program includes live interviews and a heavier emphasis on consumer tips. The local newscast broadcast just before or after the network news program usually has a "harder," more substantive edge.[9]

Late fringe local newscasts present a dilemma to stations operating in the Eastern and Pacific time zones. By 11 p.m. the prime-time audience has fallen away. Moreover, as increasing numbers of viewers go to bed earlier and get up earlier, the audience for the 11 p.m. newscast is eroding. Consequently, some stations that are not winning their time periods with local news may decide that another form of programming would be more feasible, especially since the Federal Communications Commission no longer presses licensees to program news in order to achieve license renewal.[10]

Double-Access Scheduling

Borrowing a counterprogramming ploy long used by independent stations, some affiliates have altered the time when they schedule network news so that they can counterprogram with syndicated shows. Instead of scheduling local and network news, a station will offer viewers an alternative program such as a game show or a situation comedy during a time slot in which the choices offered by the competing affiliated stations are news programs.

One strategy is to schedule the news a half hour earlier than its traditional start to create a **double-access** period from 7 p.m. to 8 p.m. As illustrated in Figure 17-1, this permits a station to schedule 2 half hours of profitable syndicated programming during this time period and avoid face-to-face competition with the news. Such a strategy may benefit the affiliate if its local news does not compete strongly against the other local news programs. Furthermore, the network news may provide a poor lead-in to the syndicated programming that is scheduled after it, and this provides an incentive to change the program schedule. Moreover, since network compensation may not be nearly as lucrative as the income from selling all the available advertising inventory in a syndicated program, preempting or rescheduling network news may generate greater revenue for the station.

A double-access strategy involves either reducing news programming or scheduling the news block earlier in the afternoon, say, from 5:30 to 7 p.m., as shown in Figure 17-1. Thus, if producing a half hour or so of news programming is cheaper than obtaining a show from a syndication source, it can be more profitable for the affiliate to expand its local news programming if the demographic segments being targeted by advertisers can be attracted to the audience.

In Figure 17-1, the CBS affiliate has scheduled local news opposite *Inside Edition,* the second half hour of *Geraldo,* and *Monkees* reruns on the Fox affiliate. Even if this station can do no better than third during the period from 5:30 to 6 p.m.,

Eastern Time	ABC Affiliate	CBS Affiliate	NBC Affiliate	Fox/ Independent
4:00	General Hospital	Sally Jesse Raphael	Donohue	Jetsons
4:30				Ducktales
	Oprah Winfrey			
5:00		Cosby		Alvin & the Chipmunks
			Geraldo	
5:30	Inside Edition			Monkees
		Local News		
6:00				Webster
	Local News		Local News	
6:30		CBS Evening News		Andy Griffith
7:00	ABC World News Tonight	Family Feud	NBC Nightly News	Beverly Hillbillies
7:30 Prime Time Access	Wheel of Fortune	Jeopardy	Hard Copy	Newhart
8:00 Prime Time				

FIGURE 17-1 Double access and counterprogramming: Monday–Friday afternoon schedule.

it may be ahead of the game in terms of revenues, particularly if it can build an appreciable audience during the second half hour of local news at 6 p.m., when it competes head to head with the other network affiliates. During the afternoon the Fox affiliate has targeted children and teens, and so there is little concern for attracting adult viewers to that station. Leading out of the *CBS Evening News,* the station has scheduled *Jeopardy* to counterprogram network news on ABC and NBC. As with the earlier programs on the Fox affiliate, reruns of *Beverly Hillbillies* should not constitute much competition for the audience that does not wish to watch a

news program. During the prime-time access period, the CBS affiliate has scheduled *Entertainment Tonight,* which competes against other first-run syndicated programming on the network affiliates and *Newhart* on the Fox/independent station.

An added consideration for scheduling local news a half hour or so earlier is that the news audience may be built up during that time period as viewers arrive home in the afternoon. Whether that strategy is workable depends on how late the bulk of working men and women, who are among the heaviest news viewers, arrive home. However, as was noted earlier in this discussion, a double-access strategy will probably be most appealing to an affiliate whose news programming does not compete well against that of the other affiliated stations.

Independent Station News

Major-market affiliates that schedule syndicated programs during the early fringe period provide an opportunity for the independent stations in those markets to schedule local news.[11] News not only can be profitable for a large-market independent, it can bolster the independent station's image and impact in the market. Furthermore, if major-market independent stations are able to garner good news ratings, this offers them an alternative to acquiring off-network sitcoms, which are expensive.[12]

So far, most of the growth in independent station news has been limited to the largest TV markets, where nearly 60 independent stations program news. The costs to a station for launching a news program are considerable. For instance, about $100,000 in start-up costs was incurred by an independent station in Omaha, which launched a Monday–Friday 9 p.m. newscast. In San Diego, a 10 p.m. newscast had start-up costs of about $2.5 million. The justification for this investment is that independent station newscasts attract viewers who stay for the local news if they are already tuned to the station for a sporting event or movie. Moreover, advertising in the newscasts is easily sold because it offers a positive identification. In the larger markets, local news programming on independent stations is considered to be clearly tied to profitability.[13]

As a supplement to their local news, independent stations are able to pick up a nightly nationally distributed program comparable to those offered by ABC, CBS, and NBC. *USA Tonight* is fed by satellite 365 days a year to over 100 stations. This program, which originates at WPIX TV in New York, is made available to stations on a barter basis.

Stations schedule *USA Tonight* at 10 Eastern time to attract viewers who want to watch the news before retiring but do not wish to stay up until 11 p.m., when the network affiliates run local news. Regardless of whether an independent also broadcasts a locally produced news program, it can capitalize on this early-evening news schedule to beat the affiliates with late-evening news and then counterprogram entertainment while the affiliates are presenting their local newscasts.

News Program Lead-Ins

The program that precedes an affiliate's local news has a considerable influence on the success of the news program's ratings. Even though some programs attract substantial audiences, they may not be appropriate early-evening news lead-ins because of their demographic **skew,** or the relative size of the audience segments that are attracted.

Some of the stations that bought *The Cosby Show* as a news lead-in did poorly because large numbers of *Cosby* viewers tuned out when the news program came on. The dilemma was most dramatically demonstrated in the spring and summer of 1990, when many network affiliates, that had paid high prices for *Cosby* sold the broadcast rights to the show to other, mostly independent, stations in their markets. These stations cut their losses because of the poor numbers of prime demographics the show was attracting.

Although *Cosby* is a high-rated off-network stripped program, its audience is dominated by children, teens, and young women, who are not heavy news viewers. Moreover, *Cosby* does poorly among men and women 50 and over, the two consistently largest segments in news audiences. Conversely, stations that have placed *Jeopardy* as their news lead-in have been very successful, as that program has delivered over 70 percent of its audience to the succeeding news programs. Another program that has worked well as a lead-in is *People's Court,* since its demographics skew toward men and women 50 and over.[14]

Some stations schedule early-afternoon newscasts because they have determined that a large proportion of viewers in the available audience do not like to watch syndicated talk shows such as *Geraldo, Oprah Winfrey,* and *Donahue.* Such talk shows have not proved to be good lead-ins because their audiences include many young women who do not watch early-evening news. Although *Donahue,* for example, attracts a considerable number of women 50 and over, its skew away from men constitutes a disadvantage as a lead-in. Consequently, some programmers have decided that news programming provides the best lead-in to another news program.[15]

Impact of News on Other Programs

Both stations and their networks influence the success of each other's news program ratings. A network's prime-time ratings can affect the number of viewers who watch an affiliate's late-evening news program. Suppose ABC scheduled a dramatic series from 10 p.m. to 11 p.m. that failed to attract a competitive share of the audience on Wednesday evening. Although a reasonable proportion of the small audience from the network program could be expected to flow into the ABC affiliates' late-evening local newscasts at 11 p.m., the CBS and NBC affiliates would have a built-in advantage because of the audiences they inherited from their prime-time network shows.

Since the 11 p.m. newscast represents a lucrative time period, it is little wonder that station managers are concerned about the strength of the network lead-in. Affiliates are quick to criticize network prime-time schedules when they perceive that these schedules will not deliver the audience to the late-evening local news. The ABC Television Network's *Monday Night Football* has been a source of consternation to affiliates because the games frequently run over their scheduled times, often continuing past midnight. This results in the preemption of the local newscast and the loss of revenues from advertising sales. Similarly, when ABC announced a change in its schedule that moved *20/20* from Thursday to Friday from 10 p.m. to 11 p.m., a

number of affiliates were concerned that the news magazine would provide a weak lead-in to the local news. Happily for both the stations and ABC Television, this prediction did not come true, but it illustrates the affiliates' sensitivity to threats to their revenue centers.

The networks are similarly sensitive to the performance of their affiliates' local news, as it affects the national ratings for the network evening news. The smaller audiences gathered by major-market affiliates, for instance, are felt to have hurt the ratings competitiveness of the *NBC Nightly News* during the 1988 season. Conversely, the high lead-in ratings provided by affiliates in the top markets for ABC's *World News Tonight* are credited with helping that program achieve its high ratings in competition with CBS and NBC.[16] One research study indicated that audience size for network news is more dependent on the success of affiliates' local news than the local programs are on network news ratings.[17] Other research has shown that when stations switch their network affiliations, most of the benefit accrues to the network nightly news.[18]

In a few markets affiliates have opted not to program local news. In some cases a network has threatened the loss of affiliation if the station did not include local news in its schedule, providing a larger audience for the network news program that followed it.

NEWS PROGRAM STRUCTURE

At most television stations in the United States decisions about program structure and judgment about the content of news programs are the purview of the news director. However, while news departments are largely autonomous, station management is sure to become involved when the ratings success of news programs is in doubt. Although the news director is usually consulted about the scheduling of news programs, the station's general manager or program director is responsible for the station's program schedule. Programmers make the final decisions about where and when news programs are placed in the lineup of programs.[19]

Understanding of the structure of a news program therefore is important in making program decisions. Even though the programming department usually has little to do with its content, the news nevertheless involves programming decisions.

As has been emphasized in other chapters, information about audience ratings is used to develop programming strategies. When programmers monitor the influx and departure of audience segments, some of the strengths and weaknesses in a news program's structure may be identified.

Audience Ratings

Television audience ratings are reported in half-hour program increments during most of the broadcast day except when news is scheduled, at which time audience measurement is reported in quarter-hour increments. This gives a programmer an opportunity to assess the effectiveness of a news program's structure by comparing the ratings of competing programs. Audiences may be attracted to one station because of an especially appealing weather report, for instance. If the weather or sports segment is scheduled during the first quarter hour of the broadcast, it may be discovered that audience members tune out in favor of a competing newscast or entertainment program if their need for weather information or sports scores is satisfied early. This is why the weather segment in half-hour newscasts usually starts at a quarter past the hour and sports begins at 20 or 25 minutes past the hour.

Building

Building is a way to provide audience members with a reason for staying with the program. To illustrate, in drama, tension builds as the protagonist and antagonist move toward the climax. When the outcome is predictable, the audience is less inclined to remain in attendance.

News programs are not dramas or contests, but building provides their audiences with incentives to stay tuned. Tradition and logic dictate that the most important news be presented during the earliest part of the broadcast, but other stories can be promoted or teased to create anticipation for what is to come later.

By virtue of their importance or interest, some stories serve as interest builders, offering "miniclimaxes," even though their newsworthiness is surpassed by that of the lead stories. In a network news program, for instance, an uneventful day during a presidential vacation is of marginal news interest, and so a report on the President's golf outing or fishing expedition would not be one of the early stories. Still, most newspeople consider what the President of the United States does to be newsworthy. Scheduled later in the newscast, a story of *some* interest offers a climactic report before the end of the program.

If the final story is a feature or "soft news" story, the newscast is brought to a close after a peak created by the next to last story. A light story about a dog that swims in the family hot tub provides a pleasant ending to a program largely filled with serious news. Besides giving the newscast an upbeat ending, a final story of little consequence causes the preceding story to be more climactic, assuming that it has greater news value.

Still another way to create the perception of building is to schedule segments of specific interest, such as sports and weather, during the second half of the program. When various stories are teased during earlier portions of the newscast, the viewer's anticipation of these reports is heightened.

Previewing a report of great interest such as the weather or sports by including a brief segment early in the newscast serves a similar purpose. Some news programs include brief segments in which the sportscaster and weather reporter are introduced and present a headline for a sports story or a highlight of the weather report. The bulk of the weather or sports follows later in the program.

Pacing

Pacing (Chapter 9) is the impression of forward movement in the development of a program. It may be jerky, as occurs when the anchors who share the presentation of a news story botch their transitions, which are sometimes called the *handoff* or *toss.* In contrast, the transition can be handled smoothly, as occurs when one anchor presents the lead or introductory sentence and the second anchor immediately picks up with the presentation of the story.

Some news anchors seem to have a better chemistry in that they react to each other more effectively, but virtually any newscaster will have a more polished presentation if nothing is left to chance. Smooth transitions that contribute positively to pacing in news programs are written so that the anchors know exactly what they should say.

The pacing of the program is also controlled by the length of the events included in the broadcast. A way to quicken the pacing is to present more stories by reducing their average length. This solution has engendered considerable criticism among people who argue that broadcast news can and should be more than a headline service. The briefer the story, the more limited its ability to convey information of sufficient depth to inform audiences.

Advances in electronic news-gathering and editing technology have provided journalists with the ability to weave a large number of excerpts from interviews with different sources into a single story. This variety is one way to broaden the story, but it can also result in a more shallow report. Running brief *sound bites,* or snippets excerpted from taped interviews, past viewers at a frantic pace can diminish viewer understanding of the story. By contrast, well-chosen sound bites add both credibility and variety to the story.

Variety

The different stories included in a news program provide variety, but the programmer must also consider the blend of personalities. The princi-pal performers—the anchors—usually change from time period to time period when the station schedules more than an hour's worth of local news. There are usually two anchors, most often a man and a woman. With the addition of sports, weather, and staff reporters, the number of different personalities featured during a newscast can be large. There is even greater variety in both personalities and subject treatment in larger-market newscasts, since consumer interest and health beat reporters are often regulars. In addition, some programs feature entertainment, restaurant, and movie critics as well as political analysts and commentators. Of course, if a newscast includes a syndicated advice piece from someone like Dr. Dean Edell, yet another personality is added to the mix.

Unity

Perhaps the major contributor to unity is the anchors, who tie the disparate elements of the news program together. In addition, the anchors typically discuss the lead sports story and the highlights of the weather with those segments' reporters; this is yet another means of integrating personalities and stories to make the program more cohesive.

In both local and network news, the anchor may question reporters who are shown on a monitor built into the news set. This practice not only conveys an impression that the anchor is drawing out information from the reporter but ties the story more closely to the anchor and the unifying news set rather than presenting it as a detached or unrelated information package.

Most news reports present a preview or *tease* of the major news, weather, and sports stories just before the standard opening of the news program. This not only entices viewers to stay tuned but provides them with an orientation to what will follow in the news program. During the introduction, each of the principal personalities, including the anchors and sports and weather personnel, is introduced. This step establishes who they are and gives them a familiarity to the viewer when they appear during the broadcast.

Teasing or billboarding forthcoming events is also a unifying factor in the broadcast. Typically, the anchor will talk to the weather or sports reporter on the set about the information to be presented during the segment to follow a commercial break. During other breaks, teases recorded on location by reporters are aired. In many programs, graphics that announce forthcoming stories are superimposed on the screen just before commercial breaks.

The practice of teasing stories during the program introduction, presenting those stories, and then summarizing them at the end of the broadcast further unifies the news program. It can be argued that these devices are repetitious and take time that could be used to present other information, but it can also be said that they contribute to audience awareness by alerting viewers and listeners and then reinforcing what has been presented since recall of news by viewers has been demonstrated to be low.

A related unifying device, the **bumper,** is often read by an anchor just before a commercial break. A bumper is a brief news item such as the stock market averages or a "Date in History" pictorial. It serves as a transition to move the viewer smoothly into the commercial break. Whereas a tease is intended to interest viewers in information yet to be presented in the newscast and generally contains no actual news, a bumper is a complete story, even though brief and relatively unimportant.[20]

On radio and television, assembling related stories so that they are presented in a cluster is another unifying factor. If the lead story is on the economy, the next story often deals with another facet of that topic. For example, a story on rising unemployment in the market may be followed by a report on the impact of the closing of a local factory on area businesses. This can be followed by a report on job counseling for unemployed workers or a "help line" feature on jobs available through unemployment offices.

The news set makes an integral contribution to program structure. If appropriately constructed, it permits a variety of camera angles, and picture composition can communicate important subtle messages. Before the sports segment, for instance, the anchor can be seen talking with the sports reporter; this communicates that the program's principal personality is effecting a transition to a subordinate segment of the program. If there are two anchors, both are usually shown discussing something about the first sports story with the sports reporter.

Variety is only one pictorial function of the set. Unity can also be enhanced through over-the-shoulder shots showing a reporter who has come onto the set looking at the anchors as they discuss the story. This indicates that the anchors are involved while also notifying viewers that a separate aspect of the news program is being presented. This device is similar to showing the anchor addressing a television monitor during an exchange with a reporter or guest who is at a remote location.

Role of Personalities

Keeping the anchors in a dominant position on the news set is important since they provide the principal identity for the program. In fact, news program consultant Al Primo has described the anchor as being worth 8 of the 10 possible points in weighing all the factors that make up a news program.[21]

The anchors' role is integral to the unity of the news program, but the most important attribute of successful anchors is their ability to establish a rapport with viewers. Thus, at both the local and network levels, the battle for ratings often seems to come down to a battle of personalities. The anchors are "stars" who attract viewers. They are heavily promoted and serve as the identities of their programs—indeed, of their stations or networks.[22] TvQ ratings and focus group research (Chapter 4) are used widely to test the appeal and credibility of news personalities.

PROGRAM CONTENT SOURCES

Broadcasting stations obtain material for their newscasts from a variety of sources outside their own reporting staffs. Much of this material is used in expanded news programming to supplement the reports gathered by local reporters.

The number of staff members in television news departments varies with the size of the market. In very small markets as few as two full-time people may constitute the staff. WGAL in Lancaster, Pennsylvania, the 44th market, has 32 news staff members.[23] WPBN TV in Traverse City, Michigan, the 139th market, has 18 news employees, whereas KRON TV in San Francisco has a staff of 140 people.[24] In the smallest markets, reporters virtually always shoot their own video footage. If the station has enough reporters, they may trade off so that one serves as the videographer for another reporter. Stations in larger markets, however, usually employ full crews, at least during the week. Weekend reporters are more likely to have to carry their own equipment and resort to a trade-off with a colleague to serve as camera operator, if one is available. In the largest markets, union rules usually dictate that a reporter be accompanied by a crew.

Even with these local resources for gathering and reporting the news, stations still seek supplementary material for their news programs. Part of the consideration is variety or a fresh perspective. Another factor is the cost of filling the time.

Syndicated Material

When stations expand their local news programming, they do not necessarily hire more reporters and video crews, as was noted above, but instead recycle material from other broadcasts. Still, new material is needed to add interest, especially for newscasts presented during dayparts when different demographic segments predominate. Syndicated program inserts can often be purchased for less than it would cost to hire the additional news staff members required to produce material to fill the same amount of time.

Much syndicated material consists of "news you can use" consumer information and health and medical reports. Typical of the latter are the medical advice features of Dr. Dean Edell (available on both radio and television) and Dr. Red Duke. These personalities dispense medical advice, report on medical advances, and explain various ailments. Other syndicated programs present a pharmacist's health information, pet care advice from a veterinarian, and consumer information reports.

Network Extra Feeds

Network affiliates can tape stories broadcast on their networks' news programs for rebroadcast on their local newscasts. At some stations these stories are repeated as they have been received from the network, but other stations overdub the network reporter's narration of the visual portion of the report with that of a local anchor or another local reporter to give the reports a more local effect. Stories that do not make the network newscasts are offered through the *delayed extra feeds* sent to affiliates. This service offers some network-level reports on national events for local news programs.

Network Overnight News Programs

ABC, CBS, and NBC offer their affiliates an overnight news program in order to maintain their presence as important sources of national and world news and preempt the competition offered by other sources. NBC launched *Nightside* in November 1991; ABC's *World News Now* made its debut in early 1992 and was followed by CBS with a revamped overnight news service called *Up to the Minute* a few weeks later.

Although some stations sign off during the early-morning hours, many others broadcast on a 24-hour basis. The overnight news programming that affiliates can offer appeals not only to night owls but to people who work late hours and might have missed newscasts earlier in the evening. Furthermore, stations that clear the network program feed do not have to purchase programming to fill that time period.

SATELLITE NETWORKS

The proliferation of satellite-distributed signals has brought about a new order in television news. One survey has determined that about 74 percent of all television stations in the United States subscribe to satellite news networks. Among the network-affiliated stations 86 percent subscribe, compared with only 31 percent of independent stations.[25] A new system of news gathering and dissemination has developed, and so stations are no longer dependent on the traditional networks for key national and international stories.

Most network affiliates have access to a variety of regularly scheduled news sources and choose the version best suited to their needs. Even small-market stations receive at least 20 separate satellite feeds a day from network and independent sources.[26] Some stations have developed contacts to embellish the feature stories they receive by satellite. For example, stories on medical news have been "localized" by appearances of medical personnel who practice in the markets where the stories are shown.[27]

If a major news story breaks anywhere in the world, a station can receive a video report in time for its earliest afternoon local news program or can preempt regular programming and go live with reports. For example, if an airliner were hijacked in a foreign country and some of its passengers were from a station's market, the station not only could provide a local angle by interviewing relatives of the captives but could show live shots of the airplane as it sat on the tarmac in the airport where the situation was unfolding. This kind of localized coverage can be put together wherever news breaks.

Satellite News Cooperatives

One of the sources of news that has changed the relationship between stations and their networks is cooperatives through which stations exchange taped and live news coverage and collaborate on the coverage of breaking and planned news events. Although most of the material is exchanged on a regional basis, stations can also receive reports from across the nation and around the world.

In 1981, Group W Television began its Newsfeed Network, which had grown to over 100 affiliates when it was sold to CNN in 1992. Daily feeds of news, sports, and features are coordinated centrally to distribute content supplied by member stations. Newsfeed also produces reports from Washington, D.C., and will include pieces tailored to stations' needs, such as an interview with a district's congressional representative or one of a state's senators.

In 1984, Hubbard Broadcasting of Minneapolis started CONUS, which enables member stations to share coverage of events in their area by uplinking those reports to satellite for distribution. Since its inception, CONUS has grown to over 100 domestic and more than 50 overseas members. In addition to custom news coverage for affiliates from Washington, D.C., a full-time crew reports from the White House and covers Congress and other newsmakers in the nation's capital.

Other state or regional satellite cooperatives share stories that a member station covers in its own market. For example, the Florida News Network provides its member stations with reports from the largest markets in that state.[28] If an important political official makes a speech in one city, coverage can be provided to the other stations, saving them the time and expense of sending their own reporters to the scene. Thus, satellite cooperatives enable stations to provide coverage of their state capitals and other cities without having to maintain expensive news bureaus.

Broadcast Network Satellite News Services

The wide adoption of satellite news services has forced the networks to greatly expand their offerings to affiliated stations for use in local newscasts. Each broadcast network provides its affiliates with a regional news service as well as early reports on major national and world events for use in local broadcasts.

The growth in satellite sources suggests that network news services may be expendable at stations that expand their local news programming. Some people have even predicted that network news will ultimately become a "video wire service" like that provided to newspapers by the Associated Press, in which the affiliate chooses some of the product that is sent out for inclusion in its local productions. Such a dramatic change in network status may or may not come to pass, but as a consequence of that threat, the networks will continue to stress the incentives to affiliates to continue their relationship. Network satellite news services have been developed largely in response to the competition from the satellite news cooperatives described above and from the other satellite-distributed news services that are discussed below.

In addition to its News One satellite feeds, ABC offers its affiliated stations six regional feeds, sending out an average of 180 stories daily. The CBS affiliate satellite feed, Newsnet, also makes regional feeds available to its affiliates, as does NBC's News Channel, which serves its affiliates 24 hours a day with videos of late-breaking news, sports, and features. Like the other networks, NBC has developed regional news feeds to provide its affiliates with news coverage in these areas. Finally, the Fox Broadcasting Company supplies its affiliates with daily news feeds; this has encouraged a number of ostensibly independent stations to develop local news programming.

A satellite service that has had a great impact on network news organizations is CNN. TV stations widely use CNN Newsource, which is marketed as a "video news wire." Newsource provides national and international news reports and live feeds for use on local newscasts. CNN's status as a news service was given a great boost by its coverage of the U.S. attack on Iraq during the Persian Gulf war of 1991. As important as the extremely favorable reviews of its journalistic performance[29] was the fact that at least 26 network affiliates preempted their networks' coverage of the war in favor of CNN's, citing its superior coverage.[30]

After buying Group W's Newsfeed in 1992, CNN now serves more than 350 stations nationally. Another service that expands stations' ability to offer coverage of breaking stories from around the world is Hubbard Broadcasting's All News Channel, a 24-hour news program. Stations can carry the service on the air in half-hour segments or use the material as inserts in programs. The news material, which is gathered through the CONUS system, is also being marketed to cable systems.

Other services include the Local Program Network, which serves about 50 stations with reports on breaking news, features, magazine material, and access to newsmakers who can be interviewed by local reporters or anchors. Potomac News provides interview and feature packages to over 80 stations from Washington, D.C. The News and Information Weekly Service (NIWS) delivers reports to over 125 stations twice a week.[31] In addition to news reports, NIWS also offers stations its MEDNEWS service, which provides medical reports, along with the Parenting Network, which features reports on family issues that are designed to appeal to adults age 18 to 49.

Medstar Communications is another source of medical reports with its Med*Source news service and a medical news headline service called Advances. Another satellite service featuring stories on the lifestyles and issues concerning viewers age 50 and over is Newsage, which offers a weekly feed. Stations can get customized news coverage from Capitol Hill through Newslink, which feeds "packages," which are complete video reports, to stations from Washington, D.C. Finally, stations can obtain feeds of sports highlights from Sports Newsatellite on a daily basis.

CABLE TELEVISION SYSTEM NEWS

Local Cable System News Channels

While most cable systems are not large enough to warrant news programs that originate locally, the pioneer programming of some systems may be a harbinger of a greater number of local and regional news services. Although some of their efforts lack the production polish of the local broadcast stations, regularly scheduled cable channel newscasts provide coverage of community events that are ignored by television stations that serve larger coverage areas.

The first and largest local 24-hour cable news channel serves New York City suburbanites on Long Island, where News 12 Long Island is distributed on the seven cable systems serving the area. News 12 provides local area news in addition to world and national news, which it receives through its affiliation with CONUS and Worldwide Television News. A high-powered staff is employed. For instance, the original producer of News 12 was a former ABC News *20/20* executive producer. The main anchors are a former ABC News correspondent and a former anchor at WABC TV in New York City. Because News 12 owns a satellite news-gathering truck, it has provided its cable viewers with coverage of congressional hearings from Washington, D.C., and major trials in New York City.

News 12 Long Island has proved successful by meeting some important criteria. First, the geographic area is large enough to offer subscriber fee and advertising revenue potential for a news service. Long Island, with a population over 2 million, has more households served by cable than do many TV markets. Second, the area must have high cable penetration to make access to households feasible, and it must be underserved by broadcast television, at least in the sense that broadcast news does not focus on the local news and events that are of interest to viewers in communities within the metro area. Typical of many suburban areas, Long Island does not receive regular news coverage by broadcast stations, whose local newscasts cover a much wider geographic area.[32]

A 24-hour local cable news service that also meets these criteria is offered to cable subscribers in the Los Angeles metropolitan area. Orange County NewsChannel, which reaches about 500,000 subscribers, could eventually serve 400,000 households in that county.[33] Another 24-hour "hyperlocal" news channel is the Chicago News Channel. This service relies on raw footage from independent WFLD TV and shares its studios and stories but has a separate staff of 50 persons.[34] A more ambitious project is under way in the Washington, D.C. metro area, where Albritton Communications' News Channel 8 employs a staff of 200 to provide a 24-hour service that sends targeted news feeds to distinct local markets in the Maryland and Virginia suburbs. A majority of the cable system operators in the area have agreed to carry News Channel 8 as a basic cable service for at least 10 years.[35]

Other cable news services are originated by individual cable system operators. Although these are not 24-hour news operations, they provide highly localized news programming for their subscribers. Such operations are serving cable systems in locations as diverse as Louisiana, Massachusetts, New Jersey, and Guam with news programming ranging from 2-minute "newsbreaks" to full half-hour newscasts.[36] One such cable news service has been serving subscribers in Fall River, New Bedford, and Dartmouth, Massachusetts, since 1981. A seven-member staff covers the communities for a daily half-hour cablecast that serves the Fall River system's 50,000 subscribers. Although it was being watched by 40 percent of the subscribers, focus group sessions indicated that viewers didn't like the style and polish of the newscast. Consequently, news consultant Al Primo was hired to advise the system on how to structure the program to make it more appealing.[37]

The latest variation on locally originated cable news is provided on the Rochester, New York, cable system's WGRC TV, a channel that is programmed like an independent TV station. WGRC TV has allocated several hundred thousand dollars to support its 10 p.m. nightly local newscast in the 68th largest Nielsen market. Twenty-four full-time news staff members are supported by the cable system's production staff in presenting a nightly half-hour news show.[38]

Cable and Broadcast News Coventures

TV station managers have recognized the importance of cable and have taken a variety of steps to capitalize on it. For broadcasters, local or regional newscast carriage on cable systems represents a way to expand their audiences and promote their local broadcasts to a wider audience. Cable operators have enjoyed unparalleled economic success as their systems have encroached on broadcast audiences. From their perspective, local news services offer a rejoinder to critics and a way to fend off the possibility of government regulation.

An increasingly popular arrangement between cable systems and broadcast stations is for the station to produce local news segments that are inserted in the broadcast that is fed to subscribers in specific areas. Some stations produce local news inserts for suburbs that a larger station, with its much wider coverage area, cannot cover, including high school sports, town meetings, traffic conditions, school lunch menus, community calendar items, and personality profiles. These segments are substituted for station newscast features and other soft news in the cable feeds.[39]

A different kind of arrangement has been made by Cox Cable. The local newscasts broadcast by WWL TV in New Orleans and WNEM in Saginaw, Michigan, are carried simultaneously on a cable channel in their markets. Each newscast is repeated continuously until the next live broadcast. Thus, the audience has access to a local news program when it is convenient, and the station expands its potential news audience. The Cox arrangement calls for the cable system and the station to split advertising revenues.[40]

Each broadcast TV network is positioning itself to become involved in a cable news service. At this writing, NBC is in discussion with cable operators and affiliates about launching a number of local 24-hour cable services for which its affiliated stations would produce news programming supplemented by news feeds from NBC News. ABC and CBS are engaged in similar talks. The networks are concerned that the many competing satellite news supplement services may usurp affiliates' reliance on the networks as the primary source for national and world news. They see the establishment of cable services as a way to expand their news service and revenue base while maintaining a strong relationship with affiliates.

Cable News and Information Networks

A variety of cable networks have changed the concept of television news and information. Whereas broadcast stations and their networks offer distinctive packages of news within specific time periods, cable services have adapted the concept of 24-hour news and information used by some radio stations. These services are designed not to be watched all the time, but to provide an update on the latest news.

Cable News Network CNN, the first 24-hour television news service, has grown in stature and is now considered on a par with ABC, CBS, and NBC in its coverage of world and national events. As was described earlier, CNN's Persian Gulf war coverage was highly acclaimed. Not only were the critics complimentary, but CNN dominated the prime-time ratings during first few days of the brief war.[41]

Although the Gulf war brought an unusual amount of attention from consumers as well as cable operators, CNN's day-to-day operation has contributed mightily to its present success. In addition to its regular newscasts, CNN schedules reports on sports, business, entertainment, weather, fashion, and other topics. When events warrant, regular programming is suspended to concentrate on the major news story. The Gulf war coverage was only one instance. CNN carried gavel-to-gavel coverage of the Senate Judiciary Committee hearings on the confirmation of Clarence Thomas and, along with Court TV, fully covered the William Kennedy Smith rape trial in 1991. When an Air Florida jetliner crashed into a bridge over the Potomac River in Washington, D.C., on January 14, 1982, CNN telecast uninterrupted coverage of the crisis. Thus, viewers across the country and the world have become accustomed to turning to CNN when major news events occur because they know that regular programming will be preempted.

CNN and its sister service, Headline News, continue to encroach on the network evening news programs' share of viewing audiences.[42] In October 1989 CNN began a new hour-long nightly newscast, *The World Today,* that competes with not only local news but also the network evening news programs for audience. In addition, CNN began a new 10 a.m. daily newscast and another hour news program that begins at noon.[43]

CNN Headline News Headline News, which also offers 24-hour news programming, is available to commercial TV stations as well as cable systems. While it does not have the emphasis on personality of the traditional broadcast network news programs, Headline News offers a credible package of information. The half-hour program keeps viewers up to date on the latest news in a fast-moving half-hour format, covering international, national, business, sports, and weather news. Cable systems typically recycle the reports, while stations can use Headline News to fill any time slot. Affiliates can preempt the weather and features segment with local news headlines.

Consumer News and Business Channel Although NBC already had a financial interest in the Arts and Entertainment Network, the broadcast network's full-fledged entry into cable networking came in April 1989 with the launch of the Consumer News and Business Channel (CNBC), which offered business and financial news. In 1991, CNBC absorbed its direct competitor, the Financial News Network (FNN), and reconfigured its programming.

The greatest difference between FNN and CNBC was CNBC's greater orientation to small cable systems, which meant that its audiences resided in smaller municipalities. CNBC also gave more emphasis to general consumer and business information, whereas FNN emphasized harder information that appealed more to seri-

ous investors. In its new configuration, CNBC absorbed FNN's daytime services, including its talent and programming.

CNBC has attempted to position its service with the title "Smart TV," based on the premise that information makes people feel smarter. Daytime programming is called "Smart Business," nighttime programming is labeled "Smart Living," and weekend programming is identified as "Smart Talk."

A business roundtable discussion program, *Business Insiders,* is presented live at 6 p.m. each day. During prime time, a live magazine show, *The Real Story,* covers political, social, and cultural issues as well as arts, entertainment, medical, lifestyle, and personal finance topics. On the weekend CNBC supplies a number of talk programs, including one featuring Dick Cavett, a longtime television talk show personality. A talk/call-in program that consists of two 90-minute programs is scheduled on Friday and Saturday nights.[44]

The Weather Channel The Weather Channel provides continuously updated weather reports on world and national conditions along with special reports for sports participants, travelers, gardeners, and farmers. Local weather conditions are inserted by affiliates. The Weather Channel has expanded its programming by scheduling hour-long documentaries on weather-related subjects such as hurricanes.

C-SPAN Cable-Satellite Public Affairs Network (C-SPAN) is a nonprofit service funded by cable operators. It is a haven for news junkies, who can watch the uninterrupted proceedings of the U.S. House of Representatives. Coverage of the Senate is provided on C-SPAN-II. When Congress is not in session, a wide range of speeches, congressional hearings, academic conferences, and other meetings are televised. In addition to discussions with politicians and experts on various issues, call-in programs give viewers an opportunity to participate. The service is noted for its unedited coverage of every event it carries. For instance, C-SPAN provides gavel-to-gavel coverage of political conventions and congressional hearings. The network recently began carrying coverage of the British House of Commons.[45]

PROGRAMMING CONSULTANTS

Because local news programs are so important in television station programming, efforts to maximize audiences are handled separately by station management. As a result, "news doctors" have become an established force in television news. Since the 1960s companies have been offering consultation to stations and networks to help them improve their ratings.

News consultants provide their client stations with statistical research on viewing traits in their markets. They analyze and summarize the research and make specific recommendations regarding news format, story presentation, and personnel.

Consultants spend time in client stations' newsrooms to identify problems involving personnel and equipment. They review videotapes of their clients' news programs and then critique them. Some firms provide copies of tapes of newscasts or news personalities in other markets to their clients to enable them to scout for new techniques and personalities who might deliver the news more effectively.

Perhaps of greatest concern to those who must bear the brunt of news consultants' recommendations is the strong possibility that their station managers, who pay for the advice, are unlikely to discount it. Broadcast journalists have been critical of news doctors' approach from the outset, largely because of the differences in the objectives of the two camps. Although many former news personnel have been hired, the orientation of consultants comes from their backgrounds in advertising or social science research. Their purpose is to seek objective solutions to the problem of increasing the audience size for news programs, a management-oriented goal. Journalists, by contrast, generally consider informing audiences to be the principal purpose of news programs.

Consultants have been accused by their detractors of dispensing virtually the same advice to all their clients (change anchors and news sets, limit story length, and revise story blocks). The research methods they employ have been criticized, including charges that sample size has been insufficient and that the questions used in surveys have been biased. Critics have suggested that the advice to stations will be the same whether or not an audience survey had been conducted. For example, Barbara Matusow has concluded that the following constants seem to be offered to consulted stations: "(1) a greater emphasis on personality; (2) a cast of characters that made viewers feel comfortable; (3) more material that appeared relevant to viewers' lives; (4) an attempt to counter the average person's growing feelings of helplessness and alienation from society; (5) relief from the steady recital of bad news . . . (6) a more entertaining presentation."[46]

Consultants have been brutal in recommending changes in anchors, advising station management to replace those who are competent as journalists with individuals who "communicate" more effectively. These consultants have sometimes gone beyond recommendations on news sets and other advice on style to urge the shortening of news stories and even to give advice about the kinds of subjects audiences may find more appealing. Little wonder that those in broadcast news who adhere to journalistic traditions are made uncomfortable by the influence of marketing researchers.

The first news consultant firm was McHugh-Hoffman, which began in 1962 and now has over 50 stations as clients. The owners are former advertising agency employees, and the firm specializes in interpreting marketing research. The company dispenses advice to client stations on the kinds of stories and the treatments that audiences want. Stations are also given advice on how their anchors can convey more warmth and personality.

The largest news consulting firm, with over 100 clients, is Magid and Associates. Frank Magid, a former college statistics instructor, founded his firm to conduct opinion research and got into broadcast news advising in 1970. Magid and Associates provides advice to on-air news personnel on dress and appearance, including clothing colors and hairstyles. They also give advice on body language, such as how to avoid squinting, and coach newscasters on enunciation and pronunciation. Makeup techniques can be imparted either at the station or after a review of videotapes sent to the Marion, Iowa, headquarters. Magid also dispenses advice on news story organization, transitional techniques, and interviewing tips.[47]

Primo Newservice, Inc. founder Al Primo, the former news director at WABC TV, New York, is credited with developing the "Eyewitness News" format employed successfully by that station and now syndicated nationally. He also served as executive producer of ABC TV's *The Reasoner Report,* a half-hour magazine program, before forming his company to advise stations on their news programs.

Audience Research & Development (ARD) in Dallas, Texas, provides audience research, news and marketing consultation, talent development, and talent placement services. ARD specializes in news programs that emphasize the local angle in stories.[48]

Another news consulting company is the Virgil Mitchell Group, which is based in North Hollywood, California. The company's head is a former news director who teaches the basics of news judgment, writing, producing, reporting, and anchoring in his clients' newsrooms.[49]

The tension between managements' quest for increased ratings and broadcast journalists' desire to be protective of the integrity of the news and information they are responsible for dispensing has not been caused by consultants, but it may contribute to the rift and makes a convenient scapegoat. Many news directors say that consultants' advice is worthwhile, although others assert that they do not accept all of it. Even longtime detractors say that as long as consultants stick to the cosmetic attributes of news programming, they can find no fault in their association with their stations. Others say that regardless of the similarity of advice given to clients in different markets, successful operations will be imitated. Virtually all concerned have at least acknowledged that the audience is more likely to tune in a newscast that is attractive and that includes production elements that make the presentation of information more compelling and unified.

SUMMARY

News programming is one of the most important aspects of a television station's operation, because it is a key to positioning the station in its market and makes a considerable contribution to profits. There has been an increase in the number of hours of news programmed by stations in recent years, particularly in the larger markets. At the same time, a tendency to schedule network news a half hour earlier in order to create a double-access time period has emerged in some markets. This creates an hour period before prime time that can be filled with syndicated shows in which advertising time can be sold for greater profits.

Most independent stations counterprogram entertainment programs against network affiliates' local news. In some large markets, though, independents have found that they can successfully schedule local news during the periods when the affiliated stations are running entertainment programs.

Networks and their affiliates have a mutual dependency on program ratings, but the networks seem to be more affected by the ratings of local news than the other way around. If affiliates do not provide a strong lead-in audience, the networks' news ratings suffer. Consequently, the networks want their affiliates to provide the best possible audience flow into their nightly news programs and encourage them to lead in with local news.

News content is the purview of the station's news director, but newscast structure can affect the audience and thus affect other programs. The news program can be structured to build audience interest through the placement of stories and the teasing of segments yet to come. Viewer interest can be maintained by the pacing of the program, which may involve alternating between anchors and presenting stories of varying lengths.

Pacing, and thus viewer interest, can also be heightened through variety in the program, which occurs naturally because news on different topics occurs in different locations. The number of anchors and other reporters on the set who present information adds variety. At the same time, unity is increased through the use of a central anchor desk and anchormen and anchorwomen, who serve to connect the disparate elements of the program. It is further enhanced by clustering the presentation of stories that are related by a common theme, such as city news or sports.

The variety and scope of news programs can be expanded by airing syndicated segments in which a medical, food, or other expert presents information. The broadcast networks provide their affiliates with world, national, and regional reports that can be included in local newscasts, as do satellite consortiums such as CONUS and CNN Newsource.

The satellite news sources used by local news programs constitute a threat to the dominance of broadcast networks in national and world news. Perhaps a greater threat is offered by the various cable news and information services that may someday overtake both the national networks and their affiliated stations. A number of specialized channels provide information 24 hours a day to cable subscribers, who no longer have to wait for a scheduled broadcast of news, weather, or financial information. Larger cable systems have developed successful local news operations that serve their subscribers with truly local news from their immediate areas.

Regardless of whether the news service is provided by a station, by a network, or via cable, news consultants have provided suggestions for improving the program in order to attract a larger audience. While there is still criticism of consultants, they have become a fixture in television news, providing advice on camera presence and appearance and suggesting how to make the program structure more appealing to viewers.

SUGGESTED READINGS

Jacobs, Jerry: *Changing Channels: Issues and Realities in Television News,* Mayfield, Mountain View, Calif., 1990.

Jacobs provides an overview of the major influences on broadcast news, with particular emphasis on local news, concentrating on the forces that make news the way it is. The most important of these influences is profitability, translated as ratings, which drives all other decisions. Technology is an ancillary influence. New delivery systems allow for wider coverage in the effort to beat the competition in attracting audiences. The changing relationship of stations and their networks, the influence of consultants, and the growing influence of anchors are discussed. In addition to providing a better understanding of these and related issues, Jacobs points to examples where news directors and their stations have resisted some of the negative influences. Thus, he shows that journalistic integrity can prevail. Similarly, Jacobs points to alternative approaches followed in other countries that result in higher-quality broadcast news and thus greater audience understanding.

Goedkoop, Richard J.: *Inside Local Television News,* Sheffield Publishing Co., Salem, Wis., 1988.

Where Jacobs concentrates mostly on large TV market news, Goedkoop uses a participant-observer approach at a medium-size market station. Here the reader is oriented to the procedures used in producing a local daily newscast. The various staff members and their duties are described, and the reader is given insight into how they make daily decisions. Thus, the reader is carried from the assignment of stories through the building and presentation of the newscast. A case study in news decision making describes how the news staff handled the story of the Pennsylvania state treasurer, R. Budd Dwyer, who committed suicide while conducting a press conference.

NOTES

1. Vernon A. Stone, "News Makes Money in TV, Pays Way in Radio," *RTNDA Communicator,* April 1991, pp. 32–33.

2. Frank Graham, "Local News Builds Stations' Image," *Electronic Media,* Dec. 17, 1990, p. 20.

3. Gary Cummings, "When Less Is More," *Washington Journalism Review,* September 1986, p. 12; Janet Stilson, "When More Is Really More," *Channels,* July 16, 1990, p. 22.

4. "Affiliates Waking Up to Early Morning News," *NAB TV Today,* Sept. 19, 1988, p. 2.

5. Jerry Jacobs, *Changing Channels: Issues and Realities in Television News,* Mayfield, Mountain View, Calif., 1990, pp. 93–94.

6. "The Fragmenting of Local TV News," *Broadcasting,* Sept. 24, 1990, p. 42.

7. Alfred J. Jaffe, "Early News Surge Continues," *Television/Radio Age,* May 16, 1988, pp. 39–40.

8. "Affiliates' Early Evening Local News Increases in Past Year," *NAB TV Today,* Aug. 8, 1988, p. 2.

9. Jacobs, op. cit., pp. 91–92.

10. Merrill Brown, "Is Local TV News at Risk?" *Channels,* July/August 1989, p. 20.

11. Elizabeth Guider, "Local Indie Newscasts Gaining on Affils, per Study of 1982–89," *Variety,* Nov. 1, 1989, p. 53.

12. Kevin O'Brien, "Independents Filling Local Newscast Void," *Electronic Media,* Nov. 7, 1988, p. 34.

13. "Independents Raise News Profiles," *Broadcasting,* Dec. 31, 1990, p. 46.

14. John Dempsey, "The Leading News Lead-Ins: 'Jeopardy' Tops 'Cosby,'" *Variety,* July 12, 1989, pp. 41–42.

15. "The Fragmenting of Local TV News," p. 42; Dick Mallary, "TV Stations Expanding Local News to Battle Competition," *Gannetteer,* February 1990, pp. 16–17.

16. "ABC News on Top of the World—And the Ratings," *Television/Radio Age,* June 1, 1988, pp. 30, 32.

17. James G. Webster and Gregory D. Newton, "Structural Determinants of the Television News Audience," *Journal of Broadcasting & Electronic Media, 32:* Fall 1988, pp. 381–389.

18. "Affiliation Switches Impact Network News," *Broadcasting,* Jan. 7, 1991, pp. 97–99, 108.

19. Richard J. Goedkoop, *Inside Local Television News,* Sheffield, Salem, Wis., 1988, p. 25.

20. Ibid., pp. 85, 100–101.

21. Barbara Matusow, *The Evening Stars,* updated ed., Ballantine, New York, 1984, pp. 191–192.

22. Jacobs, op. cit., pp. 101–109; "The Fragmenting of Local TV News," p. 42.

23. Goedkoop, op. cit., p. 105.

24. Jacobs, op. cit., p. 10.

25. Stephen Lacy, Tony Atwater, and Angela Powers, "Use of Satellite Technology in Local Television News," *Journalism Quarterly, 65,* Winter 1988, p. 927.

26. Jacobs, op. cit., p. 10.

27. Bob Puglisi, "Satellite News Feeds: Many New Sources," *RTNDA Communicator,* November 1988, pp. 10–17.

28. Brian McKernan, "Star Trucks," *Broadcast Management/Engineering,* January 1987, p. 28.

29. David Kissinger, "CNN Reigns in Desert Storm," *Variety,* Jan. 21, 1991, pp. 1, 31; Connie Malko, "Acclaimed War Coverage Wins CNN Record Ratings," *Multichannel News,* Jan. 21, 1991, pp. 1, 32.

30. "Affiliates Weigh Networks, CNN War Coverage," *Broadcasting,* Jan. 28, 1991, p. 57.

31. "Key Satellite News-Gathering Players," *Electronic Media,* Aug. 25, 1986, p. J2.

32. Chuck Reece, "The Home Town Report," *Channels,* September 1989, p. 60.

33. William Mahoney, "Calif News Channel Adds Subscribers," *Electronic Media,* Dec. 3, 1990, p. 50; Linda Haugsted, "Orange County Newschannel to Launch Sept. 17," *Multichannel News,* Sept. 3, 1990, p. 19.

34. "TCI and WFLD Making News in Chicago," *Broadcasting,* Sept. 17, 1990, p. 26.

35. "Allbritton to Launch All News Cable Channel in D.C.," *Broadcasting,* Nov. 19, 1990, p. 21; Doug Halonen, "Allbritton to Launch Cable News Channel in D.C.," *Electronic Media,* Nov. 19, 1990, p. 3; Dennis Wharton, "All-News Cable Channel Comes to Capital," *Variety,* Nov. 19, 1990, p. 24; Michael Burgi, "News Channels Struggle to Find Advertisers," *Multichannel News,* Jan. 13, 1992, p. 16.

36. Laurence Zuckerman, "Cable News Hits the Small Time," *Columbia Journalism Review,* September/October 1982, pp. 35–38.

37. Jean B. Grillo, "New Style Nets Local News Operation Big Ad Bucks," *Multichannel News,* Sept. 10, 1990, p. 4.

38. "Rochester Gets Its First 10 p.m. Newscast," *Broadcasting,* April 16, 1990, p. 75.

39. Kate Oberlander, "WMAQ-TV Offering Local News on Cable," *Electronic Media,* Feb. 4, 1991, p. 16; "Philly to Get Cable-Broadcast News Channel," *Broadcasting,* Aug. 6, 1990, p. 53.

40. Lou Prato, "Broadcast News Goes Cable," *Washington Journalism Review,* September 1990, pp. 37–42.

41. Richard Huff, "CNN Beats All in Gulf," *Variety,* Jan. 1, 1991, p. 30; Rod Granger, "CNN Ratings Fall, but Top '90," *Electronic Media,* March 18, 1991, p. 2; Ed Cohen, *How America Found Out about the Gulf War,* Birch Scarborough Research, Coral Springs, Fla., August 1991, p. 9.

42. "CNN's Got Some News," *Channels,* May 1989, p. 52.

43. "CNN Adds 6 p.m. Hour News Show," *Broadcasting,* Sept. 18, 1989, p. 32.

44. Jane Greenstein, "CNBC Readies New Program Lineup," *Multichannel News,* March 11, 1991, p. 20.

45. Jeannine Aversa, "C-SPAN, 10 Years Old, Sees Continued Growth," *Multichannel News,* April 3, 1989, p. 41; "C-SPAN: Documenting a Decade of Public Affairs," *Broadcasting,* April 3, 1989, pp. 62–64; Molly Ivins, "Attention News Junkies: You Don't Have to Rely on the Brokaw/Jennings/Rather Versions," *TV Guide,* Dec. 3, 1988, pp. 49–52; Merrill Brown, "C-SPAN, almost Ten Years Old, Continues to Broaden Its Vision," *Channels,* November 1988, p. 16.

46. Matusow, op. cit., p. 192.

47. Karl Vick, "Grooming the News: A Peek at What a Station Was Told by One Consultant," *Electronic Media,* Jan. 13, 1986, pp. 1, 28, 112.

48. Jacobs, op. cit., p. 58.

49. Ibid.

Public Television

The joke goes that the public television industry has only three problems: money, money, and money. That is an oversimplification, but it is largely true. To understand the issue of funding, it is necessary to start at the beginning.

The public television (PTV) system in the United States evolved from a loose amalgamation of noncommercial educational TV licensees. Most of these stations were licensed to school systems or universities, which meant they had tight operating budgets, and they relied on government funding to support many of their operations. Most of these stations broadcast instructional programs to elementary and high school classrooms, and many offered home viewers an opportunity to earn college credits through a cooperating university by watching televised courses and completing the class work at home. The stations usually worked separately but sometimes worked together to produce general educational programs that were offered as an alternative to commercial broadcasting's entertainment fare.

The educational television (ETV) system was seen as a vehicle for educating the American public, and the narrow mission espoused by many of these stations virtually guaranteed a small audience. Their underfunded productions were designed by educators rather than television producers, and the result was rather staid and didactic programming that failed to attract or hold many viewers.

The FCC had set aside allocations for noncommercial educational TV licensees, many of them plum VHF channels, but no one knew exactly what these stations should do. That was phase 1 of the life of public television. Out of this sea of confusion and directionlessness some goal had to come. That happened in the form of the Carnegie Commission on Educational Television.

This Commission was created in 1967 and charged with defining goals and a future for educational television. It made recommendations that, if followed, might well have led to a healthy and thriving system today, but politics intervened.

Basically the Commission made three recommendations:

1 Change the name from educational television because that limited the scope of production, the vision of the future, and people's perceptions of the programming that was created. The use of the term "public television" would allow for greater diversity of programming and define a more appropriate mission.
2 Develop a strong organization to guide the new public television enterprise in developing and executing a mission.
3 Massively increase funding to the new entity so that it could attract the best and brightest personnel to produce quality programming for the American public.

The first recommendation was simple enough, but the third was a major problem. The government was uncertain about funding levels and chose to move slowly. As a hedge against uncontrolled creativity, Congress created an unusual organizational structure in the Public Broadcasting Act of 1967. The Public Broadcasting Service (PBS) would develop interconnections between stations and would be the programming arm of the system, but there would be something called the Corporation for Public Broadcasting (CPB), a nonprofit nongovernmental organization which would deliver funds to PBS and control their use.[1] What Congress had created was what it knew best—a bureaucracy. Inevitably, CPB and PBS squabbled over money, duplicated departments, and fought over territory. Thus, what the Carnegie Commission had hoped for almost immediately degenerated into a decentralized collection of fiefdoms. According to Lawrence Grossman, onetime president of PBS, it was a system "at war with itself."[2]

Overriding the two competing organizations was a concern for localism. Congress and the FCC had believed for a long time that broadcasting should serve local needs, and the term "service" in PBS's name reinforced that function more than the word "system" would have. The local stations were given a tremendous degree of local autonomy, which was strengthened as the national organizations were weakened by in-fighting.

Thus, by 1990 public television was in big trouble. There was no method of creating a national schedule of programs carried by all the affiliates. Local stations scheduled anything they wanted whenever they wanted. There was not even a workable system for getting the best programs produced at the national level. While the system was in disarray, cable had become a serious competitor in the culture market and WTBS, Arts and Entertainment, the Discovery Channel, the Learning Channel, Mind Extension University, and others had moved into the education, arts, and informational programming that had long been the province of PBS. PBS thus had two choices: change or die. It changed (Box 18-1).

Phase 3, the current incarnation of public television, began in 1990 with the appointment of a programming "czar," Jennifer Lawson, someone who would develop programs, put together a national schedule, and create a streamlined, centralized organization to lead public television stations to the promised land.

This chapter is about the second and third phases of public television's life. It looks at how programming was organized previously, how it was implemented, and how things worked out. It then looks at the same issues after the dramatic changes of 1990. Finally, the chapter deals with the sources of programs and economic issues of the past, present, and future.

PUBLIC TELEVISION'S MISSION

The mission of post–Carnegie Commission public television was varied. While many stations delivered instructional content to schools, the more general mandate was to offer alternative programs that commercial stations and networks could not or would not create. Given that creative impetus, PTV was in a position to create a multitude of programs. The "golden age" of 1950s commercial television had passed. The *Beverly Hillbillies* was grabbing more viewers than had *Omnibus,* and *I Dream of Jeannie* was more financially successful than the high-quality dramas presented on *Studio One.* Thus, there was a culture gap in television that PTV, it seemed, could readily fill.

Public television became involved in developing ballet and opera for television. Music, drama, and dance were presented in a variety of forms. Children's television blossomed on public television as commercial networks and stations cut back on such fare. Programs for special-interest

---

**BOX 18-1
A PROGRAMMING
QUIZ**

Try to guess where the following programs and series aired:

1 *American Originals,* a profile of Thomas Edison, produced by MacNeil/Lehrer Productions and hosted by Roger Mudd.
2 Naturalist David Attenborough's *The Trials of Life.* Hint: This was the third in a series, the first two of which, *Life on Earth* and *The First Eden,* played on PBS.
3 New episodes of *All Creatures Great and Small.*
4 *Karsh: The Searching Eye,* a profile of the famous photographer Yousuf Karsh.

ANSWERS

1 The Disney Channel
2 Turner Broadcasting
3 Arts and Entertainment
4 The Discovery Channel

This should make one think about where quality programming is turning up these days.[3] ∎

groups and minorities were developed and aired, and news and public affairs programs of very high quality were created. PTV did become a cultural alternative to commercial broadcasting, but its existence has always been a difficult one. The culprit was, is, and will be the lack of sufficient funds to produce first-class programming. However, there was also an organizational problem involving the way in which programs were developed and scheduled.

PROGRAMMING

Public television's national network, the Public Broadcasting Service, does not own stations or produce any of its own shows as commercial networks do. Instead, stations used to work through a **station program cooperative (SPC)** where ideas for shows were presented to the stations in the fall each year. The stations chose the shows to be produced by committing certain amounts of money to their development. They voted with their pocketbooks: The greater the number of participating stations in a potential new program, the lower each station's cost for that program.

Although very democratic, this process led to very conservative decision making. Series with funding in place automatically rose to a higher priority level, while good but underfunded ideas did not gain support. As governmental funding fell and corporate and private giving grew soft, only the sure and safe programs were cleared by the SPC. If WQED walked into the SPC with funding for *National Geographic,* it got produced. If an independent producer pitched a wonderful but unfunded idea, it got only a polite listen.

There was another problem with the SPC system: It depended largely on producing stations to create new programs. Rather than working together through a centralized network office to hire producers and commission projects, the individual stations accounted for most of the national shows. Thus, only the largest, best funded stations were continuing contributors and a pro-

duction caste system developed. The big producers produced, while the rest of the stations helped mostly by choosing from the menu placed in front of them. This also made program funding the responsibility of the producing stations, which had to knock on corporate doors to get their shows made.

Thus, several trends began to develop. First, only bankable shows were developed. Very little cutting-edge programming could be made. Who would fund it? Second, these stations began to step on each other as they trekked to the same potential sponsors to gather the millions of dollars needed to make a series such as *Nature.* It was the norm for the producers of three or four nature shows to compete with each other for program support from the same corporations. Thus there was no networklike cohesiveness with everybody pulling on the same oars. Each station had its own agenda, production team, fund-raisers, and sense of purpose. That made corporate support even more important and allowed the sponsoring corporations to call the shots and determine what programs would be produced.

With a continuing mandate to provide an alternative to commercial TV, public stations were more and more at the mercy of funders who wanted safe shows that would not offend anyone, especially in their own companies.

The other part of the mission was in good shape, however. The mandate to produce instructional television was being met.

Instructional Television

The first and most obvious program type in public television that specifically set it apart was instructional television (ITV) designed for classrooms during school hours. In most cases a public station has contracts with the local school district or the state educational system to pay for such program delivery. Many programs are created, housed, and distributed by the Agency for Instructional Television in Bloomington, Indiana, and by the Great Plains National Instructional Television Library in Lincoln, Nebraska. Subjects range from reading and mathematics to art, history, science, and social studies. The station receives money from the schools and pays one of these program libraries for the use of the shows in an arrangement analogous to a syndication deal.

ITV also produces courses for college credit. In those offerings, programs such as Jacob Bronowski's *Ascent of Man* are accompanied by materials that students use to complete a course based on the series. The program can be viewed for general interest by the public as well as for college credit by those who enroll in a cooperating institution. Similar materials were developed to be used in conjunction with *Vietnam: A Television History* and *Eyes on the Prize,* a history of the civil rights movement.

About 23 million students in 42 states watch about 1300 hours of in-school programming, mostly via satellite. Educational programs use music videos, game shows, and animation to attract students' attention. "Square 1 TV," with its popular spoof of *Dragnet* called *Mathnet,* has been a major success in the mathematics area. Through the Satellite Educational Resources Consortium (SERC), another 1900 hours of programming are made available to schools.[4]

Children's Programs

Some of public television's most noteworthy achievements have occurred in children's programming. *Sesame Street* has been watched by millions of children and their parents and has received awards for its production quality and ability to help youngsters develop reading, math, and social skills.

While targeted to minority and poor children who are deficient in these areas, the show is a magnet for all children. *Sesame Street* uses the techniques of commercial television—fast pacing, interesting characters, and bright colors—to convey its educational message. *Sesame Street'* s success with preschoolers was extended to older children with *The Electric Company,* a program designed to help viewers expand their vocabulary and reading skills, and to science with *3-2-1 Contact.*

Another widely viewed series, but with a very different approach to communicating with young children, is *Mr. Rogers' Neighborhood.* Host Fred Rogers gently and quietly discusses the difficulties children face in growing up, including their fears and their relationships. With a clear distinction made between reality and make-believe, Rogers and his supporting cast create characters who help convey the theme of each program to young viewers.

Science and Nature

Nova, Cosmos, Scientific Frontiers, and *Newton's Apple* have brought the wonders of science into the home. Animal and nature shows such as *National Geographic, All Creatures Great and Small, Wild America, Adventure,* and *Nature* are still among the most popular offerings of the system.

Their appeals are wide, and so is their viewership. The exploration motif appeals to young and old alike and has made these programs favorites with many viewers.

Music

Evening at Symphony has been a boon to classical music lovers. Opera programs have become a mainstay and a great service to opera fans who are not able to attend live performances.

However, classical music has not been the only form of music PTV has presented seriously. In addition to various documentaries highlighting the careers of prominent jazz musicians, a regular weekly program, *Austin City Limits,* features concerts by both established and up-and-coming country-and-western performers. Similarly, jazz, rhythm and blues, soul, rock 'n' roll, and new age music have been featured.

News and Public Affairs

As commercial TV newscasts have reached out for larger audiences, many critics have attacked them for emphasizing the visual and sensational. The network evening news programs provide a thin accounting of major news events because of the severe time restrictions of the half-hour format. For viewers who have a negative impression of local or network television news, *The MacNeil/Lehrer Newshour* has provided an oasis of reasoned thought. Public affairs programs, from conservative author William F. Buckley's *Firing Line* to *Tony Brown's Journal,* which deals with issues important to African-Americans, provide interested viewers with social and political perspectives that are not available on the commercial networks. *Washington Week in Review* is a weekly discussion of national politics by some of the top Washington correspondents for major newspapers. Financial affairs are discussed each Friday on *Wall Street Week.* Several series featuring Bill Moyers have received awards, and Moyers has covered everything from intelligence to mythology with a view to how each topic interacts with the social structure. *Frontline* has been in the forefront of current issues with evenhanded and intelligent presentations and analyses.

Information

The diversity of programming on public television goes far beyond cultural and public affairs. The offerings have included instruction on house renovation and repair in a weekly series, *This Old House,* and tips on cooking from Justin Wilson, a Cajun chef. Whatever the interest of the viewer, it has been covered on PTV.

PROGRAM SOURCES

Programs have come from a variety of sources, mostly stations but also regional and state associations of stations, independent producers, the foreign market, and commercial television.

Stations

Many stations are prolific producers of shows. WGBH TV in Boston provides many shows, some acquired from the British Broadcasting Corporation (BBC). Many of the public affairs programs produced in the nation's capital come from WETA TV, Washington, D.C. WQED, Pittsburgh, is known for *National Geographic* (nature programs), and WTTW, Chicago, has produced *The Frugal Gourmet* (cooking) and *Sneak Previews* (movie reviews). In each case the individual station took responsibility for seeking funding for the show, producing it, and then making it available to other stations.

Regional Networks

There are four regional networks or associations that provide programming and secure product for their members. They include the Eastern Educational Television Network (EEN), the Southern Educational Telecommunications Association (SECA), the Central Educational Network (CEN), and the Pacific Mountain Network (PMN). These regional networks develop programming for use by member stations and possible sale to out-of-region stations. Because they are locally focused, they can provide programming that reflects regional interests and tastes.

State Associations

Many states have associations that help secure product for PTV stations within the state and generate new programs to be shared by member stations. For example, the decision making for all public TV stations in Georgia is centralized in the Atlanta office of the Georgia Public Telecommunication Authority. In Pennsylvania public stations have more autonomy, but the Pennsylvania Public Television Network coordinates their efforts and serves as an information clearinghouse that helps avoid duplication of effort and expense.

Independent Producers and Specialized Companies

Independent producers who made shows for public television had to pitch their shows to the stations rather than to the network. This "democratic" system frustrated producers because most decisions were made on the basis of cost.

Thus, independent producers were not the force in public broadcasting that they have always been in commercial broadcasting. One problem was that stations had to secure funds from corporate sources that shied away from anything controversial. Producers learned what to pitch and what to avoid, and creativity suffered.[5]

The Children's Television Workshop (CTW), which supplied *Sesame Street, The Electric Company,* and other series, and other specialized houses produce shows for public television. These shows are among the longest running programs on television (Box 18-2).[6] CTW is a nonprofit organization that derives a large percentage of its funds from product licensing agreements involving characters such as Big Bird. The licensing income has been so high that most of the production costs are covered.

Foreign Productions

Public television has made extensive use of British product over the years. In the past most BBC product seen in the United States was distributed by PBS, but now, cable networks such as Arts and Entertainment and the Discovery Channel aggressively compete with public television for this product. Shows such as *Upstairs Downstairs* were successful for PBS because they received funding from major corporations and were highly acclaimed by critics and a loyal audience. British comedy series such as *Fawlty*

Towers and *Monty Python's Flying Circus* were similarly successful.

However, PBS no longer owns the franchise on British product. In fact, Arts and Entertainment has first choice on some of the better BBC product.[7]

Commercial Television

In one notable case, a show came to public television from commercial television. *The Paper Chase,* a critically acclaimed CBS show based on the movie of the same name, was never able to secure a substantial audience by network standards and was canceled after one season, but its small audience was intensely loyal. It was a high-quality series, but very few episodes were available, and it had no chance for syndication.

The time was right for an experiment, and the show was picked up by public television for repeat showings. Although the producers did not make much money, they gained added attention for the show. Public television had obtained a series that had received favorable critical reviews. It had the potential to attract large audiences by public television standards and gave viewers a chance to watch it again. Its audience, though minuscule by CBS standards, was huge for PBS, and so the show was a ratings success in public TV terms. Later the pay-cable network Showtime acquired the rights to *The Paper Chase,* a decision based partly on the successful PBS

**BOX 18-2
LONGEST RUNNING
PUBLIC TELEVISION
SERIES**

Program	Premiere Date
Mister Rogers' Neighborhood	January 19, 1968
Tony Brown's Journal	June 12, 1968
Washington Week in Review	January 9, 1969
Sesame Street	November 10, 1969
Masterpiece Theatre	January 10, 1971
Firing Line	May 26, 1971
Wall Street Week	November 10, 1971
Nova	March 3, 1974
Great Performances	October 16, 1974
Austin City Limits	March 12, 1975

SOURCE: "Longest Running Public Television Series," *Electronic Media,* March 21, 1988, p. 62. ■

record, and produced new episodes that featured many members of the original cast.

PROGRAMMING STRATEGIES

The diversity of programming that is the strength of PTV is also a weakness. The blocking of similar programs, which increases the potential for audience flow, cuts down on the number of program types that can be used. In public television, few programs are very much like the others. As a result, public TV programmers cannot block shows as effectively as their commercial counterparts do. Each show is a potential programming island unto itself, dependent on tune-in rather than flow.

In the Sunday prime-time lineup on one public station, for instance, *The Lawrence Welk Show,* a music program appealing to older viewers (age 55 and over), led into *The Undersea World of Jacques Cousteau* (nature content), which led into *Dr. Who* (a low-budget British science-fiction program aimed at a younger audience). Little demographic or content consistency exists between these shows. The group that would tune in for *Cousteau* might not be much inclined to watch *Dr. Who,* although *Lawrence Welk* might provide some flow to *Cousteau.* More often than not, programs are placed in the schedule without much chance of delivering audiences from one show to the next.

The schedule for Sunday through Friday shown in Table 18-1 illustrates a similar pattern. On Sunday the lead show for the night is *Wonderworks,* an "umbrella" title that houses a multitude of programs for younger viewers, such as *Anne of Green Gables.* Given its younger audience appeal, this show would not be expected to lead *National Geographic* well. There is some consistency, though, between *National Geographic* and *Nature,* which both focus on nature subjects and appeal to an older, more educated audience. The following program, *Masterpiece Theatre,* represents a content shift (but not so much of a demographic shift) from the prior shows.

With this diversity, flow-related strategies lose some of their effectiveness. It is difficult to apply a hammocking strategy, for example, when the post programs have no relationship to each other or to the show in the hammock. Similarly, tentpoling becomes nearly impossible because of the lack of consistency of theme. Of course, certain individual placements are useful and represent an attempt to schedule similar programs together whenever possible.

Monday's schedule of *Miracle Planet, Eyes on the Prize,* and *American Artist* moves from science to public affairs to art/biography. Other days show similar jumps in content and audience.

Friday, however, seems to have content and demographic consistency. *The McLaughlin Group* (current political and social issues), *Wall Street Week* (investment and economics), *Washington Week in Review* (politics and government), *World of Ideas* (Bill Moyers's look at in-

TABLE 18-1 PBS Prime-Time Schedule

Day	7 p.m.	8 p.m.	8:30 p.m.	9 p.m.	9:30 p.m.	10 p.m.
Monday		Miracle Planet		Eyes on the Prize		American Artist
Tuesday		Nova		Frontline		Louis Rukyser
Wednesday		Tax Questions				Business
Thursday		This Old House	Frugal Gourmet	Mystery		Orchestra
Friday		McLaughlin Group	Wall Street Week	Washington Week	World of Ideas	South American Journey
Saturday		Lawrence Welk		Cousteau	Odyssey	Dr. Who
Sunday	Wonderworks	National Geographic		Nature		Masterpiece Theatre

teresting people and ideas), and *South American Journey* blend together as well as any network cluster could.

Still, without specific flow mechanisms on most nights, strategies are limited. One of the best ploys that PTV programmers can implement to compete with commercial and cable channels is counterprogramming. For example, on Tuesday *Nova* runs against a network comedy and two network movies. As a science show it can appeal to younger *and* older audiences. Thus, it has flexibility, and none of the networks is running a reality show during that time slot. It effectively counters the four broadcast networks. Equally important, as a science show *Nova* is in a class by itself vis-à-vis the networks in terms of type and quality.

The other strategy that PTV programmers have used effectively is stunting. There *are* shows on public television that draw larger audiences than others. The most notable are *National Geographic* specials, which have been so successful that they often turn up in video stores. PBS often stunts with such specials, especially during sweeps, when public television offerings might otherwise be obscured by large numbers of blockbuster programs on the networks.

Gaining Attention for New Programs

Before 1990 there was no fall rollout of new programs to promote sampling. That fall saw two monumental events: the *Civil War* miniseries, which became the most watched program in PBS history,[8] and the institution of Showcase Week, a time when all new series were rolled out for viewer sampling. The Showcase Week of September 30–October 6 saw premier episodes of signature series such as *Frontline, Masterpiece Theatre, Mystery, Great Performances, Live from Lincoln Center, Nova,* and *Nature.* Actor Paul Winfield served as the host and provided promotions and program introductions.[9] The one-two punch of the *Civil War* and Showcase Week gave PBS an unusually strong start for the season and signaled a new way of doing business.

FINANCIAL SUPPORT FOR PROGRAMMING

Fund-raising is an ongoing and occasionally embarrassing fact of life for PTV outlets. Pledge drives, which have been dubbed "begathons," cover as many as 60 days a year.[10] Since government and corporate sources of money have been unreliable, viewer donations now make up the largest portion of the economic pie, supplying 22 percent of station expenses.[11]

A few very creative methods have been developed to raise money. Some stations use auctions. Companies and individuals donate goods and services to the station, and an on-air bidding process is completed, with the proceeds going to the station. In North Dakota 20 percent of the public broadcasting budget is raised through a string of blackjack and bingo parlors. A Sacramento, California, station even tried running a restaurant.

Corporations have dropped out of sponsorship arrangements, sometimes after years of participation. Exxon pulled its $8 million to $10 million of support per year from such shows as *Great Performances.* The explanation was that the new management had no interest in public broadcasting, which "doesn't interest them—never did."[12]

Corporate comings and goings may constitute a form of censorship as sponsors stay away from issue-oriented programs. A 1986 study of public television in Great Britain and the United States concluded that corporate sponsorship "tends to bias provision toward noncontroversial projects and programmes."[13]

Congress passed the Public Broadcasting Act in 1967, creating the Corporation for Public Broadcasting as the funding agency for public television, but the CPB had to turn to Congress each year for money to be dispersed to public stations. The amount of government support has dwindled over the years. Aside from a growing disinclination to use public monies to support television, Congress has reacted negatively to public television programs that have broached politically sensitive subjects (Box 18-3).

**BOX 18-3
RICHARD NIXON AND
PUBLIC TELEVISION**

Public television had a habit of being critical of Presidents of the United States. It hectored President Johnson about the Vietnam war, and it needled President Nixon as well. The difference was that Nixon took it personally and complained that public television had a liberal, elitist bias. While that helped turn public opinion against public television in 1971, it was in 1973 that the President first played the card everyone had always feared—funding. During that time Nixon was besieged on all sides by Watergate questions and allegations that he had done something wrong. He was largely helpless against much of the criticism because there was no effective way to strike back at the networks, but he could punish public television. He vetoed the funding bill Congress had passed, throwing the whole system into a panic. While concerned with its own survival, public broadcasting was in no position to badger the President. More than that, Nixon had established a precedent of political interference in the workings of the PTV system and had used withdrawal of funds to silence criticism. Since one of public television's principal skills was political analysis, it was vulnerable. Later administrations would learn how to keep PTV in poverty and thus more quiet. ■

Viewer Pledge Drives

Even during the best years public stations are hard pressed to support program development. These stations have responded by scheduling pledge drives several times a year in which viewers are urged to make a donation to help keep the station on the air and continue to provide quality programs. During program breaks, station staff members and volunteers ask for contributions. Such drives are usually tied to stunting strategies that save the best programs for pledge weeks. This scheduling provides the on-air solicitors with something tangible to point out to potential contributors.

Programs aired during fund-raising drives have included replays of *The Civil War* and *Of Moose and Men: The Rocky and Bullwinkle Story* and marathons of other favorites. One station ran 10 straight hours of *Homecoming,* a series featuring popular family therapist John Bradshaw.

Underwriters

Not enough public viewers actually donate money, and so for most stations pledge drives are not a sufficient source of funds for program development. An alternative solution has Faustian overtones. A number of foundations and corporations will **underwrite** (pay for) production costs, but most are unwilling to support controversial programs, especially programs that are critical of them. As a consequence, many of the programs that receive funding are "safe" either because a potential underwriter volunteers its support or because producers feel that it would be futile to propose topics that might be deemed sensitive.

Going into the 1990s, the future for PTV was clouded. Companies that once had funded programs had found other, cheaper means of bolstering a positive public image. Because of mergers and acquisitions and the resulting debt structures, many companies reduced or eliminated corporate donations of any kind. Having come to depend on corporate America for survival, public broadcasting was being deserted by its benefactors, and the government had already served notice that more money would not be forthcoming.

PUBLIC TELEVISION'S IDENTITY

After all that time PTV was still not certain about its identity. There existed, and still exists, great variety in station ownership and direction. Public stations are owned and operated by municipal and state agencies, public schools, colleges and universities, communities, and library boards. Thus there are many opinions about what public television should be. At one end of the spectrum are those who still think that it should be a teaching tool and harken back to the days of educational television for its mission. The opposite viewpoint holds that PTV should be more commercial and strive for larger audiences by presenting more mainstream shows. Other perspectives fall somewhere in between, with a popular one being that PTV should provide "culture."

The mission of public television had never been adequately defined, and no centralized authority had emerged before 1990 to impose a mission on the system. The public stations marched on, rarely in step with each other, each making its own decisions in creating a schedule that might or might not have included all the programs offered by PBS. Then things changed.

NEW DIRECTIONS FOR PUBLIC TELEVISION

A Czar Is Born

Jennifer Lawson was named PBS vice president of national programming and promotion services in 1990 and was immediately nicknamed "the czar." In a bold stroke, PBS's National Program Policy Committee suspended the SPC and turned over programming decisions to one person for the first time. No more would decisions come out of large and anonymous committees; for good or ill, everything could be tracked to one person.

Lawson's first two programming decisions were auspicious by any standard. She chose the miniseries *The Civil War* to lead off the 1990 season and decided to concentrate its 12 hours into 5 nights rather than space them out in weekly segments. The results gave her the big victory that every new "coach" needs.[14]

Without the SPC, she was free to develop shows much as a network does by dealing directly with producers, commissioning scripts, and concentrating control. That allowed her the freedom to make decisions quickly and seize opportunities which the old PBS would have lost through slow, bureaucratic movement.

Perhaps the most important element of the change was the reduction of the CPB's functions and the raising of PBS's profile and degree of control. Former PBS president Lawrence Grossman had said that CPB could be reduced by 80 percent and be run "with about five accountants."[15] The reduction was not 80 percent but 50, and CPB was not taken entirely out of the programming business. However, the message was clear: PBS would be running the show, and money would not have to be pried out of the CPB. Lawson's early record of success all but assured the new direction of the restructured network.

Lawson's first goal was to centralize funding and programming. Once PBS had shifted out of the SPC model, about $100 million of programming money would be centrally administered to develop programming.[16]

Programs and Promotion

The original Showcase Week idea was kept and expanded in the 1991 season. Premieres that fall included *Longtime Companion* on *American Playhouse* and *The Life and Times of LBJ* on *The American Experience* in addition to the rest of the season premieres.

New ways of promoting PBS were developed. The most interesting and effective might have been the advertisements run on broadcast and cable networks. Buying time on a competitor was unusual but proved to be an excellent vehicle for alerting viewers to particular shows.

New programs were also developed. One of the most ambitious was *Columbus and the Age of Discovery,* a miniseries which aired on *The Civil War* principle of concentrated evenings. After a 4-day initial airing in early October 1991, it was repeated as a marathon on Columbus Day, October 12, 1991.

Other new programs were wondrously diverse. Lawson wanted what PBS was known for and more. She even wanted an educational game show. That she got in the form of *Where in the World Is Carmen Sandiego?*, PBS's first game show, modeled on the popular children's geography game. Other programs in the 1991–1992 season included Ken Burns's (*Civil War* producer) *The History of Baseball; Cracking the Code,* a series of eight 1-hour programs on the impact of scientific advances on civilization; *The Other Side of the News,* a 9-hour series on news reporting; *The 90s,* a series about how people get information and the accuracy of news reports; and *Critical Condition,* a series about medical science.

Opportunities in Cable Television

PBS had missed one boat that it regretted. Originally offered the opportunity to program what eventually became C-SPAN, it turned down the offer.[17] Not wishing to make the same mistake twice, PBS began talks with the Discovery Channel about developing a basic cable network for noncommercial programming, working together on a re-formation of the Learning Channel, and doing coproductions that would air on both services. While the outcomes of these discussions are not known, the important fact is that they are being held at all. With cable moving to a 200-channel environment, PBS will be lost in the shuffle unless it finds a way to turn cable to its own advantage.

Seeking Funds

Just because an idea is old does not mean that it is bad. The Carnegie Commission recommended in 1967 that a way to generate money for public broadcasting, free of political influences, would be an excise tax on television sets paid by buyers at the time of purchase. That would create a pool of money that would fund public broadcasting forever. It did not happen.

However, this idea is being revived. About 33 million television sets and VCRs are purchased in the United States each year. If each carried a modest tax of $10, the amount raised would be $330 million, which would easily fund all the programming requirements of PBS without the need to raise federal allocations.[18]

Another tack was tried in 1987 and may be tried again. Since commercial broadcasters use the public spectrum to make profits yet do not

pay for the privilege, they could support public broadcasting. The mechanism would be a 2 or 5 percent tax on transfers of stations from one owner to another. Since the 1980s was marked by a flurry of sales, including the sale of all three networks, a small tax on such sales would provide the money needed. In a show of force, the commercial broadcasters lobbied successfully to defeat the bill in the U.S. Senate. Senators were considerably more frightened of angering commercial broadcasters than they were concerned about finding new methods to fund public broadcasters.[19]

An innovative fund-raising mechanism has grown up over the past 5 years. Public broadcasters cannot accept advertising as we know it on commercial television, but they can accept underwriting where the donor's name is mentioned. In an effort to encourage corporate support of public broadcasting, rules on underwriting were relaxed so that products and services could be described at some length in underwriting mentions. Some of these announcements are almost indistinguishable from advertisements. Still, underwriters were accustomed to thinking in terms of program sponsorship, and so Broadcast Marketing was formed to act as a rep firm for public stations, working on the commercial principle of mentions within shows as opposed to sponsorship of the entire program. Since multiple underwriting for shows is not unusual, further segmenting along the commercial model of ads within blocks might work. One 2½-minute break per hour is allowed for underwriting in most public programming. If that time could be used for underwriters' messages, a considerable amount of money could be raised.

There is no telling if this idea will work, but Broadcast Marketing has taken on 60 public television stations and has added the New Jersey and Nebraska networks to the list. This will not solve public television's funding problem, but it could be part of the solution. Whatever the case, without some long-term solution to public television's money woes, we may not need a chapter on public television in the future, except as a historical reference.

SUMMARY

Public television evolved from the old educational television system. The change of name was more than cosmetic as it allowed for the production of a wider variety of programs.

Public television has moved into areas abandoned (quality children's television) or ignored (the arts, science, and in-depth public affairs) by the networks. In doing so, it has provided an alternative to traditional broadcast networks by offering quality programming. In some areas it has been accused of "stooping to conquer" by airing movies and programs such as *Lawrence Welk* and *Lassie.*

With the rise of cable networks such as Discovery and Arts and Entertainment, many programs that had been the province of public television are now being distributed through commercial outlets. Not only are these networks competing for the same audience and for funds to support original programming, they are vying for program product as well.

Sources of programming include producing stations, regional and state networks, specialty producers, and the foreign market. There has been a steady supply of available programming, although funding is often a problem.

PTV's strength is also its weakness in that the program offerings are so diverse that it is difficult to make a schedule using traditional flow strategies. The lack of blocking capacity on most evenings renders the traditional strategies moot.

Public television's funding problems continue, as can be seen in frequent pledge drives, auctions, and other attempts at fund-raising. With the government withdrawing funds, corporations reducing support, and cable competitors seeking some of the same programming, the future of public television became uncertain in the 1980s.

A dramatic change of direction in 1990 may have changed public television's fate. The appointment of programming czar Jennifer Lawson opened up new opportunities. Program development and scheduling were moved from the stations to the network, creating a strong central organization and decision-making structure. PBS was finally operating like a network, not a collection of feudal empires.

New programs were developed and new ways to fund programming were realized as CPB was downsized and half its monies were used for programming at PBS. Basic cable television was explored as an outlet mechanism for public television programming and an avenue for raising the system's profile. Coproductions with cable networks were also explored.

By 1992 public television's fortunes seemed much improved. Its future, given the competitive environment in which it operates, is still uncertain, but the dark clouds have given way a bit for the first time in years.

SUGGESTED READINGS

Fuller, John: *Who Watches Public Television?,* Public Broadcasting Service, Alexandria, Va., 1986.

Fuller is the director of research for PBS and is very knowledgeable about programming the service. In this book he explains the diversity of the PBS audience and of the service's programming. The fractionalization of the audience and its flow problems are compounded by this diversity. In a Catch-22 situation, PBS must offer real alternatives to fill its mandate and appeal to all segments of society, but to accomplish those goals, PBS gives up flow and the strategies that go with it. Still, Fuller outlines a number of programming strategies that PBS can use to compete with broadcast stations and cable networks.

NOTES

1. Robert Blakely, *To Serve the Public Interest: Educational Broadcasting in the United States,* Syracuse University Press, Syracuse, New York, 1977.

2. John Weisman, "Public TV in Crisis," *TV Guide,* Aug. 8, 1987, p. 26.

3. Judy Flander, "Public Television Hits a Mid-Life Crisis," *Washington Journalism Review,* July/August 1989, p. 32.

4. Jennifer Grossman and Mary Maguire, "Beaming the Three R's," CPB news release, Aug. 3, 1989, pp. 1–3.

5. Weisman, op. cit., p. 28.

6. "Longest Running Public Television Series," *Electronic Media,* March 21, 1988, p. 62.

7. Flander, op. cit.

8. Richard Zoglin, "The Civil War Comes Home," *Time,* Oct. 8, 1990, p. 78.

9. "PBS Packs Some Fall Fireworks," *Broadcasting,* Sept. 10, 1990, p. 63.

10. Colette Hiller, "Appeal to Public Intelligence," *Television Week,* Jan. 19, 1989, p. 17.

11. "March: Like Lion for PBS," *Broadcasting,* March 25, 1991, p. 93.

12. Weisman, op. cit., p. 27.

13. Ibid., p. 28.

14. Zoglin, op. cit.

15. Weisman, op. cit., p. 38.

16. Christopher John Farley, "PBS' Path to Success," *USA Today,* Oct. 3, 1990, pp. D1–D2; see also Janet Stilson, "PBS Changes Its Ways," *Television Business International,* February 1991, pp. 26–28.

17. Flander, op. cit.

18. Weisman, op. cit., p. 36.

19. J. J. Yore, "Public Broadcasting Trust Fund Killed," *Current,* Dec. 22, 1987, p. 1.

PART FOUR

Cable Television

Cable is no longer a luxury but is considered a necessity. How did something as simple as getting access to a few stations' signals turn into a booming industry? In this section we will find out. Cable brings everything into the home that television can offer, and all at one time. Do you want to watch wrestling? It's on somewhere. Drama? Stand-up comedy? Cartoons? Movies? You'd have to duck to miss getting hit by all the choices. Talk shows? Game shows? Half-hour programs in praise of gadgets and gimmicks? You want Gilligan? You get Gilligan.

But there's more. With whole channels devoted to trials and science fiction, cable offers a way for specialists to get their fill of their favorite topics. If you love sports, you do not have to wait for the weekend: Several channels will give you sports 24 hours a day. Never before has television presented so much specialized programming. However, as with broadcast television, there is a method to organizing cable schedules. The cable programmer thinks about much the same issues that the broadcaster considers, but with some important differences. In this section we will look at the world of cable and see what it has to offer, to whom it is offered, and how those offerings are ordered.

Chapter 19, "Assessing the Cable Television Environment," lays out the cable environment, paying special attention to viewership, technology, ownership, economics, competitors, and regulation. By every account, cable viewership is up. More homes have cable, there is more cable viewing than ever, and more cable networks are coming. Cable is an entertainment-rich environment, and profits are up. As more subscribers and advertisers come to cable, its profit profile will continue to be positive.

Chapter 20, "Cable System Programming," focuses on local systems and their organization. Programming at the system level is also discussed.

More traditional programming strategies and practices return in Chapter 21, "Basic Cable Programming," which looks at basic cable networks. Like their broadcast counterparts, cable networks seek viewers in targeted dayparts. In this chapter we explore programming practices and detail the major basic cable networks.

In Chapter 22, "Premium Cable Networks," we discuss premium and pay cable. Generally, "premium" cable refers to established services which offer 24-hour schedules for a monthly price. HBO, Showtime, and the Disney Channel are the largest ones. "Pay" is used to refer to pay-per-view cable, where the viewer pays a set price to see a single sports event, concert, or movie. All forms of premium and pay cable will be discussed.

CHAPTER 19

The Cable Environment

KEY TERMS AND CONCEPTS

Access Channel
Basic Cable
Basic Tier
Cable Headend
Cable-Ready Television
Channel Clustering
Consistent Channel Numbering
Direct Broadcast Satellite
Earth Station
Fiber Optics
Forced Tier
Headend
Home Cable Drop
If Carry/Must Pay
Interconnects
Leased Access Channel
Local-Origination Programming
Multichannel Multipoint Distribution System
Multiple System Operator
Pay-per-View
Premium/Pay Channel
Reverse Tiering
Satellite Dish
Satellite Master Antenna Television
Syndicated Exclusivity
Telcos
Tiering
Trunk Line
Television Receive-Only System
Vertical Integration

Cable TV may be the ultimate "new technology" that will compete with broadcast television. Although it is hardly new, cable provides a wide variety of programming sources.

Cable is now in more than 60 percent of the households in the United States (Table 19-1 illustrates **cable penetration.**) The potential seems promising, with 86 percent of U.S. households already passed by cable. By 1998, it is estimated that 92 percent of U.S. households will be passed.[1]

Whereas the goal of a broadcast station or network programmer is to attract and maintain audiences for programs, the goal of a cable system is to attract subscribers. Whether they watch or not is of only secondary concern since the bulk of a cable system's revenue is derived from monthly subscription fees. Consequently, a cable system is concerned with offering the kinds of services that will attract as many subscribers as possible and keep them hooked to the system.

The local cable system's management determines which broadcast station and cable-only network signals will be carried on the system. At the same time, the managers have to decide which services will be assigned to which cable channels. There is aggressive competition for the desirable VHF spaces.

Some large **multiple system operators** (MSOs)—companies that own and manage many cable systems—dictate which services will be carried on each owned system. That is the method favored by the largest American MSO, Tele-Communications, Inc. (TCI), a corporation that operates many cable systems nationwide. Since essentially the same lineup of channels is offered on all cable systems, the task of selection is minimized. The advantage is efficiency; the disadvantage is an inability to tailor systems to fit individual communities' characteristics. However, even if some decisions are left to the local system's management, because of its size, an MSO is in a position to negotiate a better rate for cable network services than a single system can.

As is the case in broadcast television, where managers take on much of the responsibility for programming, so it is in cable. There are relatively few programmers in cable systems. MSOs may have a programmer who makes decisions

TABLE 19-1   Cable Penetration

Year	Households with Cable	Percentage of U.S. Households
1992	56,234,290	61.1
1991	55,786,390	60.6
1990	54,871,330	59.0
1989	52,564,470	57.1
1988	48,636,520	53.8
1987	44,970,880	50.5
1986	42,237,140	48.1
1985	41,534,651	47.3
1984	37,290,870	43.7
1983	34,113,790	40.5
1982	29,340,570	35.0
1981	23,219,200	28.3
1980	17,671,490	22.6
1979	14,814,380	19.4
1978	13,391,910	17.9
1977	12,168,450	16.6

SOURCE: Nielsen Media Research, Northbrook, Ill., 1992.

about which cable networks to carry, but even in larger companies those decisions are often made by the general manager.

This chapter will examine the cable landscape. First we will examine cable ownership, paying special attention to the growth of large cable companies. Then we will establish how cable signals are captured by cable systems and distributed to subscribers. Related to both points is the area of cable economics. Cable economics are different in some ways from the economics of broadcast television, and these differences are important. Next we will examine cable's primary competitors. While they program the same networks and services, these competitors deliver them in different ways. We will then look at the different sources for content brought into the home via cable and examine how networks and services are organized on the cable system. Regulation is important in any industry, and cable is no exception. A few primary areas of importance will be discussed. Finally, we will focus on how technology, regulation, and economics come together to determine success or failure in program delivery systems and what to reasonably expect in the future.

CABLE OWNERSHIP

The United States has about 53,900,000 cable households, and the 20 largest MSOs account for about two-thirds of the subscribers, some 35,331,000 homes.[2] This leaves over 18 million homes in systems that are not served by the 20 largest MSOs.

Multisystem Operators

The cable industry has come to be characterized by bigness. The 20 largest MSOs provide cable service to two of every three cable households, and they are growing by acquiring new cable systems every day (Table 19-2). There are several reasons for this trend, most of them economic.

When it comes to operating a cable system, there are many tasks to be completed. Homes

TABLE 19-2 The 20 Largest Cable MSOs and Their Subscribers

Rank	Multiple System Operator	Subscribers
1	Tele-Communications, Inc.	8,375,000
2	American TV & Communications	4,400,000
3	UA Entertainment	2,715,391
4	Continental Cablevision	2,675,000
5	Warner Cable	1,851,000
6	Comcast	1,618,986
7	Cox Cable	1,598,417
8	Storer Cable	1,574,248
9	Jones Intercable	1,569,102
10	Cablevision Systems	1,537,624
11	Newhouse Broadcasting	1,241,820
12	Times Mirror Cable	1,100,000
13	Cablevision Industries	1,075,085
14	Heritage Communication	1,072,000
15	Viacom Cable	1,045,369
16	Adelphia Communication	1,022,891
17	Sammons Communication	906,251
18	Century Communications	865,000
19	Falcon Cable TV	844,100
20	Paragon Communication	812,658

SOURCE: *Cablevision,* Jan. 14, 1991

have to be wired, and that requires people, supplies, coordination with government and utilities, and capital. Small companies, unaccustomed to political ins and outs and sometimes short on capital, cannot afford unpleasant turns of events.

Another set of tasks has to do with receiving and organizing signals. That is the work of the headend, which must be designed and built with a view to the future. Building it for present capacity may mean rebuilding it later, when more networks are available or when technology has made older systems obsolete. Early cable systems were built to accommodate the 12 VHF channels, but with the weedlike growth of cable networks and the increased expectations of subscribers for expanded services, 12-channel systems soon became dinosaurs and had to be rebuilt. Access to top technology and research is more likely for a large MSO.

Once the system is built, it has to offer channels to subscribers. As was outlined in the prior section, mom-and-pop operators do not have the advantages of an MSO when it comes to negotiating contracts with cable networks. Strong networks such as MTV have the upper hand in negotiating carriage with small system operators because potential subscribers are going to demand that channel, and so the operator's chance of getting a favorable price is reduced. By contrast, an MSO speaks for hundreds of thousands, sometimes millions, of homes. It is to the advantage of the network to be carried in all those homes, and so it is likely to make a concession or two in exchange for that carriage.

Many day-to-day tasks must be performed at all local systems. Accounting, word processing, repair, management, and marketing are just a few. But does *each* cable system need all the people necessary to get these tasks done? No. One general manager, for example, can manage several systems. The accounting and legal work for many different local systems can be done by a small staff. In short, personnel do not have to be duplicated in each system. A single-system operator simply does not have this advantage. The tasks have to get done, and so certain inefficiencies are inevitable.

Mom-and-Pop Systems

As with a small store, smaller cable systems have survived next to the giant companies. Small so-called mom-and-pop cable systems have been making a go of it despite competition from the major companies, but their problems are many.

In the first place, small operators are not in a strong bargaining position with major cable network suppliers when it comes to acquiring services. Because it represents 20 percent of cable homes, TCI can "buy in bulk" from cable network suppliers and thus can negotiate a better price.

However, an industry has grown up around the small operators, giving them some of the clout they have traditionally lacked. Companies such as the National Cable Television Cooperative now represent many of the 11,000 cable systems and negotiate packages of services for

cable operators.[3] By banding together in specific ways, smaller cable systems have enjoyed some of the advantages of large companies without losing their local identity. Still, smaller operators find themselves in a difficult financial position when they compete with larger companies. Susquehanna Cable of Pennsylvania, which operated several systems in the central portion of the state, was sold to TCI in 1991, part of a trend over the past 10 years of larger MSOs taking over most of the task of delivering cable services.

CABLE TECHNOLOGY: HOW CABLE WORKS

Cable television works by capturing and distributing signals from a variety of sources. Broadcast stations in a cable system's area are received over the air just as they are in homes. Satellite networks such as TNT, MTV, and Lifetime must come in through a satellite dish, and some distant stations are delivered to the cable system by way of microwave transmission systems.

The Cable Headend

The **headend** is the nerve center of a cable system. It is here that all the channels made available to subscribers are received and prepared for delivery. Reception occurs through over-the-air antennas, satellite dishes, and microwave receivers; each captures a different kind of signal.[4]

Local and regional broadcast channels are received through antennas that are larger and more sophisticated versions of a home rooftop antenna. As stations move farther away, their signals are harder to get. Thus, to receive high-quality signals, cable systems use powerful antennas.

Almost all cable networks are now delivered by satellite. Thus, to receive those signals, the cable system uses satellite dishes, also known as earth stations or **television receive-only systems (TVROs).**

Distant signals of broadcast stations may be delivered to the cable headend by microwave.

Microwave systems nationwide deliver a variety of signals, including television, radio, and business, communications, and industrial data. If the station a cable company wishes to offer is available by microwave, that signal can be delivered to the headend.

At the headend, signals are converted to the specific channel the cable system has assigned. Since any signal can be converted to any channel, the cable system has great flexibility about what services to offer on which channels. This means that stations may not be carried on their "normal" channels. For example, channel 5 may show up on cable as channel 27 if that is deemed desirable. In any event, the signals from satellites, over-the-air antennas, and microwave are assigned to channels, converted appropriately, and sent out of the headend through the distribution system, eventually arriving at subscribers' television sets.

The Distribution System

As the word suggests, in a cable system the signals are carried along a wire from the headend to the individual home. Thus, the signals leave the headend on one of two kinds of cable: coaxial cable and fiber-optic cable. **Coaxial cable,** which has been used for decades, consists of copper wire surrounded by a protective sheath coated with aluminum. **Fiber-optic cable** is newer and is made of glass fibers that carry information much as coaxial cable does.

The difference is that fiber-optic strands can be much smaller and carry a signal much farther before the signal begins to erode and has to be amplified. For these reasons, new systems and newly rebuilt systems are increasingly using fiber-optic cable.[5]

The cable can be carried through the service area in several ways. It can be attached to power poles and telephone poles or can be buried underground. In some neighborhoods all power, telephone, and cable lines must be buried. Often cable is carried through combinations of methods from the headend to individual homes. The **trunk line** is a main cable line which runs down each street in the area, passing homes in the same way water, sewer, gas, telephone, and electrical systems do. If someone wishes to subscribe and is passed by the cable, a home drop is installed.

A **home cable drop** is an individual connection to the cable system. A coaxial cable line runs from the trunk cable to the home and is connected to one or more television sets there. The home drop is the last stop for channels received, processed, and sent out from the headend. As shown in Figure 19-1, the system is designed to deliver channels efficiently from one place to another.

Satellite distribution to cable systems One of the most profound changes in the American television industry has permitted a multitude of high-quality television signals to be distributed efficiently across the nation. Whereas cable TV was touted as the system of video abundance, its potential did not begin to be fulfilled until signals were distributed via satellite.

This is the case for several reasons. Satellites are placed in geostationary orbits, which means that they orbit the Earth in the same direction that the Earth turns and at the same speed. Thus, they stay in the "same place" in the sky, making them functionally stationary. It is easy to send signals to the satellite, since it stays in the same place. Next, sending signals through the atmosphere makes them erode and weaken. When signals are sent horizontally, across a section of the Earth, they move through the atmosphere and therefore degrade. By contrast, signals delivered to a satellite are sent up through the atmosphere, which thins out quickly, allowing the signals to travel nearly unimpeded to their targets. As the signals are sent back to earth, the same advantage of minimal atmospheric travel is realized. This produces better signals and a more efficient system as signals do not have to be relayed from one antenna or cable system to the next.

Signals coming from satellites to the Earth cover a wide area called a **footprint.** The footprint for satellites over the United States in-

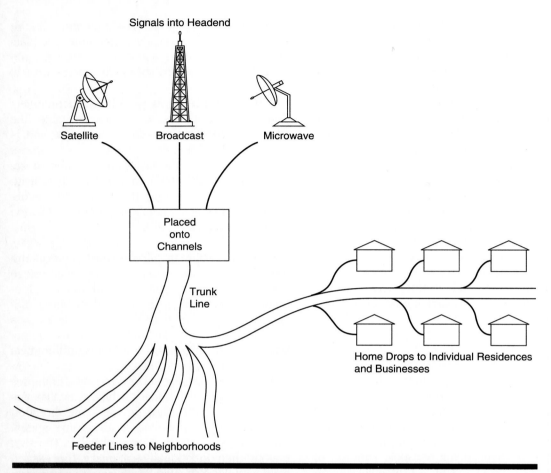

Signals into Headend

Satellite   Broadcast   Microwave

Placed onto Channels

Trunk Line

Home Drops to Individual Residences and Businesses

Feeder Lines to Neighborhoods

FIGURE 19-1   A cable distribution system.

cludes most of North America. That makes distribution simpler and more economical compared with Earth-based microwave, wire, and over-the-air systems, which require amplifiers and considerable retransmission to cover large areas.

Fiber-optic distribution from cable systems to homes
A developing technology that could revolutionize the way television is delivered to the home is on the doorstep of the electronic media industry. Fiber optics could deliver a virtually unlimited range of services to households with much higher quality and reliability than coaxial cable can provide.

Fiber-optic cable uses laser technology to send signals through flexible glass conduits. It has a number of important advantages over copper coaxial cable. First, a very small fiber-optic cable, roughly the diameter of a pencil lead, can handle many times the bandwidth of a much thicker copper coaxial cable. It is misleading, however, to consider only the physical size of the fiber-optic strand, since protective covering adds to its bulk, but several strands can be bundled to provide a bandwidth capacity that far exceeds that of a comparably sized copper coaxial cable. In addition to the small size, the cost of the cable should eventually be lower.

The most important attribute of fiber optics is

its efficiency. Because the laser-carried signal can travel much farther by fiber-optic cable than it can by coaxial cable, fewer amplifiers are needed to distribute the signal throughout the system. In addition, coaxial cable is susceptible to interference (static) from outside the system. Therefore, subscribers who are at the end of a fiber-optic cable system will receive a much sharper picture than is possible with coaxial systems. Moreover, operators can save on their power bills because they do not have to operate nearly as many amplifiers.

While satellite communication seems unlikely to be abandoned, fiber-optic cable offers an efficient terrestrial alternative for communicating over long distances. Some users of fiber optics have noted an advantage over satellite transmission in that the delay between the transmission and the reception of signals caused by the long distances they must travel is eliminated with fiber optics. Furthermore, because there are a limited number of places for satellites in orbit, fiber optics constitutes an alternative means of interconnecting the wired systems that serve the nation. One of the implications of fiber-optic technology is its potential to provide broadband services to virtually all households in the country. The efficiency of fiber optics makes it a good way to provide cable to the rural areas of the United States.

CABLE ECONOMICS

Subscribers

The primary revenue source for cable systems has always been the subscribers. The average household spends about $25 a month on cable, and with 54 million cable households nationwide, the revenues run to over $1 billion.[6]

The two traditional types of subscription are basic and pay. In **basic cable** the cable company delivers broadcast stations and a variety of cable networks focusing on sports, news, general-interest programming, and other topics for one set price.

Subscribers have the option of premium, or pay, television. A **premium service** is one for which the subscriber pays an additional amount over the basic subscription cost. For about $10 extra a month, the subscriber can enjoy films, sports, and special programming on Home Box Office (HBO), Showtime, Cinemax, and the Movie Channel or children's and family programming on the Disney Channel.

These revenue sources were sufficient in the early boom days of cable but of late have been insufficient to meet the needs of an industry that is looking to grow and expand. Additional forms of revenue have included advertising, supplemental services, and new pricing structures. Advertising is dealt with below. More specific information on new services and pricing is outlined in Chapter 20.

Cable System Advertising

Over time, local operators have discovered an important revenue source: advertising. There had been a need in many local communities for television outlets for advertising, but the size of most television markets (a 60- or 70-mile radius) made such advertising inefficient. The owner of a video store in a small town 60 miles from a major television market such as Detroit could not afford to advertise on any of the Detroit stations. Not only would such a venture be too expensive for a small business, the store owner would be paying to reach millions of people who would be too far away to rent from the store.

Cable ads, though, reach just the local area of the cable system—individual towns—rather than sprawling metropolitan areas. That puts a local, smaller business in a position to use television advertising. Also, cable delivers the best demographic groups, including a higher percentage of VCR owners, than would be possible with any other advertising vehicle.[7] Thus, $10 ads on cable would do more good for the video store owner than would $1000 ads on a station 60 miles away.

There are other opportunities to exploit. Cable

networks such as ESPN, CNN, and MTV have made ad **windows** available each hour to the cable operators, meaning that they can sell and insert local advertisements into the networks' programs. In smaller towns without television stations, this provided the first opportunity for local advertisers to use national programming as an advertising vehicle. Since the coverage area was limited to the franchise boundaries, the advertising was locally focused and inexpensive.

However, most cable companies, especially smaller ones, were unaccustomed to making money this way; they were used to receiving their income through subscription fees. During the period of cable's expansion and as the subscriber base continued to grow, increased subscriber revenues were realized yearly. Thus, cable systems did not seem to need ad sales offices, salespersons, or an advertising system. However, as cable penetration slowed down, operators started to look for other sources of revenue. Advertising was promising, but developing the necessary infrastructure was difficult and expensive.

Many cable operators in smaller towns cautiously looked around for someone who was familiar with advertising, knew who the clients were, and could sell the ad slots. That was often the local newspaper, which had a sales staff and advertising expertise. A lack of familiarity with television advertising led to some awkward-looking ads, but production talent could be hired.

In return for a percentage of the revenues, a newspaper could take over the advertising slots, and the cable company could benefit without any capital outlay for a sales staff or related resources. Given the slowed growth of cable, advertising became attractive because it could generate revenue almost immediately.

To increase the area which advertising on cable could reach, **interconnects** have been established between cable systems, allowing an advertiser to place an ad on several cable systems simultaneously. This gives the advertiser the ability to reach a larger area, even one the size of an entire television market. While parallel to the local broadcast station's reach in area, a cable interconnect offers the advantage of cable's attractive demographic composition.

More and more money is flowing into cable from advertising agencies, and the differences between broadcast and cable audiences are important. For one thing, cable audiences are more affluent. They make more money, buy more products, and own more television-related items such as VCRs and video games.[8] They thus are prime targets for advertisers.

Additionally, a trend in advertising has been toward efficiency, or reaching more desired viewers and fewer less desirable ones. Ad medium efficiency has become increasingly important to advertisers as rates have climbed. So-called waste exposures, or presentations of an ad to viewers who are unlikely to buy the product, can be more easily avoided on cable. Since the lower end of the economic scale is not represented as heavily among cable subscribers as it is in the total broadcast audience, advertising of larger-ticket items is more efficient since a greater proportion of the people exposed to the ad on cable are likely to be able to afford the item. An advertiser of a big-ticket product can make a more efficient buy on USA's showing of *Murder She Wrote* than would be possible on the same show carried on CBS.

This creates a dual revenue stream for cable, an advantage over broadcast networks and stations which have only advertising income. Cable systems realize revenues from subscribers *and* advertisers. If one stream is weak, the other is there to help.

Pay-per-View

A promising area of economic expansion in the cable industry is **pay-per-view (PPV),** in which viewers pay to watch television on an item-by-item basis. If the viewer wants to watch a championship boxing match, wrestling extravaganza, blockbuster film, or concert, he or she can select the desired event and watch it for an advertised price, as opposed to paying a monthly fee for a host of programming on HBO, Showtime, or the Disney Channel.

Pay television services that charge customers for each program or event watched are beginning to emerge as competitors of home videotape rentals. PPV owed much of its start to the success of the automatic charge systems installed on sets in many hotels.

While the concept of PPV has been around since the 1970s, advances in cable-addressable technology have enabled cable operators to allow viewers to order individual programs either through the signal converter box attached to the set or by calling a special number with a touch-tone phone. In either kind of system, a computer receives the order and locates the unique "address" of the cable subscriber's converter, sends a signal that allows an unscrambled picture to be seen on the set, and automatically bills the subscriber.

Movies are always an attractive program offering. Rental customers must often wait to get the movie of their preference because the video store does not have enough copies. PPV operators face a problem in relying on movies at the present time, though, because the revenues for home video rental far exceed the current potential for PPV. Therefore, studios release titles on video before they release them to PPV and the video stores have a head start. At present, there is a 45- to 60-day window that movie studios leave between home video release and PPV release of titles.

Special events thus seem to be the most successful type of PPV programming at present. PPV can attract many customers who watch these offerings on impulse. Some events, such as the 1988 New Year's Eve concert by the Grateful Dead, fared poorly, but the small audience was attributed to the lack of addressability available at the time. Without the ability to respond quickly to requests for service, cable operators were unable to attract nearly as many viewers as they would have liked. That technology has at last been developed.

Wrestlemania is a very successful continuing PPV series, with subscribers paying $29.95 or more to watch each special event. In late 1991 two wrestling extravaganzas were scheduled

within 6 days of each other, and both achieved buy rates in excess of 1.5.[9] Typical prices are $4 to $5 for movies and $15 to $20 for concerts.

In 1989, 12 million cable subscribers had access to PPV, with growth projected at about 3 million to 4 million a year. By 1995, PPV is expected to reach over 40 million homes.[10]

CABLE AND ITS COMPETITORS

Erosion of Network Audiences and the Rise of Cable Audiences

Both premium and advertiser supported cable networks have made significant inroads in television viewing habits. Prime-time viewing of broadcast networks declined from a 91 share in the 1976–1977 season to a 62 share in the 1990–1991 season, with even lower shares during other dayparts (Table 19-3).[11]

Although a number of the alternatives that will be discussed in this chapter have encroached on broadcast television audiences, cable TV gets much of the credit for this decline. Increasingly, off-network series such as *Murder She Wrote* are

TABLE 19-3 Broadcast Network Prime-Time Shares, 1979–1992

Year	Share of Broadcast Networks (rounded)
1979	91
1980	90
1981	83
1982	81
1983	80
1984	78
1985	76
1986	76
1987	75
1988	70
1989	67
1990	65
1991	63
1992	64*

*Fox Network viewership included for the first time.
SOURCE: Nielsen Media Research, Northbrook, Ill., 1992.

being picked up by cable networks, where they compete with the broadcast networks on which they originally ran. Some shows, such as *The Days and Nights of Molly Dodd,* have continued in first-run production after being picked up by a cable network. Consumer perceptions of differences between cable and broadcast networks are further blurred because cable services are originating programming that includes news, political analysis, comedy, situation comedies, documentaries, drama, and concerts.

Thus, an increasing number of viewers have less reason to differentiate between the big four networks and television service brought directly to the cable system.

Cable's audience is attractive because of its demographic composition. Cable subscribers are 40 percent more likely to earn $40,000 a year or more. They are 40 percent more likely to have attended college than are nonsubscribers. They are 54 percent more likely to have high-level employment than are nonsubscribers.[12] Not only is the cable audience growing, it is a very attractive audience which can be sold to advertisers. Thus, advertising revenues are increasing. However, cable is not alone in competing with broadcasters; there are other alternatives in the television environment.

Cable's Competitors

Satellite master antenna television   In many cities, apartment buildings, mobile home parks, and condominium complexes have not been wired by cable systems. Instead, many owners of these complexes serve their occupants with **satellite master antenna television (SMATV)** systems. Signals are captured at a headend that serves the building or apartment complex, and then the signals are distributed to the units. Master antenna systems are exempt from FCC regulations for cable systems. As long as they do not cross city or county streets, cable franchises are not required. With the addition of satellite signals, an SMATV system typically provides subscribers with local signals and satellite-distributed premium networks and cable network services such as ESPN.[13]

SMATV operators have been permitted to serve dwelling units because they give landlords a percentage of the subscriber fees. Court rulings have decreed that cable operators in some states can have access to private property housing units such as apartments whether the owners approve or not. When access to previously unavailable subscriber groups is opened, SMATV may lose out because cable systems generally offer a greater number of signals at a lower monthly cost.[14]

The greatest economic threat to SMATVs is the reluctance of cable networks to make their programming available, primarily for fear of offending their big customers, the MSOs. As a result, a number of SMATVs are consolidating, forming partnerships with cable operators, or selling out to them. In some cases cable operators are installing SMATV systems in areas where they are also building cable systems to prevent independent operators from gaining a foothold in the market before the system is built.[15]

An estimated 2.2 million subscribers receive SMATV services. In addition, over a million guests at more than 20,000 hotels use SMATV services yearly.[16]

MMDS: "wireless cable"   A so-called wireless cable service, the **multichannel multipoint distribution system (MMDS),** also has potential in areas where cable has not been established. Transmitted over a 20- to 25-mile radius, over-the-air MMDS signals are received by special antennas mounted on the rooftops of homes. The signals are converted at the receiving site to unused VHF channels. Using an A/B switch, the subscriber chooses between signals fed from the MMDS and those of the standard VHF/UHF antenna.[17]

One clear advantage of MMDS is its cost-effectiveness. The signals are distributed over the air, eliminating the high cost of a cable plant. This means that an operator can get into the business with a much lower initial investment.

Single-channel MDS systems can program a subscription service such as HBO. MMDS systems offer subscription services and satellite-delivered programming such as CNN, MTV, and the USA Network.

MMDS systems can use up to 33 channels in a market. Ten are allocated to multipoint distribution systems. Another 20 were originally allocated to **instructional television fixed service (ITFS),** where they were reserved for school instruction, and 3 more were allocated to the operational fixed service (OFS) originally reserved for business and similar uses. When converted to MMDS use, they carry a lineup essentially similar to what a cable system offers. For these channels, subscribers are typically charged about $20 a month.[18]

The limitations in the development of MMDS include the reluctance of program suppliers to deal with competitors of cable operators. Cable program suppliers such as HBO, Showtime, CNN, and ESPN have refused to deal with MMDS operators. Also, if a cable system has already been established in a market, MMDS is not likely to be able to compete effectively. Furthermore, when areas served by MMDS are wired for cable, a great many subscribers switch to cable. The service that delivers the widest variety of programming at the lowest cost is most likely to win the competition.

Unpassed cable homes are the primary market for MMDS services, but in spite of limited access to cable programming, wireless cable operations are beginning to compete with coaxial cable systems by offering their service at a lower cost. Although wireless cable offers fewer signals, some operators have marketed them as "fat-free" services to subscribers who don't want to pay higher fees for channels they won't watch anyway. The least viewed channels are simply not included.

Direct broadcast satellite Direct broadcast satellite (DBS) television involves the transmission of satellite-fed channels for a fee, to small home dishes mounted on rooftops. The types of content offered include premium services such as HBO and basic services such as ESPN. It has yet to come to flower, but it remains a potential

alternative. Experiments in Great Britain, Japan, and the United States have shown that DBS can work and that a satellite receiver dish about the size of an umbrella can be mass-produced for around $200. Another type of receiver is the flat plate, or phase-array, antenna, which measures about 15 by 26 inches. These receivers can be mounted on rooftops as easily as broadcast TV antennas can, and the flat plate is small enough to be kept near the TV set without being obtrusive.[19] These antennas can be small because the satellites being developed will send much stronger signals.

While DBS may be considered a potential threat to the television broadcasting system in the United States, it may turn out to be the salvation of the traditional networks as cable services siphon off more audience members. One option for DBS is to incorporate **high-definition television (HDTV)** signals which can deliver crisper pictures. With all the discussion of HDTV, direct satellite transmission remains an option for the transmission of signals to homes. This would give DBS a unique product to offer to consumers. With the availability of a small flat antenna, it could become an important service, particularly in uncabled areas.[20]

Cost is still a problem. Cable is entrenched in many of the most heavily populated areas and can deliver the same programming more cheaply. DBS has fared better in Europe and Japan, where cable has developed slowly.

Another limitation of DBS is the need for powerful satellites to deliver its signals. As a rule of thumb, the smaller the receiver, the more difficult the reception of the highly directional weak signals of most current satellites. A new generation of more powerful satellites could make DBS a competitive player in the television marketplace.

Neither a clear programming offering nor a consumer base for DBS has been established yet. DBS entrepreneurs assert that there are between 15 million and 20 million uncabled households and that many of them will never be wired. As few as 2 million subscribers could make DBS a profitable business.[21]

Television receive-only home satellite dishes During the 1980s backyard satellite dishes began springing up in suburban and rural areas where homeowners did not have the opportunity to subscribe to cable. The attraction was the low cost (around $2000 to $3000) for a dish that would receive signals ranging from pay services to network feeds.

With the scrambling of most signals, the owners of home satellite receivers have been cut off from *free* access to satellite-delivered services, but they still can receive service that is often cheaper than cable subscription. Several packagers of television services, including HBO, sell scrambled signals to home dish owners for a fee that ranges between $210 and $250 a year. Turner Broadcasting, for example, offers a package of five basic channels (CNN, Headline News, TNT, Lifetime, and the Weather Channel) and two premium services (HBO and Cinemax) for $210 a year.[22]

Telcos The Bell Operating Companies (BOCs), or "Baby Bells," created by the breakup of AT&T include Ameritech, Bell Atlantic, Bell-South, NYNEX, Pacific Telesis, Southwestern Bell, and U.S. West. The BOCs and the major independent **telcos** (telephone companies), including GTE, are vying to enter the television business in their service areas. As it now stands, telcos are prohibited by the FCC from operating cable systems in their service areas. If they are allowed to become players, these companies will bring great financial resources with which to build systems. Their background has been in delivery systems, not programming, and so it remains to be seen how effectively they can compete.

Eventually, broadband systems will probably be delivered by fiber-optic cable. It is not known when this transformation will take place, but it is unlikely before the turn of the century. One factor that could accelerate the very costly conversion of telephone lines to fiber optics is whether telcos are allowed to deliver television signals. The telcos and their opponents concur that the delivery of video programming will probably be the motivating force behind the conversion of telephone systems from twisted-pair copper wires to fiber optics.

Both broadcasting and cable interests claim that if the telcos are allowed to enter the competition, their use of broadband systems to bring television and radio signals into the home would end broadcasting as it is known. However, others argue that the resources of the BOCs could be used to develop improved telecommunications services whereas they are not now permitted to do so.

CABLE REGULATION ISSUES

The last major piece of cable regulatory legislation was the Cable Act of 1984. We will briefly review its provisions and also look at recent FCC efforts to make cable companies good corporate citizens in their communities. There are several movements afoot which promise changes in the near future. The first is the issue of carriage of local broadcast stations. How is that to be handled? The next is reregulation of cable, especially in terms of the rates charged for basic service. Finally, there is the question of syndex. How can cable respond to syndex, and what effect is syndex having on cable?

Regulation

Regulation plays an important role in the life of cable systems. The most recent sweeping aspects of cable legislation are contained in the Cable Communications Policy Act of 1984. On the FCC front, the most recent regulations have been aimed at making cable companies good corporate citizens in their communities.

Cable Act of 1984 Cable companies operate mostly as monopolies governed by franchise agreements with local municipalities. Typically, the local city or county, through elected supervisors or hired boards and/or consultants, sets guidelines for cable service in the area. In the case of new systems, several cable companies (often

MSOs) compete for the contract (franchise). The politicians or experts choose the company which seems to offer the best projected service to the community.[23] This is typically determined by finding out what services the cable company plans to carry, how many access channels will be made available to the community, what kind of local-origination programming will be produced, what other services the cable company will provide to its subscribers, and the prices to be charged. In the case of systems that already have been built, the municipality negotiates with the cable company to renew the franchise for a specified period. If the company has performed to the general expectations of the community, renewal is likely, but other companies can compete and sometimes offer very attractive packages. The subscribers are usually the beneficiaries as companies compete to serve them with better packages at attractive prices.

In exchange for its services, the cable company gets a monopoly for the area in question and does not have to face the rigors of competition. That encourages the cable operator to spread its services by passing more homes, leading to more subscribers and higher revenues.

Sometimes cable companies made promises which were impossible to keep. In some cases municipalities made unreasonable demands, forcing cable companies into arrangements they could not carry out. The promises and demands became more reasonable as each side learned about the needs and problems of the other. The Cable Act of 1984 dealt directly with the issue of franchising.

This bill permitted the development of public, educational, and government channels (PEGs). This was a change from earlier regulation which required such channels. The new act left the question to negotiation. It also made leased access channels available in systems with 36 channels or more. Such a system had to make at least 10 percent of its channels available for commercial use by entities other than the cable company. Cable operators could exercise no control over the content on those channels.

The bill also limited what municipalities could demand of cable operators. They could not specify specific program services or even general areas of programming as a requirement for winning a franchise.

Finally, municipalities were not allowed to set cable rates. Many systems had been feeling the effects of building expensive systems but charging artificially low rates because of earlier franchise agreements. Cable rates were in effect deregulated.

The upshot of this act was that subscription fees rose sharply after 1984. Operators blamed mounting expenses. Subscribers and politicians thought cable operators were raising their rates more than necessary. By 1992 several proposals were in the works to control the rates once again.

Senator Albert Gore (D-Tenn.) made a series of public statements critical of the rise in cable rates.[24] The United States Telephone Association commissioned a study which reported a 68 percent rise in cable rates from 1986 to 1989. Since 1990, there has been legislative pressure to regulate local monthly rates.[25] As this book goes to press, a Senate-House conference committee works on a final bill to regulate cable subscription rates as well as force traditional cable networks like HBO, ESPN, and the rest, to make their services available to cable competitors such as MMDS, SMATV, and DBS.

Most legislative efforts are aimed at reducing cable costs by returning some level of rate control to municipalities that have granted franchises to cable companies to provide local service. If the cable systems are made more answerable to local authorities, rates may be better controlled.

Cable operators are averse to such legislation. They point out the cost of converting old systems to provide greater channel space and of replacing coaxial cable with fiber-optic cable. Doubtless the issue will be settled in the courts at some point.

Good actor guidelines   In 1991 the FCC floated "good actor" guidelines intended to bring cable systems into line on rates and customer service without having congressional legislation enacted. A good actor would be a cable system that kept its rates reasonable by offering at least 18 channels for no more than $11.52 a month.

Systems subject to "effective" competition were exempted from the good actor guidelines. Effective competition was defined as: (1) competition from six or more unduplicated broadcast signals with less than 50 percent subscribership in the franchise area and (2) competition from another multichannel provider (usually an MMDS) with at least 10 percent penetration.

Essentially, the good actor guidelines fostered more tiering, a process which was already under way at the time. Since it was clear that only basic services would be affected by good actor guidelines, MSOs began organizing tiers called lifeline, broadcast, or subsistence.[26] Such tiers were synonyms and austere by cable standards and contained all the broadcast stations and cable networks such as C-SPAN and, occasionally, the Discovery Channel. By bundling the least expensive channels, operators could charge very low prices for lifeline tiers and meet the good actor guidelines at the same time. The better channels (ESPN, CNN, MTV) are bundled with others and offered, for an additional price, on a tier called expanded basic or basic plus. Thus, the tier most likely to be regulated is the least important tier.

Must Carry for Broadcasters

Before the Cable Act of 1984, cable systems were forced to carry all local broadcast stations on their systems; this provision was called **must carry.** After must carry was eliminated, cable systems continued to carry most broadcast stations anyway because of their popularity. However, they did not always carry all of them, and that became a sticking point for some segments of the television industry. Independent stations, especially weaker ones, were the most likely to lose channel space to increasingly popular cable networks. That further damaged their position in the community and with advertisers by shrinking the audience they could reach. These entities have been lobbying to have must carry reinstated in a form that will ensure their carriage on cable systems. Such carriage increases the likelihood that their station signals will get into more homes and will look their best since cable systems go to great lengths to deliver high-quality signals.

For affiliated stations, the issue is less about survival and more about compensation. From the affiliates' perspective, their signals are the most important ones that cable systems carry. It is network programming that helps cable market itself, especially in outlying areas. Thus, affiliates reason, not only should they be carried on cable systems, they should be compensated by cable systems for the use of their signals. This proposition has come to be called if carry/must pay, meaning that cable systems have a choice about affiliate carriage and that the exercise of that choice should be coupled with direct compensation. Not surprisingly, this idea is not popular with cable operators.

Syndex from the Cable Side

For cable executives, complaining about the restrictions of syndex is akin to complaining about the weather. Everyone in the industry does it, but there is little anyone can do. The problem syndex poses for cable is that distant signals lose some of their appeal. For example, since a local station has syndex precedence over, say, a superstation, the cable system must black out the signal of the superstation when shows are duplicated. If *Cheers* is coming into a market on WGN TV and the local syndicated rights are owned by an area station, that station will file for its syndex rights and the WGN presentation of *Cheers* will be blacked out. That creates two problems. First, the cable system doesn't want the channel to be blacked out during that time. Therefore, it must have "syndex-proof" programs, locally created or syndicated, that will not interfere with the rights of any station in the market. The more stations in the market, the more programming they have under contract, and this makes finding unused product more difficult.

The second problem is that people in the market will blame the cable system for their inability to watch *Cheers*. While *TV Guide* or the local newspaper tells them that the program is running on WGN, they find something completely different when they tune in. Not understanding the complexities of syndex, they blame the cable system. Operators have fought back with campaigns to educate the public while trying to purchase or create original programming that will not be affected by syndex considerations.

A syndex response   There is much disagreement about just what happened, but a dispute over an NFL game arose in Miami between an independent station and a local operator. On December 9, 1990, the local independent WDZL TV acquired the rights to a game between the Miami Dolphins and the Philadelphia Eagles. The game was also being carried on ESPN.

According to the station's general manager, the station's signal was cut off on cable while the ESPN signal was kept. The cable system said that no such thing occurred, that the station had been on the air the whole time.[27]

The point this raises is more than philosophical. If cable operators are presented with the same program on two channels but have advertising windows in the one that should be blacked out for syndex reasons, will they instead black out the local signal and preserve the cable signal? Of course this would violate the law, but what if it were an accident? That brings up the danger involved when regulation runs head-on into economic self-interest in an atmosphere characterized by uncertainty.

CONVERGENCE OF FORCES

Most so-called new technologies were in place for some time before they began to have a notable influence on mass communication systems, and the impact of many technologies is less apparent than their potential. Regardless, the programmer can afford to ignore neither impact nor potential. To do so may mean discovering too late that an opportunity to attract and maintain an audience has passed.

Developing a technology such as cable is not enough. For any innovation to make a real impact on electronic communication and its audiences, three circumstances must converge: technological development, favorable economic conditions, and a permissive political environment.

Technological Development

Innovation cannot proceed without having the proper technology in place or at least developed so that it can be put into place. There are many "blue-sky" proposals describing what might be, but until the requisite equipment has been manufactured and distributed, they cannot be realized.

Currently, for example, technology promises a **broadband** communications service (a distribution service that carries a large number of channels spread out over a wide frequency range), but this is only in the developmental stage. The possibilities for fiber optics are great, but fiber has not supplanted copper-core, aluminum-sheathed coaxial cable as a means of transmitting messages. At this writing, telephone companies have been using fiber-optic cables in their operations and a few cable companies have announced that they will build fiber-optic systems, but most of the plant (distribution system) still consists of paired copper wires for telephone companies and coaxial cable for cable operators.

Favorable Economic Conditions

Whether a technology is fully developed or only in the talking stages, it must be attractive enough to create consumer demand or render another technology obsolete. Compact disc technology replaced records in only a few years. VCRs spread to most homes and support a huge home video industry. Even though a new form may be superior to what is already in place, if it is rejected by consumers, it will die from lack of interest.

A few years ago quadraphonic sound was introduced, and reviewers hailed it as the system that would replace stereo. According to some, quad's four channels could provide much more realistic reproduction of music. Its admirers described the difference between quad and stereo as being as great as that between stereo and monaural sound.

Few consumers were excited by the prospect, however. Quad systems can simulate sound moving about the room, but most people are not concerned about re-creating the acoustics of a concert hall. The great majority of music consumers want popular music, which is usually produced in a studio rather than in a natural acoustical environment. Moreover, listeners are accustomed to hearing sound and music from the front.

Interest was limited by cost as well. Instead of the customary two speakers, audiophiles would have to purchase four speakers, along with a new amplifier. They bought none of it.

Permissive Political Environment

Before consumers can embrace a technology, it must be permissible to make it available. Any number of services have been stalled in their development by government regulations. Simply put, any established medium wants to protect itself and will exert any political influence it has to minimize regulation on itself while it attempts to stall the development of competitors.

Pay television is a good example of a service in which the three elements of technological development finally converged to permit its development and growth. The original pay TV, called **subscription television (STV),** or broadcast pay television, was made available to subscribers through descrambling devices that permitted the reception of an over-the-air TV signal. Although STV experiments were conducted as early as the 1950s, it had weak market potential. Commercial television was experiencing rapid growth, and "free" programming was being made available to more and more audiences. Furthermore, the regulatory climate was hostile, fueled by opposition from commercial broadcast-

ers who felt threatened by the competition posed by STV in terms of bidding for programming. The predominant stance was that the public would be deprived of viewing opportunities. Movie theater owners also strongly opposed STV, feeling that audiences would stay away if a comparable product were available in their homes. Owners went so far as to make petitions available, which they encouraged their patrons to sign at the box office or concession counter.

STV's marketplace opportunities were stymied by a set of rules issued in 1968 by the FCC that protected the status quo (commercial broadcasters). Before a broadcast station could send a scrambled pay signal, at least four other commercial channels had to be available in the market. Even then, the STV station was required to broadcast a minimum of 28 hours a week of "free" programming that was available to all viewers without commercials.[28]

Even more constraining were FCC restrictions on broadcasting programs that most viewers would want to pay for. Feature films in release for more than 2 years could not be shown. Sporting events televised on a regular basis on free television during any one of the 5 years before a proposed pay airing could not be shown. The same restriction applied to series with interconnected plots or a continuing cast of characters. The FCC rules also limited feature films and sporting events to 90 percent of total subscription services.[29]

Considering the restrictions placed on broadcast television pay operations, it is easy to see why cable TV became the medium for pay services. With its abundant channels, this newer delivery system had the capacity to deliver pay signals in markets not served by independent stations, a situation that limited the opportunity for STV to the larger markets. Furthermore, cable systems did not become established because they offered pay or premium services. The earlier systems made a profit by offering subscribers improved reception and a wider variety of off-the-air signals. Thus, the revenue from premium services was an extra, since basic subscriber service fees were counted on to pay for building and operating the system. Later, as cable became established and larger television markets were wired, premium services and other cable-exclusive networks provided the incentive to subscribe.

During the earlier years of development, though, the political environment was not conducive to cable's expansion of pay services. In 1970, 2 years after restricting STV, the FCC applied its rules to pay cable, which had grown much more rapidly than over-the-air pay services (by the mid-1970s over 500,000 households were subscribing to premium cable).[30]

In 1975 the FCC removed restrictions on series-type programs and relaxed the limitations on feature movies by expanding the window for pay broadcast from 2 to 3 years and adding exemptions for movies more than 3 years old. The rules on sporting events were also loosened to permit telecasts of certain sports events even though there was also coverage by free TV. Home Box Office challenged these new rules, and in 1977 the U.S. Court of Appeals overturned the restrictive FCC regulations, allowing pay TV services to acquire product desired by potential subscribers.[31]

HBO had begun distributing its service to cable systems by satellite in 1975. The high cost of the receiving stations (about $100,000) restricted dissemination to the largest systems until 1976, when the FCC approved the use of a smaller, cheaper satellite receiving dish. This meant that smaller cable systems could afford the equipment, which now could be obtained for under $10,000.

Convergence

HBO's success demonstrated that there was a ready market of subscribers willing to pay for a premium service, and the demand for premium cable revived slumping cable systems. Equally important, the largest markets could be wired because cable systems could offer a service that was not available over the air. The economic incentive to wire those areas was in place.

The three necessary elements that permitted pay television to flourish had converged: The economic conditions were right, and HBO had a product that was in demand. The technology of satellite communication made distribution economically feasible, particularly when lower-cost receivers were made available. Satellite communication, linked with cable TV systems, removed any argument that channel scarcity precluded offering a service only to those willing to pay for it. The political environment had at last become hospitable, permitting the other two conditions to be met.

THE FUTURE

The future is now, of course, but with the increasing likelihood that the technology of cable television will continue to bring changes, a prediction of the programmer's future seems to be in order here.

Technological changes have influenced viewers' habits. Network shares have continued to erode in spite of predictions by network officials that broadcast TV will continue to dominate cable services.

There is reason to doubt their optimism. Television audiences have become less habitual in their viewing. With the diffusion of remote control devices and the proliferation of programming choices, it may no longer be a programmer's medium in which a mass audience can be manipulated by predicting its desires. Just as radio audiences have become increasingly segmented, so have television viewers. Consequently, the broadcast media, like their cable counterparts, have become narrowcasting services.

There is little doubt that people will continue to use their television sets, but there is growing reason to believe that the traditional sources of programming will continue to decline. The history of virtually all the broadcast media has shown that a new medium borrows heavily from its predecessors until it establishes its own unique form of content. Radio drama, for instance, began when a microphone was placed among the actors in stage plays. Later, radio drama scripts, complete with sound effects, evolved. Newspapers were read over the air in the early days as filler, but news organizations were eventually developed to gather and report the news. When radio news personalities had become established, the technology of sound recording was advanced enough to permit the inclusion of actualities and interview excerpts on a regular basis. When television was introduced, virtually all its major entertainment and journalistic figures came over from radio. As radio was forced to reinvent itself, television formats evolved from the base provided by radio performers.

Later, cable TV came along, offering its subscribers improved reception and a wider variety of signals. Some time elapsed before cable began to develop original programming. Even today, the burgeoning cable networks mostly offer content that originally appeared on the traditional networks.

As the cable medium matures, the content it offers will evolve and become identifiable with the service. Even as it does, more recent media such as SMATV and MMDS will fight to survive by establishing themselves as offering the same program services that are carried on cable. DBS and fiber-optic technology are ready to be marketed, but if either of these newer technologies does develop, it will be on the basis of carrying the same kind of programming as cable.

With the increasing penetration of cable television and the growing independence of TV viewers, network TV has been searching for solutions. One solution that is touted by network programmers is an emphasis on quality programs that will compel the viewer to tune in rather than bypassing the network for an alternative. Quality is costly, but the networks' survival may require investing in programs that will increase viewer interest. In a less oligopolistic era where viewers had only three choices, low-quality fare was often justified by television's voracious appetite. That hunger has not been sated, but other, richer alternatives are offered on alternative cable networks and by video rental stores. Clearly, many viewers do not mind paying for entertainment that they can select.

One of the attributes of successful radio formats is consistency. If listeners cannot depend on WXXX sounding like it did in the morning, they may not bother listening to it in the afternoon. Similarly, if viewers cannot count on a station or channel carrying a program each day or every week, they will not form loyalties or habits that are grounded in program dependability. The TV networks and their affiliated stations may have to offer more narrow programming services rather than the general array of entertainment and information that is now the norm.

In the 1970s, when cable television began to expand into larger cities and towns across the United States, considerable attention was paid to its potential as a two-way interactive system, delivering signals that would enable its users to purchase goods in the home, pay for screenings of movies on an individual basis (pay-per-view), and do their banking and shopping from home. Municipal governments were to be transformed by electronic town meetings in which the citizenry could vote directly on issues. During the two decades since such blue-sky predictions had begun to be made, few have been realized. In the mid-1980s cable began at last to demonstrate that the promises seen in earlier years were being fulfilled, even if in ways somewhat different from what was originally forecast.

We must go back to the discussion in the previous section, in which it was noted that three things are crucial to the success of a medium: government sanction, technological capability, and economic inducement. At this writing, pay-per-view programming seems finally to be on the threshold of success, but it has not yet demonstrated consumer acceptance. Only when enough cable subscribers have access to the service will it become an economic threat to existing services such as home video rentals. If subscriber interest can be achieved, PPV may eventually take over major sports events such as the Super Bowl and college bowl games. This would cause even further erosion of the broadcast TV audience, assuming that one of the cable networks does not preempt PPV by acquiring the rights first.

SUMMARY

Cable television has grown tremendously and now reaches over 60 percent of American homes. Technologically, it uses the distribution model of utilities, in which lines are run from a central source through neighborhoods and to individual homes.

Cable ownership is following the model of media ownership in general, moving in the direction of fewer companies owning increasing percentages of the business. Among multiple system operators, Tele-Communications, Inc., is the largest, accounting for about 20 percent of cable homes.

Cable enjoys a dual revenue stream. Money comes to cable operators on a monthly basis from subscribers, and money also flows through advertising. Increasingly, as subscription growth slows as a result of industry maturity, advertising is supplying a greater portion of revenues. Pay-per-view looms as a potential gold mine for cable if the technology required to make it work is distributed to systems nationwide.

Cable has a series of competitors of variable strength. Direct broadcast satellite may be more promise than reality at present, but the chance to distribute programming directly to as many as 20 million noncable homes may bring sufficient capital into play. Multichannel multipoint distribution systems can deliver signals to homes without cable. While convenient and cost-efficient to install, MMDS suffers from networks' reluctance to provide service for fear of angering much larger cable customers. Satellite dishes have appeared in many backyards, especially in rural areas. While not a major threat to cable, dish ownership has taken away some potential cable subscribers. Also, telephone companies (telcos) may become involved in delivering video signals to homes. If they are given permission by the FCC to do so, they will pose a formidable threat to existing cable systems.

Cable programming comes from a variety of sources. First are broadcast stations, both affiliates and independents. Local-origination and access television from the cable system account

for varying amounts of programming from system to system. Basic and premium networks supply the bulk of cable programming.

Determining which signals to carry and on which channels is a growing problem as cable networks proliferate and the costs of carriage rise. Operators usually cannot offer everything available because of space limitations and cost requirements. A way to maximize revenues for channels that are made available to subscribers is tiering, the practice of bundling channels together and charging an additional fee to receive them.

Regulation is an issue of current importance in cable, as there are bills in Congress to regulate various aspects of the industry. Chief among these are attempts to control the rates charged to subscribers. Also important are the issues of must carry and syndex.

Cable, like any technology, is a product of the forces which operate in the marketplace. Technological development and availability are not enough to ensure public acceptance of a service; economic conditions and regulation also figure into that equation. Thus the three converging forces tend to define levels of success for newer technologies.

SUGGESTED READINGS

Cablevision

This biweekly periodical is one of the mainstays of the cable industry. As the cable version of *Broadcasting,* it supplies information about programming, ad sales, marketing, technology, pay-per-view, and operations. In addition, feature stories provide in-depth analyses of industry trends. A student can become reasonably cable-literate by reading this periodical carefully on a regular basis.

Cable World

This weekly publication provides a continuing overview of major areas of interest in the cable industry. Especially useful are the information on international cable issues, discussions of technology, and programming information. The "Business Extra" section at the end of each issue provides up-to-the-minute information on economics, mergers, and the business trends of major companies.

Baldwin, Thomas: *Cable Communication,* 2d ed., Prentice-Hall, New York, 1988.

This is the best source book for cable in print, providing an excellent history of the cable industry and cable programming. Also contained within its pages is an excellent discussion of technical issues from headends to fiber optics. Baldwin provides in-depth discussions of the cable networks and explains how they interact with MSOs. Every student of cable should start with this book.

Broadcasting

This magazine has been included in several chapters' suggested readings because its coverage is first rate. Despite its name, it covers cable exceptionally well, devoting several pages to a special cable section each week. It is particularly strong on legislative issues and the interface between broadcasting and cable. As with broadcasting issues, the treatment of cable issues is comprehensive, fair, and well written. This is a publication that does much good work in a variety of areas.

NOTES

1. "Cable TV's Ten Year Forecast," *Multichannel News,* May 8, 1989, p. 1

2. Janet Stilson, "Cable Changes the System from Within," *Channels Field Guide,* December 1990, p. 91.

3. National Cable Television Cooperative, Lenexa, Kan., promotional literature.

4. Thomas Baldwin and D. Stevens McVoy, *Cable Communications,* 2d ed., Prentice-Hall, Englewood Cliffs, N.J., 1988, pp. 11–14.

5. Gary Slutsker, "Good-Bye Cable TV, Hello Fiber Optics," *Forbes,* Sept. 19, 1988, pp. 174–179.

6. "CAB: Growing the 'Other' Revenue Stream," *Broadcasting,* April 8, 1991, p. 50.

7. "The Unsure Reality of Ratings and Value," *Cablevision,* Jan. 30, 1989, p. 34.

8. "Cable Subscribers Have Greater Purchasing Power," *Advertising Age,* Feb. 20, 1989, p. 30.

9. "Compression, Boxing Light Operators' PPV Fire," *Broadcasting,* May 20, 1991, p. 50.

10. "PPV Keeps Pace," *Channels Field Guide,* December 1990, p. 50.

11. "NBC Primed to Recapture Prime Time Sweeps," *Broadcasting,* May 13, 1991, p. 27.

12. "Cable Subscribers," op. cit.

13. Fleming Meeks, "The Wireless Wonder," *Forbes,* Feb. 19, 1990, p. 57.

14. Ibid.

15. Ibid.

16. Ibid.

17. Ibid.

18. Ibid.

19. Michael J. Hirrel, "Making HDTV Viable via Direct Broadcast Satellite," *Broadcasting,* Oct. 31, 1988, p. 26.

20. Ibid.

21. Harry Jessell and Peter Lambert, "The Uncertain Future of DBS," *Broadcasting,* March 13, 1989, p. 44

22. Ibid.

23. Baldwin and McEvoy, op. cit., p. 194.

24. "Gore Seeks More Review of Cable Rates," *Broadcasting,* Aug. 14, 1989, p. 60.

25. "NCTA, MSO's Oppose FCC Adoption of Customer Service Standards," *Broadcasting,* Feb. 25, 1991, p. 53.

26. Larry Jaffe, "Broadcast Tiers to Hit Big Apple," *Cablevision,* Feb. 11, 1991, p. 9.

27. Eileen Becker Salmas, "Station-System Tiff Centers on NFL Game," *Cable World,* Jan. 14, 1991, p. 24.

28. "STV: Going, Going, Going," *NAB Broadcast Marketing and Technology News,* May-June 1988, p. 2.

29. *Home Box Office, Inc. v. FCC,* 567 F.2d O, certiorari denied, 434 U.S. 829, 98 S.Ct. 111, 54 L.Ed.2d 89 (1977).

30. "STV," op. cit.

31. "HBO," op. cit.

CHAPTER 20

Cable System Programming

This chapter focuses on local cable system operators and the forces, problems, and opportunities they face. The forces operating in cable systems have a direct impact on what these systems can offer. Thus, they have an impact on programming.

The biggest controlling forces in cable are the multiple system operators (MSOs). We will look at the MSOs and examine how they have exercised control in various areas of the industry.

Next we will explore the economic realities of cable, with a special focus on the rise of interconnects. Related to that is the need for cable systems to find and exploit sources of revenue beyond subscriptions and advertising. Several of these sources are outlined.

Then we will discuss how cable operators have responded to environmental pressures. Finally, we will examine cable's future, including expansion, cable radio, and independent cable systems.

FORCES IN CABLE PROGRAMMING DECISION MAKING

Many forces make their influence felt in cable television programming. As one might expect, most of them have a financial core. One of the most important developments in cable has been the rise of the MSO and its effect on subscribers, cable networks, and cable systems. Regulation and economic conditions also play an important role in cable programming. Many practices and policies are spurred by regulatory and economic conditions.

Multiple System Operators

As was pointed out in Chapter 19, MSOs are efficient because they share resources and personnel between cable systems. They have the capacity to negotiate the best rates from suppliers and to influence the cable networks.

Of the 22 most widely distributed cable networks, TCI owns portions of CNN, the Discovery Channel, WTBS, Turner Network Television

(TNT), CNN Headline, and the Family Channel. TCI also owns portions of Black Entertainment Television (BET), Bravo, the QVC Network, American Movie Classics, the Learning Channel, the Video Jukebox Network, and Affiliated Regional Communications, which operates a series of regional sports networks.[1] This means that TCI has an influence on the networks which its own systems carry.

TCI is not the only MSO that has an **equity interest** in cable networks. Time Warner Cable owns part of CNN, WTBS, CNN Headline, TNT, the QVC Network, and Entertainment Television (E!).

This pattern of ownership is unusual in television. As was outlined in Chapter 16, broadcast networks are considered distribution systems and are not engaged in production and delivery. While broadcast networks may own a limited number of owned and operated stations, their control over affiliated stations is limited. Between 1971 and 1991 the networks could not share in the syndication revenues of the programs they carried. Thus, in the broadcast industry, production, distribution, and delivery have been kept separate. In cable, though, the MSOs, which are owners of local systems, can own the networks they carry. They can also have equity in the production companies that create programs carried on cable networks. This ownership at multiple levels of programming is called vertical integration.

A vertically integrated company has some advantages in terms of controlling product creation and distribution. Imagine that you own a film production company; that gives you the ability to produce movies. Then you acquire a company with considerable experience in the distribution of films. Finally, you buy a string of movie theaters across the country. You are now vertically integrated because you make, distribute, and exhibit films. How might this run counter to the public good? You may limit engagements in your theaters to films your company produces and distributes. If you own enough theaters, you may have an inordinate influence over what is seen. In total control of film budgets, you may opt for films that make money instead of more "artistic" films. In that environment films such as *Dances with Wolves* and *Driving Miss Daisy* might never be made. For these reasons the film industry has ownership limits, analogous to those of television, that prevent total vertical integration.

Cable, however, is largely unregulated, and vertical integration is a fact of life. Since the MSOs have seats on the boards of many cable networks, they have the power to influence the content carried by those channels as well.

The Encore challenge to premium networks   TCI created Encore, a purveyor of movies at a low monthly charge.[2] Founded in 1991, Encore represented an alternative to movie and special-event services such as HBO that typically charged $10 or more a month. Marketed to consumers for $1 to $5 a month, it was designed to cut into a premium market that had already been made "soft" by PPV and the rise of video rentals.

While the MSOs had majority ownership of the shopping channel QVC Network and thus had control of its content and profits, most basic network stakes were minority ones. Encore represented two changes. First, an MSO was founding a new service that would compete with existing basic services in which it had a stake. TCI was part owner of AMC and TNT, and some of Encore's viewers could be expected to be drawn from those two networks. In reality, TCI was competing with itself.

Second, an MSO was creating the first new premium service since the Disney Channel had been founded in 1983. Time Warner owned both HBO and Cinemax, and TCI owned a small part of Showtime and the Movie Channel. With premium subscriptions starting to slip, another service was being introduced as a price-attractive alternative. Again, the MSO was in effect competing with itself.

This self-competition indicated how many enterprises the MSOs shared. By diversifying their holdings throughout a series of different channels, the MSOs were able to influence what they did not own and start up channels they thought could compete effectively.

As one might expect, the reaction of HBO and Showtime to Encore was not entirely rosy. Encore responded by promoting HBO's and Showtime's recent films on its own programs. By giving the competing services free mentions, Encore managed to blunt fears about its territorial ambitions.

CABLE PROGRAMMING

There are several sources of cable programming for local cable systems. The first is traditional over-the-air broadcasts carried on the cable system. That system provides news, public affairs, sports, and entertainment programming for viewers of all ages. Cable systems can also originate programming. **Local-origination (LO) programming** is produced by the cable system and can focus on local sporting events, political and community meetings and activities, and local personalities. Of course, both basic and premium cable networks provide a wide variety of programming.

Broadcast Stations

While network shares have fallen, the networks still account for most viewing in the television environment.[3] Thus, one of the most popular programming sources for cable systems is the local network affiliates. Some cable subscribers sign up primarily to enhance the quality of the signals they receive from local broadcast stations. Local affiliated stations bring national network programs to the local screen as well as providing local news programs. Their local focus makes them popular with cable subscribers.

Independent stations are also heavily viewed. Their mix of movies, children's programming, and sports, along with their local orientation, makes them appealing to cable viewers as well. Many independent stations carry local professional and collegiate sports programming.

Local Origination

In the early days of cable, operators set aside channels to carry locally produced programs as a way to appease municipalities and satisfy FCC rules and regulations. Community groups wanted some local orientation, and local channels on a cable system seemed a good way to make that happen. Since that helped solidify the franchise awards which cable companies needed, they were willing to supply such channels and the time and resources required to manage them. In exchange, the cable companies were given franchises (effective monopolies for providing cable to the community) for a specific number of years. Such financial protection from competition made it possible for cable companies to afford to build their systems.

Local-origination channels can be outlets for community issues and activities. A popular LO programming type is the city council meeting or school board meeting. These events usually are not covered by other television media, but they are full of local interest and flavor.

Other forms of LO programming include local high school and small college sports which would otherwise go untelevised, sports talk/call-in shows, local talk/call-in shows, and discussions of controversial local issues. There are as many options for LO as there are communities.

These programs tend to require talent and assistance beyond the resources of the local cable company. Thus, another facet of successful LO programming is help from volunteer talent and production assistants. Systems that galvanize local interest, volunteerism, and support tend to be the most successful.

When LO succeeds in stirring interest in a community, it starts to attract advertising revenue since advertisers follow viewers wherever they go. For the corner business and even for regional or national firms, interesting LO programs can serve as a local vehicle for commercials. The goodwill inspired by the program can be transferred to a product.

Access Television

Another form of LO is access, in which the cable company gives control of a channel for some time period to a local group to program, giving that group access to television to spread its messages. The difference between access and LO is that the cable company maintains control over the content of an LO channel by writing and producing for it but does not exercise that form of control over the content of an access channel. Those who use **access channels** receive technical advice and production support from the cable company but choose their own content. Such groups may represent issues such as conservation or government, ethnic minorities, crafts practitioners, hobbyists, and the like. There is no end to the groups that would like to ballyhoo their particular interests on television.

Originally designed for use by the public, educational institutions, and government, these channels are often turned over to local institutions to run. Usually that institution is a college or public school system where educational goals can be fostered by students whose work is distributed to an audience outside the campus. Other institutions, such as hospitals, have developed increasingly sophisticated television systems and can use an access channel to deliver health information.

Leased access channels are rented by a cable company to organizations and businesses which in turn use such a channel to accomplish an organizational goal or make a profit. The typical content on such channels includes at-home shopping services, movies, sports, and information. One useful format that has grown in popularity is televised classified ads in which people place items they want to sell on the air for a period of time.

LO and access television have the same audience problems that characterize other television formats. There may be more reasons for not watching than for watching. If people do not like a show, they do not watch. Even if they are interested, potential viewers who cannot find a show don't watch it. If scheduling is inconvenient, they do not watch. Finally, since the television landscape is increasingly crowded with program offerings, standing out in LO and access requires the same skills as standing out as an affiliated or independent station. The stakes may be lower, but the rules of the game are the same.

Cable Television "Stations"

A development that has caused great consternation among broadcast TV station operators, particularly independents, has been the inauguration of cable system LO channel services that emulate the programming service and style of independent stations.[4] An idea whose time has apparently arrived has been carried out on channel 5 of the Rochester, New York, cable system. The operator even gives the service call letters (WGRC TV) and offers viewers costly off-network syndicated shows such as *Alf* and *Perfect Strangers* along with first-run product including *Divorce Court,* older comedies such as *I Dream of Jeannie,* and movie packages. The cable system has even hired a former broadcast TV personality, "Ranger Bob," to host a children's show.

In Toledo, Buckeye Cablevision inaugurated its own channel 5, called ToledoVision which is programmed in a similar manner. ToledoVision carries the Travel Channel during the day and offers local professional sports, including the Cleveland Indians, the Cincinnati Reds, and the Toledo Mud Hens (baseball), along with local college teams at night.

In addition, this channel programs older off-network syndicated product such as *The Andy Griffith Show* and has acquired a library of movies. The 6 p.m. news from local affiliate WTVG TV is rebroadcast on TV5 at 7:30 p.m.

Cable systems that program an LO channel can give their services optimum channel positions, as is the case with both the Rochester and Toledo operations. Broadcasters fear that their stations could be relegated to high channel positions, which would leave them at a competitive disadvantage.

At this juncture it is unclear how successful LO programming that emulates independent station programming can be. The prospects appear to be fairly good both for generating advertising revenue and for opening up the syndication marketplace as more systems get into the programming business.

Channel Assignments

All these sources of programming raise several issues for cable systems. The first is **shelf space,** or the number of channels available to carry all the broadcast and cable services desired. While cable systems can be built to carry more than 100 channels, most have been built to carry far fewer. Thus, in a 36-channel system, choices have to be made about what signals to carry. Additionally, when choosing the signals, operators must decide where to place each service and need to consider some plan of organization for those channels. Assigning services to channels is an organizational task. When the system bundles certain channels together and charges subscribers for receiving them, it becomes an economic issue.

Using shelf space Cable systems can accommodate only so many channels. The typical system has a 36-channel capacity, and there are many services competing for those spaces. To understand the programming issues involved, let's look at a typical system and the programming choices that have to be made.

Four channel spaces go to the affiliated stations: CBS, ABC, NBC, and Fox. Another goes to public television. Allowing for a local independent station brings the local broadcast total to six stations.

The cable system has at least one channel for LO and about three channels for access and leased access. One or two channels may be allocated for educational use, with a local school system or college developing programming for that channel. Another will be reserved for a text service such as AP News Plus. That comes to six more channels.

Now comes the creative part. The sensitive cable manager-programmer wants to keep the major demographic groups happy, and so for young people there is Nickelodeon. For women, Lifetime is a popular choice, and ESPN appeals to men. Of course, teens want their MTV. CNN and CNN Headline are among the highest-rated cable networks and probably will be selected. CNBC/FNN makes a good partner for CNN, adding a strong financial emphasis to the lineup. Superstations are popular with all viewers as they offer a mix of movies, sports, and general entertainment. Perhaps WTBS (Atlanta) and WGN (Chicago) will be chosen. The USA Network has a mix of programming that appeals to a wide range of viewers as well and is a highly rated network. We have filled 22 channels to this point.

For educational and informational programming we will probably choose between the Learning Channel and Mind Extension University. We will probably also choose Arts and Entertainment and the Discovery Channel, both of which are highly prized by subscribers. To fill out our general information category, we may want to add Entertainment Television, the Weather Channel, the Travel Channel, C-SPAN I and C-SPAN II, and the Preview Guide (an on-line guide to what shows are on). We now have 31 channels.

To solidify our film offerings, we choose American Movie Classics and TNT. We may also add the Family Channel, which shows a substantial number of movies. That makes 34 channels.

To round out our music services, we may choose VH-1 for viewers age 25 and over and either the Nashville Network or Country Music Television for country fans. That will balance the youth-oriented MTV. That fills our 36 channels.

While we have filled our spaces with a series of good and defensible choices, we have major problems. The first is the premium channels. We haven't offered Showtime, HBO, Cinemax, the Movie Channel, or the Disney Channel. Not only are they very popular choices, they bring in additional revenues for the system operator. We must have those five, and so we have to eliminate five channels we have already chosen. But there's more. We have no shopping or religious channels. Both are highly popular with segments of the viewing audience and so we must choose among the Eternal Word Television Network, the Trinity Broadcasting Network, the ACTS-Satellite Network, the Vision Interfaith Satellite Network, and the Inspirational Network. Which do we choose, and what do we get rid of to free the necessary shelf space? Among the shopping networks, do we want the Home Shopping Network, the Quality Value Network, or the J.C. Penney Shopping Network?

We haven't addressed minority audiences either. Black Entertainment Television is very popular with these audiences. In markets with a sizable Hispanic population, Univision, Bravo, and Galavision offer Spanish-language programming. Which do we need, and how do we make space?

Missing also are sports networks such as SportsChannel America and all its regional channels, Prime, and Madison Square Garden. How many sports channels should we have, and where do we get the space?

Some highly regarded and popular channels are missing from our lineup. Is there support in the community for adding the Nostalgia Network, Comedy Central, the Video Jukebox Network, the Science Fiction Network, the Cowboy Channel, and the Silent Network/Disability Channel? Again, where can we find the space?

Of course, we have not addressed the subject of PPV. We know it is coming and know that some systems are being designed to offer up to 40 PPV channels.[5] How many do we need for our subscribers and for our own profitability?

What about the future? We have not left any room for the next generation of cable networks, which are already in development. Thus, we seem to have plenty of space with 36 channels, but in fact we are faced with a series of extremely difficult choices. That is the nature of trying to program a cable system.

Consistent channel numbers How and where to place all the services being offered is a problem for cable system programmers. As has always been the case, VHF placements (channels 2 through 13) are the most desirable because many televisions are not **cable-ready** (able to receive all cable channels without a converter). If the system charges for the converter, some subscribers may opt not to pay the additional monthly fee even though they will then receive only 12 channels. Some subscribers are confused by converters and tend to use only the VHF channels. In any case, services assigned to the higher channel numbers are at a disadvantage because most viewers won't rotate through all the channels when searching for programs to watch. Thus, accidental sampling is minimized when you are assigned to, say, channel 32.

A network affiliate that broadcasts on channel 5 wants to have its "normal" channel in the cable system. That helps in promoting the station and avoids viewer confusion about where channel 5 is and what it offers. However, the cable operator, who understands the advantages of channel placement, may want the VHF channel numbers for cable-only services.

Such preemption of channel assignments is usually done to draw attention to what separates cable from broadcasting. Large MSOs such as TCI are part owners of channels such as WTBS. This **vertical integration** (ownership of more than one level of production, distribution, or delivery) occurs when the program deliverer (in this case TCI) is part owner of one or more program suppliers (cable networks). Such operators are more likely to give good channel positions to networks in which they have a financial interest. In this example, the television station broadcasting over the air on channel 5 may end up with a different cable channel assignment if the carriage of its signal offers no special economic advantage to the cable system.

All program services prefer VHF placements, but obviously, most will be assigned higher channel numbers. The cable programmer has to have a scheme for allocating channels. Whatever the basis for making these assignments, it is certain that economics will be an important influence in the decision-making process. The allocation of many of the best channel positions may favor the MSO and any cable networks in which it has a financial interest. Because local systems share in their revenues, one or more premium channels may well be placed in the VHF band.

Clustering cable networks Since many cable channel converters and some remote control devices are linear, the channel changer is forced to go through the channels in numerical order. Regardless of how many channels they can receive, most people watch only 8 to 12 channels regularly. In a system with 36 channels or more, a viewer may be required to leap from channel 15 to 32 and back to 17 to watch consecutive programs. That inconvenience can be avoided since there is usually a clustering pattern in the viewing of channels.

From the perspective of both the operator and the cable network, giving the more popular cable networks the same channel designation on systems nationwide offers advantages. If all cable systems carried Lifetime on, say, channel 4, the network could promote that channel number nationwide, along with the programs offered, allowing people to identify a channel number with the service and maintain that channel identity when they move or travel. Local cable operators could cooperate in network promotional campaigns and share centrally produced advertising materials. Such consistent channel numbering could stimulate viewership and thus advertising.

Type Clustering The programmer can practice **type clustering,** in which cable channels are grouped by the type of content they offer. Thus, ESPN, SportsChannel America, Sports South, and other national and regional sports services can be placed on consecutive channels. That natural blocking allows sports fans to move from event to event without such a dramatic change in channel numbers. News and information networks, shopping services, and religious channels also make natural clusters.

Compatibility Clustering Most viewers, however, do not watch one type of channel all the time.

A second form of clustering is called **compatibility clustering,** in which channels are placed in groups because they tend to share many of the same viewers. For example, viewers in an upscale household may watch Arts and Entertainment, CNN, CNBC, public television, and C-SPAN with some frequency. Placing these channels next to each other can limit that family's channel changing.

Tiering   Channels can be offered in **tiers** or clusters, with each cluster offered at a set price. In a *forced tier,* a subscriber must buy each subsequent tier to get to the remaining tiers. For example, the *basic tier,* containing the off-air local signals and selected basic channels such as the USA Network and Lifetime, can be provided for the basic monthly subscription fee. Tier 2 may include popular networks such as ESPN, CNN, and MTV. Segregating these desirable channels forces subscribers to elect the second tier in order to get them. A third tier may include premium movie channels such as HBO, Showtime, Cinemax, and the Movie Channel. The subscriber can make one or more choices from this tier, and many operators offer discounts for **multipay** subscriptions, in which the customer orders more than one premium channel.

A newer strategy is **reverse tiering,** in which consumers can buy any service or tier individually. In some cases subscribers take a premium service such as HBO without subscribing to anything else, including the basic tier.

Economics and Cable

Cable's traditional revenue stream has come from subscriptions, but the maturation of the cable industry, which resulted in a dramatic slowing of new subscriptions and rising monthly subscriber charges, forced operators to seek additional sources of income. The most obvious was advertising. As the industry has shifted from a growth period to one of service and retention, advertising has become more important.

Increasing sophistication in selling advertising time has come to cable through the growth of the industry and the arrival of salespersons from other media. Print, radio, and television account executives (salespeople) have been moving to cable because it represents a growth area. They bring proven selling strategies with them, and this helps generate revenues. For example, a sales drive in the Omnicon system in Michigan raised revenues 25 percent.[6]

Since people in the industry view rate hikes as unwise because of the potential for unwanted regulation, advertising revenues loom as the answer. Time Warner signed a 1991 pact with General Motors in which GM committed approximately $80 million in ad revenue to a variety of Time Warner media companies including *Time, Fortune,* and *People* magazines as well as home video, film, and book enterprises.[7] Some of that money was targeted for cable systems and may be a harbinger of things to come, especially for MSOs. The influx of advertising dollars will have a positive effect in the area of cable advertising.

During the Persian Gulf war of 1991, Los Angeles cable systems took advantage of ad windows in the CNN and CNN Headline networks. Spots on CNN sold for $700 even when they ran as early as 6 a.m. or as late as midnight. The month of February 1991, the height of the war, was sold out. As cable operators see these opportunities, they can be expected to capitalize on them.

Regional interconnects   As its advertising potential has grown, cable has continued to offer an appealing, upscale audience to advertisers. At the local level, its success has been boosted by local businesses that have been brought to cable advertising for the first time. Local businesses benefit from cable's tight geographic reach and ability to deliver a truly local audience. However, larger advertisers can use cable to reach those desirable audiences without being restricted by geography. Regional interconnects such as Adlink/NCA in Los Angeles can deliver a variety of cable systems to an advertiser depending on the advertiser's geographic needs. Local and regional chains may be strong in some areas but not in others. Adlink/NCA and other similar groups can tailor a variety of packages of systems to advertisers. In the case of national companies that are accustomed to buying ADIs, all cable systems in an ADI can be connected to emulate a broadcast station buy. The selling point for an ADI-like interconnect is the quality of cable's audiences.

As interconnects have shown more flexibility, they have achieved the capacity to compete effectively with broadcast outlets. By concentrating on local areas, they can serve local advertisers more efficiently. By connecting certain municipalities for local and regional clients, cable makes available the power of television advertising and the efficiency of coordinated geographic areas. For regional and national advertisers, cable offers a variety of programming targeted to specific demographic groups as well as a desirable overall audience. Areas characterized by higher incomes can be targeted, and low-income areas can be avoided. Broadcast entities simply cannot carve up their service areas this effectively.

Other Revenue Sources

The 900 number telephone services are a booming business. Such services advertise widely but keep their costs down by purchasing unsold avails at a discount. Thus, many of their spots air late at night, and this is a wise strategy for some of the more adult-oriented services. This buying strategy also meets the needs of cable systems which have avails to sell. A 1991 study of cable systems conducted by the Cable Advertising Bureau found that few cable systems were selling more than half their avails.[8] Even if they were sold at a discounted rate, that income often represented dollars which would otherwise go unclaimed. The 900 services, ranging from soap opera updates to horoscopes to updated sports scores, have been rejected by some affiliated stations and can now turn to cable as an alternative.

Another source of income for cable systems is the rental of remote control devices to subscribers. Many homes still lack remote control capability, and wireless remotes supplied by the cable operator can overcome that problem. These remote control units are relatively inexpensive and thus can be rented at reasonable rates and still yield profits. About 91 percent of cable systems obtain additional revenue from subscribers by providing an additional service.[9] If these services are aggressively marketed, the income can be substantial.

Shopping channels are also a source of revenue for cable operators. Carriage deals with the shopping channels usually contain a clause providing that a percentage of the purchases in the system's coverage area will be paid to the cable system operator. When several such channels are available, the combined revenues can be quite useful to the operator.

A major revenue source for the future appears to be PPV. Revenues for events and movies are shared with local operators. In the case of championship boxing matches and popular events such as *Wrestlemania,* the ticket prices are high (up to $40) and the revenue potential is great. Getting a portion of that money encourages cable system operators to obtain the technology needed to offer additional PPV services.

Marketing Cable Tiers to Subscribers

Tiering has become an important trend in recent years for several reasons. First, cable operators have heard the footsteps of the regulatory wolf at the door and are therefore reluctant to raise their rates. Second, maturation of subscriptions has been approached, and other revenue sources are needed. Third, regulatory moves appear to be aimed at broadcast and lifeline tiers. For a cable company, after creating one tier, it is a simple process to create others.

Economy tiers Lifeline, broadcast, or **economy tiers** are made up of broadcast channels, LO and access channels, and some satellite services, especially those which cost the operator the least to provide. When shopping services, C-SPAN, and the Discovery Channel are added to broadcast services, a lifeline tier can be created. Aimed at lower-income households, it can be sold to subscribers at a modest rate since its cost is minimal. In New York such a tier was offered in early 1991 for $14.95. It contained broadcast commercial and public television stations; the QVC Network; public, municipal, and educational access channels; C-SPAN; and PPV channels.

Economy tiers have a second advantage: enhanced revenues. Shopping channels help generate revenue for the operator, and PPV also is a source of funds. Thus the economy tier is profitable.

Finally, economy tiers have political advantages. Whenever rate regulation is discussed, the discussion focuses only on the lowest basic tier offered by a system. Therefore, if municipalities or legislative bodies regulated rates, only the lifeline tier would be counted. While not accounting for a large percentage of subscribers, it would take the brunt of political pressure.[10]

Basic tiers With an economy tier in place, a cable system can add popular cable networks and market the second tier as basic or standard cable. The basic tier usually includes the bulk of cable networks, those in the middle price range. Missing are the higher-cost, more popular channels such as Lifetime, Nickelodeon, MTV, and the Weather Channel.

As with the economy tier, pricing is linked to the types of services provided. The subscriber may pay an extra $4 and receive an additional 20 channels—an attractive bargain. Because the channels provided are less expensive to the operator, the cost is lower than the revenue, and so basic tiers also make money.

Expanded basic tiers Expanded basic is the top-of-the-line basic tier. The most expensive and most popular cable networks are included for an additional price. Services such as CNN, ESPN, AMC, TNT, USA, A&E, and regional sports networks are added. Since these are the most popular services, the expanded basic tier is a best-seller. Even a nominal additional price of $4 makes this tier profitable.

Expanded basic is the tier of choice for operators because it generates the highest rev-

enues. Another reason operators want expanded basic to be dominant is local advertising. When one is making use of windows on the most popular channels, it is necessary to have the greatest possible number of viewers to offer to advertisers.

Negative option tiers Negative option tiers allow subscribers to save money on their cable bills by discounting the charge if they choose not to take certain services. If subscribers are willing to give up a package of ESPN, CNN, USA, TNT, and the Comedy Channel, for example, they may realize a saving of $1.20 a month. Since the total refunded to the subscriber is lower than the cost of the combined services to the operator, negative options save the operator as well as the subscriber money.

Negative option tiers are sometimes billed as "satellite value packages" to emphasize the attractiveness and popularity of the channels they offer. MTV is usually not included on negative option tiers, though, because it has a negative image with older viewers and might spur defections, reducing potential ad revenues and alienating the younger members of cable families.

A la carte selection A radical version of tiering is called **cable segmentation** in Cablevision of New York's system. This means that all choices are placed in groups and that subscribers purchase the group or groups they want. Unlike tiers, which must be ordered in sequence, subscribers can take any combination of channels.

Table 20-1 shows the basic combinations offered in an a la carte system. The sports segment sells for $9.95 a month and includes SportsChannel America, SportsChannel New York, and Madison Square Garden Network. Note that ESPN is missing; it is included in the news and information cluster along with CNN, the Weather Channel, the Discovery Channel, CNBC, and C-SPAN I and II for $5 a month. Individual subscribers can choose among movies, children's, arts/music, and home shopping clusters as well. This gives subscribers maximum freedom of choice, but it also lowers the penetration rate for important cable networks such as CNN and ESPN.

TABLE 20-1 Basic Segments of Service for Cablevision New York*

Sports Segment, $9.95/month	News/Information, $5/month
SportsChannel America SportsChannel New York Madison Square Garden Network	CNN ESPN Weather Channel Discovery Channel CNBC/FNN C-SPAN I C-SPAN II
Movies/Entertainment, $6/month	
Family Channel USA Network Lifetime Black Entertainment TV Movietime TNT TBS WVIA TV (Scranton)	Home Shopping, $2/month
	QVC Network J.C. Penney TV Home Shopping Network
Children's/Education, $3/month	Family Cable A, $21.95/month
Discovery Channel Learning Channel Nickelodeon Mind Extension University	Primary outlet service Religious channels All segments except sports and ESPN
	Family Cable B, $25.95/month
Arts/Music, $6/month	
MTV VH-1 Country Music Television Nashville Network A&E	Primary outlet service Religious channels ESPN All segments except SportsChannel

*All segments require a $9.95/month primary outlet connection.

Disadvantages of tiering While tiering offers immediate financial advantages, it has a downside as well. The primary problem is that it reduces the viewing of some of cable's most popular networks. That is annoying to the networks, which fight tiering at every turn, especially when they are placed on the highest tier. American Movie Classics stipulates in its contracts that operators must pay for at least 95 percent of all subscribers on the monthly per-subscriber basis regardless of the percentage of penetration. Hypothetically,

if this network were placed on an expanded basic tier that was accepted by only 50 percent of viewers, the operator would still have to pay at the 95 percent level. Thus, there would be no economic advantage to an operator who tiered AMC. All networks, not surprisingly, want to be placed on the lowest tiers to keep their subscriber bases high and their advertising rates at a maximum.

The operator also loses in tiering. If the operator is taking advantage of ad windows in the most popular services, those ad revenues will shrink as the subscriber base shrinks. By tiering a service and cutting its base, the operator loses out because of decreased ad rates and revenues.

Cable Operators' Responses to Economic Pressures

Two important pressures which threaten cable operators' bottom lines are building: shelf space allocation and syndex problems. There are other problems, but these two are especially thorny.

Allocation of shelf space   Even in a cable environment with 36 channels or more, it is possible to be overwhelmed with channels. New services are experiencing carriage problems because operators are offering so many channels already. Since most of these channels cost the operators money, the operators are not eager to offer more costly channels. After all, they are paying for a host of services already. The Science Fiction Channel faced that challenge in 1992. While some operators liked the concept, many others threw up their hands and offered the no-channel-space argument. The Monitor Channel faced the same problem.[11]

Operators sometimes keep some channels empty even when they have room for more networks. A 1990 survey found that 50 percent of operators had three or more channels empty. The reason went beyond economics. These cable operators were looking to the future and wondering what would prove to be the next ESPN or CNN. They reasoned that having their shelf space full might prevent them from offering a wonderful service when it came along. In filling their systems, they would have to remove a service to add another, a practice that always causes public relations problems. Thus, it was more prudent to keep some space open.

THE FUTURE OF CABLE

Expansion and Diversification

Cable will continue to add subscribers, particularly in the cities. The last places to be wired, the cities are growing quickly in terms of cable subscriptions. Among the 20 largest cities, Pittsburgh is the most heavily wired at 73 percent and St. Louis is the least at 46 percent. Since the populations of the largest cities are moving toward cable, penetration will doubtless rise.[12] However, the rate of growth, even in the cities, is decreasing and has slowed to a crawl in areas where subscription rates exceed 80 percent.

Another problem for cable operators may well be shorter franchise periods.[13] Municipalities are more sophisticated now than they were when many cable contracts were first negotiated. They may increase the franchise fees paid by cable operators, require better customer service, or even deny franchise renewal. This could throw cable operators into chaos, especially those which are financially extended because of the cost of building their systems.

A very bright spot for operators is personal communication networks (PCNs). PCNs make use of cellular telephone technology, although they do not have the range of cellular phones; they do have much more range than cordless phones, however. This midrange product would allow an individual carrying a unit to range up to a mile from his or her cable system's fiber-optic nodes, which could still carry voice, data, and other telcolike services. Capturing even a small portion of the lucrative telephone business would prove highly profitable and ease rate hikes and regulatory worries about monthly rates.

Cable has been beset by potential competition from telcos in the delivery of television signals via fiber-optic cable. With PCNs, cable is actually reversing its position and posing a threat to the telcos. The symbolic value of this for the cable industry has been very positive.[14]

Cable radio   Since they already deliver television signals via satellite, cable operators have found the prospect of delivering cable radio promising as well. Several radio formats are already available via cable, ranging from Jazz to Country, Rock 'n' Roll to Classical.

Cable systems that offer this service have

been providing 5 to 30 different signals. Each is format-specific and runs without commercials. The early response has been positive, and some projections indicate that cable radio will be a $100 million industry in its third year.

Cable radio services have found that listeners like the lack of commercials but still prefer hearing some talk. Thus many services use disc jockeys to provide song and artist identifications and occasional low-key chatter.[15]

One of the better known services is DMX Digital Music Express. For about $5 a month, the subscriber receives 30 audio music channels without commercials. The subscriber also has to buy a digital converter to make the system work. This $200 one-time expense item becomes part of the stereo system and can be taken along if the subscriber moves to another area. This system offers compact disc–quality digital sound and a large variety of music.

Independent cable systems   Cable services do not have to be delivered by cable companies. We have already seen that MMDS and DBS systems have offered or may offer similar programming. SMATV and STV systems have also enjoyed some success in certain locations. The new star on the horizon may be an independent cable system that is run privately and not for profit but serves substantial numbers of people.

A system of this type has been developed at the University of Georgia. When the university replaced its telephone lines in the late 1980s, its administrators decided to bury cable lines, along with the phone lines, for future use. When the wiring was done, it was possible to hook up a dormitory and deliver 36-channel cable. There

were two problems to be worked out. The first was programming. Would cable networks risk the ill will of cable companies by selling services to an organization which otherwise would get its cable programming from a local system operator? The second problem involved how the cost of the system would be recovered.

Gaining access to networks took considerable negotiating. The director of the Instructional Resources Center, who also was the developer of the cable system, tied the system in to educational channels that would be fed from the resources center. Then he contacted each service separately and negotiated prices. As a smaller system, University Cablevision paid more than a large MSO would have paid on a per-subscriber, per-month basis, but not so much as to make the project unworkable. In early 1991 the system signed on to several dormitories, and the remaining buildings were wired by mid-1992. By the end of 1991 the system was offering 10 educational and data channels and 20 cable networks.

Because theft of service had been a major problem when students subscribed to local cable systems, all students' rooms were connected to all the channels. The individual buildings and/or organizations paid for the cost of wiring. Then each student subscriber had the cost added to his or her housing bill. Since cable became part of the basic student fee structure, the system was available to all students and there was no reason to tinker with the wiring in an attempt to steal service. Many other colleges and universities have studied University Cablevision with the goal of building their own systems. This may be a path for many nonprofit systems in the future.

SUMMARY

The 900-pound gorillas in cable are the MSOs. Over the years they have spread their holdings and vertically integrated to an extent rare in American business. The areas of production, distribution, and delivery are all within the purview

of the MSOs. The latest move by TCI was the founding of Encore, its own low-cost premium movie service.

Regulation is minimal in cable, explaining the degree of vertical integration in its ownership. The regulation that does exist tends to deal with franchises and municipality–cable system relations. At this writing there is reason to expect a move in the area of rate regulation, probably by Congress.

Cable economics have become more complex as the industry has moved from a subscriber base to advertising. Now cable has moved beyond traditional advertising vehicles to establish complex arrangements between MSOs and major advertisers such as General Motors. Cable has also taken in 900 number advertising, developed a profitable side business in the rental of remote control devices and cable radio hookups, and promoted shopping channels which return a portion of their sales revenues to operators.

Tiering has bloomed over the past few years. Lifeline or economy tiers have been developed to attract customers who are price holdouts. Such tiers, which are subject to regulation, may keep more substantive rate regulation at bay. Basic and expanded basic tiers have also proved popular. Negative option tiers offer additional choices to subscribers, while a la carte systems give subscribers a great deal of selection control.

As cable services have proliferated, operators have held back channels and left them unused. In part, that is a response to the rising per-subscriber fees levied by the networks; in part, it is a strategy to hold room in reserve for the next generation of highly popular cable networks.

Cable appears to have a bright future. Along with increases in subscribers and ad revenues, other areas are opening up, including cable radio and personal communication networks.

Some organizations, especially colleges and universities, may break away from operators to found their own services. The experimental systems in operation now may pave the way for hospitals and governmental agencies to follow.

SUGGESTED READINGS

Cablevision

This biweekly periodical is one of the mainstays of the cable industry. As the cable version of *Broadcasting*, it supplies information about programming, ad sales, marketing, technology, pay-per-view, and operations. In addition, feature stories provide in-depth analyses of industry trends. A student can become reasonably cable-literate by reading this periodical carefully on a regular basis.

Cable World

This weekly publication provides a continuing overview of the major areas of interest in the cable industry. Especially useful is the information it provides on international cable issues, technology, and programming. The "Business Extra" section at the end of each issue gives up-to-the-minute information on economics, mergers, and business trends.

Baldwin, Thomas: *Cable Communication,* 2d ed., Prentice-Hall, New York, 1988.

This is the best source book for cable in print, providing an excellent history of the cable industry and cable programming. Also contained within its pages is an excellent discussion of technical issues from headends to fiber optics. Baldwin provides in-depth discussions of the cable networks and explains how they interact with MSOs. Every student of cable should start with this book.

Broadcasting

This magazine has been included in several chapters' suggested readings because its coverage is first rate. Despite its name, it covers cable exceptionally well, devoting several pages to a special cable section each week. It is particularly strong on legislative issues and the interface between broadcasting and cable. As with broadcasting issues, the treatment of cable issues is comprehensive, fair, and well written. This is a publication that does much good work in a variety of areas.

NOTES

1. "Basic Cable Networks," *Channels Field Guide,* December 1990, pp. 48–49

2. "Cable Giving Encore Warm Reception," *Broadcasting,* Feb. 25, 1991, p. 23.

3. "NBC Primed to Recapture Prime Time Sweeps," *Broadcasting,* May 13, 1991, p. 27.

4. "Cable Indies Fall Victim to Economy," *Cable World,* Jan. 14, 1991, p. 14.

5. "Pay per View: Swinging for the Fences?" *Channels Field Guide,* December 1989, p. 82.

6. Harvey Solomon, "Learning from Print," *Cablevision,* Feb. 11, 1991, p. 9.

7. Pat Guy, "Time Warner, GM Reach Pact on Ads," *USA Today,* March 20, 1991, p. 2B.

8. Stewart Schley, "What's in a Number," *Cable World,* Feb. 18, 1991, p. 10.

9. "Remotes Reap Revenue," *Cablevision,* Feb. 11, 1991, p. 50.

10. Carl Weinschenk, "How Unbundling Is Working," *Cable World,* May 14, 1990, p. 8.

11. Tom Kerver, "To Fill or Not to Fill," *Cablevision,* pp. 25–27.

12. "Top 20 Market Cable Universe Comparison," *Cablevision,* Feb. 11, 1991, p. 53.

13. Vincente Pasdeloup, "Cable Franchise Wars: Shorter Terms Coming?" *Cable World,* Jan. 7, 1991, p. 1.

14. "It's Cable vs. Telcos, Again, on PCS," *Broadcasting,* Jan. 28, 1991, p. 53.

15. "Cable Radio: Gauging the Potential Market," *Marketing New Media,* Feb. 18, 1991, p. 5.

Basic Cable Programming

Cable has come a long way since it was used to bring broadcast signals to unserved areas. It has become a player in the television industry and has changed the viewing habits of large numbers of Americans. Cable has also changed the economic balance of power as it has pulled viewers and advertising dollars from the broadcast segment of the television industry.

Cable networks enjoyed a fine year in 1990, following on the heels of continuous growth throughout the 1980s. In 1990 the Turner networks TNT and WTBS increased their earnings 72 percent from 1989.[1] The MTV networks, including MTV, VH-1, and Nickelodeon/Nick at Night, increased their revenues 23 percent over 1989.

While not every cable network enjoyed the same good fortune, consistent increases in subscribers were evident. Fully 13 networks had more than 50 million subscribing homes, and two others had over 40 million. Another six basic cable networks had in excess of 30 million subscribers.[2] Basic cable is healthy.

As shown in Table 21-1, more than 55 basic services are in operation at the present time. The more widely distributed ones, such as ESPN, CNN, and USA, appear in almost all cable homes, while highly specialized services such as BET and Univision appear in fewer homes. Each is valued by some segment of the viewing audience, and if that support is sufficiently strong, smaller and more focused services can survive.

In this chapter we look at basic cable programming strategies, the cable networks, and their economic impact. We begin by describing how basic cable programming follows formulas developed over the years by broadcast television. We then discuss the major basic cable networks and give a brief description of each one. The economic aspects of the cable industry are outlined next, with special attention paid to the growth of cable penetration and the concurrent shrinkage of the broadcast market. Finally, a brief discussion of coming trends sets the stage for the future.

TABLE 21-1 Basic Cable Networks and Subscribers

Network	Subscribing Homes, millions
ESPN	61.0
CNN	56.5
USA	53.8
TBS	53.3
Discovery Channel	52.9
Nickelodeon	52.9
Nick at Nite	52.9
MTV	52.4
Family Channel	51.8
C-SPAN I and II	51.5
Nashville Network	51.0
TNT	50.0
Lifetime	50.0
A&E	48.0
Weather Channel	46.0
Headline News	44.0
VH-1	38.8
CNBC/FNN	35.4
WGN	32.5
Black Entertainment TV	29.1
AMC	28.0
Comedy Central	23.0
Learning Channel	20.9
Travel Channel	16.0
Entertainment TV	15.6
WWOR	13.5
Trinity Broadcasting Network	13.0
SportsChannel America	11.0
Nostalgia Channel	10.0
Video Jukebox Network	10.0
WPIX	9.6
Univision	6.1
Bravo	5.0
KTLA	4.7
KTVT	2.2
WSBK	2.0

SOURCE: *Television Business International,* February 1991, pp. 36–37.

PROGRAMMING TRENDS IN BASIC CABLE

Broadcasters have spent years figuring out who is available to watch television, what degree of program modularity is needed to appeal to the available audience, and which kinds of content viewers want during different dayparts and days of the week. Their research into these marketplace characteristics has led broadcasters to create certain scheduling and strategic conventions (Chapter 11) that are widely used in cable as well.

Cable networks tend to be more specialized than broadcast stations, but their programming strategies are similar. For example, viewers have come to expect programs to begin on the hour and the half hour, and so almost all cable channels use those starting times. This would normally present a problem for services such as HBO and Showtime, whose events do not always follow the half-hour and hour format, but these services use fillers between programs so that movies and events begin on the hour or half hour. Superstation WTBS is a notable exception in that it starts programs at 5 and 35 minutes past the hour.

Cable networks program not only against one another but against independent and affiliated stations and broadcast networks. They follow the programming conventions of the broadcast industry especially during prime time, when the greatest number of viewers is available.

An example is Nickelodeon, whose primary target audience is children, but after 8 p.m. Nick at Nite targets adults. The evening programming consists primarily of nostalgic appeal product such as *Mork and Mindy, Get Smart,* and *Alfred Hitchcock.* Opposite the late news, Nick at Nite runs comedy programs, emulating the strategies of independent stations.

Lifetime, targeted to women and utilizing several talk shows, also schedules off-network product such as *L.A. Law* during prime time. In the late news slot at 11 p.m., syndicated programming appears as an alternative to the news.

This tendency to program aggressively during prime time extends to other specialized cable networks as well. ESPN schedules its Sunday night National League Football games at 8 p.m. so that the contest runs through the remainder of the prime-time period. MTV debuts new videos in prime time with much buildup and promotion.

As the prime-time lineups shown in Table 21-2 illustrate, there is no appreciable difference between the program order and style of cable networks and those of independent broadcast stations.

The prime-time schedules of cable services as diverse as Arts and Entertainment, the USA Network, and the Discovery Channel have no dramatic strategic differences. Program blocking on Bravo and A&E is similar, with both running three 1-hour blocks. The Discovery Channel's content is similar to that of A&E except that the blocks are composed of half hours. CNN blocks by the hour, whereas ESPN blocks by the half hour. None of these shows is off-network. All have been created for cable or have been taken from alternative sources, but the scheduling and flow patterns are quite similar to those on affiliated and independent stations.

Lifetime, Nickelodeon, the Nostalgia Channel, and the USA Network all schedule off-network product as independent television stations do. Lifetime runs a 1-hour drama show to lead into its prime-time movie. Nickelodeon runs sitcoms that counterprogram the movies carried on many competitors' channels. The Nostalgia Channel runs two adventure shows that lead into its movie. The USA Network, like Lifetime, runs a recent off-network hour program as a lead into its movie.

Just as many independent stations do, A&E, Nickelodeon, and the Discovery Channel program comedy shows as alternatives to the 11 p.m. broadcast affiliates' news programs. Lifetime and USA offer hour-long action/adventure shows. The Nostalgia Network goes with a movie, and CNN follows its 10 p.m. news hour with a program about the financial world.

This pattern of shows has been emulated even on specialized services such as the Weather Channel, which regularly schedules programs on travel weather, sports weather, skiing conditions, aviation weather, and other pertinent topics. The Travel Channel programs half-hour and hour shows on scuba diving and beach resorts.

The shows on all these channels are scheduled in specific time slots so that viewers can develop habits based on their favorite content, just as they do when watching broadcast networks and independent stations. The *Wakin' Up* show

TABLE 21-2 Prime-Time Cable Schedules

Network	8 p.m.	8:30 p.m.	9 p.m.	9:30 p.m.
Bravo	*The Haunted Heroes*		*Carols at Christmas*	
A&E	*Birds of the World*		*Our Century*	
CNN	*Prime News*		*Larry King Live*	
ESPN	*NFL Matchup*	*NFL Trivia*	Basketball	
Lifetime	*Cagney and Lacey*	Movie		
Nick	*Mr. Ed*	*Patty Duke*	*My Three Sons*	*Donna Reed*
Discovery	*Animal World*		*Orphans of Wild*	*Wildlife*
Nostalgia	*Mr. D.A.*	*Defender*	Movie	
USA	*Murder She Wrote*	Movie		

Network	10 p.m.	10:30 p.m.	11 p.m.
Bravo	*Mozart in Salzburg*		Off
A&E	*Short Stories*		*Evening at the Improv*
CNN	Evening News		*Moneyline*
ESPN	*Basketball* (continued)		*Sportscenter*
Lifetime	Movie (continued)		*Cagney and Lacey*
Nick	*Sat. Night Live*	*Second City TV*	*Laugh-In*
Discovery	*Water Highways*	*Rendezvous*	*Ozzie & Harriet*
Nostalgia	Movie (continued)		*11 p.m. movie*
USA	Movie (continued)		*Miami Vice*

on the Weather Channel, for example, comes on at the same time each day with specific weather information that the rising person wants.

The daytime programming of other specialized services is aimed at the available demographics as well (Table 21-3). ESPN, for example, runs a business show early in the morning as an alternative to talk and children's programs. This is followed during the daytime by exercise programs that are aimed primarily at women viewers.

Lifetime also programs to women during the day with shows on exercise, food, and contemporary women's issues. The hour before prime time contains comedy shows because the audience includes more men.

In terms of appealing to audiences, basic networks can go in two directions in regard to content. They can appeal to the mass audience and try to build large audiences through general-appeal programs, or they can focus specifically on one kind of product and appeal to a more defined and smaller group.[3] The first strategy is practiced by networks such as USA and the Family Channel, which program general-appeal shows to a large potential audience. The second, more specialized type of network is analogous to a formatted radio station which plays one kind of music all day. ESPN and MTV are examples of this trend toward specialization on cable. However, the specialized channels sometimes reach for larger, broadcastlike audiences with general-appeal programming. Lifetime, Nickelodeon, and most other basic networks carry off-network comedies, drama shows, and movies, and ESPN carries NFL football and major league baseball.

It is important to remember that no matter what content is offered, cable networks struc-

TABLE 21-3   Daytime Schedules for Selected Cable Networks

Network	10 a.m.	10:30 a.m.	11 a.m.
A&E	Movie		Fugitive
CNN	World Day		Daywatch
ESPN	Sports Center		Body Jake
Lifetime	Frugal Gourmet	E.N.G.	
Nickelodeon	Eureeka's Castle		Sharon . . . Elephant
Discovery	Travel	Chefs of New Orleans	Gourmet
USA	Murder She Wrote		Divorce Court

	11:30 a.m.	12	12:30 p.m.
A&E		Letterman	
CNN	Crier & Co.	News Hour	
ESPN	Getting Fit	Bodies in Motion	Body Shape
Lifetime		Tracey Ullman	E.R.
Nickelodeon	Fred Penner	David the Gnome	Little Koala
Discovery	Pasquale's Kitchen	Homeworks	Easy Does It
USA		The Judge	

Network	1 p.m.	1:30 p.m.	2 p.m.
A&E	Avengers		Movie
CNN	Sonya Live		Newsday
ESPN	Basketball		
Lifetime	Supermarket Sweep	Shop Till You Drop	thirtysomething
Nickelodeon	Noozles	Maya the Bee	Little Bits
Discovery	Best of Europe	Chefs of New Orleans	Gourmet
USA	Superior Court		Joker's Wild

	2:30 p.m.	3 p.m.	3:30 p.m.
A&E			
CNN		Int'l Hour	
ESPN		Yacht Racing	
Lifetime		Attitudes	
Nickelodeon	Jeff's Collie	Flipper	Looney Toons
Discovery	Pasquale's Kitchen	Homeworks	Easy Does It
USA	Win, Lose, Draw	Hollywood Squares	Scrabble

ture their schedules along the lines established over the years by the broadcast channels. They follow the same strategies.

BASIC CABLE SERVICES

More than 50 basic cable services are available today. This glut may be diminished by a financial shakeout in which some services merge and others fall by the wayside. But for now, the field is crowded and promises to become more so as new services vie for channel positions.

To make better sense of the cable environment, we will briefly discuss each major cable service and categorize those which have similar programs into groups for easy comparison.

Educationally Oriented Networks

The Discovery Channel focuses on science, nature, and travel information in its programming. Among its better known shows are *Mother Nature, Natural World,* and *Wildlife Tales.* Its two primary sources of revenue are national advertising and a monthly charge per subscriber paid by cable systems that carry the service. Because of partial ownership by major MSOs such as Cox Cable, Newhouse Cable, TCI, and United, it is carried on many systems.

The Learning Channel (TLC) programs educational and informational programming and self-improvement shows to adults. Some courses for college credit are carried as well. Among its better known programs are *Art Is Fun, Gardening from the Ground Up,* and *The Do It Yourself Show.* TLC derives its revenue from per-subscriber charges to cable systems, national advertising, and fees from college credit courses. It was acquired by the Discovery Channel in 1991.

A competitor of the Learning Channel is the Mind Extension University (MEU), owned by the MSO Jones Intercable. MEU is offered free to cable operators and derives its revenues from college course fees.

Foreign-Language Networks

Galavision is a Spanish-language service that offers movies, Spanish soap operas (called *novellas,*) and variety programming. Cable operators pay for the service according to the number of persons with Hispanic surnames in the cable system's area. The network carries no advertising at this time.

Univision, another Spanish-language service, is the new incarnation of the Spanish International Network (SIN). **Advertiser-supported,** it supplies newscasts, movies, *novellas,* sports programs, and children's programs.

SCOLA is a service that brings foreign newscasts to cable systems. The newscasts are aired in the original languages with English subtitles. Newscasts from Russia, Mexico, Germany, Italy, France, and Spain predominate.

The Asia Network carries programs from Pacific rim countries in the original languages. RAI News delivers news and some entertainment programming from Italy. French TV makes available French news and entertainment programs. JISO carries Japanese-language programs, mostly from the Japanese network NHK.

Sports Networks

The Entertainment and Sports Programming Network (ESPN) is the best known sports network and carries primarily sports and exercise programs. It has expanded over the years from an emphasis on minor sports such as lacrosse and track and field to include mainstream sports such as college basketball, professional and college football, and major league baseball.

In 1991 ESPN moved strongly into the international arena, bringing programs to Japan, Mexico, and Europe. Its deal with NHK called for ESPN to supply substantial amounts of sports programming for Japan's first all-sports 24-hour cable service.[4] It is advertiser-supported and charges cable systems a per-subscriber fee each month.

Score, the evening service of the Consumer

News and Business Channel (CNBC), features sports information and events. It carries national advertising and comes free to cable services that carry CNBC.

SportsChannel America provides sporting events of a regional and national nature. These events are made available to a series of regional and local sports channels, such as SportsChannel New York and SportsChannel New England, for airplay in areas where they draw the greatest interest.

There are many local and regional sports services, some of which may eventually go national. SportsChannel New York, SportsChannel Florida, SportsChannel Ohio, SportsChannel New England, Sportsvision, Home Team Sports, Prime Sports Network, Prime Ticket, Sports South, and the Madison Square Garden Network are the largest regionals. They are offered on a variety of bases to operators; some are premium networks, some are basic, and still others are hybrids that have features of basic and premium.

In the category of sports, it is important to mention the superstations. Since superstations are basically independent stations, one thing which sets them apart and makes them attractive to national audiences is their sports packages. WTBS, Atlanta, carries Atlanta Braves baseball and Atlanta Hawks basketball. The Turner Broadcasting System–originated Goodwill Games are carried on WTBS, and a deal with CBS delivered a sizable portion of the rights to the 1992 Olympics to Turner's TNT cable network. WGN, Chicago, features Cubs baseball and Big Ten college football games. WWOR, New Jersey, carries New York Mets baseball, New York Knicks and New Jersey Nets basketball, and Islanders, Rangers, and Devils hockey. In addition, WWOR carries Big East college basketball. WPIX, New York, carries New York Yankees baseball. WSBK, Boston, carries Red Sox baseball and Bruins hockey. KTLA, Los Angeles, shows the basketball Clippers and baseball Angels. KTVT, Dallas, televises Texas Rangers baseball games and college basketball and football.

News and Information Networks

At the head of this class is CNN, a wide-ranging and credible television news organization that operates on a par with the big three broadcast networks' news services. CNN and CNN Headline News are offered as a package to operators for a monthly per-subscriber fee, and each carries advertising. CNN offers programs on money, sports, business, health, and other topics in addition to its newscasts. Headline News presents the news in continuous 30-minute repeatable blocks. This service has also found its way to a number of broadcast stations, where it is often used late at night as an alternative to old movies, comedies, and dramatic shows.

CNBC is an upscale business-oriented news and special information channel. It carries advertising and charges a per-subscriber monthly fee for carriage. CNBC acquired the Financial News Network in 1991, raising its subscriber base from 17 million homes to over 50 million.

The Monitor Channel is an outgrowth of the *Christian Science Monitor* and makes use of many programs from its Boston television station. Its signature news program, *Worldwatch,* is repeated throughout the day. Other programs include various interview, opinion, and information shows, *50 Years Ago Today, Feature Story,* and *Opinion Page.* With an editorial advisory board that includes Peggy Charren, former president of Action for Children's Television, the service also tackles children's issues and interests with programs such as *The Children's Room* and *The Good Green Earth.*[5]

Prevue Guide provides continuous listings of programs on the various services. Scrolling through about 3 hours of programs on a continuous basis, it serves the casual viewer who wants to know what is on without reaching for the newspaper or a printed guide. One advantage is that it is tailored to the channel number scheme of each cable system on which it runs. While a print publication such as *TV Guide* may provide information about content, its geographic area includes many cable systems; thus, it does not contain channel numbers, just network names.

Music Networks

Music video channels started with MTV (Music Television), which is still the most prominent music service. The videos are most often given to the network free in exchange for play, just as promotional CDs are given to radio stations for airplay. MTV charges a monthly subscriber fee to cable operators and carries advertising.

Its sister service, VH-1 (Video Hits-1), is aimed at a slightly older audience and offers videos that feature established stars. Services that carry MTV receive VH-1 free.

The Nashville Network (TNN) carries country music videos (which are absent on MTV) as well as talk, quiz, and concert programming. The network charges operators a monthly fee and sells advertising. It is most popular in the south.

Country Music Television is a competitor of TNN and programs country music videos almost exclusively. Unlike the mix of program forms on TNN, it provides a "more music" alternative. The service charges operators a monthly fee and carries advertising.

Video Jukebox charges a per-subscriber monthly fee to cable operators and carries advertising to generate revenue. An alternative to MTV, it offers fewer interruptions of the music, eschewing the syndicated programs and interview shows seen on MTV.

Film and Variety Networks

American Movie Classics (AMC) began as a premium channel but switched to basic service when competition with major premium-movie channels became increasingly difficult. Its stable of classic films appeals to many households. AMC runs no advertisements, but systems must pay a per-subscriber, per-month fee for the service. Fifty percent of AMC is owned by TCI, giving the service wide carriage.

The Nostalgia Channel offers older films and television programs and occasional nostalgic variety programming. Like AMC, it carries no advertising but charges cable operators a per-subscriber, per-month fee. It can be offered as a basic service, or the cost can be passed to con-

sumers by including it as part of a tier above the basic service.

The Family Channel (formerly the Christian Broadcasting Network) provides religious programming along with comedy, drama, movies, children's programs, and documentaries. Its lineup is much more varied than those of most other religious networks as it tries to cater to families. In many dayparts it is programmed much as an independent station is. It is offered free to cable systems and gathers revenue from advertising and viewer donations.

Turner Network Television (TNT) provides a large number of films and has an increasingly strong sports lineup with NBA games, the Goodwill Games, and events from the 1992 Olympic Games. TNT had one of the largest start-up audiences in cable history, about 20 million homes, at its 1988 launch. Advertiser-supported and charging per-subscriber monthly fees, TNT was an immediate economic success.

The USA Network presents a broad range of comedy, drama, action, sports, films, and other programs and is indistinguishable from an independent station. One of the most widely distributed cable networks, USA has a very strong lineup. By aggressively pursuing syndicated product such as *Murder She Wrote, Miami Vice,* and other off-network programs, USA built itself into one of the most watched cable networks. Advertiser-supported, it also charges operators a monthly per-subscriber fee.

Bravo programs primarily international films and performing arts specials. Formerly a premium service, Bravo found a move to basic to be advantageous. Positioning itself against competitors such as A&E and Discovery has proved less formidable than positioning itself against HBO and Disney.

Special-Interest Networks

Arts and Entertainment (A&E) offers a mix of documentary, performing arts, comedy, and drama programs. The service charges operators a monthly fee for each subscriber and takes advertising. An upscale cable version of public television, it competes for high quality-programming. It is partly owned by the ABC Network.

Black Entertainment Television (BET) has helped attract minority households as cable subscribers. The service provides a mix of music videos that feature black artists, sports, films, comedy, news, public affairs, and specials. Part ownership by TCI has helped it gain space on systems. Advertising and monthly per-subscriber fees from operators provide its revenues.

Lifetime is the only cable network that expressly targets women. Its lineup is typified by talk programs that emphasize contemporary women's issues and health (Lifetime evolved from the Health Network). In prime time, however, Lifetime programs more generally with programs such as *L.A. Law* and movies. Monthly per-subscriber fees and advertising are its sources of revenue.

Comedy Central represents a merger of the old Ha! Network and Comedy Network. By merging, the two were able to increase their subscribership and eliminate costly competition in a specialized area. Its content includes reruns of old sitcoms and comedy compilation programs, stand-up comedy performances, and original programs such as *Mystery Science 2000, Sports Monster,* and *Clash.*[6]

The latest entry from Turner Broadcasting is the Cartoon Channel. Drawing on a library of Hanna-Barbera product, it provides a steady stream of animated entertainment to children of all ages.

The Science Fiction Channel, as the name suggests, carries science-fiction and horror programs. By developing a deal with the Disney Company and locating its studios at the Disney World/MGM complex in Florida, the Science Fiction Channel has given itself both visibility and a link to future original programming.[7]

Nickelodeon and Nick at Night are companion services. Nickelodeon fills the daytime hours with children's programming, while Nick at Night programs to adults after 8 p.m. primarily with older syndicated comedy series. Monthly subscriber fees from operators and advertising form its revenue base.

The Cowboy Channel carries western reruns, films, and occasional talk and information shows ranging from a discussion of Zane Grey's works to a look at the art of Remington. Highly specialized, it tries to appeal strongly to its target audience.

Courtroom Television (CT) owes its roots to such programs as *L.A. Law* and *The People's Court.* CT covers trials live during the day and often jumps between two or three different proceedings. The William Kennedy Smith rape trial in late 1991 was carried live and brought much attention to CT. Weekends and evenings are given over to recaps, replays, and talk and information by and about lawyers and the legal profession. At this writing, a decision on the televising of federal trials is imminent. If that decision is favorable, it will prove invaluable to CT's efforts.[8]

The Cable Satellite Public Affairs Network (C-SPAN) supplies television coverage of the U.S. House of Representatives, allowing Americans to see their government in action. C-SPAN II was developed to provide similar coverage of the Senate. Neither network carries advertising. C-SPAN charges operators a per-subscriber monthly fee, and C-SPAN II is provided free to systems that carry C-SPAN.

The Silent Network/America's Disability Channel is a specialized service for hearing-impaired and otherwise disabled people. Voice, sign, and closed caption information are all carried simultaneously so that the entertainment and information programming provided will have maximum utility. Advertiser-supported, it is offered free to cable systems to encourage carriage.

The Weather Channel specializes in weather information on an international, national, regional, and local basis. This is narrowcasting at its most specific, but the daily audience is substantial since viewers check in often, if only for short periods of time. It is advertiser-supported, and operators pay a monthly per-subscriber fee.

The Travel Channel provides information that is directed toward frequent travelers. While reaching a small, upscale primary audience, this service has appeal to casual viewers as well. It derives its revenue from advertising and from products sold directly on the service. Rather than charge operators for carriage, the Travel Channel provides a commission to system operators from the merchandise sales generated in each cable service area.

Movietime features current feature film previews, with clips, interviews, and background information about theatrical movies and other films being shown on cable. Its ownership includes the MSOs ATC, Continental, and Cox as well as HBO and Warner. Advertising and monthly fees provide its revenue.

Entertainment Television (E!) covers celebrities and the entertainment industry. It functions as a hybrid of *People* magazine and *Entertainment Tonight.* Its focus on interviews, entertainment events, and reviews makes it viewer-friendly and modular. One can view the reasonably short modules for any length of time with any starting and stopping point without having to worry about plot or context. Elements are repeated throughout the day, and some pieces are repeated for several days depending on their timeliness and importance.

NuStar is a creation of several MSOs and functions as a cross between the Prevue Guide and E!. NuStar carries cross-channel tune-in promotions for basic cable networks. Similar to movie trailers, these extended promos seek to elicit interest in shows and services. By watching NuStar, viewers get more than a preview guide of what is on; they get a taste of the program itself.

Superstations

Because their signals are distributed nationally, it is easy to think of superstations as network services although they are actually independent stations. Syndicated exclusivity has brought some problems to superstations as they are blacked out when their programs duplicate those run on local stations. Thus, they have more original product, especially sports, than do most strictly local independents. Syndicators have sold fewer shows to the superstations. Con-

sequently, superstations have to rely even more on movies, sports, and original programming to fill their schedules. They program comedy and children's blocks just as independents do.

The superstations have solid sports lineups and strong film packages, making them appealing to viewers in far-flung areas. Their delivery to cable systems is indirect. **Common carriers**—organizations that deliver signals from one place to another without influencing the content (the telephone company is a common carrier)—uplink the signal to a satellite for distribution to cable systems. In exchange, the distributor receives a monthly per-subscriber fee from those cable systems.

Some stations like the idea of being superstations, WTBS being the foremost among them. The advantage offered by superstation status is that higher rates can be charged to national advertisers to reflect the number of potential households these stations reach through national distribution on cable systems. The common carrier gets income from the cable operators, the superstation receives increased advertising revenues, and cable operators receive a highly popular service to encourage subscription.

WTBS was the first of the superstations and remains the best known. It offers a strong sports package as well as movies, documentaries, and syndicated programming. The other superstations—WGN, WWOR, WPIX, KTVT, WSBK, KTLA, and WSBK—offer similar lineups of sports, movies, and syndicated programs.

Religious Networks

Most religious networks pay cable operators for carriage and rely on donations to generate operating capital. Whether on broadcast or on cable, religion is big business. In 1987 the top six televised ministries took in $600 million. However, the Jim Bakker and Jimmy Swaggert scandals cut into those revenues substantially, and by the early 1990s revenues were down. Thus, unpaid bills to cable operators led to some networks being dropped.

PTL, which stands for both Praise the Lord

and People That Love, is one of the best known religious networks. While the Family Channel carries considerable religious content, it has diversified to the point where it is not considered to be dominated by religious programming. PTL, by contrast, carries religious programming almost exclusively. After the fall of Jim and Tammy Bakker in 1987, PTL was renamed the Inspirational Network, and control fell to former Bakker associates.

The largest religious cable service is Vision Interfaith Satellite Network (VISN), which specializes in religious and values-oriented programming.

Eternal Word Television Network (EWTN) is a Catholic nonprofit service that is offered on a part-time basis during the evening. The content generally consists of family programming with a Catholic point of view. The service is provided free to cable operators, and donations provide the revenues.

The Trinity Broadcasting Network (TBN) offers a range of religious programs, along with talk, exercise, music, and children's programs. Like the Inspirational Network, TBN pays cable operators for carriage and earns its revenues through donations.

The American Christian Television Service (ACTS), run by the Southern Baptist Convention, programs family and inspirational materials.

Home Shopping Networks

When home shopping networks were introduced in the mid-1980s, the sky seemed to be the limit. Caught up in a powerful combination of convenience—a big electronic catalog piped directly to the home—and hype, many viewers went on electronic buying binges. That success prompted others to get into the game, and the home shopping field became crowded. However, by the late 1980s many home shopping networks had folded or merged. While there is still much buying (about $1 billion a year), there has been very little growth. The major players have held on, and new shopping services seem less likely.

The Home Shopping Network (HSN) originated the cable home shopping craze and still dominates the market. By selling jewelry, electronics, housewares, cosmetics, clothing, health products, and collectibles at steep discounts, HSN defined the home shopping inventory and style. HSN pays cable operators a 5 percent commission on sales from each operator's franchise area in exchange for carriage and also makes money from item sales.

The Cable Value Network (CVN) has a distinct advantage in the cable world: It is partly owned by some of the largest MSOs, including TCI, ATC, and United. This assures carriage on many systems and makes CVN number two behind HSN. As with HSN, CVN pays cable operators 5 percent of the sales in each operator's area.

The QVC network is slightly different from its competitors in that it tends to focus on higher-quality merchandise. It uses the same 5 percent compensation plan employed by the other home shopping networks.

Telshop also tends toward better product lines and shares income with cable operators on a scale that increases as purchases increase in an operator's area. That motivates the operator to find good channel spaces for the service and provide local follow-up on promotion attempts.

The J.C. Penney Company has been operating the J.C. Penney Shopping Network with limited carriage and may look to television merchandising more aggressively in the future. A smaller service is Shop TV from Ltd., Inc. The future of these two services will most likely be linked to establishing relationships with major MSOs and finding a niche in the television sales industry.

There are many cable networks with a variety of areas of specialization. More services are being contemplated, but the field is already crowded. As in the home shopping area, a shakeout is inevitable in sports, news and information, and other areas. The major players are probably here to stay because they have entrenched themselves with the public and have paid back their initial start-up debts. The newer services face greater odds against survival as cable growth slows and the industry looks to other areas for profits.

ECONOMIC ASPECTS OF BASIC CABLE

The economic aspects of basic cable have never been more positive. The ratings increases of the past few years have brought increased advertising revenues and higher per-subscriber fees from operators. As a result, basic network programmers have been able to pursue more popular programs and create original programming. The improved programming attracts more viewers, and the positive cash flow process continues.

Ratings Increases

In terms of ratings, basic cable networks as a group moved from a 16 percent share in prime time and late night in 1989 to 21 percent in

1990.[9] In 1991 their share rose to 23 percent. At the same time, broadcast networks' late-night shares fell to 51 and prime-time shares dropped to 62 in 1990.[10] The increase in audience share led to increased revenues as well. As an example, Lifetime increased its revenues 30 percent in 1990.[11]

High-Quality Demographics of Cable Audiences

These audience increases were good news for cable in more ways than audience size. Cable demographics have come to be very attractive to advertisers who are increasingly appreciative of the upscale nature of cable audiences. Table 21-4 illustrates the differences among the income levels of broadcast network and cable network audiences. Looking at homes with incomes under $30,000, we find that with a few exceptions the percentages of the broadcast networks' audiences are higher. As we move up the income scale, the

TABLE 21-4 Cable and Broadcast Audiences by Income

Network	Under $30,000	$30,000–$40,000	$40,000–$50,000	$50,000–$60,000	$60,000+
TBS	57	15	11	8	11
USA	56	15	10	8	11
ESPN	41	16	13	11	19
CNN	45	15	13	8	19
TNT	43	16	13	11	17
Nashville Network	63	17	8	4	8
Discovery	43	18	13	11	15
Nick at Nite	41	19	15	8	17
Lifetime	52	14	13	7	14
Family Channel	64	14	9	5	8
A&E	32	19	13	9	27
MTV	42	19	13	11	15
Headline News	38	14	15	9	24
Black Entertainment TV	54	14	13	8	11
Weather Channel	37	22	13	9	19
VH-1	34	17	18	12	19
NBC	53.7	14.6	11.3	7.8	12.6
ABC	46.9	15.6	13.0	8.5	15.8
CBS	52.7	15.2	11.3	7.8	13.0

NOTE: Income levels for prime-time viewing numbers indicate percentages of the viewing audience.

broadcast percentages fall off and the cable percentages are generally higher. There are exceptions—most notably TNN, the Family Channel, BET, WTBS, and USA—but the trend is significant. Cable channels with 40 percent or more of their household audiences made up of families with an income over $40,000 include CNN, CNN Headline News, ESPN, VH-1, and A&E. There are no broadcast networks in this group.[12]

Increased Advertising Rates and Revenues

As one would expect, basic cable's quality demographics have translated to increased advertiser interest and increased advertiser dollars for basic cable networks. Double-digit revenue increases were experienced in all the years from 1988 to 1992. This also has increased the value of the local ad spots sold by operators. Adlink/NCA has been charging prime-time rates for CNN for all time periods from 6 a.m. to midnight. The spots have sold out.[13]

Table 21-5 illustrates what has happened to advertising revenues. The 10 companies that advertise the most on basic cable networks increased their expenditures by as much as 689 percent between 1988 and 1989. In the case of major advertisers such as Proctor & Gamble, Annheuser-Busch, General Motors, Sears, and Chrysler, the trend was strongly upward.

TABLE 21-5 Top Advertisers on Cable Networks

Advertiser	Spending, millions
1. Proctor & Gamble	15.4
2. Time Warner	11.4
3. Phillip Morris	7.8
4. General Mills	7.8
5. Annheuser-Busch	6.8
6. Kohlberg Kravis Roberts	5.7
7. Pepsico	5.1
8. AT&T	4.8
9. General Motors	4.6
10. Sears	4.5

SOURCE: *Cable World,* Feb. 18, 1991, p. 10

Perceived Value of Cable Networks

Since subscriber bases are critical to ad sales for networks and since consumer interest in networks is important to operators who must select channels for carriage, how persons perceive cable networks is important. Two recent studies have cast some light on this subject.

In a study completed by Beta Research and reported in *Cable World,* the Discovery Channel was given the highest marks by respondents. Nonsubscribers to cable were provided with brief descriptions of cable services and then were asked to rate them on their potential interest and perceived value. They were also asked to assess how likely they would be to subscribe to each of the services listed.

As shown in Table 21-6, the top services in *perceived* value were the Discovery Channel, ESPN, AMC, CNN, and the Family Channel. The ratings according to *interest* were similar, with the top five being the Discovery Channel, CNN, ESPN, AMC, and the Family Channel. Most services' perceived values ran parallel to their interest values, but there were some disparities. The Weather Channel was rated much higher on interest than on value, as was the Nashville Network.[14]

Generally speaking, these results can be interpreted as supporting rising cable service prices and consumers' willingness to pay for the channels received. However, a study commissioned by the Cable Television Administration and Marketing Society (CTAM) showed consumer restlessness over cable costs. Looking at cable subscribers as well as nonsubscribers, the study found that consumers' perceptions of the value of cable subscription had not kept pace with the rate of price increases.[15]

Cable's Increased Acceptance and Credibility

While the perceived value of cable may wax and wane with economic conditions, basic cable has made strides in convincing consumers that it is a viable source of television. Increasing ratings for cable services are part of that equation and have

TABLE 21-6 Perceived Value of Cable Networks

Network	Perceived Value, $ per month	Network	Percentage with High Interest
Discovery	2.80	Discovery	43
ESPN	2.37	CNN	35
AMC	2.25	ESPN	35
CNN	2.25	AMC	33
Family Channel	2.14	Family Channel	32
TBS	2.03	TBS	32
A&E	1.91	Comedy Central	27
Nickelodeon	1.89	A&E	25
Comedy Central	1.85	TNT	25
TNT	1.74	Nickelodeon	25
Learning Channel	1.66	MTV	23
MTV	1.66	SportsChannel America	23
Sci-Fi Channel	1.57	TNN	21
USA Network	1.54	Nick at Nite	21
SportsChannel America	1.47	WGN	21
Nick at Nite	1.43	Weather Channel	21
WGN	1.39	Learning Channel	21
Travel Channel	1.32	Sci-Fi Channel	20
Nostalgia Channel	1.32	Headline News	19
TNN	1.28	USA Network	19
Lifetime	1.28	Nostalgia	18
Headline News	1.24	WWOR	18
WWOR	1.21	Travel Channel	16
VH-1	1.21	VH-1	15
E!	1.19	Lifetime	15
Weather Channel	1.15	E!	14
C-SPAN	0.77	C-SPAN	8
Home Shopping	0.74	Home Shopping	6

SOURCE: *Cable World,* May 14, 1990.

come about as a result of cable's continuing efforts to upgrade content quality.

ESPN took a calculated risk by spending large sums to acquire National Football League games. The move required operators to accept rate increases to cover the network's costs, but it made ESPN a much more serious player in the sports telecasting game. By carrying the country's most popular sport at the college and professional levels, ESPN was signaling a commitment to bring cable viewers the best. It was also giving football aficionados a reason to subscribe to cable in order to get an additional pro game every week. Following on the heels of this ex-

periment was the acquisition of major league baseball by ESPN. Although not successful in terms of ad revenues, the contract for big league baseball solidly entrenched ESPN as a major force in the sports world.[16]

TNT also made an entrance into big-time sports with contracts for NBA basketball and professional football. As with ESPN, the benefits were tied more to reputation than to financial gain.

The image of cable has also been helped immeasurably by CNN, especially by that network's coverage of the Persian Gulf war. During the war CNN came to be a dominant force in war reporting partly because during the opening moments of the air war the telephone connections of the broadcast network news operations were lost. CNN was buoyed by an early jump in war reporting and garnered a 20.7 rating in cable households during the first hours of the air war, compared to ABC's 17.2, NBC's 15.2, and CBS' 12.6.[17] Writing about the comparison between CNN's reporting of the war and that of the broadcast networks, *Broadcasting* editorialized that "ABC, CBS, and NBC beat the competition hands down, graphicswise. At least some of the time, CNN beat the competition hands down newswise. It tells you something."[18]

An indication of CNN's prestige and news power was provided by the fact that 26 network affiliates in markets such as San Francisco, Minneapolis, Detroit, and Dallas made substantial use of CNN feeds, often ignoring their own networks' feeds to do so.[19] Said one affiliate news director when asked about this practice, "My loyalty is first to the viewer and second to the network."[20] While these stations and others in markets such as New York, Los Angeles, and Atlanta had the right to take CNN feeds on any breaking story, an unknown number of other stations pirated the CNN signal, especially in the early days of the war.[21]

Because of its general news quality and especially its war performance, operators came to see CNN as a force in subscriber gains. They saw it as reinforcing the value of cable in the eyes of the public and the politicians.[22]

Hollywood produces for cable Another measure of cable's rising fortunes has been the creative community's willingness to develop original programming for cable. While broadcast networks have been cutting back on costly pilot development, cable has shown an increased interest in the production of original product.[23] Writers, producers, and directors who have been hurt by network cutbacks have found an outlet in cable. Thus, the development of movies, comedies, and action and drama shows for cable is at an all-time high.[24]

One indicator of cable's commitment to new programming is the rise of programming budgets at basic cable networks. Spending for programming by basic networks was twice as high in 1990 as it was in 1987 and more than three times as high as in 1984. In dollars, that amounted to an increase of $456 million from 1989 to 1990.[25]

One content area of particular concentration is movies. TNT has moved from one original movie a month to one a week. Successful films such as *Cold Sassy Tree* have found their way to subsequent theatrical runs and the video sales and rental market. The Family Channel has produced *Mother's Day* with Malcolm Jamal-Warner and is currently producing one new film a month. USA's *The Forgotten* got a 3.8 rating, and *The Haunting of Sarah Hardy* received a 4.9. Those results have helped solidify USA's resolve to develop original films.[26]

Cable's entry into the syndication market has become more aggressive as revenues have grown to support the acquisition of better programs. Cable's increasing fortunes in advertising, per-subscriber fees to networks, and subscriber fees to operators have moved cable from acquiring older programs to making deals for the likes of *L.A. Law, MacGyver, Miami Vice,* and *Murder She Wrote.* The success of these programs has fed the economic engine of cable, making future high-profile acquisitions possible.[27]

FUTURE DIRECTIONS

Further specialization seems to be the name of the game in cable. The most recent services have been testimonies to fragmentation. The Science Fiction Channel, for example, appeals to a reasonably narrow group of viewers. Perhaps even more specialized are the Cowboy Channel and the Cartoon Channel.

A recently developed channel, the Chicago Channel, is a case in point. Backed by TCI and Fox Broadcasting, the Chicago Channel is the ultimate in specialization. It features Chicago-focused newscast, interview, sports, and specialty programs. What may be even more interesting is that there are two such channels: A second channel, backed by Tribune Broadcasting, is also available in the Chicago area.

With increased interest in fragmented services, the move toward specialization may be the wave of the future. As magazines and radio stations moved from general-interest content to more highly specialized fare, television is going through the evolutionary path followed by all the mass media throughout history. The charge is being led by basic cable.

SUMMARY

Basic cable offers a cornucopia of content choices, ranging from education and information to music and comedy. Like the broadcast networks and stations which preceded cable, basic cable networks program according to time-honored practices. Programs are created in 30- and 60-minute blocks and scheduled on the hour and half hour. Great care is taken with prime-time schedules to attract the large audiences available during that period.

Revenues for some basic cable networks come from advertising. Some networks are offered free to operators, and money is made from advertisements, donations, and direct purchases from the service. However, most follow the pattern of charging operators fees each month for each subscriber and then carrying commercials to supplement the revenue stream.

Basic cable's prospects are very good at this time. Viewership is up, and thus revenues are up as well. With the increase of subscriber and advertising dollars, basic networks have begun to purchase more desirable programming in the syndication market. This has led to greater success with viewers and increased revenues. In addition to becoming bigger players in syndication, basic cable networks have begun to commission more original programming. This allows cable networks to offer unique programming and maintain the repeat and subsequent distribution control that comes with product ownership.

The quality of the cable audience has brought increased interest from advertisers. While cable audiences are small by broadcast standards, they are made up of the viewers advertisers wish most to reach. The increased appreciation of cable audiences by advertisers has led to greater commitments from major advertisers to basic cable.

This growth in audience size, advertising interest, and original and upgraded programming has helped give cable a better image. Basic cable has more acceptance and credibility than it did in the past. Some is due to prestige content such as professional sports; some is due to high-quality efforts such as that made by CNN during the Persian Gulf war. In any event, cable's image has improved as much as its fortunes.

SUGGESTED READINGS

Multi-Channel News
This trade publication is one of the best sources of information about cable programming. Each week, the cable industry is examined in detail and programming issues are treated in depth. Its articles highlight trends in programming and examine specific programs in terms of everything from management to economics. It deals with important questions of policy not often found in publications designed for more general purposes.

Broadcasting
Long the primary trade magazine, this publication has expanded its agenda to include cable and newer technologies. While newer to covering cable than more specialized cable publications, the old flagship of the broadcast industry has done an excellent job. Each week there is substantial coverage of cable issues, including programming, economics, and regulation. As with any trade publication, it tries to stay on top of breaking stories, such as when the Science-Fiction Channel was being developed, sold, and launched. Thus, information about new basic services is plentiful and accurate.

Electronic Media

Like *Broadcasting, Electronic Media* has expanded its coverage to include cable. The magazine always covered the major cable issues in its earlier years, but the growth of cable's size and importance was accompanied by a change in coverage. Stories became more frequent and detailed. Today some of the best and most readable stories about basic cable programming are carried here.

Dominick, Joseph R., Barry Sherman, and Gary Copeland: *Broadcasting, Cable and Beyond,* McGraw-Hill, New York, 1992.

While not designed as a cable book, this text does a good job of covering basic cable issues succinctly. It provides a good starting point for students who want to understand the basic issues of cable's development, growth, and future prospects.

Heeter, Carrie, and Bradley Greenberg: *Cableviewing,* Ablex, Norwood, N.J., 1988.

This is a wonderful companion book for serious students of cable. Heeter and Greenberg are researchers who are more interested in the audience for cable and its viewing habits than with cable as an industry. However, their sophisticated examination of the audience is unparalleled and supplies a different perspective from which to view the cable industry. This is perhaps *the* book for more advanced students of cable.

NOTES

1. "Cable Networks Post Strong 1990 Results," *Broadcasting,* Feb. 25, 1991, p. 21.

2. "The Cable Network Programming Universe," *Broadcasting,* Jan. 7, 1991, p. 94.

3. Thomas F. Baldwin and F. Stevens McVoy, *Cable Communication,* 2d ed., Prentice-Hall, Englewood Cliffs, N.J., 1988.

4. Risa W. King and Richard A. Melcher, "ESPN Is Playing in an International Arena Now," *Business Week,* Aug. 14, 1989, p. 71.

5. "Monitoring 'Monitor,'" *Broadcasting,* Dec. 30, 1990, p. 64.

6. Al Stewart, "Comedy Truce Raises Questions," *Cable World,* Jan. 7, 1991, p. 3.

7. "Sci-Fi Channel Gathers Subscribers for Launch," *Broadcasting,* Feb. 25, 1991, p. 40.

8. Richard Tedesco, "Courtroom TV Pleads Its Case," *Cablevision,* Feb. 11, 1991, p. 12.

9. Kevin Goldman, "Cable TV's Ratings and Ad Revenues Grow," *Wall Street Journal,* Nov. 5, 1990, p. 21.

10. Ibid.

11. Ibid.

12. "Reaction Mixed to New Nielsen Report," *Broadcasting,* June 18, 1990, pp. 52–53.

13. "Operators Resist CNN Surcharge," *Cable World,* Feb. 4, 1991, p. 7.

14. Peggy Ziegler, "Discovery Wins in Survey," *Cable World,* May 14, 1990, p. 34.

15. "Cable Rates Rising Faster Than Perceived Value," *Broadcasting,* Jan. 14, 1991, pp. 108–109.

16. John Steinbreder "ESPN's Baseball Ratings Blues," *Sports Illustrated,* Aug. 20, 1990, p. 63.

17. "Television's War, and CNN's," *Broadcasting,* Jan. 21, 1991, pp. 23–26.

18. "Editorials: The Old Order Changeth," *Broadcasting,* Jan. 21, 1991, p. 90.

19. "Affiliates Weigh Networks, CNN War Coverage," *Broadcasting,* Jan. 29, 1991, p. 57.

20. Ron Bilek, WXIA TV Atlanta, quoted in ibid.

21. "Operators Resist CNN Surcharge," *Cable World,* Feb. 4, 1991, p. 7.

22. "CNN's MSO Contribution No Sure Thing," *Broadcasting,* Feb. 11, 1991, p. 31.

23. "Broadcast Networks' Loss Is Cable's Gain," *Broadcasting,* Feb. 4, 1991, p. 31.

24. Ibid.

25. "Marketing New Media," *Cable World,* Feb. 18, 1991, p. S7.

26. "Made for Cable: Reaching for Stars and Viewers," *Broadcasting,* Aug. 14, 1989, pp. 51–52.

27. Mark Ivey and Ronald Grover, "Suddenly Basic Cable Is Offering More Than Basic Fare," *Business Week,* March 7, 1988, p. 36.

CHAPTER 22

Premium Cable Networks

Premium service subscribers pay an additional fee for extra channels. The most prominent premium services are Home Box Office, Showtime, Cinemax, the Movie Channel, Encore, and the Disney Channel. While their growth has slowed, these services are still viewed by many people. For example, in 1990 Impact Resources found that the percentages of adults watching the premium channels were substantial. The results were HBO, 17 percent; Showtime, 9 percent; Cinemax, 8 percent; the Movie Channel, 7 percent; and Disney, 5 percent.[1]

There are problems with premium services, though. These services have lost two competitive advantages that they held in the past. First, they used to be the only way for viewers to see unedited movies outside a theater. Not only did the advent of video stores nullify that advantage, the video stores could offer adult films that premium services could not air. Second, premium services became less of a bargain for movie viewers as basic cable prices rose dramatically in the late 1980s. When basic service could be acquired inexpensively, the additional outlay for a premium channel did not push the bill up very high. However, when rates climbed for basic cable, which functions as premium cable's entry point, the total bill went into the range of $25 a month for basic and one premium channel. Suddenly the package did not look so inexpensive, and one way for cost-cutting consumers to lower the bill was to bail out of premium services and rent movies on a title-specific basis.[2]

Pay-per-view may revolutionize all current theories of pay television. Before PPV, subscriptions to premium services were maintained on a month-to-month basis, with the subscriber choosing what to watch from the service offerings as the month rolled along. By paying the monthly bill, the consumer was in effect ordering another month's worth of what the service had to offer. PPV is based on a very different procedural and attitudinal foundation. In PPV the consumer elects to watch one event, which can be a movie, concert, sporting event, or special. In exchange for that experience, the consumer pays an established fee.

No monthly cornucopia of offerings here, just pay as you go.

PPV has come along at the right time for the cable industry. Increasing competition from video store chains has given consumers more choices. Price-focused video services are also offered as ancillary segments of stores that specialize in selling other products. Some drug stores, for example, offer 2-night rentals of videos and video games for as little as 69 cents each, three for $1.50.

The pressure this places on HBO, Showtime, and the rest is considerable. Fighting back for survival and growth is an ongoing concern for premium services. Occupied as they are with maintaining their place in cable, they no longer are the core draw for new subscribers. The development of myriad basic services (Chapter 21) has made basic a draw for more new subscribers. Still, the premium services represent an area of great importance and profit for operators, and the health of premium is of concern to the industry. About half of premium revenues stay with operators: If an operator charges $12 for HBO, he or she is keeping $6 a month. That is a strong incentive for paying attention to premium television's pulse.

Another facet of premium television in all its forms is the development of new technologies for delivery. In the old days of satellite delivery, each satellite had about 24 transponders, or channels. One signal was sent to each, and each sent one signal back to the Earth. **Video compression**—the process of packing signals so that transponders can each handle from 4 to 10 signals—changed all that. At a 4:1 compression ratio, a 24-transponder satellite can handle 96 channels of programming.

This has made possible the delivery of an almost unlimited number of channels to households. The 200-channel environment is here and will no doubt lead to increased fragmentation on the basic cable side. On the pay side other possibilities exist. A 1991 test in New York City included 40 different PPV channels. The test was performed to determine which forms of PPV work best, how PPV can be marketed most effectively, and how events can be scheduled for the maximum convenience of consumers. With video compression and 200 channels, using 40 channels for one branch of cable service presents no problem.

This chapter will examine the premium (pay) television environment. First we will look at PPV and what it means to the cable industry. As with any other television product, there are important programming questions that need answering. Issues such as addressability and content will be discussed as well.

Then we will look into the fortunes of the six mainstream premium services: HBO, Showtime, Cinemax, the Movie Channel, Encore, and the Disney Channel. Other services, such as Spice and the Playboy Channel, will also be discussed.

Finally, we will delve into the strategies of programming a premium channel. While not as beholden to ratings as advertiser-supported television is, pay TV still borrows many of its strategies from tried and true sources. It also adds enough of its own wrinkles to keep us interested.

PAY-PER-VIEW

Video Compression and PPV

Technology leaders such as General Instrument, Scientific Atlanta, and the cable industry–supported Cable Labs have been working to develop compression technology. As compression will make possible the delivery of hundreds of channels to subscribers, much is at stake. The development of multitudes of PPV and niche channels seems certain.[3]

One possibility that arises from multiple PPV channels is increased cable competition with video stores. When hit movies are played every 15 minutes, easy access to the most popular renters will be established. Other, less current movies may be scheduled with less frequency on additional channels. This will effectively move the video store inside the consumer's home. The big difference is that there will al-

ways be a copy of the desired movie available, and trips to the video store to search for and return films will be eliminated.[4]

PPV Content

PPV has in its brief history offered two kinds of programming: events and movies. Events have included concerts, boxing matches, and wrestling extravaganzas in the main. There is much disagreement about which kind of content works best on PPV. The consistent measure used to determine success is the **buy rate,** or the percentage of available consumers who elect to buy an event or movie. Typical buy rates run from less than 1 (percent) to as high as 14.

Many people see event programming as the mainstay of PPV. The logic in this approach is that event prices are consistently higher. A boxing match of great interest, such as the Holyfield-Forman match in the spring of 1991, can command $35 per home. The typical movie goes for $3.95, with a high of $4.95 and occasional specials as low as 99 cents.

There is research evidence for this point of view. Paul Kagan Research looked into PPV gross revenues for 1990 and found some startling results. During that calendar year boxing and wrestling events accounted for 89 percent of PPV gross revenues nationally. Of the cumulative gross of $136.5 million, wrestling accounted for $72.5 million and boxing brought in $48.6 million. Live concerts took in $11 million, and movies and entertainment specials contributed $4.4 million. While movies and entertainment contributed about 3 percent of PPV's revenues, they constituted 38 percent of the programming.[5]

Wrestling's big events have centered on a series of *Wrestlemanias* which include many of the sport's biggest stars and much pageantry. The last three have earned from $23 million to $27 million each.[6]

In an effort to determine just what the PPV market would bear, TitanSports, the producer of World Wrestling Federation events, undertook a study of pricing for a 1990 event. The spectacular was offered at $19.95 in 10 markets, $29.95 in 10 others, and $24.95 in the rest of the country. The buy rate was 5.7 percent in the $19.95 markets, 5.7 percent in the $24.95 markets, and 5.2 percent in the $29.95 markets. While the buy rate was a bit lower in the $29.95 markets, the extra revenue from the higher price more than outweighed the lower level of participation. Thus, TitanSports was convinced that higher prices would not have a negative effect on distribution.[7]

On the flip side of the coin, Warner Pay TV initiated a study showing that movies are viable PPV content. Looking at buy rates rather than gross dollars raised, the Warner study listed the most successful events in PPV from August 1987 to June 1990 (Table 22-1). In this study 6 of the top 10 events, including 5 of the top 6, were movies.[8] That is heartening for the PPV movie industry. However, it is important to remember that buy rates are not much of an indicator of income, as movies are priced at a fraction of event prices.

To see what the relationship between price and buy rate was for movies, 29 cable systems participated in a 1990 pricing experiment for the film *Look Who's Talking*. Instead of the usual price, the film was offered at $1.99. The average buy rate was above 13 on some systems and the

TABLE 22-1 Movie and Event Buy Rates for PPV

Movie/Event	Buy Rate, %
Spinks-Tyson boxing	12.7
Witches of Eastwick	9.7
Lethal Weapon	9.5
Color Purple	9.1
Beetlejuice	8.9
Full Metal Jacket	8.4
Wrestlemania IV	7.3
Lethal Weapon 2	6.6
Wrestlemania V	6.2
Leonard-Hearns 2 boxing	6.0

SOURCE: Paul Sweeting, "Warner Study Says That PPV Movie Market Is Viable," *Billboard*, Sept. 29, 1990, p. 49.

experiment was labeled a tentative success,[9] but a problem remained. Since prices had been slashed more than 50 percent, the movie would have had to achieve a buy rate more than 100 percent above average to achieve the financial results of a higher price and a lower buy rate. Allowing for the disparities in buy rate and price, the figures were about even in the final analysis.

Discounting has also been used to increase interest in and use of PPV in dayparts where PPV performance has been especially weak. One MSO offered movies at $2.99, a dollar below the usual price, for all movies shown before 5 p.m. United Artists Cable of Baton Rouge charged only $1.01 for movies on Mondays. For Tuesday viewers the system gave out coupons for a hamburger chain.

These circumstances fueled a central question in PPV film pricing: Should the price be kept down to be competitive? Lower prices offer the immediate benefit of higher participation and awareness for the PPV industry. At the same time, discounting gets users accustomed to lower prices, and they may balk at a return to "normal" prices later. In any event, price may indeed be central to PPV.[10]

Boxing is still king as far as revenues per event are concerned. The revenue from one boxing match is equal to 3 or 4 months of movie revenues.[11]

Don King, the boxing promoter, developed a deal with Showtime's PPV arm, Showtime Event Television (SET), and made the point that a 1 percent buy rate for monthly bouts would produce a profit. He also noted that an extremely small buy rate of 0.2 percent for a boxing match would generate the same revenue as a movie with an average buy rate of 5 percent or more. That, coupled with wrestling's success, opens the issue of other sports on PPV.

The National Hockey League, National Football League, National Basketball Association, and major league baseball are all experimenting with PPV or looking into the possibilities. Given the revenue potentials and rising costs for salaries and franchises, PPV seems like the solution to a building problem.[12]

The potential drawback of PPV sports is damage to the home attendance at regular season games. This could be controlled by showing only away games, but sellouts at home offer another opportunity. If home games were sold out, they could be shown on PPV as they are now shown on free television under the same circumstances. That way, PPV would not interfere with the attendance revenue and would add a substantial second stream.

There is an another revenue idea for PPV. Large numbers of displaced fans grew up in one city and rooted for its teams but now live in other cities. If they could be given access to their favorite teams via PPV, goes the argument, they might very well be willing to pay. One problem is that local attendance might suffer and that saturation of a market with additional games might lower overall attendance. If there is a game in the local stadium and another on network television, would a third game on PPV water down the effectiveness of the first two?

A partial answer to this problem lies in choosing packages from widely different time zones. For example, a package of basketball games featuring the Los Angeles Lakers could be offered in the Eastern time zone (New York, Boston, Baltimore/Washington, Atlanta, and other major metropolitan centers) without any disruption of the local game, which would be over before the West Coast game started. The same strategy would work in baseball for the Oakland Athletics and Los Angeles Dodgers. Since both of those teams moved west (from New York and Kansas City/Philadelphia) and still enjoy a following back east, they might be naturals for PPV packages in the east. Similarly, the football Los Angeles Raiders and San Francisco 49ers might sell well in the east. The hockey Los Angeles Kings, popular because of their star player, Wayne Gretzky, might earn substantial PPV revenues in the east.

The coastal strategy works both ways. Eastern teams in all sports could be beamed west, with the games showing up 3 clock hours earlier. That might mean watching football at 10 a.m. or night baseball at 5 p.m., but these tendencies have already been established through broadcast television.

The biggest fears that these possibilities engender are political ones. Fans have been receiving games on free television for decades, and politicians fear that PPV will force people to pay stiff prices for what was always free. Several politicians, including Maryland Representative Tom McMillan and New Jersey Senator Bill Bradley (both are former professional basketball stars), have readied legislation to prevent the **migration** of sporting events from free television to cable or PPV. Their thinking is that one of the nation's most enjoyed pastimes might be removed from the hands of the most ardent fans. Of course, with cable penetration not expected to exceed 70 percent, cable carriage automatically excludes at least 30 percent of homes. This process is also called **siphoning;** that is, cable siphons sports events away from free television because of its ability to pay higher fees to the owners of teams.

PPV has also penetrated the Olympics. For the Olympic Summer Games of 1992 in Barcelona, Spain, NBC created a PPV apparatus so that some or all events could be delivered to consumers via PPV. Because there were three levels of purchase, it was called the Triplecast. The limitations of time make it impossible for any single channel to carry all events. In fact, in the normally covered events, emphasis is usually placed on individuals who are favored to win medals. If several PPV channels were available, people could watch the events they like best in great depth.

The concept has worked better than the practice. NBC had problems gaining clearances from high-profile cable channels to carry the games. One idea was to use existing networks with consumer bases in excess of 50 million households. The Discovery Channel was mentioned as a possibility. The problem for NBC was that channels that were approached with the plan expressed concern that this might do irreparable harm to their image with audiences. If they changed format suddenly and for an extended period, viewers might become confused or lose the habit of watching. Similar concerns were expressed by smaller networks. The large PPV services Request TV and Select TV were also approached and had the same reservations. NBC also looked into the possibility of using Showtime as a base for the operation, but this did not go beyond the discussion phase.[13] Another option was government, educational, and public access channels. The network's ace in the hole was CNBC, which could be used as an Olympic channel and whose large subscriber base made it an attractive candidate.

In the end the Triplecast went the traditional PPV route despite some concern that not enough homes had the technology in place for such an event. MSOs and local cable operators used various versions of PPV to deliver the events. While it proved technologically bumpy to get the Triplecast up and running and despite a $30 million loss, a precedent was set that no doubt will be followed in future Olympics.

The concept of a PPV Olympics is appealing. CBS entered into an agreement with TNT which placed a major portion of the 1992 Olympic Winter Games on cable. The potential here is for a major sporting event to find its way to cable and generate event revenues from persons who formerly watched such events free of charge. Thus, the migration of bigger events, even the Super Bowl or World Series, cannot be ruled out in the future.

Another area of PPV content is adult fare. The Playboy Channel is offered on both a monthly and a nightly basis. It is carried by fewer than 600 systems despite its economic success. A second adult service called Spice gets into under 4 million homes. The MSO KBLCOM represents an example of the relative success of adult pay television. One adult PPV option was offered on only part of one channel, and mainstream movies filled three full PPV channels. Despite the disparity in product quantity, the adult content earned more than two-thirds of the revenues earned by the mainstream movies.

Adult content suffers from legal and community problems that do not plague mainstream PPV movies. An indictment brought against the defunct Tuxxedo PPV operation in 1990 for violating Alabama's obscenity statutes was credited with putting it out of business as other systems began to avoid that channel.[14] The Cox-owned cable systems dropped Playboy and Spice in 1991 without substantial consumer protests. Observers attributed this to moral objections by the family ownership rather than business disappointments.

PPV Programming Strategies

Ed Bleier, president of domestic pay television at Warner Brothers, boiled the primary issue of PPV down into one sentence when he said that consumers "want to watch a movie when they want to watch."[15] While simple on its face, delivering movies to consumers via PPV when they want them can be a problem. For example, let's say *Home Alone II* is a hot movie and consumers want to see it. If it is scheduled for 8 p.m. on Saturday and has a running time of 100 minutes, it won't be shown again until 10 p.m. Many people might prefer it at 8:30 or 9 p.m., and some might prefer 9:30. Because of the limitations of time, the movie cannot be offered with maximum effectiveness to viewers. What about other hit movies? When can they be played if *Home Alone II* is filling the channel?

The answer is multiple channels allocated to PPV. If we have four movies that are concurrent blockbuster hits and want to get them into consumers' homes on a convenient schedule, we could use four channels for each film. On channel 20 *Home Alone II* would open at 8 p.m. It would also start at 8:30 on channel 21, 9 on channel 22, and 9:30 on channel 23. A second highly popular movie might be shown on the same schedule on channels 24 through 27, a third on channels 28 through 31, and a fourth on channels 32 through 35. Since there are rarely more than four huge hits at any one time, we could offer them on a continuous basis, serving the wants and convenience of viewers.

This is a variation of a system that was used in hotels for years. Each channel carried one film continuously, and with 6 to 10 channels several options could be offered. Very popular movies were shown on two channels to allow hourly starting times. However, this plan has two flaws: (1) Where is the cable operator going to find so many channels to allocate to PPV? (2) How will viewers remember what is being offered on which channel and when?

The answer to the first problem is video compression. A 36-channel system which is full will expand to 144 channels with 4:1 compression. At a 10:1 compression ratio it will become a 360-channel system. Hence, compression has made channel space a nonissue.

The answer to the confusion problem is a **barker channel** which continuously shows the schedules for all PPV channels. If the clutter of available movies and channels is great, two barker channels could be used. The barkers would run movie clips, announce channels and starting times, and carry the prices for movies. With an ongoing source of information, any viewer could browse through this "on-line video store" to see what would strike his or her fancy.

An experiment in multichannel PPV was carried out in the Warner Cable system in Brooklyn and Queens, New York, where 40 channels were allocated to PPV. With the most popular four movies starting every 30 minutes, 16 channels were used for top films. Second-level but still popular films were given one channel each. Typically each movie started every 2 hours, with the even hours used one day and the odd hours used the next. Other channels carried a variety of films with many channels specialized by content type. One channel might carry all science-fiction movies, another comedies, and another classic films. The experiment was designed to see which films worked best, how viewers responded to barker channels, and how specifically channels could be programmed.

Generally speaking, what works best is continuous "tune-in anytime" scheduling of the hottest films, multiple PPV channels, and barker channels. Another finding was that **cross-promotion**—the promoting of one film on another film's channel—worked well. Before airing an action film, it might be wise to preview other action films and mention their channels and schedules. Or films could be promoted to demographic groups rather than by genres. In any event, such cross-promotion has proved useful in stimulating PPV buys.[16]

PPV Networks

Pay-per-view promises to be a serious competitor to the video store for film viewers and to closed-circuit television for special-event audiences. When converters that permit cable operators to identify which households are watching events such as feature movies and boxing matches are used, customers can be billed. When such **addressable** converters are more widely used, PPV audiences will expand since impulse viewing will increase. When last-minute plans change, it will be possible to order a first-rate recent film for the evening's viewing.

Several companies are already delivering films and special events. The Cable Video Store charges viewers for older hit films on a sliding price scale, depending on the title. Taking advantage of impulse-ordering technology that allows last-minute orders to be placed directly from the home, the Jerrold Electronics Corporation has gotten an increased response from consumers. The Cable Video Store service constitutes a good test market for Jerrold's technological advances as the primary producer of addressable technology. While the service is not yet in the business of new releases and special large-scale events, as the technology that its parent company produces moves toward perfection, it is likely to become a more active player.

Request Television is the largest of the PPV providers. It provides two channels with continuous service to cable operators at no charge. The operator shares revenues with Request TV when subscribers take the service's offerings. Its strong lineup of recent films and special events makes its schedule especially attractive to operators.

Viewer's Choice supplies similar programming at similar costs to subscribers. Recent movies and special events make up the programming.

Playboy on Demand has replaced the Playboy Channel. This service allows viewers to select specific programs rather than pay a monthly fee. As with most PPV suppliers, Playboy on Demand shares revenues with cable operators.

As with basic services, there are many regional and even local PPV systems in various markets. To achieve economy of scale, these systems tend to be located in major metropolitan areas. As the technology improves, the growth of national, regional, and local PPV is almost a given.

PROGRAMMING THE PREMIUM CABLE SERVICE

Premium cable might have hit its zenith in the mid-1980s, when the cable industry approached the height of its growth and the attractiveness and timeliness of premium channels were maximized. Unedited versions of major movies appeared on cable networks within months of their theatrical release because premium-cable debuts followed closely behind theatrical release as the second viewing "window" for movies.

The rise of the local video store has spelled trouble for HBO, Showtime, and the rest. Now the second release window for feature films is videocassette sales and rental. A subscription charge of $12 a month for a premium-movie channel is about equal to the cost of four to six film rentals at a video store. Since there are about that number of major releases on videocassette in any given month, the home viewer may be tempted to cancel the cable movie service. Those movies are available on videocas-

sette several months earlier than on premium channels, and increasingly, their availability on rental cassette is promoted through television advertising. Thus, they are not as "fresh" by the time they appear on the premium-cable service. As VCRs proliferate and the selection of newer and classic films available at video stores increases, viewers will be able to program their own televisions more easily.

The premium services have responded with some strategies of their own. A common strategy before the era of video rental was **front loading,** in which the best films were all introduced during the first 10 days of the month. That kicked off each month with a bang and got people's attention. The disadvantage was that the rest of the month consisted of reruns. The end of the month was the time when bored subscribers would consider canceling the premium service. It was also when the bill came. However, the beginning of the month was just around the corner, and the excitement of new releases tended to keep subscribers connected.

Increased VCR penetration has added to the end-of-month doldrums. With the concurrent rise of video rentals, families began to fill the end-of-month void with rentals. It was only a matter of time before subscribers would ask, Why keep this premium service at all? Now film premieres on the premium services are spread out during the month in the hopes of keeping people interested in new releases each week. At the end of the month they may be less likely to evaluate their subscriptions negatively.

One service, the Movie Channel, has promoted a "VCR Theatre" in which subscribers are invited to tape films from the television. At 3 a.m. each morning, one of the new releases is scheduled. Subscribers not only can timeshift their viewing (recording programs on the VCR to be played back at a convenient time) but also can archive their favorite movies for repeat viewing.

Premium services schedule their blockbuster movie debuts on the hour in prime time in order to attract the largest possible audiences. HBO and Showtime not only schedule against each other but to some degree complement each other. Since many subscribers take both services, there is minimal duplication of programming on any given evening. Programmers have asserted that program duplication is held to 25 percent during any particular month.

Important considerations in programming a premium-movie service include promotion, demographic servicing, exposure through all dayparts, and placement of adult content.

Promotion

Premier movies have lost some of their luster since the videocassette exposure window moved ahead of the premium cable window. Even so, a premium service must ballyhoo its freshest product and attract people to it.

The running times of feature films vary, but premium networks, like other television services, start programs on the hour when possible. Since movies do not conform to 90-minute or 120-minute running times, reasonably large blocks of time are therefore available in which the premium service can aggressively sell subscribers on the benefits of the service and promote the films being programmed. Film **trailers**—clips like those played in theaters—are utilized along with prepared announcements that make each film sound exciting. Such promotion is useful for reaching subscribers, but advertising is needed to bring new people to the service.

Ads for premium services generally run on network and local television. Some print and radio spots are purchased, but it is most logical to advertise a television service on television, since that is where the primary television viewer can be found. Premium service spots emphasize excitement and glitz to attract new subscribers.

Premier films receive the bulk of the advertising emphasis as a premium service tries to lure new viewers. With VCRs as competitors, the premium services cannot put much emphasis on any given film but instead promote the availabili-

ty of many movies at one low price. While only four or five films may be mentioned by name, the number of films to be shown during the month may get some mention as well. Since viewers can quickly multiply that number by the typical $2 or $3 movie rental fee, they can see a 30-film month equaling $60 or $90 in rentals. Since they can subscribe to the premium service for $12, it looks like a bargain and a convenience, since they do not have to trek to the video store.

Premium services have been making agreements for the exclusive rights to films and even for the rights to all the product of some distribution houses. In these arrangements, the premium service makes a deal with the distributor that cuts out the other premium services, usually for 30 or 60 days. That creates an opportunity to promote exclusive premieres with a phrase like "You won't see [film title] on [competing service] this month!"

Film Content and Demographics

In the late 1940s, before television made its mark, movies attracted a wide range of patrons. In that era about 90 million theater tickets were sold each week. In 1991 the figure was about 26 million a week, a much narrower audience.

Since 70 percent of movie tickets are purchased by persons under age 30, feature films are directed to that market. As a result, many of the current hits at any given time have a youth skew. Moreover, some movies skew by sex. Although Sylvester Stallone films such as the *Rambo* and *Rocky* series appeal to a broad audience, they nonetheless are skewed mostly toward males.

Since the subscribers to a premium service are an older demographic group than the primary target for theatrical film releases, the premium networks must schedule and promote a product that will appeal to a broader range of interests. A premium service must be ready to flesh out its lineup when such clustering of product appeal occurs in film releases. To some extent, this can be accomplished with plays of popular "classic" films ranging from *Wings* (1929) to more recent classics such as *Dances with Wolves* and *Rainman*. In this way, the product promotion during any given month will not overemphasize teen or action movies.

Daypart Placement

A premium service programmer must be careful to schedule each available major film during each daypart. During premiere week, the programmer must work a film into prime time, late fringe, overnight, morning, and daytime. Some films are not *daytime-playable*, meaning that they have strong language, violence, or sexual situations deemed inappropriate for daytime play.[17] On most services only G, PG, and PG-13 films can be played before 8 p.m. The strategy of playing films in various dayparts accommodates shift workers who arrive home late at night or early in the day. It also allows for mobility. People are away at meetings and social engagements on some evenings when they might otherwise be watching television. A good rule of thumb is to schedule at least two plays in each daypart during the first 2 weeks. If viewers still cannot get to the movie when it is scheduled, they can always record it on the VCR.

Adult Movies

By "adult" movies, we mean R-rated films that contain nudity or sexually explicit language. No X-rated titles are shown on mainstream premium movie services. Premium services usually start adult movies at 9 p.m. or later. Those which have the greatest emphasis on nudity and sexual themes do not run until 11 p.m. or later.

What such films lack in artistic merit, they make up for in popularity. Many adults enjoy these movies and stay up for or record them, and many people who want to watch explicit films may be embarrassed to rent them at the video store. Therefore, these titles are important in the schedule. They just have to be kept out of the view of the young.

THE MAJOR PREMIUM NETWORKS

Home Box Office

The granddaddy of the premium cable movie services is HBO. In 1975 it was the first movie service to go to the satellite for national distribution, and cable operators and subscribers were ready to accept what it had to offer. HBO's lineup still consists mainly of recent theatrical films, but it has been increasing its diversity in many areas.

Original production The premium networks have learned that new, high-quality programming attracts an audience. When coupled with high-visibility films, such programming contributes to a powerful and attractive lineup.

Episodic programming, which once was the sole province of the broadcast networks, has established a firm foothold in pay TV. HBO's *First and Ten* and *The Hitchhiker* were syndicated to broadcast stations in the late 1980s, a sign that these productions were perceived as having audience potential. Series such as *Tales from the Crypt* have been very popular. *Sessions* premiered in 1992.

Made-for-cable movies have proliferated in the last few years. After a shaky start, services such as HBO have sharpened their production and casting skills and have turned out such movies as *Mandela* and *Oppenheimer*. Not the least of the advantages of these movies is that they are entirely new. That makes them attractive as long as they are of acceptable quality. By eliminating the license fees for theatrical releases and providing fresh content with no prior exposure, made-fors have proved successful. They can be played an unlimited number of times and sold into other markets for further distribution (**off-cable** programs).

The premium services, especially HBO, have begun to distinguish themselves by producing original documentary programs. Documentaries such as *Dear America: Letters Home from Vietnam,* a reading of actual letters from servicemen and servicewomen over video footage from the war, and *Suzi's Story,* about an Australian woman who died of AIDS, both won numerous awards for HBO. HBO's documentary production department has been favorably compared by some critics to broadcast networks' documentary departments.[18]

Sports came to HBO in the form of tennis and boxing. It has also shown up in the form of high-quality sports information programs such as *Inside the NFL,* which have earned high marks.

Comedy performances have been successful, especially since they do not have to be censored as they are on broadcast television. Comedians from Stephen Wright to Robin Williams have garnered sizable audiences for these services. HBO's irreverent *Not Necessarily the News* has proved popular with its sometimes caustic parodies of news stories.

HBO has looked to expand its horizons and spread its brand name worldwide through HBO Olé, a Spanish-language service designed for Central and South America. In a partnership with the Venezuelan firm Omnivision, HBO delivers movies, sports, and special programming to cable and SMATV systems in Latin America. By adding Portuguese-language programming to its system, HBO Olé has been able to penetrate the large Portuguese-speaking country of Brazil. Approximately 10 percent of the programming carried is produced in South America.[19]

Another way of expanding HBO's reach might be for it to become partly owned by a foreign company. In addition to the infusion of capital, a European owner could help HBO become a large player in the European Community. While that has not been done at this writing, HBO chairman Michael Fuchs has discussed the possibility of partial foreign ownership.[20]

HBO's programming strategies One of HBO's most daring strategies has been **multiplexing,** the practice of feeding its programming on three channels simultaneously. As with PPV, multiplexing depends on video compression to make the requisite channel space available. For the consumer, multiplexing means increased convenience. For the person with a busy schedule and the desire to see a particular movie or event, multiplexing means that it will be shown more often in each daypart. Since two-thirds of VCR owners cannot adequately program their machines for timeshifting, multiplexing improves access to the program.[21]

Multiplexing also allows HBO to offer a demographic mix at any given time. The first channel may run a youth-oriented movie or special that appeals to viewers age 18 to 34, the second channel may include fare aimed at viewers 35 to 49, and the third channel may have something of interest for viewers 50 and over. This kind of demographic targeting in all dayparts allows HBO to serve almost all its constituents simultaneously rather than in different dayparts or in a serial fashion.

This increased access has improved cumes for movies and events, an indication that people who want to view them are getting a better opportunity to do so. In addition to household cumes, demographic cumes have risen, especially for working men and women. As cumes increase, the service can assume greater use, an indication of greater consumer satisfaction.

HBO has become more aggressive in certain dayparts with its multiplexing capabilities. Dayparts of lesser value to broadcast networks still contain substantial numbers of viewers. Friday and Saturday evenings are an example. These are nights of the highest activity in rental stores, and Saturday especially is a day where networks often "send shows to die." However, because HBO has the product that renters are looking for and the capacity to offer more than one choice, weekend evenings have been aggressively scheduled for younger viewers with two of the three channels targeted at the audience under age 35. This has helped build viewership in this daypart.

Another move has been made in the direction of early late night and late night. The audience for David Letterman must wait until 12:30 a.m. for his program to air. Before Letterman, they are offered programs which are designed for a substantially older audience. By moving into this window of opportunity, HBO and other premium services have increased their viewership in this daypart. In late night a single premium service such as HBO can have a share as high as 25.

Other dayparts have been targeted as well. Holidays give HBO an opportunity to offer an entire day of special or thematic programming, something that is difficult to do with broadcast network schedules, which are locked into episodic content. By creating festivals and theme days, HBO can build share and thus usage on holidays when audiences are large. Since it is a premium service, the competitive share is not important as a competitive measure but serves as a measure of consumer satisfaction. When subscribers watch in large numbers, it indicates that they are happy with the programming.

Weekend daytime has also proved to be fertile ground for HBO. Sports and older movies dominate this landscape. As there is little fresh programming available outside of live sporting events, a window of opportunity exists there. By appealing to young people and women with recent movies and specials, HBO pulls in more subscribers.

Showtime

Although it has a smaller subscriber base, Showtime offers an alternative to HBO for cable operators. Showtime has used pricing as a way to attract operators' interest. Since the price charged to systems is discounted, the operators keep a larger share of revenues than is possible with HBO; this is a plus for cable companies.

Showtime's most recent pricing strategy has been called total optimization of pay services (TOPS). Under the TOPS plan, an operator pays a fee per basic subscriber rather than a fee for each Showtime or Movie Channel subscriber. The fee charged against basic subscribers is low, roughly 50 cents in the first year, compared to $3 to $5 for a premium subscriber. The fee per basic subscriber rises a few cents each year, say, from 50 cents to 53 cents and then to 56 cents. At the same time, the operator can lower prices substantially for Showtime and the Movie

Channel, encouraging increased subscribership. Only a small portion of the additional revenue goes to Showtime, and so the operator is rewarded for promoting Showtime's two services, and the lowered price is attractive to consumers.

This helps operators deal with one of pay's major problems: the rising cost of basic service. When consumers compare $5 a month for a premium service to $10 or $12 being added to a $20 basic charge, the $5 seems less foreboding.[22]

If there is a danger in TOPS, it is that it may cause **churn** in higher-priced services, especially HBO. That means that subscribers would be leaving one premium system to add another, which would mean no net gain for cable operators. Since TOPS is designed to operate on an MSO-wide basis, that element is carefully studied by MSOs, and some MSOs have not participated.

Like HBO, Showtime was active in developing original programming as early as the early 1980s, when two soap operas were developed. More recently, Showtime has scored with *The Garry Shandling Show* and *The Super Dave Osborn Show,* which was successfully spun off from *Bizarre,* a Showtime original comedy show starring comedian John Byner. Other original projects have helped diversify the service. These include music and comedy concerts, Broadway adaptations, and original dramas.

Showtime has moved into boxing in a big way, signing a major contract with Don King to produce monthly boxing matches. As boxing has proved successful on PPV, pay television companies hope that more frequent matches will draw boxing fans to their services.

As with HBO, Showtime has used multiplexing to increase convenience for subscribers. Like HBO, it has followed strategies designed to improve its draw in dayparts outside prime time, where broadcast competitors are weaker.

Showtime has taken some unique and bold steps. One was a 1991 promotion with Blockbuster Video stores nationwide. It has always been assumed that premium cable and video stores are competitors, but Showtime commissioned a study of home movie viewing that contained some unexpected and interesting results. One was that premium subscribers rented *more* videos than did nonsubscribers. Thus, rather than having their movie appetite sated by Showtime or HBO, people in premium homes were renting videos in addition to watching premium cable, not instead of watching premium cable. The corollary finding was that video rental did not hurt premium subscriptions. Thus, Showtime reasoned, the two entities—Showtime and Blockbuster—were actually compatible. They could form a symbiotic arrangement to work together to satisfy viewers' substantial appetite for movies and special programming.

In the Showtime–Blockbuster Video cross-promotion, Showtime subscribers were given free rentals at the video store while Blockbuster had point-of-purchase displays featuring Showtime and the Movie Channel. According to Showtime's senior vice-president for consumer marketing, "People who subscribe to premium services rent more tapes. People who do not subscribe to premium don't rent as much as the average person."[23]

Alternative movie services Both HBO and Showtime provide mainline premium services that are differentiated by their originality and diversity. Each also offers a more focused service that gives subscribers greater specificity in programming. HBO's alternative service is Cinemax, and Showtime offers the Movie Channel. Their strength is their single-mindedness about showing films. Since they program their alternatives differently, some subscribers can be induced to sign up for two premium services. Many cable operators offer subscribers the second service at a lower monthly rate.

The Disney Channel

The Disney Channel has been a formidable player in the premium arena. Targeted to children and their parents, it takes advantage of the Disney vaults by programming original films, spe-cials, series, classic films, and cartoons. In an era when parents are increasingly alarmed by the sexual and violent content of many films and television shows (especially on cable), the Disney Channel offers an oasis of quality product that parents feel they can trust. Nothing on the Disney Channel is likely to cause the consternation that many offerings on broadcast television or cable tend to cause. Its success has been measured by rapid subscription growth through the late 1980s and into the 1990s.

Encore

The newest premium service is TCI's Encore. Marketed as a minipay channel, or one for which subscribers pay an additional but small fee, it has wide distribution because of its parentage. While advertised as featuring hit films of the 1960s, 1970s, and 1980s, it tends to focus on more recent and better known movies. That gives its films recognizability without the cost of the most recent hits.

A partial list of Encore films includes, *All That Jazz, Butch Cassidy and the Sundance Kid, A Chorus Line, The World According to Garp, Gremlins, Rocky V, Star Trek V,* and *Superman.*[24] The service programs 30 movies a month, with a different movie in prime time each night.

As a minipay it is positioned between basic and the traditional premium services, but rather than destroy the premium environment, Encore is intended to expand and enhance premium services. Whether that will occur remains to be seen. Encore's pricing is tied to the premium services taken by subscribers. For example, in a home that subscribes to a premium channel, Encore is priced at $1 a month. For a nonpremium home, it is priced at $4.95 a month. Theoretically, Encore is used to reward premium homes with additional programming at low cost, not to encourage people to drop other premium services. It should, however, offer a price-attractive choice for those who have not chosen any premium services. The $4.95 fee places it in line with Showtime's TOPS pricing.

At Encore's inception in 1991, HBO and Showtime executives were on hand for the celebration. At that time Encore was accepted with equanimity tinged by a touch of anxiety. Showtime's president, Frank Biondi, saw Encore as more of a challenger to TNT than to HBO and Showtime because of the age of its films.

SUMMARY

Premium channels, especially those which primarily schedule feature movies, have had to deal with the arrival of home video and pay-per-view. The best defense they have found against both of these delivery systems is original product. Premium networks have begun producing made-for-cable movies, comedy programs, dramatic programs, documentaries, and educational programs. They are redefining themselves to consumers who might otherwise cancel their subscriptions.

The growth of subscriptions has slowed since most of the planned systems have been built. However, cable has found other revenue sources, and cable ratings are up as the broadcast networks' ratings continue to decline.

Video compression technology makes it possible to deliver many additional channels. How those channels will be used remains to be seen, but more channels will be dedicated to pay-per-view. The ability to multiplex schedules and offer popular movies continuously may make PPV a strong challenger to home video rentals. Through creative promotion, cross-promotion, and barker channels, PPV should experience rising buy rates for both events and movies. PPV also promises to become a force in the sports world. We may see major events migrating from broadcast television to PPV.

While premium channels are a mature industry, they have found ways to fight back against their age and against new competitors. One strategy is multiplexing schedules for the convenience of households and demographic groups. Creative promotions and continuous marketing have kept them alive and well. New channels such as Encore have shown how price can affect the premium environment, as has Showtime's TOPS program.

There are six healthy premium channels: HBO, Cinemax, Showtime, the Movie Channel, Encore, and the Disney Channel. They may evolve as technology and competition dictate, but none have the appearances of dinosaurs.

SUGGESTED READINGS

Multi-Channel News

This trade publication is one of the best sources of information about issues involving premium cable programming. Each week, the cable industry is examined in detail and programming issues are treated in depth. The articles highlight trends in programming and examine specific programs in terms of everything from management to economics. The treatment of premium channels is excellent, with comparative information about the major premium channels and pay-per-view systems.

Broadcasting

Long the primary trade publication, *Broadcasting* has broadened its agenda to include cable and newer technologies. While newer to covering cable than more specialized cable publications, the old flagship of the broadcast industry has done an excellent job. Each week there is coverage of premium channel and pay-per-view issues, including programming, economics, and regulation.

Electronic Media

Like *Broadcasting, Electronic Media* has expanded its coverage to include basic and premium cable. The magazine covered the major cable issue in its earlier years, but the growth of cable's size and importance was accompanied by a change in coverage. Stories became more frequent and detailed. Today some of the best and most readable stories concerning premium cable and pay-per-view programming are carried here.

Heeter, Carrie, and Bradley Greenberg: *Cableviewing,* Ablex, Norwood, N.J., 1988.

This is a wonderful companion book for serious students of cable. Heeter and Greenberg are researchers who are more interested in the audience for cable and its viewing habits than in cable as an industry. Their sophisticated examination of the audience is unparalleled and supplies a different perspective from which to view the cable industry. This is perhaps *the* book for more advanced students of cable.

Mair, George: *Inside HBO: The Billion Dollar War between HBO, Hollywood, and Home Video,* Dodd, Mead, New York, 1988.

This book does two things: First, it makes sense of the complicated relationships between cable, the entertainment industry, and the home video revolution. Second, it provides a thorough examination of the nation's largest premium channel. The complexities of economics and programming are especially well examined.

NOTES

1. Impact Resources Inc. survey, quoted in *USA Today,* Jan. 9, 1991, p. D-1.

2. Ted Livingston, "Monday Memo: A Pay TV Marketing Commentary," *Broadcasting,* July 16, 1990, p. 24.

3. "Cable to Pursue Compression Standard," *Broadcasting,* March 18, 1991, p. 36.

4. "Digital Compression Makes PPV Future Brighter," *Broadcasting,* May 6, 1991.

5. "PPV and DBS: Partners in an Uncertain Future," *Broadcasting,* Feb. 18, 1991, p. 49.

6. Richard Katz, "Channels Field Guide 1991," *Channels,* December 1990, p. 82.

7. "Titan Looking Beyond Wrestling: WWF Study Finds That Lower Price Points Don't Lead to Higher Buy Rates," *Broadcasting,* Feb. 18, 1991, p. 51.

8. Paul Sweeting, "Warner Study Says That PPV Movie Market Is Viable," *Billboard,* Sept. 29, 1990, p. 49.

9. Richard Katz, "Look Who's Discounting," *Channels,* Sept. 24, 1990, p. 42.

10. "Lower Priced Events Seen as a Way to Jump-Start PPV," *Broadcasting,* July 10, 1989, p. 44.

11. "Boxing Remains PPV Champion," *Broadcasting,* March 4, 1991, p. 54.

12. "Pro Leagues Readying to Enter PPV Waters," *Broadcasting,* May 13, 1991, pp. 54–55.

13. "1992 PPV Olympics: The Long Road to Barcelona," *Broadcasting,* March 25, 1991, p. 50.

14. Ibid.

15. "Testing Movie of the Week Waters in PPV," *Broadcasting,* July 16, 1990, pp. 40–41.

16. Ibid.

17. Personal conversation with David Baldwin, director of programming, HBO, May 24, 1991.

18. John Carman, television critic, *San Francisco Chronicle,* personal conversation.

19. "HBO Olé Targeted to Latin America," *Broadcasting,* Jan. 21, 1991, p. 36.

20. "HBO: Life after the Gold Rush," *Broadcasting,* March 25, 1991, pp. 43–49.

21. Conversation with David Baldwin.

22. "Biondi, Redstone Spell Out State of Viacom," *Broadcasting,* March 11, 1991, p. 51; see also, "Cablevision First in TOPS," *Broadcasting,* Feb. 18, 1991, pp. 51–52.

23. "Cable-Video Double Feature," *Broadcasting,* March 25, 1991, p. 51.

24. "Encore Is Sie's TCI Encore," *Broadcasting,* Feb. 25, 1991, p. 39.

Glossary

A.C. Nielsen Company A research firm that measures television audiences. Now called Nielsen Media Research.

Access The period between 7:30 p.m. and 8:00 p.m. was returned to local control by the FCC's prime-time access rule, which forbade network affiliates in the 50 largest markets to carry more than 3 hours of network programming during prime time.

Access Channels Cable channels set aside for public use on a first-come, first-served basis. The cable operator supplies technical help and does not control the content.

Action/Adventure A type of television show characterized by action scenes and law-and-order conflicts. Good guys vie with bad guys for the upper hand, with the bad guys eventually being brought to justice. Conflict is central, and violence and sex predominate.

Active Respondents Refers to the selection of respondents for audience research from among people who are known listeners or viewers. For instance, respondents may be identified when they call the station to participate in a contest or to request a record. See *passive respondents*.

Ad Hoc Network A temporary or occasional distribution arrangement in which stations agree to carry a program fed from a single source. College athletic conference basketball packages are an example.

Addressable Refers to a computer-controlled cable TV system in which each television set hooked to the system has a converter with a unique identification (address). When the subscriber wants to add or drop a tier or an individual service, the cable system operator can enter that information in the computer, which periodically sweeps each converter, and permits those signals to be tuned in or blocked.

Adjacencies Advertising positions that occur between network shows; they are adjacent to those programs. While the network sells internal spots, adjacencies are usually made available to the affiliates for sale.

Advertiser-Supported Refers to a basic cable network that sells advertising time.

Advertising Agencies Agencies that serve clients by producing commercial announcements and placing them on radio and television stations and networks. In return for their creative work and research into where the spots can best be placed, they keep 15 percent of the ad contract. Their share comes not from the client but from the station or network that is selling the ad positions. Since the agency tends to buy in bulk, 15 percent is a reasonable exchange for the network's ability to sell inventory in quantity without much sales cost.

Affiliate A television or radio station that has a contract with a network to carry programs and announcements; also refers to cable systems that carry programming from one or more satellite networks.

Affiliate Boards Consist of representatives (usually general managers) of network-affiliated stations who are elected by their peers. These boards represent the interests of their stations by lobbying for changes and working with the network to effect solutions to mutually perceived problems.

Aided Recall Interview A survey technique in which

respondents are given lists of programs or other prompts to stimulate their memory about what they were doing during a specified period.

Air Check A recording of a disc jockey's on-air performance that is used to generate a critique or as a sample of the disc jockey's work. The recorder is usually on during the beginning and the ending of each song but is stopped to cut out the middle. The point is to listen to the context of a music show without having to hear all the music. A recording only a few minutes long illustrates how effectively the deejay introduces songs, plays commercials, reads news and other material, and projects to listeners.

American Society of Composers, Artists, and Publishers (ASCAP) A major licensing organization for music rights. Stations and networks pay royalties for the use of music that are based on market size and frequency of use. See *Broadcast Music Incorporated* and *SESAC.*

Amortization The process of assigning a cost to each play of an episode of syndicated programming. Since the value of an episode decreases each time it is scheduled, most stations and other outlets use *accelerated amortization,* in which value decreases with each play. In the case of children's programs, where ratings do not fall with subsequent airings, the value of each play of the episode is the same; this is called *straight-line amortization.*

Anchor Shows Programs that start a lineup within a daypart. Typically, these are 8 p.m. network shows which begin in prime time. If these shows are strong, the rest of the lineup should benefit because of the flow principle. Anchor programs can occur in other dayparts, such as daytime, where the first soap opera in a set serves as the anchor for the rest.

Appeals Elements in shows that attract viewers, including sex, violence, information, and identification; sex and violence are considered the strongest appeal elements in television.

Arbitrends Arbitron Radio measurements of large markets in which respondents keep diaries during 48 weeks during the year. Arbitron's rolling average report combines data from the most recent month with data from the two previous months. Used to spot trends in a station's audience.

Arbitron Information on Demand (AID) A computer data service from Arbitron Ratings that allows clients to track radio listening on a quarter-hour basis throughout the broadcast day.

Arbitron Ratings Company A research firm that measures television and radio audiences.

Area of Dominant Influence (ADI) Arbitron's geographic market design in which every county in the United States is assigned to only one area. The assignment is made on the basis of the households in the county that limit the bulk of their TV viewing to stations in that market.

Artist Separation A way of scheduling music that avoids playing different records by the same artist within a specified period.

Audience Flow A measure of change in the audience during a program and between programs; shows the numbers or percentages of people or households who turn a program on or off, switch to or from another channel, or remain tuned to the same channel. The lead-in program provides a base of viewers, most of whom can be expected to remain in the audience for the next program.

Audience Segment See *demographic segment.*

Audimeter (Storage Instantaneous Audimeter) Nielsen's electronic measurement device. It is used to record when a television set is on and which channel is tuned in; has been supplanted by the *people meter.*

Auditorium Research Music testing in which groups of respondents are gathered in one place to rank music recordings on the basis of their appeal.

Automated System Equipment designed to play recorded program content after a controller has been programmed to specify which events should be played at a particular time and in a specified order. The equipment typically consists of reel and cartridge tape playback units that are cued by inaudible electronic signals to start and stop. Switches may also permit the routing of network signals. With desktop computers, compact disc players can be coupled to play specific songs.

Avails Advertising spots that are available for sale.

Average Quarter Hour (AQH) The average number of listeners or viewers in the audience during a specified period. Since audiences are measured on a quarter-hour basis, the number of persons in each quarter hour is divided by the number of quarter-hour periods in the daypart or hour. An *AQH rating* is an estimate of AQH persons or households expressed as a percentage of the universe.

Away-from-Home Listening Estimated listening in a location outside the home, such as in a car.

Back Announce To inform listeners about the records that were just played, as opposed to introducing recordings before they are played.

Back End Distribution Ancillary markets for programs. The primary, or front end, market for television programs is the network (station in the case of first-run syndication product). The back end includes foreign distribution, cable, and eventual syndication.

Back Load To schedule the heaviest load of commercial announcements *(stop sets)* in the third and fourth quarter hours of each hour during a radio program. See *front load.*

Barker Channel A cable channel that describes what is on other, usually PPV, channels to draw attention to events and schedules.

Barter Instead of selling a program to a station, the supplier gives the program to the station in exchange for commercial time slots during the program or during other parts of the station's schedule. See *cash plus barter.*

Basic Cable Channels received by cable subscribers at no extra charge; usually supported by advertising and small per-subscriber fees paid by cable operators.

Beats per Minute (BPM) A count of the number of beats in a musical arrangement (record) as an index of its tempo.

Bias (Research) Any influence or condition causing a distortion from the results that would have been obtained by pure chance. For example, error in an audience survey can result from including persons in the sample who do not provide information. Bias can also occur in a survey that favors a particular answer to a research question.

Billboard An announcement listing or describing some of the program events to be presented during a forthcoming time period of a radio program.

Block Booking A practice of program syndicators in which buyers are forced to purchase an inferior product in order to be able to purchase a more desirable product.

Blocking (Block Programming) The strategy of scheduling similar programs in groups within a time period to encourage viewers to watch the entire series of shows; designed to encourage audience flow. In radio, refers to the scheduling of one program type or format for long periods during the broadcast day.

Brand Character A means of making a product distinct from its competitors. In radio, the image of playing a certain kind of music or having a certain kind of personality, usually represented by the morning program personalities. In television, the brand character of the station is often based on the position its local newscasts have in the community. They may be light-hearted, serious, or authoritative and hold such an image among potential viewers.

Bridging See *front-ending.*

Broadband A wide range of frequencies, generally including the entire spectrum assigned to broadcasting. Cable TV is often referred to as broadband communication because of the frequencies it can carry.

Broadcast Music Incorporated (BMI) A major licensing organization for music rights. Stations and networks pay royalties for the use of music that are based on market size and frequency of use. See *American Society of Composers, Artists, and Publishers* and *SESAC.*

Broadcast Tier See *economy tier.*

Bumpers Phrases such as "Don't go away" and "We'll be right back" that are used to get viewers to stay with a channel through commercial breaks. By promising that the wait will not be long and that there is more content to come, they help keep viewers tuned. See *tease.*

Burnout The point when a record being aired on a station has become an *irritant* in that listeners are tired of hearing it; the decline in the popularity of a program series that occurs after repeated airings.

Buy Rate In pay-per-view television, the percentage of subscriber homes purchasing an event. If 12.2 percent of subscribers pay for a special showing of a movie, its buy rate is 12.2.

Cable Penetration The proportion of cable subscriber homes to all television homes in an area, expressed as a percentage. For example, if cable TV is in 100,000 homes in a market and the number of TV households in that market is 500,000, cable penetration is 20 percent.

Cable-Ready Refers to a television that can accept cable signals without the use of a converter box.

Cable Segmentation In cable system marketing, cable networks are placed in groups, or segments, and sold by the group to subscribers. Thus, a group including ESPN, CNN, CNBC, the Weather Channel, the Discovery Channel, and C-SPAN I and II might be sold as an "information" segment.

Cable Television (System) A television signal delivery system in which signals are distributed to households through coaxial cable for a monthly subscription fee. Additional (*premium*) services are available at an additional cost.

Call-Out Research Radio panel surveys that monitor audience acceptance of new and established records that are aired on a station.

Cash Deal The exchange of cash for episodes of a syndicated program.

Cash plus Barter (C+) The practice of exchanging cash plus one or more advertising spots within a program for episodes of that program. See *barter.*

CD (Compact Disc) A 3- or 5-inch disc on which a digital audio signal is pressed so that it can be read optically by a laser beam.

Cells In a tabulation of data, the figure that appears in the space formed by the intersection of the vertical lines on either side of a column with the horizontal lines above and below the row. For example, WXXX's AQH is reported in a row that intersects with the column for women age 18 to 24. In the row below, another cell reports AQH for women age 18 to 24 who listened to WZZZ.

Census A study in which, instead of sampling, the researcher attempts to measure every member of the population *(universe).*

Channel Capacity The number of channels or signals on a cable TV system that are available for current or future use. See *shelf space.*

Checkerboarding The practice of placing different programs in the same time slot on different days. On the program schedule for the week, the content in the time slot alternates each day, creating a checkerboardlike appearance. The opposite of *stripping.*

Churn A cable industry statistic based on a formula that measures subscriber connects, disconnects, upgrades, and downgrades.

Clearance The practice of making time available for a network program to be shown by an affiliate. If a program is not cleared, it is not broadcast in that market. The networks pay compensation to their affiliates as an incentive to clear programs.

Cliff-Hangers Dramatic crises during the plot development in shows that force viewers who are interested in the outcome to wait through a commercial or until the next episode for the resolution.

Climax The ultimate resolution of a plot development, usually near the end of a program.

Clustering The practice of placing cable channels together in groups to reflect lifestyle or content groupings. In *compatibility clusters,* channels such as CNN, Discovery, and A&E are given consecutive channel numbers because large numbers of people who watch one also watch the others. In *type clustering,* all sports channels are consecutive, as are information channels, religious channels, and the rest.

Coaxial Cable A copper wire conductor that is suspended in aluminum sheathing by plastic foam or another plastic material. Used to carry cable TV signals. Generally resistant to outside electromagnetic interference.

Coincidental Interview A survey method that asks respondents to report on what they are watching or listening to at the time of the inquiry; usually a telephone call.

Colorization The process of adding color to motion pictures and television programs that were originally produced in black and white.

Commercial Announcement (CA) See *spots.*

Common Carrier A service that carries communication messages with no restriction on or interest in the content.

Compatibility Clustering See *clustering.*

Concept An idea for a program or series. In program testing, a concept is a brief statement of the premise. See *concept testing.*

Concept Testing Research that evaluates the audience appeal of a program idea; a preliminary step in determining the feasibility of investing in the development of a program idea into a full-fledged script and eventual pilot program.

Consultant An individual or firm that provides expert services to stations in the form of customized audience research, advice on the interpretation of audience ratings, or evaluations of programming. Some consultants specialize while others provide a wide range of services, but all consultants try to increase a station's competitive position in its market.

Continuous Measurement Year-round radio audience measurement. Surveys are under way during most weeks of the year.

Cooperative Productions A program produced by two or more entities that share the telecast of the finished product. These can be single event programs or ongoing series.

Core Audience The dominant demographic segments that constitute the actual audience for a station or program as ascertained by audience ratings estimates.

Cost per Thousand (CPM) The cost of reaching 1000 households or individuals with an advertising message. A standard comparison of the cost-efficiency of different programs, stations, or other advertising media.

Counterprogramming The practice of offering an alternative to the viewing audience or trying to reach a demographic group different from the one attracted to competing programs offered during the same time slot.

Crossover Songs Recordings that generally are classified by the music and radio industry in a particular category, such as jazz or country and gain wide acceptance not only from the listeners of stations using that format but from listeners to stations using another format.

Cross-Promotion The practice of promoting one show on another show or one network on another network because the two are cooperating with each other. For example, NBC might choose to promote the *Fresh Prince of Bel-Air* on *A Different World* and vice versa because it feels the shows share audience segments and could help each other. ABC might announce ESPN events because it is a part owner of that cable network. This is common on cable pay-per-view channels, where one movie may be accompanied by an announcement about another movie of a similar type that will run later on another PPV channel.

Cume Total unduplicated listeners or households tuned in for at least 5 minutes during a specified period. See *reach*.

Curtain Time A time when large numbers of viewers are making program selections. Curtain times tend to occur at the beginnings of dayparts and are marked by tune-in rather than flow, but they can occur within dayparts. For example, the prime-time curtain occurs at 8 p.m. as the family decides what to watch. Other curtain times are 7 a.m. (morning news programs), 9 a.m. (morning talk shows and comedies), 12:30/1 p.m. (the beginning of the soap opera block), 4 p.m. (the start of early fringe), and 6 p.m. (news).

Daypart A standard period of time used by the broadcasting industry to identify periods of radio listening or TV viewing based on advertiser needs and audi-

ence habits. The basic dayparts are 6 a.m.–10 a.m., 10 a.m.–3 p.m., 3 p.m.–7 p.m., and 7 p.m.–midnight. Television includes early fringe, prime-time access, prime time, and late fringe.

Daypart Separation The practice of scheduling music for a radio program to avoid playing the same song during the same time period on successive days.

Dayparting The strategy of scheduling programs to appeal to the audiences that predominate during particular dayparts.

Daytime A daypart that spans the period between early morning and early fringe and encompasses the hours from 9 a.m. to 4 p.m. Daytime is dominated by women, but children enter near the end of this daypart.

Demographic Segment A portion of the real or potential audience, identified by sex and age. The age and sex increments generally reported in audience research reports include: children 2 to 6, children 7 to 11, teens (12 to 17), men 18 to 24, women 18 to 24, men 25 to 34, women 25 to 34, men 35 to 44, women 35 to 44, men 45 to 54, women 45 to 54, men 55 to 64, women 55 to 64, men 65 and above, and women 65 and above. By breaking the audience down in this manner, the programmer or advertiser can be as specific or general as his or her purposes require. For instance, segments of the audience can be combined into another demographic segment, such as men and women age 18 to 34.

Deregulation An ongoing policy by the Federal Communications Commission to remove requirements and restrictions on broadcasting. Part of the argument for deregulation is based on the considerable improvements in the technical reliability of equipment since the regulations were originally put in effect. The other, more important part of the argument is based on the changing basis for competition, principally the increases in alternative programming services available in broadcast markets.

Designated Market Area (DMA) Nielsen's definition of a television market: a group of counties in which commercial stations receive the largest audience share. As in Arbitron ADIs, each county is assigned exclusively to a DMA.

Diary A questionnaire in which respondents to an audience ratings survey are asked to furnish a written record of TV or radio activity for a specific period, usually 7 days.

Differential Survey Treatment (DST) Arbitron Radio's

practice of offering higher premiums as an incentive to respondents to complete and return their diaries.

Digital Audio Tape (DAT) An audio cassette format that can reproduce sound of a quality comparable to that of CDs. DAT can be reproduced with no loss in signal quality, unlike analogue or standard audiotape recordings.

Direct Broadcast Satellite (DBS) A satellite service whose signal is delivered directly to a viewer's home through the viewer's own dish or phase-array antenna.

Discretionary Income Money available for the purchase of goods or services beyond food, clothing, shelter, and transportation. This is the money families have available to take vacations, take the children out to dinner or to the movies, and purchase new VCRs and camcorders.

Distant Signal A TV broadcast signal from outside the market that is imported into the community by a local cable system.

Docudrama Dramatized versions of historical situations and events. Docudramas represent a marriage of documentaries and dramatic shows. They do not adhere tightly to fact, often taking considerable license in presenting the motives of the people involved and making events interesting to the audience.

Documentaries Nondramatic productions that rely on actuality footage to present a factual account of a situation or event.

Double Access The practice by some TV network affiliates of scheduling local and network news earlier, leaving the time slot from 7 to 7:30 p.m. adjacent to the prime-time access period (7:30 to 8 p.m. Eastern time) open. This creates a lucrative 60-minute period for programming syndicated game shows or situation comedies.

Downscale Audiences Audiences characterized by lower education, income, and social status.

Dramas Shows that focus on the relationships between people and do not have much violence. Serial dramas (soaps) develop themes over periods of time. Episodic dramas such as *St. Elsewhere* complete the resolution of themes on a weekly basis. Some themes, however, continue over time.

Drive Time *Morning drive* for radio is the 6 a.m.–10 a.m. daypart, while *afternoon drive* is the 3 p.m.–7 p.m. period. These are the times when the greatest amount of in-car listening is done. However, the majority of listening during both periods is done in homes, not in cars.

Early Fringe The time period between 4 p.m. and 8 p.m. It is more chaotic than most dayparts because so much change occurs in audiences and activities. The predominant demographic at the start of this daypart is women, supplemented by children and eventually by men and working women. In reality, there are several dayparts within early fringe: early early fringe from 4 to 6 p.m., news from 6 to 7 p.m., and the access hour from 7 to 8 p.m.

Early Morning A daypart characterized by high modularity, high activity, and audiences in flux. As television viewers go off to work between 7 a.m. and 9 a.m., the audience becomes increasingly female and program modularity declines somewhat at the end of the period.

Economy Tier The lowest-level collection of channels offered by a cable company. Generally it consists of broadcast channels with a small number of less desirable cable networks added to the package. It is sold to subscribers for a low price.

Efficiency of Target Audience (ETA) An index of the effectiveness of a station or program in attracting viewers or listeners from among all those in the target audience.

Equity Interest Where one company has part ownership of another. In the cable industry, equity interests influence which networks are allocated space on cable systems. For example, TCI's part ownership of CNN, BET, and The Discovery Channel gives these networks the carriage that makes them viable.

Event In radio programming, each separate part of the program content. Each record, commercial announcement, station jingle, and bit of banter between disc jockeys is an element in the program format.

Exclusive Listeners and Viewers Audience members who watch only one program or listen to only one radio station. A television station's news program will probably have a core of exclusive viewers who never watch the competing local news programs, for example.

Exclusivity The sole rights to air a program in a market.

Exposition The introduction to a television program; the premise is established, and the main characters and their relationships are introduced.

Fast Denouement After the climax of the show, all the plot segments must be pulled together. In television this is done especially quickly because of time limitations.

Federal Communications Commission (FCC) An independent government agency established by Congress to regulate communications by radio, television, telephone, wire, cable, and satellite.

Festival A technique, usually employed by independent stations, of showing several hours of episodes of the same program, several productions with a common theme, or several programs or films featuring the same star.

Fiber-Optic Cable A flexible glass fiber that carries laser signals. It is a highly efficient carrier of television and audio signals, capable of sending them over long distances at low amplification.

Financial Interest and Syndication Rules (Fin-Syn) Fin-syn was designed by the FCC to get the networks out of the production business and loosen their grip on the syndication market. This rule spurred the creation of independent production companies that have control over their product after network runs. Thus, the syndication market is currently controlled by those independent companies and their distribution arms. Networks were later allowed to produce news programs, and by 1988 they were allowed to produce up to 3 1/2 hours a week of nonnews, nonsports programs.

First-Run Programs Original programming that has not been aired before being sold to stations.

First-Run Syndication Programs which never appeared on a network. They are created for direct distribution to, and airing on, stations.

Flow See *audience flow*.

Focus Group Interview A technique in which groups of 8 to 10 persons are interviewed to elicit insight into problems associated with a product (station or program) or the concerns and interests of audience members.

Footprint The geographic area covered by a satellite-delivered signal. Depending on its position in the sky, a satellite's footprint may include the eastern or western portion of the United States or another area of the world.

Format A procedure or strategy used to present material in a consistent, controlled way. A television news format may call for a brief taped introduction that is followed by a live greeting by two anchors who tease the important news stories coming up after a commercial break. *Radio formats* generally specialize in a type of music (Country, Rock, etc.) or Talk (sports, news, interview, call-in). Features, music cate-

gories, commercials, and other elements are scheduled to attract and maintain the largest possible audience.

Formatics The techniques by which a radio format is executed. A format is akin to strategy, whereas formatics is equivalent to tactics. For instance, a programmer may advocate sweeping three songs over the 10-minute period that covers the end of a quarter-hour period and the beginning of the next one.

Formula The consistent application of elements that constitute a program. One of the most common formulas used in movies is "boy meets girl, girl doesn't like boy, but eventually boy gets girl." Personalities and places vary, but the elements are consistent.

Fragmentation of Audience Audiences for radio, broadcast television, and cable have many listening and viewing choices. Instead of local stations, some radio listeners tune in stations from other markets, listen to music recordings, or listen to audio services carried on cable systems. In addition to the many choices on cable TV, viewers watch rental movies. Such alternatives pull some listeners or viewers away, fragmenting the mass audience into multiple smaller audiences.

Front-Ending The practice of starting a longer program before a competitor's stronger but shorter program. If the audience is collected earlier, it may be held away from the show being front-ended.

Front Load Premium channels used to place all the new films and big events for the month in the first half of the month in order to make a splash with viewers. This practice compresses the release of new product into the first portion of the month. See *back load*.

Full-Service Radio Station A station with a full complement of news, sports, weather, music, and other entertainment components. These stations appeal to a broad range of adult demographics.

Genres Classifications of program that have consistent formulas. Standard TV program genres include westerns, situation comedies, and variety, quiz, game, crime/detective, action/adventure, documentary, and news shows.

Geodemographic Research Reports on persons based on demographic attributes such as age, sex, income, education, and location or place of residence as identified by ZIP code.

Grazing The practice by television viewers with remote control devices of rotating through the available channels instead of selecting channels purposively. Grazers stop and watch when something interests them and resume grazing when the content (such as a commercial) bores them.

Group Ownership Occurs when a corporation or individual owns and operates two or more radio or television stations. Certain tasks can be coordinated, materials can be purchased at a bulk discount, and employees can perform tasks for all the group's outlets. Economies of scale and potential profitability have led to the growth of group owners, especially among affiliated stations. These group owners can create programs, purchase syndicated product, and run the group of stations at higher profit levels than would be possible at the individual station level.

Hammocking The scheduling of a program, particularly a new show, a fading show, or a weak show, between two highly rated shows.

Headend The central distribution point of a cable TV system; the location of the satellite receiver dishes, off-air TV antenna, signal amplifiers, and other equipment needed to receive TV and radio signals and distribute them through a cable system.

Heavy Listeners and Viewers Heavy users of radio and television. These audience members devote as much time to listening or watching as they have available. While their loyalties may shift, these segments cannot be relied upon to increase radio or television audience size.

High-Definition Television (HDTV) A system that transmits TV signals with more lines per picture frame than the current U.S. standard of 525 lines per frame. The picture is wider and has higher resolution.

High-Density Black Area (HDBA) According to Arbitron, a radio market where the black population is 25 percent or greater.

High-Density Hispanic Area (HDHA) According to Arbitron, a radio market where the Hispanic population is 25 percent or greater.

Homevideo Index (HVI) Nielsen's measurement service for cable television audiences.

Hook (Music) A brief portion of the most familiar part of a recording, usually about 8 to 10 seconds. Hooks are played in call-out and auditorium music research so that respondents can rate the songs they represent.

Hook (TV Program) The technique of providing viewers with a compelling reason to stay tuned to a program. In a situation comedy, for instance, the opening scene may show one of the regular characters being dumped by his girlfriend. Viewers will want to see how he resolves this dilemma.

Horizontal Separation The practice of scheduling songs in a radio music program to avoid repeating them during the same hour on consecutive days.

Hot Clock A circular graph that represents a radio format by visualizing when each event is to be aired during an hour. Most stations use a different hot clock during each daypart.

Households Using Television (HUT) The percentage of all TV households in a survey area with one or more sets in use during a specific time period.

In-Tab The number of responses to a survey that are actually used in tabulating the results. In any survey, there is an attrition rate: Some sample units may never be contacted, and others may refuse to participate. Among those who do participate, some may provide such incomplete or erroneous responses that their responses must be discarded before the results are compiled.

Incumbent Station A station or cable outlet that currently holds the rights to a television program which is being sold again in the market. That station or outlet is usually offered the right of first refusal to renew the licensing agreement.

Independent (Indie) A television station that is not affiliated with one of the major networks (ABC, CBS, and NBC; Fox has attempted to remain exempt from network rules). The FCC defines an independent as a station that does not carry more than 10 hours of prime-time programming a week that is offered by the major networks. These stations must acquire or produce programs to fill their entire schedules, whereas affiliates can rely on a network for the bulk of their programming.

Instructional Television Fixed Service (ITFS) A TV delivery service using line-of-sight microwave that the FCC licenses to educational institutions and permits multichannel multipoint distribution system operators to use to offer potential subscribers a variety of channels.

Interactive Cable System A two-way cable system that allows viewer response and/or participation during programs.

Interactive Television Television that makes the viewer an active participant. Two current types of interactivity are call-in lines *(Donahue, Oprah)* and electronic devices that allow home viewers to play along with a game such as *Wheel of Fortune.*

Intercept Survey A survey technique in which persons are stopped on the street or, more typically, in a shopping mall and interviewed.

Interconnects In cable television, several cable systems can cooperate to run an ad at the same time. By interconnecting their systems, they can offer tailored geographic areas, from small to ADI size, to advertisers.

Irritant In radio, any program event that is disliked by a group of listeners. Irritants cause tune-out.

Jingle A short production, usually with a chorus of singers, used by radio stations to provide a distinctive musical signature. The jingle usually presents the station's call letters and perhaps a slogan such as "And now more music" or "Your kind of Country." Specialty production houses create jingle packages of various lengths for use in different time periods, for music segues, and for transitions between program events.

Late Fringe The time period between 11 p.m. and 2 a.m. The audience is typically younger, more liberal, and more accepting of unusual programming. This explains some of the success of *Letterman* and *Saturday Night Live.*

Lead-In The preceding program in a station or network's schedule. The lead-in program's audience is expected to stay tuned for the next show in the schedule. See *audience flow.*

Lead-Out The following program in a station or network's schedule. If the lead-out program has strong appeal, it should help the audience of the show that precedes it in the schedule. See *audience flow.*

Leased Access Channels Cable channels rented by businesses that seek to profit through the use of such a channel.

License Fee Money paid by a broadcast or cable entity to a syndicator in exchange for the rights to air a program for a specified number of plays over a specified number of years.

Lifeline Tier See *economy tier.*

Lifestyle Measurable qualitative traits of audiences that indicate their social status and interests. These traits can include income, sex, and other standard demographic attributes but go beyond those descriptors to include occupation, residence, and the like. A yuppie and a blue collar worker may both be men age 25 to 34 who have similar incomes, but most people would recognize the differences between the interests and purchasing habits of people who are members of double-income professional households, have no children, and live in high-rise condominiums and the interests of those who reside in small towns, have two children, and work in skilled-labor jobs.

Light Viewers and Listeners Light users of radio or television. These audience members are more selective and use more of their discretionary time for purposes other than watching or listening.

Linear Clock A radio programming strategy in which events are scheduled sequentially instead of according to clock time.

Liner At most radio stations, an event other than music, news, sports, and commercials. Typical liners include skits and humorous events and syndicated features such as commentaries and consumer information.

Live Assist An override use of automated equipment by a live disc jockey, who interjects comments and introduces recordings that are started and stopped manually.

Local-Origination (LO) Programming Programming carried on a cable system that is acquired independently of a network or by carriage of an over-the-air broadcast signal. Typically used by a channel devoted to locally produced programs or to syndicated programming.

Loyalty An audience's habit of tuning in one station or dividing its listening or viewing between several. In television, viewers are loyal to early-evening and late-evening newscasts.

Made-Fors Feature-length movies that are produced specifically for broadcast television or cable.

Make-Goods Commercial spots given free to a client to make up for a station, broadcast network, or cable network's mistake in running a scheduled spot.

Mall Survey See *intercept survey.*

Market The specific geographic area that has been determined to be the service area of a station or group of stations. The extent of the market is determined by population density and signal reach but most importantly by the frequency with which stations are listened to or watched by people residing in specific counties. See *ADI, DMA, metropolitan survey area, and total survey area.* A broadcast market is defined by its metro survey area and the surrounding counties. In radio markets, these counties can overlap; in television, they are assigned exclusively to one market.

Market Segmentation The practice of identifying groups of listeners or viewers according to their demographic and qualitative attributes. Stations that can attract older, more affluent viewers or listeners who are inclined to change their lifestyles because they no longer have to support children but are not ready for retirement may be attractive to condominium developers and travel agents.

Mean A measure of the central tendency or central position in a population. An arithmetic mean is the simple average of the scores in a distribution; it is determined by dividing the sum of the scores by the total number of scores.

Mechanical Diary A printout of the information contained in the diaries used in Arbitron's estimates of audience listening.

Metered Market A television market in which a sample of viewing households is measured with people meters to report overnight ratings.

Metromail Inc. A Lincoln, Nebraska, company that maintains telephone listings by state, county, and ZIP code. These lists form the basis for the sample frames used by Nielsen Media Research and Arbitron.

Metropolitan Statistical Area (MSA) A geographic area as defined by the U.S. Office of Management and Budget, that includes a city with a population of 50,000 or more and the county or counties surrounding it. Also includes contiguous counties if the social and economic relationships between them and the central county or counties meet the criterion of metropolitan character and integration. Formerly called a Standard Metropolitan Statistical Area (SMSA).

Metropolitan Survey Area The central part of a broadcast market, usually corresponding to the Metropolitan Statistical Area (MSA). This is the densely populated heart of the market.

Migration See *siphoning*.

Minicrisis A plot device that creates a conflict that will be resolved after a commercial break; it is used to hold viewers through commercial interruptions.

Miniseries A dramatic program that is broadcast in several episodes over several evenings, preempting the regularly scheduled programming on a TV network. A successful miniseries can attract unusually large audiences for several evenings, thus diminishing the ratings of competitors.

Modularity An approach to producing a television program that takes into account a short attention span and viewer movement into and out of the audience. The program is structured as a series of short segments or modules to maximize viewer interest by controlling pacing and gaining the immediate interest of viewers who tune in.

Multichannel Multipoint Distribution System (MMDS) A TV delivery system using line-of-sight microwave with four or more channels operated by a single company. Often called wireless cable.

Multipay The purchase of more than one premium channel by a cable household.

Multiple System Operator (MSO) A company that owns more than one cable system.

Multiplexing The practice by cable networks of offering their service on more than one channel. In the most common three-channel system, three program elements can be offered simultaneously, appealing to different demographic groups. HBO might run a movie aimed at older audiences on one channel, a concert aimed at the young on the second, and a sports talk show aimed at men on the third. Thus, several groups can be appealed to at all viewing times.

Music Bed Music used as background, such as underneath an announcer's voice, in a production.

Music Director In a radio station, the individual responsible for overseeing the selection and categorization of the recordings to be aired.

Music Sweep A period of time in a radio program when several songs are played without commercial interruption, usually presented back to back with little interjection by the disc jockey.

Music Texture The production values of recorded music, taking into account all that the listener hears, including the timbre and intensity of the singer's voice, the intensity of the instrumentation, the loudness of the music, and the beat.

Must Carry No longer in effect, this rule forced cable systems to carry the signals of all television stations licensed to communities within a 35-mile radius of the municipality served by the cable system.

Nag Factor Children have little discretionary money and thus are dependent on adults to make purchases for them. To keep brand loyalty, which is felt more by youngsters than by adults, they nag adults for particular products. The higher the brand loyalty or product specificity, the higher the nag factor brought into the child-parent interaction.

Narrowcasting A cable television term that is applicable to all types of broadcasting. A program or program service that targets a narrow audience segment. With so many program choices available, programmers position their offerings to specified groups in an attempt to attract the majority of that segment of the audience.

Broadcasting has traditionally aimed at large, hetero-geneous audiences, while narrowcasting is aimed at more specifically defined viewing audiences. Cable TV services such as ESPN, MTV, and CNBC typically narrowcast. On broadcast television, such specialization has been limited by the networks to sports and special events, but more recent shows such as *thirtysomething* and *The Days and Nights of Molly Dodd* have been aimed at narrower demographic groups.

National Association of Television Programming Executives (NATPE) An organization of cable and broadcast station programmers and managers that fosters professionalism in the industry.

Negative Option Tier A system in which cable subscribers can refuse certain channels and thus realize a savings on the cable bill.

Network Compensation Payment to an affiliate by the network for each show cleared.

Niche An underserved segment of the audience that can be attracted to a program or program service.

Nielsen Media Research See A. C. Nielsen Company.

Nielsen Station Index (NSI) Nielsen's local-market reports on television viewing.

Nielsen Television Index (NTI) Nielsen's national network television audience reports.

Noncommercial Broadcasting A special class of broadcast licensees that have noncommercial, educational licenses and rely on institutional support (universities, school systems, libraries) and public and corporate donations for operating funds. Traditionally, these stations provide an alternative service to the commercial fare offered by network-affiliated stations and independent commercial broadcasters.

Off-Cable Refers to a program available for broadcast on a television network or in syndication after it has been aired on a cable network.

Off-Network Programs Programs available for TV syndication after they have been aired on a network.

Off-Network Syndication Occurs when a program is made available for syndication after it has been aired on a network.

Op-News Slots Time periods that are filled with shows that offer an alternative to competing stations' news programs. See *counterprogramming.*

Out-of-Market Station A station licensed to another market (usually adjacent) that is received off the air by listeners or viewers in the local market.

Overnight Report Reports on television viewing in metered markets. Because the data are gathered by computer, reports on one day's viewing can be generated for delivery the next morning.

Overnights Household ratings and shares provided to metered market clients the morning after a telecast.

Owned and Operated Station (O & O) A local station that is owned and operated by a network.

Pacing The forward movement of a program. The pacing of a radio program is controlled by the tempo of the music and the amount of time allocated for each event. For instance, if a hard-driving rock song which lasted 3 minutes ends and the disc jockey immediately begins talking in an excited voice while the introduction of the next song is heard under his or her voice, the pacing is quick. In contrast, an Easy Listening format may use relaxed announcers whose soothing intonations are followed by a beat or two of silence before the music starts again. It's a slower pace but much more relaxing, and this is especially appealing to older listeners. Television programs work in a similar way. When the scenes are short and contain snappy dialogue and lots of action, the pacing is quicker than is the case when characters are shown talking for long periods.

Panel A group of respondents who are surveyed periodically to measure changes in attitudes and preferences over time. The members are typically rotated after several weeks to minimize respondent sensitivity to the subject of the research.

Parsimony Principle The process of getting maximum showings of program product. There is great pressure on available programming because so many broadcast stations and cable channels have to fill time. Thus, repeating material is necessary.

Passive People Meter See *people meter.* A device that recognizes when people are in the room where a television set is located and thus does not require any overt action on the part of the viewer to indicate that he or she has entered or is leaving the audience.

Passive Respondents Respondents to a survey who are selected at random from among all possible respondents in the universe. See *active respondents.*

Pay Cable See *premium service.*

Pay Television Refers to stations licensed to broadcast scrambled signals which are received over the air by subscribers who pay a fee for the use of a descrambling device. Also called *subscription television.*

Pay-per-View (PPV) Pay TV for which subscribers pay on a program basis rather than on a monthly basis. PPV can be seen on cable or on over-the-air pay services.

Payola Under the table payments to disc jockeys by record promoters to give their product airplay.

People Meter An electronic device that measures when a set is on, which channel is tuned in, and which household members are watching (if they remember to push the buttons).

Perceptual Study Also known as an image study. An evaluation of the audience's perception of a station or program to evaluate its position in the market.

Persons Using Radio (PUR) The percentage of all persons in the potential audience who are listening to the radio at a specified time.

Persons Using Television (PUT) The percentage of all persons in a given demographic category in the survey area who are viewing television during a specific time period.

Pilot Program A prototype show designed to demonstrate a program concept and introduce the characters and situations.

Playlist The categorization scheme, based on popularity with listeners, of music aired during a specified period on a radio station. The playlist is an internal information source used to direct the frequency of music airplay, but it is shared with record promoters, who are interested in the amount of exposure their product is receiving.

Pledge Weeks Fund-raising weeks in public broadcasting; listeners and viewers are asked to contribute money to support the station.

Plugola The acceptance of under the table payments by on-air personalities to mention or otherwise promote products or services.

Population See *universe.*

Positioning The strategy of establishing a place (the image of a station or program) in a listener's or viewer's mind. A station may be considered boring or very professional, depending on who is asked. One station may be perceived as having the most accurate weather forecasts by viewers who tune in because they "know" it is correct information. Another station may counter by having a weatherperson with a pleasant, mellow personality. The audience for this forecast may perceive this station's weather forecaster as being more likable and thus may consider him or her more believable.

Positioning Line A statement of the unique benefit provided to the listener, such as "TV channel 10, with the coast's most accurate weather forecast" or "KBIM . . . playing the music you like to party with."

Posts Strong shows scheduled on the hour that feed audiences to weaker shows scheduled on the half hour.

Preemption The substitution of a network program by another offering chosen by an affiliate. See *clearance.*

Premium Service Cable services or channels, such as HBO, Showtime, and the Disney Channel, for which subscribers pay a monthly fee in addition to a basic cable service charge.

Prime Time The hours from 8 p.m. to 11 p.m. Monday through Saturday and 7 p.m. to 11 p.m. Sunday in the Eastern and Pacific time zones (7 to 10 and 6 to 10, respectively, Central and Mountain time). This is when viewing audiences are largest and when networks bring out their highest-priced, best-produced programming.

Prime-Time Access Rule (PTAR) The FCC passed PTAR in 1971 as a way of lessening network control over slots when the most viewing occurs. In addition, PTAR was seen as a way of spurring the first-run syndication industry or even local production (the latter never panned out). When network programming was limited to 3 hours during prime time (7 to 11 p.m.), the hour from 7 to 8 p.m. reverted to local stations. An exception to the 3-hour rule was made for news and public affairs programs such as *60 Minutes* on CBS. Stations can run network newscasts in access as long as they are preceded by a local newscast. Thus, the half hour from 7:30 to 8 p.m. is the real access slot.

Probability Sample A sample in which the elements (respondents) in a sample frame have an equal likelihood of selection. In a simple random sample, each element and all possible equal-size combinations of elements have an equal chance of being selected.

Product Whether produced in-house or purchased, programs available to broadcast stations or networks. Since most series are produced in an assembly-line fashion, using variations based on a formula that appeals to audiences, the name is apt. Shows are considered filler material between commercials, and so this term indicates the function accorded to programs by industry professionals.

Product Differentiation Promotion and emphasis of the differences between a media outlet's programming and that of the competition.

Production Values The inclusion and execution of elements such as music, interesting voices, dialogue, sound effects, and compelling dramatic situations—the things that make a program or commercial more or less interesting.

Program Log The schedule of all programs, commercial announcements, and other items that a station presents on the air during each broadcast day. The operator on duty is responsible for following the log and indicating any changes in the schedule. The FCC no longer requires radio stations to maintain program logs, but most continue to use them as a record of what was broadcast.

Promotion A strategy to attract and maintain an audience. One way to do this is to create awareness of program offerings. It is also possible to create an image for a program or electronic media outlet, while other promotional efforts are intended to reinforce viewer or listener loyalty. See *positioning* and *product differentiation.*

Psychographics Identification of audience members by personality type (lifestyle).

Public Broadcasting Noncommercial, educational licensees of radio and television stations.

Public File Documents that station licensees must assemble and make available during business hours to any member of the public who asks to see them. The items include the station's construction permit or license application, license renewal applications, equal employment opportunity reports if the number of full-time employees exceeds four, a copy of the FCC's *The Public and Broadcasting—a Procedural Manual,* a record of requests for political broadcasting time, and a quarterly list of programs the licensee feels have provided the most significant treatment of community issues.

Q-Ratings A measure of the popularity of a performer or program. See *TvQ.*

Qualitative Research Descriptors of audiences that go beyond age and sex, the two standard demographic attributes; includes attitudinal, economic, and lifestyle variables that describe how groups live and spend their money.

Quantitative Research The standard demographic characteristics, primarily age and sex, with some measurement of ethnic groups.

Quarter-Hour Audience Individuals viewing or listening to a station for at least 5 minutes in a 15-minute period.

Quarter-Hour Maintenance Strategy A strategy for attracting and keeping radio listeners through successive quarter-hour periods to maximize audience size. To be counted in a quarter hour, an individual must listen for at least 5 minutes.

Quarter Separation A radio music schedule in which plays of a song are rotated from one quarter hour to another on successive days.

Quota Sample A sample in which desired sample sizes, or quotas, for various groups are established. Selections of sample elements are not random, and the probability of selecting an element is often unknown. Some elements may not have any chance of being selected.

Random-Digit Dialing A situation in which the last four digits of telephone numbers are drawn from a table of random numbers so that any combination of those numbers has an equally likely chance of being selected. The sample is selected by adding the prefixes used in a market and drawing a sample size that is proportionate to the number of working telephone numbers assigned to each prefix.

Random Selection Occurs when every member of the population (universe) being studied has an equally likely chance of being selected as a member of the sample.

Rating An estimate of the size of a television or radio audience relative to the universe, expressed as a percentage; the estimated percentage of all TV households or radio listeners tuned to a specific station at a specified time.

Rating Points A rating is the percentage of audience members in the possible audience who are actually listening or watching at a specific time. The total possible audience equals 100 percent, and so the rating points for a particular program in a time period are its percentage of all possible viewers. If a single program garners 100 rating points, it has attracted all the viewers or listeners in the entire viewing or listening area.

Reach The number of different (unduplicated) households or persons in the audience for a program during a specified time period. See *cume.*

Reality Programs Programs that emphasize actuality footage in focusing on real events and people. Examples include *60 Minutes, Hard Copy,* and *Inside Edition.*

Recall Interview An interview in which respondents are asked to report on their viewing or listening activity during a specified period, usually the previous 24 hours.

Recycling The proportion of the audience for a daypart or program that is also in the audience for another daypart or program.

Release Windows Feature films can reach the public through a number of vehicles: theatrical release, pay-per-view showings on cable, videocassette, pay cable showings, network broadcast, and airing on a local station. Each of these represents a window of opportunity to reach potential viewers. With the rising popularity of videocassette rentals and the growth of pay-per-view, the order of the windows has changed.

Remote Control A small electronic device that transmits a low-level infrared signal to control the power, volume, and channel selection of a television receiver or VCR. Most VCR remote control devices permit the user to change channels as well as to start and stop the VCR and engage the record, pause, and fast-forward functions.

Rep Firm A company that specializes in representing stations to national advertisers, allowing a station to sell its available inventory at the best rate. Since the rep firm's income is derived from the advertising time it sells, it is worthwhile for it to become involved in the client station's programming in order to increase audience size and thus ad rates.

Repeat Tolerance An audience's willingness to continue watching multiple plays of the same episode in a program series; typically highest in children.

Representativeness The quality of a sample that has the same distribution of characteristics as the population from which it was selected. Thus, results observed in a sample are assumed to represent similar characteristics in the population.

Respondent A person who provides information as part of a survey.

Response Rate Sometimes called a cooperation rate; reflects the difference between the initially designated sample and the final, or in-tab, sample.

Reverse Tiering A cable marketing practice in which households are allowed to select and pay for cable networks on an individual basis rather than subscribing to basic packages or tiered bundles.

Reward A programming concept in which the members of an audience are presented with a desirable program event that gives them an incentive to stay tuned. If the audience endures the commercials, for instance, it will be rewarded with a song it likes or information it wants, such as sports scores or the weather forecast.

Rising Action Rising action contributes to the building of a climax through events designed to hold viewers' attention. A series of minicrises is typically assembled, each helping the plot build to the point where a confrontation must occur.

Rolling Average Report Arbitron's rolling average report combines data from the most recent month with data for the two previous months. Used to spot trends in a station's audience.

Rotation The frequency with which a record is aired. Most radio stations use several categories, placing the most popular records in a rotation to ensure that they receive several airings each day. Older records, including those declining in popularity, are given a less frequent rotation.

Sample One or more elements (persons or households) selected from a universe to represent the universe.

Sample Frame A listing of the known population of a universe from which a sample is drawn.

Sampling Occurs when viewers watch a show for the first time or the first few times, thus becoming acquainted with a new program offering. Shows that get sufficient sampling have the best chance of reaching their intended audiences.

Sampling Error The theoretical degree to which the measurements taken in a sample differ from those which would have resulted from a census of the whole population.

Satellite Master Antenna Television (SMATV) Also called private cable. A miniature cable system that receives programming by satellite and serves a housing complex or hotel.

Satellite Station A television station that transmits programs and commercials received from another station to extend the coverage area of the parent station.

ScanAmerica Arbitron's single-source people meter; a laser wand with which participating household members record their purchases by waving the wand over the Universal Product Code (UPC) bars on each item. Until the service was canceled in 1992, it was Arbitron's combination of audience viewing and purchasing data.

Second Season After the fall shows have been on for a few weeks, the ratings indicate which are attracting an audience. The failures are eventually pulled from the lineup, and new shows are introduced at around the first of the new year. This second season serves as a fresh start, giving viewers new program choices and a chance to adapt to new schedules. The second season starts in January or February.

Segmentation Identification of a subset of the potential audience and the development of a programming strategy to attract it. Instead of attempting to appeal to the widest possible audience, the media outlet targets specific demographic groups.

SESAC A licensing organization for music rights. SESAC originally represented European music publishers, but its repertory now consists primarily of American works. Stations and networks pay royalties for the use of music based on market size and the spot advertising rate. See *American Society of Composers, Artists, and Publishers* and *Broadcast Music Incorporated.*

Sets in Use The percentage of all TV sets in the survey area that are being viewed during a specific time period. Sometimes used erroneously as a synonym for *households using television (HUT).*

Share The percentage of the households using television (HUT) or persons using television (PUT) or the percentage of persons using radio (PUR) tuned to a specific program or station in the market at a specified time.

Shelf Space The number of channels a cable operator has available for use.

Short Run A program that has relatively few episodes. Such series have not lived the normal program life span or accumulated enough episodes to be a force in the syndication market.

Single-Source Measurement A combination of television viewing and audience purchasing statistics from the same households. Ideally, single-source data enable researchers to discover clear relationships between what people watch on television and what they buy.

Siphoning The process by which cable television draws events away from free broadcast television, most often in the area of sports.

Situation Comedies (Sitcoms) Television shows that follow a family or group through a series of situations which allow for comedic occurrences. The humor can be derived from jokes, sight gags, slapstick routines, interpersonal interactions, plot twists, and ongoing themes.

Skew Synonymous with lean or slant. Used to indicate that audiences (as described in demographic terms) lean toward some characteristic. For example, MTV is said to "skew young," meaning that its audience is disproportionately young. *Murder She Wrote* skews older. Shows can skew along any demographic or psychographic characteristic.

Slivercasting An extreme form of narrowcasting. The show *Moonlighting* is aimed at a young upscale audience, and golf tournaments are even more narrowly focused. The National Jewish Channel (NJT) and the Eternal Word Network are aimed at very specific audience segments.

Soft Format Diary Arbitron's radio diary, which uses an open format in which respondents indicate the length of time spent listening by drawing a line down the page. Also includes a place for the respondent to indicate listening "at work" in addition to "at home," "in the car," and in "other places."

Sound Bite A brief excerpt from a taped interview or speech that is included in a news report. In radio sound bites are also called voicers.

Special A one-time-only entertainment program featuring major stars which preempts a network's regular offering. Sometimes referred to as a blockbuster program, it is intended to attract audience members from the competition's regular programming.

Spinoffs Shows that are born from other shows; characters from one series become the central figures in a new show. *Happy Days* gave birth to *Laverne and Shirley* and *Mork and Mindy,* spinning them off from the parent show and giving them their own half hours and unique settings. Spinoffs are popular with producers and networks because they are based on audience responses to existing characters. Since the failure rate for new shows is so high, spinoffs allow for a measured response before entering into production.

Spot A commercial advertising message or public service announcement. Spots are usually 30 or 60 seconds long, although some may be only 10 or 15 seconds long. The name derived from the practice of spot placement of messages in various programs scheduled at different times during the day or week as an alternative to concentrating the advertising through sole sponsorship of a single program.

Spot Load The number of commercial announcements a station carries per hour during various dayparts. Since commercials are generally considered a listener or viewer irritant, a heavy spot load detracts from the appeal of the programming.

Spot Rate The rate charged by a station, cable system, or network for advertising time. Rates vary according to audience size, flexibility of placement, number of spots purchased, and length of contract.

Spot Set Groupings of commercials that are scheduled during a radio program. Some programmers differentiate between spot sets for scheduling commercials (spots) and *stop sets,* which can include announcements and other noncommercial matter.

Standard Metropolitan Statistical Area (SMSA) See *Metropolitan Statistical Area.*

Station Group Production Programs produced by a station group for use by its member stations and potentially for syndication to nongroup stations.

Station Identifier A brief phrase, such as "Q-102" or "Hot Hits 96," by which a radio station is known to listeners. The identifier may be easier to remember than the call letters; this is very important when the listener makes an entry in a diary in response to an Arbitron audience survey. The identifier is often an abbreviated combination of the positioning line or slogan and the station's call letters or frequency.

Station Program Cooperative A program fair organized by PBS during which new shows are offered to public television stations. Shows that receive the most station support get on the air.

Station Rep See *rep firm.*

Stop Set A grouping of commercials and other announcements scheduled during a radio program. See *spot set.*

Straight-Voice (Talk) Commercial A commercial announcement read by an announcer without the accompaniment of music or other sound.

Strategy A plan to achieve an overall objective; consists of a number of steps, or tactics, that are carried out to achieve the strategy.

Stripping The practice of placing the same show in the same slot each day (Monday through Friday, Sunday through Friday). In the program schedule, it appears as a strip across the days.

Strong Slots Time periods filled by strong shows that can generate their own audiences. They not only contribute to flow, but can start it by fostering tune-in.

These slots occur on the hour in prime time and most other dayparts. Exceptions include the access slot and the news lead slot, which occur on the half hour.

Stunting The practice of scheduling blockbuster specials and movies to attract a larger than usual number of viewers and weaken opponents' strong shows and disrupt their flow, especially during *sweeps.*

Subscription TV (STV) An over-the-air TV station that uses a standard broadcast channel to transmit scrambled signals to subscribers whose sets are equipped with decoders. The subscribers pay a monthly fee.

Superstation A term originally coined for and copyrighted by WTCG (later WTBS), Channel 17, Atlanta. Now it generically refers to a station whose signal is available to cable systems across the country via satellite transmission. Other superstations include WOR TV, New York, and WGN TV, Chicago.

Survey Research A study of a population based on a sample in which each member of the population (universe) has an equally likely chance to be selected for the sample. The persons selected are contacted by mail, by telephone, or in person and asked to respond to questions.

Sustaining Programs Programs that run without commercial support. They are scheduled in spite of the lack of advertiser support because a network considers them sufficiently important. The practice is increasingly rare.

Sweep A time period when the audience in every radio or television market is being measured. While sweeps are actually national aggregates of local-market measurements, the term is sometimes used loosely to indicate a period when some markets are being measured, since larger television and radio markets are measured more frequently than others are.

Syndicated Exclusivity (Syndex) Buyers of syndicated shows receive exclusive rights to air a program in a market so they don't have to compete against the same show on another channel. In order to protect local stations, cable operators are required to black out other stations that carry the same programs.

Syndicated Program A program, generally a filmed or taped series, that is sold to individual stations for broadcast.

Syndication The practice of selling exclusive market rights to broadcast a program to stations.

Syndicators Companies that make programming available to stations and cable networks in first-run and off-network forms. Some syndicators are arms of production houses that create programs. Others are sales specialists responsible for moving product for a production company that has no syndication sales division.

Tactic A step in executing a programming plan (strategy). Whereas strategy is the grand design, each tactic represents one of several attempts to carry out the strategy.

Target Audience A portion of the TV or radio audience seen by an advertiser as most likely to purchase its product; for radio or TV programmers, the segments of the total audience that a station is specifically attempting to attract.

Tease An incentive for the viewer or listener to stay tuned. In radio, the listener may be told that a song by a popular artist is to be played "right after the news." See *bumpers*.

Telco A telephone company. Generally, any of the Bell Operating Companies (BOCs), including Ameritech, Bell Atlantic, BellSouth, NYNEX, Pacific Telesis, Southwestern Bell, and U.S. West, along with independent phone companies such as GTE.

Television Receive-Only System (TVRO) A satellite receiving antenna, also known as a downlink or a backyard dish.

Tentpoling Very strong programs tend to raise the ratings of the shows that precede and follow them in the schedule. Like a tentpole, these shows raise the programs around them closer to their own height. Loyal viewers tune in early to make sure they don't miss the show and are counted in the ratings for the previous show. Tuning inertia leads to flow, which helps the following shows. The stronger the show, the greater the tentpoling effect.

Theater Testing A process in which pilot programs are watched by a group of respondents who use electronic devices to indicate points during the program when they like or dislike the characters or situations. Respondents are usually interviewed in groups after the screening.

Tier (Cable) The practice of charging cable TV subscribers separately for additional packages of cable channels. A tier may include additional pay-TV channels such as HBO and Showtime.

Tier Deal An agreement between a syndicator and a station for a program in which several possible times of the day for the show to air are listed. Because each time slot develops more or less revenue depending on available audience sizes, the prices charged by the syndicator reflect the time slots.

Tier (Movie) A level of quality of a movie package. The best film packages are tier 1, and successively lower-quality product is assigned to lower tiers, such as tier 2 or tier 3.

Time Spent Listening (TSL) An index of listener or viewer loyalty to a station or program calculated on the basis of the number of quarter hours. TSL equals AQH (multiplied by the quarter hours in the time period) divided by cume.

Timeshifting The recording of TV programs on VCRs to be watched at a later time. Among the most frequent users are working women, who record soap operas while they are at work and replay the programs during the evening.

Total Survey Area (TSA) A geographic area encompassing the counties of the metro survey area and certain counties outside of it. The TSA includes counties where a significant number of households or persons tune to stations of the home market.

Track Record The record that a broadcast or cable network program amasses during its lifetime. It is measured by ratings, viewer demographics, and the strength of competing shows.

Traffic The scheduling of commercial announcements and program events in a station's broadcast day. Stations usually have a traffic department that is responsible for this activity.

Traffic Director The person responsible for scheduling commercial announcements and other matter in a station's program schedule.

Trailers Extended previews of films that run in movie theaters. They contain scene segments, usually the most exciting ones, to lure audiences.

Trunk Line In cable television distribution systems, the trunk line runs down streets much as utility lines do, making cable available to residents.

Tuning Inertia Viewers' tendency to leave the set tuned to a channel for an extended period rather than change the channel. Before remote control devices became popular, tuning inertia was a more important factor because it was troublesome to get up, walk across the room, and change the channel.

Turnover An index of the stability of the audience during a time period. It is a mirror of time spent listening (a long TSL indicates a low turnover). Turnover equals cume divided by AQH. Turnover is an index of reach, while TSL is an indication of the frequency with which messages may have to be presented in order to reach audience members.

TvQ A measurement of how well the audience likes programs and performers based on their familiarity and appeal.

Type Clustering See *clustering*.

Underwriting Occurs when an institution or company contributes part or all of the funds necessary to cover the costs of producing a program or operating a non-commercial broadcast program service or station.

Universe A population chosen for study. The estimated total number of people in the age or sex group and geographic area being reported, for example, all households or all women age 18 to 49.

Upscale Consumers Viewers with high levels of income, education, and purchasing power. These viewers are the most coveted by advertisers, especially those selling premium products. Shows are designed to appeal to this audience segment whenever possible.

Validity The essential characteristic of good research: measuring what it is supposed to measure. For example, the discrepencies between the viewing patterns of metered households and those of diary households may suggest that the meter is a better indicator of the length of time the set is on than of the amount of time someone is watching it.

Variety Program A television genre that features different kinds of content, including short dramatic segments, comedy sketches, songs, and dance numbers, under the umbrella of a single show. Examples include *Dolly Parton, The Smothers Brothers* and, much earlier, *Ed Sullivan*.

Vertical Integration The ownership of elements at more than one level of production, distribution, and delivery. Some MSOs, for example, own cable systems (delivery) and have a financial interest in cable networks (production and distribution).

Vertical Separation A scheduling plan of radio sta-

tions to avoid replaying a song for a specified period of time, usually 1 or 2 hours, after it has aired.

Video Compression The process of delivering four or more signals on what was previously a single channel. It makes possible hundreds of channels where there may have been only 50 or 100.

Warehousing The practice of acquiring the rights to broadcast a program in a market in order to prevent a competitor from scheduling it. The station avoids the problem of dealing with the series as a competitor by buying the show without intending to air it.

Waste Exposures Advertisers target particular demographic groups and place messages in programs that reach them. Although the advertiser pays for all viewers, some groups are not considered likely to purchase the product or service and thus constitute wasted exposures.

Weak Slots Time periods beginning on the half hour in prime time and other dayparts. Weak slots are filled by shows that are not strong in pulling their own audiences (tune-in) but can facilitate audience flow through to the second post in the hammock. New and aging shows tend to find their way to weak slots.

Weekly A program aired once a week rather than stripped.

Windows In local cable system advertising, an open spot on a major network which the local cable company can sell to local advertisers. Many cable networks make a 1-minute window available each hour for local cable companies to fill.

Wireless Cable See *multichannel multipoint distribution system*.

Zapping The practice by users of remote control devices of bypassing programs or commercials by muting the sound, changing channels, or not recording those segments on videotape recorders.

ZIP Code A means of identifying groups of viewers or listeners based on where they reside in the market; can provide an indication of socioeconomic status.

Zipping The practice by users of home VCRs of fast-forwarding through commercial messages or other parts of programs that were recorded for playback.

References

ANDERSON, J. R.: "More Radio Stations Trying 'Picture Painting' Call Letters," *Electronic Media,* Sept. 14, 1987, pp. 30, 46.

"AOR, Black/Urban Gain in New Diary," *NAB Radio Week,* April 3, 1989, p. 8.

"Arbitron Compares Meters and Diaries," *Broadcasting,* Feb. 27, 1989, pp. 38–39.

Arbitron Radio Market Report Reference Guide, Arbitron Ratings Company, Laurel, Md., 1987.

BAKER, JERI: "The Maturing of Marketing," *Channels,* October 1987, p. 18.

BALON, ROB: "Asking Questions Listeners Can Answer," *Radio & Records,* Aug. 11, 1989, p. 38.

———: "Building a Better Contest," *Radio & Records,* July 14, 1989, p. 38.

———: "The Feast and Famine Fallacy," *Radio & Records,* Jan. 6, 1988, p. 37.

———: "Fine-Tuning Positioning Liners: You Are What You Say You Are," *Radio & Records,* Sept. 7, 1990, p. 52.

———: "Straight Talk on Auditorium Testing," *Radio & Records,* Feb. 3, 1989, p. 52.

———: "Think Like a Listener," *Radio & Records,* June 8, 1990, p. 38.

———: "Understanding Psychographics," *Radio & Records,* Sept. 8, 1989, p. 64.

———: "What the Average Listener Knows about Radio," *Radio & Records,* April 8, 1988, p. 48.

BARNOUW, ERIK: *The Sponsor: Notes on a Modern Potentate,* Oxford University Press, New York, 1978.

BARTOLINI, WILLIAM F.: "Market Planning as a Team Effort," *BPME Image,* April/May 1989, pp. 8–10.

BEHRENS, STEVE: "A Finer Grind from the Ratings Mill," *Channels,* January 1988, pp. 10–16.

BELDEN, JOE: *A Broadcast Research Primer,* National Association of Broadcasters, Washington, D.C., 1980.

BELLAMY, ROBERT V., DANIEL G. McDONALD, and JAMES R. WALKER: "The Spin-Off as Television Program Form and Strategy," *Journal of Broadcasting & Electronic Media, 34,* Summer 1990, pp. 283–297.

BERCOVICI, LIZA: "The Moving Needle Stops," *TV Guide,* Dec. 21, 1974, pp. 23–26.

BESCHLOSS, STEVEN: "Making the Rules in Prime Time," *Channels,* May 7, 1990, pp. 22–27.

BEVILLE, HUGH MALCOLM, Jr.: *Audience Ratings: Radio, Television, Cable,* 2d ed. Lawrence Erlbaum, Hillsdale, N.J., 1988.

———: "People Meter Will Impact All Segments of TV Industry," *Television/Radio Age,* Oct. 27, 1986, pp. 53–57.

BIRCH, TOM: "Anatomy of the Birch Radio Telephone Interview," *Radio & Records,* Dec. 8, 1989.

———: "Understanding and Using Qualitative Research," *Radio & Records,* April 28, 1989, p. 62.

———: "Understanding the Numbers," *Radio & Records,* July 28, 1989, p. 36.

BOEMER, MARILYN LAWRENCE: "Correlating Lead-In Show Ratings with Local Television News Ratings," *Journal of Broadcasting & Electronic Media, 31,* Winter 1987, pp. 89–94.

BORTZ, PAUL I., MARK C. WYCHE, and JAMES M. TRAUTMAN: *Great Expectations: A Television Manager's Guide to the Future,* National Association of Broadcasters, Washington, D.C., 1986.

BOSLEY, RHODY: "Make Your Station a Brand Name," *Radio & Records,* Sept. 15, 1989, p. 72.

BREEN, GEORGE, and A. B. BLANKENSHIP: *Do-It-Yourself Marketing Research,* 2d ed., McGraw-Hill, New York, 1982.

BUCKMAN, ADAM: "FCC Tightens Focus in Fight on Indecency," *Electronic Media,* Sept. 7, 1987, pp. R5–R6.

———: "Radio News Tries to Please Listeners," *Electronic Media,* Aug. 25, 1986, p. J8.

———: "Radio Officials Confused by Federal 'Payola' Probe," *Electronic Media,* Jan. 4, 1988, p. 24.

———: "'Shock Radio' Battle Dominates Radio News," *Electronic Media,* Jan. 4, 1988, p. 50.

———: "Study: Viewers Back Boycotts," *Electronic Media,* June 5, 1988, p. 2.

BUELL, VICTOR P.: *Marketing Management: A Strategic Planning Approach,* McGraw-Hill, New York, 1984.

BUZZARD, KAREN S.: *Chains of Gold: Marketing the Ratings and Rating the Markets,* Scarecrow Press, Metuchen, N.J., 1990.

CAMPBELL, LARRY: "Lessons Learned for Success," *Radio & Records,* May 24, 1985, p. 18.

CHAMBERS, EVERETT: *Producing TV Movies,* Prentice-Hall, Englewood Cliffs, N.J., 1986.

CLARK, GINGER: "Eliminating the Risks from Prime Time Schedules," *Feedback,* Spring 1991, pp. 1, 10–15.

COATES, COLBY: "Popular Personalities: 'Cosby' Stars Top 'Performer Q' Ratings," *Electronic Media,* July 28, 1986, p. 3.

COHEN, EDWARD: *How America Found Out about the Gulf War,* Birch Scarborough Research, Coral Springs, Fla., 1991.

———: "A Primer for Managers on Qualitative Research," *NAB News,* Sept. 4, 1989, pp. 26–28.

———, THOMAS BALDWIN, and BRADLEY SAMUELS: "The Effect of Sampling Error on Radio Market Rankings," paper presented to the Sales and Management Division, Broadcast Education Association Annual Convention, Dallas, March 1987.

COUZENS, MICHAEL: "Demos Do the Talking," *Channels,* March 1989, p. 20.

———: "Nielsen under Pressure," *Channels,* Sept. 10, 1990, pp. 30–32.

COX, MEG: "Is NBC Putting Ratings before Taste?" *Wall Street Journal,* April 11, 1989, sec. B, p. 1.

DANNER, TERRY: "Executive Guide to Custom Radio Research," *NAB Research & Planning Memorandum,* July/August 1988.

DAVIS, DONALD M., and JAMES R. WALKER: "Countering the New Media: The Resurgence of Share Maintenance in Primetime Network Television," *Journal of Broadcasting & Electronic Media, 34,* Fall 1990, pp. 487–493.

DAVIS, E. ALVIN: "Maximizing Your Promotion Strategy," *NAB RadioWeek,* Dec. 12, 1988, p. 8.

"D.C. Court Backs FCC on Smut but Questions 'Indecency Hours,'" *Variety,* Aug. 3, 1988, p. 66.

DENISOFF, R. SERGE: *Solid Gold: The Popular Record Industry,* Transaction, New Brunswick, N.J., 1975.

DENVER, JOEL: "Callout Research—A Primer," *Radio & Records,* Oct. 8, 1982, pp. 19–22.

Description of Methodology: Arbitron Ratings Company Market Reports—Radio, Arbitron Ratings Company, New York, 1987.

Description of Methodology: Arbitron Ratings Company Market Reports—Television, Arbitron Ratings Company, New York, 1989.

"Does New Arbitron Diary Help AOR? Yes and No," *Television/Radio Age,* May 1, 1989, p. 36.

DUCEY, RICHARD V.:"Qualitative Audience Research: A New Tool for Marketing Your Station," *NAB Research Memo,* Washington, D.C., December 1983.

DUCEY, RICK: "Radio Listening Stable, AM Slip Slows," *NAB RadioWeek,* Jan. 1, 1990, p. 8.

DUNCAN, JAMES H., JR.: *American Radio: Tenth Anniversary Issue 1976–1986: A Prose and Statistical History,* Duncan's American Radio, Kalamazoo, Mich., 1986.

————: *The Relationship between Radio Audience Shares and Revenue Shares,* Duncan's American Radio, Indianapolis, 1991.

DUNLAP, JOY: "Making the Programming-Management Transition," *NAB RadioWeek,* Dec. 12, 1988, p. 4.

EASTMAN, SUSAN TYLER, and ROBERT A. KLEIN (eds.): *Strategies in Broadcast and Cable Promotion,* 2d ed., Waveland Press, Prospect Heights, Ill., 1991.

FEINSTEIN, STEVE: "The Right Stuff: What a GM Looks For in a PD," *Radio & Records,* April 27, 1984, pp. 78, 80.

FIELD, SYD: *Screenplay: The Foundations of Screenwriting,* Delacorte, New York, 1982.

FLANDER, JUDY: "Public Television Hits a Midlife Crisis," *Washington Journalism Review,* July/August 1989, pp. 32–34.

FLETCHER, JAMES E.: *Handbook of Radio and TV Broadcasting: Research Procedures in Audience, Program and Revenues,* Van Nostrand Reinhold, Florence, Ky., 1981.

————: *Music & Program Research,* National Association of Broadcasters, Washington, D.C., 1987.

————: *Profiting from Radio Ratings,* National Association of Broadcasters, Washington, D.C., 1989.

————(ed.): *Broadcast Research Definitions,* National Association of Broadcasters, Washington, D.C., 1988.

———— and ROGER D. WIMMER: *Focus Group Interviews in Radio Research,* National Association of Broadcasters, Washington, D.C., 1981.

FORKAN, JAMES P.: "TvQ Ratings Serve 'Fish' & 'CHiPs,'" *Advertising Age,* Dec. 19, 1977, p. 27.

Glossary of Cable & TV Terms, A. C. Nielsen, Northbrook, Ill., 1981.

GOEDKOOP, RICHARD J.: *Inside Local Television News,* Sheffield, Salem, Wis., 1988.

GOLDSTEIN, STEVEN: "Keeping Pace with the Marketplace," *Radio & Records,* April 8, 1988, pp. 36–38.

GRIFFIN, BENNETT M.: "Psychographics . . . the Next Step," *NAB Research Memorandum,* September 1984.

Guidelines for Radio Promotion, National Association of Broadcasters, Washington, D.C., 1981.

A Guide to Media Planning & Buying for Agencies & Advertisers, Arbitron Ratings Company, New York, 1989.

A Guide to Understanding and Using Radio Audience Estimates, Arbitron Ratings Company, New York, 1987.

HALL, ROBERT W.: *Media Math: Basic Techniques of Media Evaluation,* NTC Business Books, Lincolnwood, Ill., 1989.

HALONEN, DOUG: "FCC Study: Cable Jilted 704 Stations," *Electronic Media,* Sept. 5, 1988, pp. 1, 43.

————: "Senate OKs Bill to Clean Up TV Fare," *Electronic Media,* June 5, 1989, p. 3.

HALPER, DONNA L.: *Full-Service Radio: Programming for the Community,* Focal Press, Boston, 1991.

————: *Radio Music Directing,* Focal Press, Boston, 1991.

HANSON, KURT: "All Contests Are Not Equal," *Radio & Records,* April 20, 1990, p. 44.

————: "Living and Dying by Ratings Roulette," *Radio & Records,* Feb. 9, 1990, p. 34.

HARTSHORN, GERALD G. (ed.): *Audience Research Sourcebook,* National Association of Broadcasters, Washington, D.C., 1991.

HEETER, CARRIE, and BRADLEY S. GREENBERG: "A Theoretical Overview of the Program Choice Process," in Carrie Heeter and Bradley S. Greenberg (eds.), *Cableviewing,* Ablex, Norwood, N.J., 1988, pp. 33–50.

HELTON, LON: "Getting Down to Research Basics: Answers to PDs' Most Frequently Asked Questions," *Radio & Records,* June 16, 1989, p. 54.

————: "What Today's PD Needs to Know," *Radio & Records,* June 9, 1989, p. 58.

HESBACKER, PETER, NANCY CLASBY, BRUCE ANDERSON, and DAVID G. BERGER: "Radio Format Strategies," *Journal of Communication, 26,* Winter 1976, pp. 110–119.

HIBER, JAHN: *Winning Radio Research: Turning Research into Ratings & Revenues,* National Association of Broadcasters, Washington, D.C., 1987.

HORNIK, JACOB, and SHMUEL ELLIS: "Strategies to Secure Compliance for a Mall Intercept Interview," *Public Opinion Quarterly, 52,* pp. 539–551, 1988.

HOWARD, HERBERT H., and MICHAEL S. KIEVMAN: *Radio and TV Programming,* Grid, Columbus, Ohio, 1983.

How Birch Measures Radio: The Complete Birch Radio Sourcebook, Birch/Scarborough Research Corp., Coral Springs, Fla., 1990.

How to Read Your Arbitron Television Market Report, Arbitron Ratings Company, Laurel, Md., 1987.

How to Read Your Arbitron Television Market Report, Arbitron Ratings Company, New York, 1989.

How to Understand Television Measurement, General Television Corporation, Victoria, Australia, 1971.

HULLEBERG, ELLEN: "Helping Yourself with Home-Grown Research," *Broadcasting,* June, 11, 1979, p. 10.

HURLEY, DAN: "Those Hush-Hush Q Ratings—Fair or Foul?" *TV Guide,* Dec. 10, 1988, pp. 2–6.

JACOBS, JERRY: *Changing Channels: Issues and Realities in Television News,* Mayfield, Mountain View, Calif., 1990.

JAFFE, ALFRED J.: "Outlook Not Good on Closing the Meter-Diary Gap," *Television/Radio Age,* June 27, 1988, pp. 33–36.

JOHNSON, JOSEPH S., and KENNETH K. JONES: *Modern Radio Station Practices,* 2d ed., Wadsworth, Belmont, Calif., 1982.

KATZ, RICHARD: "Exploring Home Video," *Channels,* September 1989, p. 26.

KEEGAN, CAROL A. V.: "Qualitative Audience Research in Public Television," *Journal of Communication, 30,* Summer 1980, pp. 164–172.

KEITH, MICHAEL C.: *Radio Programming: Consultancy and Formatics,* Focal Press, Boston, 1987.

KOJAN, HARVEY: "Musical Musings Dominate Joint AOR Workshop," *Radio & Records,* May 19, 1989, pp. 55–56.

———: "The Ultimate PD," *Radio & Records,* Dec. 7, 1990, pp. 39–40.

KUHNS, WILLIAM: *Why We Watch Them: Interpreting TV Shows,* Benziger, New York, 1970.

LICHTY, LAWRENCE W., and JOSEPH M. RIPLEY II: *American Broadcasting: Introduction and Analysis: Readings,* College Printing & Publishing Co., Madison, Wis., 1969.

LOVECE, FRANK: "Muddling through the Must-Carry Mess," *Channels,* September 1988, pp. 48–51.

LULL, JAMES, LAWRENCE M. JOHNSON, and DONALD EDMOND: "Radio Listeners' Electronic Media Habits," *Journal of Broadcasting, 25,* Winter 1981, pp. 25–36.

———,———, and CAROL E. SWEENY: "Audiences for Contemporary Radio Formats," *Journal of Broadcasting, 22,* Fall 1978, pp. 439–453.

MACFARLAND, DAVID T.: *Contemporary Radio Programming Strategies,* Lawrence Erlbaum, Hillsdale, N.J., 1990.

———: "The Development of the Top 40 Radio Format," Ph.D. dissertation, University of Wisconsin-Madison, 1972, reprinted as *The Development of the Top 40 Radio Format,* Arno, New York, 1979.

———: "Up from Middle America: The Development of Top 40," in Lawrence W. Lichty and Malachi C. Topping (eds.), *American Broadcasting: A Source Book on the History of Radio and Television,* Hastings House, New York, 1975, pp. 399–403.

MARIN, RICK: "Loved the Pilot, Hate the Show," *Channels,* Sept. 10, 1990, pp. 43–45.

MAY, MICHAEL: *Building with the Basics: Radio Personality Development,* Michael May Enterprises, Billings, Mont., 1979.

McDONOUGH, JOHN: "What Happened to Those Old TV Formats?" *Electronic Media,* Jan. 15, 1990, pp. 57–64.

McGUIRE, BERNADETTE (ed.): *Radio in Search of Excellence: Lessons from America's Best-Run Radio Stations,* National Association of Broadcasters, Washington, D.C., 1985.

McLEAN, AUSTIN J. (ed.): *RadiOutlook II: New Forces Shaping the Industry,* National Association of Broadcasters, Washington, D.C., 1991.

MILLER, CHRIS: "AM Stereo: After All These Years, Is the Marketplace Ready?" *Feedback,* Winter 1984, pp. 14–18.

MITCHELL, KIM: "TCI, Fox Sign Affiliation Pact," *Multichannel News,* Sept. 10, 1990, pp. 1, 43.

Nielsen Media Research: *What the Ratings Really Mean,* A. C. Nielsen Co., Northbrook, Ill. 1987.

Nielsen Station Index Reference Supplement 1990-91: NSI Methodology, Techniques and Data Interpretation, Nielsen Media Research, Northbrook, Ill., 1990.

"Nielsen Study: Lower Dial Position = Higher Ratings," *Broadcasting/Cable,* Jan. 8, 1990, p. 12.

OTT, RICK: "The Quest for Your Station's Operating Level," *Radio & Records,* April 8, 1988, p. 40.

PARIKHAL, JOHN: "Need-Driven Marketing," *Radio & Records,* Oct. 27, 1989, p. 35.

——— and DAVID OAKES: *Programming Radio to Win in the New America,* National Association of Broadcasters, Washington, D.C., 1987.

PENNYBACKER, JOHN H., and DONALD R. MOTT: "AM Stereo: Broadcasters' Acceptance," *Feedback*, Winter 1984, pp. 19–21.

POLLACK, JEFF: "Anticipating the Competition," *Radio & Records,* April 28, 1989, p. 56.

POLTRACK, DAVID F.: *Television Marketing: Network/Local/Cable,* McGraw-Hill, New York, 1983.

PRICE, CYNTHIA: "How to Beat the Record Service Catch-22," *NAB RadioWeek,* July 25, 1988, p. 4.

PRIZM Geo-Demographic Market Segmentation & Targeting: An Introduction, Claritas Corporation, New York, 1982.

Programmers Guide to Birch Radio Research, Birch/Scarborough Research Corp., Coral Springs, Fla., 1990.

"Pushing the Right Buttons in Radio Syndication," *Broadcasting,* June 24, 1991, pp. 29–44.

"A Qualitative Research Service," Marketing Evaluation/TvQ, Inc., 1980.

"Radio's Promotional Efforts on the Rise," *Broadcasting,* Oct. 3, 1988, pp. 53–54.

Radio Year-Round: The Medium for All Seasons, Arbitron Ratings, New York, 1987.

"Rating the Stars," *Newsweek,* May 27, 1974, p. 89.

RIES, AL, and JACK TROUT: *Marketing Warfare,* McGraw-Hill, New York, 1986.

——— and ———: *Positioning: The Battle for Your Mind,* McGraw-Hill, New York, 1981.

ROSE, BRIAN G. (ed.): *TV Genres: A Handbook and Reference Guide,* Greenwood, Westport, Conn., 1985.

ROUTT, ED, JAMES B. McGRATH, and FREDRIC A. WEISS: *The Radio Format Conundrum,* Hastings House, New York, 1978.

RUBENS, WILLIAM S.: "Program Research at NBC, or Type I Error as a Way of Life," *Journal of Advertising Research,* June/July 1985, pp. 12–15.

RUST, R.T.: "Scheduling Network Television Programs: A Heuristic Audience Flow Approach to Maximizing Audience Share," *Journal of Advertising, 19,* 1989, pp. 11–18.

SCHATZER, LEW: "Revving Up TV Promo with Research," *BPME Image,* April/May 1989, pp. 13–14.

SCOTT, JAMES D., MARTIN R. WARSHAW, and JAMES R. TAYLOR: *Introduction to Marketing Management,* 5th ed., Richard D. Irwin, Homewood, Ill., 1985.

SHANE, ED.: *Programming Dynamics: Radio's Management Guide,* Globecom, Overland Park, Kans., 1984.

SHANKS, BOB: *The Cool Fire: How to Make It in Television,* Norton, New York, 1976.

SHERER, JILL: "Psychographics Define Audience's Values," *Electronic Media,* Dec. 18, 1989, p. 70.

SPEARS, RICHARD W.: "The Changing Face of Marketing Information and the Implications for Broadcasters," *National Association of Broadcasters Research Memo,* Washington, D.C., May 1986.

SPILLMAN, SUSAN: "Some Listeners Will Do Anything for a Buck," *Electronic Media,* May 16, 1988, p. 17.

———: "Tacky Promotions Can Gain Publicity for Radio Stations," *Electronic Media,* Feb. 8, 1988, p. 40.

STANTON, WILLIAM J., MICHAEL J. ETZEL, and BRUCE J. WALKER: *Fundamentals of Marketing,* 9th ed., McGraw-Hill, New York, 1991.

STERLING, CHRISTOPHER H.: "Second Service: Some Keys to the Development of FM Broadcasting," *Journal of Broadcasting, 15,* Spring 1971, pp. 181–194.

STOW, RUPERT L.: "Catalyst for Human Change," *FEEDBACK,* Fall 1982, pp. 3–6.

"Surrey Surveys PD Attitudes toward Job," *Radio & Records,* Aug. 5, 1988, p. 16.

TAYLOR, MARLIN RAYMOND: "How to Promote FM," *Broadcast Management/Engineering,* February 1970, pp. 28–31.

TIEDGE, JAMES T., and KENNETH J. KSOBIECH: "Counterprogramming Primetime Network Television," *Journal of Broadcasting & Electronic Media, 31,* Winter 1987, pp. 41–55.

—— and ——: "The 'Lead-In' Strategy for Prime-Time TV: Does It Increase the Audience?" *Journal of Communication, 36,* Summer 1986, pp. 51–63.

—— and ——: "The Sandwich Programming Strategy: A Case of Audience Flow," *Journalism Quarterly, 65,* Summer 1988, pp. 376–383.

TRAUB, JAMES: "The World According to Nielsen: Who Watches Television—And Why," *Channels,* January/February 1985, pp. 26–32, 70–71.

"TV Program Director: Endangered Species?" *Broadcasting,* Aug. 27, 1990, pp. 32–33.

"Two Record Promoters Indicted over Payola," *Broadcasting,* March 14, 1988, p. 45.

Understanding Broadcast Ratings, Broadcast Rating Council, New York, 1981.

WALKER, JAMES R.: "Inheritance Effects in the New Media Environment," *Journal of Broadcasting & Electronic Media, 32,* Fall 1988, pp. 391–401.

—— and ROBERT V. BELLAMY, Jr.: "Remote Control Grazing as Diversionary Viewing," *Feedback,* Winter 1991, pp. 2–4.

WALLACE, EILEEN: "Radio Promos: Where Dreams Do Come True," *Gannetteer,* October 1987, pp. 8–11.

WARRENS, BOB: "Consumers of the World, Segment!" *A.C. Nielsen AIM,* 1989, pp. 19–21.

WEBSTER, JAMES: "People Meters," *NAB Research & Planning Memo,* Washington, D. C., April 1984.

—— and LAWRENCE W. LICHTY: *Ratings Analysis: Theory and Practice,* Lawrence Erlbaum, Hillsdale, N.J., 1991.

WEBSTER, JAMES G.: "Audience Behavior in the New Media Environment," *Journal of Communication, 36,* Summer 1986, pp. 77–91.

——: Program Audience Duplication: "A Study of Television Inheritance Effects," *Journal of Broadcasting & Electronic Media, 29,* Spring 1985, pp. 121–133.

—— and GREGORY D. NEWTON: "Structural Determinants of the Television News Audience," *Journal of Broadcasting & Electronic Media, 32,* Fall 1988, pp. 381–389.

WHETMORE, EDWARD JAY: *The Magic Medium: An Introduction to Radio in America,* Wadsworth, Belmont, Calif., 1981.

WIMMER, ROGER: "The Dangers of Being Too Selective," *Radio & Records,* Jan. 12, 1990, p. 42.

WIMMER, ROGER D., and JOSEPH R. DOMINICK: *Mass Media Research: An Introduction,* 3d ed., Wadsworth, Belmont, Calif., 1991.

WOLLERT, JAMES A.: "Radio: Technology and the Next Decade," *Feedback,* Fall 1982, pp. 14–16.

Your Guide to Nielsen Reports and Services, A.C. Nielsen Co., Northbrook, Ill., 1987.

ZOGLIN, RICHARD: "The Fox Trots Faster," *Time,* Aug. 27, 1990, pp. 64–66.

Index